ST/ESA/SER.A/254

DEPARTMENT OF ECONOMIC AND SOCIAL AFFAIRS
POPULATION DIVISION

World Population Policies 2005

The work is published for
and on behalf of the
United Nations

ACADEMIC FOUNDATION

DESA

The Department of Economic and Social Affairs of the United Nations Secretariat is a vital interface between global policies in the economic, social and environmental spheres and national action. The Department works in three main interlinked areas: (i) it compiles, generates and analyses a wide range of economic, social and environmental data and information on which States Members of the United Nations draw to review common problems and take stock of policy options; (ii) it facilitates the negotiations of Member States in many intergovernmental bodies on joint courses of action to address ongoing or emerging global challenges; and (iii) it advises interested Governments on the ways and means of translating policy frameworks developed in United Nations conferences and summits into programmes at the country level and, through technical assistance, helps build national capacities.

Note

The designations employed and the presentation of the material in this publication do not imply the expression of any opinion whatsoever on the part of the Secretariat of the United Nations concerning the legal status of any country, city or area or of its authorities, or concerning the delimitation of its frontiers or boundaries.

The designations "developed" and "developing" countries and "more developed" and "less developed" regions are intended for statistical convenience and do not necessarily express a judgment about the stage reached by a particular country or area in the development process.

The term "country" as used in the text of this publication also refers, as appropriate, to territories or areas.

This publication has been issued without formal editing.

ST/ESA/SER.A/254

UNITED NATIONS PUBLICATION

The work is published for and
on behalf of the United Nations
by

ACADEMIC FOUNDATION

4772 / 23, Bharat Ram Road, (23 Ansari Road),
Darya Ganj, New Delhi - 110 002.

Tel : +91-11-23245001 / 02 / 03 / 04
Fax : +91-11-23245005
e-mail : academic@vsnl.com
www.academicfoundation.com

ISBN 81-7188-570-5

This edition is printed in India in 2006

PREFACE

This report delineates Governments' views and policies concerning population and development for the 194 Member States and non-member States of the United Nations. In particular, it itemizes policies in the areas of population size and growth, population age structure, fertility and family planning, health and mortality, spatial distribution and internal migration and international migration. Prior to 2003, the publication was issued as *National Population Policies 2001* (Sales No. E.02.XIII.12) and *National Population Policies 1998* (Sales No. E.99.XIII.3). Prior to 1998, the data were published as the *Global Review and Inventory of Population Policies (GRIPP).*

A major characteristic of United Nations international population conferences during the past three decades has been the emphasis placed on the monitoring of the implementation of their goals and recommendations. Accordingly, the Programme of Action adopted by the International Conference on Population and Development held at Cairo in 1994 recommended that actions should be taken "to measure, assess, monitor and evaluate progress towards meeting the goals of the present Programme of Action".[1]

The monitoring of population policies at the international level has a long history that goes back to the World Population Plan of Action[2] adopted at the World Population Conference held at Bucharest in 1974. The Plan of Action was the first international instrument on population policy. Within the framework of the Plan of Action, population policies were defined in terms of all policies and programmes—including social and economic policies—concerned with the major population variables: fertility, mortality, internal migration and geographical distribution of population, and international migration.

The Population Division of the Department of Economic and Social Affairs is responsible for providing the international community with up-to-date, accurate and scientifically objective information on population and development. The Population Division provides guidance to the United Nations General Assembly, the Economic and Social Council and the Commission on Population and Development on population and development issues. In addition, the Division undertakes studies on population levels and trends, population estimates and projections, population policies, and population and development interrelationships.

Responsibility for *World Population Policies 2005* rests with the Population Division. Preparation of this publication was facilitated by the collaboration of the Member States and non-member States of the United Nations, the regional commissions, and the United Nations programmes, funds and agencies.

The data presented in this publication are also being released in a user-friendly electronic form on a CD-ROM. An order form is included in this volume. Selected parts of this publication, as well as other population information, may be accessed on the Population Division website at http://www.unpopulation.org.

Questions and comments concerning this publication may be addressed to the office of Ms. Hania Zlotnik, Director, Population Division, Department of Economic and Social Affairs, United Nations, New York, NY 10017, fax number 212-963-2147.

[1] *Report of the International Conference on Population and Development, Cairo, 5-13 September 1994* (United Nations publication, Sales No. E.95.XIII.18), chap. I, resolution 1, annex, para. 13.6.

[2] *Report of the United Nations World Population Conference, Bucharest, 19-30 August 1974* (United Nations publication, Sales No. E.75.XIII.3), chap. I.

CONTENTS

BOXES

TEXT TABLES

FIGURES

Explanatory notes

Symbols of United Nations documents are composed of capital letters combined with figures.

Various symbols have been used in the tables throughout this report, as follows:

Two dots (..) indicate that data are not available or are not separately reported.

An em dash (—) indicates that the population is less than 500 persons.

A hyphen (-) indicates that the item is not applicable.

A minus sign (-) before a figure indicates a decrease.

A full stop (.) is used to indicate decimals.

Years given begin with 1 July.

Use of a hyphen (-) between years, for example, 2000-2005, signifies the full period involved, from 1 July of the beginning year to 1 July of the end year.

Percentages in tables and figures do not necessarily add to 100 per cent because of rounding.

Countries and areas are grouped geographically into six major areas: Africa; Asia; Europe; Latin America and the Caribbean; Northern America; and Oceania. Those major areas are further divided geographically into 21 regions. In addition, the regions are classified as belonging, for statistical convenience, to either of two general groups: more developed and less developed regions. The less developed regions include all regions of Africa, Asia (excluding Japan), Latin America and the Caribbean, Melanesia, Micronesia and Polynesia. The more developed regions comprise Northern America, Japan, Europe and Australia/New Zealand.

The group of least developed countries currently comprises 50 countries: Afghanistan, Angola, Bangladesh, Benin, Bhutan, Burkina Faso, Burundi, Cambodia, Cape Verde, Central African Republic, Chad, Comoros, Democratic Republic of Timor-Leste, Democratic Republic of the Congo, Djibouti, Equatorial Guinea, Eritrea, Ethiopia, Gambia, Guinea, Guinea-Bissau, Haiti, Kiribati, Lao People's Democratic Republic, Lesotho, Liberia, Madagascar, Malawi, Maldives, Mali, Mauritania, Mozambique, Myanmar, Nepal, Niger, Rwanda, Samoa, Sao Tome and Principe, Senegal, Sierra Leone, Solomon Islands, Somalia, Sudan, Togo, Tuvalu, Uganda, the United Republic of Tanzania, Vanuatu, Yemen and Zambia.

INTRODUCTION

A major characteristic of United Nations international population conferences during the past three decades has been the emphasis placed on the monitoring of the implementation of their goals and recommendations. Accordingly, the Programme of Action adopted by the International Conference on Population and Development held at Cairo in 1994 recommended that actions should be taken "to measure, assess, monitor and evaluate progress towards meeting the goals of the present Programme of Action".[1]

The monitoring of population policies at the international level has a long history that dates back to the World Population Plan of Action[2] adopted at the World Population Conference held at Bucharest in 1974. The Plan of Action was the first international instrument on population policy. Within the framework of the Plan of Action, population policies were defined in terms of all policies and programmes—including social and economic policies—concerned with the major population variables: fertility, mortality, internal migration and geographical distribution of population, and international migration.

The United Nations Department of Economic and Social Affairs, through its Population Division, is responsible for the global monitoring of the implementation of the Programme of Action emanating from the 1994 International Conference on Population and Development, as it was for the Plan of Action of the 1974 World Population Conference. From the very beginning, the reporting format adopted for the monitoring of implementation has been guided by the principles of objectivity and non-advocacy. Reports have been descriptive and concise, focusing on analytical comparisons among countries and regions over time.

The present publication is part of the effort of the Population Division to disseminate the information resulting from its monitoring activities. It provides an overview of population policies and dynamics for each of the Member States and non-member States for which data are available at mid-decade for the 1970s, 1980s and 1990s—that is, at the time of the convening of the population conferences at Bucharest, Mexico City and Cairo—as well as for 2005.

The core information included in the monitoring of population policies encompasses three basic components:

Government perceptions of population size and growth, population age structure and spatial distribution, and of the demographic components of fertility, mortality and migration that affect them. For each of these variables, is the level or trend viewed as a significant policy issue, and is the prevailing level or rate of change seen as too high, too low or acceptable/satisfactory in relation to other social and economic conditions?

Government objectives with respect to each variable. Is the objective of the Government to raise or to lower the level of the variable or to maintain its current level?

Government policies concerning interventions to influence each variable. Does the Government view intervention to alter levels and trends as a legitimate exercise of its authority? Has the Government actively intervened to influence the variable?

World Population Policies 2005 differs somewhat in format from *World Population Policies 2003* (Sales No. E.04.XIII.3). Several additional policy variables have been included in *World Population Policies 2005,* while other policy variables have been dropped. Box 1 summarizes the changes which have been incorporated in *World Population Policies 2005.*

---

[1] *Report of the International Conference on Population and Development, Cairo, 5-13 September 1994* (United Nations publication, Sales No. E.95.XIII.18), chap. I, resolution 1, annex, para. 13.6.

[2] *Report of the United Nations World Population Conference, Bucharest, 19-30 August 1974* (United Nations publication, Sales No. E.75.XIII.3), chap. I.

BOX 1. WHAT'S NEW IN *WORLD POPULATION POLICIES 2005*

Population policy variable	*Variables dropped from World Population Policies 2005*	*Variables added to World Population Policies 2005*
Health and mortality		Measures implemented to control HIV/AIDS
Policies on spatial distribution	Policy on spatial distribution Between regions Between rural and urban places Policy on internal migration Into metropolitan areas From rural areas to other locations	Policy on internal migration From rural to urban areas From rural to rural areas From urban to rural areas From urban to urban areas Into urban agglomerations
Policies on international migration	Policy on migrants workers Policy on dependents of migrant workers	Policy on temporary workers Policy on highly skilled workers Policy on family reunification

The Population Policy Data Bank maintained by the Population Division was established to compile the requisite information for monitoring the implementation of the Plan of Action and later the Programme of Action. The major sources of information contained in the databank may be classified into four broad types (see box 2). The first type of information comprises official Government responses to the *United Nations Inquiry among Governments on Population and Development*, of which there have been nine separate rounds since 1963. The eighth round, the first directed towards the Programme of Action of the 1994 International Conference on Population and Development, was initiated in 1997. The ninth round was undertaken in 2003. Each round of the *Inquiry* has consisted of a detailed request for information sent to all Member States and non-member States of the United Nations. The second type of information consists of publications, documents, speeches and other materials issued by Governments, including development plans, laws, regulations and proclamations. These materials are a particularly important source of data as they reflect the official positions taken by countries. The third category of information is comprised of materials provided by international organizations, such as regional commissions, funds, programmes and agencies of the United Nations system, as well as other regional intergovernmental organizations. As countries collectively are the source of these materials, an official status may be attached to them. The fourth type of information consists of non-governmental materials, including clippings from the world press, articles in academic journals, proceedings of conferences and seminars, reports and studies prepared by research centres and non-governmental organizations, as well as correspondence and personal communications with experts.

The successive monitoring reports have pointed to significant changes since 1974 in Government views of population issues as well as in population policy formulation. The monitoring exercise itself contributes to this evolution by increasing worldwide awareness of population issues and the need for appropriate policy responses.

Part One of the present publication offers a global perspective on the evolution of selected aspects of population policies between 1976 and 2005 with respect to each of the major population variables, based on the country profiles. Part Two presents, on a country-by-country basis, the evolution of Government views and policies from 1976 to 2005 with respect to population size and growth, population age structure, fertility and family planning, health and mortality, spatial distribution and internal migration and international migration, within the context of demographic and social and economic change. Country profiles are included for 194 Member States and non-member States of the United Nations. The material is presented in the form of data sheets, containing population policy data for each country around the dates 1976, 1986, 1996 and 2005, and population indicators for the corresponding years.

The data included in the publication were based on information available as of 31 December 2005.

BOX 2. SOURCES FOR MONITORING GOVERNMENT VIEWS AND POLICIES ON POPULATION

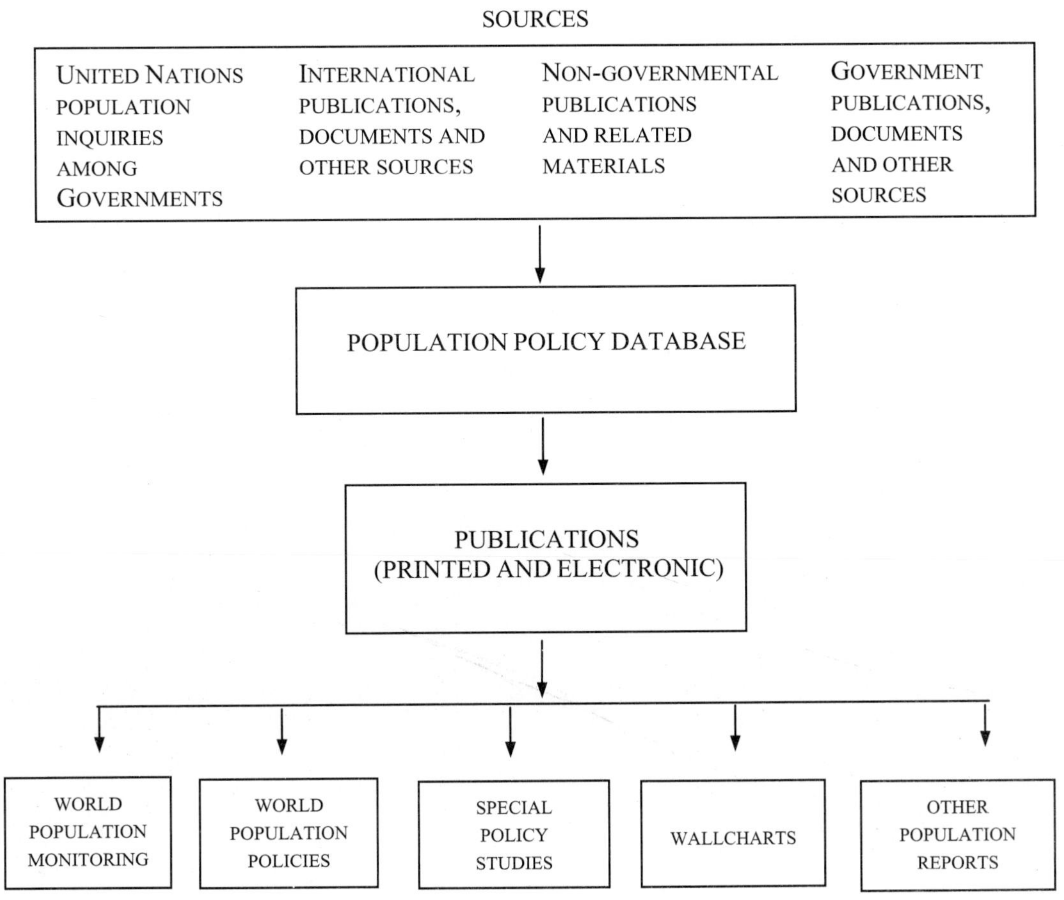

Source: Trends in Population Policy (United Nations publication, Sales No. E.89.XIII.13).

Part One

GOVERNMENT VIEWS AND POLICIES

GOVERNMENT VIEWS AND POLICIES

HIV/AIDS stands out as the most significant population issue in the world. According to this 2005 survey of population policies, 88 per cent of developing countries and 79 per cent of developed countries considered HIV/AIDS as the most pressing population and development issue (box 3). Among the developing countries, high mortality related to infant and child mortality and maternal mortality were the second and third most important issues. The large size of the working age population, high adolescent fertility, low life expectancy, the undesirable pattern of spatial distribution, high fertility and high population growth round out the other concerns for developing countries.

In contrast, in developed countries, the other population concerns were related to low fertility and included population ageing, low fertility itself and the small size of the working age population

It is interesting to note that both developing and developed countries shared their concern with the working age population. However, in developed countries, the issues related to the shortage of workers (due to low fertility and population ageing); whereas, in developing countries the issue usually related to a surplus of workers due to a history of high fertility and population growth.

I. Population size and growth

More than half of the developing countries continued to view their population growth as being too high in 2005 (table 1). This is despite declining rates of population growth in the less developed regions from an average annual rate of 2.4 per cent during 1970-1975 to 1.5 per cent in 2000-2005 (United Nations, 2005a). Among the 50 least developed countries, the proportion of countries that viewed population growth as too high rose from 50 per cent in 1986 to 80 per cent in 2005. Many developing countries have realized the importance of reducing high rates of population growth in order to ease the mounting pressure on renewable and non-renewable resources, environmental pollution and degradation and food insufficiency and to provide employment and basic social services.

Africa was the region with the greatest proportion of countries that viewed growth as too high, almost three fourths of countries do so, up from 35 per cent in 1976. In Asia, which has experienced substantial declines in fertility, more than 40 per cent of countries viewed population growth as too high. Latin America and the Caribbean was the only region where the proportion of Governments that viewed population growth as too high has continuously decreased, from 48 per cent in 1986 to 27 per cent in 2005.

To a great extent, concerns with the detrimental consequences of high population growth translated into policy interventions. In 2005, 48 cent of developing countries and 70 per cent of the least developed countries had policies aimed at reducing their population growth rate (table 2). One of the most significant population policy developments of the second half of the 1990s was the continued rise in the number of African Governments that reported policies aimed at reducing the rapid growth of their population: 66 per cent in 2005, up from 60 per cent in 1996, 39 per cent in 1986 and 25 per cent in 1976.

BOX 3. MAJOR POPULATION CONCERNS OF GOVERNMENTS IN 2005

ISSUES OF SIGNIFICANCE TO AT LEAST ONE HALF OF GOVERNMENTS IN 2005, BY LEVEL OF DEVELOPMENT

Region and Issues	*Percentage of Governments reporting it is significant*
World	
HIV/AIDS	86
Infant and child mortality	72
Maternal mortality	69
Size of the working-age population	66
Adolescent fertility	59
Low life expectancy	57
Population ageing	52
Pattern of spatial distribution	50
More developed regions	
HIV/AIDS	79
Population ageing	76
Low fertility	65
Size of the working-age population	57
Less developed regions	
HIV/AIDS	88
Infant and child mortality	85
Maternal mortality	81
Size of the working-age population	70
Adolescent fertility	65
Low life expectancy	64
Pattern of spatial distribution	55
High fertility	54
High rates of population growth	52

Conversely, the proportion of African Governments which did not intervene with respect to population growth continued to decline from 60 per cent in 1976 to only 21 per cent in 2005. Many African Governments have realized that effective population policy implementation requires the creation of an institutional framework that ensures the integration of population variables into the planning process with adequate mechanisms for its monitoring and evaluation (box 4). In contrast, in Latin America and the Caribbean,. the proportion of non-interventionist Governments increased from 52 per cent in 1996 to 61 per cent in 2005.

Box 4. Population growth and government policies on population growth in Africa

During the past three decades, Government support for population policies has increased substantially in Africa. An increasing number of African Governments viewed the rate of population growth as too high. This was a major change in the view held by most African Governments at the time of 1974 Population Conference in Bucharest. At that time, it was felt that economic development would in the long run bring about lower fertility and population growth. In 1976, only one third of African Governments perceived that the population growth rate was too high. As of 2005, three fourths of African Governments viewed their population growth as being too high and the majority of Governments adopted policies to lower the growth rate. Of the 53 African countries, 35 enacted policies aimed at lowering their population growth rate. The policy stance was to a large extent determined by the level of growth.

During the period 2000-2005, 10 countries in Africa experienced population growth of 3 per cent or more. Nine of these countries felt that the growth rate was too high and seven implemented a policy to lower it (see table). The remaining three did not intervene with respect to the growth rate (Benin, Sierra Leone and Somalia). Of the 21 countries with a growth rate between 2 and 3 per cent, 15 felt that the growth rate was too high and implemented measures to lower it. Six countries felt that the population growth rate was satisfactory and either had programmes designed to maintain the current level (three countries) or did not intervene (three countries).

Among the 15 countries with a growth rate between 1 to 2 per cent, 10 countries felt that the growth rate was too high and enacted policy aimed at lowering it. Four countries either had no policy or aimed to maintain the current level. Gabon is the only country in Africa with a policy to raise its population growth.

Within the group of seven countries with a growth rate less than 1 per cent, four viewed the growth rate as too high and three had policies to lower it (Botswana, Lesotho and Zimbabwe). It is, however, important to stress that these countries are among those most affected by the HIV/AIDS epidemic and so the decline in population growth in these countries was largely due to the AIDS epidemic. Still, these countries aimed to lower population growth and fertility, regardless of the country's level of mortality.

By 2003, 52 African countries (excepting the Libyan Arab Jamahiriya) had either formulated or were in the process of formulating comprehensive population policies covering demographic, social, economic and environmental issues with objectives, targets and strategies similar to those recommended by the Programme of Action of the International Conference on Population and Development (United Nations Economic Commission for Africa, 2004).

Government views and policies on population growth in 2005 by the level of population growth, 2000-2005, Africa (Number of countries)

Growth rate	*Government views*			
	Too low	*Satisfactory*	*Too high*	*Total*
Less than 1 per cent	0	3	4	7
1-2 per cent	1	4	10	15
2-3 per cent	0	6	15	21
3 per cent or more	0	1	9	10
Total	1	14	38	53

Growth rate	*Government policies*				
	Raise	*Maintain*	*Lower*	*No intervention*	*Total*
Less than 1 per cent	0	2	3	2	7
1-2 per cent	1	1	10	3	15
2-3 per cent	0	3	15	3	21
3 per cent or more	0	0	7	3	10
Total	1	6	35	11	53

In response to the persistence of low population growth, a growing number of countries particularly in the more developed regions, have expressed concern about the consequences of low or negative population growth, resulting from very low fertility, and in some cases sharply higher mortality and substantial out-migration. Forty-four percent of Governments in more developed regions considered their population growth to be too low, up from one third in 1976. Consequently, the proportion of developed countries with policies aimed at raising the growth of their population climbed from 23 per cent in 1996 to 35 per cent in 2005. Twenty of the 21 developed countries that viewed their population growth as too low are in Europe. The proportion of Governments in Europe that did not have policies to modify their population growth rate decreased from 72 per cent in 1976 to 44 per cent in 2005.

The changes in Government views and policies described above have been matched by a slowdown in population growth in many countries. Whereas during the period 1970-1975, 36 countries had population growth rates of 3 per cent or more and 76 countries had growth rates between 2 to 3 per cent, corresponding figures for the period 2000-2005 were 10 and 23 respectively. Nevertheless, 11 countries with population growth less than 1 per cent in 2000-2005, still considered the growth rate as too high, while Israel and Kuwait, two countries with growth rates above 2 per cent considered their growth rate as satisfactory. Eight countries which considered the rate of growth as too high did not intervene and six countries which viewed population growth as too low did not intervene. Of the 19 countries with negative population growth during 2000-2005, 18 countries felt that the growth rate was too low; 16 countries have established policies to raise it. Latvia and Poland considered the growth rate to be too low but did not intervene.

II. Population age structure

One of the inevitable consequences of the demographic transition from high to low fertility and high to low mortality has been the evolution in the age structure of world population. Many socictics, particularly in the more developed regions, have attained older population age structures than have ever been seen in the past. In developed countries, 20 per cent of the population was aged 60 years or older and by 2050 one in three persons will be aged 60 or older (United Nations, 2005a). The number of older persons was larger than the number of children (persons under age 15) in developed countries; by 2050, there will be two older persons for every child. Many developing countries in the midst of the demographic transition have experienced rapid shifts in the relative numbers of children, working-age population and older persons. The proportion of the population aged 60 or older in the less developed regions is expected to rise from 8 per cent in 2005 to close to 20 per cent by 2050.

As of 2005, more than half of reporting countries viewed population ageing as a major concern, and another half as a minor concern (table 3, figure I). Although concerns with population ageing were much more pronounced among developed countries, where three quarters of Governments considered it a major concern, a number of Governments in developing countries became concerned with this demographic phenomenon as well. Forty-two per cent of developing countries expressed major concern over population ageing in 2005. In Latin America and the Caribbean, about two-thirds of the countries considered population ageing to be a major concern, while more than one third of reporting countries in Africa and in Asia saw it as a major concern.

The size of the working-age population was also a source of concern: two-thirds of reporting countries viewed the size of the population aged 15 to 59 years as a major concern (table 4). Developed and developing countries, however, differ in terms of the nature of the concern. Whereas developed countries were concerned that the size of the working-age population was too small, thus creating labour shortages, most developing countries felt that the working age population was too large, posing problems of high unemployment.

In order to deal with the consequences of population ageing (decrease of the working age population, pension system viability and provision of care for the growing older population), many Governments in more developed regions implemented measures such as increasing the retirement age, eliminating incentives for early retirement and encouraging more women to enter the workforce.

Figure I. Government level of concern about the ageing of the population, 2005

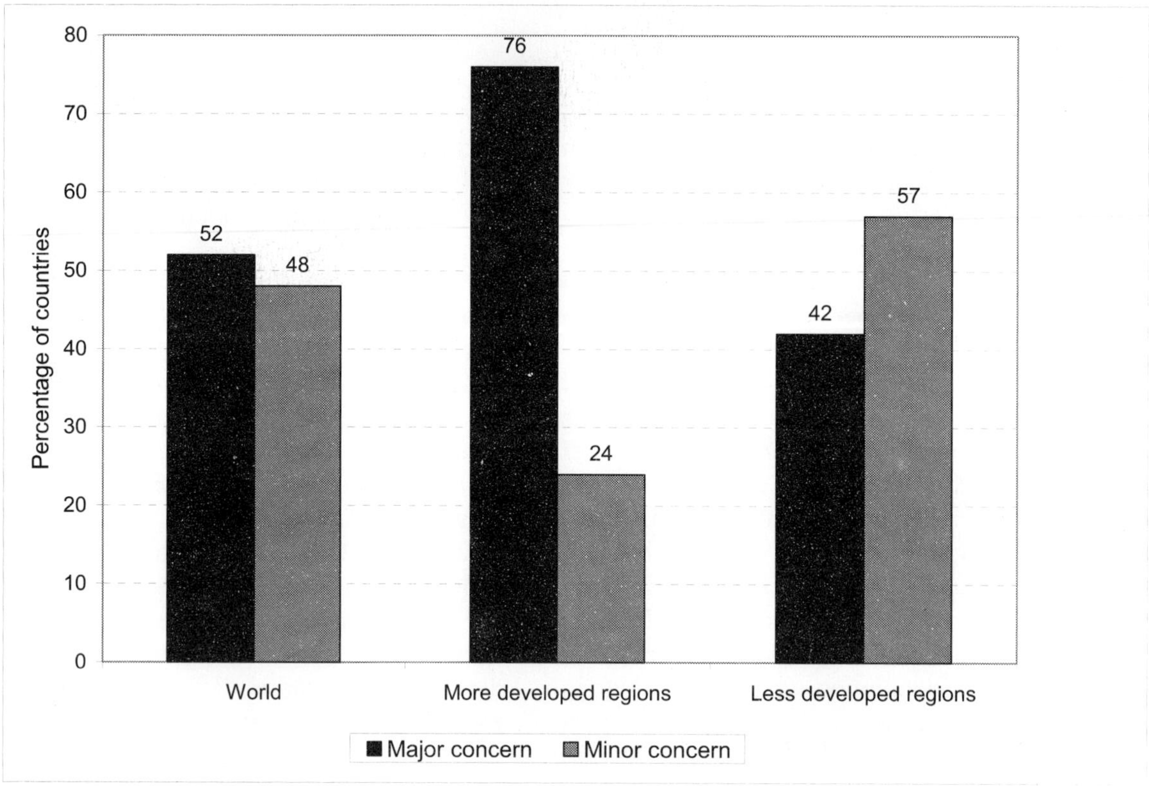

III. Fertility and family planning

The wealth of information collected on fertility trends provides ample evidence of the decline in fertility in most parts of the world. From 1975 to 2005, the number of countries with total fertility of four or more births per woman decreased from 129 to 56. As a consequence, global total fertility declined from an average of 4.5 births per woman in 1970-1975 to 2.6 births in 2000-2005 (United Nations, 2005a).

Governments' views and policies concerning fertility contributed to the fertility decline in developing countries. In 1976, 37 per cent of Governments viewed their fertility as too high (table 5). This figure rose to 45 per cent in 1996 and then decreased slightly to 41 per cent in 2005. Unlike in the past, when perceptions of high fertility were usually not accompanied by policy intervention, virtually all countries which viewed fertility as too high in 2005 intervened to lower it. In 1976, more than half of the countries did not intervene to modify the level of fertility. By 2005, the percentage of non-interventionist countries had fallen to less than one quarter. As a consequences, the proportion of countries in less developed regions that had policies to lower fertility rose from 34 per cent in 1976 to 56 per cent in 1996 and declined slightly to 53 per cent in 2005 (table 6, figure II). Among the countries that viewed fertility as too high were most developing countries, including much of Africa, South-central and South-eastern Asia.

Figure II. Government policies on the level of fertility, 1976, 1986, 1996 and 2005

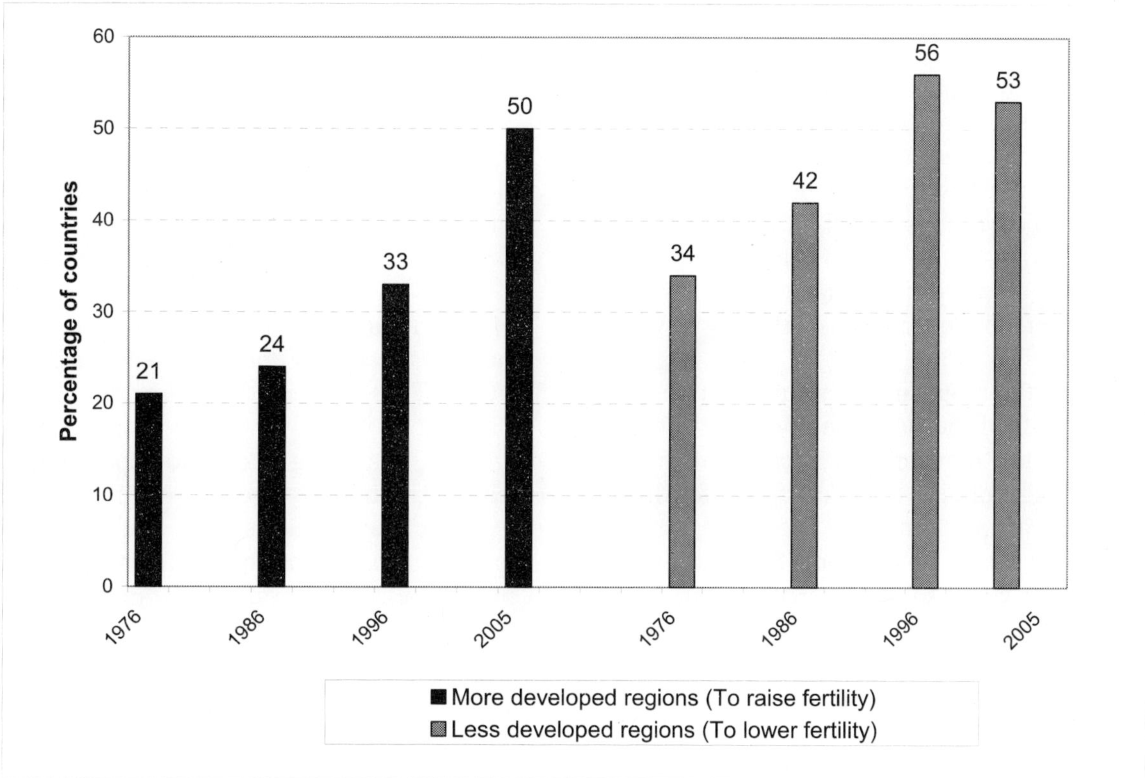

Figure III. Government views on the level of fertility, Africa, 1976 and 2005

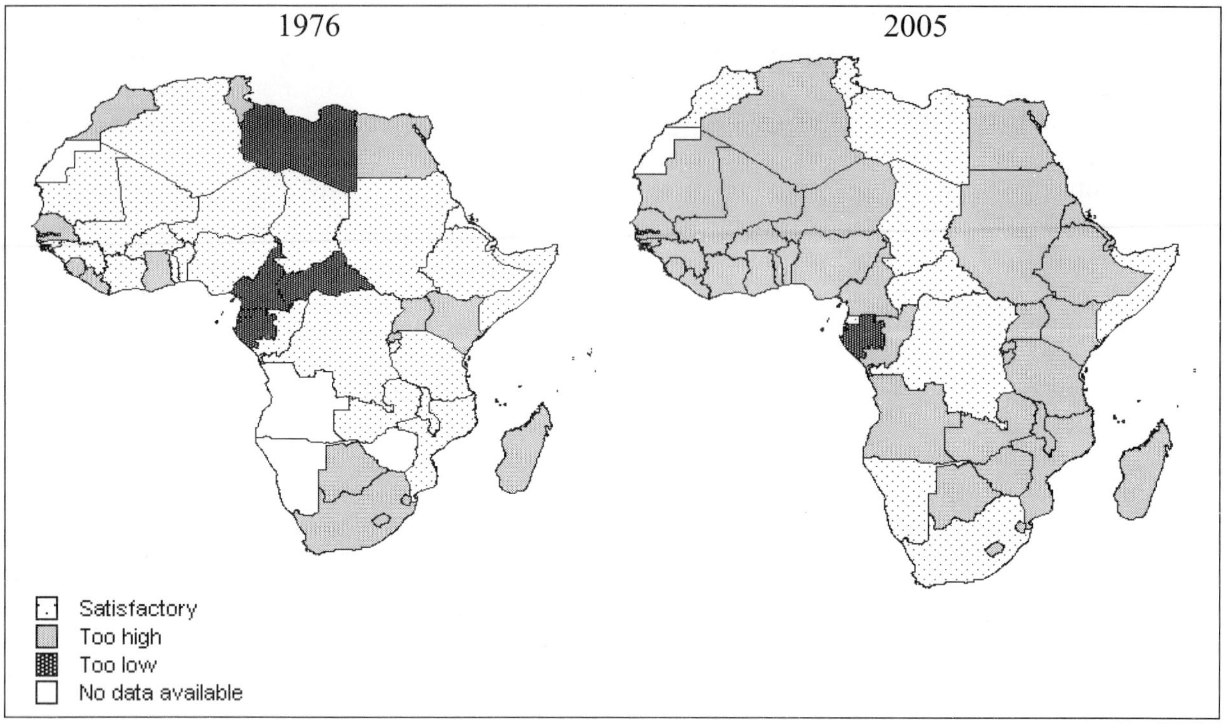

Among the countries in the less developed regions, 54 per cent considered their fertility too high in 2005. More than four fifths of the least developed countries held that view. The evolution of fertility perceptions in Africa is clearly visible in figure III. In 1976, one third of African countries viewed fertility as too high; by 2005, three quarters of Governments held this view.

One of the most significant population policy developments of the second half of the 1990s was the rise in the number of African Governments that reported policies to reduce their fertility. In 1986, only 41 per cent of African Governments had policies aimed at lowering their fertility. By 2005, 74 per cent of Governments pursued lower fertility.

However, as with population growth, there was no direct correspondence between the level of fertility and Government views and policies on fertility. Four countries in Africa with total fertility of six births or more per woman viewed their level of fertility as satisfactory, while Gabon, a country with total fertility of four births, considered its fertility as too low (United Nations, 2005a). In addition, of the countries that considered their total fertility to be too high, seven did not intervene with respect to fertility, while one country (Angola) aimed to maintain its high fertility.

Governments implemented a variety of measures to directly and indirectly affect fertility levels. These included the integration of family planning and safe motherhood into primary care systems, providing access to reproductive health services, enhancing the role of men in sexual and reproductive health, raising the minimum legal age at marriage, improving female education and employment opportunities, discouraging son preference and providing low cost, safe and effective contraception.

The persistence of low fertility was a concern for a growing number of countries. Total fertility for more developed regions feel well below replacement level to 1.6 births per woman in 2000-2005. Whereas in 1976, only one quarter of countries in Europe felt that fertility was too low, about two-thirds held this view by 2005 (figure IV). By 1967, 67 countries had already introduced family allowance schemes, although it is not known in how many of these countries the objective was to raise fertility (United Nations, 1972). Of the 46 countries that viewed fertility as too low in 2005, more than three quarters had policies to boost fertility. To raise fertility, Governments offered a host of measures, such as baby bonuses, family allowances, maternal and paternal leave, subsidized child care, tax breaks, subsidized housing, flexible work schedules, and promoting the sharing of parenting and household work among spouses. A public opinion conducted by the European Union's Eurobarometer in 2004, however, revealed that 84 percent of the men surveyed either had not taken parental leave or did not intend to do so, even when informed of their rights (European Union, 2005). In Eastern Europe, profound economic and political changes were accompanied by a sharp decline in fertility, resulting in some of the lowest fertility in the world. Factors to account for this trend included: political instability-induced "fear of the future" and reluctance to have children; declining per capita income and living standards; and major transformations in family formation and dissolution (Economic Commission for Europe, 2002).

Figure IV. Government views on the level of fertility, Europe, 1976 and 2005

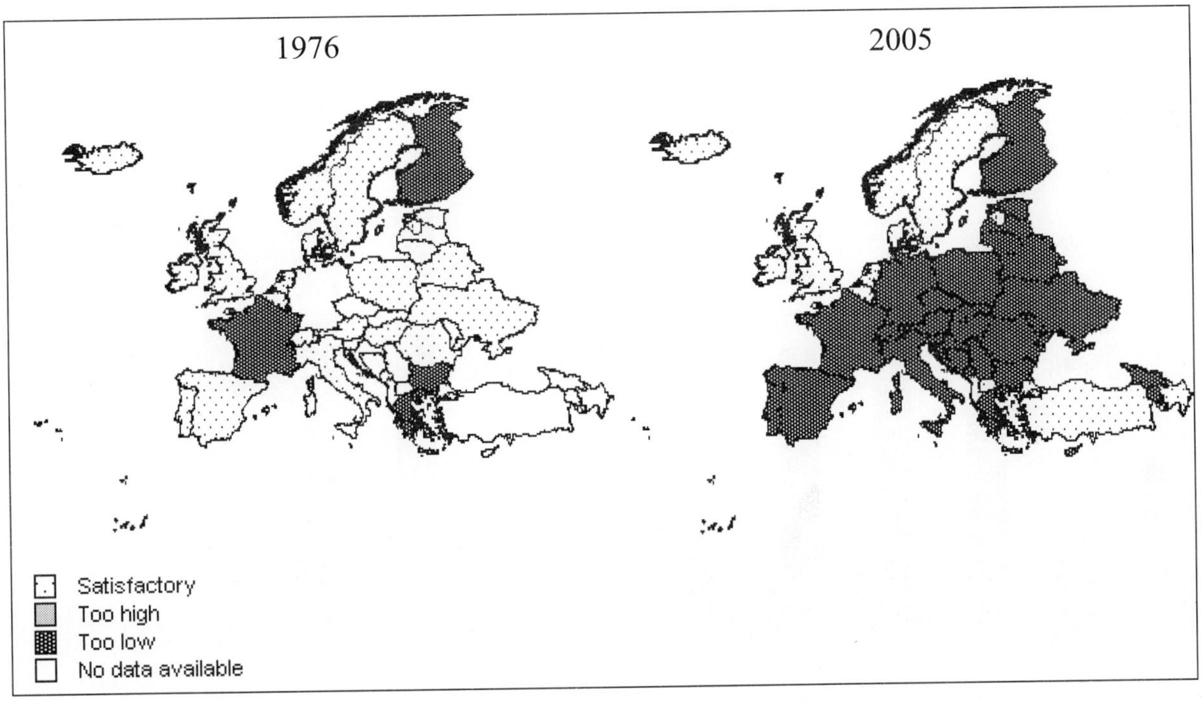

An important determinant of reproductive behaviour, as well as of maternal and child health, are Government policies on providing access to contraceptive methods. Direct support entailed the provision of family planning services through Government-run facilities, such as hospitals, clinics, health posts and health centres and through Government fieldworkers. Government support for methods of contraception has steadily increased. By 2005, 92 per cent of countries supported contraceptive provision, either directly (74 per cent) or indirectly (18 per cent), by supporting non-governmental activities, such as those operated by family planning associations (table 7). Despite widespread Government support for contraceptives, demand was believed to outstrip supply. It was estimated that as of 2000, some 123 million women lacked ready access to safe and effective means of contraception (Ross and Winfrey, 2002).

Nearly all developing countries shifted their policies in favour of increased direct support for contraceptive methods during the last 30 years (figures V and VI). Even previously pronatalist Governments, which in the past had wanted to maintain or even increase population growth, gradually changed their stance and accepted family planning and contraception as an integral part of maternal and child health programmes. Examples included Cameroon, Cambodia, Côte d'Ivoire, the Lao's People Republic, Oman and the United Arab Emirates. At the same time, some countries, particularly in Europe (for example, Austria, Denmark, France, Italy and Switzerland) reduced their support for contraceptive methods, possibly as a response to below-replacement fertility, or an acknowledgement that the private sector was meeting demands for contraception without more Government subsidies.

Figure V. Governments providing direct support for contraceptive methods, 1976, 1986, 1996 and 2005

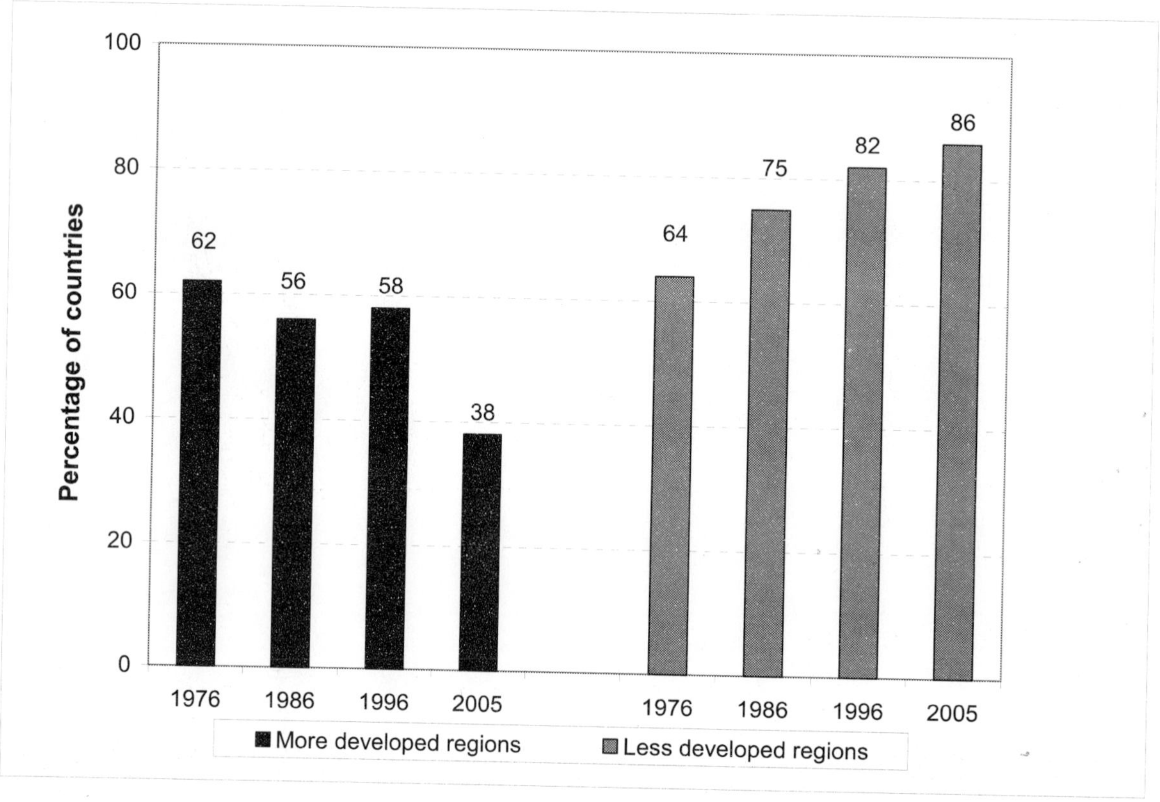

Figure. VI. Governments policies on providing access to contraceptive methods, Africa, 1976 and 2005

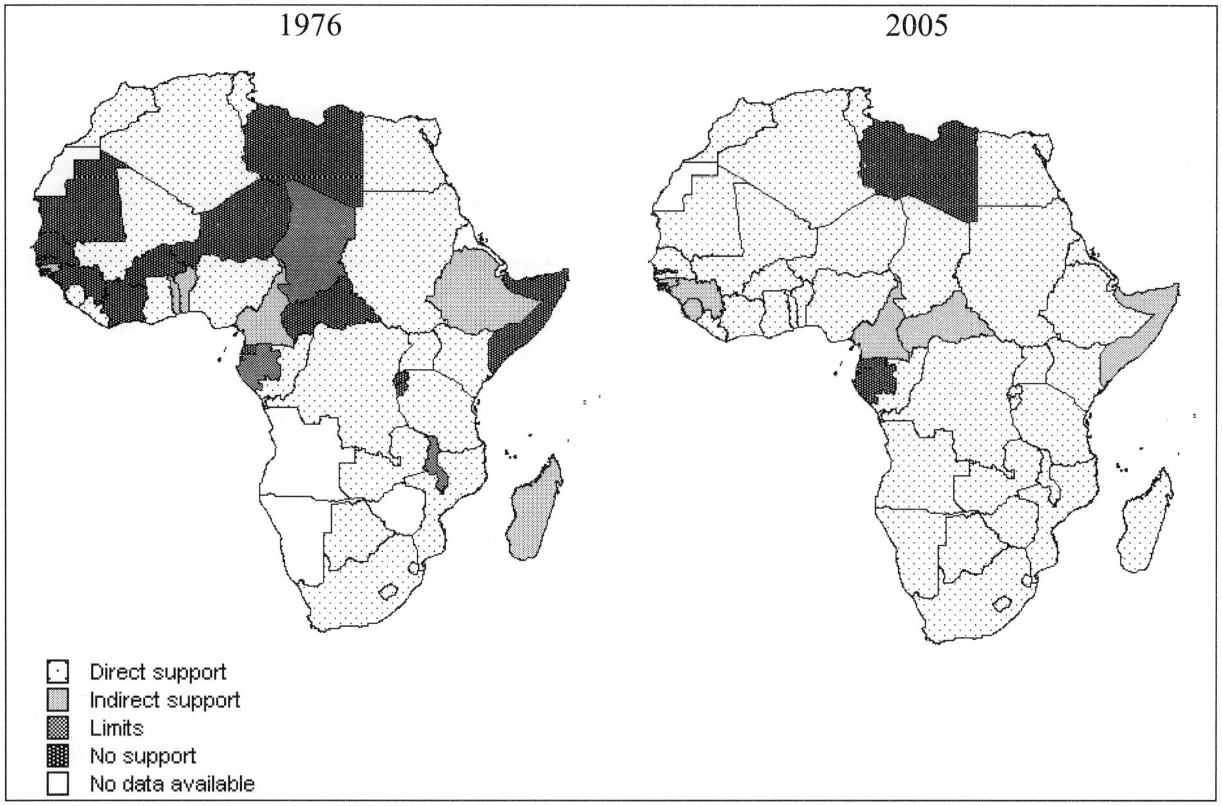

Adolescent fertility (births to women under 20 years of age) was a concern for Governments, particularly in the less developed regions. Early childbearing entails a much greater risk of maternal death, while the children born to young mothers have higher levels of morbidity and mortality. Of the 181 Governments whose views regarding fertility among adolescents were known, 162 (90 per cent) expressed concern regarding the level (table 8). They included virtually all countries in Latin America and the Caribbean and most countries in Africa. While slightly more than one third of Governments in the more developed regions viewed the level of adolescent fertility as a major concern, two-thirds of Governments in the less developed regions considered it a major concern.

Of the 180 countries with information available, 77 per cent reported having policies and programmes to address adolescent fertility (table 9). They included 40 countries in Africa, 31 countries in Asia and 31 countries in Latin America and the Caribbean.

VI. Health and mortality

The pursuit of health and longevity are among the fundamental pillars of development. Life expectancy has improved substantially in the last few decades, as attention to health concerns and reduction of infant and child mortality have increased the average length of life. Correspondingly, the percentage of Governments in developing countries that viewed their mortality level as acceptable increased from one quarter to 36 per cent between 1976 and 2005 (table 10, figure VII). However, there were still major gaps, between the more and less developed regions. During 2000-2005, life expectancy averaged 76 years in the more developed regions compared to 63 years in the less developed regions. In the least developed countries, life expectancy at birth was only 51 years (United Nations, 2005a). Due, among other things to the HIV/AIDS epidemic, the transition to low mortality stagnated or even reversed in a number of African countries. It was therefore not surprising that Governments' views of the country's mortality level differed according to development level. In 2005, two-thirds of countries in more developed regions considered the level of life expectancy to be acceptable, whereas only slightly more than one third of less developed countries did so. No least developed country viewed the mortality level as acceptable.

While 98 countries, representing 51 per cent of the world's population, met the Programme of Action goal of life expectancy at birth higher than 70 years by 2000-2005, 96 countries had life expectancies of less than 70 years. Of these countries, 50 (13 per cent of world population), mostly in sub-Saharan Africa fell far short of this benchmark (United Nations, 2005a). Life expectancy in these countries was less than 60 years of age. A number of factors explained this low level of life expectation, including military and political conflict, economic crises, socio-economic restructuring, unhealthy lifestyles, the re-emergence of diseases such as malaria, tuberculosis and cholera and the impact of the HIV/AIDS epidemic. For many low income countries, the cost of providing a minimum package of cost-effective public-health and clinical services exceeded levels of Government expenditures on health. In 2001, per capita health expenditures were US$ 75 in less developed regions and US$ 25 in the least developed countries. This compares with US$ 2,200 for more developed regions (United Nations, 2005b). Aggravating the situation in a number of countries was the lack of capacity to absorb additional resources, as well as shortages of health care providers due to inadequate salaries and emigration.

At the world level, infant and child mortality and maternal mortality were the second and third principal concerns after the HIV/AIDS epidemic. More than four fifths of countries in the less developed regions cited mortality under age 5 as a major concern; one third of countries in the more developed regions did so. While dissatisfaction with the level of infant and child mortality decreased since 1996 in the more developed regions, when just over half of the Governments considered its level as unacceptable, concern over the level of infant and child mortality remained unchanged in the less developed regions (table 11). This was because, rapid improvements observed before 1990 in child mortality in these regions gave way to a stagnation in progress during the 1990s. It was estimated that some 11 million children under 5 years of age die each year, half from preventable diseases such as acute respiratory infection, diarrhea, measles and malaria (World Bank, 2005). Lack of basic sanitation, safe water and food accounted for the high death toll among children. Lack of progress in achieving health objectives, for example those cited in the Programme of Action and the Millennium Development Goals may have been due as much to wide inequalities within countries – wealthy and poor populations, urban and rural, male and female, as to inequalities between countries.

Figure VII. Governments that view their mortality level as acceptable, less developed regions, 1976, 1986, 1996 and 2005

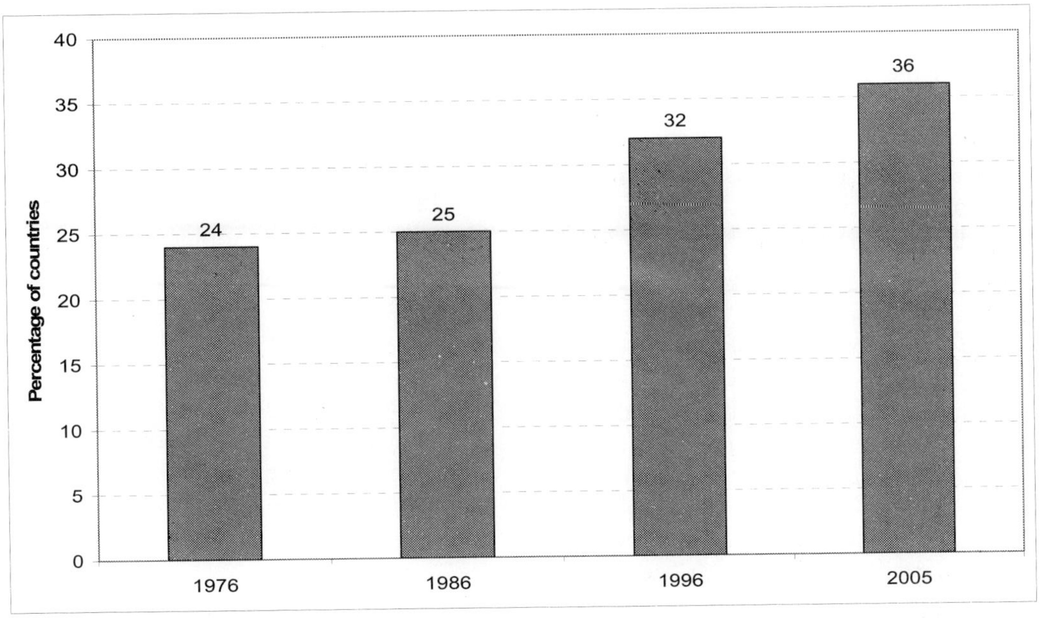

Maternal mortality was a major concern in the less developed regions. Indeed, their inclusion in the Millennium Development Goals (MDGs) heightened the awareness of Governments to the need to provide reproductive health services. Of 192 countries, 132 (69 per cent) considered the level of maternal mortality as unacceptable (table 12). The proportion of countries dissatisfied with the level of maternal mortality increased to 81 per cent in the less developed regions and 98 per cent in the least developed countries.

In contrast, among developed countries, health concerns included: the prevention of non-communicable diseases (cardiovascular disease, cancer, diabetes and respiratory disorders); unhealthy life styles (drug and tobacco use, alcohol abuse, obesity); efficiency in hospital care; cost-effective provision of primary care; disability; the costs of health and long-term care for older persons, communicable diseases and inadequate health systems in transition countries (Organization for Economic Co-operation and Development, 2004).

The AIDS epidemic was one of the greatest challenges confronting the international community. It was the most important concern stated by countries from both more and less developed regions, with 79 and 88 per cent of countries, respectively, viewing it as a major concern (table 13). With more than 25 million deaths to date and 40 million people living with HIV, the epidemic has erased decades of socio-economic progress and has had a devastating impact on population in terms of increased morbidity and mortality (UNAIDS, 2005). Furthermore, the epidemic has undermined households and families, firms, agriculture, the education and health sectors and national economies. Although Governments began formulating policies concerning HIV/AIDS by the mid-1980s, these policies were frequently fragmented and had a narrow health focus. However, in recent years, the epidemic has spawned an unprecedented array of global, regional and national responses. Governments have pursued a multi-pronged strategy to combat HIV/AIDS by focusing on a) prevention; b) care and treatment; c) protection from discrimination and stigmatization; d) development of multi-sectoral strategies; e) creation of HIV/AIDS coordination bodies and f) establishment of partnerships with civil society, people living with

HIV/AIDS, community-based groups, non-governmental organizations and the private sector (United Nations, 2004c).

Prevention is the foundation of measures to respond to HIV/AIDS and many countries introduced prevention strategies, as well as care, support and treatment programmes. Governments have raised public awareness by promoting information, education and communication (IEC) programmes through print media, theatre, radio, television and other public messages. The participation of non-governmental organizations, people living with HIV/AIDS, religious institutions and international and bilateral donors are important to ensure the success of IEC activities. Although antiretroviral treatment has significantly prolonged life and alleviated the suffering, access remained extremely low. Despite concerted international and national efforts to slash the price of these medicines, only around 1 million of the 6 million people in developing countries and countries in transition needing treatment received antiretroviral therapy as of mid-2005. While programmes to promote condom provision were widespread, supply shortages and poor quality persisted. Condom supplies were estimated to be 40 per cent below the number required (United Nations, 2005b).

By 2005, 171 of 189 countries reported having measures to screen national blood supplies for the HIV virus (table 14, figure VIII). Among the developing countries, 125 (89 per cent) reported that they had implemented blood screening measures. In the wake of the Declaration of Commitment on HIV/AIDS, an increasing number of African countries have implemented such measures bringing to 44 countries (88 per cent) the number which screened the blood supply. In Oceania, blood screening for HIV was the lowest, with only half of Governments reporting that they screened blood. However, it is important to stress that blood screening programmes differ in coverage and comprehensiveness across countries. Whereas Botswana strengthened blood screening and supported blood donation programmes among low risk groups, in India, there was mandatory testing of all blood.

In nearly all reporting countries (99 per cent), Governments have implemented information and education (IEC) campaigns on HIV/AIDS. These programmes took various forms, including news papers and other print media, theatre, radio, television, direct mailings and other public service messages. But much remains to be done to improve the effectiveness of Government strategies with respect to changes in behaviour of the population in some of the most affected countries.

The provision of antiretroviral therapy was still limited in most developing countries. Although three quarters of Governments in the less developed regions reported that they provided access to antiretroviral treatment for AIDS patients, in many of these countries, the coverage was less than 10 per cent of those who require it. For example, Zimbabwe, which has the world's fourth highest rate of HIV infection and which was experiencing a severe economic crisis, has recently seen the cost of antiretroviral therapies quadruple (IRIN News, 2005).

Governments have increasingly enacted laws to protect people affected by the HIV/AIDS epidemic. As of 2005, 63 per cent of reporting countries banned discrimination against AIDS patients. Three quarters of Governments in the more developed regions implemented such policies, whereas only 57 per cent of countries in the less developed regions had done so. In Africa, where the epidemic was most widespread, only half of countries reported that they had undertaken such measures.

Figure VIII. Distribution of countries according to the implementation of measures to control HIV/AIDS, 2005

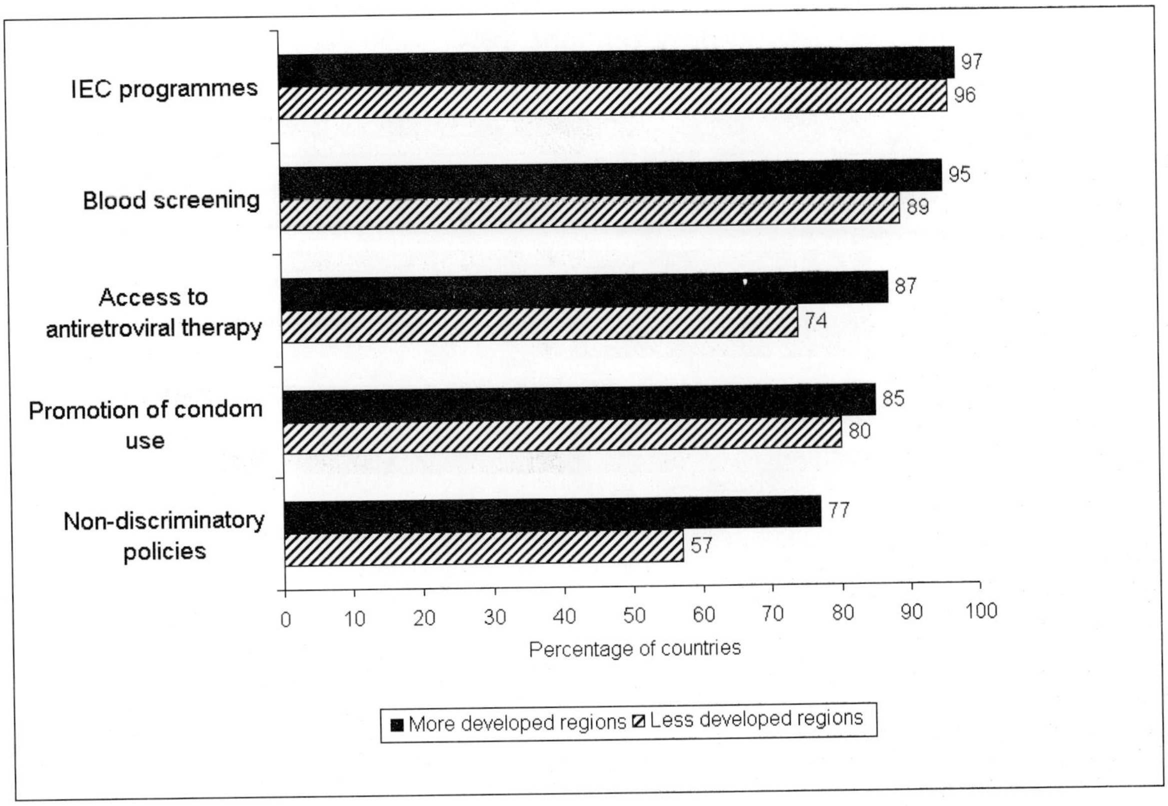

The promotion of condom use was high; 83 per cent of Governments worldwide promoted its use. In Africa, 86 per cent of Governments did so. Oceania was the region where the promotion of condoms by Governments was lowest (50 per cent).

According to the World Health Organization, some 46 million pregnancies are voluntarily terminated each year - 27 million legally and 19 million outside the legal system (World Health Organization, 2004). In a strict sense, abortion was legal in most of the world. The overwhelming majority of countries, 98 per cent, permitted abortion to save the pregnant woman's life (figure IX). In four countries, Chile, El Salvador, Holy See, and Malta abortion was not permitted. In the last quarter century, there has been a global trend towards expanding the grounds on which abortion was permitted. Between 1980 and 2005, the percentage of countries permitting abortion to save the woman's life increased from 86 to 98 per cent and from 25 to 47 per cent on grounds of rape or incest. The percentage of countries permitting abortion on request more than doubled from 11 to 28 per cent. The breadth of conditions under which abortion may legally be performed varied widely. Abortion laws and policies were significantly more restrictive in the developing world than in the developed world. In developed countries, abortion was permitted for economic or social reasons in three quarters of countries and on request in two-thirds of the countries. In contrast, one in five developing counties permitted abortion for economic or social reasons and one in seven developing countries on request. Between 2003 and 2005, eight countries (Benin, Chad, Cook Islands, Ethiopia, Jordan, the Lao People's Democratic Republic, Mali, and Swaziland) modified the grounds on which abortion was permitted. All eight developing countries expanded the grounds for permitting abortion.

Figure IX. Grounds on which abortion is permitted by level of development, 2005

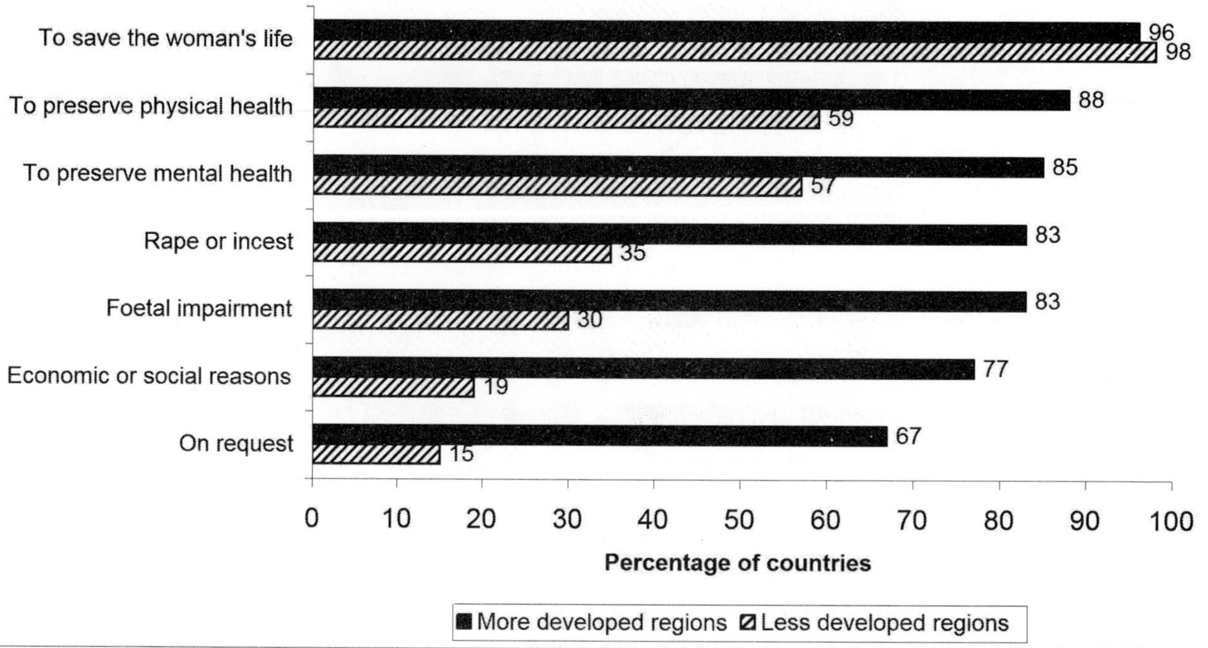

V. SPATIAL DISTRIBUTION AND INTERNAL MIGRATION

One of the major demographic trends during the latter half of the twentieth century was the rapid growth of urban agglomerations. Half of the world's population are now urban dwellers. Whereas, in 1950, only two urban agglomerations, New York and Tokyo had 10 million or more inhabitants, by 2005, 20 urban agglomerations, of which 16 were in developing countries had at least 10 million inhabitants (United Nations, 2004d). Governments have expressed concern about the pattern of spatial distribution for many years. This concern usually arose from the large movement of persons from rural to urban areas and the uncontrolled growth of primate cities and large urban agglomerations, especially in the developing countries.

After a long period (1976 to 1996) of increasing satisfaction among Governments with their spatial distribution, the recent period has been marked by a reversal in this trend. Between 1996 and 2005, the desire to modify the spatial pattern climbed from 77 per cent to 87 per cent among developing countries. Among developed countries, the increase was even greater; the proportion of developed countries which wanted a change in spatial distribution rose from 54 to 73 per cent between 1996 and 2005 (table 15, figure X).

Dissatisfaction regarding patterns of spatial distribution was highest among African Governments. Of the 53 African Governments, 38 desired major changes in their population distribution, while 13 Governments wanted minor changes. In Asia, a large majority of Governments - 39 out of 47 - expressed dissatisfaction with patterns of spatial distribution: 23 Governments desired major changes in their population distribution, whereas 16 Governments wanted minor changes.

In Latin America and the Caribbean, about 80 per cent of Governments were dissatisfied with patterns of spatial distribution: 13 Governments desired major changes in their population distribution and an equal number of Governments wanted minor changes.

Spatial distribution patterns have been remarkably resilient to change. Governments have employed an arsenal of measures since the 1970s to modify the distribution, including redirecting growth from large urban agglomerations to small and medium-sized cities, establishing sustainable rural development, undertaking land re-distribution schemes, creating regional development zones, imposing internal migration controls and moving the national capital. Most of these attempts failed to achieve their objectives.

The great majority of Governments in developing countries feared that rapid urban growth would hamper their ability to provide basic urban services such as safe drinking water, sanitation, affordable housing, public transportation and employment. There were estimated to be one billion slum-dwellers in the world (UN-Habitat, 2004).

In developed countries, which were somewhat more satisfied with the spatial distribution of their populations than the developing countries, spatial distribution policies have not been vigorously pursued. Those policies undertaken have generally focused on achieving a balanced regional development. This took the form of recognizing the interdependence between rural and urban areas, shifting from a sector or agriculture-based focus to a more integrated approach by promoting rural diversification and competitiveness, mobilizing investment (instead of distributing subsidies) and improving the living conditions of rural dwellers (OECD, 2003). Another approach to stem rural depopulation (for example, in Australia and Canada) was to encourage newly admitted immigrants to settle in rural areas experiencing labour shortages.

Figure X. Governments that view a change in the spatial distribution of the population as desired, 1976, 1986, 1996 and 2005

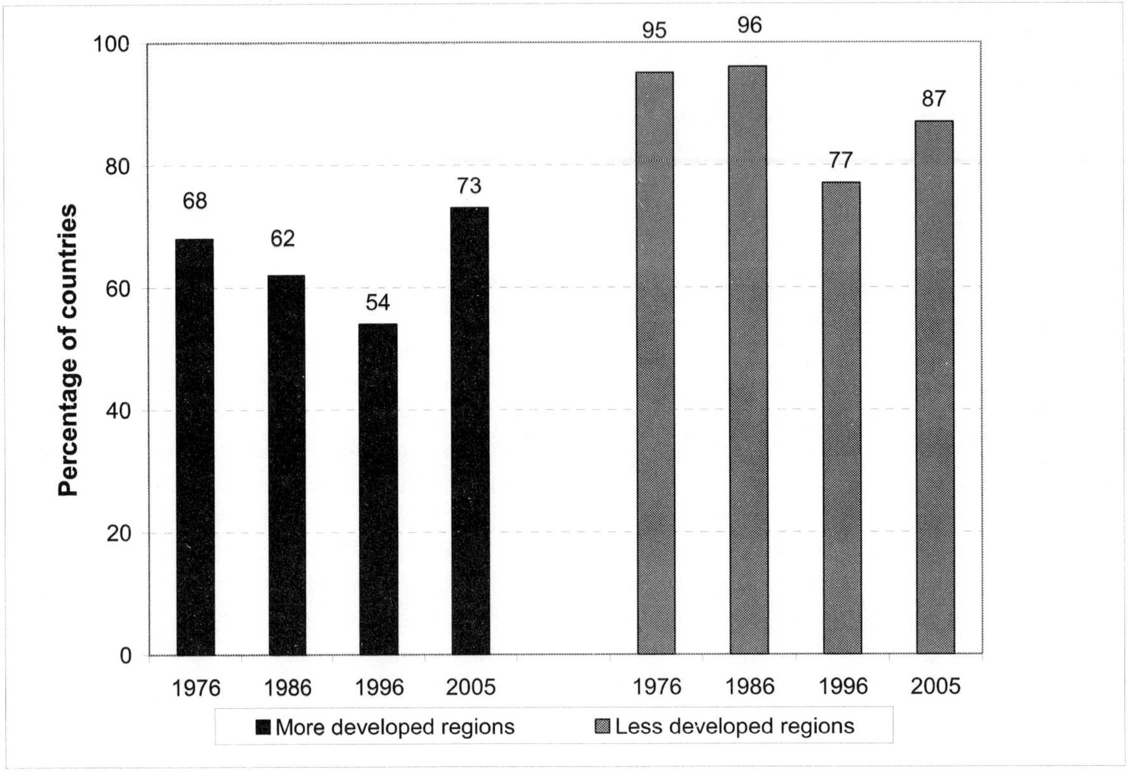

Among the 164 countries for which information on rural to urban migration policies was available, 70 per cent of countries in 2005 aimed to lower migration from rural to urban areas, while 4 per cent of countries implemented policies to raise it (table 16). While the more developed and the less developed regions were similar with respect to the proportion of countries with policies aimed at raising migration from rural to urban areas (around 2 to 4 per cent), countries in less developed regions were somewhat more likely to implement policies to lower it, with almost three of every four countries having such measures. Three of every five countries in more developed regions implemented policies to decrease this type of migration.

In many developing countries, spatial distribution policies were largely synonymous with measures to reduce or even reverse rural-urban migration, with the aim of controlling the growth of primate cities or large urban agglomerations. The previously noted upsurge after 1996, in the proportion of Governments which wanted to modify spatial distribution, was also reflected in the trend to implement policies to reduce migration to urban agglomerations. The proportion of developing countries with policies to lower migration to urban agglomeration rose from 51 per cent to in 1996 to 73 per cent in 2005. Among developed countries this trend was less apparent. The proportion of developed countries with policies to reduce migration to urban agglomerations rose slightly from 26 per cent in 1996 to 32 per cent in 2005 (table 18). In practice, policies to slow the growth of urban agglomerations were often ineffective.

In addition to slowing the growth of urban agglomerations, many Governments throughout the developing world vigourously endorsed the concept of promoting small and intermediate-sized cities. However, while there was broad consensus for such a strategy, how to pursue it was far less clear. A number of countries have promoted the development of new towns; however, the pace of development of these towns was generally slow. Similarly, a few developing countries attempted to relocate the capital. Regional development policies for lagging regions, border-region strategies and land colonization schemes were also employed in a number of developing countries, although the impact on overall population distribution was almost negligible.

VI. INTERNATIONAL MIGRATION

International migration was given a more complete and comprehensive treatment in this publication because of the importance of migration issues at this time. National and international issues related to migration such as brain drain, brain gain and brain circulation, remittances, diasporas, asylum, trafficking and undocumented movements have intersected with national concerns of low fertility and population ageing, unemployment, human rights and citizen rights, social integration, xenophobia, and national security. All together, these concerns have led to a re-examination of international migration policies and the potential benefits and disadvantages accruing to origin and destination countries.

Many Governments and intergovernmental organizations have called for greater coherence in international migration policies. However, migration policies often lacked clear objectives and were not effectively implemented. These outcomes stem from the fact that policy-makers are confronted with competing priorities from policies dealing with employment, trade, development and national security. By undertaking a systematic and forthright examination of migration policies and their outcomes, Governments may gain a better understanding of the policy options open to them.

In this regard, there have been two important recent initiatives. The first was the creation of the Global Commission on International Migration by several Governments in 2003. With a mandate to provide the framework for the formulation of a coherent, comprehensive and global response to the issue of international migration, the Commission presented its report to the Secretary-General in 2005. The report focused on issues of current concern to the international community, especially related to the economic, social, human rights, and governance dimensions of international migration. This initiative has already borne fruit. Based on a Commission proposal, the Secretary-General took action to establish a broader and more formal coordination mechanism.

The second initiative was the decision of the General Assembly, in its resolution 58/208 of 23 December 2003, to devote a high-level dialogue on international migration and development during its sixty-first session in 2006. The purpose of the dialogue was to discuss the multidimensional aspects of international migration and development in order to identify appropriate ways and means to maximize its development benefits and minimize its negative impacts.

When the United Nations began monitoring Government views and policies on population in 1976, international migration was not a topic of major concern for most Governments. However, substantial changes in Government perceptions of migration trends and migration policies took place beginning late in the 1970s, as Governments' concerns with the demographic, economic, social and political consequences of migration grew. While in 1976, only 7 per cent of Governments aimed to lower immigration levels, the proportion of countries which expressed that policy goal increased to around one in five countries by the mid-1980s and to 40 per cent by the mid-1990s. However, since the late 1990s, a number of Governments have moved away from policies to restrict migration by focusing on the better management of migration flows. Consequently, the proportion of countries wishing to lower immigration fell to 22 per cent in 2005 (table 20, figure XI).

Since the mid-1990s, major changes were observed in international migration policies. Most significantly, Governments have become increasingly likely to maintain the level of immigration and less inclined to restrict it. As of 2005, 22 per cent of countries wanted to lower immigration, down from 40 per cent in 1996. At the same time, there was an upturn in the proportion of countries seeking to maintain (or to not intervene) the prevailing level of immigration from 55 per cent in 1996 to 72 per cent in 2005. For the most part, those countries not intervening with respect to immigration were countries in Africa with negative migration balances and often borders which were difficult to supervise. The proportion of countries aiming to raise the immigration levels remained unchanged at around 5 per cent.

Of the 78 countries which in 1996 wanted to lower immigration, 35 wanted to maintain the current level of immigration, 7 reported no intervention and 5 countries aimed to increase the level in 2005. The remaining 31 countries continued to pursue the goal of lower immigration in 2005.

This shift away from restricting immigration was attributable to a number of factors, including an improved understanding of the consequences of international migration; the growing recognition on the part of Governments for the need to better manage migration, rather than limit it; the smaller than anticipated emigration from the former Union of Soviet Socialist Republics and Eastern Europe in the wake of the political changes of the early 1990s; the persistence of labour shortages in certain sectors; regional harmonization of migration policies; an expanding global economy and long-term trends in population ageing.

The trend toward less restrictive immigration was even more pronounced among developed countries, where the percentage of countries with policies to lower immigration fell from 60 per cent in 1996 to 12 per cent by 2005. Only six developed countries wanted to reduce overall immigration; Denmark, Estonia, France, Italy, the Netherlands and Romania. Despite the goal of lower overall immigration, three of the countries, Denmark, France and the Netherlands hoped to increase the migration of skilled workers, while Italy promoted the migration of workers on a temporary basis. Four developed countries, namely Australia, Canada, the Czech Republic and the Russian Federation, actively promoted immigration with the aim of increasing overall immigration in line with national needs.

Figure XI. Government policies on immigration, 1976, 1986, 1996, 2003 and 2005

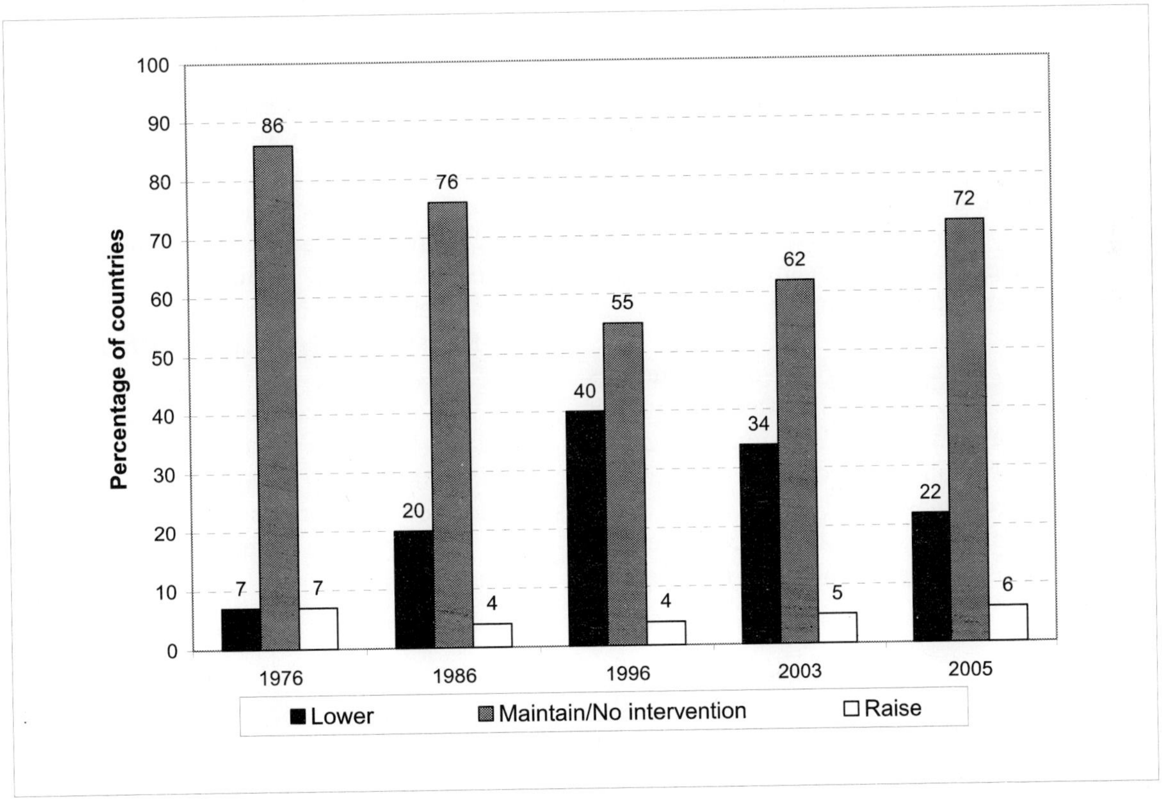

In the less developed regions, the proportion of countries with policies to lower immigration also declined, from one third of countries in 1996 to one quarter in 2005. In Latin America and the Caribbean, only four countries wanted to restrict migration - Bahamas, Belize, Ecuador and Panama. In Asia, the continent with the highest proportion of countries reporting policies to lower immigration, the shift in migration policies was very recent. While one in two Asian countries aimed at lower immigration in 2003, one in three countries wanted lower immigration in 2005.

With the advent of less costly and more rapid forms of transport, countries became more diverse with respect to immigration policies, and in particular, to the length of stay of migrants. At the world level, half of the 153 reporting countries desired to maintain the current level of migration for permanent settlement, while one quarter of countries wanted to lower it (table 21). In more developed regions, two-thirds of countries aimed at maintaining the level of permanent settlement, and another one-fifth had policies to lower migration for permanent settlement. One of ten countries in the developed regions aimed to increase permanent settlement. In contrast, countries in the less developed regions were somewhat more likely to have policies to lower permanent settlement (one quarter). Another quarter of countries in less developed regions did not intervene with respect to permanent settlement, while 6 per cent of countries in these regions had policies to raise migration for permanent settlement. The remaining 43 per cent of countries wished to maintain the level.

Migration policy in receiving countries reflected an evolution towards greater selectiveness, favouring the admission of migrants who met specific labour needs such as those in science and technology and those with skills considered in short supply. Some 30 countries out of 134 countries with available information, had policies in place promoting the migration of highly skilled workers in 2005. While more than 40 per cent of developed countries aimed to increase the immigration of the highly skilled, only 14 per cent of developing countries pursued such a strategy (table 22, figure XII).

By either preferential categories as in the United States, or point systems in Australia and Canada, traditional countries of immigration enacted legislation placing greater emphasis on migrant skills. By the early 1990s, point systems to recruit highly skilled workers were also in place in Europe (for example, the Czech Republic and the United Kingdom). The selection of immigrants based on skills had a significant impact on the origin and nature of overall migration flows. For instance, under the preference system, new migrants to the United States were more likely to come from Asia and Europe, while in Australia and Canada, the numerical weight attached to education, training, occupation and language skills reduced the proportion of immigrants dependent on family relationship.

Labour migration has become increasingly complex, as the skills that migrants possess to a large extent determined the likelihood of their being admitted in receiving countries. Many host countries amended their legislation in the late 1990s to facilitate the entry of skilled foreign workers and launched specific recruitment programmes. In addition to immigration policy measures, some countries provided fiscal incentives for highly skilled migrants – income-tax-free status or large tax deductions.

Only five countries (Bhutan, Botswana, Jordan, Saudi Arabia and the United Arab Emirates) wanted to reduce the entry of highly skilled foreign workers in 2005, the aim of which was to improve employment prospects for nationals.

Figure XII. Government policies on the migration of highly skilled workers, 2005

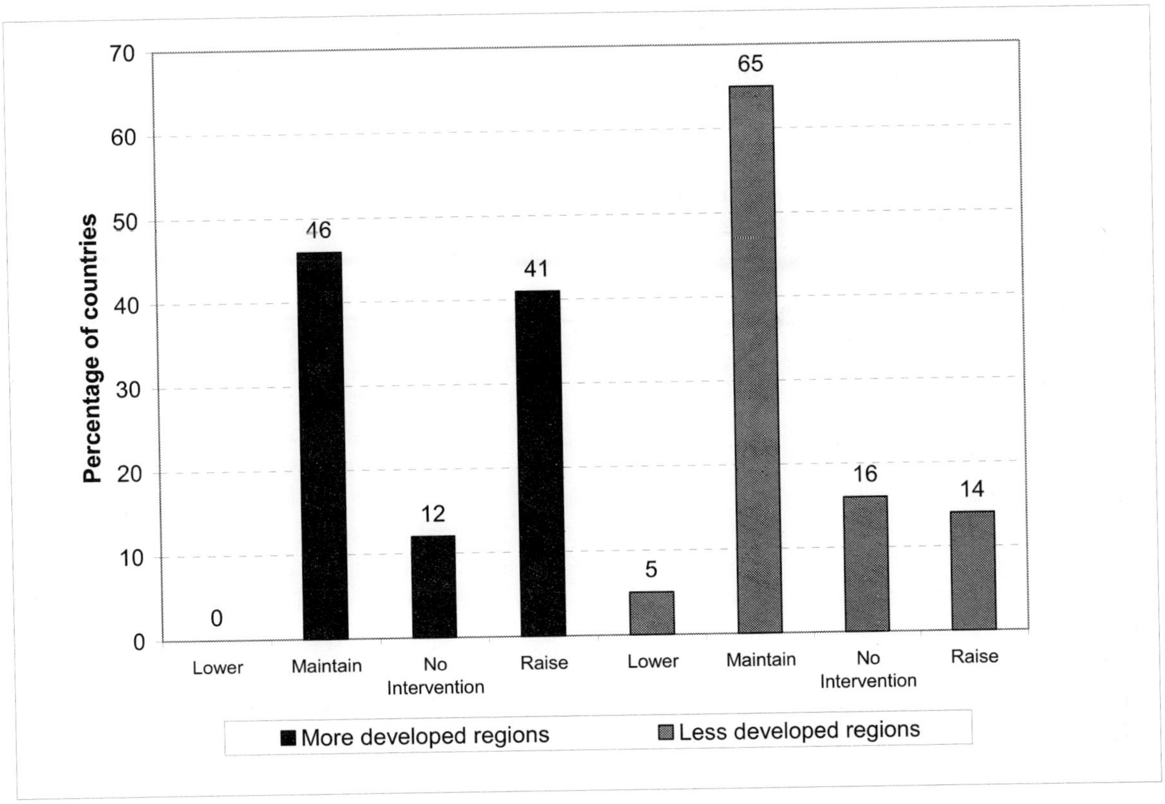

Although countries of destination have emphasized the need to attract highly skilled workers, population ageing and rising job expectations also produced labour shortages in low-skilled sectors such as agriculture, construction and domestic services. Demand for low-skilled labour was generally filled on a temporary basis. Several receiving countries established specific annual quotas and signed bilateral agreements with countries of origin. These bilateral agreements usually covered seasonal workers, contract and project-linked workers, guest workers and cross-border workers. Many of these workers migrate on the basis of temporary labour contracts and were generally admitted in host countries for a fixed period without an expectation of obtaining permanent residence status. In 2005, 11 per cent of the reporting Governments in the more developed regions had policies to increase the number of temporary workers, whereas 4 per cent of countries in the less developed regions adopted such policies (table 23). In addition, 31 per cent of the reporting Governments in the less developed regions aimed to lower the number of temporary workers, compared to 17 per cent of reporting Governments in more developed regions.

Most countries of destination have some basic provision for family reunification, which allowed individuals to join family members already in the country. At the same time, family reunification was not universally accepted. Many contract labour arrangements precluded admission of family members. In a number of labour-importing countries, debate focused on the cost of providing migrants' dependants with health, education and welfare benefits.

Since the 1980s, family reunification has been the major basis for immigration in a significant number of countries, particularly in Europe. Most migrants to Canada, Denmark, France, Norway, Sweden and the United States were admitted on family reunification grounds. High levels of migration for family reunification was a contentious issue in many European countries. In recent years, several European countries sought to limit entry by family members, for example, Denmark, France, Italy, and Ireland. While family reunification ensures the integrity of the family unit, it is a type of migration that is difficult to manage. It is open to potential abuse through sham marriages that use family reunification provisions as a means of trafficking. Such abuses led some countries to tighten requirements for the immigration of spouses, for instance by raising the minimum age requirement for reunification of spouses or granting permanent status to the immigrant spouse only after a specified period and proven successful integration.

Of the 135 countries for which information on immigration for family reunification was available in 2005, 12 per cent aimed to lower immigration for this purpose, 62 per cent to maintain it, and 5 per cent implemented policies to raise it (table 24). Twenty-one per cent did not intervene with respect to family reunification. While the more developed regions and the less developed regions were similar with respect to the proportion of countries in each group with policies aimed at reducing migration for family reunification (around 12 per cent), countries in more developed regions were somewhat more likely to implement policies to increase family reunification, with almost 1 of 10 countries having such measures. Only 3 per cent of countries in less developed regions implemented policies to increase this type of migration.

Destination countries increasingly adopted policies that focused on the integration of migrants. In 2005, 75 countries reported programmes to integrate non-nationals, up from 52 countries in 1996 (table 25). Integration policies were found in 37 developed countries and 38 developing countries. While assimilation has been the accepted means of integration, many developed countries recognized and promoted the benefits that diversity brings to their society. To ensure that minimal human rights standards were respected, many countries adopted non-discrimination provisions to protect religious freedom and the use of other languages. Many developed countries undertook initiatives to make it easier for migrants to become a part of society – in particular through language training and courses to inform immigrants on the life and culture of the country. These integration policies were based on the principle of offering more support for integration efforts, while making requirements for successful integration stricter. The integration process has not always been smooth, particularly in countries where the foreign-born were more prone to unemployment than nationals, thus leading to welfare dependency. To improve migrants' access to labour markets, some countries introduced education and employment training programmes.

In most countries, non-nationals did not enjoy the same basic rights as were enjoyed by citizens; thus preventing them from participating fully in the civil and political life of the country in which they lived. Only upon being granted citizenship, do migrants fully share the same responsibilities and enjoy the same privileges as nationals. Many Governments have historically not regarded themselves as countries of permanent immigration and thus have not encouraged non-nationals to obtain permanent residence and eventual citizenship. In some countries, citizenship laws may disadvantage migrant women, as well as women marrying non-nationals (United Nations, 2004a). A growing number of countries – both of destination and origin – offered dual citizenship. Such provisions reflected migrants' dual loyalties, and enabled origin countries to benefit from their diaspora. Some countries modified the legal provisions with respect to granting citizenship to immigrant children, so as to enable them to hold the citizenship of both their parents' country and their birth country.

With respect to emigration, despite the significant increase in the number of migrants, the proportion of countries in less developed regions which wanted to lower emigration has remained at about one quarter since the 1980s (table 27, figure XIII). A number of countries, both in more and less developed regions, were concerned by the level of emigration, especially of highly skilled workers. In contrast, 11 countries – 9 of which were in Asia - had policies to increase emigration. These were countries with young population age structures, high unemployment, particularly of young people, and a tradition of emigration. Several countries established Government units to manage emigration flows, or entered into bilateral agreements with receiving States to ensure minimum labour standards (for example, the Philippines, Thailand and Vietnam).

A sharp rise in the emigration of skilled workers prompted some countries to address the challenges posed by the brain drain through initiatives to encourage the return of skilled workers living abroad. Overall, 72 countries had policies and programmes in place in 2005 to encourage their nationals to return, up from 59 countries in 1996. Of the countries that promoted the return of their nationals, 59 were developing countries (table 28).

Emigration created both opportunities and difficulties for developing countries. Concerns have often been raised about the loss of highly skilled human resources that may hinder the development process. The provision of medical care in Africa has been particularly hard-hit, as a result of the emigration of significant numbers of health care providers. On the other hand, for many countries of origin, remittances played an important role in sustaining national and local economies. A number of Governments undertook initiatives to facilitate remittance transfers, as well as to maximize the positive impact of remittances on development. Technologies of communication and transportation have facilitated active contacts between emigrants and their countries of origin. The potential positive impact on the home country through the transfer of knowledge and technology, as well as through investments and trade was widely recognized. Governments, therefore, increasingly encouraged diasporas to invest in their countries of origin and to participate in transnational knowledge networks.

Figure XIII. Governments with policies to lower emigration, 1976, 1986, 1996 and 2005

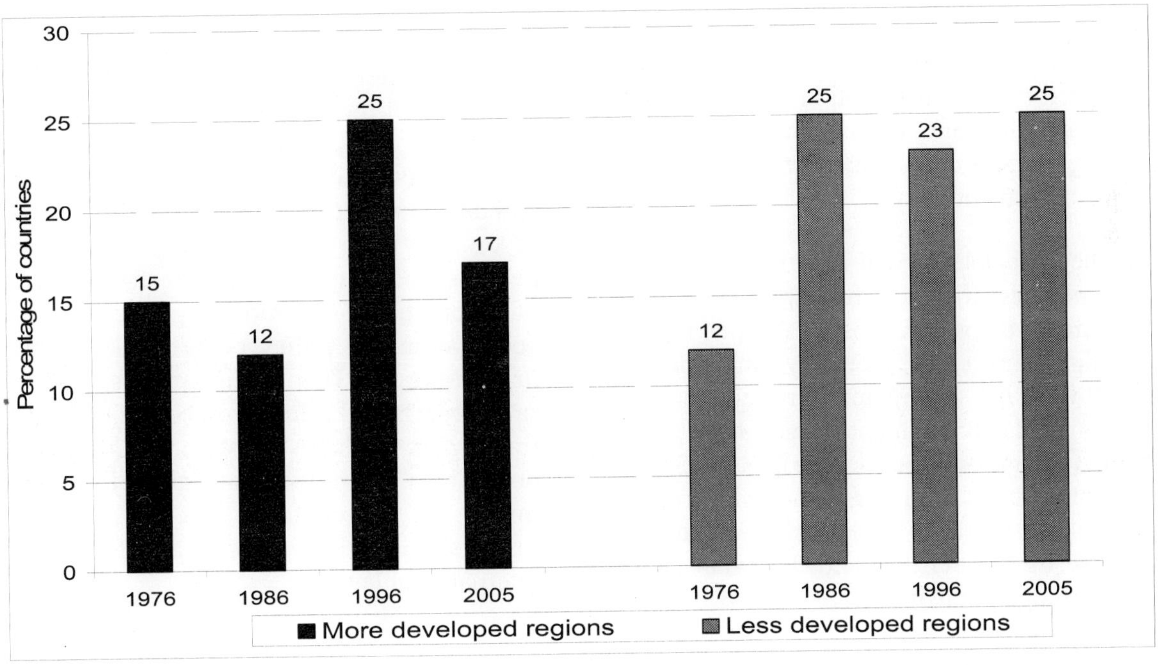

VII. SUMMARY AND CONCLUSIONS

World Population Policies 2005 tracks the evolution of Governments views and policies on population and development that has taken place since the convening of the World Population Conference in 1974. The major conclusion of this study is that Governments have become increasingly concerned with the consequences of population trends. Furthermore, Governments are more inclined to view population as a legitimate area of Government action and to act upon these concerns by formulating and implementing policies which address these issues.

Population policies and programmes in many countries have been reoriented towards the Programme of Action of the 1994 International Conference on Population and Development, the goals of the ICPD + 5 year review undertaken in 1999 and the ICPD + 10 year review undertaken in 2004, as well as the series of regional conferences and reviews held in the wake of the ICPD. For example, in the area of family planning, policies focusing on women of reproductive age have given way to a life-cycle oriented reproductive health approach encompassing both sexes. Targets to reduce the unmet need for contraception have replaced fertility reduction and contraceptive-use targets. Improving method choice and the quality of care have also become priorities.

At the global level, the HIV/AIDS epidemic was the most significant demographic issue in the world. Among the world's less developed regions, high infant and child mortality and maternal mortality were the second and third most pressing population and development issues. In the more developed regions, besides HIV/AIDS, the demographic issues of greatest concern were those related to low fertility (population ageing, the persistence of low fertility and the small size of the working-age population).

In the less developed regions and especially in Africa, an increasing number of Governments felt that both population growth and fertility were too high and implemented measures to lower them.

As regards international migration, countries of destination increasingly recognized the need and benefits of international migration and adopted policies and measures to tailor migration to national needs. Fewer countries aimed at lower immigration, while a growing number of countries promoted the migration of skilled workers. In the longer term, immigration is likely to grow, given long-term trends in declining fertility and population ageing, even if in the short term, reversals in immigration policies take place in response to immediate political considerations. Despite the increased volume of migration, the proportion of countries which sought to lower emigration has remained at about one in four since the mid-1980s. At the same time, countries have become more inclined to encourage the return of nationals living abroad, to create links with their diasporas and to harness the positive impact of migration on development and poverty reduction in the countries of origin. As the migration and development discourse gains momentum, policies concerning emigrants will be an important issue, especially for countries of origin.

Since the adoption of the Programme of Action of the International Conference on Population and Development, there has been growing recognition that international migration and development were inexorably linked and were of key relevance to the global agenda. To reap the benefits and minimize the adverse consequences of international migration, greater international cooperation and policy coherence are considered to be essential. This requires the establishment of safe, orderly and rule-governed migration within a framework where States understand their obligations and protect the rights of migrants, and migrants recognize their rights and responsibilities, as well as respect for national and international laws.

Adopting a population policy, however, was only the initial step in ensuring the achievement of population and development objectives. Other essential elements included the implementation of appropriate programmes, sufficient political commitment and adequate financial resources. Respect for traditional cultural values, partnerships with non-governmental organizations, civil society, the business community and international donors, good governance and the maintenance of peace and security were also crucial.

REFERENCES

European Union (2005). Results available from http://www.europarl.eu.int/press/Eurobarometer/index_en.htm.

Organization for Economic Co-operation and Development (2003). The Future of Rural Policy: From Sectoral to Place-based Policies in Rural Areas. OECD Publications, Paris: OECD.

______ (2004). Towards High-Performing Health Systems. Paris: Organization for Economic Cooperation and Development.

Ross, John, and William L. Winfrey (2002). Unmet need for contraception in the developing world and the former Soviet Union: an updated estimate. International Family Planning Perspectives, Vol. 28, No. 3, September.

United Nations (1972). Measures, Policies and Programmes Affecting Fertility, with Particular Reference to National Family Planning Programmes. Population Studies No. 51, United Nations Publication, Sales No. E.72.XIII.3.

______ (1995). *Population Consensus at Cairo, Mexico City and Bucharest: An Analytical Comparison.* United Nations publication, Sales No. E.96.XIII.2.

______ (2004a). 2004 World Survey on the Role of Women in Development: Women and Migration. Sales No. E.04.IV.4.

______ (2004b). *Review and Appraisal of the Progress Made in Achieving the Goals and Objectives of the Programme of Action of the International Conference on Population and Development. The 2004 Report.* United Nations publication, Sales No. E.04.XIII.8.

______ (2004c). *The Impact of AIDS.* United Nations publication, Sales No. E.04.XIII.7.

______ (2004d). World Urbanization Prospects. The 2003 Revision. United Nations publication, Sales No. E.04.XIII.6.

______ (2005a). World Population Prospects: The 2004 Revision. United Nations publication, Sales No. E.05.XIII.5.

______ (2005b). *Population and HIV/AIDS 2005.* Wall chart. ST/ESA/SER/A/241. United Nations publication, Sales No. E.05.XIII.2.

United Nations, Economic Commission for Africa (2004). *ICPD + 10 Anniversary: Africa Regional Review Report*, Addis Ababa, Ethiopia, Available from: http://www.uneca.org/popia/ ICPD+10/doc/Implementationtarget_Eng_Final.pdf (accessed 29 November 2005).

United Nations, Economic Commission for Europe (2002). *Economic Survey of Europe, 2002, No. 1.* United Nations, New York and Geneva.

United Nations Human Settlements Programme (2004). State of the World's Cities 2004/2005 – Globalization and Urban Culture. UN-HABITAT, ISBN No. 92-1-131705-3.

United Nations Integrated Regional Information Network (IRIN News) (2005), ZIMBABWE: ARV price hikes a concern for people living with HIV/AIDS, 24 October 2005, Available from: http://www.irinnews.org/AIDSreport.asp?ReportID=5361 (accessed 17 November 2005).

United Nations, Joint United Nations Programme on HIV/AIDS (2005). AIDS Epidemic Update, December 2005. UNAIDS/05.19E. Geneva.

World Bank (2005). *World Development Indicators 2005.* Washington D.C.

World Health Organization (2004). Unsafe abortion. *Global and regional estimates of the incidence of unsafe abortion and associated mortality in 2000.* Fourth edition. Geneva.

TABLES

1 - 28

TABLE 1. GOVERNMENT VIEWS ON THE RATE OF POPULATION GROWTH: 1976, 1986, 1996 AND 2005

A. By level of development

Year	(Number of countries)				(Percentage)			
	Too low	Satisfactory	Too high	Total	Too low	Satisfactory	Too high	Total
					World			
1976	34	67	49	150	23	45	33	100
1986	26	73	65	164	16	45	40	100
1996	31	83	79	193	16	43	41	100
2005	37	81	76	194	19	42	39	100
					More developed regions			
1976	11	22	1	34	32	65	3	100
1986	6	28	0	34	18	82	0	100
1996	13	34	1	48	27	71	2	100
2005	21	27	0	48	44	56	0	100
					Less developed regions			
1976	23	45	48	116	20	39	41	100
1986	20	45	65	130	15	35	50	100
1996	18	49	78	145	12	34	54	100
2005	16	54	76	146	11	37	52	100
					Least developed countries			
1976	6	25	11	42	14	60	26	100
1986	4	20	24	48	8	42	50	100
1996	2	11	36	49	4	22	73	100
2005	0	10	40	50	0	20	80	100

TABLE 1. (CONTINUED)

B. By major area

Year	(Number of countries) Too low	Satisfactory	Too high	Total	(Percentage) Too low	Satisfactory	Too high	Total
Africa								
1976	7	24	17	48	15	50	35	100
1986	3	18	30	51	6	35	59	100
1996	1	13	39	53	2	25	74	100
2005	1	14	38	53	2	26	72	100
Asia								
1976	11	12	14	37	30	32	38	100
1986	13	13	12	38	34	34	32	100
1996	11	16	19	46	24	35	41	100
2005	12	15	20	47	26	32	43	100
Europe								
1976	11	18	0	29	38	62	0	100
1986	6	23	0	29	21	79	0	100
1996	13	29	1	43	30	67	2	100
2005	20	23	0	43	47	53	0	100
Latin America and the Caribbean								
1976	4	10	13	27	15	37	48	100
1986	3	14	16	33	9	42	48	100
1996	2	18	13	33	6	55	39	100
2005	1	23	9	33	3	70	27	100
Northern America								
1976	0	2	0	2	0	100	0	100
1986	0	2	0	2	0	100	0	100
1996	0	2	0	2	0	100	0	100
2005	0	2	0	2	0	100	0	100
Oceania								
1976	1	1	5	7	14	14	71	100
1986	1	3	7	11	9	27	64	100
1996	4	5	7	16	25	31	44	100
2005	3	4	9	16	19	25	56	100

TABLE 2. GOVERNMENT POLICIES ON THE RATE OF POPULATION GROWTH: 1976, 1986, 1996 AND 2005

A. By level of development

Year	Raise (Number of countries)	Maintain (Number of countries)	Lower (Number of countries)	No intervention (Number of countries)	Total (Number of countries)	Raise (Percentage)	Maintain (Percentage)	Lower (Percentage)	No intervention (Percentage)	Total (Percentage)
World										
1976	28	0	39	83	150	19	0	26	55	100
1986	26	12	53	73	164	16	7	32	45	100
1996	25	16	71	81	193	13	8	37	42	100
2005	29	32	70	63	194	15	16	36	32	100
More developed regions										
1976	8	0	0	26	34	24	0	0	76	100
1986	8	8	0	18	34	24	24	0	53	100
1996	11	6	1	30	48	23	12	2	62	100
2005	17	8	0	23	48	35	17	0	48	100
Less developed regions										
1976	20	0	39	57	116	17	0	34	49	100
1986	18	4	53	55	130	14	3	41	42	100
1996	14	10	70	51	145	10	7	48	35	100
2005	12	24	70	40	146	8	16	48	27	100
Least developed countries										
1976	5	0	6	31	42	12	0	14	74	100
1986	4	3	14	27	48	8	6	29	56	100
1996	1	1	27	20	49	2	2	55	41	100
2005	0	4	35	11	50	0	8	70	22	100

TABLE 2. (CONTINUED)

B. By major area

Year	(Number of countries)					(Percentage)				
	Raise	Maintain	Lower	No intervention	Total	Raise	Maintain	Lower	No intervention	Total
					Africa					
1976	7	0	12	29	48	15	0	25	60	100
1986	4	3	20	24	51	8	6	39	47	100
1996	2	2	32	17	53	4	4	60	32	100
2005	1	6	35	11	53	2	11	66	21	100
					Asia					
1976	9	0	14	14	37	24	0	38	38	100
1986	13	1	12	12	38	34	3	32	32	100
1996	8	5	18	15	46	17	11	39	33	100
2005	10	12	19	6	47	21	26	40	13	100
					Europe					
1976	8	0	0	21	29	28	0	0	72	100
1986	8	6	0	15	29	28	21	0	52	100
1996	11	6	1	25	43	26	14	2	58	100
2005	16	8	0	19	43	37	19	0	44	100
					Latin America and the Caribbean					
1976	3	0	9	15	27	11	0	33	56	100
1986	0	0	15	18	33	0	0	45	55	100
1996	1	2	13	17	33	3	6	39	52	100
2005	0	5	8	20	33	0	15	24	61	100
					Northern America					
1976	0	0	0	2	2	0	0	0	100	100
1986	0	1	0	1	2	0	50	0	50	100
1996	0	0	0	2	2	0	0	0	100	100
2005	0	0	0	2	2	0	0	0	100	100
					Oceania					
1976	1	0	4	2	7	14	0	57	29	100
1986	1	1	6	3	11	9	9	55	27	100
1996	3	1	7	5	16	19	6	44	31	100
2005	2	1	8	5	16	12	6	50	31	100

TABLE 3. GOVERNMENT LEVEL OF CONCERN ABOUT THE AGEING OF THE POPULATION, 2005

(Number of countries)				(Percentage)			
Major concern	*Minor concern*	*Not a concern*	*Total*	*Major concern*	*Minor concern*	*Not a concern*	*Total*
A. By level of development							
World							
85	79	1	165	52	48	1	100
More developed regions							
34	11	0	45	76	24	0	100
Less developed regions							
51	68	1	120	42	57	1	100
Least developed countries							
9	25	1	35	26	71	3	100
B. By major area							
Africa							
15	27	1	43	35	63	2	100
Asia							
16	25	0	41	39	61	0	100
Europe							
30	10	0	40	75	25	0	100
Latin America and the Caribbean							
21	12	0	33	64	36	0	100
Northern America							
2	0	0	2	100	0	0	100
Oceania							
1	5	0	6	17	83	0	100

TABLE 4. GOVERNMENT LEVEL OF CONCERN ABOUT THE SIZE OF THE WORKING-AGE POPULATION, 2005

(Number of countries)				(Percentage)			
Major concern	*Minor concern*	*Not a concern*	*Total*	*Major concern*	*Minor concern*	*Not a concern*	*Total*
A. By level of development							
World							
102	40	12	154	66	26	8	100
More developed regions							
25	14	5	44	57	32	11	100
Less developed regions							
77	26	7	110	70	24	6	100
Least developed countries							
28	3	0	31	90	10	0	100
B. By major area							
Africa							
28	6	0	34	82	18	0	100
Asia							
31	9	1	41	76	22	2	100
Europe							
21	14	4	39	54	36	10	100
Latin America and the Caribbean							
12	10	6	28	43	36	21	100
Northern America							
2	0	0	2	100	0	0	100
Oceania							
8	1	1	10	80	10	10	100

TABLE 5. GOVERNMENT VIEWS ON THE LEVEL OF FERTILITY: 1976, 1986, 1996 AND 2005

A. By level of development

Year	(Number of countries)				(Percentage)			
	Too low	*Satisfactory*	*Too high*	*Total*	*Too low*	*Satisfactory*	*Too high*	*Total*
				World				
1976	16	79	55	150	11	53	37	100
1986	22	75	67	164	13	46	41	100
1996	28	78	87	193	15	40	45	100
2005	46	69	79	194	24	36	41	100
				More developed regions				
1976	7	27	0	34	21	79	0	100
1986	9	25	0	34	26	74	0	100
1996	19	28	1	48	40	58	2	100
2005	31	17	0	48	65	35	0	100
				Less developed regions				
1976	9	52	55	116	8	45	47	100
1986	13	50	67	130	10	38	52	100
1996	9	50	86	145	6	34	59	100
2005	15	52	79	146	10	36	54	100
				Least developed countries				
1976	3	26	13	42	7	62	31	100
1986	2	20	26	48	4	42	54	100
1996	0	11	38	49	0	22	78	100
2005	0	6	44	50	0	12	88	100

TABLE 5. (CONTINUED)

B. By major area

Year	Too low (Number of countries)	Satisfactory (Number of countries)	Too high (Number of countries)	Total (Number of countries)	Too low (Percentage)	Satisfactory (Percentage)	Too high (Percentage)	Total (Percentage)
				Africa				
1976	5	25	18	48	10	52	38	100
1986	3	17	31	51	6	33	61	100
1996	1	11	41	53	2	21	77	100
2005	1	12	40	53	2	23	75	100
				Asia				
1976	2	18	17	37	5	49	46	100
1986	7	17	14	38	18	45	37	100
1996	7	20	19	46	15	43	41	100
2005	11	17	19	47	23	36	40	100
				Europe				
1976	7	22	0	29	24	76	0	100
1986	9	20	0	29	31	69	0	100
1996	18	24	1	43	42	56	2	100
2005	28	15	0	43	65	35	0	100
				Latin America and the Caribbean				
1976	2	9	16	27	7	33	59	100
1986	3	15	15	33	9	45	45	100
1996	1	14	18	33	3	42	55	100
2005	2	19	12	33	6	58	36	100
				Northern America				
1976	0	2	0	2	0	100	0	100
1986	0	2	0	2	0	100	0	100
1996	0	2	0	2	0	100	0	100
2005	1	1	0	2	50	50	0	100
				Oceania				
1976	0	3	4	7	0	43	57	100
1986	0	4	7	11	0	36	64	100
1996	1	7	8	16	6	44	50	100
2005	3	5	8	16	19	31	50	100

TABLE 6. GOVERNMENT POLICIES ON THE LEVEL OF FERTILITY: 1976, 1986, 1996 AND 2005

A. By level of development

Year	(Number of countries)					(Percentage)				
	Raise	Maintain	Lower	No intervention	Total	Raise	Maintain	Lower	No intervention	Total
					World					
1976	13	19	40	78	150	9	13	27	52	100
1986	19	16	54	75	164	12	10	33	46	100
1996	27	19	82	65	193	14	10	42	34	100
2005	38	31	78	47	194	20	16	40	24	100
					More developed regions					
1976	7	7	0	20	34	21	21	0	59	100
1986	8	6	0	20	34	24	18	0	59	100
1996	16	4	1	27	48	33	8	2	56	100
2005	24	8	0	16	48	50	17	0	33	100
					Less developed regions					
1976	6	12	40	58	116	5	10	34	50	100
1986	11	10	54	55	130	8	8	42	42	100
1996	11	15	81	38	145	8	10	56	26	100
2005	14	23	78	31	146	10	16	53	21	100
					Least developed countries					
1976	1	2	6	33	42	2	5	14	79	100
1986	2	4	15	27	48	4	8	31	56	100
1996	0	3	32	14	49	0	6	65	29	100
2005	0	3	38	9	50	0	6	76	18	100

TABLE 6. (CONTINUED)

Year	Raise	Maintain	Lower	No intervention	Total	Raise	Maintain	Lower	No intervention	Total
	(Number of countries)					*(Percentage)*				
B. By major area										
Africa										
1976	2	2	12	32	48	4	4	25	67	100
1986	3	3	21	24	51	6	6	41	47	100
1996	2	3	36	12	53	4	6	68	23	100
2005	1	4	39	9	53	2	8	74	17	100
Asia										
1976	2	9	14	12	37	5	24	38	32	100
1986	8	6	13	11	38	21	16	34	29	100
1996	7	9	19	11	46	15	20	41	24	100
2005	11	12	17	7	47	23	26	36	15	100
Europe										
1976	7	7	0	15	29	24	24	0	52	100
1986	8	6	0	15	29	28	21	0	52	100
1996	16	4	1	22	43	37	9	2	51	100
2005	22	7	0	14	43	51	16	0	33	100
Latin America and the Caribbean										
1976	2	0	10	15	27	7	0	37	56	100
1986	0	0	15	18	33	0	0	45	55	100
1996	1	0	18	14	33	3	0	55	42	100
2005	1	5	13	14	33	3	15	39	42	100
Northern America										
1976	0	0	0	2	2	0	0	0	100	100
1986	0	0	0	2	2	0	0	0	100	100
1996	0	0	0	2	2	0	0	0	100	100
2005	0	0	0	2	2	0	0	0	100	100
Oceania										
1976	0	1	4	2	7	0	14	57	29	100
1986	0	1	5	5	11	0	9	45	45	100
1996	1	3	8	4	16	6	19	50	25	100
2005	3	3	9	1	16	19	19	56	6	100

TABLE 7. GOVERNMENT POLICIES ON PROVIDING ACCESS TO CONTRACEPTIVE METHODS: 1976, 1986, 1996 AND 2005

A. By level of development

Year	(Number of countries)					(Percentage)				
	Limits	No support	Indirect support	Direct support	Total	Limits	No support	Indirect support	Direct support	Total
					World					
1976	10	28	17	95	150	7	19	11	63	100
1986	7	18	22	117	164	4	11	13	71	100
1996	2	26	18	143	189	1	14	10	76	100
2005	1	15	35	143	194	1	8	18	74	100
					More developed regions					
1976	3	4	6	21	34	9	12	18	62	100
1986	3	4	8	19	34	9	12	24	56	100
1996	1	12	7	28	48	2	25	15	58	100
2005	1	9	20	18	48	2	19	42	38	100
					Less developed regions					
1976	7	24	11	74	116	6	21	9	64	100
1986	4	14	14	98	130	3	11	11	75	100
1996	1	14	11	115	141	1	10	8	82	100
2005	0	6	15	125	146	0	4	10	86	100
					Least developed countries					
1976	4	14	6	18	42	10	33	14	43	100
1986	2	4	7	35	48	4	8	15	73	100
1996	0	3	3	42	48	0	6	6	88	100
2005	0	2	5	43	50	0	4	10	86	100

TABLE 7. (CONTINUED)

B. By major area

Year	(Number of countries) Limits	No support	Indirect support	Direct support	Total	(Percentage) Limits	No support	Indirect support	Direct support	Total
Africa										
1976	3	14	7	24	48	6	29	15	50	100
1986	0	7	6	38	51	0	14	12	75	100
1996	0	4	5	43	52	0	8	10	83	100
2005	0	3	6	44	53	0	6	11	83	100
Asia										
1976	3	7	2	25	37	8	19	5	68	100
1986	4	5	4	25	38	11	13	11	66	100
1996	1	9	3	32	45	2	20	7	71	100
2005	0	2	6	39	47	0	4	13	83	100
Europe										
1976	3	4	5	17	29	10	14	17	59	100
1986	3	4	6	16	29	10	14	21	55	100
1996	1	12	6	24	43	2	28	14	56	100
2005	1	9	17	16	43	2	21	40	37	100
Latin America and the Caribbean										
1976	1	3	2	21	27	4	11	7	78	100
1986	0	2	4	27	33	0	6	12	82	100
1996	0	1	3	29	33	0	3	9	88	100
2005	0	0	2	31	33	0	0	6	94	100
Northern America										
1976	0	0	0	2	2	0	0	0	100	100
1986	0	0	0	2	2	0	0	0	100	100
1996	0	0	0	2	2	0	0	0	100	100
2005	0	0	1	1	2	0	0	50	50	100
Oceania										
1976	0	0	1	6	7	0	0	14	86	100
1986	0	0	2	9	11	0	0	18	82	100
1996	0	0	1	13	14	0	0	7	93	100
2005	0	1	3	12	16	0	6	19	75	100

TABLE 8. GOVERNMENT LEVEL OF CONCERN ABOUT ADOLESCENT FERTILITY, 1996 AND 2005

Year	(Number of countries) Major concern	Minor concern	Not a concern	Total	(Percentage) Major concern	Minor concern	Not a concern	Total
A. By level of development								
World								
1996	59	39	30	128	46	30	23	100
2005	106	56	19	181	59	31	10	100
More developed regions								
1996	9	12	12	33	27	36	36	100
2005	16	19	7	42	38	45	17	100
Less developed regions								
1996	50	27	18	95	53	28	19	100
2005	90	37	12	139	65	27	9	100
Least developed countries								
1996	16	9	8	33	48	27	24	100
2005	30	12	5	47	64	26	11	100
B. By major area								
Africa								
1996	24	8	9	41	59	20	22	100
2005	32	15	5	52	62	29	10	100
Asia								
1996	7	12	8	27	26	44	30	100
2005	20	15	7	42	48	36	17	100
Europe								
1996	7	9	12	28	25	32	43	100
2005	13	17	7	37	35	46	19	100
Latin America and the Caribbean								
1996	18	6	1	25	72	24	4	100
2005	30	3	0	33	91	9	0	100
Northern America								
1996	1	1	0	2	50	50	0	100
2005	2	0	0	2	100	0	0	100
Oceania								
1996	2	3	0	5	40	60	0	100
2005	9	6	0	15	60	40	0	100

TABLE 9. GOVERNMENT POLICIES AND PROGRAMMES ADDRESSING ADOLESCENT FERTILITY, 1996 AND 2005

Year	(Number of countries)			(Percentage)		
	Yes	No	Total	Yes	No	Total
			A. By level of development			
			World			
1996	76	51	127	60	40	100
2005	138	42	180	77	23	100
			More developed regions			
1996	16	15	31	52	48	100
2005	26	18	44	59	41	100
			Less developed regions			
1996	60	36	96	62	38	100
2005	112	24	136	82	18	100
			Least developed countries			
1996	18	12	30	60	40	100
2005	36	9	45	80	20	100
			B. By major area			
			Africa			
1996	24	14	38	63	37	100
2005	40	10	50	80	20	100
			Asia			
1996	16	13	29	55	45	100
2005	31	12	43	72	28	100
			Europe			
1996	13	15	28	46	54	100
2005	22	17	39	56	44	100
			Latin America and the Caribbean			
1996	18	6	24	75	25	100
2005	31	0	31	100	0	100
			Northern America			
1996	2	0	2	100	0	100
2005	2	0	2	100	0	100
			Oceania			
1996	3	3	6	50	50	100
2005	12	3	15	80	20	100

TABLE 10. GOVERNMENT VIEWS ON THE ACCEPTABILITY OF THE MORTALITY LEVEL: 1976, 1986, 1996 AND 2005

A. By level of development

Year	*(Number of countries)*			*(Percentage)*		
	Acceptable	*Unacceptable*	*Total*	*Acceptable*	*Unacceptable*	*Total*
			World			
1976	55	95	150	37	63	100
1986	60	104	164	37	63	100
1996	77	116	193	40	60	100
2005	83	111	194	43	57	100
			More developed regions			
1976	27	7	34	79	21	100
1986	27	7	34	79	21	100
1996	30	18	48	62	38	100
2005	31	17	48	65	35	100
			Less developed regions			
1976	28	88	116	24	76	100
1986	33	97	130	25	75	100
1996	47	98	145	32	68	100
2005	52	94	146	36	64	100
			Least developed countries			
1976	2	40	42	5	95	100
1986	3	45	48	6	94	100
1996	1	48	49	2	98	100
2005	0	50	50	0	100	100

TABLE 10. (CONTINUED)

Year	(Number of countries) Acceptable	Unacceptable	Total	(Percentage) Acceptable	Unacceptable	Total
B. By major area						
Africa						
1976	2	46	48	4	96	100
1986	4	47	51	8	92	100
1996	7	46	53	13	87	100
2005	6	47	53	11	89	100
Asia						
1976	13	24	37	35	65	100
1986	15	23	38	39	61	100
1996	19	27	46	41	59	100
2005	22	25	47	47	53	100
Europe						
1976	22	7	29	76	24	100
1986	22	7	29	76	24	100
1996	28	15	43	65	35	100
2005	27	16	43	63	37	100
Latin America and the Caribbean						
1976	11	16	27	41	59	100
1986	13	20	33	39	61	100
1996	17	16	33	52	48	100
2005	19	14	33	58	42	100
Northern America						
1976	2	0	2	100	0	100
1986	2	0	2	100	0	100
1996	1	1	2	50	50	100
2005	1	1	2	50	50	100
Oceania						
1976	5	2	7	71	29	100
1986	4	7	11	36	64	100
1996	5	11	16	31	69	100
2005	8	8	16	50	50	100

TABLE 11. GOVERNMENT VIEWS ON THE ACCEPTABILITY OF THE LEVEL OF UNDER-FIVE MORTALITY, 1996 AND 2005

Year	(Number of countries)			(Percentage)		
	Acceptable	Unacceptable	Total	Acceptable	Unacceptable	Total
A. By level of development						
World						
1996	26	87	113	23	77	100
2005	53	138	191	28	72	100
More developed regions						
1996	13	15	28	46	54	100
2005	32	16	48	67	33	100
Less developed regions						
1996	13	72	85	15	85	100
2005	21	122	143	15	85	100
Least developed countries						
1996	0	34	34	0	100	100
2005	0	49	49	0	100	100
B. By major area						
Africa						
1996	2	39	41	5	95	100
2005	2	51	53	4	96	100
Asia						
1996	8	17	25	32	68	100
2005	10	37	47	21	79	100
Europe						
1996	13	11	24	54	46	100
2005	30	13	43	70	30	100
Latin America and the Caribbean						
1996	3	16	19	16	84	100
2005	5	27	32	16	84	100
Northern America						
1996	0	1	1	0	100	100
2005	1	1	2	50	50	100
Oceania						
1996	0	3	3	0	100	100
2005	5	9	14	36	64	100

TABLE 12. GOVERNMENT VIEWS ON THE ACCEPTABILITY OF THE LEVEL OF MATERNAL MORTALITY, 2005

(Number of countries)			(Percentage)		
Acceptable	*Unacceptable*	*Total*	*Acceptable*	*Unacceptable*	*Total*
A. By level of development					
World					
60	132	192	31	69	100
More developed regions					
33	15	48	69	31	100
Less developed regions					
27	117	144	19	81	100
Least developed countries					
1	48	49	2	98	100
B. By major area					
Africa					
1	52	53	2	98	100
Asia					
12	35	47	26	74	100
Europe					
30	13	43	70	30	100
Latin America and the Caribbean					
9	24	33	27	73	100
Northern America					
1	1	2	50	50	100
Oceania					
7	7	14	50	50	100

TABLE 13. GOVERNMENT LEVEL OF CONCERN ABOUT HIV/AIDS, 1996 AND 2005

Year	(Number of countries) Major concern	Minor concern	Not a concern	Total	(Percentage) Major concern	Minor concern	Not a concern	Total
A. By level of development								
World								
1996	89	34	2	125	71	27	2	100
2005	165	26	1	192	86	14	1	100
More developed regions								
1996	21	12	0	33	64	36	0	100
2005	37	10	0	47	79	21	0	100
Less developed regions								
1996	68	22	2	92	74	24	2	100
2005	128	16	1	145	88	11	1	100
Least developed countries								
1996	26	8	0	34	76	24	0	100
2005	48	1	0	49	98	2	0	100
B. By major area								
Africa								
1996	34	7	0	41	83	17	0	100
2005	46	5	1	52	88	10	2	100
Asia								
1996	17	7	2	26	65	27	8	100
2005	39	8	0	47	83	17	0	100
Europe								
1996	17	11	0	28	61	39	0	100
2005	32	10	0	42	76	24	0	100
Latin America and the Caribbean								
1996	16	8	0	24	67	33	0	100
2005	30	3	0	33	91	9	0	100
Northern America								
1996	2	0	0	2	100	0	0	100
2005	2	0	0	2	100	0	0	100
Oceania								
1996	3	1	0	4	75	25	0	100
2005	16	0	0	16	100	0	0	100

TABLE 14. GOVERNMENT MEASURES IMPLEMENTED TO CONTROL HIV/AIDS, 2005

(Number of countries)					(Percentage)				
IEC programmes	Blood Screening	Promotion of condom use	Access to antiretroviral therapy	Non discriminatory policies	IEC programmes	Blood Screening	Promotion of condom use	Access to antiretroviral therapy	Non discriminatory policies
A. By level of development									
World									
183	171	154	148	117	99	93	83	80	63
More developed regions									
47	46	41	42	37	97	95	85	87	77
Less developed regions									
136	125	113	106	80	96	89	80	74	57
Least developed countries									
43	39	36	26	18	92	84	77	55	38
B. By major area									
Africa									
48	44	43	40	25	96	88	86	80	50
Asia									
45	47	38	31	32	96	100	82	66	68
Europe									
42	41	36	37	32	97	95	84	86	74
Latin America and the Caribbean									
33	30	28	29	20	100	91	85	88	61
Northern America									
2	2	2	2	2	100	100	100	100	100
Oceania									
13	7	7	9	6	92	50	50	64	43

TABLE 15. GOVERNMENT VIEWS ON THE SPATIAL DISTRIBUTION OF THE POPULATION: 1976, 1986, 1996 AND 2005

A. By level of development

Year	(Number of countries) Major change desired	Minor change desired	Satisfactory	Total	(Percentage) Major change desired	Minor change desired	Satisfactory	Total
World								
1976	78	55	17	150	52	37	11	100
1986	75	71	18	164	46	43	11	100
1996	80	57	55	192	42	30	29	100
2005	97	64	33	194	50	33	17	100
More developed regions								
1976	4	19	11	34	12	56	32	100
1986	3	18	13	34	9	53	38	100
1996	11	15	22	48	23	31	46	100
2005	17	18	13	48	35	38	27	100
Less developed regions								
1976	74	36	6	116	64	31	5	100
1986	72	53	5	130	55	41	4	100
1996	69	42	33	144	48	29	23	100
2005	80	46	20	146	55	32	14	100
Least developed countries								
1976	27	15	0	42	64	36	0	100
1986	26	22	0	48	54	46	0	100
1996	30	12	6	48	62	25	12	100
2005	31	17	2	50	62	34	4	100

TABLE 15. (CONTINUED)

B. By major area

Year	(Number of countries) Major change desired	Minor change desired	Satisfactory	Total	(Percentage) Major change desired	Minor change desired	Satisfactory	Total
				Africa				
1976	36	12	0	48	75	25	0	100
1986	34	17	0	51	67	33	0	100
1996	33	13	6	52	63	25	12	100
2005	38	13	2	53	72	25	4	100
				Asia				
1976	14	19	4	37	38	51	11	100
1986	11	24	3	38	29	63	8	100
1996	17	18	11	46	37	39	24	100
2005	23	16	8	47	49	34	17	100
				Europe				
1976	2	17	10	29	7	59	34	100
1986	2	15	12	29	7	52	41	100
1996	10	13	20	43	23	30	47	100
2005	16	15	12	43	37	35	28	100
				Latin America and the Caribbean				
1976	22	4	1	27	81	15	4	100
1986	24	8	1	33	73	24	3	100
1996	16	7	10	33	48	21	30	100
2005	13	13	7	33	39	39	21	100
				Northern America				
1976	0	1	1	2	0	50	50	100
1986	0	1	1	2	0	50	50	100
1996	0	0	2	2	0	0	100	100
2005	0	1	1	2	0	50	50	100
				Oceania				
1976	4	2	1	7	57	29	14	100
1986	4	6	1	11	36	55	9	100
1996	4	6	6	16	25	38	38	100
2005	7	6	3	16	44	38	19	100

TABLE 16. GOVERNMENT POLICIES ON INTERNAL MIGRATION FROM RURAL AREAS TO URBAN AREAS, 2005

(Number of countries)					(Percentage)				
Lower	*Maintain*	*No intervention*	*Raise*	*Total*	*Lower*	*Maintain*	*No intervention*	*Raise*	*Total*
A. By level of development									
World									
115	2	41	6	164	70	1	25	4	100
More developed regions									
25	1	13	2	41	61	2	32	5	100
Less developed regions									
90	1	28	4	123	73	1	23	3	100
Least developed countries									
32	0	8	1	41	78	0	20	2	100
B. By major area									
Africa									
38	0	7	0	45	84	0	16	0	100
Asia									
30	0	7	3	40	75	0	18	8	100
Europe									
23	1	10	2	36	64	3	28	6	100
Latin America and the Caribbean									
16	1	13	0	30	53	3	43	0	100
Northern America									
0	0	2	0	2	0	0	100	0	100
Oceania									
8	0	2	1	11	73	0	18	9	100

TABLE 17. GOVERNMENT POLICIES ON INTERNAL MIGRATION FROM URBAN AREAS TO URBAN AREAS, 2005

(Number of countries)					(Percentage)				
Lower	Maintain	No intervention	Raise	Total	Lower	Maintain	No intervention	Raise	Total
A. By level of development									
World									
4	22	69	10	105	4	21	66	10	100
More developed regions									
2	2	25	0	29	7	7	86	0	100
Less developed regions									
2	20	44	10	76	3	26	58	13	100
Least developed countries									
1	6	9	2	18	6	33	50	11	100
B. By major area									
Africa									
2	4	13	2	21	10	19	62	10	100
Asia									
0	14	13	3	30	0	47	43	10	100
Europe									
2	2	20	0	24	8	8	83	0	100
Latin America and the Caribbean									
0	2	17	4	23	0	9	74	17	100
Northern America									
0	0	2	0	2	0	0	100	0	100
Oceania									
0	0	4	1	5	0	0	80	20	100

TABLE 18. GOVERNMENT POLICIES ON INTERNAL MIGRATION INTO URBAN AGGLOMERATIONS: 1976, 1986, 1996 AND 2005

A. By level of development

Year	(Number of countries)					(Percentage)				
	Raise	*Maintain*	*Lower*	*No intervention*	*Total*	*Raise*	*Maintain*	*Lower*	*No intervention*	*Total*
					World					
1976	4	0	39	40	83	5	0	47	48	100
1986	2	1	50	41	94	2	1	53	44	100
1996	3	5	55	60	123	2	4	45	49	100
2005	4	5	107	55	171	2	3	63	32	100
					More developed regions					
1976	2	0	11	7	20	10	0	55	35	100
1986	1	1	8	9	19	5	5	42	47	100
1996	3	3	8	17	31	10	10	26	55	100
2005	2	2	14	26	44	5	5	32	59	100
					Less developed regions					
1976	2	0	28	33	63	3	0	44	52	100
1986	1	0	42	32	75	1	0	56	43	100
1996	0	2	47	43	92	0	2	51	47	100
2005	2	3	93	29	127	2	2	73	23	100
					Least developed countries					
1976	0	0	11	15	26	0	0	42	58	100
1986	0	0	7	19	26	0	0	27	73	100
1996	0	0	17	17	34	0	0	50	50	100
2005	0	0	30	12	42	0	0	71	29	100

TABLE 18. (CONTINUED)

Year	Raise	Maintain	Lower	No intervention	Total	Raise	Maintain	Lower	No intervention	Total
	B. By major area									
	(Number of countries)					*(Percentage)*				
						Africa				
1976	0	0	18	19	37	0	0	49	51	100
1986	0	0	16	17	33	0	0	48	52	100
1996	0	1	22	18	41	0	2	54	44	100
2005	0	0	35	10	45	0	0	78	22	100
						Asia				
1976	1	0	4	0	5	20	0	80	0	100
1986	1	0	12	6	19	5	0	63	32	100
1996	0	0	18	9	27	0	0	67	33	100
2005	2	3	29	8	42	5	7	69	19	100
						Europe				
1976	2	0	11	6	19	11	0	58	32	100
1986	1	1	8	6	16	6	6	50	38	100
1996	3	3	7	13	26	12	12	27	50	100
2005	2	2	13	22	39	5	5	33	56	100
						Latin America and the Caribbean				
1976	1	0	6	13	20	5	0	30	65	100
1986	0	0	13	6	19	0	0	68	32	100
1996	0	0	8	15	23	0	0	35	65	100
2005	0	0	20	11	31	0	0	65	35	100
						Northern America				
1976	0	0	0	1	1	0	0	0	100	100
1986	0	0	0	2	2	0	0	0	100	100
1996	0	0	0	2	2	0	0	0	100	100
2005	0	0	0	2	2	0	0	0	100	100
						Oceania				
1976	0	0	0	1	1	0	0	0	100	100
1986	0	0	1	4	5	0	0	20	80	100
1996	0	1	0	3	4	0	25	0	75	100
2005	0	0	10	2	12	0	0	83	17	100

TABLE 19. GOVERNMENT VIEWS ON THE LEVEL OF IMMIGRATION: 1976, 1986, 1996 AND 2005

A. By level of development

Year	(Number of countries)				(Percentage)			
	Too low	*Satisfactory*	*Too high*	*Total*	*Too low*	*Satisfactory*	*Too high*	*Total*
				World				
1976	11	129	10	150	7	86	7	100
1986	6	125	33	164	4	76	20	100
1996	4	148	41	193	2	77	21	100
2005	10	151	33	194	5	78	17	100
				More developed regions				
1976	1	27	6	34	3	79	18	100
1986	0	26	8	34	0	76	24	100
1996	1	31	16	48	2	65	33	100
2005	4	40	4	48	8	83	8	100
				Less developed regions				
1976	10	102	4	116	9	88	3	100
1986	6	99	25	130	5	76	19	100
1996	3	117	25	145	2	81	17	100
2005	6	111	29	146	4	76	20	100
				Least developed countries				
1976	2	39	1	42	5	93	2	100
1986	1	40	7	48	2	83	15	100
1996	0	41	8	49	0	84	16	100
2005	0	44	6	50	0	88	12	100

TABLE 19. (CONTINUED)

Year	(Number of countries) Too low	Satisfactory	Too high	Total	(Percentage) Too low	Satisfactory	Too high	Total
B. By major area								
Africa								
1976	5	41	2	48	10	85	4	100
1986	1	39	11	51	2	76	22	100
1996	0	46	7	53	0	87	13	100
2005	0	43	10	53	0	81	19	100
Asia								
1976	4	32	1	37	11	86	3	100
1986	1	30	7	38	3	79	18	100
1996	1	35	10	46	2	76	22	100
2005	4	30	13	47	9	64	28	100
Europe								
1976	0	24	5	29	0	83	17	100
1986	0	22	7	29	0	76	24	100
1996	0	27	16	43	0	63	37	100
2005	2	37	4	43	5	86	9	100
Latin America and the Caribbean								
1976	1	25	1	27	4	93	4	100
1986	4	23	6	33	12	70	18	100
1996	2	26	5	33	6	79	15	100
2005	1	28	4	33	3	85	12	100
Northern America								
1976	0	2	0	2	0	100	0	100
1986	0	1	1	2	0	50	50	100
1996	0	2	0	2	0	100	0	100
2005	1	1	0	2	50	50	0	100
Oceania								
1976	1	5	1	7	14	71	14	100
1986	0	10	1	11	0	91	9	100
1996	1	12	3	16	6	75	19	100
2005	2	12	2	16	12	75	12	100

TABLE 20. GOVERNMENT POLICIES ON IMMIGRATION: 1976, 1986, 1996 AND 2005

A. By level of development

Year	*(Number of countries)*				*(Percentage)*			
	Raise	*Maintain/No intervention*	*Lower*	*Total*	*Raise*	*Maintain/No intervention*	*Lower*	*Total*
				World				
1976	11	129	10	150	7	86	7	100
1986	6	125	33	164	4	76	20	100
1996	8	107	78	193	4	55	40	100
2005	11	140	43	194	6	72	22	100
				More developed regions				
1976	1	27	6	34	3	79	18	100
1986	0	21	13	34	0	62	38	100
1996	1	18	29	48	2	37	60	100
2005	4	38	6	48	8	78	12	100
				Less developed regions				
1976	10	102	4	116	9	88	3	100
1986	6	104	20	130	5	80	15	100
1996	7	89	49	145	5	61	34	100
2005	7	102	37	146	5	70	25	100
				Least developed countries				
1976	2	39	1	42	5	93	2	100
1986	1	43	4	48	2	90	8	100
1996	1	35	13	49	2	72	27	100
2005	1	39	10	50	2	78	20	100

TABLE 20. (CONTINUED)

B. By major area								
	(Number of countries)				(Percentage)			
Year	Raise	Maintain/No intervention	Lower	Total	Raise	Maintain/No intervention	Lower	Total
				Africa				
1976	5	41	2	48	10	85	4	100
1986	1	41	9	51	2	80	18	100
1996	2	35	16	53	4	66	30	100
2005	1	39	13	53	2	73	25	100
				Asia				
1976	4	32	1	37	11	86	3	100
1986	1	30	7	38	3	79	18	100
1996	2	23	21	46	4	50	46	100
2005	4	26	17	47	9	55	36	100
				Europe				
1976	0	24	5	29	0	83	17	100
1986	0	16	13	29	0	55	45	100
1996	0	15	28	43	0	35	65	100
2005	2	35	6	43	5	81	14	100
				Latin America and the Caribbean				
1976	1	25	1	27	4	93	4	100
1986	4	25	4	33	12	76	12	100
1996	3	20	10	33	9	60	30	100
2005	1	28	4	33	3	85	12	100
				Northern America				
1976	0	2	0	2	0	100	0	100
1986	0	2	0	2	0	100	0	100
1996	0	1	1	2	0	50	50	100
2005	1	1	0	2	50	50	0	100
				Oceania				
1976	1	5	1	7	14	71	14	100
1986	0	11	0	11	0	100	0	100
1996	1	13	2	16	6	81	12	100
2005	2	11	3	16	12	69	19	100

TABLE 21. GOVERNMENT POLICIES ON MIGRATION FOR PERMANENT SETTLEMENT, 2005

(Number of countries)					(Percentage)				
Lower	Maintain	No intervention	Raise	Total	Lower	Maintain	No intervention	Raise	Total
A. By level of development									
World									
37	77	28	11	153	24	50	18	7	100
More developed regions									
9	31	2	5	47	19	66	4	11	100
Less developed regions									
28	46	26	6	106	26	43	25	6	100
Least developed countries									
5	5	15	0	25	20	20	60	0	100
B. By major area									
Africa									
8	5	16	0	29	28	17	55	0	100
Asia									
11	19	5	4	39	28	49	13	10	100
Europe									
9	29	2	2	42	21	69	5	5	100
Latin America and the Caribbean									
6	21	4	1	32	19	66	12	3	100
Northern America									
0	1	0	1	2	0	50	0	50	100
Oceania									
3	2	1	3	9	33	22	11	33	100

TABLE 22. GOVERNMENT POLICIES ON THE MIGRATION OF HIGHLY SKILLED WORKERS, 2005

(Number of countries)					(Percentage)				
Lower	*Maintain*	*No intervention*	*Raise*	*Total*	*Lower*	*Maintain*	*No intervention*	*Raise*	*Total*
A. By level of development									
World									
5	79	20	30	134	4	59	15	22	100
More developed regions									
0	19	5	17	41	0	46	12	41	100
Less developed regions									
5	60	15	13	93	5	65	16	14	100
Least developed countries									
1	8	8	1	18	6	44	44	6	100
B. By major area									
Africa									
1	6	12	1	20	5	30	60	5	100
Asia									
4	26	1	8	39	10	67	3	21	100
Europe									
0	18	5	13	36	0	50	14	36	100
Latin America and the Caribbean									
0	24	1	4	29	0	83	3	14	100
Northern America									
0	1	0	1	2	0	50	0	50	100
Oceania									
0	4	1	3	8	0	50	12	38	100

TABLE 23. GOVERNMENT POLICIES ON THE MIGRATION OF TEMPORARY WORKERS, 2005

(Number of countries)					(Percentage)				
Lower	Maintain	No intervention	Raise	Total	Lower	Maintain	No intervention	Raise	Total
A. By level of development									
World									
42	83	21	9	155	27	54	14	6	100
More developed regions									
8	32	2	5	47	17	68	4	11	100
Less developed regions									
34	51	19	4	108	31	47	18	4	100
Least developed countries									
3	11	10	1	25	12	44	40	4	100
B. By major area									
Africa									
7	6	12	0	25	28	24	48	0	100
Asia									
16	23	1	2	42	38	55	2	5	100
Europe									
8	29	2	3	42	19	69	5	7	100
Latin America and the Caribbean									
4	19	6	1	30	13	63	20	3	100
Northern America									
0	1	0	1	2	0	50	0	50	100
Oceania									
7	5	0	2	14	50	36	0	14	100

TABLE 24. GOVERNMENT POLICIES ON MIGRATION FOR FAMILY REUNIFICATION, 2005

Lower	Maintain	No intervention	Raise	Total	Lower	Maintain	No intervention	Raise	Total
A. By level of development									
(Number of countries)					*(Percentage)*				
World									
16	84	28	7	135	12	62	21	5	100
More developed regions									
5	33	3	4	45	11	73	7	9	100
Less developed regions									
11	51	25	3	90	12	57	28	3	100
Least developed countries									
1	6	12	1	20	5	30	60	5	100
B. By major area									
Africa									
2	5	15	1	23	9	22	65	4	100
Asia									
6	23	5	1	35	17	66	14	3	100
Europe									
4	30	3	3	40	10	75	8	8	100
Latin America and the Caribbean									
2	22	4	1	29	7	76	14	3	100
Northern America									
0	1	0	1	2	0	50	0	50	100
Oceania									
2	3	1	0	6	33	50	17	0	100

TABLE 25. GOVERNMENT POLICIES ON THE INTEGRATION OF NON-NATIONALS, 2005

(Number of countries)			(Percentage)		
No	*Yes*	*Total*	*No*	*Yes*	*Total*
A. By level of development					
World					
50	75	125	40	60	100
More developed regions					
7	37	44	16	84	100
Less developed regions					
43	38	81	53	47	100
Least developed countries					
14	5	19	74	26	100
B. By major area					
Africa					
14	11	25	56	44	100
Asia					
17	14	31	55	45	100
Europe					
6	33	39	15	85	100
Latin America and the Caribbean					
13	10	23	57	43	100
Northern America					
0	2	2	0	100	100
Oceania					
0	5	5	0	100	100

TABLE 26. GOVERNMENT VIEWS ON THE LEVEL OF EMIGRATION: 1976, 1986, 1996 AND 2005

A. By level of development

Year	*(Number of countries)* Too low	Satisfactory	Too high	Total	*(Percentage)* Too low	Satisfactory	Too high	Total
				World				
1976	6	125	19	150	4	83	13	100
1986	9	124	31	164	5	76	19	100
1996	5	133	55	193	3	69	28	100
2005	10	131	53	194	5	68	27	100
				More developed regions				
1976	1	28	5	34	3	82	15	100
1986	2	29	3	34	6	85	9	100
1996	1	35	12	48	2	73	25	100
2005	0	39	9	48	0	81	19	100
				Less developed regions				
1976	5	97	14	116	4	84	12	100
1986	7	95	28	130	5	73	22	100
1996	4	98	43	145	3	68	30	100
2005	10	92	44	146	7	63	30	100
				Least developed countries				
1976	0	39	3	42	0	93	7	100
1986	1	39	8	48	2	81	17	100
1996	1	37	11	49	2	76	22	100
2005	2	40	8	50	4	80	16	100

TABLE 26. (CONTINUED)

Year	(Number of countries)				(Percentage)			
	Too low	Satisfactory	Too high	Total	Too low	Satisfactory	Too high	Total
B. By major area								
Africa								
1976	1	44	3	48	2	92	6	100
1986	3	41	7	51	6	80	14	100
1996	2	40	11	53	4	75	21	100
2005	2	42	9	53	4	79	17	100
Asia								
1976	4	31	2	37	11	84	5	100
1986	3	28	7	38	8	74	18	100
1996	2	31	13	46	4	67	28	100
2005	7	25	15	47	15	53	32	100
Europe								
1976	1	23	5	29	3	79	17	100
1986	1	26	2	29	3	90	7	100
1996	1	31	11	43	2	72	26	100
2005	0	34	9	43	0	79	21	100
Latin America and the Caribbean								
1976	0	18	9	27	0	67	33	100
1986	2	17	14	33	6	52	42	100
1996	0	18	15	33	0	55	45	100
2005	0	18	15	33	0	55	45	100
Northern America								
1976	0	2	0	2	0	100	0	100
1986	0	2	0	2	0	100	0	100
1996	0	2	0	2	0	100	0	100
2005	0	2	0	2	0	100	0	100
Oceania								
1976	0	7	0	7	0	100	0	100
1986	0	10	1	11	0	91	9	100
1996	0	11	5	16	0	69	31	100
2005	1	10	5	16	6	62	31	100

TABLE 27. GOVERNMENT POLICIES ON EMIGRATION: 1976, 1986, 1996 AND 2005

A. By level of development

Year	(Number of countries) Raise	Maintain/ No intervention	Lower	Total	(Percentage) Raise	Maintain/ No intervention	Lower	Total
				World				
1976	6	125	19	150	4	83	13	100
1986	8	120	36	164	5	73	22	100
1996	6	142	45	193	3	74	23	100
2005	11	139	44	194	6	71	23	100
				More developed regions				
1976	1	28	5	34	3	82	15	100
1986	2	28	4	34	6	82	12	100
1996	1	35	12	48	2	73	25	100
2005	0	40	8	48	0	84	17	100
				Less developed regions				
1976	5	97	14	116	4	84	12	100
1986	6	92	32	130	5	71	25	100
1996	5	107	33	145	3	74	23	100
2005	11	99	36	146	8	68	25	100
				Least developed countries				
1976	0	39	3	42	0	93	7	100
1986	0	39	9	48	0	81	19	100
1996	1	39	9	49	2	79	18	100
2005	4	37	9	50	8	74	18	100

TABLE 27. (CONTINUED)

B. By major area

Year	(Number of countries) Raise	Maintain/ No intervention	Lower	Total	(Percentage) Raise	Maintain/ No intervention	Lower	Total
Africa								
1976	1	44	3	48	2	92	6	100
1986	2	41	8	51	4	80	16	100
1996	2	42	9	53	4	79	17	100
2005	1	42	10	53	2	79	19	100
Asia								
1976	4	31	2	37	11	84	5	100
1986	5	25	8	38	13	66	21	100
1996	3	32	11	46	7	70	24	100
2005	9	24	14	47	19	51	30	100
Europe								
1976	1	23	5	29	3	79	17	100
1986	1	24	4	29	3	83	14	100
1996	1	30	12	43	2	70	28	100
2005	0	35	8	43	0	81	19	100
Latin America and the Caribbean								
1976	0	18	9	27	0	67	33	100
1986	0	18	15	33	0	55	45	100
1996	0	23	10	33	0	70	30	100
2005	0	25	8	33	0	76	24	100
Northern America								
1976	0	2	0	2	0	100	0	100
1986	0	2	0	2	0	100	0	100
1996	0	2	0	2	0	100	0	100
2005	0	2	0	2	0	100	0	100
Oceania								
1976	0	7	0	7	0	100	0	100
1986	0	10	1	11	0	91	9	100
1996	0	13	3	16	0	82	19	100
2005	1	11	4	16	6	69	25	100

TABLE 28. GOVERNMENT POLICIES ON ENCOURAGING THE RETURN OF MIGRANTS, 2005

(Number of countries)			(Percentage)		
No	*Yes*	*Total*	*No*	*Yes*	*Total*
A. By level of development					
World					
69	72	141	49	51	100
More developed regions					
29	13	42	69	31	100
Less developed regions					
40	59	99	40	60	100
Least developed countries					
9	17	26	35	65	100
B. By major area					
Africa					
15	18	33	45	55	100
Asia					
12	21	33	36	64	100
Europe					
25	12	37	68	32	100
Latin America and the Caribbean					
12	16	28	43	57	100
Northern America					
2	0	2	100	0	100
Oceania					
3	5	8	38	62	100

Part Two

COUNTRY PROFILES

VIII. Definitions and Sources

A. Glossary

1. Government views and policies

Population size and growth

View on growth - Government views on the level of the total population's prevailing rate of growth

Too high	The Government has indicated population growth to be too high;
Satisfactory	The Government has indicated that the rate of population growth is acceptable or has not expressed a view;
Too low	The Government has indicated population growth to be too low.

Policy on growth - Government policies on the rate of population growth

Raise	The Government has policies in place to raise population growth;
Maintain	The Government has policies in place to maintain population growth;
Lower	The Government has policies in place to lower population growth;
No intervention	The Government does not intervene with regard to population growth.

Population age structure

Size of the working-age population - Government level of concern regarding the current size of the population aged 15 to 59 years in relation to the domestic labour market

Major concern	The Government has expressed serious concern that the working-age population is either too small or too large for the present labour market;
Minor concern	The Government has expressed some concern that the working-age population is either too small or too large for the present labour market;
Not a concern	The Government has indicated that the size of the working-age population is not a concern;
..	The Government's view on the working-age population is not known.

Ageing of the population - Government level of concern regarding the transformation of the age structure of the population, especially the growing proportion of the population aged 60 years or older

Major concern	The Government has expressed serious concern about the ageing of the population and/or increased burden on health and welfare provisions due to the number of people aged 60 years or older;
Minor concern	The Government has expressed some concern about the ageing of the population and/or increased burden on health and welfare provisions due to the number of people aged 60 years or older;
Not a concern	The Government has indicated that population ageing is not a concern;
..	The Government's view on population ageing is not known.

Fertility and family planning

View on fertility level - Government views on the level of fertility

Too high	The Government has indicated that the fertility level is too high;
Satisfactory	The Government has indicated that the fertility level is acceptable or has not expressed a view;
Too low	The Government has indicated that the fertility level is too low.

Policy on fertility - Government policies on the level of fertility

Raise	The Government has policies in place to raise fertility levels;
Maintain	The Government has policies to maintain fertility levels;
Lower	The Government has policies in place to lower fertility levels;
No intervention	The Government has no stated policy on fertility levels.

Access to contraceptive methods - Government level of support for modern methods of contraception (e.g. the pill, IUD, injectables, hormonal implants, condoms and female barrier methods)

Direct support	The Government directly supports the dissemination of information, guidance and materials through Government facilities;
Indirect support	The Government indirectly supports provision of information, guidance and materials by non-governmental sources;
No support	The Government permits the provision of information, guidance and materials by non-governmental sources but provides no support to such organizations;
Limits	The Government prevents access to information, guidance and materials in respect to modern methods of contraception.

Adolescent fertility - Government level of concern regarding the fertility of women under 20 years of age

Major concern	The Government has expressed serious concern about the level of adolescent fertility;
Minor concern	The Government has expressed some concern about the level of adolescent fertility;
Not a concern	The Government has indicated that adolescent fertility is not a concern;
..	The Government's view is not known.

Policies and programmes addressing adolescent fertility - Government policies and programmes that support activities to lower fertility among women under 20 years of age

Yes	The Government has policies in place and/or supports programmes to lower adolescent fertility rates (e.g. counselling and family planning services, education programmes);
No	The Government has no policies in place or does not support programmes to lower adolescent fertility rates;
..	It is not known whether the Government has a policy or supports programmes to lower adolescent fertility.

Health and mortality

Expectation of life - Government views on the current level of life expectancy at birth

Acceptable	The Government considers the present life expectancy at birth as acceptable;
Unacceptable	The Government considers the present life expectancy at birth as unacceptable.

Under-five mortality - Government views on the current level of mortality of children under five years of age:

Acceptable	The Government considers the present level of under-five mortality as acceptable;
Unacceptable	The Government considers the present level of under-five mortality as unacceptable.

Maternal mortality - Government views on the current level of maternal mortality

Acceptable	The Government considers the present maternal mortality level as acceptable;
Unacceptable	The Government considers the present maternal mortality level as unacceptable.

HIV/AIDS - Government level of concern regarding the incidence of HIV/AIDS

Major concern	The Government has expressed serious concern about the level of HIV/AIDS and/or the risk that it poses to the country;
Minor concern	The Government has expressed some concern about the level of HIV/AIDS and/or the risk that it poses to the country;
Not a concern	The Government has indicated that HIV/AIDS is not a concern;
..	The Government's view on HIV/AIDS is not known.

Measures implemented to control HIV/AIDS – Government policies on selected approaches to tackling HIV/AIDS

1. Blood screening
2. Information, education and communication (IEC) campaigns
3. Access to antiretroviral (ART) treatment
4. Non-discriminatory policies
5. Promoting condom use

Grounds on which abortion is permitted - Government's legally permissible grounds for an abortion

1. To save the life of the woman;
2. Preservation of the physical health of the woman;
3. Preservation of the mental health of the woman;
4. Rape or incest;
5. Foetal impairment;
6. Economic or social reasons;
7. Available on request (abortion permitted on all grounds).

Spatial distribution and internal migration

View on spatial distribution - Government level of desire in modifying the spatial distribution of population

Major change desired	The Government has indicated a desire to significantly alter the spatial distribution of the population;
Minor change desired	The Government has indicated a desire to somewhat alter the spatial distribution of the population;
Satisfactory	The Government has indicated that the spatial distribution of the population is acceptable, or has not expressed a view.

Policies on internal migration

From rural to urban areas – Government policies to alter internal migration from rural to urban areas

Raise	The Government has policies in place to raise internal migration from rural to urban areas;
Maintain	The Government has policies in place to maintain internal migration from rural to urban areas;
Lower	The Government has policies in place to lower internal migration from rural to urban areas;
No intervention	The Government has no stated policy to alter the internal migration from rural to urban areas;
..	It is not known whether the Government has a policy to alter the internal migration from rural to urban areas.

From rural to rural areas – Government policies to alter internal migration from rural to rural areas

Raise	The Government has policies in place to raise internal migration from rural to rural areas;
Maintain	The Government has policies in place to maintain internal migration from rural to rural areas;
Lower	The Government has policies in place to lower internal migration from rural to rural areas;
No intervention	The Government has no stated policy to alter the internal migration from rural to rural areas;
..	It is not known whether the Government has a policy to alter the internal migration from rural to rural areas;

From urban to rural areas – Government policies to alter internal migration from urban to rural areas

Raise	The Government has policies in place to raise internal migration from urban to rural areas;
Maintain	The Government has policies in place to maintain internal migration from urban to rural areas;
Lower	The Government has policies in place to lower internal migration from urban to rural areas;
No intervention	The Government has no stated policy to alter the internal migration from urban to rural areas;

..	It is not known whether the Government has a policy to alter the internal migration from urban to rural areas.

From urban to urban areas – Government policies to alter internal migration from urban to urban areas

Raise	The Government has policies in place to raise internal migration from urban to urban areas;
Maintain	The Government has policies in place to maintain internal migration from urban to urban areas;
Lower	The Government has policies in place to lower internal migration from urban to urban areas;
No intervention	The Government has no stated policy to alter the internal migration from urban to urban areas;
..	It is not known whether the Government has a policy to alter the internal migration from urban to urban areas.

Policy on internal migration into urban agglomerations

Raise	The Government has policies in place to raise internal migration into urban agglomerations;
Maintain	The Government has policies in place to maintain internal migration into urban agglomerations;
Lower	The Government has policies in place to lower internal migration into urban agglomerations;
No intervention	The Government has no stated policy to alter the internal migration into urban agglomerations;
..	It is not known whether the Government has a policy to alter the internal migration into urban agglomerations.

International migration

View on immigration - Government views on the level of documented immigration into the country, including immigration for permanent settlement, temporary and highly skilled work and family reunification. Government views towards asylum-seekers, refugees and undocumented migrants are not taken into consideration.

Too high	The Government has indicated that the level of immigration is too high;
Satisfactory	The Government has indicated that the level of immigration is acceptable or has not expressed a view;
Too low	The Government has indicated that the level of immigration is too low.

Policies on immigration

Policies on immigration - Government policies regarding the overall level of immigration

Raise	The Government has policies in place to raise the overall level of immigration;
Maintain	The Government has policies in place to maintain the overall level of immigration;

Lower	The Government has policies in place to lower the overall level of immigration;
No intervention	The Government has no stated policy on the overall level of immigration;

Permanent settlement - Government policies on migration for the purpose of permanent settlement

Raise	The Government has policies in place to raise migration for permanent settlement;
Maintain	The Government has policies in place to maintain migration for permanent settlement;
Lower	The Government has policies in place to lower migration for permanent settlement;
No intervention	The Government has no stated policy regarding migration for permanent settlement;
..	It is not known whether the Government has a policy towards migration for permanent settlement.

Temporary workers – Government policies on the migration of temporary workers

Raise	The Government has policies in place to raise the migration of temporary workers;
Maintain	The Government has policies in place to maintain the migration of temporary workers;
Lower	The Government has policies in place to lower the migration of temporary workers;
No intervention	The Government has no stated policy regarding the migration of temporary workers;
..	It is not known whether the Government has a policy towards the migration of temporary workers.

Highly skilled workers – Government policies on the migration of highly skilled workers

Raise	The Government has policies in place to raise the migration of highly skilled workers;
Maintain	The Government has policies in place to maintain the migration of highly skilled workers;
Lower	The Government has policies in place to lower the migration of highly skilled workers;
No intervention	The Government has no stated policy regarding the migration of highly skilled workers;
..	It is not known whether the Government has a policy towards the migration of highly skilled workers.

Family reunification – Government policies concerning migration for the family reunification of migrant workers

Raise	The Government has policies in place to raise migration for family reunification;
Maintain	The Government has policies in place to maintain migration for family reunification;
Lower	The Government has policies in place to lower migration for family reunification;
No intervention	The Government has no stated policy regarding migration for family reunification;
..	It is not known whether the Government has a policy towards migration for family reunification.

Integration of non-nationals - Government policies and/or programmes to foster the integration of non-nationals into society

Yes	The Government has policies and/or programmes to foster the integration of non-nationals (e.g. language classes, provision of social services);
No	The Government has no policies or programmes to foster the integration of non-nationals;
..	It is not known whether the Government has a policy and/or programme to foster the integration of non-nationals.

Emigration

View on emigration - Government views of the current level of emigration from the country

Too high	The Government has indicated that the level of emigration is too high;
Satisfactory	The Government has indicated that the level of emigration is acceptable, or has not expressed a view;
Too low	The Government has indicated that the level of emigration is too low.

Policies on emigration - Government policies towards nationals leaving to establish residency outside of the country

Raise	The Government has policies in place to raise emigration;
Maintain	The Government has policies in place to maintain emigration;
Lower	The Government has policies in place to lower emigration;
No intervention	The Government has no stated policy on emigration.

Encouraging the return of nationals - Government policies designed to encourage nationals to return to the country

Yes	The Government has policies to encourage nationals to return (e.g. tax incentives, financial inducements);
No	The Government has no policies to encourage nationals to return;
..	It is not known whether the Government has a policy to encourage nationals to return.

2. Demographic indicators

Annual population growth rate reflects the exponential average annual rate of population growth, expressed as a percentage.

Total fertility measures the average number of children that would be born per woman if all women lived to the end of their childbearing years and if current age-specific fertility rates remained constant during their childbearing years.

Teenage fertility rate is the number of births occurring during a calendar year to women aged 15-19 years per women of that age group in that calendar year.

Percentage of married women using contraception is the percentage of women aged 15-49 years in a marital or consensual union using a modern contraceptive method (sterilization, the pill, injectables, IUD, condom, vaginal barrier method or implant) or any method (modern contraceptive method, rhythm, withdrawal or other traditional methods).

Life expectancy at birth reflects the expected average number of years to be lived by a newly born baby if current age-specific mortality rates remained constant.

Infant mortality rate is the probability of dying before age 1 per 1,000 newborns.

Mortality under age 5 reflects the probability of a child dying before age 5, per 1,000 newborns.

Maternal mortality ratio is the number of deaths of women occurring over a year while pregnant, or within 42 days of termination of pregnancy, regardless of the cause of death, per 100,000 live births in that year.

Number of adults infected with HIV/AIDS is the estimated number of adults aged 15-49 years with HIV infection, whether or not they have developed symptoms of AIDS, alive at the end of 2003. For some countries, because of a lack of data, no country specific estimates were produced. For additional information, see *Report on the global HIV/AIDS epidemic, 2004.*

Urban population refers to the estimated population living in urban areas as a percentage of the total mid-year population in a country.

International migrant stock refers to the estimated mid-year number of persons born outside the country.

B. SOURCES

Population indicators. Sources: *World Population Prospects: The 2004 Revision* (United Nations publication, *Vol. I, Comprehensive Tables,* Sales No. E.05.XIII.5) and Vol. II, *Sex and Age Distribution of the World Population* (Sales No. E.05.XIII.6); *World Urbanization Prospects: The 2003 Revision* (United Nations publication, Sales No. E.04.XIII.6). As regards demographic indicators, the rate indicators, such as annual growth rate, total fertility and infant mortality rate, the percentages of births to women under age 20 and aged 35 or older and life expectancy at birth are calculated for the periods 1970-1975, 1980-1985, 1990-1995 and 2000-2005.

Contraceptive prevalence. Sources: *World Contraceptive Use 2005, Wall Chart* (United Nations publication, ST/ESA/SER.A/227); United *Nations World Contraceptive Use 2005 Database* (United Nations Population Division). Annual indicators are given for 1975, 1985, 1995 and 2003, or the closest year.

International migrant stock. Sources: *Database on Trends in Total Migrant Stock by Sex, 1990-2005, 2005 Revision* (United Nations, forthcoming). Annual indicators are given for 1975, 1985, 1995 and 2005, or the closest year.

Maternal mortality ratio. Source: *Maternal Mortality in 2000: Estimates developed by WHO, UNICEF and UNFPA* prepared by the World Health Organization, the United Nations Children's Fund and the United Nations Population Fund (2004).

HIV/AIDS. Source: *Report on the global HIV/AIDS epidemic, 2004* prepared by the Joint United Nations Programme on HIV/AIDS (UNAIDS).

C. ORDERING THE DATA ON CD-ROM

UNITED NATIONS

Department of Economic and Social Affairs
POPULATION DIVISION

World Population Policies 2005
Data in Digital Form

Date ____________________

Order form

World Population Policies 2005 *(data formatted for Windows 95 or higher)*	*Unit price (in US $)*	*Quantity*	*Total price (in US $)*
One CD-ROM disk	$100.00		

SHIP TO:

Name: ....

Institution: ....

Address: ....

Telephone: .... Fax No: ....

For overnight or express mail delivery, please provide a billing account number: ....

Notes

1. Data contained in the above data sets are copyrighted by the United Nations. No portion of the data files contained on disk can be reproduced, distributed or used to prepare derivative works or for commercial purposes without the express permission of the United Nations, to be obtained from the Secretary of the United Nations Publications Board. For further information, please contact the Director, Population Division, Department of Economic and Social Affairs, United Nations (Room DC2-1950), New York, NY 10017, United States of America; fax number (212) 963-2147.

2. The order form should be accompanied by a cheque or an international money order in **United States dollars drawn on a United States bank** for the correct amount, payable to the UNITED NATIONS POPULATION DIVISION, and mailed to: The Director, Population Division/DESA, United Nations, DC2-1950, New York, NY 10017, USA. **Credit cards are not accepted.**

IX. PROFILES OF NATIONAL POPULATION POLICIES

Government views and policies

Population policy variable	*1976*	*1986*	*1996*	*2005*
Population size and growth				
View on growth	Satisfactory	Too high	Too high	Satisfactory
Policy on growth	No intervention	No intervention	No intervention	No intervention
Population age structure				
Level of concern about				
Size of the working-age population	..	..	..	..
Ageing of the population	..	..	..	Minor concern
Fertility and family planning				
View on fertility level	Too high	Too high	Too high	Too high
Policy	No intervention	No intervention	No intervention	No intervention
Access to contraceptive methods	Direct support	Direct support	Direct support	Direct support
Adolescent fertility				
Level of concern	..	..	..	Major concern
Policies and programmes	..	..	..	..
Health and mortality				
View				
Expectation of life	Unacceptable	Unacceptable	Unacceptable	Unacceptable
Under-five mortality	..	..	..	Unacceptable
Maternal mortality	..	..	..	Unacceptable
Level of concern about HIV/AIDS	..	..	..	Major concern
Measures implemented to control HIV/AIDS*	..	..	..	1,2,5
Grounds on which abortion is permitted**	..	..	1	1
Spatial distribution and internal migration				
View on spatial distribution	Minor change desired	Minor change desired	Minor change desired	Minor change desired
Policies on internal migration				
From rural to urban areas	..	..	..	Lower
From rural to rural areas	..	..	..	..
From urban to rural areas	..	..	..	..
From urban to urban areas	..	..	..	..
Into urban agglomerations	..	No intervention	..	Lower
International migration				
Immigration				
View	Satisfactory	Satisfactory	Satisfactory	Satisfactory
Policy	Maintain	Maintain	Maintain	Maintain
Permanent settlement	..	..	..	..
Temporary workers	..	..	..	..
Highly skilled workers	..	..	..	..
Family reunification	..	..	..	..
Integration of non-nationals	..	..	..	..
Emigration				
View	Satisfactory	Too high	Too high	Too high
Policy	Maintain	Lower	Lower	Lower
Encouraging the return of nationals	Yes	..	..	Yes

* Measures implemented to control HIV/AIDS: (1) blood screening; (2) information/education campaigns; (3) access to antiretroviral treatment; (4) non-discriminatory policies; (5) promoting condom use.
** Grounds on which abortion is permitted: (1) to save the woman's life; (2) to preserve physical health; (3) to preserve mental health; (4) rape or incest; (5) foetal impairment; (6) economic or social reasons; (7) on request.

Population indicators

Indicator	*1975*	*1985*	*1995*	*2005*
Population size and growth				
Population size (thousands)	14 319	13 912	20 669	29 863
Annual growth rate (percentage)*	2.6	-1.8	6.9	4.6
Population age structure				
Percentage of population under age 15	44	45	46	46
Percentage of population aged 60 or older	5	5	5	4
Fertility and family planning				
Total fertility (births per woman)*	7.7	7.8	8.0	7.5
Teenage fertility rate (per 1,000 women, aged 15 - 19)*	136	146	166	132
Percentage of births to women under age 20*	13	14	16	13
Percentage of births to women aged 35 or older*	21	20	18	15
Percentage of married women using contraception				
Modern methods	2[a]	..	..	4[b]
All methods	2[a]	..	..	5[b]
Health and mortality				
Life expectancy at birth (years)*				
Males	40	44	45	46
Females	40	44	46	46
Both sexes combined	40	44	46	46
Infant mortality rate (per 1,000 births)*	179	159	151	149
Mortality under age 5 (per 1,000 births)*	316	275	257	252
Maternal mortality ratio (per 100,000 births) (2000)	..	..	..	1 900
HIV/AIDS (2003)				
Number of infected adults (thousands)	..	..	..	..
Adult prevalence rate (percentage)	..	..	..	..
Spatial distribution				
Population density (per sq. km)	22	21	32	46
Urban population (percentage)	13	17	20	24
Annual urban growth rate (percentage)*	6.1	-0.7	8.4	6.0
Annual rural growth rate (percentage)*	1.9	-2.5	6.2	3.3
International migration				
International migrant stock				
Number of migrants (thousands)	28	28	35	43
Percentage of total population	0.2	0.2	0.2	0.1

* For the periods 1970-1975, 1980-1985, 1990-1995 and 2000-2005.
[a] For 1973.
[b] For 2000.

Government views and policies

Population policy variable	*1976*	*1986*	*1996*	*2005*
Population size and growth				
View on growth	Satisfactory	Satisfactory	Satisfactory	Satisfactory
Policy on growth	No intervention	Maintain	Maintain	Maintain
Population age structure				
Level of concern about				
Size of the working-age population	..	..	..	Minor concern
Ageing of the population	..	..	..	Minor concern
Fertility and family planning				
View on fertility level	Satisfactory	Satisfactory	Satisfactory	Satisfactory
Policy	Maintain	Maintain	Maintain	Maintain
Access to contraceptive methods	Direct support	Direct support	Direct support	Direct support
Adolescent fertility				
Level of concern	..	..	..	Minor concern
Policies and programmes	..	..	..	..
Health and mortality				
View				
Expectation of life	Unacceptable	Unacceptable	Acceptable	Acceptable
Under-five mortality	..	..	..	Unacceptable
Maternal mortality	..	..	..	Unacceptable
Level of concern about HIV/AIDS	..	..	..	Major concern
Measures implemented to control HIV/AIDS*	..	..	..	1,2,4,5
Grounds on which abortion is permitted**	..	..	1,2,3,4,5,6,7	1,2,3,4,5,6,7
Spatial distribution and internal migration				
View on spatial distribution	Minor change desired	Minor change desired	Satisfactory	Major change desired
Policies on internal migration				
From rural to urban areas	..	..	..	Lower
From rural to rural areas	..	..	..	..
From urban to rural areas	..	..	..	..
From urban to urban areas	..	..	..	..
Into urban agglomerations	..	..	..	Lower
International migration				
Immigration				
View	Satisfactory	Satisfactory	Satisfactory	Satisfactory
Policy	Maintain	Maintain	Maintain	Maintain
Permanent settlement	..	..	..	Maintain
Temporary workers	..	..	..	Maintain
Highly skilled workers	..	..	..	Maintain
Family reunification	..	..	..	Maintain
Integration of non-nationals	..	..	..	No
Emigration				
View	Satisfactory	Satisfactory	Satisfactory	Satisfactory
Policy	Maintain	Maintain	No intervention	Maintain
Encouraging the return of nationals	..	..	..	Yes

* Measures implemented to control HIV/AIDS: (1) blood screening; (2) information/education campaigns; (3) access to antiretroviral treatment; (4) non-discriminatory policies; (5) promoting condom use.

** Grounds on which abortion is permitted: (1) to save the woman's life; (2) to preserve physical health; (3) to preserve mental health; (4) rape or incest; (5) foetal impairment; (6) economic or social reasons; (7) on request.

Population indicators

Indicator	*1975*	*1985*	*1995*	*2005*
Population size and growth				
Population size (thousands)	2 401	2 957	3 133	3 130
Annual growth rate (percentage)*	2.3	2.0	-1.0	0.4
Population age structure				
Percentage of population under age 15	40	35	32	27
Percentage of population aged 60 or older	7	7	9	12
Fertility and family planning				
Total fertility (births per woman)*	4.7	3.4	2.8	2.3
Teenage fertility rate (per 1,000 women, aged 15 - 19)*	27	19	16	16
Percentage of births to women under age 20*	4	4	3	4
Percentage of births to women aged 35 or older*	10	8	10	10
Percentage of married women using contraception				
Modern methods	..	..	..	8[a]
All methods	..	..	..	75[a]
Health and mortality				
Life expectancy at birth (years)*				
Males	66	68	69	71
Females	70	73	75	77
Both sexes combined	68	70	72	74
Infant mortality rate (per 1,000 births)*	58	45	32	25
Mortality under age 5 (per 1,000 births)*	91	68	47	34
Maternal mortality ratio (per 100,000 births) (2000)	..	..	..	55
HIV/AIDS (2003)				
Number of infected adults (thousands)	..	..	..	..
Adult prevalence rate (percentage)	..	..	..	..
Spatial distribution				
Population density (per sq. km)	84	103	109	109
Urban population (percentage)	33	35	39	45
Annual urban growth rate (percentage)*	2.9	2.6	0.9	2.1
Annual rural growth rate (percentage)*	2.1	1.7	-1.6	-0.4
International migration				
International migrant stock				
Number of migrants (thousands)	57	63	71	83
Percentage of total population	2.4	2.1	2.3	2.6

* For the periods 1970-1975, 1980-1985, 1990-1995 and 2000-2005.
[a] For 2002.

Government views and policies

Population policy variable	*1976*	*1986*	*1996*	*2005*
Population size and growth				
View on growth	Satisfactory	Too high	Too high	Too high
Policy on growth	No intervention	Lower	Lower	Lower
Population age structure				
Level of concern about				
Size of the working-age population	..	..	..	Major concern
Ageing of the population	..	..	..	Minor concern
Fertility and family planning				
View on fertility level	Satisfactory	Too high	Too high	Too high
Policy	No intervention	Lower	Lower	Lower
Access to contraceptive methods	Direct support	Direct support	Direct support	Direct support
Adolescent fertility				
Level of concern	..	..	Not a concern	Minor concern
Policies and programmes	..	..	No	No
Health and mortality				
View				
Expectation of life	Unacceptable	Unacceptable	Unacceptable	Unacceptable
Under-five mortality	..	..	Unacceptable	Unacceptable
Maternal mortality	..	..	..	Unacceptable
Level of concern about HIV/AIDS	..	..	Major concern	Minor concern
Measures implemented to control HIV/AIDS*	..	..	..	1,2,3,5
Grounds on which abortion is permitted**	..	..	1,2,3,4	1,2,3
Spatial distribution and internal migration				
View on spatial distribution	Major change desired	Major change desired	Major change desired	Major change desired
Policies on internal migration				
From rural to urban areas	..	..	..	Lower
From rural to rural areas	..	..	..	..
From urban to rural areas	..	..	..	..
From urban to urban areas	..	..	..	Raise
Into urban agglomerations	..	Lower	Lower	Lower
International migration				
Immigration				
View	Satisfactory	Satisfactory	Satisfactory	Satisfactory
Policy	Maintain	Maintain	Maintain	Maintain
Permanent settlement	..	..	..	..
Temporary workers	..	..	..	Maintain
Highly skilled workers	..	..	..	..
Family reunification	..	..	..	Maintain
Integration of non-nationals	..	..	..	..
Emigration				
View	Too low	Satisfactory	Satisfactory	Satisfactory
Policy	Raise	Lower	Lower	No intervention
Encouraging the return of nationals	..	..	Yes	Yes

* Measures implemented to control HIV/AIDS: (1) blood screening; (2) information/education campaigns; (3) access to antiretroviral treatment; (4) non-discriminatory policies; (5) promoting condom use.

** Grounds on which abortion is permitted: (1) to save the woman's life; (2) to preserve physical health; (3) to preserve mental health; (4) rape or incest; (5) foetal impairment; (6) economic or social reasons; (7) on request.

Population indicators

Indicator	*1975*	*1985*	*1995*	*2005*
Population size and growth				
Population size (thousands)	16 018	22 097	28 271	32 854
Annual growth rate (percentage)*	3.1	3.2	2.2	1.5
Population age structure				
Percentage of population under age 15	48	45	40	30
Percentage of population aged 60 or older	6	5	6	6
Fertility and family planning				
Total fertility (births per woman)*	7.4	6.5	4.1	2.5
Teenage fertility rate (per 1,000 women, aged 15 - 19)*	61	53	24	9
Percentage of births to women under age 20*	7	7	5	2
Percentage of births to women aged 35 or older*	22	18	22	20
Percentage of married women using contraception				
Modern methods	..	31[a]	49	50[b]
All methods	..	36[a]	52	64[b]
Health and mortality				
Life expectancy at birth (years)*				
Males	54	60	67	70
Females	56	63	69	72
Both sexes combined	55	61	68	71
Infant mortality rate (per 1,000 births)*	131	84	54	37
Mortality under age 5 (per 1,000 births)*	158	106	61	41
Maternal mortality ratio (per 100,000 births) (2000)	..	..	..	140
HIV/AIDS (2003)				
Number of infected adults (thousands)	..	..	..	9
Adult prevalence rate (percentage)	..	..	..	0.1
Spatial distribution				
Population density (per sq. km)	7	9	12	14
Urban population (percentage)	40	48	54	60
Annual urban growth rate (percentage)*	3.5	5.0	3.3	2.6
Annual rural growth rate (percentage)*	2.8	1.5	0.9	0.3
International migration				
International migrant stock				
Number of migrants (thousands)	160	289	299	242
Percentage of total population	1	1.3	1.1	0.7

* For the periods 1970-1975, 1980-1985, 1990-1995 and 2000-2005.
[a] For 1986.
[b] For 2000.

Government views and policies

Population policy variable	*1976*	*1986*	*1996*	*2005*
Population size and growth				
View on growth	..	..	Satisfactory	Satisfactory
Policy on growth	..	..	Maintain	Maintain
Population age structure				
Level of concern about				
Size of the working-age population	..	..	..	Not a concern
Ageing of the population	..	..	..	Minor concern
Fertility and family planning				
View on fertility level	..	..	Satisfactory	Satisfactory
Policy	..	..	Maintain	Maintain
Access to contraceptive methods	..	..	No support	No support
Adolescent fertility				
Level of concern	..	..	..	Minor concern
Policies and programmes	..	..	..	Yes
Health and mortality				
View				
Expectation of life	..	..	Acceptable	Acceptable
Under-five mortality	..	..	..	Acceptable
Maternal mortality	..	..	..	Acceptable
Level of concern about HIV/AIDS	..	..	..	Major concern
Measures implemented to control HIV/AIDS*	..	..	..	2
Grounds on which abortion is permitted**	..	..	Not permitted	1
Spatial distribution and internal migration				
View on spatial distribution	..	..	Satisfactory	Satisfactory
Policies on internal migration				
From rural to urban areas	..	..	..	No intervention
From rural to rural areas	..	..	..	..
From urban to rural areas	..	..	..	..
From urban to urban areas	..	..	..	..
Into urban agglomerations	..	..	..	No intervention
International migration				
Immigration				
View	..	..	Satisfactory	Satisfactory
Policy	..	..	Maintain	Maintain
Permanent settlement	..	..	Maintain	Maintain
Temporary workers	..	..	..	Maintain
Highly skilled workers	..	..	..	No intervention
Family reunification	..	..	..	Maintain
Integration of non-nationals	..	..	..	Yes
Emigration				
View	..	..	Satisfactory	Satisfactory
Policy	..	..	Maintain	Maintain
Encouraging the return of nationals	..	..	..	No

* Measures implemented to control HIV/AIDS: (1) blood screening; (2) information/education campaigns; (3) access to antiretroviral treatment; (4) non-discriminatory policies; (5) promoting condom use.

** Grounds on which abortion is permitted: (1) to save the woman's life; (2) to preserve physical health; (3) to preserve mental health; (4) rape or incest; (5) foetal impairment; (6) economic or social reasons; (7) on request.

Population indicators

Indicator	*1975*	*1985*	*1995*	*2005*
Population size and growth				
Population size (thousands)	31	47	64	67
Annual growth rate (percentage)*	4.7	4.8	4.1	0.4
Population age structure				
Percentage of population under age 15	..	..	..	..
Percentage of population aged 60 or older	..	..	..	..
Fertility and family planning				
Total fertility (births per woman)*	..	..	..	..
Teenage fertility rate (per 1,000 women, aged 15 - 19)*	..	..	..	..
Percentage of births to women under age 20*	..	..	..	..
Percentage of births to women aged 35 or older*	..	..	..	..
Percentage of married women using contraception				
Modern methods	..	..	..	..
All methods	..	..	..	..
Health and mortality				
Life expectancy at birth (years)*				
Males	..	..	..	..
Females	..	..	..	..
Both sexes combined	..	..	..	..
Infant mortality rate (per 1,000 births)*	..	..	..	..
Mortality under age 5 (per 1,000 births)*	..	..	..	..
Maternal mortality ratio (per 100,000 births) (2000)	..	..	..	..
HIV/AIDS (2003)				
Number of infected adults (thousands)	..	..	..	..
Adult prevalence rate (percentage)	..	..	..	..
Spatial distribution				
Population density (per sq. km)	66	100	137	143
Urban population (percentage)	96	95	93	91
Annual urban growth rate (percentage)*	6.1	5.2	3.7	2.3
Annual rural growth rate (percentage)*	6.2	7.9	7.3	5.3
International migration				
International migrant stock				
Number of migrants (thousands)	18	33	50	52
Percentage of total population	58.3	70.6	77.6	77.9

* For the periods 1970-1975, 1980-1985, 1990-1995 and 2000-2005.

Government views and policies

Population policy variable	*1976*	*1986*	*1996*	*2005*
Population size and growth				
View on growth	..	Satisfactory	Satisfactory	Satisfactory
Policy on growth	..	No intervention	No intervention	Maintain
Population age structure				
Level of concern about				
Size of the working-age population	..	..	..	..
Ageing of the population	..	..	..	Minor concern
Fertility and family planning				
View on fertility level	..	Satisfactory	Too high	Too high
Policy	..	No intervention	No intervention	Maintain
Access to contraceptive methods	..	Direct support	Direct support	Direct support
Adolescent fertility				
Level of concern	..	..	Major concern	Major concern
Policies and programmes	..	..	Yes	Yes
Health and mortality				
View				
Expectation of life	..	Unacceptable	Unacceptable	Unacceptable
Under-five mortality	..	..	Unacceptable	Unacceptable
Maternal mortality	..	..	..	Unacceptable
Level of concern about HIV/AIDS	..	..	Minor concern	Major concern
Measures implemented to control HIV/AIDS*	..	..	..	1,2,3,4,5
Grounds on which abortion is permitted**	..	..	1	1
Spatial distribution and internal migration				
View on spatial distribution	..	Major change desired	Satisfactory	Major change desired
Policies on internal migration				
From rural to urban areas	..	..	..	No intervention
From rural to rural areas	..	..	..	..
From urban to rural areas	..	..	..	..
From urban to urban areas	..	..	..	..
Into urban agglomerations	..	..	No intervention	No intervention
International migration				
Immigration				
View	..	Satisfactory	Satisfactory	Satisfactory
Policy	..	Maintain	No intervention	No intervention
Permanent settlement	..	..	No intervention	..
Temporary workers	..	..	No intervention	..
Highly skilled workers	..	..	..	..
Family reunification	..	..	No intervention	..
Integration of non-nationals	..	..	Yes	..
Emigration				
View	..	Satisfactory	Satisfactory	Satisfactory
Policy	..	Maintain	No intervention	No intervention
Encouraging the return of nationals	..	..	No	No

* Measures implemented to control HIV/AIDS: (1) blood screening; (2) information/education campaigns; (3) access to antiretroviral treatment; (4) non-discriminatory policies; (5) promoting condom use.

** Grounds on which abortion is permitted: (1) to save the woman's life; (2) to preserve physical health; (3) to preserve mental health; (4) rape or incest; (5) foetal impairment; (6) economic or social reasons; (7) on request.

Population indicators

Indicator	*1975*	*1985*	*1995*	*2005*
Population size and growth				
Population size (thousands)	6 813	9 276	12 280	15 941
Annual growth rate (percentage)*	2.3	3.4	3.1	2.8
Population age structure				
Percentage of population under age 15	46	47	47	46
Percentage of population aged 60 or older	5	4	4	4
Fertility and family planning				
Total fertility (births per woman)*	7.2	7.2	7.1	6.8
Teenage fertility rate (per 1,000 women, aged 15 - 19)*	229	229	226	143
Percentage of births to women under age 20*	23	23	23	16
Percentage of births to women aged 35 or older*	13	12	12	15
Percentage of married women using contraception				
Modern methods	..	..	..	5[a]
All methods	..	..	..	6[a]
Health and mortality				
Life expectancy at birth (years)*				
Males	36	38	38	39
Females	39	42	42	42
Both sexes combined	38	40	40	41
Infant mortality rate (per 1,000 births)*	173	160	155	139
Mortality under age 5 (per 1,000 births)*	287	277	270	245
Maternal mortality ratio (per 100,000 births) (2000)	..	..	..	1 700
HIV/AIDS (2003)				
Number of infected adults (thousands)	..	..	..	220
Adult prevalence rate (percentage)	..	..	..	3.9
Spatial distribution				
Population density (per sq. km)	5	7	10	13
Urban population (percentage)	17	23	30	37
Annual urban growth rate (percentage)*	5.0	6.0	5.5	5.4
Annual rural growth rate (percentage)*	1.5	2.5	2.1	2.0
International migration				
International migrant stock				
Number of migrants (thousands)	31	109	38	56
Percentage of total population	0.5	1.2	0.3	0.4

* For the periods 1970-1975, 1980-1985, 1990-1995 and 2000-2005.
[a] For 2001.

Government views and policies

Population policy variable	*1976*	*1986*	*1996*	*2005*
Population size and growth				
View on growth	..	Too high	Satisfactory	Satisfactory
Policy on growth	..	Lower	Maintain	No intervention
Population age structure				
Level of concern about				
Size of the working-age population	..	..	..	..
Ageing of the population	..	..	..	Major concern
Fertility and family planning				
View on fertility level	..	Too high	Satisfactory	Satisfactory
Policy	..	Lower	No intervention	No intervention
Access to contraceptive methods	..	Direct support	Direct support	Direct support
Adolescent fertility				
Level of concern	..	..	..	Minor concern
Policies and programmes	..	..	..	Yes
Health and mortality				
View				
Expectation of life	..	Unacceptable	Acceptable	Acceptable
Under-five mortality	..	..	..	Acceptable
Maternal mortality	..	..	..	Acceptable
Level of concern about HIV/AIDS	..	..	..	Major concern
Measures implemented to control HIV/AIDS*	..	..	..	1,2,5
Grounds on which abortion is permitted**	..	..	1	1
Spatial distribution and internal migration				
View on spatial distribution	..	Minor change desired	Major change desired	Satisfactory
Policies on internal migration				
From rural to urban areas	..	..	..	No intervention
From rural to rural areas	..	..	..	No intervention
From urban to rural areas	..	..	..	No intervention
From urban to urban areas	..	..	..	No intervention
Into urban agglomerations	..	..	..	No intervention
International migration				
Immigration				
View	..	Satisfactory	Satisfactory	Satisfactory
Policy	..	Maintain	Maintain	Maintain
Permanent settlement	..	..	..	Maintain
Temporary workers	..	..	..	Maintain
Highly skilled workers	..	..	..	Maintain
Family reunification	..	..	..	..
Integration of non-nationals	..	..	..	..
Emigration				
View	..	Satisfactory	Satisfactory	Too high
Policy	..	Maintain	Lower	No intervention
Encouraging the return of nationals	..	..	..	Yes

* Measures implemented to control HIV/AIDS: (1) blood screening; (2) information/education campaigns; (3) access to antiretroviral treatment; (4) non-discriminatory policies; (5) promoting condom use.

** Grounds on which abortion is permitted: (1) to save the woman's life; (2) to preserve physical health; (3) to preserve mental health; (4) rape or incest; (5) foetal impairment; (6) economic or social reasons; (7) on request.

Population indicators

Indicator	*1975*	*1985*	*1995*	*2005*
Population size and growth				
Population size (thousands)	62	64	70	81
Annual growth rate (percentage)*	-1.2	0.1	1.9	1.3
Population age structure				
Percentage of population under age 15	..	..	..	..
Percentage of population aged 60 or older	..	..	..	..
Fertility and family planning				
Total fertility (births per woman)*	..	..	..	..
Teenage fertility rate (per 1,000 women, aged 15 - 19)*	..	..	..	..
Percentage of births to women under age 20*	..	..	..	..
Percentage of births to women aged 35 or older*	..	..	..	..
Percentage of married women using contraception				
Modern methods	..	51[a]	..	..
All methods	..	53[a]	..	..
Health and mortality				
Life expectancy at birth (years)*				
Males	..	..	..	..
Females	..	..	..	..
Both sexes combined	..	..	..	..
Infant mortality rate (per 1,000 births)*	..	..	..	..
Mortality under age 5 (per 1,000 births)*	..	..	..	..
Maternal mortality ratio (per 100,000 births) (2000)	..	..	..	..
HIV/AIDS (2003)				
Number of infected adults (thousands)	..	..	..	..
Adult prevalence rate (percentage)	..	..	..	..
Spatial distribution				
Population density (per sq. km)	140	144	157	184
Urban population (percentage)	34	35	36	38
Annual urban growth rate (percentage)*	-0.8	0.4	1.6	1.4
Annual rural growth rate (percentage)*	-1.2	0.0	1.2	0.0
International migration				
International migrant stock				
Number of migrants (thousands)	8	10	14	18
Percentage of total population	12.8	16.5	19.9	22.4

* For the periods 1970-1975, 1980-1985, 1990-1995 and 2000-2005.
[a] For 1988.

Government views and policies

Population policy variable	*1976*	*1986*	*1996*	*2005*
Population size and growth				
View on growth	Too low	Satisfactory	Satisfactory	Satisfactory
Policy on growth	Raise	No intervention	No intervention	No intervention
Population age structure				
Level of concern about				
Size of the working-age population	..	..	..	Not a concern
Ageing of the population	..	..	..	Minor concern
Fertility and family planning				
View on fertility level	Too low	Satisfactory	Satisfactory	Satisfactory
Policy	Raise	No intervention	No intervention	No intervention
Access to contraceptive methods	Limits	No support	No support	Direct support
Adolescent fertility				
Level of concern	..	..	Major concern	Major concern
Policies and programmes	..	..	Yes	Yes
Health and mortality				
View				
Expectation of life	Unacceptable	Acceptable	Unacceptable	Acceptable
Under-five mortality	..	..	Unacceptable	Unacceptable
Maternal mortality	..	..	..	Unacceptable
Level of concern about HIV/AIDS	..	..	Minor concern	Major concern
Measures implemented to control HIV/AIDS*	..	..	..	1,2,3,4,5
Grounds on which abortion is permitted**	..	..	1,2	1,2,3,4
Spatial distribution and internal migration				
View on spatial distribution	Major change desired	Major change desired	Satisfactory	Minor change desired
Policies on internal migration				
From rural to urban areas	..	..	..	No intervention
From rural to rural areas	..	..	..	No intervention
From urban to rural areas	..	..	..	No intervention
From urban to urban areas	..	..	..	No intervention
Into urban agglomerations	Lower	Lower	No intervention	No intervention
International migration				
Immigration				
View	Too low	Satisfactory	Satisfactory	Satisfactory
Policy	Raise	Maintain	Maintain	Maintain
Permanent settlement	..	..	Maintain	Maintain
Temporary workers	..	..	Maintain	Maintain
Highly skilled workers	..	..	..	Maintain
Family reunification	..	..	Lower	Maintain
Integration of non-nationals	..	..	Yes	Yes
Emigration				
View	Satisfactory	Too high	Satisfactory	Too high
Policy	Maintain	Lower	No intervention	Lower
Encouraging the return of nationals	Yes	..	No	Yes

* Measures implemented to control HIV/AIDS: (1) blood screening; (2) information/education campaigns; (3) access to antiretroviral treatment; (4) non-discriminatory policies; (5) promoting condom use.
** Grounds on which abortion is permitted: (1) to save the woman's life; (2) to preserve physical health; (3) to preserve mental health; (4) rape or incest; (5) foetal impairment; (6) economic or social reasons; (7) on request.

Population indicators

Indicator	*1975*	*1985*	*1995*	*2005*
Population size and growth				
Population size (thousands)	26 049	30 305	34 835	38 747
Annual growth rate (percentage)*	1.7	1.5	1.3	1.0
Population age structure				
Percentage of population under age 15	29	31	29	26
Percentage of population aged 60 or older	11	12	13	14
Fertility and family planning				
Total fertility (births per woman)*	3.1	3.2	2.9	2.4
Teenage fertility rate (per 1,000 women, aged 15 - 19)*	68	74	73	61
Percentage of births to women under age 20*	13	13	16	15
Percentage of births to women aged 35 or older*	14	13	13	13
Percentage of married women using contraception				
Modern methods	..	..	..	..
All methods	..	..	..	..
Health and mortality				
Life expectancy at birth (years)*				
Males	64	67	69	71
Females	71	74	76	78
Both sexes combined	67	70	72	74
Infant mortality rate (per 1,000 births)*	48	32	24	15
Mortality under age 5 (per 1,000 births)*	58	38	28	17
Maternal mortality ratio (per 100,000 births) (2000)	..	..	..	82
HIV/AIDS (2003)				
Number of infected adults (thousands)	..	..	..	120
Adult prevalence rate (percentage)	..	..	..	0.7
Spatial distribution				
Population density (per sq. km)	9	11	13	14
Urban population (percentage)	81	85	88	91
Annual urban growth rate (percentage)*	2.2	2.0	1.6	1.4
Annual rural growth rate (percentage)*	-0.4	-1.2	-0.9	-0.9
International migration				
International migrant stock				
Number of migrants (thousands)	2 064	1 780	1 590	1 500
Percentage of total population	7.9	5.9	4.6	3.9

* For the periods 1970-1975, 1980-1985, 1990-1995 and 2000-2005.

Government views and policies

Population policy variable	*1976*	*1986*	*1996*	*2005*
Population size and growth				
View on growth	..	..	Satisfactory	Too low
Policy on growth	..	..	Maintain	Raise
Population age structure				
Level of concern about				
Size of the working-age population	..	..	..	Minor concern
Ageing of the population	..	..	..	Major concern
Fertility and family planning				
View on fertility level	..	..	Satisfactory	Too low
Policy	..	..	Raise	Raise
Access to contraceptive methods	..	..	Direct support	Indirect support
Adolescent fertility				
Level of concern	..	..	..	Minor concern
Policies and programmes	..	..	No	Yes
Health and mortality				
View				
Expectation of life	..	..	Acceptable	Acceptable
Under-five mortality	..	..	..	Unacceptable
Maternal mortality	..	..	..	Unacceptable
Level of concern about HIV/AIDS	..	..	..	Major concern
Measures implemented to control HIV/AIDS*	..	..	..	1,2,3,4,5
Grounds on which abortion is permitted**	..	..	1,2,3,4,5,6,7	1,2,3,4,5,6,7
Spatial distribution and internal migration				
View on spatial distribution	..	..	Major change desired	Major change desired
Policies on internal migration				
From rural to urban areas	..	..	..	Lower
From rural to rural areas	..	..	..	No intervention
From urban to rural areas	..	..	..	Raise
From urban to urban areas	..	..	..	No intervention
Into urban agglomerations	..	..	..	Maintain
International migration				
Immigration				
View	..	..	Satisfactory	Too low
Policy	..	..	No intervention	Raise
Permanent settlement	..	..	No intervention	Raise
Temporary workers	..	..	No intervention	Maintain
Highly skilled workers	..	..	..	Maintain
Family reunification	..	..	No intervention	No intervention
Integration of non-nationals	..	..	No	Yes
Emigration				
View	..	..	Too high	Too high
Policy	..	..	Lower	Lower
Encouraging the return of nationals	..	..	No	Yes

* Measures implemented to control HIV/AIDS: (1) blood screening; (2) information/education campaigns; (3) access to antiretroviral treatment; (4) non-discriminatory policies; (5) promoting condom use.

** Grounds on which abortion is permitted: (1) to save the woman's life; (2) to preserve physical health; (3) to preserve mental health; (4) rape or incest; (5) foetal impairment; (6) economic or social reasons; (7) on request.

Population indicators

Indicator	*1975*	*1985*	*1995*	*2005*
Population size and growth				
Population size (thousands)	2 826	3 339	3 227	3 016
Annual growth rate (percentage)*	2.3	1.5	-1.9	-0.4
Population age structure				
Percentage of population under age 15	34	30	30	21
Percentage of population aged 60 or older	8	8	13	15
Fertility and family planning				
Total fertility (births per woman)*	3.0	2.4	2.4	1.3
Teenage fertility rate (per 1,000 women, aged 15 - 19)*	97	76	76	31
Percentage of births to women under age 20*	22	17	16	14
Percentage of births to women aged 35 or older*	5	3	5	5
Percentage of married women using contraception				
Modern methods	..	..	..	22[a]
All methods	..	..	..	61[a]
Health and mortality				
Life expectancy at birth (years)*				
Males	68	68	65	68
Females	74	74	72	75
Both sexes combined	71	71	69	71
Infant mortality rate (per 1,000 births)*	63	53	41	30
Mortality under age 5 (per 1,000 births)*	73	62	49	35
Maternal mortality ratio (per 100,000 births) (2000)	..	..	..	55
HIV/AIDS (2003)				
Number of infected adults (thousands)	..	..	..	3
Adult prevalence rate (percentage)	..	..	..	0.1
Spatial distribution				
Population density (per sq. km)	95	112	108	101
Urban population (percentage)	63	67	66	64
Annual urban growth rate (percentage)*	3.5	1.8	-1.6	-0.8
Annual rural growth rate (percentage)*	0.5	1.0	-0.7	0.1
International migration				
International migrant stock				
Number of migrants (thousands)	..	..	455	235
Percentage of total population	..	..	14.1	7.8

* For the periods 1970-1975, 1980-1985, 1990-1995 and 2000-2005.
[a] For 2000.

Government views and policies

Population policy variable	*1976*	*1986*	*1996*	*2005*
Population size and growth				
View on growth	Satisfactory	Satisfactory	Satisfactory	Satisfactory
Policy on growth	No intervention	Maintain	No intervention	No intervention
Population age structure				
Level of concern about				
Size of the working-age population	..	..	..	Major concern
Ageing of the population	..	..	..	Major concern
Fertility and family planning				
View on fertility level	Satisfactory	Satisfactory	Satisfactory	Too low
Policy	No intervention	No intervention	No intervention	Raise
Access to contraceptive methods	Indirect support	Indirect support	Indirect support	Indirect support
Adolescent fertility				
Level of concern	..	..	Minor concern	Minor concern
Policies and programmes	..	..	..	Yes
Health and mortality				
View				
Expectation of life	Acceptable	Acceptable	Unacceptable	Acceptable
Under-five mortality	..	..	Unacceptable	Acceptable
Maternal mortality	..	..	..	Acceptable
Level of concern about HIV/AIDS	..	..	Major concern	Major concern
Measures implemented to control HIV/AIDS*	..	..	..	1,2,3,4,5
Grounds on which abortion is permitted**	..	..	1,2,3,4,5,6	1,2,3,4,5,6,7
Spatial distribution and internal migration				
View on spatial distribution	Major change desired	Major change desired	Minor change desired	Minor change desired
Policies on internal migration				
From rural to urban areas	..	..	..	Lower
From rural to rural areas	..	..	..	No intervention
From urban to rural areas	..	..	..	No intervention
From urban to urban areas	..	..	..	No intervention
Into urban agglomerations	..	..	No intervention	Lower
International migration				
Immigration				
View	Too low	Satisfactory	Satisfactory	Too low
Policy	Raise	Maintain	Maintain	Raise
Permanent settlement	..	..	Maintain	Raise
Temporary workers	..	..	Maintain	Raise
Highly skilled workers	..	..	..	Raise
Family reunification	..	..	Maintain	Lower
Integration of non-nationals	..	..	Yes	Yes
Emigration				
View	Satisfactory	Satisfactory	Satisfactory	Satisfactory
Policy	Maintain	Maintain	No intervention	No intervention
Encouraging the return of nationals	..	..	No	No

* Measures implemented to control HIV/AIDS: (1) blood screening; (2) information/education campaigns; (3) access to antiretroviral treatment; (4) non-discriminatory policies; (5) promoting condom use.

** Grounds on which abortion is permitted: (1) to save the woman's life; (2) to preserve physical health; (3) to preserve mental health; (4) rape or incest; (5) foetal impairment; (6) economic or social reasons; (7) on request.

Population indicators

Indicator	1975	1985	1995	2005
Population size and growth				
Population size (thousands)	13 625	15 669	17 941	20 155
Annual growth rate (percentage)*	1.4	1.4	1.2	1.1
Population age structure				
Percentage of population under age 15	28	24	22	20
Percentage of population aged 60 or older	13	15	15	17
Fertility and family planning				
Total fertility (births per woman)*	2.5	1.9	1.9	1.7
Teenage fertility rate (per 1,000 women, aged 15 - 19)*	27	21	20	16
Percentage of births to women under age 20*	7	6	5	4
Percentage of births to women aged 35 or older*	12	13	15	17
Percentage of married women using contraception				
Modern methods	..	72[a]	..	..
All methods	..	76[a]	..	..
Health and mortality				
Life expectancy at birth (years)*				
Males	68	72	75	78
Females	75	79	81	83
Both sexes combined	72	75	78	80
Infant mortality rate (per 1,000 births)*	17	10	7	5
Mortality under age 5 (per 1,000 births)*	19	12	8	6
Maternal mortality ratio (per 100,000 births) (2000)	..	..	..	8
HIV/AIDS (2003)				
Number of infected adults (thousands)	..	..	..	14
Adult prevalence rate (percentage)	..	..	..	0.1
Spatial distribution				
Population density (per sq. km)	2	2	2	3
Urban population (percentage)	86	85	88	93
Annual urban growth rate (percentage)*	2.2	1.3	2.0	1.4
Annual rural growth rate (percentage)*	1.0	1.8	-2.7	-3.8
International migration				
International migrant stock				
Number of migrants (thousands)	2 694	3 432	4 068	4 097
Percentage of total population	19.8	21.9	22.7	20.3

* For the periods 1970-1975, 1980-1985, 1990-1995 and 2000-2005.
[a] For 1986.

Government views and policies

Population policy variable	*1976*	*1986*	*1996*	*2005*
Population size and growth				
View on growth	Satisfactory	Satisfactory	Satisfactory	Too low
Policy on growth	No intervention	No intervention	Maintain	Raise
Population age structure				
Level of concern about				
Size of the working-age population	..	..	..	Major concern
Ageing of the population	..	..	..	Major concern
Fertility and family planning				
View on fertility level	Satisfactory	Satisfactory	Satisfactory	Too low
Policy	No intervention	No intervention	No intervention	Raise
Access to contraceptive methods	Direct support	Direct support	Direct support	No support
Adolescent fertility				
Level of concern	..	..	Not a concern	Minor concern
Policies and programmes	..	..	No	No
Health and mortality				
View				
Expectation of life	Acceptable	Acceptable	Acceptable	Acceptable
Under-five mortality	..	..	Acceptable	Acceptable
Maternal mortality	..	..	..	Acceptable
Level of concern about HIV/AIDS	..	..	Minor concern	Minor concern
Measures implemented to control HIV/AIDS*	..	..	..	1,2,3,4,5
Grounds on which abortion is permitted**	..	..	1,2,3,4,5,6,7	1,2,3,4,5,6,7
Spatial distribution and internal migration				
View on spatial distribution	Minor change desired	Minor change desired	Minor change desired	Satisfactory
Policies on internal migration				
From rural to urban areas	..	..	..	Lower
From rural to rural areas	..	..	..	No intervention
From urban to rural areas	..	..	..	No intervention
From urban to urban areas	..	..	..	No intervention
Into urban agglomerations	Lower	..	..	No intervention
International migration				
Immigration				
View	Satisfactory	Satisfactory	Too high	Satisfactory
Policy	Maintain	Lower	Lower	Maintain
Permanent settlement	..	..	Lower	Maintain
Temporary workers	..	..	Lower	Maintain
Highly skilled workers	..	..	..	Maintain
Family reunification	..	..	Lower	Maintain
Integration of non-nationals	..	..	Yes	Yes
Emigration				
View	Satisfactory	Satisfactory	Satisfactory	Satisfactory
Policy	Maintain	Maintain	No intervention	No intervention
Encouraging the return of nationals	No	..	..	Yes

* Measures implemented to control HIV/AIDS: (1) blood screening; (2) information/education campaigns; (3) access to antiretroviral treatment; (4) non-discriminatory policies; (5) promoting condom use.

** Grounds on which abortion is permitted: (1) to save the woman's life; (2) to preserve physical health; (3) to preserve mental health; (4) rape or incest; (5) foetal impairment; (6) economic or social reasons; (7) on request.

Population indicators

Indicator	*1975*	*1985*	*1995*	*2005*
Population size and growth				
Population size (thousands)	7 579	7 578	8 047	8 189
Annual growth rate (percentage)*	0.3	0.1	0.8	0.2
Population age structure				
Percentage of population under age 15	23	18	18	16
Percentage of population aged 60 or older	20	20	20	23
Fertility and family planning				
Total fertility (births per woman)*	2.0	1.6	1.5	1.4
Teenage fertility rate (per 1,000 women, aged 15 - 19)*	23	18	17	14
Percentage of births to women under age 20*	6	6	4	4
Percentage of births to women aged 35 or older*	9	9	9	13
Percentage of married women using contraception				
Modern methods	..	56[a]	47[b]	..
All methods	..	71[a]	51[b]	..
Health and mortality				
Life expectancy at birth (years)*				
Males	67	70	73	76
Females	74	77	79	82
Both sexes combined	71	73	76	79
Infant mortality rate (per 1,000 births)*	24	12	7	5
Mortality under age 5 (per 1,000 births)*	25	14	8	6
Maternal mortality ratio (per 100,000 births) (2000)	..	..	..	4
HIV/AIDS (2003)				
Number of infected adults (thousands)	..	..	..	10
Adult prevalence rate (percentage)	..	..	..	0.3
Spatial distribution				
Population density (per sq. km)	90	90	96	98
Urban population (percentage)	65	66	66	66
Annual urban growth rate (percentage)*	0.3	0.1	0.8	0.0
Annual rural growth rate (percentage)*	0.2	0.0	0.8	0.0
International migration				
International migrant stock				
Number of migrants (thousands)	217	283	717	1 234
Percentage of total population	2.9	3.7	8.9	15.1

* For the periods 1970-1975, 1980-1985, 1990-1995 and 2000-2005.
[a] For 1982.
[b] For 1995/1996.

Government views and policies

Population policy variable	*1976*	*1986*	*1996*	*2005*
Population size and growth				
View on growth	..	..	Too low	Satisfactory
Policy on growth	..	..	Maintain	Raise
Population age structure				
Level of concern about				
Size of the working-age population	..	..	..	Major concern
Ageing of the population	..	..	..	Major concern
Fertility and family planning				
View on fertility level	..	..	Satisfactory	Satisfactory
Policy	..	..	Maintain	Maintain
Access to contraceptive methods	..	..	Indirect support	Direct support
Adolescent fertility				
Level of concern	..	..	..	Major concern
Policies and programmes	..	..	No	No
Health and mortality				
View				
Expectation of life	..	..	Unacceptable	Unacceptable
Under-five mortality	..	..	..	Unacceptable
Maternal mortality	..	..	..	Unacceptable
Level of concern about HIV/AIDS	..	..	..	Major concern
Measures implemented to control HIV/AIDS*	..	..	..	1,2,4,5
Grounds on which abortion is permitted**	..	..	1,2,3,4,5,6,7	1,2,3,4,5,6,7
Spatial distribution and internal migration				
View on spatial distribution	..	..	Satisfactory	Major change desired
Policies on internal migration				
From rural to urban areas	..	..	..	Lower
From rural to rural areas	..	..	..	..
From urban to rural areas	..	..	..	..
From urban to urban areas	..	..	..	..
Into urban agglomerations	..	..	..	Lower
International migration				
Immigration				
View	..	..	Satisfactory	Satisfactory
Policy	..	..	Maintain	Maintain
Permanent settlement	..	..	No intervention	No intervention
Temporary workers	..	..	..	Maintain
Highly skilled workers	..	..	..	..
Family reunification	..	..	..	..
Integration of non-nationals	..	..	Yes	Yes
Emigration				
View	..	..	Satisfactory	Satisfactory
Policy	..	..	No intervention	Lower
Encouraging the return of nationals	..	..	No	Yes

* Measures implemented to control HIV/AIDS: (1) blood screening; (2) information/education campaigns; (3) access to antiretroviral treatment; (4) non-discriminatory policies; (5) promoting condom use.

** Grounds on which abortion is permitted: (1) to save the woman's life; (2) to preserve physical health; (3) to preserve mental health; (4) rape or incest; (5) foetal impairment; (6) economic or social reasons; (7) on request.

Population indicators

Indicator	*1975*	*1985*	*1995*	*2005*
Population size and growth				
Population size (thousands)	5 689	6 670	7 791	8 411
Annual growth rate (percentage)*	1.9	1.6	1.5	0.6
Population age structure				
Percentage of population under age 15	40	33	34	26
Percentage of population aged 60 or older	8	7	8	9
Fertility and family planning				
Total fertility (births per woman)*	4.3	3.0	2.9	1.9
Teenage fertility rate (per 1,000 women, aged 15 - 19)*	80	57	54	32
Percentage of births to women under age 20*	15	12	9	10
Percentage of births to women aged 35 or older*	8	4	6	8
Percentage of married women using contraception				
Modern methods	..	..	..	12[a]
All methods	..	..	..	55[a]
Health and mortality				
Life expectancy at birth (years)*				
Males	62	61	62	63
Females	69	69	69	70
Both sexes combined	66	65	66	67
Infant mortality rate (per 1,000 births)*	100	90	81	76
Mortality under age 5 (per 1,000 births)*	124	110	98	91
Maternal mortality ratio (per 100,000 births) (2000)	..	..	..	94
HIV/AIDS (2003)				
Number of infected adults (thousands)	..	..	..	1
Adult prevalence rate (percentage)	..	..	..	<0.1
Spatial distribution				
Population density (per sq. km)	66	77	90	97
Urban population (percentage)	51	54	52	50
Annual urban growth rate (percentage)*	2.5	1.9	1.0	0.6
Annual rural growth rate (percentage)*	1.3	1.2	2.3	1.2
International migration				
International migrant stock				
Number of migrants (thousands)	..	..	292	182
Percentage of total population	..	..	3.7	2.2

* For the periods 1970-1975, 1980-1985, 1990-1995 and 2000-2005.
[a] For 2001.

Government views and policies

Population policy variable	*1976*	*1986*	*1996*	*2005*
Population size and growth				
View on growth	Too low	Satisfactory	Satisfactory	Satisfactory
Policy on growth	Raise	No intervention	No intervention	Maintain
Population age structure				
Level of concern about				
Size of the working-age population	..	..	..	Minor concern
Ageing of the population	..	..	..	Major concern
Fertility and family planning				
View on fertility level	Satisfactory	Satisfactory	Satisfactory	Satisfactory
Policy	No intervention	No intervention	No intervention	No intervention
Access to contraceptive methods	Indirect support	Indirect support	Indirect support	Direct support
Adolescent fertility				
Level of concern	..	..	Minor concern	Major concern
Policies and programmes	..	..	..	Yes
Health and mortality				
View				
Expectation of life	Unacceptable	Acceptable	Acceptable	Acceptable
Under-five mortality	..	..	..	Unacceptable
Maternal mortality	..	..	..	Unacceptable
Level of concern about HIV/AIDS	..	..	Major concern	Major concern
Measures implemented to control HIV/AIDS*	..	..	..	1,2,3,4,5
Grounds on which abortion is permitted**	..	..	1,2,3	1,2,3
Spatial distribution and internal migration				
View on spatial distribution	Minor change desired	Major change desired	Satisfactory	Satisfactory
Policies on internal migration				
From rural to urban areas	..	..	..	No intervention
From rural to rural areas	..	..	..	No intervention
From urban to rural areas	..	..	..	No intervention
From urban to urban areas	..	..	..	No intervention
Into urban agglomerations	..	No intervention	No intervention	No intervention
International migration				
Immigration				
View	Satisfactory	Too high	Too high	Too high
Policy	Maintain	Maintain	Lower	Lower
Permanent settlement	..	..	Lower	Lower
Temporary workers	..	..	Lower	Maintain
Highly skilled workers	..	..	..	Maintain
Family reunification	..	..	Lower	Maintain
Integration of non-nationals	..	..	No	No
Emigration				
View	Satisfactory	Too low	Satisfactory	Satisfactory
Policy	Maintain	Maintain	No intervention	No intervention
Encouraging the return of nationals	..	..	No	Yes

* Measures implemented to control HIV/AIDS: (1) blood screening; (2) information/education campaigns; (3) access to antiretroviral treatment; (4) non-discriminatory policies; (5) promoting condom use.

** Grounds on which abortion is permitted: (1) to save the woman's life; (2) to preserve physical health; (3) to preserve mental health; (4) rape or incest; (5) foetal impairment; (6) economic or social reasons; (7) on request.

Population indicators

Indicator	*1975*	*1985*	*1995*	*2005*
Population size and growth				
Population size (thousands)	189	233	279	323
Annual growth rate (percentage)*	2.1	2.1	1.8	1.4
Population age structure				
Percentage of population under age 15	41	36	31	28
Percentage of population aged 60 or older	6	6	7	9
Fertility and family planning				
Total fertility (births per woman)*	3.4	3.2	2.6	2.3
Teenage fertility rate (per 1,000 women, aged 15 - 19)*	91	83	69	61
Percentage of births to women under age 20*	17	18	14	14
Percentage of births to women aged 35 or older*	10	9	10	13
Percentage of married women using contraception				
Modern methods	..	60[a]	..	..
All methods	..	62[a]	..	..
Health and mortality				
Life expectancy at birth (years)*				
Males	63	64	63	66
Females	70	72	73	73
Both sexes combined	67	68	68	69
Infant mortality rate (per 1,000 births)*	38	30	19	14
Mortality under age 5 (per 1,000 births)*	51	39	26	16
Maternal mortality ratio (per 100,000 births) (2000)	..	..	..	60
HIV/AIDS (2003)				
Number of infected adults (thousands)	..	..	..	5
Adult prevalence rate (percentage)	..	..	..	3.0
Spatial distribution				
Population density (per sq. km)	14	17	20	23
Urban population (percentage)	73	80	86	90
Annual urban growth rate (percentage)*	2.6	3.3	2.7	1.5
Annual rural growth rate (percentage)*	0.9	-2.0	-1.8	-1.6
International migration				
International migrant stock				
Number of migrants (thousands)	27	25	28	32
Percentage of total population	14.4	10.9	10.2	9.8

* For the periods 1970-1975, 1980-1985, 1990-1995 and 2000-2005.
[a] For 1988.

Government views and policies

Population policy variable	*1976*	*1986*	*1996*	*2005*
Population size and growth				
View on growth	Satisfactory	Satisfactory	Satisfactory	Too high
Policy on growth	No intervention	No intervention	No intervention	Lower
Population age structure				
Level of concern about				
Size of the working-age population	..	..	..	Minor concern
Ageing of the population	..	..	..	Minor concern
Fertility and family planning				
View on fertility level	Too high	Satisfactory	Satisfactory	Too high
Policy	No intervention	No intervention	Lower	Lower
Access to contraceptive methods	Indirect support	Direct support	Direct support	Direct support
Adolescent fertility				
Level of concern	..	..	Not a concern	Not a concern
Policies and programmes	..	..	No	No
Health and mortality				
View				
Expectation of life	Unacceptable	Acceptable	Acceptable	Acceptable
Under-five mortality	..	..	Unacceptable	Unacceptable
Maternal mortality	..	..	..	Acceptable
Level of concern about HIV/AIDS	..	..	..	Minor concern
Measures implemented to control HIV/AIDS*	..	..	..	1,2,3
Grounds on which abortion is permitted**	..	..	1,2,3,5	1,2,3,4,5,6,7
Spatial distribution and internal migration				
View on spatial distribution	Satisfactory	Satisfactory	Satisfactory	Satisfactory
Policies on internal migration				
From rural to urban areas	..	..	..	..
From rural to rural areas	..	..	..	..
From urban to rural areas	..	..	..	..
From urban to urban areas	..	..	..	..
Into urban agglomerations	..	Raise	No intervention	..
International migration				
Immigration				
View	Satisfactory	Too high	Satisfactory	Satisfactory
Policy	Maintain	Lower	No intervention	Maintain
Permanent settlement	..	..	No intervention	..
Temporary workers	..	..	No intervention	Lower
Highly skilled workers	..	..	..	..
Family reunification	..	..	No intervention	Maintain
Integration of non-nationals	..	..	..	..
Emigration				
View	Satisfactory	Satisfactory	Satisfactory	Satisfactory
Policy	Maintain	Maintain	No intervention	No intervention
Encouraging the return of nationals	..	..	No	..

* Measures implemented to control HIV/AIDS: (1) blood screening; (2) information/education campaigns; (3) access to antiretroviral treatment; (4) non-discriminatory policies; (5) promoting condom use.

** Grounds on which abortion is permitted: (1) to save the woman's life; (2) to preserve physical health; (3) to preserve mental health; (4) rape or incest; (5) foetal impairment; (6) economic or social reasons; (7) on request.

Population indicators

Indicator	*1975*	*1985*	*1995*	*2005*
Population size and growth				
Population size (thousands)	272	413	584	727
Annual growth rate (percentage)[*]	4.3	3.5	3.4	1.6
Population age structure				
Percentage of population under age 15	43	32	30	27
Percentage of population aged 60 or older	4	4	4	4
Fertility and family planning				
Total fertility (births per woman)[*]	5.9	4.6	3.4	2.5
Teenage fertility rate (per 1,000 women, aged 15 - 19)[*]	42	33	24	18
Percentage of births to women under age 20[*]	7	4	3	4
Percentage of births to women aged 35 or older[*]	20	18	20	28
Percentage of married women using contraception				
Modern methods	..	30[a]	31	..
All methods	..	53[a]	62	..
Health and mortality				
Life expectancy at birth (years)[*]				
Males	62	67	70	73
Females	65	71	74	76
Both sexes combined	63	69	72	74
Infant mortality rate (per 1,000 births)[*]	52	22	20	14
Mortality under age 5 (per 1,000 births)[*]	74	29	26	17
Maternal mortality ratio (per 100,000 births) (2000)	..	..	..	28
HIV/AIDS (2003)				
Number of infected adults (thousands)	..	..	..	<1
Adult prevalence rate (percentage)	..	..	..	0.2
Spatial distribution				
Population density (per sq. km)	392	596	842	1 047
Urban population (percentage)	86	87	89	90
Annual urban growth rate (percentage)[*]	4.5	3.7	3.8	2.3
Annual rural growth rate (percentage)[*]	2.8	2.3	2.3	0.9
International migration				
International migrant stock				
Number of migrants (thousands)	60	137	219	295
Percentage of total population	22.1	33.1	37.5	40.7

[*] For the periods 1970-1975, 1980-1985, 1990-1995 and 2000-2005.
[a] For 1989.

Government views and policies

Population policy variable	*1976*	*1986*	*1996*	*2005*
Population size and growth				
View on growth	Too high	Too high	Too high	Too high
Policy on growth	Lower	Lower	Lower	Lower
Population age structure				
Level of concern about				
Size of the working-age population	..	..	..	Major concern
Ageing of the population	..	..	..	Major concern
Fertility and family planning				
View on fertility level	Too high	Too high	Too high	Too high
Policy	Lower	Lower	Lower	Lower
Access to contraceptive methods	Direct support	Direct support	Direct support	Direct support
Adolescent fertility				
Level of concern	..	..	Minor concern	Major concern
Policies and programmes	..	..	Yes	Yes
Health and mortality				
View				
Expectation of life	Unacceptable	Unacceptable	Unacceptable	Unacceptable
Under-five mortality	..	..	Unacceptable	Unacceptable
Maternal mortality	..	..	..	Unacceptable
Level of concern about HIV/AIDS	..	..	Minor concern	Major concern
Measures implemented to control HIV/AIDS*	..	..	..	1,2,5
Grounds on which abortion is permitted**	..	..	1	1
Spatial distribution and internal migration				
View on spatial distribution	Minor change desired	Minor change desired	Major change desired	Satisfactory
Policies on internal migration				
From rural to urban areas	..	..	..	Lower
From rural to rural areas	..	..	..	..
From urban to rural areas	..	..	..	..
From urban to urban areas	..	..	..	Maintain
Into urban agglomerations	..	No intervention	No intervention	Lower
International migration				
Immigration				
View	Satisfactory	Satisfactory	Satisfactory	Satisfactory
Policy	Maintain	Maintain	Lower	Lower
Permanent settlement	..	..	No intervention	No intervention
Temporary workers	..	..	No intervention	Maintain
Highly skilled workers	..	..	..	..
Family reunification	..	..	No intervention	Maintain
Integration of non-nationals	..	..	No	No
Emigration				
View	Satisfactory	Satisfactory	Satisfactory	Too low
Policy	Maintain	Maintain	No intervention	Raise
Encouraging the return of nationals	..	..	No	No

* Measures implemented to control HIV/AIDS: (1) blood screening; (2) information/education campaigns; (3) access to antiretroviral treatment; (4) non-discriminatory policies; (5) promoting condom use.

** Grounds on which abortion is permitted: (1) to save the woman's life; (2) to preserve physical health; (3) to preserve mental health; (4) rape or incest; (5) foetal impairment; (6) economic or social reasons; (7) on request.

Population indicators

Indicator	*1975*	*1985*	*1995*	*2005*
Population size and growth				
Population size (thousands)	73 178	92 818	116 455	141 822
Annual growth rate (percentage)*	2.4	2.4	2.3	1.9
Population age structure				
Percentage of population under age 15	44	42	40	35
Percentage of population aged 60 or older	6	5	5	6
Fertility and family planning				
Total fertility (births per woman)*	6.2	5.3	4.1	3.2
Teenage fertility rate (per 1,000 women, aged 15 - 19)*	223	189	170	132
Percentage of births to women under age 20*	26	25	26	25
Percentage of births to women aged 35 or older*	12	11	7	9
Percentage of married women using contraception				
Modern methods	5	18	42[a]	47[b]
All methods	8	25	49[a]	58[b]
Health and mortality				
Life expectancy at birth (years)*				
Males	46	50	56	62
Females	45	50	57	63
Both sexes combined	45	50	56	63
Infant mortality rate (per 1,000 births)*	148	120	88	59
Mortality under age 5 (per 1,000 births)*	222	178	124	79
Maternal mortality ratio (per 100,000 births) (2000)	..	..	..	380
HIV/AIDS (2003)				
Number of infected adults (thousands)	..	..	..	..
Adult prevalence rate (percentage)	..	..	..	..
Spatial distribution				
Population density (per sq. km)	508	645	809	985
Urban population (percentage)	10	17	21	25
Annual urban growth rate (percentage)*	7.7	5.8	4.1	3.5
Annual rural growth rate (percentage)*	2.0	1.9	2.0	1.5
International migration				
International migrant stock				
Number of migrants (thousands)	769	842	1 006	1 032
Percentage of total population	1.1	0.9	0.9	0.7

* For the periods 1970-1975, 1980-1985, 1990-1995 and 2000-2005.
[a] For 1996.
[b] For 2004.

Government views and policies

Population policy variable	*1976*	*1986*	*1996*	*2005*
Population size and growth				
View on growth	Too high	Too high	Satisfactory	Satisfactory
Policy on growth	Lower	Lower	No intervention	No intervention
Population age structure				
Level of concern about				
Size of the working-age population	..	..	..	Minor concern
Ageing of the population	..	..	..	Major concern
Fertility and family planning				
View on fertility level	Too high	Too high	Satisfactory	Too low
Policy	Lower	Lower	No intervention	Raise
Access to contraceptive methods	Direct support	Direct support	Direct support	Direct support
Adolescent fertility				
Level of concern	..	..	Minor concern	Major concern
Policies and programmes	..	..	Yes	Yes
Health and mortality				
View				
Expectation of life	Acceptable	Acceptable	Acceptable	Acceptable
Under-five mortality	..	..	..	Acceptable
Maternal mortality	..	..	..	Unacceptable
Level of concern about HIV/AIDS	..	..	..	Major concern
Measures implemented to control HIV/AIDS*	..	..	..	1,2,3,4
Grounds on which abortion is permitted**	..	..	1,2,3,4,5,6	1,2,3,4,5,6
Spatial distribution and internal migration				
View on spatial distribution	Satisfactory	Satisfactory	Satisfactory	Satisfactory
Policies on internal migration				
From rural to urban areas	..	..	..	No intervention
From rural to rural areas	..	..	..	No intervention
From urban to rural areas	..	..	..	No intervention
From urban to urban areas	..	..	..	No intervention
Into urban agglomerations	No intervention	..	..	No intervention
International migration				
Immigration				
View	Satisfactory	Satisfactory	Satisfactory	Satisfactory
Policy	Maintain	Maintain	Lower	Maintain
Permanent settlement	..	..	..	Lower
Temporary workers	..	..	..	Maintain
Highly skilled workers	..	..	..	Raise
Family reunification	..	..	..	Maintain
Integration of non-nationals	..	..	..	No
Emigration				
View	Satisfactory	Satisfactory	Satisfactory	Satisfactory
Policy	Maintain	Maintain	No intervention	No intervention
Encouraging the return of nationals	No	..	No	Yes

* Measures implemented to control HIV/AIDS: (1) blood screening; (2) information/education campaigns; (3) access to antiretroviral treatment; (4) non-discriminatory policies; (5) promoting condom use.

** Grounds on which abortion is permitted: (1) to save the woman's life; (2) to preserve physical health; (3) to preserve mental health; (4) rape or incest; (5) foetal impairment; (6) economic or social reasons; (7) on request.

Population indicators

Indicator	*1975*	*1985*	*1995*	*2005*
Population size and growth				
Population size (thousands)	246	253	262	270
Annual growth rate (percentage)*	0.6	0.3	0.4	0.3
Population age structure				
Percentage of population under age 15	31	27	23	19
Percentage of population aged 60 or older	14	15	14	13
Fertility and family planning				
Total fertility (births per woman)*	2.7	1.9	1.6	1.5
Teenage fertility rate (per 1,000 women, aged 15 - 19)*	80	56	47	43
Percentage of births to women under age 20*	23	17	14	13
Percentage of births to women aged 35 or older*	7	6	9	11
Percentage of married women using contraception				
Modern methods	..	53[a]	..	..
All methods	..	55[a]	..	..
Health and mortality				
Life expectancy at birth (years)*				
Males	67	70	71	71
Females	72	75	78	78
Both sexes combined	69	73	75	75
Infant mortality rate (per 1,000 births)*	33	17	14	11
Mortality under age 5 (per 1,000 births)*	40	20	16	12
Maternal mortality ratio (per 100,000 births) (2000)	..	..	..	95
HIV/AIDS (2003)				
Number of infected adults (thousands)	..	..	..	3
Adult prevalence rate (percentage)	..	..	..	1.5
Spatial distribution				
Population density (per sq. km)	571	588	609	627
Urban population (percentage)	41	42	47	53
Annual urban growth rate (percentage)*	0.2	1.4	1.5	1.5
Annual rural growth rate (percentage)*	0.8	-0.5	-0.5	-0.8
International migration				
International migrant stock				
Number of migrants (thousands)	16	20	23	26
Percentage of total population	6.5	7.9	8.7	9.7

* For the periods 1970-1975, 1980-1985, 1990-1995 and 2000-2005.
[a] For 1988.

Government views and policies

Population policy variable	*1976*	*1986*	*1996*	*2005*
Population size and growth				
View on growth	Too low	Satisfactory	Too low	Too low
Policy on growth	Raise	Maintain	Raise	Raise
Population age structure				
Level of concern about				
Size of the working-age population	..	..	..	Major concern
Ageing of the population	..	..	..	Major concern
Fertility and family planning				
View on fertility level	Satisfactory	Satisfactory	Satisfactory	Too low
Policy	Maintain	Maintain	Raise	Raise
Access to contraceptive methods	Direct support	Direct support	Direct support	Direct support
Adolescent fertility				
Level of concern	..	..	Major concern	Major concern
Policies and programmes	..	..	No	No
Health and mortality				
View				
Expectation of life	Unacceptable	Unacceptable	Acceptable	Unacceptable
Under-five mortality	..	..	Unacceptable	Unacceptable
Maternal mortality	..	..	..	Unacceptable
Level of concern about HIV/AIDS	..	..	Major concern	Major concern
Measures implemented to control HIV/AIDS*	..	..	..	1,2,3,4,5
Grounds on which abortion is permitted**	..	..	1,2,3,4,5,6,7	1,2,3,4,5,6,7
Spatial distribution and internal migration				
View on spatial distribution	Minor change desired	Minor change desired	Satisfactory	Major change desired
Policies on internal migration				
From rural to urban areas	..	..	..	Lower
From rural to rural areas	..	..	..	Maintain
From urban to rural areas	..	..	..	Raise
From urban to urban areas	..	..	..	Maintain
Into urban agglomerations	..	..	Maintain	Lower
International migration				
Immigration				
View	Satisfactory	Satisfactory	Satisfactory	Satisfactory
Policy	Maintain	Maintain	Maintain	Maintain
Permanent settlement	..	..	Maintain	Maintain
Temporary workers	..	..	Maintain	Maintain
Highly skilled workers	..	..	..	Maintain
Family reunification	..	..	Maintain	Maintain
Integration of non-nationals	..	..	No	Yes
Emigration				
View	Satisfactory	Satisfactory	Satisfactory	Satisfactory
Policy	Maintain	Maintain	Lower	Lower
Encouraging the return of nationals	..	..	Yes	Yes

* Measures implemented to control HIV/AIDS: (1) blood screening; (2) information/education campaigns; (3) access to antiretroviral treatment; (4) non-discriminatory policies; (5) promoting condom use.
** Grounds on which abortion is permitted: (1) to save the woman's life; (2) to preserve physical health; (3) to preserve mental health; (4) rape or incest; (5) foetal impairment; (6) economic or social reasons; (7) on request.

Population indicators

Indicator	*1975*	*1985*	*1995*	*2005*
Population size and growth				
Population size (thousands)	9 367	9 999	10 249	9 755
Annual growth rate (percentage)*	0.7	0.7	0.0	-0.6
Population age structure				
Percentage of population under age 15	26	23	22	15
Percentage of population aged 60 or older	14	15	18	19
Fertility and family planning				
Total fertility (births per woman)*	2.3	2.1	1.7	1.2
Teenage fertility rate (per 1,000 women, aged 15 - 19)*	59	54	44	28
Percentage of births to women under age 20*	16	13	13	12
Percentage of births to women aged 35 or older*	5	4	5	6
Percentage of married women using contraception				
Modern methods	..	..	42	..
All methods	..	..	50	..
Health and mortality				
Life expectancy at birth (years)*				
Males	67	66	64	62
Females	76	75	75	74
Both sexes combined	72	71	70	68
Infant mortality rate (per 1,000 births)*	21	20	13	15
Mortality under age 5 (per 1,000 births)*	25	23	17	18
Maternal mortality ratio (per 100,000 births) (2000)	..	..	..	35
HIV/AIDS (2003)				
Number of infected adults (thousands)	..	..	..	..
Adult prevalence rate (percentage)	..	..	..	..
Spatial distribution				
Population density (per sq. km)	45	48	49	47
Urban population (percentage)	50	62	68	72
Annual urban growth rate (percentage)*	3.5	2.5	0.5	0.1
Annual rural growth rate (percentage)*	-1.7	-1.9	-1.2	-1.7
International migration				
International migrant stock				
Number of migrants (thousands)	..	..	1 269	1 191
Percentage of total population	..	..	12.4	12.2

* For the periods 1970-1975, 1980-1985, 1990-1995 and 2000-2005.

Government views and policies

Population policy variable	*1976*	*1986*	*1996*	*2005*
Population size and growth				
View on growth	Satisfactory	Satisfactory	Satisfactory	Satisfactory
Policy on growth	No intervention	Maintain	No intervention	No intervention
Population age structure				
Level of concern about				
Size of the working-age population	..	..	..	Major concern
Ageing of the population	..	..	..	Major concern
Fertility and family planning				
View on fertility level	Satisfactory	Satisfactory	Satisfactory	Satisfactory
Policy	No intervention	Maintain	No intervention	No intervention
Access to contraceptive methods	Indirect support	Indirect support	Indirect support	Direct support
Adolescent fertility				
Level of concern	..	..	Minor concern	Minor concern
Policies and programmes	..	..	..	Yes
Health and mortality				
View				
Expectation of life	Acceptable	Acceptable	Acceptable	Acceptable
Under-five mortality	..	..	Acceptable	Acceptable
Maternal mortality	..	..	..	Acceptable
Level of concern about HIV/AIDS	..	..	Minor concern	Minor concern
Measures implemented to control HIV/AIDS*	..	..	..	1,2,3,4,5
Grounds on which abortion is permitted**	..	..	1,2,3,4,5,6	1,2,3,4,5,6,7
Spatial distribution and internal migration				
View on spatial distribution	Satisfactory	Satisfactory	Satisfactory	Minor change desired
Policies on internal migration				
From rural to urban areas	..	..	..	Raise
From rural to rural areas	..	..	..	No intervention
From urban to rural areas	..	..	..	Lower
From urban to urban areas	..	..	..	No intervention
Into urban agglomerations	..	..	Raise	Raise
International migration				
Immigration				
View	Satisfactory	Satisfactory	Too high	Satisfactory
Policy	Maintain	Maintain	Lower	Maintain
Permanent settlement	..	..	Lower	Maintain
Temporary workers	..	..	Lower	Maintain
Highly skilled workers	..	..	..	Maintain
Family reunification	..	..	Lower	Maintain
Integration of non-nationals	..	..	Yes	Yes
Emigration				
View	Satisfactory	Satisfactory	Satisfactory	Satisfactory
Policy	Maintain	Maintain	No intervention	No intervention
Encouraging the return of nationals	..	..	No	No

* Measures implemented to control HIV/AIDS: (1) blood screening; (2) information/education campaigns; (3) access to antiretroviral treatment; (4) non-discriminatory policies; (5) promoting condom use.

** Grounds on which abortion is permitted: (1) to save the woman's life; (2) to preserve physical health; (3) to preserve mental health; (4) rape or incest; (5) foetal impairment; (6) economic or social reasons; (7) on request.

Population indicators

Indicator	*1975*	*1985*	*1995*	*2005*
Population size and growth				
Population size (thousands)	9 801	9 858	10 137	10 419
Annual growth rate (percentage)*	0.3	0.0	0.3	0.2
Population age structure				
Percentage of population under age 15	22	19	18	17
Percentage of population aged 60 or older	19	20	21	22
Fertility and family planning				
Total fertility (births per woman)*	1.9	1.6	1.6	1.7
Teenage fertility rate (per 1,000 women, aged 15 - 19)*	11	9	10	9
Percentage of births to women under age 20*	3	3	2	2
Percentage of births to women aged 35 or older*	9	7	9	12
Percentage of married women using contraception				
Modern methods	47[a]	63[b]	74[c]	..
All methods	87[a]	81[b]	78[c]	..
Health and mortality				
Life expectancy at birth (years)*				
Males	68	70	73	76
Females	75	77	80	82
Both sexes combined	71	74	77	79
Infant mortality rate (per 1,000 births)*	19	11	7	4
Mortality under age 5 (per 1,000 births)*	36	19	11	6
Maternal mortality ratio (per 100,000 births) (2000)	..	..	..	10
HIV/AIDS (2003)				
Number of infected adults (thousands)	..	..	..	10
Adult prevalence rate (percentage)	..	..	..	0.2
Spatial distribution				
Population density (per sq. km)	321	323	332	341
Urban population (percentage)	94	96	97	97
Annual urban growth rate (percentage)*	0.4	0.1	0.4	0.2
Annual rural growth rate (percentage)*	-1.9	-2.5	-2.0	-0.8
International migration				
International migrant stock				
Number of migrants (thousands)	772	888	909	719
Percentage of total population	7.9	9	9	6.9

* For the periods 1970-1975, 1980-1985, 1990-1995 and 2000-2005.
[a] For 1976.
[b] For 1983.
[c] For 1991/1992.

Government views and policies

Population policy variable	*1976*	*1986*	*1996*	*2005*
Population size and growth				
View on growth	..	Satisfactory	Too low	Too high
Policy on growth	..	No intervention	No intervention	No intervention
Population age structure				
Level of concern about				
Size of the working-age population	..	..	..	Minor concern
Ageing of the population	..	..	..	Major concern
Fertility and family planning				
View on fertility level	..	Satisfactory	Too high	Too high
Policy	..	No intervention	No intervention	No intervention
Access to contraceptive methods	..	No support	Indirect support	Indirect support
Adolescent fertility				
Level of concern	..	..	Major concern	Major concern
Policies and programmes	..	..	Yes	Yes
Health and mortality				
View				
Expectation of life	..	Acceptable	Acceptable	Acceptable
Under-five mortality	..	..	Unacceptable	Unacceptable
Maternal mortality	..	..	..	Acceptable
Level of concern about HIV/AIDS	..	..	Major concern	Major concern
Measures implemented to control HIV/AIDS*	..	..	..	1,2,3,5
Grounds on which abortion is permitted**	..	..	1,2,3,4,5,6	1,2,3,5,6
Spatial distribution and internal migration				
View on spatial distribution	..	Minor change desired	Minor change desired	Minor change desired
Policies on internal migration				
From rural to urban areas	..	..	..	No intervention
From rural to rural areas	..	..	..	No intervention
From urban to rural areas	..	..	..	No intervention
From urban to urban areas	..	..	..	No intervention
Into urban agglomerations	..	No intervention	No intervention	No intervention
International migration				
Immigration				
View	..	Satisfactory	Too high	Too high
Policy	..	Maintain	Lower	Lower
Permanent settlement	..	..	Lower	Lower
Temporary workers	..	..	Maintain	Lower
Highly skilled workers	..	..	..	Maintain
Family reunification	..	..	Maintain	Lower
Integration of non-nationals	..	..	Yes	No
Emigration				
View	..	Too high	Too high	Satisfactory
Policy	..	Lower	Lower	No intervention
Encouraging the return of nationals	..	..	No	No

* Measures implemented to control HIV/AIDS: (1) blood screening; (2) information/education campaigns; (3) access to antiretroviral treatment; (4) non-discriminatory policies; (5) promoting condom use.

** Grounds on which abortion is permitted: (1) to save the woman's life; (2) to preserve physical health; (3) to preserve mental health; (4) rape or incest; (5) foetal impairment; (6) economic or social reasons; (7) on request.

Population indicators

Indicator	*1975*	*1985*	*1995*	*2005*
Population size and growth				
Population size (thousands)	134	163	214	270
Annual growth rate (percentage)*	1.7	2.5	2.8	2.1
Population age structure				
Percentage of population under age 15	47	45	42	37
Percentage of population aged 60 or older	7	6	6	6
Fertility and family planning				
Total fertility (births per woman)*	6.3	5.4	4.4	3.2
Teenage fertility rate (per 1,000 women, aged 15 - 19)*	175	151	122	87
Percentage of births to women under age 20*	24	23	20	17
Percentage of births to women aged 35 or older*	9	8	8	9
Percentage of married women using contraception				
Modern methods	..	..	42[a]	..
All methods	..	..	47[a]	..
Health and mortality				
Life expectancy at birth (years)*				
Males	67	70	71	69
Females	68	72	74	75
Both sexes combined	68	71	72	72
Infant mortality rate (per 1,000 births)*	52	39	34	31
Mortality under age 5 (per 1,000 births)*	73	54	45	41
Maternal mortality ratio (per 100,000 births) (2000)	..	..	..	140
HIV/AIDS (2003)				
Number of infected adults (thousands)	..	..	..	4
Adult prevalence rate (percentage)	..	..	..	2.4
Spatial distribution				
Population density (per sq. km)	6	7	9	12
Urban population (percentage)	50	49	48	49
Annual urban growth rate (percentage)*	1.4	2.3	2.7	2.3
Annual rural growth rate (percentage)*	2.0	2.8	2.8	1.8
International migration				
International migrant stock				
Number of migrants (thousands)	11	25	29	41
Percentage of total population	8.2	15.6	13.7	15

* For the periods 1970-1975, 1980-1985, 1990-1995 and 2000-2005.
[a] For 1991.

Government views and policies

Population policy variable	*1976*	*1986*	*1996*	*2005*
Population size and growth				
View on growth	Satisfactory	Satisfactory	Satisfactory	Too high
Policy on growth	No intervention	No intervention	No intervention	No intervention
Population age structure				
Level of concern about				
Size of the working-age population	..	..	..	Major concern
Ageing of the population	..	..	..	Minor concern
Fertility and family planning				
View on fertility level	Satisfactory	Satisfactory	Satisfactory	Too high
Policy	No intervention	No intervention	No intervention	Lower
Access to contraceptive methods	Indirect support	Indirect support	Direct support	Direct support
Adolescent fertility				
Level of concern	..	..	Minor concern	Major concern
Policies and programmes	..	..	No	Yes
Health and mortality				
View				
Expectation of life	Unacceptable	Unacceptable	Unacceptable	Unacceptable
Under-five mortality	..	..	Unacceptable	Unacceptable
Maternal mortality	..	..	..	Unacceptable
Level of concern about HIV/AIDS	..	..	Major concern	Major concern
Measures implemented to control HIV/AIDS*	..	..	..	1,2,3,4,5
Grounds on which abortion is permitted**	..	..	1	1,2,3,4,5
Spatial distribution and internal migration				
View on spatial distribution	Major change desired	Major change desired	Major change desired	Major change desired
Policies on internal migration				
From rural to urban areas	..	..	..	Lower
From rural to rural areas	..	..	..	Maintain
From urban to rural areas	..	..	..	Raise
From urban to urban areas	..	..	..	Maintain
Into urban agglomerations	No intervention	..	No intervention	Lower
International migration				
Immigration				
View	Satisfactory	Satisfactory	Satisfactory	Too high
Policy	Maintain	Maintain	No intervention	No intervention
Permanent settlement	..	..	No intervention	No intervention
Temporary workers	..	..	No intervention	No intervention
Highly skilled workers	..	..	..	No intervention
Family reunification	..	..	No intervention	No intervention
Integration of non-nationals	..	..	No	No
Emigration				
View	Satisfactory	Satisfactory	Satisfactory	Satisfactory
Policy	Maintain	Maintain	No intervention	Lower
Encouraging the return of nationals	..	..	Yes	No

* Measures implemented to control HIV/AIDS: (1) blood screening; (2) information/education campaigns; (3) access to antiretroviral treatment; (4) non-discriminatory policies; (5) promoting condom use.

** Grounds on which abortion is permitted: (1) to save the woman's life; (2) to preserve physical health; (3) to preserve mental health; (4) rape or incest; (5) foetal impairment; (6) economic or social reasons; (7) on request.

Population indicators

Indicator	*1975*	*1985*	*1995*	*2005*
Population size and growth				
Population size (thousands)	3 212	4 393	6 201	8 439
Annual growth rate (percentage)*	2.5	3.4	3.6	3.2
Population age structure				
Percentage of population under age 15	44	47	47	44
Percentage of population aged 60 or older	6	5	4	4
Fertility and family planning				
Total fertility (births per woman)*	7.1	7.1	6.6	5.9
Teenage fertility rate (per 1,000 women, aged 15 - 19)*	73	188	166	136
Percentage of births to women under age 20*	8	18	18	18
Percentage of births to women aged 35 or older*	20	15	15	13
Percentage of married women using contraception				
Modern methods	..	1[a]	3[b]	7[c]
All methods	..	9[a]	16[b]	19[c]
Health and mortality				
Life expectancy at birth (years)*				
Males	45	49	52	53
Females	49	52	55	55
Both sexes combined	47	51	54	54
Infant mortality rate (per 1,000 births)*	145	129	116	105
Mortality under age 5 (per 1,000 births)*	244	212	183	161
Maternal mortality ratio (per 100,000 births) (2000)	..	..	..	850
HIV/AIDS (2003)				
Number of infected adults (thousands)	..	..	..	62
Adult prevalence rate (percentage)	..	..	..	1.9
Spatial distribution				
Population density (per sq. km)	29	39	55	75
Urban population (percentage)	22	31	38	46
Annual urban growth rate (percentage)*	7.8	5.4	5.4	4.4
Annual rural growth rate (percentage)*	1.1	2.0	2.0	1.3
International migration				
International migrant stock				
Number of migrants (thousands)	50	68	146	175
Percentage of total population	1.6	1.5	2.4	2.1

* For the periods 1970-1975, 1980-1985, 1990-1995 and 2000-2005.
[a] For 1982.
[b] For 1996.
[c] For 2001.

Government views and policies

Population policy variable	*1976*	*1986*	*1996*	*2005*
Population size and growth				
View on growth	Too low	Too low	Too low	Too high
Policy on growth	No intervention	No intervention	No intervention	Lower
Population age structure				
Level of concern about				
Size of the working-age population	..	..	..	Major concern
Ageing of the population	..	..	..	..
Fertility and family planning				
View on fertility level	Satisfactory	Satisfactory	Satisfactory	Too high
Policy	No intervention	No intervention	No intervention	Lower
Access to contraceptive methods	Direct support	Direct support	Direct support	Direct support
Adolescent fertility				
Level of concern	..	..	..	..
Policies and programmes	..	..	..	No
Health and mortality				
View				
Expectation of life	Unacceptable	Unacceptable	Unacceptable	Unacceptable
Under-five mortality	..	..	..	Unacceptable
Maternal mortality	..	..	..	Unacceptable
Level of concern about HIV/AIDS	..	..	..	Major concern
Measures implemented to control HIV/AIDS*	..	..	..	1,2,5
Grounds on which abortion is permitted**	..	..	1	1
Spatial distribution and internal migration				
View on spatial distribution	Minor change desired	Minor change desired	Minor change desired	Minor change desired
Policies on internal migration				
From rural to urban areas	..	..	..	Lower
From rural to rural areas	..	..	..	..
From urban to rural areas	..	..	..	..
From urban to urban areas	..	..	..	Raise
Into urban agglomerations	..	..	..	Lower
International migration				
Immigration				
View	Satisfactory	Satisfactory	Too high	Satisfactory
Policy	Maintain	Maintain	Lower	Lower
Permanent settlement	..	..	Lower	Lower
Temporary workers	..	..	..	Maintain
Highly skilled workers	..	..	..	Lower
Family reunification	..	..	..	..
Integration of non-nationals	..	..	..	..
Emigration				
View	Satisfactory	Satisfactory	Satisfactory	Satisfactory
Policy	Maintain	Maintain	Maintain	Lower
Encouraging the return of nationals	..	..	..	..

* Measures implemented to control HIV/AIDS: (1) blood screening; (2) information/education campaigns; (3) access to antiretroviral treatment; (4) non-discriminatory policies; (5) promoting condom use.
** Grounds on which abortion is permitted: (1) to save the woman's life; (2) to preserve physical health; (3) to preserve mental health; (4) rape or incest; (5) foetal impairment; (6) economic or social reasons; (7) on request.

Population indicators

Indicator	*1975*	*1985*	*1995*	*2005*
Population size and growth				
Population size (thousands)	1 161	1 447	1 733	2 163
Annual growth rate (percentage)*	2.1	2.3	1.1	2.2
Population age structure				
Percentage of population under age 15	41	41	43	38
Percentage of population aged 60 or older	6	6	6	7
Fertility and family planning				
Total fertility (births per woman)*	5.9	5.9	5.6	4.4
Teenage fertility rate (per 1,000 women, aged 15 - 19)*	87	85	73	38
Percentage of births to women under age 20*	10	10	10	7
Percentage of births to women aged 35 or older*	16	16	16	15
Percentage of married women using contraception				
Modern methods	..	..	19[a]	..
All methods	..	..	19[a]	..
Health and mortality				
Life expectancy at birth (years)*				
Males	41	45	55	61
Females	42	47	57	64
Both sexes combined	42	46	56	63
Infant mortality rate (per 1,000 births)*	151	128	82	56
Mortality under age 5 (per 1,000 births)*	252	213	129	84
Maternal mortality ratio (per 100,000 births) (2000)	..	..	..	420
HIV/AIDS (2003)				
Number of infected adults (thousands)	..	..	..	..
Adult prevalence rate (percentage)	..	..	..	..
Spatial distribution				
Population density (per sq. km)	25	31	37	46
Urban population (percentage)	3	5	6	9
Annual urban growth rate (percentage)*	4.5	5.4	4.8	6.3
Annual rural growth rate (percentage)*	2.0	2.3	1.1	2.7
International migration				
International migrant stock				
Number of migrants (thousands)	7	8	9	10
Percentage of total population	0.6	0.5	0.5	0.5

* For the periods 1970-1975, 1980-1985, 1990-1995 and 2000-2005.
[a] For 1994.

Government views and policies

Population policy variable	*1976*	*1986*	*1996*	*2005*
Population size and growth				
View on growth	Satisfactory	Too low	Satisfactory	Satisfactory
Policy on growth	No intervention	No intervention	No intervention	No intervention
Population age structure				
Level of concern about				
Size of the working-age population	..	..	..	Not a concern
Ageing of the population	..	..	..	Major concern
Fertility and family planning				
View on fertility level	Satisfactory	Too low	Satisfactory	Satisfactory
Policy	No intervention	No intervention	No intervention	No intervention
Access to contraceptive methods	Direct support	Indirect support	Direct support	Direct support
Adolescent fertility				
Level of concern	..	..	Minor concern	Major concern
Policies and programmes	..	..	Yes	Yes
Health and mortality				
View				
Expectation of life	Unacceptable	Unacceptable	Unacceptable	Unacceptable
Under-five mortality	..	..	Unacceptable	Unacceptable
Maternal mortality	..	..	..	Unacceptable
Level of concern about HIV/AIDS	..	..	Minor concern	Minor concern
Measures implemented to control HIV/AIDS*	..	..	..	2,3,5
Grounds on which abortion is permitted**	..	..	1,2,4	1,2,3,4
Spatial distribution and internal migration				
View on spatial distribution	Major change desired	Major change desired	Satisfactory	Major change desired
Policies on internal migration				
From rural to urban areas	..	..	..	Lower
From rural to rural areas	..	..	..	..
From urban to rural areas	..	..	..	..
From urban to urban areas	..	..	..	..
Into urban agglomerations	..	Lower	No intervention	Lower
International migration				
Immigration				
View	Satisfactory	Too low	Satisfactory	Satisfactory
Policy	Maintain	Raise	No intervention	Maintain
Permanent settlement	..	..	No intervention	Maintain
Temporary workers	..	..	No intervention	No intervention
Highly skilled workers	..	..	..	Maintain
Family reunification	..	..	No intervention	Maintain
Integration of non-nationals	..	..	No	No
Emigration				
View	Satisfactory	Too high	Satisfactory	Satisfactory
Policy	Maintain	Lower	No intervention	No intervention
Encouraging the return of nationals	..	..	No	..

* Measures implemented to control HIV/AIDS: (1) blood screening; (2) information/education campaigns; (3) access to antiretroviral treatment; (4) non-discriminatory policies; (5) promoting condom use.

** Grounds on which abortion is permitted: (1) to save the woman's life; (2) to preserve physical health; (3) to preserve mental health; (4) rape or incest; (5) foetal impairment; (6) economic or social reasons; (7) on request.

Population indicators

Indicator	*1975*	*1985*	*1995*	*2005*
Population size and growth				
Population size (thousands)	4 759	5 964	7 482	9 182
Annual growth rate (percentage)*	2.4	2.2	2.3	2.0
Population age structure				
Percentage of population under age 15	43	42	41	38
Percentage of population aged 60 or older	6	6	6	7
Fertility and family planning				
Total fertility (births per woman)*	6.5	5.3	4.8	4.0
Teenage fertility rate (per 1,000 women, aged 15 - 19)*	95	89	89	84
Percentage of births to women under age 20*	11	12	13	14
Percentage of births to women aged 35 or older*	20	17	17	15
Percentage of married women using contraception				
Modern methods	..	12[a]	18[b]	27[c]
All methods	..	26[a]	45[b]	53[c]
Health and mortality				
Life expectancy at birth (years)*				
Males	45	52	58	62
Females	49	56	62	66
Both sexes combined	47	54	60	64
Infant mortality rate (per 1,000 births)*	151	109	75	56
Mortality under age 5 (per 1,000 births)*	245	165	100	72
Maternal mortality ratio (per 100,000 births) (2000)	..	..	..	420
HIV/AIDS (2003)				
Number of infected adults (thousands)	..	..	..	5
Adult prevalence rate (percentage)	..	..	..	0.1
Spatial distribution				
Population density (per sq. km)	4	5	7	8
Urban population (percentage)	41	51	59	64
Annual urban growth rate (percentage)*	3.2	4.3	3.6	2.7
Annual rural growth rate (percentage)*	1.9	0.2	0.5	0.6
International migration				
International migrant stock				
Number of migrants (thousands)	57	59	70	116
Percentage of total population	1.2	1	0.9	1.3

* For the periods 1970-1975, 1980-1985, 1990-1995 and 2000-2005.
[a] For 1983.
[b] For 1994.
[c] For 2000.

Government views and policies

Population policy variable	*1976*	*1986*	*1996*	*2005*
Population size and growth				
View on growth	..	..	Too low	Too low
Policy on growth	..	..	No intervention	No intervention
Population age structure				
Level of concern about				
Size of the working-age population	..	..	..	Major concern
Ageing of the population	..	..	..	Major concern
Fertility and family planning				
View on fertility level	..	..	Too low	Too low
Policy	..	..	No intervention	No intervention
Access to contraceptive methods	..	..	Indirect support	Indirect support
Adolescent fertility				
Level of concern	..	..	..	..
Policies and programmes	..	..	..	No
Health and mortality				
View				
Expectation of life	..	..	Unacceptable	Unacceptable
Under-five mortality	..	..	..	Unacceptable
Maternal mortality	..	..	..	Acceptable
Level of concern about HIV/AIDS	..	..	..	Major concern
Measures implemented to control HIV/AIDS*	..	..	..	1,2
Grounds on which abortion is permitted**	..	..	1,2,3,4,5,6,7	1,2,3,4,5,6,7
Spatial distribution and internal migration				
View on spatial distribution	..	..	Major change desired	Major change desired
Policies on internal migration				
From rural to urban areas	..	..	..	Lower
From rural to rural areas	..	..	..	..
From urban to rural areas	..	..	..	Raise
From urban to urban areas	..	..	..	..
Into urban agglomerations	..	..	..	Lower
International migration				
Immigration				
View	..	..	Satisfactory	Satisfactory
Policy	..	..	No intervention	Maintain
Permanent settlement	..	..	..	Maintain
Temporary workers	..	..	..	Maintain
Highly skilled workers	..	..	..	..
Family reunification	..	..	..	Maintain
Integration of non-nationals	..	..	..	..
Emigration				
View	..	..	Too high	Too high
Policy	..	..	Lower	Lower
Encouraging the return of nationals	..	..	Yes	Yes

* Measures implemented to control HIV/AIDS: (1) blood screening; (2) information/education campaigns; (3) access to antiretroviral treatment; (4) non-discriminatory policies; (5) promoting condom use.

** Grounds on which abortion is permitted: (1) to save the woman's life; (2) to preserve physical health; (3) to preserve mental health; (4) rape or incest; (5) foetal impairment; (6) economic or social reasons; (7) on request.

Population indicators

Indicator	*1975*	*1985*	*1995*	*2005*
Population size and growth				
Population size (thousands)	3 747	4 122	3 420	3 907
Annual growth rate (percentage)*	1.0	1.0	-4.6	0.3
Population age structure				
Percentage of population under age 15	31	25	22	17
Percentage of population aged 60 or older	8	9	13	19
Fertility and family planning				
Total fertility (births per woman)*	2.6	2.0	1.5	1.3
Teenage fertility rate (per 1,000 women, aged 15 - 19)*	55	42	32	24
Percentage of births to women under age 20*	14	11	9	9
Percentage of births to women aged 35 or older*	6	5	7	8
Percentage of married women using contraception				
Modern methods	..	..	..	16[a]
All methods	..	..	..	48[a]
Health and mortality				
Life expectancy at birth (years)*				
Males	65	68	70	71
Females	70	73	75	77
Both sexes combined	67	71	72	74
Infant mortality rate (per 1,000 births)*	51	27	17	14
Mortality under age 5 (per 1,000 births)*	57	31	20	16
Maternal mortality ratio (per 100,000 births) (2000)	..	..	..	31
HIV/AIDS (2003)				
Number of infected adults (thousands)	..	..	..	1
Adult prevalence rate (percentage)	..	..	..	<0.1
Spatial distribution				
Population density (per sq. km)	73	81	67	76
Urban population (percentage)	31	38	41	45
Annual urban growth rate (percentage)*	3.8	2.2	-3.8	2.2
Annual rural growth rate (percentage)*	-0.2	0.4	-5.2	0.3
International migration				
International migrant stock				
Number of migrants (thousands)	..	..	73	41
Percentage of total population	..	..	2.1	1

* For the periods 1970-1975, 1980-1985, 1990-1995 and 2000-2005.
[a] For 2000.

Government views and policies

Population policy variable	*1976*	*1986*	*1996*	*2005*
Population size and growth				
View on growth	Too high	Too high	Too high	Too high
Policy on growth	Lower	Lower	Lower	Lower
Population age structure				
Level of concern about				
Size of the working-age population	..	..	..	..
Ageing of the population	..	..	..	Minor concern
Fertility and family planning				
View on fertility level	Too high	Too high	Too high	Too high
Policy	Lower	Lower	Lower	Lower
Access to contraceptive methods	Direct support	Direct support	Direct support	Direct support
Adolescent fertility				
Level of concern	..	..	Major concern	Major concern
Policies and programmes	..	..	No	Yes
Health and mortality				
View				
Expectation of life	Unacceptable	Unacceptable	Unacceptable	Unacceptable
Under-five mortality	..	..	Unacceptable	Unacceptable
Maternal mortality	..	..	..	Unacceptable
Level of concern about HIV/AIDS	..	..	Major concern	Major concern
Measures implemented to control HIV/AIDS*	..	..	..	1,2,3,4,5
Grounds on which abortion is permitted**	..	..	1,2,3,4,5	1,2,3,4,5
Spatial distribution and internal migration				
View on spatial distribution	Major change desired	Major change desired	Major change desired	Major change desired
Policies on internal migration				
From rural to urban areas	..	..	..	Lower
From rural to rural areas	..	..	..	..
From urban to rural areas	..	..	..	..
From urban to urban areas	..	..	..	..
Into urban agglomerations	Lower	No intervention	Lower	Lower
International migration				
Immigration				
View	Satisfactory	Satisfactory	Satisfactory	Too high
Policy	Maintain	Maintain	No intervention	Lower
Permanent settlement	..	..	No intervention	No intervention
Temporary workers	..	..	No intervention	Lower
Highly skilled workers	..	..	..	Lower
Family reunification	..	..	No intervention	No intervention
Integration of non-nationals	..	..	No	Yes
Emigration				
View	Too high	Satisfactory	Satisfactory	Satisfactory
Policy	Lower	Lower	No intervention	No intervention
Encouraging the return of nationals	No	..	No	No

* Measures implemented to control HIV/AIDS: (1) blood screening; (2) information/education campaigns; (3) access to antiretroviral treatment; (4) non-discriminatory policies; (5) promoting condom use.

** Grounds on which abortion is permitted: (1) to save the woman's life; (2) to preserve physical health; (3) to preserve mental health; (4) rape or incest; (5) foetal impairment; (6) economic or social reasons; (7) on request.

Population indicators

Indicator	*1975*	*1985*	*1995*	*2005*
Population size and growth				
Population size (thousands)	885	1 236	1 616	1 765
Annual growth rate (percentage)*	3.3	3.3	2.5	0.1
Population age structure				
Percentage of population under age 15	49	48	42	38
Percentage of population aged 60 or older	4	4	4	5
Fertility and family planning				
Total fertility (births per woman)*	6.8	5.8	4.1	3.2
Teenage fertility rate (per 1,000 women, aged 15 - 19)*	170	145	101	79
Percentage of births to women under age 20*	21	19	19	18
Percentage of births to women aged 35 or older*	16	15	15	13
Percentage of married women using contraception				
Modern methods	..	32[a]	..	39[b]
All methods	..	33[a]	..	40[b]
Health and mortality				
Life expectancy at birth (years)*				
Males	54	61	62	36
Females	58	65	67	37
Both sexes combined	56	63	64	37
Infant mortality rate (per 1,000 births)*	90	56	46	51
Mortality under age 5 (per 1,000 births)*	128	78	62	106
Maternal mortality ratio (per 100,000 births) (2000)	..	..	..	100
HIV/AIDS (2003)				
Number of infected adults (thousands)	..	..	..	330
Adult prevalence rate (percentage)	..	..	..	37.3
Spatial distribution				
Population density (per sq. km)	2	2	3	3
Urban population (percentage)	13	29	48	53
Annual urban growth rate (percentage)*	12.5	12.0	5.1	1.8
Annual rural growth rate (percentage)*	2.3	0.7	0.8	-0.1
International migration				
International migrant stock				
Number of migrants (thousands)	13	20	39	80
Percentage of total population	1.5	1.6	2.4	4.5

* For the periods 1970-1975, 1980-1985, 1990-1995 and 2000-2005.
[a] For 1988.
[b] For 2000.

Government views and policies

Population policy variable	*1976*	*1986*	*1996*	*2005*
Population size and growth				
View on growth	Satisfactory	Satisfactory	Satisfactory	Satisfactory
Policy on growth	No intervention	No intervention	No intervention	No intervention
Population age structure				
Level of concern about				
Size of the working-age population	..	..	..	Minor concern
Ageing of the population	..	..	..	Major concern
Fertility and family planning				
View on fertility level	Satisfactory	Satisfactory	Satisfactory	Satisfactory
Policy	No intervention	No intervention	No intervention	No intervention
Access to contraceptive methods	Indirect support	Direct support	Direct support	Direct support
Adolescent fertility				
Level of concern	..	..	Major concern	Major concern
Policies and programmes	..	..	Yes	Yes
Health and mortality				
View				
Expectation of life	Unacceptable	Unacceptable	Unacceptable	Unacceptable
Under-five mortality	..	..	Unacceptable	Unacceptable
Maternal mortality	..	..	..	Unacceptable
Level of concern about HIV/AIDS	..	..	Major concern	Major concern
Measures implemented to control HIV/AIDS*	..	..	..	2,3,4,5
Grounds on which abortion is permitted**	..	..	1,4	1,4
Spatial distribution and internal migration				
View on spatial distribution	Minor change desired	Minor change desired	Minor change desired	Major change desired
Policies on internal migration				
From rural to urban areas	..	..	..	Lower
From rural to rural areas	..	..	..	Raise
From urban to rural areas	..	..	..	Raise
From urban to urban areas	..	..	..	No intervention
Into urban agglomerations	Raise	..	Lower	Lower
International migration				
Immigration				
View	Satisfactory	Satisfactory	Satisfactory	Satisfactory
Policy	Maintain	Maintain	Maintain	Maintain
Permanent settlement	..	..	Maintain	Maintain
Temporary workers	..	..	Maintain	Maintain
Highly skilled workers	..	..	..	Maintain
Family reunification	..	..	Maintain	Maintain
Integration of non-nationals	..	..	No	Yes
Emigration				
View	Satisfactory	Satisfactory	Too high	Satisfactory
Policy	Maintain	Maintain	No intervention	No intervention
Encouraging the return of nationals	No	..	No	No

* Measures implemented to control HIV/AIDS: (1) blood screening; (2) information/education campaigns; (3) access to antiretroviral treatment; (4) non-discriminatory policies; (5) promoting condom use.

** Grounds on which abortion is permitted: (1) to save the woman's life; (2) to preserve physical health; (3) to preserve mental health; (4) rape or incest; (5) foetal impairment; (6) economic or social reasons; (7) on request.

Population indicators

Indicator	*1975*	*1985*	*1995*	*2005*
Population size and growth				
Population size (thousands)	108 124	136 063	161 376	186 405
Annual growth rate (percentage)*	2.4	2.2	1.5	1.4
Population age structure				
Percentage of population under age 15	40	37	33	28
Percentage of population aged 60 or older	6	6	7	9
Fertility and family planning				
Total fertility (births per woman)*	4.7	3.8	2.6	2.3
Teenage fertility rate (per 1,000 women, aged 15 - 19)*	68	75	84	90
Percentage of births to women under age 20*	11	13	19	21
Percentage of births to women aged 35 or older*	17	12	10	10
Percentage of married women using contraception				
Modern methods	..	57[a]	70[b]	..
All methods	..	66[a]	77[b]	..
Health and mortality				
Life expectancy at birth (years)*				
Males	57	60	63	66
Females	62	67	71	74
Both sexes combined	60	63	67	70
Infant mortality rate (per 1,000 births)*	91	63	43	27
Mortality under age 5 (per 1,000 births)*	126	80	56	35
Maternal mortality ratio (per 100,000 births) (2000)	..	..	..	260
HIV/AIDS (2003)				
Number of infected adults (thousands)	..	..	..	650
Adult prevalence rate (percentage)	..	..	..	0.7
Spatial distribution				
Population density (per sq. km)	13	16	19	22
Urban population (percentage)	61	71	78	84
Annual urban growth rate (percentage)*	4.2	3.5	2.3	2.0
Annual rural growth rate (percentage)*	-0.2	-0.6	-1.1	-2.4
International migration				
International migrant stock				
Number of migrants (thousands)	1 206	978	730	641
Percentage of total population	1.1	0.7	0.5	0.3

* For the periods 1970-1975, 1980-1985, 1990-1995 and 2000-2005.
[a] For 1986.
[b] For 1996.

Government views and policies

Population policy variable	*1976*	*1986*	*1996*	*2005*
Population size and growth				
View on growth	..	Satisfactory	Satisfactory	Satisfactory
Policy on growth	..	No intervention	No intervention	No intervention
Population age structure				
Level of concern about				
Size of the working-age population	..	..	..	..
Ageing of the population	..	..	..	Minor concern
Fertility and family planning				
View on fertility level	..	Satisfactory	Satisfactory	Satisfactory
Policy	..	No intervention	No intervention	No intervention
Access to contraceptive methods	..	No support	No support	No support
Adolescent fertility				
Level of concern	..	..	Not a concern	Not a concern
Policies and programmes	..	..	No	No
Health and mortality				
View				
Expectation of life	..	Acceptable	Acceptable	Acceptable
Under-five mortality	..	..	Acceptable	Acceptable
Maternal mortality	..	..	..	Acceptable
Level of concern about HIV/AIDS	..	..	Minor concern	Minor concern
Measures implemented to control HIV/AIDS*	..	..	..	1,2
Grounds on which abortion is permitted**	..	..	1	1
Spatial distribution and internal migration				
View on spatial distribution	..	Minor change desired	Minor change desired	Minor change desired
Policies on internal migration				
From rural to urban areas	..	..	..	..
From rural to rural areas	..	..	..	..
From urban to rural areas	..	..	..	..
From urban to urban areas	..	..	..	..
Into urban agglomerations	..	..	No intervention	..
International migration				
Immigration				
View	..	Satisfactory	Satisfactory	Satisfactory
Policy	..	Maintain	Lower	Maintain
Permanent settlement	..	..	Lower	No intervention
Temporary workers	..	..	Maintain	Maintain
Highly skilled workers	..	..	..	Raise
Family reunification	..	..	Lower	No intervention
Integration of non-nationals	..	..	No	No
Emigration				
View	..	Satisfactory	Satisfactory	Satisfactory
Policy	..	Maintain	No intervention	No intervention
Encouraging the return of nationals	..	..	No	No

* Measures implemented to control HIV/AIDS: (1) blood screening; (2) information/education campaigns; (3) access to antiretroviral treatment; (4) non-discriminatory policies; (5) promoting condom use.

** Grounds on which abortion is permitted: (1) to save the woman's life; (2) to preserve physical health; (3) to preserve mental health; (4) rape or incest; (5) foetal impairment; (6) economic or social reasons; (7) on request.

Population indicators

Indicator	*1975*	*1985*	*1995*	*2005*
Population size and growth				
Population size (thousands)	161	223	295	374
Annual growth rate (percentage)*	4.3	2.9	2.8	2.3
Population age structure				
Percentage of population under age 15	40	38	33	30
Percentage of population aged 60 or older	6	4	4	5
Fertility and family planning				
Total fertility (births per woman)*	5.4	3.8	3.1	2.5
Teenage fertility rate (per 1,000 women, aged 15 - 19)*	68	48	39	31
Percentage of births to women under age 20*	10	8	6	5
Percentage of births to women aged 35 or older*	19	13	17	17
Percentage of married women using contraception				
Modern methods	..	..	..	..
All methods	..	..	..	..
Health and mortality				
Life expectancy at birth (years)*				
Males	67	70	72	74
Females	70	74	77	79
Both sexes combined	68	72	74	76
Infant mortality rate (per 1,000 births)*	54	14	8	6
Mortality under age 5 (per 1,000 births)*	57	16	9	7
Maternal mortality ratio (per 100,000 births) (2000)	..	..	..	37
HIV/AIDS (2003)				
Number of infected adults (thousands)	..	..	..	<1
Adult prevalence rate (percentage)	..	..	..	<0.1
Spatial distribution				
Population density (per sq. km)	28	39	51	65
Urban population (percentage)	62	62	70	78
Annual urban growth rate (percentage)*	4.4	3.7	4.0	3.2
Annual rural growth rate (percentage)*	4.1	1.7	0.2	-0.7
International migration				
International migrant stock				
Number of migrants (thousands)	41	61	87	124
Percentage of total population	25.6	27.5	29.6	33.2

* For the periods 1970-1975, 1980-1985, 1990-1995 and 2000-2005.

Government views and policies

Population policy variable	*1976*	*1986*	*1996*	*2005*
Population size and growth				
View on growth	Too low	Too low	Too low	Too low
Policy on growth	Raise	Raise	No intervention	Raise
Population age structure				
Level of concern about				
Size of the working-age population	..	..	..	Major concern
Ageing of the population	..	..	..	Major concern
Fertility and family planning				
View on fertility level	Too low	Too low	Too low	Too low
Policy	Raise	Raise	Raise	Raise
Access to contraceptive methods	Direct support	Direct support	No support	Indirect support
Adolescent fertility				
Level of concern	..	..	Not a concern	Major concern
Policies and programmes	..	..	No	No
Health and mortality				
View				
Expectation of life	Acceptable	Acceptable	Unacceptable	Unacceptable
Under-five mortality	..	..	Unacceptable	Unacceptable
Maternal mortality	..	..	..	Unacceptable
Level of concern about HIV/AIDS	..	..	Minor concern	Major concern
Measures implemented to control HIV/AIDS*	..	..	..	1,2,3,5
Grounds on which abortion is permitted**	..	..	1,2,3,4,5,6,7	1,2,3,4,5,6,7
Spatial distribution and internal migration				
View on spatial distribution	Minor change desired	Minor change desired	Major change desired	Minor change desired
Policies on internal migration				
From rural to urban areas	..	..	..	Lower
From rural to rural areas	..	..	..	..
From urban to rural areas	..	..	..	..
From urban to urban areas	..	..	..	..
Into urban agglomerations	Lower	Lower	No intervention	No intervention
International migration				
Immigration				
View	Satisfactory	Satisfactory	Too high	Satisfactory
Policy	Maintain	Maintain	Maintain	Maintain
Permanent settlement	..	..	Maintain	Maintain
Temporary workers	..	..	Maintain	Maintain
Highly skilled workers	..	..	..	Maintain
Family reunification	..	..	Maintain	Maintain
Integration of non-nationals	..	..	No	Yes
Emigration				
View	Satisfactory	Satisfactory	Too high	Satisfactory
Policy	Maintain	Maintain	Lower	Maintain
Encouraging the return of nationals	..	..	No	..

* Measures implemented to control HIV/AIDS: (1) blood screening; (2) information/education campaigns; (3) access to antiretroviral treatment; (4) non-discriminatory policies; (5) promoting condom use.

** Grounds on which abortion is permitted: (1) to save the woman's life; (2) to preserve physical health; (3) to preserve mental health; (4) rape or incest; (5) foetal impairment; (6) economic or social reasons; (7) on request.

Population indicators

Indicator	*1975*	*1985*	*1995*	*2005*
Population size and growth				
Population size (thousands)	8 721	8 960	8 297	7 726
Annual growth ratc (pcrccntagc)*	0.5	0.2	-1.0	-0.7
Population age structure				
Percentage of population under age 15	22	21	18	14
Percentage of population aged 60 or older	16	17	21	22
Fertility and family planning				
Total fertility (births per woman)*	2.2	2.0	1.5	1.2
Teenage fertility rate (per 1,000 women, aged 15 - 19)*	90	83	61	46
Percentage of births to women under age 20*	21	20	22	18
Percentage of births to women aged 35 or older*	4	4	4	4
Percentage of married women using contraception				
Modern methods	8[a]	..	26[b]	..
All methods	76[a]	..	42[b]	..
Health and mortality				
Life expectancy at birth (years)*				
Males	69	68	68	69
Females	73	74	75	76
Both sexes combined	71	71	71	72
Infant mortality rate (per 1,000 births)*	26	18	16	13
Mortality under age 5 (per 1,000 births)*	33	22	20	17
Maternal mortality ratio (per 100,000 births) (2000)	..	..	..	32
HIV/AIDS (2003)				
Number of infected adults (thousands)	..	..	..	<1
Adult prevalence rate (percentage)	..	..	..	<0.1
Spatial distribution				
Population density (per sq. km)	79	81	75	70
Urban population (percentage)	58	65	68	70
Annual urban growth rate (percentage)*	2.6	1.3	-0.3	-0.3
Annual rural growth rate (percentage)*	-2.0	-1.6	-1.6	-2.0
International migration				
International migrant stock				
Number of migrants (thousands)	22	22	47	104
Percentage of total population	0.2	0.2	0.6	1.3

* For the periods 1970-1975, 1980-1985, 1990-1995 and 2000-2005.
[a] For 1976.
[b] For 1997.

Government views and policies

Population policy variable	*1976*	*1986*	*1996*	*2005*
Population size and growth				
View on growth	Satisfactory	Satisfactory	Too high	Too high
Policy on growth	No intervention	No intervention	No intervention	Lower
Population age structure				
Level of concern about				
Size of the working-age population	..	..	..	Minor concern
Ageing of the population	..	..	..	Minor concern
Fertility and family planning				
View on fertility level	Satisfactory	Satisfactory	Too high	Too high
Policy	No intervention	No intervention	Lower	Lower
Access to contraceptive methods	No support	Indirect support	Direct support	Direct support
Adolescent fertility				
Level of concern	..	..	Major concern	Major concern
Policies and programmes	..	..	Yes	Yes
Health and mortality				
View				
Expectation of life	Unacceptable	Unacceptable	Unacceptable	Unacceptable
Under-five mortality	..	..	Unacceptable	Unacceptable
Maternal mortality	..	..	..	Unacceptable
Level of concern about HIV/AIDS	..	..	Major concern	Major concern
Measures implemented to control HIV/AIDS*	..	..	..	1,2,3,5
Grounds on which abortion is permitted**	..	..	1,2	1,2,3,4,5
Spatial distribution and internal migration				
View on spatial distribution	Major change desired	Major change desired	Major change desired	Minor change desired
Policies on internal migration				
From rural to urban areas	..	..	..	Lower
From rural to rural areas	..	..	..	Lower
From urban to rural areas	..	..	..	Maintain
From urban to urban areas	..	..	..	No intervention
Into urban agglomerations	No intervention	No intervention	Lower	Lower
International migration				
Immigration				
View	Satisfactory	Satisfactory	Satisfactory	Satisfactory
Policy	Maintain	Maintain	No intervention	No intervention
Permanent settlement	..	..	No intervention	No intervention
Temporary workers	..	..	No intervention	No intervention
Highly skilled workers	..	..	..	No intervention
Family reunification	..	..	No intervention	No intervention
Integration of non-nationals	..	..	No	No
Emigration				
View	Too high	Satisfactory	Too high	Too high
Policy	Lower	Maintain	Lower	No intervention
Encouraging the return of nationals	No	..	No	Yes

* Measures implemented to control HIV/AIDS: (1) blood screening; (2) information/education campaigns; (3) access to antiretroviral treatment; (4) non-discriminatory policies; (5) promoting condom use.

** Grounds on which abortion is permitted: (1) to save the woman's life; (2) to preserve physical health; (3) to preserve mental health; (4) rape or incest; (5) foetal impairment; (6) economic or social reasons; (7) on request.

Population indicators

Indicator	*1975*	*1985*	*1995*	*2005*
Population size and growth				
Population size (thousands)	5 947	7 386	9 832	13 228
Annual growth rate (percentage)*	2.2	2.3	2.8	3.2
Population age structure				
Percentage of population under age 15	45	47	48	47
Percentage of population aged 60 or older	6	6	5	4
Fertility and family planning				
Total fertility (births per woman)*	7.8	7.7	7.2	6.7
Teenage fertility rate (per 1,000 women, aged 15 - 19)*	167	136	182	165
Percentage of births to women under age 20*	17	15	20	19
Percentage of births to women aged 35 or older*	17	19	15	13
Percentage of married women using contraception				
Modern methods	..	..	4[a]	9[b]
All methods	..	..	8[a]	14[b]
Health and mortality				
Life expectancy at birth (years)*				
Males	43	46	45	47
Females	45	49	48	48
Both sexes combined	44	48	47	47
Infant mortality rate (per 1,000 births)*	159	142	125	121
Mortality under age 5 (per 1,000 births)*	274	240	208	196
Maternal mortality ratio (per 100,000 births) (2000)	..	..	..	1 000
HIV/AIDS (2003)				
Number of infected adults (thousands)	..	..	..	270
Adult prevalence rate (percentage)	..	..	..	4.2
Spatial distribution				
Population density (per sq. km)	22	27	36	48
Urban population (percentage)	6	11	15	19
Annual urban growth rate (percentage)*	4.3	8.5	5.1	5.0
Annual rural growth rate (percentage)*	2.1	1.9	2.5	2.5
International migration				
International migrant stock				
Number of migrants (thousands)	106	273	464	773
Percentage of total population	1.8	3.7	4.7	5.8

* For the periods 1970-1975, 1980-1985, 1990-1995 and 2000-2005.
[a] For 1993.
[b] For 2003.

Government views and policies

Population policy variable	*1976*	*1986*	*1996*	*2005*
Population size and growth				
View on growth	Satisfactory	Too high	Too high	Too high
Policy on growth	No intervention	Lower	Lower	Lower
Population age structure				
Level of concern about				
Size of the working-age population	..	..	..	..
Ageing of the population	..	..	..	..
Fertility and family planning				
View on fertility level	Satisfactory	Too high	Too high	Too high
Policy	No intervention	Lower	Lower	Lower
Access to contraceptive methods	No support	Direct support	Direct support	Direct support
Adolescent fertility				
Level of concern	..	..	Not a concern	Not a concern
Policies and programmes	..	..	No	No
Health and mortality				
View				
Expectation of life	Unacceptable	Unacceptable	Unacceptable	Unacceptable
Under-five mortality	..	..	Unacceptable	Unacceptable
Maternal mortality	..	..	..	Unacceptable
Level of concern about HIV/AIDS	..	..	Major concern	Major concern
Measures implemented to control HIV/AIDS*	..	..	..	1,2,3,4,5
Grounds on which abortion is permitted**	..	..	1,2	1,2,3
Spatial distribution and internal migration				
View on spatial distribution	Minor change desired	Minor change desired	Minor change desired	Major change desired
Policies on internal migration				
From rural to urban areas	..	..	..	Lower
From rural to rural areas	..	..	..	Raise
From urban to rural areas	..	..	..	..
From urban to urban areas	..	..	..	..
Into urban agglomerations	No intervention	..	Lower	Lower
International migration				
Immigration				
View	Satisfactory	Satisfactory	Satisfactory	Satisfactory
Policy	Maintain	Maintain	No intervention	No intervention
Permanent settlement	..	..	No intervention	No intervention
Temporary workers	..	..	..	..
Highly skilled workers	..	..	..	..
Family reunification	..	..	..	..
Integration of non-nationals	..	..	No	..
Emigration				
View	Satisfactory	Satisfactory	Satisfactory	Satisfactory
Policy	Maintain	Maintain	No intervention	No intervention
Encouraging the return of nationals	No	..	Yes	..

* Measures implemented to control HIV/AIDS: (1) blood screening; (2) information/education campaigns; (3) access to antiretroviral treatment; (4) non-discriminatory policies; (5) promoting condom use.

** Grounds on which abortion is permitted: (1) to save the woman's life; (2) to preserve physical health; (3) to preserve mental health; (4) rape or incest; (5) foetal impairment; (6) economic or social reasons; (7) on request.

Population indicators

Indicator	*1975*	*1985*	*1995*	*2005*
Population size and growth				
Population size (thousands)	3 680	4 885	6 159	7 548
Annual growth rate (percentage)*	0.9	3.4	1.7	3.0
Population age structure				
Percentage of population under age 15	45	44	47	45
Percentage of population aged 60 or older	6	5	4	4
Fertility and family planning				
Total fertility (births per woman)*	6.8	6.8	6.8	6.8
Teenage fertility rate (per 1,000 women, aged 15 - 19)*	50	50	50	50
Percentage of births to women under age 20*	6	6	5	7
Percentage of births to women aged 35 or older*	23	20	23	21
Percentage of married women using contraception				
Modern methods	..	1[a]	..	10[b]
All methods	..	9[a]	..	16[b]
Health and mortality				
Life expectancy at birth (years)*				
Males	42	46	41	42
Females	46	49	44	44
Both sexes combined	44	47	42	43
Infant mortality rate (per 1,000 births)*	137	118	128	106
Mortality under age 5 (per 1,000 births)*	244	206	220	187
Maternal mortality ratio (per 100,000 births) (2000)	..	..	..	1 000
HIV/AIDS (2003)				
Number of infected adults (thousands)	..	..	..	220
Adult prevalence rate (percentage)	..	..	..	6.0
Spatial distribution				
Population density (per sq. km)	132	176	221	271
Urban population (percentage)	3	5	8	11
Annual urban growth rate (percentage)*	6.9	7.0	5.0	6.5
Annual rural growth rate (percentage)*	0.8	3.1	1.2	2.7
International migration				
International migrant stock				
Number of migrants (thousands)	140	343	295	100
Percentage of total population	3.8	7	4.8	1.3

* For the periods 1970-1975, 1980-1985, 1990-1995 and 2000-2005.
[a] For 1987.
[b] For 2000.

Government views and policies

Population policy variable	*1976*	*1986*	*1996*	*2005*
Population size and growth				
View on growth	Too low	Too low	Too high	Too high
Policy on growth	Raise	Raise	Lower	Lower
Population age structure				
Level of concern about				
Size of the working-age population	..	..	..	Major concern
Ageing of the population	..	..	..	Minor concern
Fertility and family planning				
View on fertility level	Too low	Too low	Too high	Too high
Policy	Raise	Raise	Lower	Lower
Access to contraceptive methods	Limits	Limits	Direct support	Direct support
Adolescent fertility				
Level of concern	..	..	..	Not a concern
Policies and programmes	..	..	..	No
Health and mortality				
View				
Expectation of life	Unacceptable	Unacceptable	Unacceptable	Unacceptable
Under-five mortality	..	..	..	Unacceptable
Maternal mortality	..	..	..	Unacceptable
Level of concern about HIV/AIDS	..	..	..	Major concern
Measures implemented to control HIV/AIDS*	..	..	..	1,2,3,4,5
Grounds on which abortion is permitted**	..	..	1,2,3,4,5,6,7	1,2,3,4,5,6,7
Spatial distribution and internal migration				
View on spatial distribution	Major change desired	Major change desired	Major change desired	Major change desired
Policies on internal migration				
From rural to urban areas	..	..	..	Lower
From rural to rural areas	..	..	..	No intervention
From urban to rural areas	..	..	..	Raise
From urban to urban areas	..	..	..	Maintain
Into urban agglomerations	..	..	..	Lower
International migration				
Immigration				
View	Satisfactory	Satisfactory	Satisfactory	Satisfactory
Policy	Maintain	Maintain	Maintain	Maintain
Permanent settlement	..	..	Maintain	No intervention
Temporary workers	..	..	..	No intervention
Highly skilled workers	..	..	..	Maintain
Family reunification	..	..	..	No intervention
Integration of non-nationals	..	..	..	No
Emigration				
View	Satisfactory	Too high	Too high	Satisfactory
Policy	Maintain	Lower	Lower	No intervention
Encouraging the return of nationals	..	..	Yes	No

* Measures implemented to control HIV/AIDS: (1) blood screening; (2) information/education campaigns; (3) access to antiretroviral treatment; (4) non-discriminatory policies; (5) promoting condom use.
** Grounds on which abortion is permitted: (1) to save the woman's life; (2) to preserve physical health; (3) to preserve mental health; (4) rape or incest; (5) foetal impairment; (6) economic or social reasons; (7) on request.

Population indicators

Indicator	*1975*	*1985*	*1995*	*2005*
Population size and growth				
Population size (thousands)	7 098	8 101	11 368	14 071
Annual growth rate (percentage)*	0.5	4.1	3.1	2.0
Population age structure				
Percentage of population under age 15	42	44	46	37
Percentage of population aged 60 or older	5	5	5	6
Fertility and family planning				
Total fertility (births per woman)*	5.5	6.6	5.4	4.1
Teenage fertility rate (per 1,000 women, aged 15 - 19)*	133	158	88	51
Percentage of births to women under age 20*	16	16	9	10
Percentage of births to women aged 35 or older*	8	8	19	18
Percentage of married women using contraception				
Modern methods	..	..	7	19[a]
All methods	..	..	13	24[a]
Health and mortality				
Life expectancy at birth (years)*				
Males	39	50	53	52
Females	42	54	57	60
Both sexes combined	40	52	55	56
Infant mortality rate (per 1,000 births)*	181	124	110	95
Mortality under age 5 (per 1,000 births)*	303	205	170	140
Maternal mortality ratio (per 100,000 births) (2000)	..	..	..	450
HIV/AIDS (2003)				
Number of infected adults (thousands)	..	..	..	170
Adult prevalence rate (percentage)	..	..	..	2.6
Spatial distribution				
Population density (per sq. km)	39	45	63	78
Urban population (percentage)	10	13	14	20
Annual urban growth rate (percentage)*	-2.1	4.5	5.6	5.5
Annual rural growth rate (percentage)*	0.8	4.1	2.9	1.7
International migration				
International migrant stock				
Number of migrants (thousands)	15	13	116	304
Percentage of total population	0.2	0.2	1	2.2

* For the periods 1970-1975, 1980-1985, 1990-1995 and 2000-2005.
[a] For 2000.

Government views and policies

Population policy variable	*1976*	*1986*	*1996*	*2005*
Population size and growth				
View on growth	Too low	Too high	Too high	Too high
Policy on growth	Raise	No intervention	Lower	Lower
Population age structure				
Level of concern about				
Size of the working-age population	..	..	..	Major concern
Ageing of the population	..	..	..	..
Fertility and family planning				
View on fertility level	Too low	Too high	Too high	Too high
Policy	No intervention	No intervention	Lower	Lower
Access to contraceptive methods	Indirect support	Direct support	Indirect support	Indirect support
Adolescent fertility				
Level of concern	..	..	Major concern	Major concern
Policies and programmes	..	..	Yes	Yes
Health and mortality				
View				
Expectation of life	Unacceptable	Unacceptable	Unacceptable	Unacceptable
Under-five mortality	..	..	Unacceptable	Unacceptable
Maternal mortality	..	..	..	Unacceptable
Level of concern about HIV/AIDS	..	..	Major concern	Major concern
Measures implemented to control HIV/AIDS*	..	..	..	1,2,3,5
Grounds on which abortion is permitted**	..	..	1,2,4	1,2,3,4
Spatial distribution and internal migration				
View on spatial distribution	Major change desired	Minor change desired	Major change desired	Major change desired
Policies on internal migration				
From rural to urban areas	..	..	..	Lower
From rural to rural areas	..	..	..	..
From urban to rural areas	..	..	..	..
From urban to urban areas	..	..	..	..
Into urban agglomerations	Lower	Lower	Lower	Lower
International migration				
Immigration				
View	Satisfactory	Satisfactory	Satisfactory	Satisfactory
Policy	Maintain	Maintain	Lower	Lower
Permanent settlement	..	..	Lower	Lower
Temporary workers	..	..	Lower	..
Highly skilled workers	..	..	..	..
Family reunification	..	..	Maintain	..
Integration of non-nationals	..	..	Yes	..
Emigration				
View	Satisfactory	Satisfactory	Satisfactory	Satisfactory
Policy	Maintain	Maintain	No intervention	No intervention
Encouraging the return of nationals	Yes	..	No	..

* Measures implemented to control HIV/AIDS: (1) blood screening; (2) information/education campaigns; (3) access to antiretroviral treatment; (4) non-discriminatory policies; (5) promoting condom use.

** Grounds on which abortion is permitted: (1) to save the woman's life; (2) to preserve physical health; (3) to preserve mental health; (4) rape or incest; (5) foetal impairment; (6) economic or social reasons; (7) on request.

Population indicators

Indicator	*1975*	*1985*	*1995*	*2005*
Population size and growth				
Population size (thousands)	7 563	10 067	13 302	16 322
Annual growth rate (percentage)*	2.6	2.8	2.7	1.9
Population age structure				
Percentage of population under age 15	43	45	44	41
Percentage of population aged 60 or older	6	6	5	6
Fertility and family planning				
Total fertility (births per woman)*	6.3	6.4	5.7	4.6
Teenage fertility rate (per 1,000 women, aged 15 - 19)*	190	186	160	122
Percentage of births to women under age 20*	20	21	21	19
Percentage of births to women aged 35 or older*	16	15	14	12
Percentage of married women using contraception				
Modern methods	1[a]	..	7[b]	13[c]
All methods	2[a]	..	19[b]	26[c]
Health and mortality				
Life expectancy at birth (years)*				
Males	44	49	50	45
Females	47	52	54	47
Both sexes combined	46	51	52	46
Infant mortality rate (per 1,000 births)*	128	103	93	94
Mortality under age 5 (per 1,000 births)*	214	176	154	163
Maternal mortality ratio (per 100,000 births) (2000)	..	..	..	730
HIV/AIDS (2003)				
Number of infected adults (thousands)	..	..	..	520
Adult prevalence rate (percentage)	..	..	..	6.9
Spatial distribution				
Population density (per sq. km)	16	21	28	34
Urban population (percentage)	27	36	45	53
Annual urban growth rate (percentage)*	8.2	5.4	4.9	3.4
Annual rural growth rate (percentage)*	0.9	1.5	1.3	0.2
International migration				
International migrant stock				
Number of migrants (thousands)	215	185	159	137
Percentage of total population	2.8	1.8	1.2	0.8

* For the periods 1970-1975, 1980-1985, 1990-1995 and 2000-2005.
[a] For 1978.
[b] For 1998.
[c] For 2004.

Government views and policies

Population policy variable	*1976*	*1986*	*1996*	*2005*
Population size and growth				
View on growth	Satisfactory	Satisfactory	Satisfactory	Satisfactory
Policy on growth	No intervention	Maintain	No intervention	No intervention
Population age structure				
Level of concern about				
Size of the working-age population	..	..	..	Major concern
Ageing of the population	..	..	..	Major concern
Fertility and family planning				
View on fertility level	Satisfactory	Satisfactory	Satisfactory	Too low
Policy	No intervention	No intervention	No intervention	No intervention
Access to contraceptive methods	Direct support	Direct support	Direct support	Indirect support
Adolescent fertility				
Level of concern	..	..	Minor concern	Major concern
Policies and programmes	..	..	Yes	Yes
Health and mortality				
View				
Expectation of life	Acceptable	Acceptable	Acceptable	Acceptable
Under-five mortality	..	..	..	Acceptable
Maternal mortality	..	..	..	Acceptable
Level of concern about HIV/AIDS	..	..	Major concern	Major concern
Measures implemented to control HIV/AIDS*	..	..	..	1,2,3,4,5
Grounds on which abortion is permitted**	..	..	1,2,3,4,5,6,7	1,2,3,4,5,6,7
Spatial distribution and internal migration				
View on spatial distribution	Minor change desired	Minor change desired	Satisfactory	Minor change desired
Policies on internal migration				
From rural to urban areas	..	..	..	No intervention
From rural to rural areas	..	..	..	No intervention
From urban to rural areas	..	..	..	No intervention
From urban to urban areas	..	..	..	No intervention
Into urban agglomerations	No intervention	No intervention	No intervention	No intervention
International migration				
Immigration				
View	Satisfactory	Satisfactory	Satisfactory	Too low
Policy	Maintain	Maintain	Lower	Raise
Permanent settlement	..	..	Lower	Raise
Temporary workers	..	..	Maintain	Raise
Highly skilled workers	..	..	..	Raise
Family reunification	..	..	Lower	Raise
Integration of non-nationals	..	..	Yes	Yes
Emigration				
View	Satisfactory	Satisfactory	Satisfactory	Satisfactory
Policy	Maintain	Maintain	No intervention	No intervention
Encouraging the return of nationals	No	..	No	No

* Measures implemented to control HIV/AIDS: (1) blood screening; (2) information/education campaigns; (3) access to antiretroviral treatment; (4) non-discriminatory policies; (5) promoting condom use.
** Grounds on which abortion is permitted: (1) to save the woman's life; (2) to preserve physical health; (3) to preserve mental health; (4) rape or incest; (5) foetal impairment; (6) economic or social reasons; (7) on request.

Population indicators

Indicator	*1975*	*1985*	*1995*	*2005*
Population size and growth				
Population size (thousands)	23 142	25 843	29 302	32 268
Annual growth rate (percentage)*	1.3	1.1	1.1	1.0
Population age structure				
Percentage of population under age 15	26	21	20	18
Percentage of population aged 60 or older	12	15	16	18
Fertility and family planning				
Total fertility (births per woman)*	2.0	1.6	1.7	1.5
Teenage fertility rate (per 1,000 women, aged 15 - 19)*	25	21	22	15
Percentage of births to women under age 20*	8	6	5	5
Percentage of births to women aged 35 or older*	9	10	13	16
Percentage of married women using contraception				
Modern methods	..	70[a]	73	..
All methods	..	73[a]	75	..
Health and mortality				
Life expectancy at birth (years)*				
Males	70	73	75	77
Females	77	80	81	82
Both sexes combined	73	76	78	80
Infant mortality rate (per 1,000 births)*	16	9	6	5
Mortality under age 5 (per 1,000 births)*	19	11	8	6
Maternal mortality ratio (per 100,000 births) (2000)	..	..	..	6
HIV/AIDS (2003)				
Number of infected adults (thousands)	..	..	..	55
Adult prevalence rate (percentage)	..	..	..	0.3
Spatial distribution				
Population density (per sq. km)	2	3	3	3
Urban population (percentage)	76	76	78	81
Annual urban growth rate (percentage)*	1.3	1.2	1.4	1.2
Annual rural growth rate (percentage)*	1.3	0.5	0.2	-1.0
International migration				
International migrant stock				
Number of migrants (thousands)	3 518	3 895	5 003	6 106
Percentage of total population	15.2	15.1	17.1	18.9

* For the periods 1970-1975, 1980-1985, 1990-1995 and 2000-2005.
[a] For 1984.

Government views and policies

Population policy variable	*1976*	*1986*	*1996*	*2005*
Population size and growth				
View on growth	Satisfactory	Satisfactory	Too high	Satisfactory
Policy on growth	No intervention	No intervention	Lower	Maintain
Population age structure				
Level of concern about				
Size of the working-age population	..	..	..	Major concern
Ageing of the population	..	..	..	Major concern
Fertility and family planning				
View on fertility level	Satisfactory	Satisfactory	Too high	Too high
Policy	No intervention	No intervention	Lower	Lower
Access to contraceptive methods	Direct support	Direct support	Direct support	Direct support
Adolescent fertility				
Level of concern	..	..	..	Major concern
Policies and programmes	..	..	No	Yes
Health and mortality				
View				
Expectation of life	Unacceptable	Unacceptable	Unacceptable	Unacceptable
Under-five mortality	..	..	..	Unacceptable
Maternal mortality	..	..	..	Unacceptable
Level of concern about HIV/AIDS	..	..	..	Minor concern
Measures implemented to control HIV/AIDS*	..	..	..	1,2
Grounds on which abortion is permitted**	..	..	1,2,3,4,5,6	1,2,3,4,5,6,7
Spatial distribution and internal migration				
View on spatial distribution	Major change desired	Major change desired	Major change desired	Major change desired
Policies on internal migration				
From rural to urban areas	..	..	..	Lower
From rural to rural areas	..	..	..	..
From urban to rural areas	..	..	..	..
From urban to urban areas	..	..	..	..
Into urban agglomerations	No intervention	..	..	Lower
International migration				
Immigration				
View	Satisfactory	Satisfactory	Satisfactory	Satisfactory
Policy	Maintain	Maintain	No intervention	No intervention
Permanent settlement	..	..	No intervention	No intervention
Temporary workers	..	..	..	No intervention
Highly skilled workers	..	..	..	No intervention
Family reunification	..	..	..	No intervention
Integration of non-nationals	..	..	..	No
Emigration				
View	Satisfactory	Satisfactory	Too low	Satisfactory
Policy	Maintain	Maintain	Maintain	Maintain
Encouraging the return of nationals	No	..	..	Yes

* Measures implemented to control HIV/AIDS: (1) blood screening; (2) information/education campaigns; (3) access to antiretroviral treatment; (4) non-discriminatory policies; (5) promoting condom use.
** Grounds on which abortion is permitted: (1) to save the woman's life; (2) to preserve physical health; (3) to preserve mental health; (4) rape or incest; (5) foetal impairment; (6) economic or social reasons; (7) on request.

Population indicators

Indicator	*1975*	*1985*	*1995*	*2005*
Population size and growth				
Population size (thousands)	278	319	401	507
Annual growth rate (percentage)*	0.8	2.0	2.4	2.4
Population age structure				
Percentage of population under age 15	47	46	46	40
Percentage of population aged 60 or older	8	7	6	6
Fertility and family planning				
Total fertility (births per woman)*	7.0	6.5	5.0	3.8
Teenage fertility rate (per 1,000 women, aged 15 - 19)*	85	79	116	94
Percentage of births to women under age 20*	13	12	17	19
Percentage of births to women aged 35 or older*	25	16	15	14
Percentage of married women using contraception				
Modern methods	..	..	46[a]	..
All methods	..	..	53[a]	..
Health and mortality				
Life expectancy at birth (years)*				
Males	56	60	64	67
Females	59	64	69	73
Both sexes combined	57	62	66	70
Infant mortality rate (per 1,000 births)*	83	63	44	30
Mortality under age 5 (per 1,000 births)*	111	86	56	36
Maternal mortality ratio (per 100,000 births) (2000)	..	..	..	150
HIV/AIDS (2003)				
Number of infected adults (thousands)	..	..	..	..
Adult prevalence rate (percentage)	..	..	..	..
Spatial distribution				
Population density (per sq. km)	69	79	99	126
Urban population (percentage)	21	33	49	58
Annual urban growth rate (percentage)*	2.6	8.5	4.2	3.5
Annual rural growth rate (percentage)*	0.3	-0.9	0.6	0.1
International migration				
International migrant stock				
Number of migrants (thousands)	8	8	10	11
Percentage of total population	2.8	2.7	2.4	2.2

* For the periods 1970-1975, 1980-1985, 1990-1995 and 2000-2005.
[a] For 1998.

Government views and policies

Population policy variable	*1976*	*1986*	*1996*	*2005*
Population size and growth				
View on growth	Too low	Too high	Too high	Satisfactory
Policy on growth	Raise	No intervention	No intervention	No intervention
Population age structure				
Level of concern about				
Size of the working-age population	..	..	..	Major concern
Ageing of the population	..	..	..	..
Fertility and family planning				
View on fertility level	Too low	Too high	Too high	Satisfactory
Policy	No intervention	No intervention	No intervention	No intervention
Access to contraceptive methods	No support	Direct support	Direct support	Indirect support
Adolescent fertility				
Level of concern	..	..	Not a concern	Minor concern
Policies and programmes	..	..	..	Yes
Health and mortality				
View				
Expectation of life	Unacceptable	Unacceptable	Unacceptable	Unacceptable
Under-five mortality	..	..	Unacceptable	Unacceptable
Maternal mortality	..	..	..	Unacceptable
Level of concern about HIV/AIDS	..	..	Major concern	Major concern
Measures implemented to control HIV/AIDS*	..	..	..	2
Grounds on which abortion is permitted**	..	..	1	1
Spatial distribution and internal migration				
View on spatial distribution	Major change desired	Minor change desired	Minor change desired	Major change desired
Policies on internal migration				
From rural to urban areas	..	..	..	Lower
From rural to rural areas	..	..	..	..
From urban to rural areas	..	..	..	..
From urban to urban areas	..	..	..	..
Into urban agglomerations	Lower	Lower	No intervention	Lower
International migration				
Immigration				
View	Satisfactory	Satisfactory	Satisfactory	Satisfactory
Policy	Maintain	Maintain	No intervention	No intervention
Permanent settlement	..	..	No intervention	No intervention
Temporary workers	..	..	No intervention	..
Highly skilled workers	..	..	..	..
Family reunification	..	..	No intervention	..
Integration of non-nationals	..	..	No	..
Emigration				
View	Satisfactory	Satisfactory	Too high	Too high
Policy	Maintain	Maintain	No intervention	No intervention
Encouraging the return of nationals	No	..	No	..

* Measures implemented to control HIV/AIDS: (1) blood screening; (2) information/education campaigns; (3) access to antiretroviral treatment; (4) non-discriminatory policies; (5) promoting condom use.

** Grounds on which abortion is permitted: (1) to save the woman's life; (2) to preserve physical health; (3) to preserve mental health; (4) rape or incest; (5) foetal impairment; (6) economic or social reasons; (7) on request.

Population indicators

Indicator	*1975*	*1985*	*1995*	*2005*
Population size and growth				
Population size (thousands)	2 060	2 677	3 414	4 038
Annual growth rate (percentage)*	1.9	2.8	2.6	1.3
Population age structure				
Percentage of population under age 15	41	42	43	43
Percentage of population aged 60 or older	7	6	6	6
Fertility and family planning				
Total fertility (births per woman)*	5.7	5.7	5.6	5.0
Teenage fertility rate (per 1,000 women, aged 15 - 19)*	174	173	167	133
Percentage of births to women under age 20*	21	21	21	20
Percentage of births to women aged 35 or older*	15	14	14	11
Percentage of married women using contraception				
Modern methods	..	..	3	7[a]
All methods	..	..	15	28[a]
Health and mortality				
Life expectancy at birth (years)*				
Males	41	45	44	39
Females	46	51	50	40
Both sexes combined	43	48	47	39
Infant mortality rate (per 1,000 births)*	141	115	106	98
Mortality under age 5 (per 1,000 births)*	235	199	181	176
Maternal mortality ratio (per 100,000 births) (2000)	..	..	..	1 100
HIV/AIDS (2003)				
Number of infected adults (thousands)	..	..	..	240
Adult prevalence rate (percentage)	..	..	..	13.5
Spatial distribution				
Population density (per sq. km)	3	4	5	6
Urban population (percentage)	34	36	39	44
Annual urban growth rate (percentage)*	4.1	3.4	3.5	2.5
Annual rural growth rate (percentage)*	0.8	2.3	2.1	0.4
International migration				
International migrant stock				
Number of migrants (thousands)	52	59	67	76
Percentage of total population	2.5	2.2	2	1.9

* For the periods 1970-1975, 1980-1985, 1990-1995 and 2000-2005.
[a] For 2000.

Government views and policies

Population policy variable	*1976*	*1986*	*1996*	*2005*
Population size and growth				
View on growth	Satisfactory	Satisfactory	Too high	Too high
Policy on growth	No intervention	No intervention	Lower	Lower
Population age structure				
Level of concern about				
Size of the working-age population	..	..	..	..
Ageing of the population	..	..	..	..
Fertility and family planning				
View on fertility level	Satisfactory	Satisfactory	Satisfactory	Satisfactory
Policy	No intervention	No intervention	No intervention	No intervention
Access to contraceptive methods	Limits	No support	Indirect support	Direct support
Adolescent fertility				
Level of concern	..	..	..	Minor concern
Policies and programmes	..	..	..	Yes
Health and mortality				
View				
Expectation of life	Unacceptable	Unacceptable	Unacceptable	Unacceptable
Under-five mortality	..	..	..	Unacceptable
Maternal mortality	..	..	..	Unacceptable
Level of concern about HIV/AIDS	..	..	..	Major concern
Measures implemented to control HIV/AIDS*	..	..	..	1,2,3,5
Grounds on which abortion is permitted**	..	..	1	1,2,5
Spatial distribution and internal migration				
View on spatial distribution	Minor change desired	Minor change desired	Minor change desired	Minor change desired
Policies on internal migration				
From rural to urban areas	..	..	..	No intervention
From rural to rural areas	..	..	..	No intervention
From urban to rural areas	..	..	..	No intervention
From urban to urban areas	..	..	..	No intervention
Into urban agglomerations	No intervention	..	..	No intervention
International migration				
Immigration				
View	Satisfactory	Satisfactory	Satisfactory	Satisfactory
Policy	Maintain	Maintain	Maintain	Maintain
Permanent settlement	..	..	Maintain	Maintain
Temporary workers	..	..	..	..
Highly skilled workers	..	..	..	..
Family reunification	..	..	..	..
Integration of non-nationals	..	..	..	..
Emigration				
View	Satisfactory	Satisfactory	Satisfactory	Satisfactory
Policy	Maintain	Maintain	Maintain	Maintain
Encouraging the return of nationals	No	..	..	..

* Measures implemented to control HIV/AIDS: (1) blood screening; (2) information/education campaigns; (3) access to antiretroviral treatment; (4) non-discriminatory policies; (5) promoting condom use.

** Grounds on which abortion is permitted: (1) to save the woman's life; (2) to preserve physical health; (3) to preserve mental health; (4) rape or incest; (5) foetal impairment; (6) economic or social reasons; (7) on request.

Population indicators

Indicator	*1975*	*1985*	*1995*	*2005*
Population size and growth				
Population size (thousands)	4 185	5 215	7 034	9 749
Annual growth rate (percentage)*	2.2	2.4	3.0	3.4
Population age structure				
Percentage of population under age 15	44	45	46	47
Percentage of population aged 60 or older	6	5	5	5
Fertility and family planning				
Total fertility (births per woman)*	6.7	6.7	6.7	6.7
Teenage fertility rate (per 1,000 women, aged 15 - 19)*	217	217	217	195
Percentage of births to women under age 20*	22	23	23	21
Percentage of births to women aged 35 or older*	14	13	12	11
Percentage of married women using contraception				
Modern methods	..	..	1[a]	2[b]
All methods	..	..	4[a]	8[b]
Health and mortality				
Life expectancy at birth (years)*				
Males	39	43	44	43
Females	42	46	48	45
Both sexes combined	41	45	46	44
Infant mortality rate (per 1,000 births)*	157	133	118	116
Mortality under age 5 (per 1,000 births)*	262	233	207	203
Maternal mortality ratio (per 100,000 births) (2000)	..	..	..	1 100
HIV/AIDS (2003)				
Number of infected adults (thousands)	..	..	..	180
Adult prevalence rate (percentage)	..	..	..	4.8
Spatial distribution				
Population density (per sq. km)	3	4	5	8
Urban population (percentage)	16	20	22	26
Annual urban growth rate (percentage)*	7.6	3.3	4.0	4.6
Annual rural growth rate (percentage)*	1.2	1.9	2.6	2.4
International migration				
International migrant stock				
Number of migrants (thousands)	64	71	78	437
Percentage of total population	1.5	1.4	1.1	4.5

* For the periods 1970-1975, 1980-1985, 1990-1995 and 2000-2005.
[a] For 1996.
[b] For 2000.

Government views and policies

Population policy variable	*1976*	*1986*	*1996*	*2005*
Population size and growth				
View on growth	Satisfactory	Too low	Satisfactory	Satisfactory
Policy on growth	No intervention	No intervention	No intervention	No intervention
Population age structure				
Level of concern about				
Size of the working-age population	..	..	..	Minor concern
Ageing of the population	..	..	..	Major concern
Fertility and family planning				
View on fertility level	Too high	Too low	Satisfactory	Satisfactory
Policy	No intervention	No intervention	No intervention	No intervention
Access to contraceptive methods	Direct support	Direct support	Direct support	Direct support
Adolescent fertility				
Level of concern	..	..	Major concern	Major concern
Policies and programmes	..	..	Yes	Yes
Health and mortality				
View				
Expectation of life	Acceptable	Acceptable	Acceptable	Acceptable
Under-five mortality	..	..	Acceptable	Unacceptable
Maternal mortality	..	..	..	Acceptable
Level of concern about HIV/AIDS	..	..	Minor concern	Major concern
Measures implemented to control HIV/AIDS*	..	..	..	1,2,3,4,5
Grounds on which abortion is permitted**	..	..	Not permitted	Not permitted
Spatial distribution and internal migration				
View on spatial distribution	Major change desired	Major change desired	Minor change desired	Satisfactory
Policies on internal migration				
From rural to urban areas	..	..	..	No intervention
From rural to rural areas	..	..	..	No intervention
From urban to rural areas	..	..	..	No intervention
From urban to urban areas	..	..	..	No intervention
Into urban agglomerations	No intervention	..	Lower	No intervention
International migration				
Immigration				
View	Satisfactory	Satisfactory	Satisfactory	Satisfactory
Policy	Maintain	Maintain	Maintain	Maintain
Permanent settlement	..	..	No intervention	Maintain
Temporary workers	..	..	Lower	Maintain
Highly skilled workers	..	..	..	Maintain
Family reunification	..	..	..	Raise
Integration of non-nationals	..	..	Yes	Yes
Emigration				
View	Satisfactory	Satisfactory	Satisfactory	Satisfactory
Policy	Maintain	Maintain	No intervention	Maintain
Encouraging the return of nationals	..	..	Yes	No

* Measures implemented to control HIV/AIDS: (1) blood screening; (2) information/education campaigns; (3) access to antiretroviral treatment; (4) non-discriminatory policies; (5) promoting condom use.
** Grounds on which abortion is permitted: (1) to save the woman's life; (2) to preserve physical health; (3) to preserve mental health; (4) rape or incest; (5) foetal impairment; (6) economic or social reasons; (7) on request.

Population indicators

Indicator	*1975*	*1985*	*1995*	*2005*
Population size and growth				
Population size (thousands)	10 413	12 102	14 395	16 295
Annual growth rate (percentage)*	1.7	1.6	1.8	1.1
Population age structure				
Percentage of population under age 15	37	31	30	25
Percentage of population aged 60 or older	8	8	9	12
Fertility and family planning				
Total fertility (births per woman)*	3.6	2.7	2.6	2.0
Teenage fertility rate (per 1,000 women, aged 15 - 19)*	84	64	68	62
Percentage of births to women under age 20*	16	15	13	17
Percentage of births to women aged 35 or older*	12	9	11	15
Percentage of married women using contraception				
Modern methods	..	..	..	..
All methods	..	..	..	..
Health and mortality				
Life expectancy at birth (years)*				
Males	60	67	71	75
Females	67	74	77	81
Both sexes combined	63	71	74	78
Infant mortality rate (per 1,000 births)*	69	24	14	8
Mortality under age 5 (per 1,000 births)*	81	28	17	10
Maternal mortality ratio (per 100,000 births) (2000)	..	..	..	31
HIV/AIDS (2003)				
Number of infected adults (thousands)	..	..	..	26
Adult prevalence rate (percentage)	..	..	..	0.3
Spatial distribution				
Population density (per sq. km)	14	16	19	22
Urban population (percentage)	78	83	84	88
Annual urban growth rate (percentage)*	2.5	1.9	1.9	1.6
Annual rural growth rate (percentage)*	-1.0	0.0	0.3	-1.4
International migration				
International migrant stock				
Number of migrants (thousands)	86	90	136	231
Percentage of total population	0.8	0.7	0.9	1.4

* For the periods 1970-1975, 1980-1985, 1990-1995 and 2000-2005.

Government views and policies

Population policy variable	*1976*	*1986*	*1996*	*2005*
Population size and growth				
View on growth	Too high	Too high	Satisfactory	Satisfactory
Policy on growth	Lower	Lower	Lower	Maintain
Population age structure				
Level of concern about				
Size of the working-age population	..	..	..	Major concern
Ageing of the population	..	..	..	Major concern
Fertility and family planning				
View on fertility level	Too high	Too high	Satisfactory	Satisfactory
Policy	Lower	Lower	Lower	Maintain
Access to contraceptive methods	Direct support	Direct support	Direct support	Direct support
Adolescent fertility				
Level of concern	..	..	Major concern	Minor concern
Policies and programmes	..	..	Yes	No
Health and mortality				
View				
Expectation of life	Unacceptable	Unacceptable	Acceptable	Acceptable
Under-five mortality	..	..	Acceptable	Acceptable
Maternal mortality	..	..	..	Acceptable
Level of concern about HIV/AIDS	..	..	Major concern	Major concern
Measures implemented to control HIV/AIDS*	..	..	..	1,2,3,4,5
Grounds on which abortion is permitted**	..	..	1,2,3,4,5,6,7	1,2,3,4,5,6,7
Spatial distribution and internal migration				
View on spatial distribution	Minor change desired	Minor change desired	Minor change desired	Minor change desired
Policies on internal migration				
From rural to urban areas	..	..	..	Raise
From rural to rural areas	..	..	..	..
From urban to rural areas	..	..	..	..
From urban to urban areas	..	..	..	Maintain
Into urban agglomerations	..	..	Lower	Raise
International migration				
Immigration				
View	Satisfactory	Satisfactory	Satisfactory	Satisfactory
Policy	Maintain	Maintain	Maintain	No intervention
Permanent settlement	..	..	Maintain	Maintain
Temporary workers	..	..	Maintain	Maintain
Highly skilled workers	..	..	..	Maintain
Family reunification	..	..	Maintain	Maintain
Integration of non-nationals	..	..	..	No
Emigration				
View	Satisfactory	Satisfactory	Satisfactory	Satisfactory
Policy	Maintain	Maintain	Maintain	Maintain
Encouraging the return of nationals	..	..	No	No

* Measures implemented to control HIV/AIDS: (1) blood screening; (2) information/education campaigns; (3) access to antiretroviral treatment; (4) non-discriminatory policies; (5) promoting condom use.

** Grounds on which abortion is permitted: (1) to save the woman's life; (2) to preserve physical health; (3) to preserve mental health; (4) rape or incest; (5) foetal impairment; (6) economic or social reasons; (7) on request.

Population indicators

Indicator	*1975*	*1985*	*1995*	*2005*
Population size and growth				
Population size (thousands)	927 808	1 070 175	1 219 331	1 315 844
Annual growth rate (percentage)*	2.2	1.4	1.1	0.6
Population age structure				
Percentage of population under age 15	39	30	26	21
Percentage of population aged 60 or older	7	8	9	11
Fertility and family planning				
Total fertility (births per woman)*	4.9	2.6	1.9	1.7
Teenage fertility rate (per 1,000 women, aged 15 - 19)*	14	7	5	5
Percentage of births to women under age 20*	2	2	1	1
Percentage of births to women aged 35 or older*	3	2	3	4
Percentage of married women using contraception				
Modern methods	..	68[a]	83[b]	..
All methods	..	71[a]	84[b]	..
Health and mortality				
Life expectancy at birth (years)*				
Males	63	65	67	70
Females	64	68	70	73
Both sexes combined	63	67	68	71
Infant mortality rate (per 1,000 births)*	61	52	47	35
Mortality under age 5 (per 1,000 births)*	73	62	56	41
Maternal mortality ratio (per 100,000 births) (2000)	..	..	..	56
HIV/AIDS (2003)				
Number of infected adults (thousands)	..	..	..	830
Adult prevalence rate (percentage)	..	..	..	0.1
Spatial distribution				
Population density (per sq. km)	97	112	127	137
Urban population (percentage)	17	23	31	41
Annual urban growth rate (percentage)*	2.2	4.5	3.8	3.2
Annual rural growth rate (percentage)*	2.2	0.5	0.0	-0.8
International migration				
International migrant stock				
Number of migrants (thousands)	302	327	441	596
Percentage of total population	0	0	0	0

* For the periods 1970-1975, 1980-1985, 1990-1995 and 2000-2005.
[a] For 1982.
[b] For 1997.

Government views and policies

Population policy variable	*1976*	*1986*	*1996*	*2005*
Population size and growth				
View on growth	Too high	Satisfactory	Satisfactory	Satisfactory
Policy on growth	Lower	No intervention	No intervention	No intervention
Population age structure				
Level of concern about				
Size of the working-age population	..	..	..	..
Ageing of the population	..	..	..	Minor concern
Fertility and family planning				
View on fertility level	Too high	Satisfactory	Satisfactory	Too high
Policy	Lower	No intervention	No intervention	Lower
Access to contraceptive methods	Direct support	Direct support	Indirect support	Direct support
Adolescent fertility				
Level of concern	..	..	Not a concern	Major concern
Policies and programmes	..	..	No	Yes
Health and mortality				
View				
Expectation of life	Unacceptable	Unacceptable	Acceptable	Acceptable
Under-five mortality	..	..	..	Unacceptable
Maternal mortality	..	..	..	Unacceptable
Level of concern about HIV/AIDS	..	..	Major concern	Major concern
Measures implemented to control HIV/AIDS*	..	..	..	1,2,3,4,5
Grounds on which abortion is permitted**	..	..	1	1
Spatial distribution and internal migration				
View on spatial distribution	Major change desired	Major change desired	Satisfactory	Satisfactory
Policies on internal migration				
From rural to urban areas	..	..	..	No intervention
From rural to rural areas	..	..	..	No intervention
From urban to rural areas	..	..	..	No intervention
From urban to urban areas	..	..	..	No intervention
Into urban agglomerations	Lower	Lower	No intervention	No intervention
International migration				
Immigration				
View	Satisfactory	Satisfactory	Satisfactory	Satisfactory
Policy	Maintain	Maintain	No intervention	Maintain
Permanent settlement	..	..	No intervention	Lower
Temporary workers	..	..	No intervention	Raise
Highly skilled workers	..	..	..	Raise
Family reunification	..	..	No intervention	Maintain
Integration of non-nationals	..	..	No	Yes
Emigration				
View	Satisfactory	Too high	Too high	Too high
Policy	Maintain	Lower	Lower	Lower
Encouraging the return of nationals	No	..	Yes	Yes

* Measures implemented to control HIV/AIDS: (1) blood screening; (2) information/education campaigns; (3) access to antiretroviral treatment; (4) non-discriminatory policies; (5) promoting condom use.

** Grounds on which abortion is permitted: (1) to save the woman's life; (2) to preserve physical health; (3) to preserve mental health; (4) rape or incest; (5) foetal impairment; (6) economic or social reasons; (7) on request.

Population indicators

Indicator	*1975*	*1985*	*1995*	*2005*
Population size and growth				
Population size (thousands)	25 381	31 659	38 542	45 600
Annual growth rate (percentage)*	2.4	2.1	1.9	1.6
Population age structure				
Percentage of population under age 15	43	38	34	31
Percentage of population aged 60 or older	6	6	7	8
Fertility and family planning				
Total fertility (births per woman)*	5.0	3.7	3.0	2.6
Teenage fertility rate (per 1,000 women, aged 15 - 19)*	90	68	100	80
Percentage of births to women under age 20*	14	13	19	17
Percentage of births to women aged 35 or older*	15	12	10	12
Percentage of married women using contraception				
Modern methods	30[a]	53[b]	59	64[c]
All methods	43[a]	65[b]	72	77[c]
Health and mortality				
Life expectancy at birth (years)*				
Males	60	64	64	69
Females	64	70	73	75
Both sexes combined	62	67	68	72
Infant mortality rate (per 1,000 births)*	73	48	35	26
Mortality under age 5 (per 1,000 births)*	101	67	47	33
Maternal mortality ratio (per 100,000 births) (2000)	..	..	..	130
HIV/AIDS (2003)				
Number of infected adults (thousands)	..	..	..	180
Adult prevalence rate (percentage)	..	..	..	0.7
Spatial distribution				
Population density (per sq. km)	22	28	34	40
Urban population (percentage)	60	65	72	77
Annual urban growth rate (percentage)*	3.5	2.9	2.9	2.2
Annual rural growth rate (percentage)*	0.7	0.7	-0.3	-0.5
International migration				
International migrant stock				
Number of migrants (thousands)	85	96	108	123
Percentage of total population	0.3	0.3	0.3	0.3

* For the periods 1970-1975, 1980-1985, 1990-1995 and 2000-2005.
[a] For 1976.
[b] For 1986.
[c] For 2000.

Government views and policies

Population policy variable	*1976*	*1986*	*1996*	*2005*
Population size and growth				
View on growth	Too high	Too high	Too high	Too high
Policy on growth	No intervention	Lower	Lower	Lower
Population age structure				
Level of concern about				
Size of the working-age population	..	..	..	Major concern
Ageing of the population	..	..	..	..
Fertility and family planning				
View on fertility level	Too high	Too high	Too high	Too high
Policy	No intervention	Lower	Lower	Lower
Access to contraceptive methods	No support	Direct support	Direct support	Direct support
Adolescent fertility				
Level of concern	..	..	Major concern	Major concern
Policies and programmes	..	..	No	Yes
Health and mortality				
View				
Expectation of life	Unacceptable	Unacceptable	Unacceptable	Unacceptable
Under-five mortality	..	..	Unacceptable	Unacceptable
Maternal mortality	..	..	..	Unacceptable
Level of concern about HIV/AIDS	..	..	Major concern	Major concern
Measures implemented to control HIV/AIDS*	..	..	..	1,2,4,5
Grounds on which abortion is permitted**	..	..	1,2	1,2,3
Spatial distribution and internal migration				
View on spatial distribution	Minor change desired	Minor change desired	Satisfactory	Major change desired
Policies on internal migration				
From rural to urban areas	..	..	..	..
From rural to rural areas	..	..	..	..
From urban to rural areas	..	..	..	..
From urban to urban areas	..	..	..	..
Into urban agglomerations	..	No intervention	No intervention	..
International migration				
Immigration				
View	Satisfactory	Too high	Satisfactory	Satisfactory
Policy	Maintain	Maintain	No intervention	No intervention
Permanent settlement	..	..	No intervention	No intervention
Temporary workers	..	..	..	..
Highly skilled workers	..	..	..	..
Family reunification	..	..	..	..
Integration of non-nationals	..	..	No	..
Emigration				
View	Satisfactory	Satisfactory	Satisfactory	Satisfactory
Policy	Maintain	Maintain	No intervention	No intervention
Encouraging the return of nationals	No	..	No	..

* Measures implemented to control HIV/AIDS: (1) blood screening; (2) information/education campaigns; (3) access to antiretroviral treatment; (4) non-discriminatory policies; (5) promoting condom use.
** Grounds on which abortion is permitted: (1) to save the woman's life; (2) to preserve physical health; (3) to preserve mental health; (4) rape or incest; (5) foetal impairment; (6) economic or social reasons; (7) on request.

Population indicators

Indicator	*1975*	*1985*	*1995*	*2005*
Population size and growth				
Population size (thousands)	318	456	607	798
Annual growth rate (percentage)*	2.9	3.3	2.8	2.6
Population age structure				
Percentage of population under age 15	48	48	45	42
Percentage of population aged 60 or older	4	4	4	4
Fertility and family planning				
Total fertility (births per woman)*	7.1	7.1	5.8	4.9
Teenage fertility rate (per 1,000 women, aged 15 - 19)*	166	166	75	59
Percentage of births to women under age 20*	17	18	11	9
Percentage of births to women aged 35 or older*	14	14	17	15
Percentage of married women using contraception				
Modern methods	..	..	11[a]	19[b]
All methods	..	..	21[a]	26[b]
Health and mortality				
Life expectancy at birth (years)*				
Males	47	51	56	61
Females	51	55	60	65
Both sexes combined	49	53	58	63
Infant mortality rate (per 1,000 births)*	127	106	80	58
Mortality under age 5 (per 1,000 births)*	188	153	113	77
Maternal mortality ratio (per 100,000 births) (2000)	..	..	..	480
HIV/AIDS (2003)				
Number of infected adults (thousands)	..	..	..	..
Adult prevalence rate (percentage)	..	..	..	..
Spatial distribution				
Population density (per sq. km)	142	204	272	357
Urban population (percentage)	21	25	30	36
Annual urban growth rate (percentage)*	4.7	5.2	4.7	4.6
Annual rural growth rate (percentage)*	2.4	2.7	2.2	1.9
International migration				
International migrant stock				
Number of migrants (thousands)	10	32	52	67
Percentage of total population	3.3	7	8.6	8.4

* For the periods 1970-1975, 1980-1985, 1990-1995 and 2000-2005.
[a] For 1996.
[b] For 2000.

Government views and policies

Population policy variable	*1976*	*1986*	*1996*	*2005*
Population size and growth				
View on growth	Satisfactory	Too low	Too high	Too high
Policy on growth	No intervention	No intervention	Lower	Lower
Population age structure				
Level of concern about				
Size of the working-age population	..	..	..	Minor concern
Ageing of the population	..	..	..	Minor concern
Fertility and family planning				
View on fertility level	Satisfactory	Too low	Too high	Too high
Policy	No intervention	No intervention	Lower	Lower
Access to contraceptive methods	Direct support	Direct support	Direct support	Direct support
Adolescent fertility				
Level of concern	..	..	Major concern	Major concern
Policies and programmes	..	..	Yes	Yes
Health and mortality				
View				
Expectation of life	Unacceptable	Unacceptable	Unacceptable	Unacceptable
Under-five mortality	..	..	Unacceptable	Unacceptable
Maternal mortality	..	..	..	Unacceptable
Level of concern about HIV/AIDS	..	..	Major concern	Major concern
Measures implemented to control HIV/AIDS*	..	..	..	1,2,3,5
Grounds on which abortion is permitted**	..	..	1,2	1
Spatial distribution and internal migration				
View on spatial distribution	Major change desired	Major change desired	Major change desired	Major change desired
Policies on internal migration				
From rural to urban areas	..	..	..	Lower
From rural to rural areas	..	..	..	..
From urban to rural areas	..	..	..	..
From urban to urban areas	..	..	..	..
Into urban agglomerations	No intervention	Lower	Lower	Lower
International migration				
Immigration				
View	Satisfactory	Satisfactory	Satisfactory	Satisfactory
Policy	Maintain	Maintain	Lower	No intervention
Permanent settlement	..	..	Maintain	..
Temporary workers	..	..	Lower	..
Highly skilled workers	..	..	..	..
Family reunification	..	..	Maintain	..
Integration of non-nationals	..	..	Yes	..
Emigration				
View	Satisfactory	Satisfactory	Satisfactory	Satisfactory
Policy	Maintain	Maintain	No intervention	No intervention
Encouraging the return of nationals	No	..	No	..

* Measures implemented to control HIV/AIDS: (1) blood screening; (2) information/education campaigns; (3) access to antiretroviral treatment; (4) non-discriminatory policies; (5) promoting condom use.

** Grounds on which abortion is permitted: (1) to save the woman's life; (2) to preserve physical health; (3) to preserve mental health; (4) rape or incest; (5) foetal impairment; (6) economic or social reasons; (7) on request.

Population indicators

Indicator	*1975*	*1985*	*1995*	*2005*
Population size and growth				
Population size (thousands)	1 544	2 114	2 916	3 999
Annual growth rate (percentage)*	3.1	3.2	3.2	3.0
Population age structure				
Percentage of population under age 15	45	46	46	47
Percentage of population aged 60 or older	5	5	5	5
Fertility and family planning				
Total fertility (births per woman)*	6.3	6.3	6.3	6.3
Teenage fertility rate (per 1,000 women, aged 15 - 19)*	146	146	146	146
Percentage of births to women under age 20*	17	17	18	18
Percentage of births to women aged 35 or older*	17	16	16	14
Percentage of married women using contraception				
Modern methods	..	..	..	..
All methods	..	..	..	..
Health and mortality				
Life expectancy at birth (years)*				
Males	53	54	50	51
Females	57	59	56	53
Both sexes combined	55	57	53	52
Infant mortality rate (per 1,000 births)*	95	86	73	72
Mortality under age 5 (per 1,000 births)*	136	126	113	108
Maternal mortality ratio (per 100,000 births) (2000)	..	..	..	510
HIV/AIDS (2003)				
Number of infected adults (thousands)	..	..	..	80
Adult prevalence rate (percentage)	..	..	..	4.9
Spatial distribution				
Population density (per sq. km)	5	6	9	12
Urban population (percentage)	35	46	50	54
Annual urban growth rate (percentage)*	4.2	5.8	4.1	3.4
Annual rural growth rate (percentage)*	2.5	1.2	2.5	1.6
International migration				
International migrant stock				
Number of migrants (thousands)	58	99	169	288
Percentage of total population	3.8	4.7	5.8	7.2

* For the periods 1970-1975, 1980-1985, 1990-1995 and 2000-2005.

Government views and policies

Population policy variable	*1976*	*1986*	*1996*	*2005*
Population size and growth				
View on growth	..	..	Too low	Too low
Policy on growth	..	..	Raise	Raise
Population age structure				
Level of concern about				
Size of the working-age population	..	..	..	Major concern
Ageing of the population	..	..	..	Minor concern
Fertility and family planning				
View on fertility level	..	..	Satisfactory	Too low
Policy	..	..	Maintain	Raise
Access to contraceptive methods	..	..	Direct support	Direct support
Adolescent fertility				
Level of concern	..	..	Minor concern	Major concern
Policies and programmes	..	..	Yes	No
Health and mortality				
View				
Expectation of life	..	..	Acceptable	Acceptable
Under-five mortality	..	..	..	Acceptable
Maternal mortality	..	..	..	Acceptable
Level of concern about HIV/AIDS	..	..	..	Major concern
Measures implemented to control HIV/AIDS*	..	..	..	1,2,3,4,5
Grounds on which abortion is permitted**	..	..	1,2,3	1,2,3,4
Spatial distribution and internal migration				
View on spatial distribution	..	..	Satisfactory	Satisfactory
Policies on internal migration				
From rural to urban areas	..	..	..	Raise
From rural to rural areas	..	..	..	No intervention
From urban to rural areas	..	..	..	No intervention
From urban to urban areas	..	..	..	No intervention
Into urban agglomerations	..	..	..	Lower
International migration				
Immigration				
View	..	..	Satisfactory	Satisfactory
Policy	..	..	No intervention	Lower
Permanent settlement	..	..	..	Lower
Temporary workers	..	..	..	Lower
Highly skilled workers	..	..	..	No intervention
Family reunification	..	..	..	No intervention
Integration of non-nationals	..	..	..	Yes
Emigration				
View	..	..	Too high	Too high
Policy	..	..	Lower	Lower
Encouraging the return of nationals	..	..	..	Yes

* Measures implemented to control HIV/AIDS: (1) blood screening; (2) information/education campaigns; (3) access to antiretroviral treatment; (4) non-discriminatory policies; (5) promoting condom use.

** Grounds on which abortion is permitted: (1) to save the woman's life; (2) to preserve physical health; (3) to preserve mental health; (4) rape or incest; (5) foetal impairment; (6) economic or social reasons; (7) on request.

Population indicators

Indicator	*1975*	*1985*	*1995*	*2005*
Population size and growth				
Population size (thousands)	20	18	20	18
Annual growth rate (percentage)*	-0.9	0.5	1.7	-1.0
Population age structure				
Percentage of population under age 15	..	..	..	..
Percentage of population aged 60 or older	..	..	..	..
Fertility and family planning				
Total fertility (births per woman)*	..	..	..	..
Teenage fertility rate (per 1,000 women, aged 15 - 19)*	..	..	..	..
Percentage of births to women under age 20*	..	..	..	..
Percentage of births to women aged 35 or older*	..	..	..	..
Percentage of married women using contraception				
Modern methods	..	..	60[a]	..
All methods	..	..	63[a]	..
Health and mortality				
Life expectancy at birth (years)*				
Males	..	..	..	..
Females	..	..	..	..
Both sexes combined	..	..	..	..
Infant mortality rate (per 1,000 births)*	..	..	..	..
Mortality under age 5 (per 1,000 births)*	..	..	..	..
Maternal mortality ratio (per 100,000 births) (2000)	..	..	..	..
HIV/AIDS (2003)				
Number of infected adults (thousands)	..	..	..	..
Adult prevalence rate (percentage)	..	..	..	..
Spatial distribution				
Population density (per sq. km)	87	77	85	76
Urban population (percentage)	54	56	59	73
Annual urban growth rate (percentage)*	-1.5	0.1	1.0	2.5
Annual rural growth rate (percentage)*	-2.1	-0.6	0.2	-5.1
International migration				
International migrant stock				
Number of migrants (thousands)	2	2	3	3
Percentage of total population	7.6	13.5	13.7	17

* For the periods 1970-1975, 1980-1985, 1990-1995 and 2000-2005.
[a] For 1996.

Government views and policies

Population policy variable	*1976*	*1986*	*1996*	*2005*
Population size and growth				
View on growth	Too high	Satisfactory	Too high	Satisfactory
Policy on growth	No intervention	No intervention	Lower	No intervention
Population age structure				
Level of concern about				
Size of the working-age population	..	..	..	Not a concern
Ageing of the population	..	..	..	Major concern
Fertility and family planning				
View on fertility level	Too high	Satisfactory	Too high	Satisfactory
Policy	No intervention	No intervention	Lower	Lower
Access to contraceptive methods	Direct support	Direct support	Direct support	Direct support
Adolescent fertility				
Level of concern	..	..	..	Major concern
Policies and programmes	..	..	..	Yes
Health and mortality				
View				
Expectation of life	Acceptable	Acceptable	Acceptable	Acceptable
Under-five mortality	..	..	..	Unacceptable
Maternal mortality	..	..	..	Acceptable
Level of concern about HIV/AIDS	..	..	..	Major concern
Measures implemented to control HIV/AIDS*	..	..	..	1,2,3,4,5
Grounds on which abortion is permitted**	..	..	1,2	1,2,3
Spatial distribution and internal migration				
View on spatial distribution	Major change desired	Major change desired	Major change desired	Minor change desired
Policies on internal migration				
From rural to urban areas	..	..	..	Lower
From rural to rural areas	..	..	..	..
From urban to rural areas	..	..	..	..
From urban to urban areas	..	..	..	Raise
Into urban agglomerations	No intervention	Lower	..	Lower
International migration				
Immigration				
View	Satisfactory	Too high	Too high	Satisfactory
Policy	Maintain	Lower	Lower	Maintain
Permanent settlement	..	..	Lower	Maintain
Temporary workers	..	..	Maintain	Maintain
Highly skilled workers	..	..	..	..
Family reunification	..	..	Maintain	Maintain
Integration of non-nationals	..	..	..	Yes
Emigration				
View	Satisfactory	Too low	Satisfactory	Satisfactory
Policy	Maintain	Maintain	No intervention	No intervention
Encouraging the return of nationals	Yes	..	Yes	No

* Measures implemented to control HIV/AIDS: (1) blood screening; (2) information/education campaigns; (3) access to antiretroviral treatment; (4) non-discriminatory policies; (5) promoting condom use.

** Grounds on which abortion is permitted: (1) to save the woman's life; (2) to preserve physical health; (3) to preserve mental health; (4) rape or incest; (5) foetal impairment; (6) economic or social reasons; (7) on request.

Population indicators

Indicator	1975	1985	1995	2005
Population size and growth				
Population size (thousands)	2 051	2 697	3 475	4 327
Annual growth rate (percentage)*	2.4	2.8	2.4	1.9
Population age structure				
Percentage of population under age 15	41	36	34	28
Percentage of population aged 60 or older	7	7	7	8
Fertility and family planning				
Total fertility (births per woman)*	4.3	3.5	2.9	2.3
Teenage fertility rate (per 1,000 women, aged 15 - 19)*	105	98	94	78
Percentage of births to women under age 20*	19	18	17	20
Percentage of births to women aged 35 or older*	13	9	11	10
Percentage of married women using contraception				
Modern methods	54[a]	59[b]	71[c]	..
All methods	64[a]	69[b]	80[c]	..
Health and mortality				
Life expectancy at birth (years)*				
Males	66	72	74	76
Females	70	76	79	81
Both sexes combined	68	73	76	78
Infant mortality rate (per 1,000 births)*	53	19	15	10
Mortality under age 5 (per 1,000 births)*	64	24	17	12
Maternal mortality ratio (per 100,000 births) (2000)	..	..	..	43
HIV/AIDS (2003)				
Number of infected adults (thousands)	..	..	..	12
Adult prevalence rate (percentage)	..	..	..	0.6
Spatial distribution				
Population density (per sq. km)	40	53	68	85
Urban population (percentage)	42	51	56	62
Annual urban growth rate (percentage)*	4.2	4.5	3.4	2.8
Annual rural growth rate (percentage)*	1.2	1.2	1.3	0.6
International migration				
International migrant stock				
Number of migrants (thousands)	29	117	228	441
Percentage of total population	1.4	4.3	6.6	10.2

* For the periods 1970-1975, 1980-1985, 1990-1995 and 2000-2005.
[a] For 1976.
[b] For 1986.
[c] For 1999.

Government views and policies

Population policy variable	*1976*	*1986*	*1996*	*2005*
Population size and growth				
View on growth	Too low	Satisfactory	Satisfactory	Too high
Policy on growth	Raise	Raise	Raise	Lower
Population age structure				
Level of concern about				
Size of the working-age population	..	..	..	..
Ageing of the population	..	..	..	Major concern
Fertility and family planning				
View on fertility level	Satisfactory	Satisfactory	Satisfactory	Too high
Policy	Maintain	Raise	Raise	Lower
Access to contraceptive methods	No support	No support	Indirect support	Direct support
Adolescent fertility				
Level of concern	..	..	..	Major concern
Policies and programmes	..	..	..	Yes
Health and mortality				
View				
Expectation of life	Unacceptable	Acceptable	Acceptable	Unacceptable
Under-five mortality	..	..	..	Unacceptable
Maternal mortality	..	..	..	Unacceptable
Level of concern about HIV/AIDS	..	..	..	Major concern
Measures implemented to control HIV/AIDS*	..	..	..	1,2,3,5
Grounds on which abortion is permitted**	..	..	1	1
Spatial distribution and internal migration				
View on spatial distribution	Major change desired	Major change desired	Major change desired	Major change desired
Policies on internal migration				
From rural to urban areas	..	..	..	Lower
From rural to rural areas	..	..	..	Maintain
From urban to rural areas	..	..	..	Raise
From urban to urban areas	..	..	..	Maintain
Into urban agglomerations	Lower	Lower	..	Lower
International migration				
Immigration				
View	Too high	Too high	Too high	Too high
Policy	Lower	Lower	Lower	Lower
Permanent settlement	..	..	Lower	Lower
Temporary workers	..	..	Lower	Lower
Highly skilled workers	..	..	..	Maintain
Family reunification	..	..	Lower	Lower
Integration of non-nationals	..	..	No	No
Emigration				
View	Satisfactory	Satisfactory	Satisfactory	Satisfactory
Policy	Maintain	Maintain	Maintain	No intervention
Encouraging the return of nationals	No	..	..	No

* Measures implemented to control HIV/AIDS: (1) blood screening; (2) information/education campaigns; (3) access to antiretroviral treatment; (4) non-discriminatory policies; (5) promoting condom use.

** Grounds on which abortion is permitted: (1) to save the woman's life; (2) to preserve physical health; (3) to preserve mental health; (4) rape or incest; (5) foetal impairment; (6) economic or social reasons; (7) on request.

Population indicators

Indicator	*1975*	*1985*	*1995*	*2005*
Population size and growth				
Population size (thousands)	6 592	10 503	14 755	18 154
Annual growth rate (percentage)*	4.3	4.6	3.1	1.6
Population age structure				
Percentage of population under age 15	45	46	46	42
Percentage of population aged 60 or older	4	4	5	5
Fertility and family planning				
Total fertility (births per woman)*	7.4	7.4	6.3	5.1
Teenage fertility rate (per 1,000 women, aged 15 - 19)*	266	300	205	133
Percentage of births to women under age 20*	25	27	24	21
Percentage of births to women aged 35 or older*	16	14	15	12
Percentage of married women using contraception				
Modern methods	..	1[a]	7[b]	..
All methods	..	3[a]	15[b]	..
Health and mortality				
Life expectancy at birth (years)*				
Males	48	52	48	45
Females	52	56	52	47
Both sexes combined	50	54	50	46
Infant mortality rate (per 1,000 births)*	133	115	113	118
Mortality under age 5 (per 1,000 births)*	217	181	177	189
Maternal mortality ratio (per 100,000 births) (2000)	..	..	..	690
HIV/AIDS (2003)				
Number of infected adults (thousands)	..	..	..	530
Adult prevalence rate (percentage)	..	..	..	7.0
Spatial distribution				
Population density (per sq. km)	20	33	46	56
Urban population (percentage)	32	37	42	46
Annual urban growth rate (percentage)*	7.2	5.8	3.7	2.6
Annual rural growth rate (percentage)*	2.7	3.5	2.1	0.8
International migration				
International migrant stock				
Number of migrants (thousands)	1 541	1 663	2 314	2 371
Percentage of total population	23.4	15.8	15.7	13.1

* For the periods 1970-1975, 1980-1985, 1990-1995 and 2000-2005.
[a] For 1981.
[b] For 1998/1999.

Government views and policies

Population policy variable	*1976*	*1986*	*1996*	*2005*
Population size and growth				
View on growth	..	..	Satisfactory	Too low
Policy on growth	..	..	Raise	Raise
Population age structure				
Level of concern about				
Size of the working-age population	..	..	..	Major concern
Ageing of the population	..	..	..	Major concern
Fertility and family planning				
View on fertility level	..	..	Too low	Too low
Policy	..	..	Raise	Raise
Access to contraceptive methods	..	..	Direct support	Direct support
Adolescent fertility				
Level of concern	..	..	Not a concern	Minor concern
Policies and programmes	..	..	..	Yes
Health and mortality				
View				
Expectation of life	..	..	Acceptable	Acceptable
Under-five mortality	..	..	..	Acceptable
Maternal mortality	..	..	..	Acceptable
Level of concern about HIV/AIDS	..	..	Major concern	Major concern
Measures implemented to control HIV/AIDS*	..	..	..	1,2,3,4,5
Grounds on which abortion is permitted**	..	..	1,2,3,4,5,6,7	1,2,3,4,5,6,7
Spatial distribution and internal migration				
View on spatial distribution	..	..	Major change desired	Major change desired
Policies on internal migration				
From rural to urban areas	..	..	..	Lower
From rural to rural areas	..	..	..	No intervention
From urban to rural areas	..	..	..	Maintain
From urban to urban areas	..	..	..	No intervention
Into urban agglomerations	..	..	No intervention	No intervention
International migration				
Immigration				
View	..	..	Satisfactory	Satisfactory
Policy	..	..	No intervention	Maintain
Permanent settlement	..	..	No intervention	Lower
Temporary workers	..	..	No intervention	Raise
Highly skilled workers	..	..	..	Raise
Family reunification	..	..	No intervention	Maintain
Integration of non-nationals	..	..	..	Yes
Emigration				
View	..	..	Too high	Too high
Policy	..	..	Lower	Lower
Encouraging the return of nationals	..	..	Yes	Yes

* Measures implemented to control HIV/AIDS: (1) blood screening; (2) information/education campaigns; (3) access to antiretroviral treatment; (4) non-discriminatory policies; (5) promoting condom use.

** Grounds on which abortion is permitted: (1) to save the woman's life; (2) to preserve physical health; (3) to preserve mental health; (4) rape or incest; (5) foetal impairment; (6) economic or social reasons; (7) on request.

Population indicators

Indicator	*1975*	*1985*	*1995*	*2005*
Population size and growth				
Population size (thousands)	4 263	4 471	4 669	4 551
Annual growth rate (percentage)*	0.4	0.4	0.7	0.2
Population age structure				
Percentage of population under age 15	21	21	19	16
Percentage of population aged 60 or older	16	16	20	22
Fertility and family planning				
Total fertility (births per woman)*	2.0	2.0	1.5	1.3
Teenage fertility rate (per 1,000 women, aged 15 - 19)*	23	23	18	15
Percentage of births to women under age 20*	7	5	6	5
Percentage of births to women aged 35 or older*	10	9	11	11
Percentage of married women using contraception				
Modern methods	..	..	..	..
All methods	..	..	..	..
Health and mortality				
Life expectancy at birth (years)*				
Males	66	66	68	71
Females	73	75	77	78
Both sexes combined	70	70	73	75
Infant mortality rate (per 1,000 births)*	27	18	11	7
Mortality under age 5 (per 1,000 births)*	29	20	12	8
Maternal mortality ratio (per 100,000 births) (2000)	..	..	..	8
HIV/AIDS (2003)				
Number of infected adults (thousands)	..	..	..	<1
Adult prevalence rate (percentage)	..	..	..	<0.1
Spatial distribution				
Population density (per sq. km)	75	79	83	81
Urban population (percentage)	45	52	56	60
Annual urban growth rate (percentage)*	2.8	1.3	-1.0	0.5
Annual rural growth rate (percentage)*	-1.3	-0.5	-2.4	-1.2
International migration				
International migrant stock				
Number of migrants (thousands)	..	..	721	661
Percentage of total population	..	..	15.4	14.5

* For the periods 1970-1975, 1980-1985, 1990-1995 and 2000-2005.

Government views and policies

Population policy variable	*1976*	*1986*	*1996*	*2005*
Population size and growth				
View on growth	Satisfactory	Satisfactory	Satisfactory	Satisfactory
Policy on growth	No intervention	No intervention	No intervention	No intervention
Population age structure				
Level of concern about				
Size of the working-age population	..	..	..	Not a concern
Ageing of the population	..	..	..	Major concern
Fertility and family planning				
View on fertility level	Satisfactory	Satisfactory	Satisfactory	Satisfactory
Policy	No intervention	No intervention	No intervention	No intervention
Access to contraceptive methods	Direct support	Direct support	Direct support	Direct support
Adolescent fertility				
Level of concern	..	..	Major concern	Major concern
Policies and programmes	..	..	Yes	Yes
Health and mortality				
View				
Expectation of life	Acceptable	Acceptable	Acceptable	Acceptable
Under-five mortality	..	..	Acceptable	Acceptable
Maternal mortality	..	..	..	Acceptable
Level of concern about HIV/AIDS	..	..	Major concern	Major concern
Measures implemented to control HIV/AIDS*	..	..	..	1,2,3,4,5
Grounds on which abortion is permitted**	..	..	1,2,3,4,5,6,7	1,2,3,4,5,6,7
Spatial distribution and internal migration				
View on spatial distribution	Minor change desired	Minor change desired	Minor change desired	Major change desired
Policies on internal migration				
From rural to urban areas	..	..	..	Lower
From rural to rural areas	..	..	..	No intervention
From urban to rural areas	..	..	..	No intervention
From urban to urban areas	..	..	..	No intervention
Into urban agglomerations	..	No intervention	Lower	Lower
International migration				
Immigration				
View	Satisfactory	Satisfactory	Satisfactory	Satisfactory
Policy	Maintain	Maintain	Maintain	Maintain
Permanent settlement	..	..	Maintain	Maintain
Temporary workers	..	..	Maintain	Maintain
Highly skilled workers	..	..	..	Maintain
Family reunification	..	..	Maintain	Maintain
Integration of non-nationals	..	..	No	No
Emigration				
View	Satisfactory	Satisfactory	Satisfactory	Satisfactory
Policy	Maintain	Lower	Maintain	Maintain
Encouraging the return of nationals	..	..	No	No

* Measures implemented to control HIV/AIDS: (1) blood screening; (2) information/education campaigns; (3) access to antiretroviral treatment; (4) non-discriminatory policies; (5) promoting condom use.

** Grounds on which abortion is permitted: (1) to save the woman's life; (2) to preserve physical health; (3) to preserve mental health; (4) rape or incest; (5) foetal impairment; (6) economic or social reasons; (7) on request.

Population indicators

Indicator	*1975*	*1985*	*1995*	*2005*
Population size and growth				
Population size (thousands)	9 251	10 041	10 867	11 269
Annual growth rate (percentage)*	1.7	0.8	0.6	0.3
Population age structure				
Percentage of population under age 15	37	27	22	19
Percentage of population aged 60 or older	10	11	12	15
Fertility and family planning				
Total fertility (births per woman)*	3.5	1.8	1.6	1.6
Teenage fertility rate (per 1,000 women, aged 15 - 19)*	141	85	67	50
Percentage of births to women under age 20*	23	30	19	14
Percentage of births to women aged 35 or older*	10	4	4	10
Percentage of married women using contraception				
Modern methods	..	67[a]	..	72[b]
All methods	..	70[a]	..	73[b]
Health and mortality				
Life expectancy at birth (years)*				
Males	69	73	73	75
Females	73	76	77	79
Both sexes combined	71	74	74	77
Infant mortality rate (per 1,000 births)*	38	17	15	6
Mortality under age 5 (per 1,000 births)*	44	21	19	8
Maternal mortality ratio (per 100,000 births) (2000)	..	..	..	33
HIV/AIDS (2003)				
Number of infected adults (thousands)	..	..	..	3
Adult prevalence rate (percentage)	..	..	..	0.1
Spatial distribution				
Population density (per sq. km)	83	91	98	102
Urban population (percentage)	64	71	75	76
Annual urban growth rate (percentage)*	3.1	1.7	0.9	0.5
Annual rural growth rate (percentage)*	-0.4	-1.1	-0.1	-0.4
International migration				
International migrant stock				
Number of migrants (thousands)	125	110	90	74
Percentage of total population	1.4	1.1	0.8	0.7

* For the periods 1970-1975, 1980-1985, 1990-1995 and 2000-2005.
[a] For 1987.
[b] For 2000.

Government views and policies

Population policy variable	*1976*	*1986*	*1996*	*2005*
Population size and growth				
View on growth	Satisfactory	Too low	Too low	Too low
Policy on growth	No intervention	Raise	Raise	Raise
Population age structure				
Level of concern about				
Size of the working-age population	..	..	..	Major concern
Ageing of the population	..	..	..	Major concern
Fertility and family planning				
View on fertility level	Satisfactory	Too low	Too low	Too low
Policy	No intervention	Raise	Raise	Raise
Access to contraceptive methods	No support	Direct support	Indirect support	Direct support
Adolescent fertility				
Level of concern	..	..	Minor concern	Minor concern
Policies and programmes	..	..	No	Yes
Health and mortality				
View				
Expectation of life	Acceptable	Acceptable	Acceptable	Acceptable
Under-five mortality	..	..	Acceptable	Acceptable
Maternal mortality	..	..	..	Acceptable
Level of concern about HIV/AIDS	..	..	Major concern	Major concern
Measures implemented to control HIV/AIDS*	..	..	..	1,2,3,4,5
Grounds on which abortion is permitted**	..	..	1,2,3,4,5	1,2,3,4,5
Spatial distribution and internal migration				
View on spatial distribution	Minor change desired	Major change desired	Major change desired	Major change desired
Policies on internal migration				
From rural to urban areas	..	..	..	Lower
From rural to rural areas	..	..	..	Maintain
From urban to rural areas	..	..	..	Raise
From urban to urban areas	..	..	..	Maintain
Into urban agglomerations	Raise	No intervention	..	Lower
International migration				
Immigration				
View	Satisfactory	Satisfactory	Satisfactory	Too high
Policy	Maintain	Maintain	Lower	Lower
Permanent settlement	..	..	Lower	Lower
Temporary workers	..	..	Lower	Lower
Highly skilled workers	..	..	..	Maintain
Family reunification	..	..	No intervention	Maintain
Integration of non-nationals	..	..	No	Yes
Emigration				
View	Too high	Satisfactory	Satisfactory	Satisfactory
Policy	Lower	Maintain	Lower	Maintain
Encouraging the return of nationals	Yes	..	Yes	Yes

* Measures implemented to control HIV/AIDS: (1) blood screening; (2) information/education campaigns; (3) access to antiretroviral treatment; (4) non-discriminatory policies; (5) promoting condom use.

** Grounds on which abortion is permitted: (1) to save the woman's life; (2) to preserve physical health; (3) to preserve mental health; (4) rape or incest; (5) foetal impairment; (6) economic or social reasons; (7) on request.

Population indicators

Indicator	*1975*	*1985*	*1995*	*2005*
Population size and growth				
Population size (thousands)	609	647	731	835
Annual growth rate (percentage)*	-0.2	1.2	1.4	1.2
Population age structure				
Percentage of population under age 15	26	25	25	20
Percentage of population aged 60 or older	14	14	15	17
Fertility and family planning				
Total fertility (births per woman)*	2.5	2.4	2.4	1.6
Teenage fertility rate (per 1,000 women, aged 15 - 19)*	21	21	20	8
Percentage of births to women under age 20*	5	4	4	3
Percentage of births to women aged 35 or older*	9	9	11	10
Percentage of married women using contraception				
Modern methods	..	..	..	..
All methods	..	..	..	..
Health and mortality				
Life expectancy at birth (years)*				
Males	70	73	75	76
Females	73	78	79	81
Both sexes combined	71	75	77	79
Infant mortality rate (per 1,000 births)*	29	16	7	6
Mortality under age 5 (per 1,000 births)*	29	17	8	7
Maternal mortality ratio (per 100,000 births) (2000)	..	..	..	47
HIV/AIDS (2003)				
Number of infected adults (thousands)	..	..	..	..
Adult prevalence rate (percentage)	..	..	..	..
Spatial distribution				
Population density (per sq. km)	66	70	79	90
Urban population (percentage)	45	59	68	69
Annual urban growth rate (percentage)*	1.9	3.6	2.7	1.0
Annual rural growth rate (percentage)*	-1.7	-1.8	-0.1	0.3
International migration				
International migrant stock				
Number of migrants (thousands)	37	41	55	116
Percentage of total population	6	6.4	7.6	13.9

* For the periods 1970-1975, 1980-1985, 1990-1995 and 2000-2005.

Government views and policies

Population policy variable	*1976*	*1986*	*1996*	*2005*
Population size and growth				
View on growth	..	..	Satisfactory	Too low
Policy on growth	..	..	No intervention	Raise
Population age structure				
Level of concern about				
Size of the working-age population	..	..	..	Major concern
Ageing of the population	..	..	..	Major concern
Fertility and family planning				
View on fertility level	..	..	Satisfactory	Too low
Policy	..	..	No intervention	Raise
Access to contraceptive methods	..	..	Indirect support	Indirect support
Adolescent fertility				
Level of concern	..	..	..	Not a concern
Policies and programmes	..	..	..	No
Health and mortality				
View				
Expectation of life	..	..	Unacceptable	Acceptable
Under-five mortality	..	..	..	Acceptable
Maternal mortality	..	..	..	Acceptable
Level of concern about HIV/AIDS	..	..	..	Major concern
Measures implemented to control HIV/AIDS*	..	..	..	1,2,3,4,5
Grounds on which abortion is permitted**	..	..	1,2,3,4,5,6,7	1,2,3,4,5,6,7
Spatial distribution and internal migration				
View on spatial distribution	..	..	Minor change desired	Minor change desired
Policies on internal migration				
From rural to urban areas	..	..	..	..
From rural to rural areas	..	..	..	..
From urban to rural areas	..	..	..	..
From urban to urban areas	..	..	..	..
Into urban agglomerations	..	..	..	No intervention
International migration				
Immigration				
View	..	..	Satisfactory	Too low
Policy	..	..	Maintain	Raise
Permanent settlement	..	..	Maintain	Raise
Temporary workers	..	..	Maintain	Maintain
Highly skilled workers	..	..	..	Raise
Family reunification	..	..	Maintain	Raise
Integration of non-nationals	..	..	Yes	Yes
Emigration				
View	..	..	Satisfactory	Satisfactory
Policy	..	..	No intervention	No intervention
Encouraging the return of nationals	..	..	..	No

* Measures implemented to control HIV/AIDS: (1) blood screening; (2) information/education campaigns; (3) access to antiretroviral treatment; (4) non-discriminatory policies; (5) promoting condom use.

** Grounds on which abortion is permitted: (1) to save the woman's life; (2) to preserve physical health; (3) to preserve mental health; (4) rape or incest; (5) foetal impairment; (6) economic or social reasons; (7) on request.

Population indicators

Indicator	*1975*	*1985*	*1995*	*2005*
Population size and growth				
Population size (thousands)	9 997	10 305	10 331	10 220
Annual growth rate (percentage)*	0.4	0.0	0.0	-0.1
Population age structure				
Percentage of population under age 15	22	24	19	15
Percentage of population aged 60 or older	18	17	18	20
Fertility and family planning				
Total fertility (births per woman)*	2.2	2.0	1.6	1.2
Teenage fertility rate (per 1,000 women, aged 15 - 19)*	32	29	24	12
Percentage of births to women under age 20*	7	7	9	4
Percentage of births to women aged 35 or older*	5	6	6	7
Percentage of married women using contraception				
Modern methods	49[a]	..	63[b]	..
All methods	95[a]	..	72[b]	..
Health and mortality				
Life expectancy at birth (years)*				
Males	67	67	69	72
Females	74	74	76	79
Both sexes combined	70	71	72	75
Infant mortality rate (per 1,000 births)*	20	15	9	6
Mortality under age 5 (per 1,000 births)*	20	15	10	6
Maternal mortality ratio (per 100,000 births) (2000)	..	..	..	9
HIV/AIDS (2003)				
Number of infected adults (thousands)	..	..	..	3
Adult prevalence rate (percentage)	..	..	..	0.1
Spatial distribution				
Population density (per sq. km)	127	131	131	130
Urban population (percentage)	64	75	75	75
Annual urban growth rate (percentage)*	4.4	0.2	-0.1	0.0
Annual rural growth rate (percentage)*	-5.2	-0.5	0.5	-0.5
International migration				
International migrant stock				
Number of migrants (thousands)	..	..	454	453
Percentage of total population	..	..	4.4	4.4

* For the periods 1970-1975, 1980-1985, 1990-1995 and 2000-2005.
[a] For 1977.
[b] For 1997.

Government views and policies

Population policy variable	*1976*	*1986*	*1996*	*2005*
Population size and growth				
View on growth	Too low	Too low	Satisfactory	Too low
Policy on growth	Raise	Raise	No intervention	Maintain
Population age structure				
Level of concern about				
Size of the working-age population	..	..	..	Not a concern
Ageing of the population	..	..	..	Minor concern
Fertility and family planning				
View on fertility level	Satisfactory	Satisfactory	Satisfactory	Too low
Policy	Maintain	Maintain	Maintain	No intervention
Access to contraceptive methods	Direct support	Direct support	Direct support	Direct support
Adolescent fertility				
Level of concern	..	..	..	Not a concern
Policies and programmes	..	..	..	No
Health and mortality				
View				
Expectation of life	Unacceptable	Unacceptable	Acceptable	Unacceptable
Under-five mortality	..	..	..	Unacceptable
Maternal mortality	..	..	..	Unacceptable
Level of concern about HIV/AIDS	..	..	..	Minor concern
Measures implemented to control HIV/AIDS*	..	..	..	1,2,5
Grounds on which abortion is permitted**	..	..	1,2,3,4,5,6,7	1,2,3,4,5,6,7
Spatial distribution and internal migration				
View on spatial distribution	Minor change desired	Minor change desired	Minor change desired	Satisfactory
Policies on internal migration				
From rural to urban areas	..	..	..	Lower
From rural to rural areas	..	..	..	Maintain
From urban to rural areas	..	..	..	Raise
From urban to urban areas	..	..	..	Maintain
Into urban agglomerations	..	..	..	Maintain
International migration				
Immigration				
View	Satisfactory	Satisfactory	Satisfactory	Satisfactory
Policy	Maintain	Maintain	Maintain	Maintain
Permanent settlement	..	..	..	Lower
Temporary workers	..	..	..	Lower
Highly skilled workers	..	..	..	Maintain
Family reunification	..	..	..	Raise
Integration of non-nationals	..	..	..	No
Emigration				
View	Satisfactory	Satisfactory	Satisfactory	Satisfactory
Policy	Maintain	Maintain	Maintain	Maintain
Encouraging the return of nationals	..	..	No	..

* Measures implemented to control HIV/AIDS: (1) blood screening; (2) information/education campaigns; (3) access to antiretroviral treatment; (4) non-discriminatory policies; (5) promoting condom use.

** Grounds on which abortion is permitted: (1) to save the woman's life; (2) to preserve physical health; (3) to preserve mental health; (4) rape or incest; (5) foetal impairment; (6) economic or social reasons; (7) on request.

Population indicators

Indicator	*1975*	*1985*	*1995*	*2005*
Population size and growth				
Population size (thousands)	16 018	18 438	20 918	22 488
Annual growth rate (percentage)*	2.1	1.4	1.2	0.6
Population age structure				
Percentage of population under age 15	38	30	27	25
Percentage of population aged 60 or older	6	7	8	11
Fertility and family planning				
Total fertility (births per woman)*	3.9	2.8	2.3	2.0
Teenage fertility rate (per 1,000 women, aged 15 - 19)*	27	9	2	2
Percentage of births to women under age 20*	4	2	0	0
Percentage of births to women aged 35 or older*	22	9	3	4
Percentage of married women using contraception				
Modern methods	..	..	53[a]	..
All methods	..	..	62[a]	..
Health and mortality				
Life expectancy at birth (years)*				
Males	61	64	62	60
Females	65	69	67	66
Both sexes combined	63	66	65	63
Infant mortality rate (per 1,000 births)*	45	35	41	46
Mortality under age 5 (per 1,000 births)*	59	44	52	59
Maternal mortality ratio (per 100,000 births) (2000)	..	..	..	67
HIV/AIDS (2003)				
Number of infected adults (thousands)	..	..	..	..
Adult prevalence rate (percentage)	..	..	..	..
Spatial distribution				
Population density (per sq. km)	133	153	174	187
Urban population (percentage)	57	58	59	62
Annual urban growth rate (percentage)*	3.0	1.8	1.6	1.0
Annual rural growth rate (percentage)*	1.0	1.1	1.0	-0.2
International migration				
International migrant stock				
Number of migrants (thousands)	30	33	35	37
Percentage of total population	0.2	0.2	0.2	0.2

* For the periods 1970-1975, 1980-1985, 1990-1995 and 2000-2005.
[a] For 1990/1992.

Government views and policies

Population policy variable	*1976*	*1986*	*1996*	*2005*
Population size and growth				
View on growth	Satisfactory	Satisfactory	Satisfactory	Satisfactory
Policy on growth	No intervention	No intervention	No intervention	No intervention
Population age structure				
Level of concern about				
Size of the working-age population	..	..	..	..
Ageing of the population	..	..	..	..
Fertility and family planning				
View on fertility level	Satisfactory	Satisfactory	Satisfactory	Satisfactory
Policy	No intervention	No intervention	No intervention	No intervention
Access to contraceptive methods	Direct support	Indirect support	Direct support	Direct support
Adolescent fertility				
Level of concern	..	..	Minor concern	Minor concern
Policies and programmes	..	..	Yes	Yes
Health and mortality				
View				
Expectation of life	Unacceptable	Unacceptable	Unacceptable	Unacceptable
Under-five mortality	..	..	Unacceptable	Unacceptable
Maternal mortality	..	..	..	Unacceptable
Level of concern about HIV/AIDS	..	..	Major concern	Major concern
Measures implemented to control HIV/AIDS*	..	..	..	1,2,3,5
Grounds on which abortion is permitted**	..	..	1	1
Spatial distribution and internal migration				
View on spatial distribution	Major change desired	Major change desired	Major change desired	Major change desired
Policies on internal migration				
From rural to urban areas	..	..	..	..
From rural to rural areas	..	..	..	..
From urban to rural areas	..	..	..	..
From urban to urban areas	..	..	..	..
Into urban agglomerations	Lower	Lower	No intervention	..
International migration				
Immigration				
View	Satisfactory	Satisfactory	Satisfactory	Satisfactory
Policy	Maintain	Maintain	Lower	Lower
Permanent settlement	..	..	No intervention	..
Temporary workers	..	..	Lower	..
Highly skilled workers	..	..	..	..
Family reunification	..	..	No intervention	..
Integration of non-nationals	..	..	Yes	..
Emigration				
View	Satisfactory	Satisfactory	Satisfactory	Satisfactory
Policy	Maintain	Maintain	No intervention	No intervention
Encouraging the return of nationals	No	..	No	..

* Measures implemented to control HIV/AIDS: (1) blood screening; (2) information/education campaigns; (3) access to antiretroviral treatment; (4) non-discriminatory policies; (5) promoting condom use.
** Grounds on which abortion is permitted: (1) to save the woman's life; (2) to preserve physical health; (3) to preserve mental health; (4) rape or incest; (5) foetal impairment; (6) economic or social reasons; (7) on request.

Population indicators

Indicator	*1975*	*1985*	*1995*	*2005*
Population size and growth				
Population size (thousands)	23 912	32 346	44 999	57 549
Annual growth rate (percentage)*	3.0	2.9	3.5	2.8
Population age structure				
Percentage of population under age 15	46	47	47	47
Percentage of population aged 60 or older	5	4	4	4
Fertility and family planning				
Total fertility (births per woman)*	6.5	6.7	6.7	6.7
Teenage fertility rate (per 1,000 women, aged 15 - 19)*	222	230	230	230
Percentage of births to women under age 20*	23	24	25	25
Percentage of births to women aged 35 or older*	14	14	13	12
Percentage of married women using contraception				
Modern methods	..	..	2[a]	4[b]
All methods	..	..	8[a]	31[b]
Health and mortality				
Life expectancy at birth (years)*				
Males	44	46	43	42
Females	48	49	46	44
Both sexes combined	46	48	45	43
Infant mortality rate (per 1,000 births)*	127	117	118	119
Mortality under age 5 (per 1,000 births)*	212	202	209	212
Maternal mortality ratio (per 100,000 births) (2000)	..	..	..	990
HIV/AIDS (2003)				
Number of infected adults (thousands)	..	..	..	1 000
Adult prevalence rate (percentage)	..	..	..	4.2
Spatial distribution				
Population density (per sq. km)	10	14	19	25
Urban population (percentage)	30	28	29	33
Annual urban growth rate (percentage)*	2.4	2.3	4.0	4.4
Annual rural growth rate (percentage)*	3.2	3.0	3.2	2.2
International migration				
International migrant stock				
Number of migrants (thousands)	1 317	931	2 049	539
Percentage of total population	5.5	2.9	4.6	0.9

* For the periods 1970-1975, 1980-1985, 1990-1995 and 2000-2005.
[a] For 1991.
[b] For 2001.

Government views and policies

Population policy variable	*1976*	*1986*	*1996*	*2005*
Population size and growth				
View on growth	..	..	..	Too high
Policy on growth	..	..	..	No intervention
Population age structure				
Level of concern about				
Size of the working-age population	..	..	..	Major concern
Ageing of the population	..	..	..	..
Fertility and family planning				
View on fertility level	..	..	..	Too high
Policy	..	..	..	No intervention
Access to contraceptive methods	..	..	..	Direct support
Adolescent fertility				
Level of concern	..	..	..	..
Policies and programmes	..	..	..	..
Health and mortality				
View				
Expectation of life	..	..	..	Unacceptable
Under-five mortality	..	..	..	Unacceptable
Maternal mortality	..	..	..	Unacceptable
Level of concern about HIV/AIDS	..	..	..	Major concern
Measures implemented to control HIV/AIDS*	..	..	..	1,5
Grounds on which abortion is permitted**	..	..	..	..
Spatial distribution and internal migration				
View on spatial distribution	..	..	..	Minor change desired
Policies on internal migration				
From rural to urban areas	..	..	..	No intervention
From rural to rural areas	..	..	..	..
From urban to rural areas	..	..	..	..
From urban to urban areas	..	..	..	..
Into urban agglomerations	..	..	..	No intervention
International migration				
Immigration				
View	..	..	..	Satisfactory
Policy	..	..	..	Maintain
Permanent settlement	..	..	..	Maintain
Temporary workers	..	..	..	Maintain
Highly skilled workers	..	..	..	Maintain
Family reunification	..	..	..	Maintain
Integration of non-nationals	..	..	..	..
Emigration				
View	..	..	..	Satisfactory
Policy	..	..	..	No intervention
Encouraging the return of nationals	..	..	..	..

* Measures implemented to control HIV/AIDS: (1) blood screening; (2) information/education campaigns; (3) access to antiretroviral treatment; (4) non-discriminatory policies; (5) promoting condom use.

** Grounds on which abortion is permitted: (1) to save the woman's life; (2) to preserve physical health; (3) to preserve mental health; (4) rape or incest; (5) foetal impairment; (6) economic or social reasons; (7) on request.

Population indicators

Indicator	*1975*	*1985*	*1995*	*2005*
Population size and growth				
Population size (thousands)	672	659	848	947
Annual growth rate (percentage)*	2.1	2.5	2.7	5.4
Population age structure				
Percentage of population under age 15	42	40	42	41
Percentage of population aged 60 or older	5	4	4	5
Fertility and family planning				
Total fertility (births per woman)*	6.2	5.4	4.8	7.8
Teenage fertility rate (per 1,000 women, aged 15 - 19)*	61	53	47	182
Percentage of births to women under age 20*	7	7	5	23
Percentage of births to women aged 35 or older*	17	15	16	17
Percentage of married women using contraception				
Modern methods	..	..	..	9[a]
All methods	..	..	..	10[a]
Health and mortality				
Life expectancy at birth (years)*				
Males	39	39	47	54
Females	41	41	49	56
Both sexes combined	40	40	48	55
Infant mortality rate (per 1,000 births)*	183	183	133	94
Mortality under age 5 (per 1,000 births)*	275	275	197	134
Maternal mortality ratio (per 100,000 births) (2000)	..	..	..	660
HIV/AIDS (2003)				
Number of infected adults (thousands)	..	..	..	..
Adult prevalence rate (percentage)	..	..	..	..
Spatial distribution				
Population density (per sq. km)	45	44	57	64
Urban population (percentage)	9	8	7	8
Annual urban growth rate (percentage)*	1.3	1.6	1.6	4.8
Annual rural growth rate (percentage)*	2.2	2.6	2.6	3.9
International migration				
International migrant stock				
Number of migrants (thousands)	5	5	6	6
Percentage of total population	0.8	0.8	0.7	0.6

* For the periods 1970-1975, 1980-1985, 1990-1995 and 2000-2005.
[a] For 2003.

Government views and policies

Population policy variable	*1976*	*1986*	*1996*	*2005*
Population size and growth				
View on growth	Satisfactory	Satisfactory	Satisfactory	Satisfactory
Policy on growth	No intervention	No intervention	No intervention	No intervention
Population age structure				
Level of concern about				
Size of the working-age population	..	..	..	Minor concern
Ageing of the population	..	..	..	Major concern
Fertility and family planning				
View on fertility level	Satisfactory	Satisfactory	Satisfactory	Satisfactory
Policy	No intervention	No intervention	No intervention	No intervention
Access to contraceptive methods	Direct support	Direct support	Direct support	Indirect support
Adolescent fertility				
Level of concern	..	..	Minor concern	Minor concern
Policies and programmes	..	..	Yes	Yes
Health and mortality				
View				
Expectation of life	Acceptable	Acceptable	Acceptable	Acceptable
Under-five mortality	..	..	Acceptable	Acceptable
Maternal mortality	..	..	..	Acceptable
Level of concern about HIV/AIDS	..	..	Major concern	Minor concern
Measures implemented to control HIV/AIDS*	..	..	..	1,2,3,4,5
Grounds on which abortion is permitted**	..	..	1,2,3,4,5,6,7	1,2,3,4,5,6,7
Spatial distribution and internal migration				
View on spatial distribution	Satisfactory	Satisfactory	Satisfactory	Satisfactory
Policies on internal migration				
From rural to urban areas	..	..	..	No intervention
From rural to rural areas	..	..	..	No intervention
From urban to rural areas	..	..	..	No intervention
From urban to urban areas	..	..	..	No intervention
Into urban agglomerations	Raise	..	No intervention	No intervention
International migration				
Immigration				
View	Satisfactory	Satisfactory	Too high	Too high
Policy	Maintain	Maintain	Lower	Lower
Permanent settlement	..	..	Lower	Lower
Temporary workers	..	..	Lower	Maintain
Highly skilled workers	..	..	..	Raise
Family reunification	..	..	Lower	Lower
Integration of non-nationals	..	..	Yes	Yes
Emigration				
View	Satisfactory	Satisfactory	Satisfactory	Satisfactory
Policy	Maintain	Maintain	No intervention	No intervention
Encouraging the return of nationals	No	..	No	No

* Measures implemented to control HIV/AIDS: (1) blood screening; (2) information/education campaigns; (3) access to antiretroviral treatment; (4) non-discriminatory policies; (5) promoting condom use.

** Grounds on which abortion is permitted: (1) to save the woman's life; (2) to preserve physical health; (3) to preserve mental health; (4) rape or incest; (5) foetal impairment; (6) economic or social reasons; (7) on request.

Population indicators

Indicator	*1975*	*1985*	*1995*	*2005*
Population size and growth				
Population size (thousands)	5 060	5 114	5 228	5 431
Annual growth rate (percentage)*	0.5	0.0	0.3	0.3
Population age structure				
Percentage of population under age 15	23	18	17	19
Percentage of population aged 60 or older	19	20	20	21
Fertility and family planning				
Total fertility (births per woman)*	2.0	1.4	1.7	1.8
Teenage fertility rate (per 1,000 women, aged 15 - 19)*	9	6	8	7
Percentage of births to women under age 20*	2	2	2	2
Percentage of births to women aged 35 or older*	11	13	13	16
Percentage of married women using contraception				
Modern methods	60	72[a]	..	..
All methods	63	78[a]	..	..
Health and mortality				
Life expectancy at birth (years)*				
Males	71	72	73	75
Females	76	78	78	79
Both sexes combined	74	75	75	77
Infant mortality rate (per 1,000 births)*	12	8	7	5
Mortality under age 5 (per 1,000 births)*	14	10	8	6
Maternal mortality ratio (per 100,000 births) (2000)	..	..	..	5
HIV/AIDS (2003)				
Number of infected adults (thousands)	..	..	..	5
Adult prevalence rate (percentage)	..	..	..	0.2
Spatial distribution				
Population density (per sq. km)	117	119	121	126
Urban population (percentage)	82	84	85	86
Annual urban growth rate (percentage)*	1.1	0.1	0.4	0.3
Annual rural growth rate (percentage)*	-2.0	-0.8	0.2	-0.4
International migration				
International migrant stock				
Number of migrants (thousands)	139	190	250	389
Percentage of total population	2.7	3.7	4.8	7.2

* For the periods 1970-1975, 1980-1985, 1990-1995 and 2000-2005.
[a] For 1988.

Government views and policies

Population policy variable	*1976*	*1986*	*1996*	*2005*
Population size and growth				
View on growth	..	Satisfactory	Satisfactory	Too high
Policy on growth	..	No intervention	No intervention	Lower
Population age structure				
Level of concern about				
Size of the working-age population	..	..	..	Major concern
Ageing of the population	..	..	..	Not a concern
Fertility and family planning				
View on fertility level	..	Satisfactory	Satisfactory	Too high
Policy	..	No intervention	No intervention	No intervention
Access to contraceptive methods	..	No support	No support	Direct support
Adolescent fertility				
Level of concern	..	..	Not a concern	Not a concern
Policies and programmes	..	..	..	No
Health and mortality				
View				
Expectation of life	..	Unacceptable	Unacceptable	Unacceptable
Under-five mortality	..	..	Unacceptable	Unacceptable
Maternal mortality	..	..	..	Unacceptable
Level of concern about HIV/AIDS	..	..	Minor concern	Major concern
Measures implemented to control HIV/AIDS*	..	..	..	1,2,5
Grounds on which abortion is permitted**	..	..	1	1
Spatial distribution and internal migration				
View on spatial distribution	..	Minor change desired	Minor change desired	Major change desired
Policies on internal migration				
From rural to urban areas	..	..	..	Lower
From rural to rural areas	..	..	..	..
From urban to rural areas	..	..	..	..
From urban to urban areas	..	..	..	..
Into urban agglomerations	..	No intervention	No intervention	Lower
International migration				
Immigration				
View	..	Too high	Too high	Too high
Policy	..	Maintain	Lower	Lower
Permanent settlement	..	..	Lower	Lower
Temporary workers	..	..	Maintain	..
Highly skilled workers	..	..	..	..
Family reunification	..	..	Maintain	..
Integration of non-nationals	..	..	No	No
Emigration				
View	..	Satisfactory	Satisfactory	Satisfactory
Policy	..	Maintain	No intervention	No intervention
Encouraging the return of nationals	..	..	No	No

* Measures implemented to control HIV/AIDS: (1) blood screening; (2) information/education campaigns; (3) access to antiretroviral treatment; (4) non-discriminatory policies; (5) promoting condom use.

** Grounds on which abortion is permitted: (1) to save the woman's life; (2) to preserve physical health; (3) to preserve mental health; (4) rape or incest; (5) foetal impairment; (6) economic or social reasons; (7) on request.

Population indicators

Indicator	*1975*	*1985*	*1995*	*2005*
Population size and growth				
Population size (thousands)	224	403	609	793
Annual growth rate (percentage)*	6.5	3.4	1.7	2.1
Population age structure				
Percentage of population under age 15	46	45	44	41
Percentage of population aged 60 or older	4	4	4	5
Fertility and family planning				
Total fertility (births per woman)*	7.2	6.6	6.1	5.1
Teenage fertility rate (per 1,000 women, aged 15 - 19)*	61	67	71	57
Percentage of births to women under age 20*	7	8	9	8
Percentage of births to women aged 35 or older*	23	22	20	18
Percentage of married women using contraception				
Modern methods	..	..	..	..
All methods	..	..	..	..
Health and mortality				
Life expectancy at birth (years)*				
Males	43	47	50	51
Females	46	50	53	54
Both sexes combined	44	49	51	53
Infant mortality rate (per 1,000 births)*	154	127	111	93
Mortality under age 5 (per 1,000 births)*	230	195	168	140
Maternal mortality ratio (per 100,000 births) (2000)	..	..	..	730
HIV/AIDS (2003)				
Number of infected adults (thousands)	..	..	..	8
Adult prevalence rate (percentage)	..	..	..	2.9
Spatial distribution				
Population density (per sq. km)	10	17	26	34
Urban population (percentage)	62	71	79	85
Annual urban growth rate (percentage)*	8.1	4.4	2.5	2.1
Annual rural growth rate (percentage)*	3.8	0.1	-1.9	-1.2
International migration				
International migrant stock				
Number of migrants (thousands)	3	21	35	20
Percentage of total population	1.2	5.2	5.8	2.6

* For the periods 1970-1975, 1980-1985, 1990-1995 and 2000-2005.

Government views and policies

Population policy variable	*1976*	*1986*	*1996*	*2005*
Population size and growth				
View on growth	..	Too high	Too high	Satisfactory
Policy on growth	..	Lower	Lower	No intervention
Population age structure				
Level of concern about				
Size of the working-age population	..	..	..	Major concern
Ageing of the population	..	..	..	Major concern
Fertility and family planning				
View on fertility level	..	Too high	Too high	Satisfactory
Policy	..	Lower	Lower	No intervention
Access to contraceptive methods	..	Direct support	Direct support	Direct support
Adolescent fertility				
Level of concern	..	..	..	Major concern
Policies and programmes	..	..	..	Yes
Health and mortality				
View				
Expectation of life	..	Unacceptable	Unacceptable	Acceptable
Under-five mortality	..	..	..	Acceptable
Maternal mortality	..	..	..	Acceptable
Level of concern about HIV/AIDS	..	..	..	Major concern
Measures implemented to control HIV/AIDS*	..	..	..	1,2,3
Grounds on which abortion is permitted**	..	..	1	1
Spatial distribution and internal migration				
View on spatial distribution	..	Minor change desired	Minor change desired	Satisfactory
Policies on internal migration				
From rural to urban areas	..	..	..	No intervention
From rural to rural areas	..	..	..	No intervention
From urban to rural areas	..	..	..	No intervention
From urban to urban areas	..	..	..	No intervention
Into urban agglomerations	..	..	..	No intervention
International migration				
Immigration				
View	..	Satisfactory	Satisfactory	Satisfactory
Policy	..	Maintain	Maintain	Maintain
Permanent settlement	..	..	Maintain	Maintain
Temporary workers	..	..	..	Maintain
Highly skilled workers	..	..	..	Maintain
Family reunification	..	..	..	Maintain
Integration of non-nationals	..	..	..	Yes
Emigration				
View	..	Too high	Too high	Satisfactory
Policy	..	Maintain	Maintain	No intervention
Encouraging the return of nationals	..	..	..	Yes

* Measures implemented to control HIV/AIDS: (1) blood screening; (2) information/education campaigns; (3) access to antiretroviral treatment; (4) non-discriminatory policies; (5) promoting condom use.

** Grounds on which abortion is permitted: (1) to save the woman's life; (2) to preserve physical health; (3) to preserve mental health; (4) rape or incest; (5) foetal impairment; (6) economic or social reasons; (7) on request.

Population indicators

Indicator	*1975*	*1985*	*1995*	*2005*
Population size and growth				
Population size (thousands)	224	403	609	793
Annual growth rate (percentage)*	6.5	3.4	1.7	2.1
Population age structure				
Percentage of population under age 15	46	45	44	41
Percentage of population aged 60 or older	4	4	4	5
Fertility and family planning				
Total fertility (births per woman)*	7.2	6.6	6.1	5.1
Teenage fertility rate (per 1,000 women, aged 15 - 19)*	61	67	71	57
Percentage of births to women under age 20*	7	8	9	8
Percentage of births to women aged 35 or older*	23	22	20	18
Percentage of married women using contraception				
Modern methods	..	..	..	..
All methods	..	..	..	..
Health and mortality				
Life expectancy at birth (years)*				
Males	43	47	50	51
Females	46	50	53	54
Both sexes combined	44	49	51	53
Infant mortality rate (per 1,000 births)*	154	127	111	93
Mortality under age 5 (per 1,000 births)*	230	195	168	140
Maternal mortality ratio (per 100,000 births) (2000)	..	..	..	730
HIV/AIDS (2003)				
Number of infected adults (thousands)	..	..	..	8
Adult prevalence rate (percentage)	..	..	..	2.9
Spatial distribution				
Population density (per sq. km)	10	17	26	34
Urban population (percentage)	62	71	79	85
Annual urban growth rate (percentage)*	8.1	4.4	2.5	2.1
Annual rural growth rate (percentage)*	3.8	0.1	-1.9	-1.2
International migration				
International migrant stock				
Number of migrants (thousands)	3	21	35	20
Percentage of total population	1.2	5.2	5.8	2.6

* For the periods 1970-1975, 1980-1985, 1990-1995 and 2000-2005.

Government views and policies

Population policy variable	*1976*	*1986*	*1996*	*2005*
Population size and growth				
View on growth	..	Too high	Too high	Satisfactory
Policy on growth	..	Lower	Lower	No intervention
Population age structure				
Level of concern about				
Size of the working-age population	..	..	..	Major concern
Ageing of the population	..	..	..	Major concern
Fertility and family planning				
View on fertility level	..	Too high	Too high	Satisfactory
Policy	..	Lower	Lower	No intervention
Access to contraceptive methods	..	Direct support	Direct support	Direct support
Adolescent fertility				
Level of concern	..	..	..	Major concern
Policies and programmes	..	..	..	Yes
Health and mortality				
View				
Expectation of life	..	Unacceptable	Unacceptable	Acceptable
Under-five mortality	..	..	..	Acceptable
Maternal mortality	..	..	..	Acceptable
Level of concern about HIV/AIDS	..	..	..	Major concern
Measures implemented to control HIV/AIDS*	..	..	..	1,2,3
Grounds on which abortion is permitted**	..	..	1	1
Spatial distribution and internal migration				
View on spatial distribution	..	Minor change desired	Minor change desired	Satisfactory
Policies on internal migration				
From rural to urban areas	..	..	..	No intervention
From rural to rural areas	..	..	..	No intervention
From urban to rural areas	..	..	..	No intervention
From urban to urban areas	..	..	..	No intervention
Into urban agglomerations	..	..	..	No intervention
International migration				
Immigration				
View	..	Satisfactory	Satisfactory	Satisfactory
Policy	..	Maintain	Maintain	Maintain
Permanent settlement	..	..	Maintain	Maintain
Temporary workers	..	..	..	Maintain
Highly skilled workers	..	..	..	Maintain
Family reunification	..	..	..	Maintain
Integration of non-nationals	..	..	..	Yes
Emigration				
View	..	Too high	Too high	Satisfactory
Policy	..	Maintain	Maintain	No intervention
Encouraging the return of nationals	..	..	..	Yes

* Measures implemented to control HIV/AIDS: (1) blood screening; (2) information/education campaigns; (3) access to antiretroviral treatment; (4) non-discriminatory policies; (5) promoting condom use.

** Grounds on which abortion is permitted: (1) to save the woman's life; (2) to preserve physical health; (3) to preserve mental health; (4) rape or incest; (5) foetal impairment; (6) economic or social reasons; (7) on request.

Population indicators

Indicator	*1975*	*1985*	*1995*	*2005*
Population size and growth				
Population size (thousands)	72	73	75	79
Annual growth rate (percentage)*	0.5	-0.2	0.8	0.3
Population age structure				
Percentage of population under age 15	..	..	..	..
Percentage of population aged 60 or older	..	..	..	..
Fertility and family planning				
Total fertility (births per woman)*	..	..	..	..
Teenage fertility rate (per 1,000 women, aged 15 - 19)*	..	..	..	..
Percentage of births to women under age 20*	..	..	..	..
Percentage of births to women aged 35 or older*	..	..	..	..
Percentage of married women using contraception				
Modern methods	..	48[a]	..	..
All methods	..	50[a]	..	..
Health and mortality				
Life expectancy at birth (years)*				
Males	..	..	..	..
Females	..	..	..	..
Both sexes combined	..	..	..	..
Infant mortality rate (per 1,000 births)*	..	..	..	..
Mortality under age 5 (per 1,000 births)*	..	..	..	..
Maternal mortality ratio (per 100,000 births) (2000)	..	..	..	..
HIV/AIDS (2003)				
Number of infected adults (thousands)	..	..	..	..
Adult prevalence rate (percentage)	..	..	..	..
Spatial distribution				
Population density (per sq. km)	96	98	100	105
Urban population (percentage)	55	66	69	73
Annual urban growth rate (percentage)*	3.8	0.6	1.3	0.8
Annual rural growth rate (percentage)*	-2.9	-1.7	-0.2	-0.9
International migration				
International migrant stock				
Number of migrants (thousands)	2	2	3	5
Percentage of total population	2.6	2.8	4.1	5.7

* For the periods 1970-1975, 1980-1985, 1990-1995 and 2000-2005.
[a] For 1987.

Government views and policies

Population policy variable	*1976*	*1986*	*1996*	*2005*
Population size and growth				
View on growth	Too high	Too high	Too high	Too high
Policy on growth	Lower	Lower	Lower	Lower
Population age structure				
Level of concern about				
Size of the working-age population	..	..	..	Major concern
Ageing of the population	..	..	..	Major concern
Fertility and family planning				
View on fertility level	Too high	Too high	Too high	Too high
Policy	Lower	Lower	Lower	Lower
Access to contraceptive methods	Direct support	Direct support	Direct support	Direct support
Adolescent fertility				
Level of concern	..	..	Major concern	Major concern
Policies and programmes	..	..	No	Yes
Health and mortality				
View				
Expectation of life	Unacceptable	Unacceptable	Unacceptable	Unacceptable
Under-five mortality	..	..	Unacceptable	Unacceptable
Maternal mortality	..	..	..	Unacceptable
Level of concern about HIV/AIDS	..	..	Minor concern	Major concern
Measures implemented to control HIV/AIDS*	..	..	..	1,2,3,4,5
Grounds on which abortion is permitted**	..	..	1	1
Spatial distribution and internal migration				
View on spatial distribution	Major change desired	Major change desired	Satisfactory	Major change desired
Policies on internal migration				
From rural to urban areas	..	..	..	Lower
From rural to rural areas	..	..	..	..
From urban to rural areas	..	..	..	..
From urban to urban areas	..	..	..	..
Into urban agglomerations	No intervention	Lower	No intervention	Lower
International migration				
Immigration				
View	Satisfactory	Too high	Too high	Satisfactory
Policy	Maintain	Lower	Lower	Maintain
Permanent settlement	..	..	No intervention	Maintain
Temporary workers	..	..	No intervention	Maintain
Highly skilled workers	..	..	..	..
Family reunification	..	..	No intervention	Maintain
Integration of non-nationals	..	..	No	No
Emigration				
View	Satisfactory	Too high	Too high	Satisfactory
Policy	Maintain	Lower	No intervention	No intervention
Encouraging the return of nationals	No	..	No	No

* Measures implemented to control HIV/AIDS: (1) blood screening; (2) information/education campaigns; (3) access to antiretroviral treatment; (4) non-discriminatory policies; (5) promoting condom use.
** Grounds on which abortion is permitted: (1) to save the woman's life; (2) to preserve physical health; (3) to preserve mental health; (4) rape or incest; (5) foetal impairment; (6) economic or social reasons; (7) on request.

Population indicators

Indicator	*1975*	*1985*	*1995*	*2005*
Population size and growth				
Population size (thousands)	5 058	6 443	7 672	8 895
Annual growth rate (percentage)*	2.7	2.4	1.6	1.5
Population age structure				
Percentage of population under age 15	46	40	38	33
Percentage of population aged 60 or older	5	5	5	6
Fertility and family planning				
Total fertility (births per woman)*	5.6	4.2	3.2	2.7
Teenage fertility rate (per 1,000 women, aged 15 - 19)*	117	119	103	93
Percentage of births to women under age 20*	16	20	19	20
Percentage of births to women aged 35 or older*	13	11	7	6
Percentage of married women using contraception				
Modern methods	26	47[a]	52[b]	66[c]
All methods	32	50[a]	56[b]	70[c]
Health and mortality				
Life expectancy at birth (years)*				
Males	58	61	64	64
Females	62	65	69	71
Both sexes combined	60	63	66	67
Infant mortality rate (per 1,000 births)*	94	63	47	35
Mortality under age 5 (per 1,000 births)*	135	90	67	51
Maternal mortality ratio (per 100,000 births) (2000)	..	..	..	150
HIV/AIDS (2003)				
Number of infected adults (thousands)	..	..	..	85
Adult prevalence rate (percentage)	..	..	..	1.7
Spatial distribution				
Population density (per sq. km)	104	133	158	183
Urban population (percentage)	46	54	57	60
Annual urban growth rate (percentage)*	5.2	3.4	2.2	2.1
Annual rural growth rate (percentage)*	0.7	1.4	1.1	0.6
International migration				
International migrant stock				
Number of migrants (thousands)	51	90	118	156
Percentage of total population	1	1.4	1.5	1.8

* For the periods 1970-1975, 1980-1985, 1990-1995 and 2000-2005.
[a] For 1986.
[b] For 1991.
[c] For 2002.

Government views and policies

Population policy variable	*1976*	*1986*	*1996*	*2005*
Population size and growth				
View on growth	Too high	Satisfactory	Satisfactory	Satisfactory
Policy on growth	No intervention	No intervention	No intervention	No intervention
Population age structure				
Level of concern about				
Size of the working-age population	..	..	..	..
Ageing of the population	..	..	..	Minor concern
Fertility and family planning				
View on fertility level	Too high	Satisfactory	Too high	Satisfactory
Policy	No intervention	No intervention	Lower	Maintain
Access to contraceptive methods	Direct support	Direct support	Direct support	Direct support
Adolescent fertility				
Level of concern	..	..	Major concern	Major concern
Policies and programmes	..	..	Yes	Yes
Health and mortality				
View				
Expectation of life	Acceptable	Unacceptable	Unacceptable	Unacceptable
Under-five mortality	..	..	Unacceptable	Unacceptable
Maternal mortality	..	..	..	Unacceptable
Level of concern about HIV/AIDS	..	..	Minor concern	Major concern
Measures implemented to control HIV/AIDS*	..	..	..	1,2,3
Grounds on which abortion is permitted**	..	..	1,2,4	1,2,3,4
Spatial distribution and internal migration				
View on spatial distribution	Major change desired	Major change desired	Major change desired	Minor change desired
Policies on internal migration				
From rural to urban areas	..	..	..	No intervention
From rural to rural areas	..	..	..	No intervention
From urban to rural areas	..	..	..	No intervention
From urban to urban areas	..	..	..	No intervention
Into urban agglomerations	No intervention	Lower	Lower	No intervention
International migration				
Immigration				
View	Satisfactory	Too high	Satisfactory	Too high
Policy	Maintain	Maintain	Lower	Lower
Permanent settlement	..	..	No intervention	Lower
Temporary workers	..	..	Lower	Lower
Highly skilled workers	..	..	..	Maintain
Family reunification	..	..	Lower	Maintain
Integration of non-nationals	..	..	No	No
Emigration				
View	Satisfactory	Satisfactory	Satisfactory	Too high
Policy	Maintain	Maintain	No intervention	Lower
Encouraging the return of nationals	Yes	..	No	Yes

* Measures implemented to control HIV/AIDS: (1) blood screening; (2) information/education campaigns; (3) access to antiretroviral treatment; (4) non-discriminatory policies; (5) promoting condom use.
** Grounds on which abortion is permitted: (1) to save the woman's life; (2) to preserve physical health; (3) to preserve mental health; (4) rape or incest; (5) foetal impairment; (6) economic or social reasons; (7) on request.

Population indicators

Indicator	*1975*	*1985*	*1995*	*2005*
Population size and growth				
Population size (thousands)	6 907	9 099	11 396	13 228
Annual growth rate (percentage)*	2.9	2.7	2.1	1.4
Population age structure				
Percentage of population under age 15	44	41	36	32
Percentage of population aged 60 or older	6	6	7	8
Fertility and family planning				
Total fertility (births per woman)*	6.0	4.7	3.4	2.8
Teenage fertility rate (per 1,000 women, aged 15 - 19)*	120	100	84	85
Percentage of births to women under age 20*	16	15	16	18
Percentage of births to women aged 35 or older*	16	14	13	13
Percentage of married women using contraception				
Modern methods	26[a]	36[b]	46[c]	50[d]
All methods	34[a]	44[b]	57[c]	66[d]
Health and mortality				
Life expectancy at birth (years)*				
Males	57	62	68	71
Females	60	67	73	77
Both sexes combined	59	64	70	74
Infant mortality rate (per 1,000 births)*	95	68	44	25
Mortality under age 5 (per 1,000 births)*	137	95	57	30
Maternal mortality ratio (per 100,000 births) (2000)	..	..	..	130
HIV/AIDS (2003)				
Number of infected adults (thousands)	..	..	..	20
Adult prevalence rate (percentage)	..	..	..	0.3
Spatial distribution				
Population density (per sq. km)	24	32	40	47
Urban population (percentage)	42	51	58	63
Annual urban growth rate (percentage)*	4.4	4.4	3.1	2.3
Annual rural growth rate (percentage)*	1.9	1.0	0.9	0.2
International migration				
International migrant stock				
Number of migrants (thousands)	59	76	88	114
Percentage of total population	0.9	0.8	0.8	0.9

* For the periods 1970-1975, 1980-1985, 1990-1995 and 2000-2005.
[a] For 1979.
[b] For 1987.
[c] For 1994.
[d] For 1999.

Government views and policies

Population policy variable	*1976*	*1986*	*1996*	*2005*
Population size and growth				
View on growth	Too high	Too high	Too high	Too high
Policy on growth	Lower	Lower	Lower	Lower
Population age structure				
Level of concern about				
Size of the working-age population	..	..	..	Major concern
Ageing of the population	..	..	..	Minor concern
Fertility and family planning				
View on fertility level	Too high	Too high	Too high	Too high
Policy	Lower	Lower	Lower	Lower
Access to contraceptive methods	Direct support	Direct support	Direct support	Direct support
Adolescent fertility				
Level of concern	..	..	Major concern	Minor concern
Policies and programmes	..	..	No	Yes
Health and mortality				
View				
Expectation of life	Unacceptable	Unacceptable	Acceptable	Acceptable
Under-five mortality	..	..	Acceptable	Unacceptable
Maternal mortality	..	..	..	Unacceptable
Level of concern about HIV/AIDS	..	..	Minor concern	Minor concern
Measures implemented to control HIV/AIDS*	..	..	..	1,2,3,4,5
Grounds on which abortion is permitted**	..	..	1	1
Spatial distribution and internal migration				
View on spatial distribution	Major change desired	Major change desired	Major change desired	Major change desired
Policies on internal migration				
From rural to urban areas	..	..	..	Lower
From rural to rural areas	..	..	..	No intervention
From urban to rural areas	..	..	..	No intervention
From urban to urban areas	..	..	..	No intervention
Into urban agglomerations	Lower	Lower	No intervention	Lower
International migration				
Immigration				
View	Satisfactory	Satisfactory	Satisfactory	Satisfactory
Policy	Maintain	Maintain	Lower	Lower
Permanent settlement	..	..	Lower	Lower
Temporary workers	..	..	Maintain	Lower
Highly skilled workers	..	..	..	Maintain
Family reunification	..	..	Lower	Maintain
Integration of non-nationals	..	..	No	Yes
Emigration				
View	Satisfactory	Satisfactory	Too low	Too low
Policy	Maintain	Maintain	Raise	Maintain
Encouraging the return of nationals	No	..	No	Yes

* Measures implemented to control HIV/AIDS: (1) blood screening; (2) information/education campaigns; (3) access to antiretroviral treatment; (4) non-discriminatory policies; (5) promoting condom use.

** Grounds on which abortion is permitted: (1) to save the woman's life; (2) to preserve physical health; (3) to preserve mental health; (4) rape or incest; (5) foetal impairment; (6) economic or social reasons; (7) on request.

Population indicators

Indicator	*1975*	*1985*	*1995*	*2005*
Population size and growth				
Population size (thousands)	39 295	49 612	61 225	74 033
Annual growth rate (percentage)*	2.2	2.5	1.9	1.9
Population age structure				
Percentage of population under age 15	41	42	39	34
Percentage of population aged 60 or older	6	6	7	7
Fertility and family planning				
Total fertility (births per woman)*	5.7	5.3	3.9	3.3
Teenage fertility rate (per 1,000 women, aged 15 - 19)*	95	89	69	46
Percentage of births to women under age 20*	13	11	12	10
Percentage of births to women aged 35 or older*	13	12	12	10
Percentage of married women using contraception				
Modern methods	22	29[a]	46	57[b]
All methods	25	30[a]	47	60[b]
Health and mortality				
Life expectancy at birth (years)*				
Males	51	55	62	67
Females	53	58	66	72
Both sexes combined	52	57	64	70
Infant mortality rate (per 1,000 births)*	136	107	65	37
Mortality under age 5 (per 1,000 births)*	184	143	82	43
Maternal mortality ratio (per 100,000 births) (2000)	..	..	..	84
HIV/AIDS (2003)				
Number of infected adults (thousands)	..	..	..	12
Adult prevalence rate (percentage)	..	..	..	<0.1
Spatial distribution				
Population density (per sq. km)	39	50	61	74
Urban population (percentage)	43	44	43	42
Annual urban growth rate (percentage)*	2.7	2.5	1.7	2.1
Annual rural growth rate (percentage)*	1.7	2.4	2.2	1.9
International migration				
International migrant stock				
Number of migrants (thousands)	196	182	172	166
Percentage of total population	0.5	0.4	0.3	0.2

* For the periods 1970-1975, 1980-1985, 1990-1995 and 2000-2005.
[a] For 1984.
[b] For 2003.

Government views and policies

Population policy variable	*1976*	*1986*	*1996*	*2005*
Population size and growth				
View on growth	Too high	Too high	Too high	Satisfactory
Policy on growth	Lower	Lower	Lower	No intervention
Population age structure				
Level of concern about				
Size of the working-age population	..	..	..	Not a concern
Ageing of the population	..	..	..	Minor concern
Fertility and family planning				
View on fertility level	Too high	Too high	Too high	Satisfactory
Policy	Lower	Lower	Lower	No intervention
Access to contraceptive methods	Direct support	Direct support	Direct support	Direct support
Adolescent fertility				
Level of concern	..	..	Minor concern	Major concern
Policies and programmes	..	..	No	Yes
Health and mortality				
View				
Expectation of life	Unacceptable	Unacceptable	Unacceptable	Unacceptable
Under-five mortality	..	..	Unacceptable	Unacceptable
Maternal mortality	..	..	..	Unacceptable
Level of concern about HIV/AIDS	..	..	Major concern	Major concern
Measures implemented to control HIV/AIDS*	..	..	..	1,2,3,4,5
Grounds on which abortion is permitted**	..	..	Not permitted	Not permitted
Spatial distribution and internal migration				
View on spatial distribution	Major change desired	Major change desired	Major change desired	Major change desired
Policies on internal migration				
From rural to urban areas	..	..	..	No intervention
From rural to rural areas	..	..	..	No intervention
From urban to rural areas	..	..	..	No intervention
From urban to urban areas	..	..	..	No intervention
Into urban agglomerations	No intervention	No intervention	No intervention	Lower
International migration				
Immigration				
View	Satisfactory	Satisfactory	Satisfactory	Satisfactory
Policy	Maintain	Maintain	No intervention	No intervention
Permanent settlement	..	..	No intervention	No intervention
Temporary workers	..	..	No intervention	No intervention
Highly skilled workers	..	..	..	Maintain
Family reunification	..	..	No intervention	Maintain
Integration of non-nationals	..	..	Yes	No
Emigration				
View	Satisfactory	Too high	Satisfactory	Too high
Policy	Maintain	Lower	No intervention	Lower
Encouraging the return of nationals	No	..	No	Yes

* Measures implemented to control HIV/AIDS: (1) blood screening; (2) information/education campaigns; (3) access to antiretroviral treatment; (4) non-discriminatory policies; (5) promoting condom use.
** Grounds on which abortion is permitted: (1) to save the woman's life; (2) to preserve physical health; (3) to preserve mental health; (4) rape or incest; (5) foetal impairment; (6) economic or social reasons; (7) on request.

Population indicators

Indicator	*1975*	*1985*	*1995*	*2005*
Population size and growth				
Population size (thousands)	4 120	4 769	5 669	6 881
Annual growth rate (percentage)*	2.7	0.8	2.1	1.8
Population age structure				
Percentage of population under age 15	46	44	37	34
Percentage of population aged 60 or older	5	6	7	8
Fertility and family planning				
Total fertility (births per woman)*	6.1	4.5	3.5	2.9
Teenage fertility rate (per 1,000 women, aged 15 - 19)*	151	130	111	87
Percentage of births to women under age 20*	19	21	22	17
Percentage of births to women aged 35 or older*	13	12	10	11
Percentage of married women using contraception				
Modern methods	18	46	54[a]	61[b]
All methods	19	48	60[a]	67[b]
Health and mortality				
Life expectancy at birth (years)*				
Males	56	51	63	68
Females	61	64	71	74
Both sexes combined	58	57	67	71
Infant mortality rate (per 1,000 births)*	105	77	40	26
Mortality under age 5 (per 1,000 births)*	152	118	51	35
Maternal mortality ratio (per 100,000 births) (2000)	..	..	..	150
HIV/AIDS (2003)				
Number of infected adults (thousands)	..	..	..	28
Adult prevalence rate (percentage)	..	..	..	0.7
Spatial distribution				
Population density (per sq. km)	196	227	269	327
Urban population (percentage)	42	47	54	60
Annual urban growth rate (percentage)*	3.7	1.9	3.9	2.1
Annual rural growth rate (percentage)*	2.0	-0.2	0.1	0.7
International migration				
International migrant stock				
Number of migrants (thousands)	31	28	26	24
Percentage of total population	0.8	0.6	0.5	0.3

* For the periods 1970-1975, 1980-1985, 1990-1995 and 2000-2005.
[a] For 1998.
[b] For 2002/2003.

Government views and policies

Population policy variable	*1976*	*1986*	*1996*	*2005*
Population size and growth				
View on growth	Too low	Too low	Satisfactory	Satisfactory
Policy on growth	Raise	Raise	Maintain	Maintain
Population age structure				
Level of concern about				
Size of the working-age population	..	..	..	..
Ageing of the population	..	..	..	Major concern
Fertility and family planning				
View on fertility level	Too low	Too low	Satisfactory	Satisfactory
Policy	No intervention	Raise	Maintain	Maintain
Access to contraceptive methods	No support	No support	No support	No support
Adolescent fertility				
Level of concern	..	..	..	Major concern
Policies and programmes	..	..	..	Yes
Health and mortality				
View				
Expectation of life	Unacceptable	Unacceptable	Unacceptable	Unacceptable
Under-five mortality	..	..	Unacceptable	Unacceptable
Maternal mortality	..	..	..	Unacceptable
Level of concern about HIV/AIDS	..	..	Major concern	Major concern
Measures implemented to control HIV/AIDS*	..	..	..	..
Grounds on which abortion is permitted**	..	..	1	1,2,3
Spatial distribution and internal migration				
View on spatial distribution	Major change desired	Major change desired	Satisfactory	Minor change desired
Policies on internal migration				
From rural to urban areas	..	..	..	Lower
From rural to rural areas	..	..	..	..
From urban to rural areas	..	..	..	..
From urban to urban areas	..	..	..	..
Into urban agglomerations	Lower	..	No intervention	Lower
International migration				
Immigration				
View	Too low	Too low	Satisfactory	Satisfactory
Policy	Raise	Raise	No intervention	No intervention
Permanent settlement	..	..	No intervention	No intervention
Temporary workers	..	..	..	Maintain
Highly skilled workers	..	..	..	..
Family reunification	..	..	..	..
Integration of non-nationals	..	..	No	..
Emigration				
View	Satisfactory	Satisfactory	Satisfactory	Satisfactory
Policy	Maintain	Maintain	No intervention	Lower
Encouraging the return of nationals	Yes	..	Yes	..

* Measures implemented to control HIV/AIDS: (1) blood screening; (2) information/education campaigns; (3) access to antiretroviral treatment; (4) non-discriminatory policies; (5) promoting condom use.
** Grounds on which abortion is permitted: (1) to save the woman's life; (2) to preserve physical health; (3) to preserve mental health; (4) rape or incest; (5) foetal impairment; (6) economic or social reasons; (7) on request.

Population indicators

Indicator	*1975*	*1985*	*1995*	*2005*
Population size and growth				
Population size (thousands)	228	314	398	504
Annual growth rate (percentage)*	-5.1	7.1	2.4	2.3
Population age structure				
Percentage of population under age 15	40	41	43	44
Percentage of population aged 60 or older	7	7	6	6
Fertility and family planning				
Total fertility (births per woman)*	5.7	5.8	5.9	5.9
Teenage fertility rate (per 1,000 women, aged 15 - 19)*	162	189	192	192
Percentage of births to women under age 20*	19	21	22	23
Percentage of births to women aged 35 or older*	14	13	14	12
Percentage of married women using contraception				
Modern methods	..	..	..	..
All methods	..	..	..	..
Health and mortality				
Life expectancy at birth (years)*				
Males	39	42	44	43
Females	42	45	48	44
Both sexes combined	41	44	46	43
Infant mortality rate (per 1,000 births)*	157	138	118	102
Mortality under age 5 (per 1,000 births)*	262	241	207	181
Maternal mortality ratio (per 100,000 births) (2000)	..	..	..	880
HIV/AIDS (2003)				
Number of infected adults (thousands)	..	..	..	..
Adult prevalence rate (percentage)	..	..	..	..
Spatial distribution				
Population density (per sq. km)	8	11	14	18
Urban population (percentage)	27	29	40	50
Annual urban growth rate (percentage)*	-4.9	8.6	5.4	4.7
Annual rural growth rate (percentage)*	-5.2	6.6	0.8	0.8
International migration				
International migrant stock				
Number of migrants (thousands)	7	4	4	6
Percentage of total population	3.2	1.2	0.9	1.2

* For the periods 1970-1975, 1980-1985, 1990-1995 and 2000-2005.

Government views and policies

Population policy variable	*1976*	*1986*	*1996*	*2005*
Population size and growth				
View on growth	..	..	Too high	Too high
Policy on growth	..	..	Lower	Lower
Population age structure				
Level of concern about				
Size of the working-age population	..	..	..	..
Ageing of the population	..	..	..	Minor concern
Fertility and family planning				
View on fertility level	..	..	Too high	Too high
Policy	..	..	Lower	Lower
Access to contraceptive methods	..	..	..	Direct support
Adolescent fertility				
Level of concern	..	..	..	Minor concern
Policies and programmes	..	..	..	Yes
Health and mortality				
View				
Expectation of life	..	..	Unacceptable	Unacceptable
Under-five mortality	..	..	..	Unacceptable
Maternal mortality	..	..	..	Unacceptable
Level of concern about HIV/AIDS	..	..	..	Major concern
Measures implemented to control HIV/AIDS*	..	..	..	1,2,5
Grounds on which abortion is permitted**	..	..	1,2,3	1,2,3
Spatial distribution and internal migration				
View on spatial distribution	..	..	..	Major change desired
Policies on internal migration				
From rural to urban areas	..	..	..	No intervention
From rural to rural areas	..	..	..	No intervention
From urban to rural areas	..	..	..	No intervention
From urban to urban areas	..	..	..	No intervention
Into urban agglomerations	..	..	..	No intervention
International migration				
Immigration				
View	..	..	Satisfactory	Satisfactory
Policy	..	..	No intervention	No intervention
Permanent settlement	..	..	..	..
Temporary workers	..	..	..	..
Highly skilled workers	..	..	..	..
Family reunification	..	..	..	..
Integration of non-nationals	..	..	..	..
Emigration				
View	..	..	Satisfactory	Satisfactory
Policy	..	..	No intervention	No intervention
Encouraging the return of nationals	..	..	Yes	Yes

* Measures implemented to control HIV/AIDS: (1) blood screening; (2) information/education campaigns; (3) access to antiretroviral treatment; (4) non-discriminatory policies; (5) promoting condom use.
** Grounds on which abortion is permitted: (1) to save the woman's life; (2) to preserve physical health; (3) to preserve mental health; (4) rape or incest; (5) foetal impairment; (6) economic or social reasons; (7) on request.

Population indicators

Indicator	*1975*	*1985*	*1995*	*2005*
Population size and growth				
Population size (thousands)	2 089	2 682	3 097	4 401
Annual growth rate (percentage)*	2.6	2.4	0.4	4.3
Population age structure				
Percentage of population under age 15	45	47	46	45
Percentage of population aged 60 or older	4	5	4	4
Fertility and family planning				
Total fertility (births per woman)*	6.5	6.5	6.2	5.5
Teenage fertility rate (per 1,000 women, aged 15 - 19)*	134	133	116	94
Percentage of births to women under age 20*	15	14	16	13
Percentage of births to women aged 35 or older*	19	21	21	17
Percentage of married women using contraception				
Modern methods	..	..	4	5[a]
All methods	..	..	5	8[a]
Health and mortality				
Life expectancy at birth (years)*				
Males	42	42	47	52
Females	46	46	52	55
Both sexes combined	44	44	49	54
Infant mortality rate (per 1,000 births)*	129	116	90	65
Mortality under age 5 (per 1,000 births)*	202	179	135	94
Maternal mortality ratio (per 100,000 births) (2000)	..	..	..	630
HIV/AIDS (2003)				
Number of infected adults (thousands)	..	..	..	55
Adult prevalence rate (percentage)	..	..	..	2.7
Spatial distribution				
Population density (per sq. km)	18	23	26	37
Urban population (percentage)	13	15	17	21
Annual urban growth rate (percentage)*	4.2	4.0	2.2	5.8
Annual rural growth rate (percentage)*	2.4	2.3	0.3	3.1
International migration				
International migrant stock				
Number of migrants (thousands)	10	11	12	15
Percentage of total population	0.5	0.4	0.4	0.3

* For the periods 1970-1975, 1980-1985, 1990-1995 and 2000-2005.
[a] For 2002.

Government views and policies

Population policy variable	*1976*	*1986*	*1996*	*2005*
Population size and growth				
View on growth	..	..	Satisfactory	Too low
Policy on growth	..	..	No intervention	Raise
Population age structure				
Level of concern about				
Size of the working-age population	..	..	..	Minor concern
Ageing of the population	..	..	..	Major concern
Fertility and family planning				
View on fertility level	..	..	Too low	Too low
Policy	..	..	Raise	Raise
Access to contraceptive methods	..	..	No support	Indirect support
Adolescent fertility				
Level of concern	..	..	Not a concern	Minor concern
Policies and programmes	..	..	No	Yes
Health and mortality				
View				
Expectation of life	..	..	Acceptable	Unacceptable
Under-five mortality	..	..	..	Acceptable
Maternal mortality	..	..	..	Acceptable
Level of concern about HIV/AIDS	..	..	Minor concern	Major concern
Measures implemented to control HIV/AIDS*	..	..	..	1,2,3
Grounds on which abortion is permitted**	..	..	1,2,3,4,5,6,7	1,2,3,4,5,6,7
Spatial distribution and internal migration				
View on spatial distribution	..	..	Satisfactory	Minor change desired
Policies on internal migration				
From rural to urban areas	..	..	..	Lower
From rural to rural areas	..	..	..	..
From urban to rural areas	..	..	..	..
From urban to urban areas	..	..	..	..
Into urban agglomerations	..	..	No intervention	Lower
International migration				
Immigration				
View	..	..	Too high	Satisfactory
Policy	..	..	Lower	Lower
Permanent settlement	..	..	Lower	Lower
Temporary workers	..	..	No intervention	Lower
Highly skilled workers	..	..	..	Maintain
Family reunification	..	..	Lower	Maintain
Integration of non-nationals	..	..	Yes	Yes
Emigration				
View	..	..	Satisfactory	Satisfactory
Policy	..	..	Maintain	Maintain
Encouraging the return of nationals	..	..	No	Yes

* Measures implemented to control HIV/AIDS: (1) blood screening; (2) information/education campaigns; (3) access to antiretroviral treatment; (4) non-discriminatory policies; (5) promoting condom use.
** Grounds on which abortion is permitted: (1) to save the woman's life; (2) to preserve physical health; (3) to preserve mental health; (4) rape or incest; (5) foetal impairment; (6) economic or social reasons; (7) on request.

Population indicators

Indicator	*1975*	*1985*	*1995*	*2005*
Population size and growth				
Population size (thousands)	1 432	1 525	1 447	1 330
Annual growth rate (percentage)*	1.0	0.7	-1.8	-0.6
Population age structure				
Percentage of population under age 15	22	22	21	15
Percentage of population aged 60 or older	17	17	19	22
Fertility and family planning				
Total fertility (births per woman)*	2.2	2.1	1.6	1.4
Teenage fertility rate (per 1,000 women, aged 15 - 19)*	59	58	45	24
Percentage of births to women under age 20*	14	13	14	9
Percentage of births to women aged 35 or older*	7	6	7	10
Percentage of married women using contraception				
Modern methods	..	..	56[a]	..
All methods	..	..	70[a]	..
Health and mortality				
Life expectancy at birth (years)*				
Males	66	65	63	65
Females	75	75	74	77
Both sexes combined	71	70	69	71
Infant mortality rate (per 1,000 births)*	21	20	15	10
Mortality under age 5 (per 1,000 births)*	26	24	20	12
Maternal mortality ratio (per 100,000 births) (2000)	..	..	..	63
HIV/AIDS (2003)				
Number of infected adults (thousands)	..	..	..	8
Adult prevalence rate (percentage)	..	..	..	1.1
Spatial distribution				
Population density (per sq. km)	32	34	32	29
Urban population (percentage)	68	71	70	70
Annual urban growth rate (percentage)*	1.8	1.0	-2.2	-1.0
Annual rural growth rate (percentage)*	-0.6	0.0	-1.0	-1.2
International migration				
International migrant stock				
Number of migrants (thousands)	..	..	309	202
Percentage of total population	..	..	21.3	15.2

* For the periods 1970-1975, 1980-1985, 1990-1995 and 2000-2005.
[a] For 1994.

Government views and policies

Population policy variable	*1976*	*1986*	*1996*	*2005*
Population size and growth				
View on growth	Satisfactory	Too high	Too high	Too high
Policy on growth	No intervention	No intervention	No intervention	Lower
Population age structure				
Level of concern about				
Size of the working-age population	..	..	..	Major concern
Ageing of the population	..	..	..	Minor concern
Fertility and family planning				
View on fertility level	Satisfactory	Too high	Too high	Too high
Policy	No intervention	No intervention	Lower	Lower
Access to contraceptive methods	Indirect support	Direct support	Direct support	Direct support
Adolescent fertility				
Level of concern	..	..	Major concern	Major concern
Policies and programmes	..	..	Yes	No
Health and mortality				
View				
Expectation of life	Unacceptable	Unacceptable	Unacceptable	Unacceptable
Under-five mortality	..	..	Unacceptable	Unacceptable
Maternal mortality	..	..	..	Unacceptable
Level of concern about HIV/AIDS	..	..	Major concern	Major concern
Measures implemented to control HIV/AIDS*	..	..	..	1,2,3,4,5
Grounds on which abortion is permitted**	..	..	1,2	1,2,3,4,5
Spatial distribution and internal migration				
View on spatial distribution	Major change desired	Minor change desired	Major change desired	Major change desired
Policies on internal migration				
From rural to urban areas	..	..	..	Lower
From rural to rural areas	..	..	..	No intervention
From urban to rural areas	..	..	..	Raise
From urban to urban areas	..	..	..	No intervention
Into urban agglomerations	No intervention	No intervention	No intervention	Lower
International migration				
Immigration				
View	Satisfactory	Satisfactory	Satisfactory	Satisfactory
Policy	Maintain	Maintain	No intervention	No intervention
Permanent settlement	..	..	..	No intervention
Temporary workers	..	..	..	No intervention
Highly skilled workers	..	..	..	No intervention
Family reunification	..	..	..	No intervention
Integration of non-nationals	..	..	..	No
Emigration				
View	Satisfactory	Satisfactory	Satisfactory	Satisfactory
Policy	Maintain	Maintain	No intervention	No intervention
Encouraging the return of nationals	..	..	..	Yes

* Measures implemented to control HIV/AIDS: (1) blood screening; (2) information/education campaigns; (3) access to antiretroviral treatment; (4) non-discriminatory policies; (5) promoting condom use.

** Grounds on which abortion is permitted: (1) to save the woman's life; (2) to preserve physical health; (3) to preserve mental health; (4) rape or incest; (5) foetal impairment; (6) economic or social reasons; (7) on request.

Population indicators

Indicator	*1975*	*1985*	*1995*	*2005*
Population size and growth				
Population size (thousands)	34 114	43 361	60 007	77 431
Annual growth rate (percentage)*	2.7	3.1	3.2	2.4
Population age structure				
Percentage of population under age 15	45	46	46	45
Percentage of population aged 60 or older	4	4	4	5
Fertility and family planning				
Total fertility (births per woman)*	6.8	6.8	6.8	5.9
Teenage fertility rate (per 1,000 women, aged 15 - 19)*	159	145	127	96
Percentage of births to women under age 20*	17	16	14	13
Percentage of births to women aged 35 or older*	16	17	18	16
Percentage of married women using contraception				
Modern methods	..	..	3[a]	6[b]
All methods	..	..	4[a]	8[b]
Health and mortality				
Life expectancy at birth (years)*				
Males	42	43	46	47
Females	45	46	49	49
Both sexes combined	44	45	47	48
Infant mortality rate (per 1,000 births)*	140	131	114	100
Mortality under age 5 (per 1,000 births)*	234	229	198	172
Maternal mortality ratio (per 100,000 births) (2000)	..	..	..	850
HIV/AIDS (2003)				
Number of infected adults (thousands)	..	..	..	1 400
Adult prevalence rate (percentage)	..	..	..	4.4
Spatial distribution				
Population density (per sq. km)	31	39	54	70
Urban population (percentage)	10	12	14	16
Annual urban growth rate (percentage)*	4.6	5.0	5.0	4.1
Annual rural growth rate (percentage)*	2.4	2.8	2.9	2.2
International migration				
International migrant stock				
Number of migrants (thousands)	392	584	795	555
Percentage of total population	1.1	1.3	1.3	0.7

* For the periods 1970-1975, 1980-1985, 1990-1995 and 2000-2005.
[a] For 1990.
[b] For 2000.

Government views and policies

Population policy variable	*1976*	*1986*	*1996*	*2005*
Population size and growth				
View on growth	Too high	Too high	Satisfactory	Satisfactory
Policy on growth	Lower	Lower	Maintain	Maintain
Population age structure				
Level of concern about				
Size of the working-age population	..	..	..	Major concern
Ageing of the population	..	..	..	Minor concern
Fertility and family planning				
View on fertility level	Too high	Too high	Too high	Satisfactory
Policy	Lower	Lower	Lower	Lower
Access to contraceptive methods	Direct support	Direct support	Direct support	Direct support
Adolescent fertility				
Level of concern	..	..	..	Minor concern
Policies and programmes	..	..	..	Yes
Health and mortality				
View				
Expectation of life	Acceptable	Acceptable	Acceptable	Acceptable
Under-five mortality	..	..	..	Unacceptable
Maternal mortality	..	..	..	Unacceptable
Level of concern about HIV/AIDS	..	..	..	Major concern
Measures implemented to control HIV/AIDS*	..	..	..	2,3,4,5
Grounds on which abortion is permitted**	..	..	1,2,3	1,2,3,6
Spatial distribution and internal migration				
View on spatial distribution	Major change desired	Major change desired	Minor change desired	Major change desired
Policies on internal migration				
From rural to urban areas	..	..	..	Lower
From rural to rural areas	..	..	..	..
From urban to rural areas	..	..	..	..
From urban to urban areas	..	..	..	..
Into urban agglomerations	No intervention	Lower	..	Lower
International migration				
Immigration				
View	Satisfactory	Satisfactory	Satisfactory	Satisfactory
Policy	Maintain	Maintain	Maintain	Lower
Permanent settlement	..	..	Maintain	Lower
Temporary workers	..	..	..	Lower
Highly skilled workers	..	..	..	..
Family reunification	..	..	..	Lower
Integration of non-nationals	..	..	..	Yes
Emigration				
View	Satisfactory	Satisfactory	Satisfactory	Too high
Policy	Maintain	Lower	No intervention	Lower
Encouraging the return of nationals	No	..	..	No

* Measures implemented to control HIV/AIDS: (1) blood screening; (2) information/education campaigns; (3) access to antiretroviral treatment; (4) non-discriminatory policies; (5) promoting condom use.
** Grounds on which abortion is permitted: (1) to save the woman's life; (2) to preserve physical health; (3) to preserve mental health; (4) rape or incest; (5) foetal impairment; (6) economic or social reasons; (7) on request.

Population indicators

Indicator	*1975*	*1985*	*1995*	*2005*
Population size and growth				
Population size (thousands)	576	709	768	848
Annual growth rate (percentage)*	2.0	2.2	1.2	0.9
Population age structure				
Percentage of population under age 15	40	39	36	32
Percentage of population aged 60 or older	4	5	5	6
Fertility and family planning				
Total fertility (births per woman)*	4.2	3.8	3.4	2.9
Teenage fertility rate (per 1,000 women, aged 15 - 19)*	70	63	55	41
Percentage of births to women under age 20*	12	10	10	9
Percentage of births to women aged 35 or older*	9	9	11	12
Percentage of married women using contraception				
Modern methods	35[a]	..	..	..
All methods	41[a]	..	..	..
Health and mortality				
Life expectancy at birth (years)*				
Males	59	63	65	66
Females	63	67	69	70
Both sexes combined	61	65	67	68
Infant mortality rate (per 1,000 births)*	52	40	35	22
Mortality under age 5 (per 1,000 births)*	68	51	44	27
Maternal mortality ratio (per 100,000 births) (2000)	..	..	..	75
HIV/AIDS (2003)				
Number of infected adults (thousands)	..	..	..	<1
Adult prevalence rate (percentage)	..	..	..	0.1
Spatial distribution				
Population density (per sq. km)	32	39	42	46
Urban population (percentage)	37	39	45	53
Annual urban growth rate (percentage)*	3.1	2.6	3.0	2.5
Annual rural growth rate (percentage)*	1.4	2.0	-0.2	-0.6
International migration				
International migrant stock				
Number of migrants (thousands)	15	13	15	17
Percentage of total population	2.6	1.8	1.9	2

* For the periods 1970-1975, 1980-1985, 1990-1995 and 2000-2005.
[a] For 1974.

Government views and policies

Population policy variable	*1976*	*1986*	*1996*	*2005*
Population size and growth				
View on growth	Too low	Satisfactory	Satisfactory	Satisfactory
Policy on growth	No intervention	No intervention	No intervention	No intervention
Population age structure				
Level of concern about				
Size of the working-age population	..	..	..	Major concern
Ageing of the population	..	..	..	Major concern
Fertility and family planning				
View on fertility level	Too low	Satisfactory	Satisfactory	Too low
Policy	Raise	No intervention	Raise	Raise
Access to contraceptive methods	Direct support	Direct support	Direct support	Direct support
Adolescent fertility				
Level of concern	..	..	Minor concern	Minor concern
Policies and programmes	..	..	No	Yes
Health and mortality				
View				
Expectation of life	Unacceptable	Acceptable	Acceptable	Unacceptable
Under-five mortality	..	..	Acceptable	Acceptable
Maternal mortality	..	..	..	Acceptable
Level of concern about HIV/AIDS	..	..	Major concern	Major concern
Measures implemented to control HIV/AIDS*	..	..	..	1,2,3,4,5
Grounds on which abortion is permitted**	..	..	1,2,3,4,5,6	1,2,3,4,5,6
Spatial distribution and internal migration				
View on spatial distribution	Minor change desired	Satisfactory	Minor change desired	Major change desired
Policies on internal migration				
From rural to urban areas	..	..	..	Lower
From rural to rural areas	..	..	..	Maintain
From urban to rural areas	..	..	..	Raise
From urban to urban areas	..	..	..	Maintain
Into urban agglomerations	Lower	Lower	Maintain	Lower
International migration				
Immigration				
View	Satisfactory	Satisfactory	Satisfactory	Satisfactory
Policy	Maintain	Maintain	Lower	Maintain
Permanent settlement	..	..	Lower	Maintain
Temporary workers	..	..	Lower	Maintain
Highly skilled workers	..	..	..	Maintain
Family reunification	..	..	No intervention	Maintain
Integration of non-nationals	..	..	Yes	Yes
Emigration				
View	Too high	Satisfactory	Satisfactory	Satisfactory
Policy	Lower	Maintain	Maintain	No intervention
Encouraging the return of nationals	Yes	..	Yes	No

* Measures implemented to control HIV/AIDS: (1) blood screening; (2) information/education campaigns; (3) access to antiretroviral treatment; (4) non-discriminatory policies; (5) promoting condom use.

** Grounds on which abortion is permitted: (1) to save the woman's life; (2) to preserve physical health; (3) to preserve mental health; (4) rape or incest; (5) foetal impairment; (6) economic or social reasons; (7) on request.

Population indicators

Indicator	*1975*	*1985*	*1995*	*2005*
Population size and growth				
Population size (thousands)	4 711	4 902	5 108	5 249
Annual growth rate (percentage)*	0.5	0.5	0.5	0.3
Population age structure				
Percentage of population under age 15	22	19	19	17
Percentage of population aged 60 or older	16	17	19	21
Fertility and family planning				
Total fertility (births per woman)*	1.6	1.7	1.8	1.7
Teenage fertility rate (per 1,000 women, aged 15 - 19)*	9	9	10	11
Percentage of births to women under age 20*	3	3	2	3
Percentage of births to women aged 35 or older*	12	14	17	19
Percentage of married women using contraception				
Modern methods	78[a]	75[b]	..	..
All methods	80[a]	77[b]	..	..
Health and mortality				
Life expectancy at birth (years)*				
Males	67	70	72	75
Females	75	78	80	82
Both sexes combined	71	74	76	78
Infant mortality rate (per 1,000 births)*	12	6	5	4
Mortality under age 5 (per 1,000 births)*	13	8	6	5
Maternal mortality ratio (per 100,000 births) (2000)	..	..	..	6
HIV/AIDS (2003)				
Number of infected adults (thousands)	..	..	..	2
Adult prevalence rate (percentage)	..	..	..	0.1
Spatial distribution				
Population density (per sq. km)	14	14	15	16
Urban population (percentage)	58	60	61	61
Annual urban growth rate (percentage)*	3.4	0.5	0.5	0.1
Annual rural growth rate (percentage)*	-3.1	0.5	0.5	0.3
International migration				
International migrant stock				
Number of migrants (thousands)	35	48	103	156
Percentage of total population	0.8	1	2	3

* For the periods 1970-1975, 1980-1985, 1990-1995 and 2000-2005.
[a] For 1977.
[b] For 1989.

Government views and policies

Population policy variable	*1976*	*1986*	*1996*	*2005*
Population size and growth				
View on growth	Too low	Too low	Satisfactory	Satisfactory
Policy on growth	Raise	Raise	Raise	Maintain
Population age structure				
Level of concern about				
Size of the working-age population	..	..	..	Major concern
Ageing of the population	..	..	..	Major concern
Fertility and family planning				
View on fertility level	Too low	Too low	Too low	Too low
Policy	Raise	Raise	Raise	Raise
Access to contraceptive methods	Direct support	Indirect support	No support	Indirect support
Adolescent fertility				
Level of concern	..	..	Major concern	Minor concern
Policies and programmes	..	..	Yes	Yes
Health and mortality				
View				
Expectation of life	Unacceptable	Acceptable	Acceptable	Acceptable
Under-five mortality	..	..	Acceptable	Acceptable
Maternal mortality	..	..	..	Unacceptable
Level of concern about HIV/AIDS	..	..	Major concern	Major concern
Measures implemented to control HIV/AIDS*	..	..	..	1,2,3,4,5
Grounds on which abortion is permitted**	..	..	1,2,3,4,5,6,7	1,2,3,4,5,6,7
Spatial distribution and internal migration				
View on spatial distribution	Major change desired	Minor change desired	Minor change desired	Minor change desired
Policies on internal migration				
From rural to urban areas	..	..	..	Lower
From rural to rural areas	..	..	..	No intervention
From urban to rural areas	..	..	..	No intervention
From urban to urban areas	..	..	..	No intervention
Into urban agglomerations	Lower	Lower	Lower	Lower
International migration				
Immigration				
View	Satisfactory	Too high	Too high	Too high
Policy	Maintain	Lower	Lower	Lower
Permanent settlement	..	..	Lower	Lower
Temporary workers	..	..	Lower	Lower
Highly skilled workers	..	..	..	Raise
Family reunification	..	..	Maintain	Maintain
Integration of non-nationals	..	..	Yes	Yes
Emigration				
View	Satisfactory	Satisfactory	Satisfactory	Satisfactory
Policy	Maintain	Maintain	Maintain	No intervention
Encouraging the return of nationals	No	..	No	No

* Measures implemented to control HIV/AIDS: (1) blood screening; (2) information/education campaigns; (3) access to antiretroviral treatment; (4) non-discriminatory policies; (5) promoting condom use.
** Grounds on which abortion is permitted: (1) to save the woman's life; (2) to preserve physical health; (3) to preserve mental health; (4) rape or incest; (5) foetal impairment; (6) economic or social reasons; (7) on request.

Population indicators

Indicator	*1975*	*1985*	*1995*	*2005*
Population size and growth				
Population size (thousands)	52 699	55 284	58 203	60 496
Annual growth rate (percentage)*	0.7	0.5	0.5	0.4
Population age structure				
Percentage of population under age 15	24	21	19	18
Percentage of population aged 60 or older	18	18	21	21
Fertility and family planning				
Total fertility (births per woman)*	2.3	1.9	1.7	1.9
Teenage fertility rate (per 1,000 women, aged 15 - 19)*	17	14	13	14
Percentage of births to women under age 20*	4	4	3	4
Percentage of births to women aged 35 or older*	10	9	11	14
Percentage of married women using contraception				
Modern methods	21[a]	67[b]	69[c]	..
All methods	64[a]	81[b]	75[c]	..
Health and mortality				
Life expectancy at birth (years)*				
Males	69	71	73	76
Females	76	79	81	83
Both sexes combined	72	75	77	79
Infant mortality rate (per 1,000 births)*	16	9	7	4
Mortality under age 5 (per 1,000 births)*	17	10	8	5
Maternal mortality ratio (per 100,000 births) (2000)	..	..	..	17
HIV/AIDS (2003)				
Number of infected adults (thousands)	..	..	..	120
Adult prevalence rate (percentage)	..	..	..	0.4
Spatial distribution				
Population density (per sq. km)	96	100	106	110
Urban population (percentage)	73	74	75	77
Annual urban growth rate (percentage)*	1.3	0.6	0.7	0.7
Annual rural growth rate (percentage)*	-0.6	0.2	-0.2	-0.3
International migration				
International migrant stock				
Number of migrants (thousands)	5 572	5 957	6 089	6 471
Percentage of total population	10.6	10.8	10.5	10.7

* For the periods 1970-1975, 1980-1985, 1990-1995 and 2000-2005.
[a] For 1972.
[b] For 1988.
[c] For 1994.

Government views and policies

Population policy variable	*1976*	*1986*	*1996*	*2005*
Population size and growth				
View on growth	Too low	Too low	Too low	Too low
Policy on growth	Raise	Raise	Raise	Raise
Population age structure				
Level of concern about				
Size of the working-age population	..	..	..	..
Ageing of the population	..	..	..	Major concern
Fertility and family planning				
View on fertility level	Too low	Too low	Too low	Too low
Policy	Raise	Raise	Raise	Raise
Access to contraceptive methods	Limits	No support	No support	No support
Adolescent fertility				
Level of concern	..	..	..	Minor concern
Policies and programmes	..	..	..	Yes
Health and mortality				
View				
Expectation of life	Unacceptable	Unacceptable	Unacceptable	Unacceptable
Under-five mortality	..	..	..	Unacceptable
Maternal mortality	..	..	..	Unacceptable
Level of concern about HIV/AIDS	..	..	..	Major concern
Measures implemented to control HIV/AIDS*	..	..	..	1,2,3,5
Grounds on which abortion is permitted**	..	..	1	1
Spatial distribution and internal migration				
View on spatial distribution	Major change desired	Major change desired	Major change desired	Major change desired
Policies on internal migration				
From rural to urban areas	..	..	..	Lower
From rural to rural areas	..	..	..	..
From urban to rural areas	..	..	..	..
From urban to urban areas	..	..	..	..
Into urban agglomerations	Lower	Lower	..	Lower
International migration				
Immigration				
View	Too low	Too high	Too high	Too high
Policy	Raise	Lower	Lower	Lower
Permanent settlement	..	..	Lower	..
Temporary workers	..	..	Lower	..
Highly skilled workers	..	..	..	..
Family reunification	..	..	..	..
Integration of non-nationals	..	..	..	..
Emigration				
View	Satisfactory	Too high	Too high	Too high
Policy	Maintain	Lower	Lower	Lower
Encouraging the return of nationals	No	..	..	No

* Measures implemented to control HIV/AIDS: (1) blood screening; (2) information/education campaigns; (3) access to antiretroviral treatment; (4) non-discriminatory policies; (5) promoting condom use.

** Grounds on which abortion is permitted: (1) to save the woman's life; (2) to preserve physical health; (3) to preserve mental health; (4) rape or incest; (5) foetal impairment; (6) economic or social reasons; (7) on request.

Population indicators

Indicator	*1975*	*1985*	*1995*	*2005*
Population size and growth				
Population size (thousands)	601	813	1 119	1 384
Annual growth rate (percentage)*	2.5	3.1	3.1	1.7
Population age structure				
Percentage of population under age 15	36	42	43	40
Percentage of population aged 60 or older	10	9	7	6
Fertility and family planning				
Total fertility (births per woman)*	5.3	5.5	5.2	4.0
Teenage fertility rate (per 1,000 women, aged 15 - 19)*	156	164	155	114
Percentage of births to women under age 20*	18	18	21	20
Percentage of births to women aged 35 or older*	16	12	13	12
Percentage of married women using contraception				
Modern methods	..	..	..	12[a]
All methods	..	..	..	33[a]
Health and mortality				
Life expectancy at birth (years)*				
Males	47	55	58	54
Females	50	58	62	55
Both sexes combined	49	56	60	55
Infant mortality rate (per 1,000 births)*	114	78	59	58
Mortality under age 5 (per 1,000 births)*	188	130	95	95
Maternal mortality ratio (per 100,000 births) (2000)	..	..	..	420
HIV/AIDS (2003)				
Number of infected adults (thousands)	..	..	..	45
Adult prevalence rate (percentage)	..	..	..	8.1
Spatial distribution				
Population density (per sq. km)	2	3	4	5
Urban population (percentage)	40	59	76	85
Annual urban growth rate (percentage)*	7.6	6.7	5.2	2.7
Annual rural growth rate (percentage)*	-0.2	-1.1	-2.6	-2.7
International migration				
International migrant stock				
Number of migrants (thousands)	62	110	164	245
Percentage of total population	10.3	13.5	14.7	17.7

* For the periods 1970-1975, 1980-1985, 1990-1995 and 2000-2005.
[a] For 2000.

Government views and policies

Population policy variable	*1976*	*1986*	*1996*	*2005*
Population size and growth				
View on growth	Satisfactory	Too high	Too high	Too high
Policy on growth	No intervention	Lower	Lower	Lower
Population age structure				
Level of concern about				
Size of the working-age population	..	..	..	Major concern
Ageing of the population	..	..	..	Minor concern
Fertility and family planning				
View on fertility level	Satisfactory	Too high	Too high	Too high
Policy	No intervention	Lower	Lower	Lower
Access to contraceptive methods	Indirect support	Direct support	Direct support	Direct support
Adolescent fertility				
Level of concern	..	..	Minor concern	Major concern
Policies and programmes	..	..	Yes	Yes
Health and mortality				
View				
Expectation of life	Unacceptable	Unacceptable	Unacceptable	Unacceptable
Under-five mortality	..	..	Unacceptable	Unacceptable
Maternal mortality	..	..	..	Unacceptable
Level of concern about HIV/AIDS	..	..	Major concern	Major concern
Measures implemented to control HIV/AIDS*	..	..	..	1,2,5
Grounds on which abortion is permitted**	..	..	1,2,3	1,2,3
Spatial distribution and internal migration				
View on spatial distribution	Minor change desired	Major change desired	Major change desired	Major change desired
Policies on internal migration				
From rural to urban areas	..	..	..	Lower
From rural to rural areas	..	..	..	No intervention
From urban to rural areas	..	..	..	Raise
From urban to urban areas	..	..	..	Lower
Into urban agglomerations	Lower	No intervention	Lower	Lower
International migration				
Immigration				
View	Satisfactory	Too high	Too high	Too high
Policy	Maintain	Lower	Lower	Lower
Permanent settlement	..	..	Lower	Lower
Temporary workers	..	..	Lower	Lower
Highly skilled workers	..	..	..	No intervention
Family reunification	..	..	Lower	No intervention
Integration of non-nationals	..	..	No	..
Emigration				
View	Satisfactory	Satisfactory	Satisfactory	Satisfactory
Policy	Maintain	Maintain	No intervention	No intervention
Encouraging the return of nationals	No	..	Yes	No

* Measures implemented to control HIV/AIDS: (1) blood screening; (2) information/education campaigns; (3) access to antiretroviral treatment; (4) non-discriminatory policies; (5) promoting condom use.

** Grounds on which abortion is permitted: (1) to save the woman's life; (2) to preserve physical health; (3) to preserve mental health; (4) rape or incest; (5) foetal impairment; (6) economic or social reasons; (7) on request.

Population indicators

Indicator	*1975*	*1985*	*1995*	*2005*
Population size and growth				
Population size (thousands)	555	773	1 115	1 517
Annual growth rate (percentage)*	3.4	3.4	3.5	2.8
Population age structure				
Percentage of population under age 15	42	43	42	40
Percentage of population aged 60 or older	5	5	5	6
Fertility and family planning				
Total fertility (births per woman)*	6.5	6.5	5.6	4.7
Teenage fertility rate (per 1,000 women, aged 15 - 19)*	205	205	155	127
Percentage of births to women under age 20*	19	20	18	18
Percentage of births to women aged 35 or older*	17	17	16	14
Percentage of married women using contraception				
Modern methods	..	..	7[a]	9[b]
All methods	..	..	12[a]	10[b]
Health and mortality				
Life expectancy at birth (years)*				
Males	36	43	50	54
Females	39	46	53	57
Both sexes combined	38	44	51	55
Infant mortality rate (per 1,000 births)*	173	135	99	77
Mortality under age 5 (per 1,000 births)*	287	238	170	129
Maternal mortality ratio (per 100,000 births) (2000)	..	..	..	540
HIV/AIDS (2003)				
Number of infected adults (thousands)	..	..	..	6
Adult prevalence rate (percentage)	..	..	..	1.2
Spatial distribution				
Population density (per sq. km)	49	68	99	134
Urban population (percentage)	17	22	26	26
Annual urban growth rate (percentage)*	5.8	6.0	4.6	2.6
Annual rural growth rate (percentage)*	2.9	2.7	3.1	2.7
International migration				
International migrant stock				
Number of migrants (thousands)	60	94	148	232
Percentage of total population	10.8	12.2	13.3	15.3

* For the periods 1970-1975, 1980-1985, 1990-1995 and 2000-2005.
[a] For 1990.
[b] For 2000.

Government views and policies

Population policy variable	*1976*	*1986*	*1996*	*2005*
Population size and growth				
View on growth	..	..	Too low	Too low
Policy on growth	..	..	No intervention	Raise
Population age structure				
Level of concern about				
Size of the working-age population	..	..	..	..
Ageing of the population	..	..	..	Minor concern
Fertility and family planning				
View on fertility level	..	..	Too low	Too low
Policy	..	..	Raise	Raise
Access to contraceptive methods	..	..	No support	Direct support
Adolescent fertility				
Level of concern	..	..	Minor concern	Minor concern
Policies and programmes	..	..	No	Yes
Health and mortality				
View				
Expectation of life	..	..	Acceptable	Unacceptable
Under-five mortality	..	..	Unacceptable	Unacceptable
Maternal mortality	..	..	..	Unacceptable
Level of concern about HIV/AIDS	..	..	Not a concern	Major concern
Measures implemented to control HIV/AIDS*	..	..	..	1,2,3,4,5
Grounds on which abortion is permitted**	..	..	1,2,3,4,5,6,7	1,2,3,4,5,6,7
Spatial distribution and internal migration				
View on spatial distribution	..	..	Minor change desired	Major change desired
Policies on internal migration				
From rural to urban areas	..	..	..	Lower
From rural to rural areas	..	..	..	..
From urban to rural areas	..	..	..	..
From urban to urban areas	..	..	..	..
Into urban agglomerations	..	..	Lower	Lower
International migration				
Immigration				
View	..	..	Satisfactory	Satisfactory
Policy	..	..	No intervention	Maintain
Permanent settlement	..	..	No intervention	Maintain
Temporary workers	..	..	No intervention	Maintain
Highly skilled workers	..	..	..	Maintain
Family reunification	..	..	No intervention	Maintain
Integration of non-nationals	..	..	No	..
Emigration				
View	..	..	Too high	Too high
Policy	..	..	No intervention	Lower
Encouraging the return of nationals	..	..	No	..

* Measures implemented to control HIV/AIDS: (1) blood screening; (2) information/education campaigns; (3) access to antiretroviral treatment; (4) non-discriminatory policies; (5) promoting condom use.
** Grounds on which abortion is permitted: (1) to save the woman's life; (2) to preserve physical health; (3) to preserve mental health; (4) rape or incest; (5) foetal impairment; (6) economic or social reasons; (7) on request.

Population indicators

Indicator	*1975*	*1985*	*1995*	*2005*
Population size and growth				
Population size (thousands)	4 908	5 287	5 033	4 474
Annual growth rate (percentage)*	0.8	0.8	-1.6	-1.1
Population age structure				
Percentage of population under age 15	28	25	24	19
Percentage of population aged 60 or older	12	13	16	18
Fertility and family planning				
Total fertility (births per woman)*	2.6	2.3	2.0	1.5
Teenage fertility rate (per 1,000 women, aged 15 - 19)*	87	76	66	35
Percentage of births to women under age 20*	20	18	16	13
Percentage of births to women aged 35 or older*	7	5	7	10
Percentage of married women using contraception				
Modern methods	..	..	..	20[a]
All methods	..	..	..	41[a]
Health and mortality				
Life expectancy at birth (years)*				
Males	64	66	67	67
Females	72	73	74	74
Both sexes combined	68	70	70	70
Infant mortality rate (per 1,000 births)*	52	47	40	40
Mortality under age 5 (per 1,000 births)*	55	49	43	43
Maternal mortality ratio (per 100,000 births) (2000)	..	..	..	32
HIV/AIDS (2003)				
Number of infected adults (thousands)	..	..	..	3
Adult prevalence rate (percentage)	..	..	..	0.1
Spatial distribution				
Population density (per sq. km)	70	76	72	64
Urban population (percentage)	50	54	54	51
Annual urban growth rate (percentage)*	1.7	1.7	-0.8	-1.4
Annual rural growth rate (percentage)*	0.0	-0.1	0.1	-0.4
International migration				
International migrant stock				
Number of migrants (thousands)	..	..	250	191
Percentage of total population	..	..	5	4.3

* For the periods 1970-1975, 1980-1985, 1990-1995 and 2000-2005.
[a] For 1999/2000.

Government views and policies

Population policy variable	*1976*	*1986*	*1996*	*2005*
Population size and growth				
View on growth	..	..	Satisfactory	Satisfactory
Policy on growth	..	..	No intervention	No intervention
Population age structure				
Level of concern about				
Size of the working-age population	..	..	..	Major concern
Ageing of the population	..	..	..	Major concern
Fertility and family planning				
View on fertility level	..	..	Too low	Too low
Policy	..	..	No intervention	No intervention
Access to contraceptive methods	..	..	No support	No support
Adolescent fertility				
Level of concern	..	..	Not a concern	Major concern
Policies and programmes	..	..	No	Yes
Health and mortality				
View				
Expectation of life	..	..	Acceptable	Acceptable
Under-five mortality	..	..	Acceptable	Acceptable
Maternal mortality	..	..	..	Acceptable
Level of concern about HIV/AIDS	..	..	Major concern	Major concern
Measures implemented to control HIV/AIDS*	..	..	..	1,2,3,4,5
Grounds on which abortion is permitted**	..	..	1,2,3,4,5,6,7	1,2,3,4,5,6,7
Spatial distribution and internal migration				
View on spatial distribution	..	..	Satisfactory	Major change desired
Policies on internal migration				
From rural to urban areas	..	..	..	Lower
From rural to rural areas	..	..	..	No intervention
From urban to rural areas	..	..	..	Lower
From urban to urban areas	..	..	..	No intervention
Into urban agglomerations	..	..	No intervention	No intervention
International migration				
Immigration				
View	..	..	Too high	Satisfactory
Policy	..	..	Lower	Maintain
Permanent settlement	..	..	Lower	Lower
Temporary workers	..	..	Lower	Maintain
Highly skilled workers	..	..	..	Raise
Family reunification	..	..	Lower	Maintain
Integration of non-nationals	..	..	Yes	Yes
Emigration				
View	..	..	Satisfactory	Satisfactory
Policy	..	..	No intervention	No intervention
Encouraging the return of nationals	..	..	No	No

* Measures implemented to control HIV/AIDS: (1) blood screening; (2) information/education campaigns; (3) access to antiretroviral treatment; (4) non-discriminatory policies; (5) promoting condom use.

** Grounds on which abortion is permitted: (1) to save the woman's life; (2) to preserve physical health; (3) to preserve mental health; (4) rape or incest; (5) foetal impairment; (6) economic or social reasons; (7) on request.

Population indicators

Indicator	*1975*	*1985*	*1995*	*2005*
Population size and growth				
Population size (thousands)	78 674	77 685	81 661	82 689
Annual growth rate (percentage)*	0.1	-0.2	0.6	0.1
Population age structure				
Percentage of population under age 15	22	16	16	14
Percentage of population aged 60 or older	20	20	21	25
Fertility and family planning				
Total fertility (births per woman)*	1.6	1.5	1.3	1.3
Teenage fertility rate (per 1,000 women, aged 15 - 19)*	16	14	12	11
Percentage of births to women under age 20*	5	5	3	4
Percentage of births to women aged 35 or older*	12	10	11	17
Percentage of married women using contraception				
Modern methods	..	68	72[a]	..
All methods	..	78	75[a]	..
Health and mortality				
Life expectancy at birth (years)*				
Males	68	70	73	76
Females	74	77	79	81
Both sexes combined	71	74	76	79
Infant mortality rate (per 1,000 births)*	21	11	6	4
Mortality under age 5 (per 1,000 births)*	22	12	7	6
Maternal mortality ratio (per 100,000 births) (2000)	..	..	..	8
HIV/AIDS (2003)				
Number of infected adults (thousands)	..	..	..	43
Adult prevalence rate (percentage)	..	..	..	0.1
Spatial distribution				
Population density (per sq. km)	220	218	229	232
Urban population (percentage)	81	84	86	88
Annual urban growth rate (percentage)*	0.5	0.2	0.8	0.3
Annual rural growth rate (percentage)*	-1.4	-1.8	-1.1	-1.5
International migration				
International migrant stock				
Number of migrants (thousands)	..	..	9 092	10 144
Percentage of total population	..	..	11.1	12.3

* For the periods 1970-1975, 1980-1985, 1990-1995 and 2000-2005.
[a] For 1992.

Government views and policies

Population policy variable	*1976*	*1986*	*1996*	*2005*
Population size and growth				
View on growth	Too high	Too high	Too high	Too high
Policy on growth	Lower	Lower	Lower	Lower
Population age structure				
Level of concern about				
Size of the working-age population	..	..	..	Major concern
Ageing of the population	..	..	..	Major concern
Fertility and family planning				
View on fertility level	Too high	Too high	Too high	Too high
Policy	Lower	Lower	Lower	Lower
Access to contraceptive methods	Direct support	Direct support	Direct support	Direct support
Adolescent fertility				
Level of concern	..	..	Major concern	Major concern
Policies and programmes	..	..	Yes	Yes
Health and mortality				
View				
Expectation of life	Unacceptable	Unacceptable	Unacceptable	Unacceptable
Under-five mortality	..	..	Unacceptable	Unacceptable
Maternal mortality	..	..	..	Unacceptable
Level of concern about HIV/AIDS	..	..	Major concern	Major concern
Measures implemented to control HIV/AIDS*	..	..	..	1,2,3,4,5
Grounds on which abortion is permitted**	..	..	1,2,3,4,5	1,2,3,4,5
Spatial distribution and internal migration				
View on spatial distribution	Major change desired	Major change desired	Minor change desired	Major change desired
Policies on internal migration				
From rural to urban areas	..	..	..	Lower
From rural to rural areas	..	..	..	No intervention
From urban to rural areas	..	..	..	Raise
From urban to urban areas	..	..	..	No intervention
Into urban agglomerations	Lower	..	Lower	Lower
International migration				
Immigration				
View	Too high	Too high	Satisfactory	Too high
Policy	Lower	Lower	No intervention	Lower
Permanent settlement	..	..	No intervention	Lower
Temporary workers	..	..	No intervention	Lower
Highly skilled workers	..	..	..	No intervention
Family reunification	..	..	No intervention	No intervention
Integration of non-nationals	..	..	No	No
Emigration				
View	Satisfactory	Satisfactory	Too high	Too high
Policy	Maintain	Maintain	Lower	Lower
Encouraging the return of nationals	No	..	No	Yes

* Measures implemented to control HIV/AIDS: (1) blood screening; (2) information/education campaigns; (3) access to antiretroviral treatment; (4) non-discriminatory policies; (5) promoting condom use.

** Grounds on which abortion is permitted: (1) to save the woman's life; (2) to preserve physical health; (3) to preserve mental health; (4) rape or incest; (5) foetal impairment; (6) economic or social reasons; (7) on request.

Population indicators

Indicator	*1975*	*1985*	*1995*	*2005*
Population size and growth				
Population size (thousands)	10 241	13 399	17 725	22 113
Annual growth rate (percentage)*	2.6	3.4	2.7	2.1
Population age structure				
Percentage of population under age 15	45	45	43	39
Percentage of population aged 60 or older	5	5	5	6
Fertility and family planning				
Total fertility (births per woman)*	6.7	6.5	5.5	4.4
Teenage fertility rate (per 1,000 women, aged 15 - 19)*	133	127	108	70
Percentage of births to women under age 20*	15	15	15	12
Percentage of births to women aged 35 or older*	22	21	19	18
Percentage of married women using contraception				
Modern methods	6[a]	5[b]	13[c]	19[d]
All methods	10[a]	13[b]	22[c]	25[d]
Health and mortality				
Life expectancy at birth (years)*				
Males	49	52	55	56
Females	51	55	58	57
Both sexes combined	50	54	57	57
Infant mortality rate (per 1,000 births)*	108	90	73	62
Mortality under age 5 (per 1,000 births)*	177	151	121	102
Maternal mortality ratio (per 100,000 births) (2000)	..	..	..	540
HIV/AIDS (2003)				
Number of infected adults (thousands)	..	..	..	320
Adult prevalence rate (percentage)	..	..	..	3.1
Spatial distribution				
Population density (per sq. km)	43	56	74	93
Urban population (percentage)	30	33	40	46
Annual urban growth rate (percentage)*	3.5	4.7	4.7	3.2
Annual rural growth rate (percentage)*	2.5	3.1	1.5	1.3
International migration				
International migrant stock				
Number of migrants (thousands)	385	494	1 038	1 669
Percentage of total population	3.8	3.7	5.9	7.5

* For the periods 1970-1975, 1980-1985, 1990-1995 and 2000-2005.
[a] For 1979.
[b] For 1988.
[c] For 1999.
[d] For 2003.

Government views and policies

Population policy variable	*1976*	*1986*	*1996*	*2005*
Population size and growth				
View on growth	Too low	Too low	Too low	Too low
Policy on growth	Raise	Raise	Raise	Raise
Population age structure				
Level of concern about				
Size of the working-age population	..	..	..	Major concern
Ageing of the population	..	..	..	Major concern
Fertility and family planning				
View on fertility level	Too low	Too low	Too low	Too low
Policy	Raise	Raise	Raise	Raise
Access to contraceptive methods	Limits	No support	No support	Indirect support
Adolescent fertility				
Level of concern	..	..	..	Major concern
Policies and programmes	..	..	..	Yes
Health and mortality				
View				
Expectation of life	Acceptable	Unacceptable	Unacceptable	Acceptable
Under-five mortality	..	..	..	Acceptable
Maternal mortality	..	..	..	Acceptable
Level of concern about HIV/AIDS	..	..	..	Major concern
Measures implemented to control HIV/AIDS*	..	..	..	1,2,3,4,5
Grounds on which abortion is permitted**	..	..	1,2,3,4,5,6,7	1,2,3,4,5,6,7
Spatial distribution and internal migration				
View on spatial distribution	Minor change desired	Major change desired	Major change desired	Major change desired
Policies on internal migration				
From rural to urban areas	..	..	..	Lower
From rural to rural areas	..	..	..	No intervention
From urban to rural areas	..	..	..	Raise
From urban to urban areas	..	..	..	No intervention
Into urban agglomerations	Lower	Lower	..	Lower
International migration				
Immigration				
View	Satisfactory	Too high	Too high	Satisfactory
Policy	Maintain	Lower	Lower	Maintain
Permanent settlement	..	..	Lower	Maintain
Temporary workers	..	..	..	Maintain
Highly skilled workers	..	..	..	Maintain
Family reunification	..	..	..	Maintain
Integration of non-nationals	..	..	..	Yes
Emigration				
View	Too high	Satisfactory	Satisfactory	Satisfactory
Policy	Lower	Lower	Lower	No intervention
Encouraging the return of nationals	Yes	..	Yes	Yes

* Measures implemented to control HIV/AIDS: (1) blood screening; (2) information/education campaigns; (3) access to antiretroviral treatment; (4) non-discriminatory policies; (5) promoting condom use.

** Grounds on which abortion is permitted: (1) to save the woman's life; (2) to preserve physical health; (3) to preserve mental health; (4) rape or incest; (5) foetal impairment; (6) economic or social reasons; (7) on request.

Population indicators

Indicator	*1975*	*1985*	*1995*	*2005*
Population size and growth				
Population size (thousands)	9 047	9 934	10 657	11 120
Annual growth rate (percentage)*	0.6	0.6	1.0	0.3
Population age structure				
Percentage of population under age 15	24	21	17	14
Percentage of population aged 60 or older	17	18	21	23
Fertility and family planning				
Total fertility (births per woman)*	2.3	2.0	1.4	1.3
Teenage fertility rate (per 1,000 women, aged 15 - 19)*	28	24	16	10
Percentage of births to women under age 20*	7	6	6	3
Percentage of births to women aged 35 or older*	11	9	9	13
Percentage of married women using contraception				
Modern methods	..	..	..	..
All methods	..	..	..	..
Health and mortality				
Life expectancy at birth (years)*				
Males	71	73	75	76
Females	74	78	80	81
Both sexes combined	72	75	77	78
Infant mortality rate (per 1,000 births)*	34	15	8	6
Mortality under age 5 (per 1,000 births)*	36	17	9	8
Maternal mortality ratio (per 100,000 births) (2000)	..	..	..	9
HIV/AIDS (2003)				
Number of infected adults (thousands)	..	..	..	9
Adult prevalence rate (percentage)	..	..	..	0.2
Spatial distribution				
Population density (per sq. km)	69	75	81	84
Urban population (percentage)	55	58	59	61
Annual urban growth rate (percentage)*	1.6	0.8	0.7	0.6
Annual rural growth rate (percentage)*	-0.6	0.3	0.4	-0.5
International migration				
International migrant stock				
Number of migrants (thousands)	123	309	549	974
Percentage of total population	1.4	3.1	5.1	8.8

* For the periods 1970-1975, 1980-1985, 1990-1995 and 2000-2005.

Government views and policies

Population policy variable	*1976*	*1986*	*1996*	*2005*
Population size and growth				
View on growth	Too high	Too high	Satisfactory	Satisfactory
Policy on growth	Lower	Lower	Maintain	No intervention
Population age structure				
Level of concern about				
Size of the working-age population	..	..	..	..
Ageing of the population	..	..	..	Minor concern
Fertility and family planning				
View on fertility level	Too high	Too high	Too high	Too high
Policy	Lower	Lower	Lower	Lower
Access to contraceptive methods	Direct support	Direct support	Direct support	Direct support
Adolescent fertility				
Level of concern	..	..	Major concern	Major concern
Policies and programmes	..	..	Yes	Yes
Health and mortality				
View				
Expectation of life	Unacceptable	Unacceptable	Unacceptable	Unacceptable
Under-five mortality	..	..	Unacceptable	Unacceptable
Maternal mortality	..	..	..	Unacceptable
Level of concern about HIV/AIDS	..	..	Major concern	Major concern
Measures implemented to control HIV/AIDS*	..	..	..	2,5
Grounds on which abortion is permitted**	..	..	1,2,3	1,2,3
Spatial distribution and internal migration				
View on spatial distribution	Major change desired	Major change desired	Satisfactory	Minor change desired
Policies on internal migration				
From rural to urban areas	..	..	..	..
From rural to rural areas	..	..	..	..
From urban to rural areas	..	..	..	..
From urban to urban areas	..	..	..	..
Into urban agglomerations	Lower	..	No intervention	..
International migration				
Immigration				
View	Satisfactory	Satisfactory	Satisfactory	Satisfactory
Policy	Maintain	Maintain	Maintain	Maintain
Permanent settlement	..	..	..	Maintain
Temporary workers	..	..	..	Maintain
Highly skilled workers	..	..	..	Maintain
Family reunification	..	..	..	Maintain
Integration of non-nationals	..	..	..	..
Emigration				
View	Satisfactory	Satisfactory	Too high	Too high
Policy	Maintain	Maintain	Lower	Lower
Encouraging the return of nationals	No	..	Yes	Yes

* Measures implemented to control HIV/AIDS: (1) blood screening; (2) information/education campaigns; (3) access to antiretroviral treatment; (4) non-discriminatory policies; (5) promoting condom use.

** Grounds on which abortion is permitted: (1) to save the woman's life; (2) to preserve physical health; (3) to preserve mental health; (4) rape or incest; (5) foetal impairment; (6) economic or social reasons; (7) on request.

Population indicators

Indicator	*1975*	*1985*	*1995*	*2005*
Population size and growth				
Population size (thousands)	92	93	99	103
Annual growth rate (percentage)*	-0.4	0.7	0.6	0.3
Population age structure				
Percentage of population under age 15	..	..	..	..
Percentage of population aged 60 or older	..	..	..	..
Fertility and family planning				
Total fertility (births per woman)*	..	..	..	..
Teenage fertility rate (per 1,000 women, aged 15 - 19)*	..	..	..	..
Percentage of births to women under age 20*	..	..	..	..
Percentage of births to women aged 35 or older*	..	..	..	..
Percentage of married women using contraception				
Modern methods	..	27	..	..
All methods	..	31	54[a]	..
Health and mortality				
Life expectancy at birth (years)*				
Males	..	..	..	..
Females	..	..	..	..
Both sexes combined	..	..	..	..
Infant mortality rate (per 1,000 births)*	..	..	..	..
Mortality under age 5 (per 1,000 births)*	..	..	..	..
Maternal mortality ratio (per 100,000 births) (2000)	..	..	..	..
HIV/AIDS (2003)				
Number of infected adults (thousands)	..	..	..	..
Adult prevalence rate (percentage)	..	..	..	..
Spatial distribution				
Population density (per sq. km)	269	271	289	299
Urban population (percentage)	33	33	35	42
Annual urban growth rate (percentage)*	-0.1	-0.6	1.1	1.6
Annual rural growth rate (percentage)*	-0.5	-0.4	-1.3	-1.5
International migration				
International migrant stock				
Number of migrants (thousands)	3	3	6	11
Percentage of total population	3	3.4	5.9	10.5

* For the periods 1970-1975, 1980-1985, 1990-1995 and 2000-2005.
[a] For 1990.

Government views and policies

Population policy variable	*1976*	*1986*	*1996*	*2005*
Population size and growth				
View on growth	Too high	Too high	Satisfactory	Too high
Policy on growth	No intervention	No intervention	No intervention	Lower
Population age structure				
Level of concern about				
Size of the working-age population	..	..	..	Major concern
Ageing of the population	..	..	..	Minor concern
Fertility and family planning				
View on fertility level	Too high	Satisfactory	Too high	Too high
Policy	No intervention	No intervention	Lower	Lower
Access to contraceptive methods	Direct support	Direct support	Direct support	Direct support
Adolescent fertility				
Level of concern	..	..	Minor concern	Major concern
Policies and programmes	..	..	No	Yes
Health and mortality				
View				
Expectation of life	Unacceptable	Unacceptable	Unacceptable	Unacceptable
Under-five mortality	..	..	..	Unacceptable
Maternal mortality	..	..	..	Unacceptable
Level of concern about HIV/AIDS	..	..	..	Major concern
Measures implemented to control HIV/AIDS*	..	..	..	1,2,3,4,5
Grounds on which abortion is permitted**	..	..	1	1
Spatial distribution and internal migration				
View on spatial distribution	Major change desired	Major change desired	Major change desired	Major change desired
Policies on internal migration				
From rural to urban areas	..	..	..	Lower
From rural to rural areas	..	..	..	Maintain
From urban to rural areas	..	..	..	Raise
From urban to urban areas	..	..	..	Maintain
Into urban agglomerations	No intervention	..	..	Lower
International migration				
Immigration				
View	Satisfactory	Satisfactory	Satisfactory	Too high
Policy	Maintain	Maintain	No intervention	No intervention
Permanent settlement	..	..	No intervention	No intervention
Temporary workers	..	..	..	No intervention
Highly skilled workers	..	..	..	Maintain
Family reunification	..	..	..	No intervention
Integration of non-nationals	..	..	..	Yes
Emigration				
View	Satisfactory	Satisfactory	Too high	Satisfactory
Policy	Maintain	Maintain	No intervention	No intervention
Encouraging the return of nationals	..	..	..	No

* Measures implemented to control HIV/AIDS: (1) blood screening; (2) information/education campaigns; (3) access to antiretroviral treatment; (4) non-discriminatory policies; (5) promoting condom use.
** Grounds on which abortion is permitted: (1) to save the woman's life; (2) to preserve physical health; (3) to preserve mental health; (4) rape or incest; (5) foetal impairment; (6) economic or social reasons; (7) on request.

Population indicators

Indicator	*1975*	*1985*	*1995*	*2005*
Population size and growth				
Population size (thousands)	6 203	7 929	9 970	12 599
Annual growth rate (percentage)*	2.7	2.5	2.3	2.4
Population age structure				
Percentage of population under age 15	45	46	45	43
Percentage of population aged 60 or older	4	5	6	6
Fertility and family planning				
Total fertility (births per woman)*	6.2	6.1	5.5	4.6
Teenage fertility rate (per 1,000 women, aged 15 - 19)*	138	139	128	115
Percentage of births to women under age 20*	16	17	18	18
Percentage of births to women aged 35 or older*	15	14	13	11
Percentage of married women using contraception				
Modern methods	15[a]	21[b]	27	34[c]
All methods	18[a]	25[b]	31	43[c]
Health and mortality				
Life expectancy at birth (years)*				
Males	52	56	59	63
Females	55	60	66	71
Both sexes combined	54	58	62	67
Infant mortality rate (per 1,000 births)*	102	79	55	39
Mortality under age 5 (per 1,000 births)*	165	122	79	52
Maternal mortality ratio (per 100,000 births) (2000)	..	..	..	240
HIV/AIDS (2003)				
Number of infected adults (thousands)	..	..	..	74
Adult prevalence rate (percentage)	..	..	..	1.1
Spatial distribution				
Population density (per sq. km)	57	73	92	116
Urban population (percentage)	37	39	43	47
Annual urban growth rate (percentage)*	3.4	3.4	3.6	3.4
Annual rural growth rate (percentage)*	2.4	2.0	1.9	1.8
International migration				
International migrant stock				
Number of migrants (thousands)	38	82	45	53
Percentage of total population	0.6	1	0.5	0.4

* For the periods 1970-1975, 1980-1985, 1990-1995 and 2000-2005.
[a] For 1978.
[b] For 1983.
[c] For 2002.

Government views and policies

Population policy variable	*1976*	*1986*	*1996*	*2005*
Population size and growth				
View on growth	Satisfactory	Satisfactory	Too high	Too high
Policy on growth	No intervention	No intervention	Lower	Lower
Population age structure				
Level of concern about				
Size of the working-age population	..	..	..	Minor concern
Ageing of the population	..	..	..	Minor concern
Fertility and family planning				
View on fertility level	Satisfactory	Too high	Too high	Too high
Policy	No intervention	No intervention	Lower	Lower
Access to contraceptive methods	No support	Direct support	Direct support	Indirect support
Adolescent fertility				
Level of concern	..	..	Major concern	Minor concern
Policies and programmes	..	..	No	No
Health and mortality				
View				
Expectation of life	Unacceptable	Unacceptable	Unacceptable	Unacceptable
Under-five mortality	..	..	Unacceptable	Unacceptable
Maternal mortality	..	..	..	Unacceptable
Level of concern about HIV/AIDS	..	..	Major concern	Major concern
Measures implemented to control HIV/AIDS*	..	..	..	2,3,4,5
Grounds on which abortion is permitted**	..	..	1,2,3	1,2,3
Spatial distribution and internal migration				
View on spatial distribution	Minor change desired	Minor change desired	Major change desired	Major change desired
Policies on internal migration				
From rural to urban areas	..	..	..	Lower
From rural to rural areas	..	..	..	No intervention
From urban to rural areas	..	..	..	Raise
From urban to urban areas	..	..	..	Maintain
Into urban agglomerations	..	..	Lower	Lower
International migration				
Immigration				
View	Satisfactory	Satisfactory	Satisfactory	Satisfactory
Policy	Maintain	Maintain	Lower	No intervention
Permanent settlement	..	..	No intervention	No intervention
Temporary workers	..	..	Lower	No intervention
Highly skilled workers	..	..	..	No intervention
Family reunification	..	..	No intervention	No intervention
Integration of non-nationals	..	..	No	No
Emigration				
View	Too high	Too high	Satisfactory	Satisfactory
Policy	Lower	Lower	No intervention	No intervention
Encouraging the return of nationals	..	..	Yes	No

* Measures implemented to control HIV/AIDS: (1) blood screening; (2) information/education campaigns; (3) access to antiretroviral treatment; (4) non-discriminatory policies; (5) promoting condom use.

** Grounds on which abortion is permitted: (1) to save the woman's life; (2) to preserve physical health; (3) to preserve mental health; (4) rape or incest; (5) foetal impairment; (6) economic or social reasons; (7) on request.

Population indicators

Indicator	*1975*	*1985*	*1995*	*2005*
Population size and growth				
Population size (thousands)	4 212	5 386	7 525	9 402
Annual growth rate (percentage)*	1.0	2.3	3.8	2.2
Population age structure				
Percentage of population under age 15	42	43	44	44
Percentage of population aged 60 or older	5	5	5	6
Fertility and family planning				
Total fertility (births per woman)*	6.9	6.8	6.4	5.9
Teenage fertility rate (per 1,000 women, aged 15 - 19)*	193	197	208	201
Percentage of births to women under age 20*	18	21	23	24
Percentage of births to women aged 35 or older*	18	18	14	13
Percentage of married women using contraception				
Modern methods	..	..	4[a]	..
All methods	..	..	6[a]	..
Health and mortality				
Life expectancy at birth (years)*				
Males	39	42	48	53
Females	40	43	49	54
Both sexes combined	39	43	49	54
Infant mortality rate (per 1,000 births)*	181	162	134	106
Mortality under age 5 (per 1,000 births)*	320	285	224	166
Maternal mortality ratio (per 100,000 births) (2000)	..	..	..	740
HIV/AIDS (2003)				
Number of infected adults (thousands)	..	..	..	130
Adult prevalence rate (percentage)	..	..	..	3.2
Spatial distribution				
Population density (per sq. km)	17	22	31	38
Urban population (percentage)	16	22	29	36
Annual urban growth rate (percentage)*	4.2	5.5	6.2	3.8
Annual rural growth rate (percentage)*	0.3	1.8	2.6	0.4
International migration				
International migrant stock				
Number of migrants (thousands)	191	222	870	406
Percentage of total population	4.5	4.1	11.6	4.3

* For the periods 1970-1975, 1980-1985, 1990-1995 and 2000-2005.
[a] For 1999.

Government views and policies

Population policy variable	*1976*	*1986*	*1996*	*2005*
Population size and growth				
View on growth	Satisfactory	Satisfactory	Satisfactory	Satisfactory
Policy on growth	No intervention	No intervention	No intervention	No intervention
Population age structure				
Level of concern about				
Size of the working-age population	..	..	..	..
Ageing of the population	..	..	..	Minor concern
Fertility and family planning				
View on fertility level	Satisfactory	Satisfactory	Too high	Too high
Policy	No intervention	No intervention	No intervention	No intervention
Access to contraceptive methods	Indirect support	Direct support	Direct support	Indirect support
Adolescent fertility				
Level of concern	..	..	Major concern	Major concern
Policies and programmes	..	..	Yes	Yes
Health and mortality				
View				
Expectation of life	Unacceptable	Unacceptable	Unacceptable	Unacceptable
Under-five mortality	..	..	Unacceptable	Unacceptable
Maternal mortality	..	..	..	Unacceptable
Level of concern about HIV/AIDS	..	..	Major concern	Major concern
Measures implemented to control HIV/AIDS*	..	..	..	..
Grounds on which abortion is permitted**	..	..	1	1
Spatial distribution and internal migration				
View on spatial distribution	Major change desired	Minor change desired	Major change desired	Major change desired
Policies on internal migration				
From rural to urban areas	..	..	..	..
From rural to rural areas	..	..	..	..
From urban to rural areas	..	..	..	..
From urban to urban areas	..	..	..	..
Into urban agglomerations	Lower	Lower	Lower	..
International migration				
Immigration				
View	Satisfactory	Satisfactory	Satisfactory	Satisfactory
Policy	Maintain	Maintain	No intervention	No intervention
Permanent settlement	..	..	No intervention	..
Temporary workers	..	..	No intervention	..
Highly skilled workers	..	..	..	..
Family reunification	..	..	No intervention	..
Integration of non-nationals	..	..	Yes	..
Emigration				
View	Satisfactory	Satisfactory	Too high	Too high
Policy	Maintain	Maintain	Lower	Lower
Encouraging the return of nationals	Yes	..	Yes	..

* Measures implemented to control HIV/AIDS: (1) blood screening; (2) information/education campaigns; (3) access to antiretroviral treatment; (4) non-discriminatory policies; (5) promoting condom use.

** Grounds on which abortion is permitted: (1) to save the woman's life; (2) to preserve physical health; (3) to preserve mental health; (4) rape or incest; (5) foetal impairment; (6) economic or social reasons; (7) on request.

Population indicators

Indicator	*1975*	*1985*	*1995*	*2005*
Population size and growth				
Population size (thousands)	651	891	1 189	1 586
Annual growth rate (percentage)*	2.2	2.3	3.2	3.0
Population age structure				
Percentage of population under age 15	43	45	46	48
Percentage of population aged 60 or older	6	6	5	5
Fertility and family planning				
Total fertility (births per woman)*	7.1	7.1	7.1	7.1
Teenage fertility rate (per 1,000 women, aged 15 - 19)*	197	197	197	197
Percentage of births to women under age 20*	19	20	21	20
Percentage of births to women aged 35 or older*	18	16	15	14
Percentage of married women using contraception				
Modern methods	..	..	..	4[a]
All methods	..	..	..	8[a]
Health and mortality				
Life expectancy at birth (years)*				
Males	35	38	41	43
Females	38	41	45	46
Both sexes combined	36	39	43	45
Infant mortality rate (per 1,000 births)*	183	164	140	120
Mortality under age 5 (per 1,000 births)*	302	288	246	211
Maternal mortality ratio (per 100,000 births) (2000)	..	..	..	1 100
HIV/AIDS (2003)				
Number of infected adults (thousands)	..	..	..	..
Adult prevalence rate (percentage)	..	..	..	..
Spatial distribution				
Population density (per sq. km)	18	25	33	44
Urban population (percentage)	16	20	28	36
Annual urban growth rate (percentage)*	3.2	5.6	6.1	5.4
Annual rural growth rate (percentage)*	2.0	1.6	2.1	1.7
International migration				
International migrant stock				
Number of migrants (thousands)	13	13	32	19
Percentage of total population	1.9	1.4	2.7	1.2

* For the periods 1970-1975, 1980-1985, 1990-1995 and 2000-2005.
[a] For 2000.

Government views and policies

Population policy variable	*1976*	*1986*	*1996*	*2005*
Population size and growth				
View on growth	Satisfactory	Satisfactory	Satisfactory	Satisfactory
Policy on growth	No intervention	No intervention	No intervention	No intervention
Population age structure				
Level of concern about				
Size of the working-age population	..	..	..	Major concern
Ageing of the population	..	..	..	Major concern
Fertility and family planning				
View on fertility level	Satisfactory	Satisfactory	Satisfactory	Satisfactory
Policy	No intervention	No intervention	No intervention	No intervention
Access to contraceptive methods	No support	Direct support	Direct support	Direct support
Adolescent fertility				
Level of concern	..	..	..	Major concern
Policies and programmes	..	..	..	Yes
Health and mortality				
View				
Expectation of life	Unacceptable	Acceptable	Unacceptable	Unacceptable
Under-five mortality	..	..	..	Unacceptable
Maternal mortality	..	..	..	Unacceptable
Level of concern about HIV/AIDS	..	..	..	Major concern
Measures implemented to control HIV/AIDS*	..	..	..	1,2,3,4,5
Grounds on which abortion is permitted**	..	..	1,2,3,4,5,6,7	1,2,3,4,5,6,7
Spatial distribution and internal migration				
View on spatial distribution	Major change desired	Major change desired	Minor change desired	Minor change desired
Policies on internal migration				
From rural to urban areas	..	..	..	Lower
From rural to rural areas	..	..	..	..
From urban to rural areas	..	..	..	..
From urban to urban areas	..	..	..	..
Into urban agglomerations	No intervention	..	..	Lower
International migration				
Immigration				
View	Satisfactory	Too low	Satisfactory	Satisfactory
Policy	Maintain	Raise	Raise	Maintain
Permanent settlement	..	..	Raise	Maintain
Temporary workers	..	..	..	..
Highly skilled workers	..	..	..	Maintain
Family reunification	..	..	..	Maintain
Integration of non-nationals	..	..	..	..
Emigration				
View	Too high	Too high	Too high	Too high
Policy	Lower	Lower	No intervention	No intervention
Encouraging the return of nationals	Yes	..	..	..

* Measures implemented to control HIV/AIDS: (1) blood screening; (2) information/education campaigns; (3) access to antiretroviral treatment; (4) non-discriminatory policies; (5) promoting condom use.

** Grounds on which abortion is permitted: (1) to save the woman's life; (2) to preserve physical health; (3) to preserve mental health; (4) rape or incest; (5) foetal impairment; (6) economic or social reasons; (7) on request.

Population indicators

Indicator	*1975*	*1985*	*1995*	*2005*
Population size and growth				
Population size (thousands)	734	754	732	751
Annual growth rate (percentage)*	0.7	-0.2	0.1	0.2
Population age structure				
Percentage of population under age 15	44	39	34	29
Percentage of population aged 60 or older	5	6	7	7
Fertility and family planning				
Total fertility (births per woman)*	4.9	3.3	2.6	2.3
Teenage fertility rate (per 1,000 women, aged 15 - 19)*	186	124	86	67
Percentage of births to women under age 20*	29	26	21	15
Percentage of births to women aged 35 or older*	6	6	7	8
Percentage of married women using contraception				
Modern methods	28	..	..	36[a]
All methods	31	..	..	37[a]
Health and mortality				
Life expectancy at birth (years)*				
Males	58	58	56	60
Females	62	64	63	66
Both sexes combined	60	61	60	63
Infant mortality rate (per 1,000 births)*	79	70	62	49
Mortality under age 5 (per 1,000 births)*	114	98	89	68
Maternal mortality ratio (per 100,000 births) (2000)	..	..	..	170
HIV/AIDS (2003)				
Number of infected adults (thousands)	..	..	..	11
Adult prevalence rate (percentage)	..	..	..	2.5
Spatial distribution				
Population density (per sq. km)	3	4	3	3
Urban population (percentage)	30	32	35	38
Annual urban growth rate (percentage)*	1.0	0.7	1.1	1.4
Annual rural growth rate (percentage)*	0.5	-0.6	-0.1	-0.5
International migration				
International migrant stock				
Number of migrants (thousands)	9	4	2	1
Percentage of total population	1.2	0.6	0.3	0.1

* For the periods 1970-1975, 1980-1985, 1990-1995 and 2000-2005.
[a] For 2000.

Government views and policies

Population policy variable	*1976*	*1986*	*1996*	*2005*
Population size and growth				
View on growth	Too high	Too high	Too high	Too high
Policy on growth	Lower	Lower	Lower	Lower
Population age structure				
Level of concern about				
Size of the working-age population	..	..	..	..
Ageing of the population	..	..	..	Minor concern
Fertility and family planning				
View on fertility level	Too high	Too high	Too high	Too high
Policy	Lower	Lower	Lower	Lower
Access to contraceptive methods	Direct support	Direct support	Direct support	Direct support
Adolescent fertility				
Level of concern	..	..	..	Minor concern
Policies and programmes	..	..	..	..
Health and mortality				
View				
Expectation of life	Unacceptable	Unacceptable	Unacceptable	Unacceptable
Under-five mortality	..	..	..	Unacceptable
Maternal mortality	..	..	..	Unacceptable
Level of concern about HIV/AIDS	..	..	..	Major concern
Measures implemented to control HIV/AIDS*	..	..	..	1,2,3,5
Grounds on which abortion is permitted**	..	..	1	1
Spatial distribution and internal migration				
View on spatial distribution	Major change desired	Major change desired	Major change desired	Major change desired
Policies on internal migration				
From rural to urban areas	..	..	..	No intervention
From rural to rural areas	..	..	..	No intervention
From urban to rural areas	..	..	..	No intervention
From urban to urban areas	..	..	..	No intervention
Into urban agglomerations	Lower	Lower	..	No intervention
International migration				
Immigration				
View	Satisfactory	Satisfactory	Satisfactory	Satisfactory
Policy	Maintain	Maintain	Maintain	Maintain
Permanent settlement	..	..	..	..
Temporary workers	..	..	..	..
Highly skilled workers	..	..	..	..
Family reunification	..	..	..	..
Integration of non-nationals	..	..	..	..
Emigration				
View	Too high	Too high	Too high	Too high
Policy	Lower	Lower	Lower	Lower
Encouraging the return of nationals	Yes	..	..	Yes

* Measures implemented to control HIV/AIDS: (1) blood screening; (2) information/education campaigns; (3) access to antiretroviral treatment; (4) non-discriminatory policies; (5) promoting condom use.

** Grounds on which abortion is permitted: (1) to save the woman's life; (2) to preserve physical health; (3) to preserve mental health; (4) rape or incest; (5) foetal impairment; (6) economic or social reasons; (7) on request.

Population indicators

Indicator	*1975*	*1985*	*1995*	*2005*
Population size and growth				
Population size (thousands)	4 920	6 129	7 391	8 528
Annual growth rate (percentage)*	1.7	2.3	1.5	1.4
Population age structure				
Percentage of population under age 15	41	43	43	37
Percentage of population aged 60 or older	7	6	6	6
Fertility and family planning				
Total fertility (births per woman)*	5.8	6.2	4.8	4.0
Teenage fertility rate (per 1,000 women, aged 15 - 19)*	66	90	76	64
Percentage of births to women under age 20*	9	11	12	13
Percentage of births to women aged 35 or older*	24	21	19	17
Percentage of married women using contraception				
Modern methods	5[a]	4[b]	13	21[c]
All methods	19[a]	7[b]	18	27[c]
Health and mortality				
Life expectancy at birth (years)*				
Males	47	50	46	51
Females	50	53	50	52
Both sexes combined	48	52	48	51
Infant mortality rate (per 1,000 births)*	152	122	76	62
Mortality under age 5 (per 1,000 births)*	194	175	134	110
Maternal mortality ratio (per 100,000 births) (2000)	..	..	..	680
HIV/AIDS (2003)				
Number of infected adults (thousands)	..	..	..	260
Adult prevalence rate (percentage)	..	..	..	5.6
Spatial distribution				
Population density (per sq. km)	177	221	266	307
Urban population (percentage)	22	26	33	39
Annual urban growth rate (percentage)*	3.6	4.4	3.6	3.0
Annual rural growth rate (percentage)*	1.2	1.6	0.7	0.3
International migration				
International migrant stock				
Number of migrants (thousands)	12	16	22	30
Percentage of total population	0.2	0.3	0.3	0.4

* For the periods 1970-1975, 1980-1985, 1990-1995 and 2000-2005.
[a] For 1977.
[b] For 1983.
[c] For 2000.

Government views and policies

Population policy variable	*1976*	*1986*	*1996*	*2005*
Population size and growth				
View on growth	Too low	Satisfactory	Satisfactory	Satisfactory
Policy on growth	No intervention	No intervention	No intervention	No intervention
Population age structure				
Level of concern about				
Size of the working-age population	..	..	..	..
Ageing of the population	..	..	..	..
Fertility and family planning				
View on fertility level	Satisfactory	Satisfactory	Satisfactory	Satisfactory
Policy	No intervention	No intervention	No intervention	No intervention
Access to contraceptive methods	Limits	Limits	Limits	Limits
Adolescent fertility				
Level of concern	..	..	..	..
Policies and programmes	..	..	..	..
Health and mortality				
View				
Expectation of life	Acceptable	Acceptable	Acceptable	Acceptable
Under-five mortality	..	..	..	Acceptable
Maternal mortality	..	..	..	Acceptable
Level of concern about HIV/AIDS	..	..	..	..
Measures implemented to control HIV/AIDS*	..	..	..	2,3,4
Grounds on which abortion is permitted**	..	..	Not permitted	Not permitted
Spatial distribution and internal migration				
View on spatial distribution	Satisfactory	Satisfactory	Satisfactory	Satisfactory
Policies on internal migration				
From rural to urban areas	..	..	..	..
From rural to rural areas	..	..	..	..
From urban to rural areas	..	..	..	..
From urban to urban areas	..	..	..	..
Into urban agglomerations	No intervention	..	..	..
International migration				
Immigration				
View	Satisfactory	Satisfactory	Satisfactory	Satisfactory
Policy	Maintain	Maintain	Maintain	Maintain
Permanent settlement	..	..	..	..
Temporary workers	..	..	..	..
Highly skilled workers	..	..	..	..
Family reunification	..	..	..	..
Integration of non-nationals	..	..	..	..
Emigration				
View	Satisfactory	Satisfactory	Satisfactory	Satisfactory
Policy	Maintain	Maintain	Maintain	Maintain
Encouraging the return of nationals	No	..	..	..

* Measures implemented to control HIV/AIDS: (1) blood screening; (2) information/education campaigns; (3) access to antiretroviral treatment; (4) non-discriminatory policies; (5) promoting condom use.

** Grounds on which abortion is permitted: (1) to save the woman's life; (2) to preserve physical health; (3) to preserve mental health; (4) rape or incest; (5) foetal impairment; (6) economic or social reasons; (7) on request.

Population indicators

Indicator	*1975*	*1985*	*1995*	*2005*
Population size and growth				
Population size (thousands)	1	1	1	1
Annual growth rate (percentage)*	2.4	0.6	0.3	-0.1
Population age structure				
Percentage of population under age 15	..	..	..	..
Percentage of population aged 60 or older	..	..	..	..
Fertility and family planning				
Total fertility (births per woman)*	..	..	..	..
Teenage fertility rate (per 1,000 women, aged 15 - 19)*	..	..	..	..
Percentage of births to women under age 20*	..	..	..	..
Percentage of births to women aged 35 or older*	..	..	..	..
Percentage of married women using contraception				
Modern methods	..	..	..	..
All methods	..	..	..	..
Health and mortality				
Life expectancy at birth (years)*				
Males	..	..	..	..
Females	..	..	..	..
Both sexes combined	..	..	..	..
Infant mortality rate (per 1,000 births)*	..	..	..	..
Mortality under age 5 (per 1,000 births)*	..	..	..	..
Maternal mortality ratio (per 100,000 births) (2000)	..	..	..	..
HIV/AIDS (2003)				
Number of infected adults (thousands)	..	..	..	..
Adult prevalence rate (percentage)	..	..	..	..
Spatial distribution				
Population density (per sq. km)	1 657	1 698	1 775	1 780
Urban population (percentage)	100	100	100	100
Annual urban growth rate (percentage)*	2.3	0.2	0.3	0.0
Annual rural growth rate (percentage)*	0.0	0.0	0.0	0.0
International migration				
International migrant stock				
Number of migrants (thousands)	1	1	1	1
Percentage of total population	100	100	100	100

* For the periods 1970-1975, 1980-1985, 1990-1995 and 2000-2005.

Government views and policies

Population policy variable	*1976*	*1986*	*1996*	*2005*
Population size and growth				
View on growth	Satisfactory	Too high	Satisfactory	Satisfactory
Policy on growth	No intervention	Lower	No intervention	No intervention
Population age structure				
Level of concern about				
Size of the working-age population	..	..	..	Minor concern
Ageing of the population	..	..	..	Minor concern
Fertility and family planning				
View on fertility level	Too high	Too high	Too high	Too high
Policy	Lower	Lower	Lower	Lower
Access to contraceptive methods	Direct support	Direct support	Direct support	Direct support
Adolescent fertility				
Level of concern	..	..	Minor concern	Major concern
Policies and programmes	..	..	Yes	Yes
Health and mortality				
View				
Expectation of life	Acceptable	Unacceptable	Unacceptable	Unacceptable
Under-five mortality	..	..	Unacceptable	Unacceptable
Maternal mortality	..	..	..	Unacceptable
Level of concern about HIV/AIDS	..	..	Major concern	Major concern
Measures implemented to control HIV/AIDS*	..	..	..	1,2,3,4,5
Grounds on which abortion is permitted**	..	..	1	1
Spatial distribution and internal migration				
View on spatial distribution	Major change desired	Major change desired	Major change desired	Major change desired
Policies on internal migration				
From rural to urban areas	..	..	..	Lower
From rural to rural areas	..	..	..	..
From urban to rural areas	..	..	..	..
From urban to urban areas	..	..	..	..
Into urban agglomerations	No intervention	Lower	No intervention	Lower
International migration				
Immigration				
View	Satisfactory	Too high	Satisfactory	Satisfactory
Policy	Maintain	Lower	Lower	Maintain
Permanent settlement	..	..	Lower	Maintain
Temporary workers	..	..	No intervention	Maintain
Highly skilled workers	..	..	..	Maintain
Family reunification	..	..	No intervention	Maintain
Integration of non-nationals	..	..	No	..
Emigration				
View	Too high	Too high	Satisfactory	Satisfactory
Policy	Lower	Lower	No intervention	No intervention
Encouraging the return of nationals	No	..	No	..

* Measures implemented to control HIV/AIDS: (1) blood screening; (2) information/education campaigns; (3) access to antiretroviral treatment; (4) non-discriminatory policies; (5) promoting condom use.

** Grounds on which abortion is permitted: (1) to save the woman's life; (2) to preserve physical health; (3) to preserve mental health; (4) rape or incest; (5) foetal impairment; (6) economic or social reasons; (7) on request.

Population indicators

Indicator	*1975*	*1985*	*1995*	*2005*
Population size and growth				
Population size (thousands)	3 016	4 182	5 625	7 205
Annual growth rate (percentage)*	3.0	3.2	2.9	2.3
Population age structure				
Percentage of population under age 15	48	46	44	39
Percentage of population aged 60 or older	4	4	5	6
Fertility and family planning				
Total fertility (births per woman)*	7.1	6.0	4.9	3.7
Teenage fertility rate (per 1,000 women, aged 15 - 19)*	151	140	127	103
Percentage of births to women under age 20*	17	18	18	19
Percentage of births to women aged 35 or older*	17	14	13	12
Percentage of married women using contraception				
Modern methods	..	30[a]	35[b]	51[c]
All methods	..	35[a]	47[b]	62[c]
Health and mortality				
Life expectancy at birth (years)*				
Males	52	59	64	66
Females	56	63	68	70
Both sexes combined	54	61	66	68
Infant mortality rate (per 1,000 births)*	104	65	44	32
Mortality under age 5 (per 1,000 births)*	163	104	64	48
Maternal mortality ratio (per 100,000 births) (2000)	..	..	..	110
HIV/AIDS (2003)				
Number of infected adults (thousands)	..	..	..	59
Adult prevalence rate (percentage)	..	..	..	1.8
Spatial distribution				
Population density (per sq. km)	27	37	50	64
Urban population (percentage)	32	38	42	46
Annual urban growth rate (percentage)*	5.1	4.8	3.9	3.3
Annual rural growth rate (percentage)*	2.1	2.3	2.2	1.6
International migration				
International migrant stock				
Number of migrants (thousands)	14	83	31	26
Percentage of total population	0.5	2	0.5	0.4

* For the periods 1970-1975, 1980-1985, 1990-1995 and 2000-2005.
[a] For 1984.
[b] For 1992.
[c] For 2001.

Government views and policies

Population policy variable	*1976*	*1986*	*1996*	*2005*
Population size and growth				
View on growth	Satisfactory	Too low	Too low	Too low
Policy on growth	No intervention	Raise	Raise	Raise
Population age structure				
Level of concern about				
Size of the working-age population	..	..	..	Minor concern
Ageing of the population	..	..	..	Major concern
Fertility and family planning				
View on fertility level	Satisfactory	Too low	Too low	Too low
Policy	Maintain	Raise	Raise	Raise
Access to contraceptive methods	Direct support	Direct support	Direct support	Indirect support
Adolescent fertility				
Level of concern	..	..	Not a concern	Minor concern
Policies and programmes	..	..	No	No
Health and mortality				
View				
Expectation of life	Acceptable	Acceptable	Unacceptable	Unacceptable
Under-five mortality	..	..	Acceptable	Unacceptable
Maternal mortality	..	..	..	Unacceptable
Level of concern about HIV/AIDS	..	..	Minor concern	Major concern
Measures implemented to control HIV/AIDS*	..	..	..	1,2,3,4
Grounds on which abortion is permitted**	..	..	1,2,3,4,5,6,7	1,2,3,4,5,6,7
Spatial distribution and internal migration				
View on spatial distribution	Satisfactory	Satisfactory	Satisfactory	Minor change desired
Policies on internal migration				
From rural to urban areas	..	..	..	..
From rural to rural areas	..	..	..	..
From urban to rural areas	..	..	..	..
From urban to urban areas	..	..	..	..
Into urban agglomerations	No intervention	No intervention	No intervention	No intervention
International migration				
Immigration				
View	Satisfactory	Satisfactory	Satisfactory	Satisfactory
Policy	Maintain	Maintain	Lower	Maintain
Permanent settlement	..	..	Lower	Maintain
Temporary workers	..	..	Lower	Maintain
Highly skilled workers	..	..	..	..
Family reunification	..	..	No intervention	Maintain
Integration of non-nationals	..	..	No	Yes
Emigration				
View	Satisfactory	Satisfactory	Satisfactory	Satisfactory
Policy	Maintain	Maintain	No intervention	No intervention
Encouraging the return of nationals	No	..	Yes	No

* Measures implemented to control HIV/AIDS: (1) blood screening; (2) information/education campaigns; (3) access to antiretroviral treatment; (4) non-discriminatory policies; (5) promoting condom use.

** Grounds on which abortion is permitted: (1) to save the woman's life; (2) to preserve physical health; (3) to preserve mental health; (4) rape or incest; (5) foetal impairment; (6) economic or social reasons; (7) on request.

Population indicators

Indicator	*1975*	*1985*	*1995*	*2005*
Population size and growth				
Population size (thousands)	10 532	10 579	10 329	10 098
Annual growth rate (percentage)*	0.4	-0.2	-0.1	-0.3
Population age structure				
Percentage of population under age 15	20	21	18	16
Percentage of population aged 60 or older	18	18	19	21
Fertility and family planning				
Total fertility (births per woman)*	2.1	1.8	1.7	1.3
Teenage fertility rate (per 1,000 women, aged 15 - 19)*	39	34	33	22
Percentage of births to women under age 20*	10	8	11	7
Percentage of births to women aged 35 or older*	7	7	9	9
Percentage of married women using contraception				
Modern methods	44[a]	62[b]	68[c]	..
All methods	74[a]	73[b]	77[c]	..
Health and mortality				
Life expectancy at birth (years)*				
Males	66	65	65	68
Females	72	73	74	77
Both sexes combined	69	69	70	73
Infant mortality rate (per 1,000 births)*	34	20	13	8
Mortality under age 5 (per 1,000 births)*	39	24	16	11
Maternal mortality ratio (per 100,000 births) (2000)	..	..	..	16
HIV/AIDS (2003)				
Number of infected adults (thousands)	..	..	..	3
Adult prevalence rate (percentage)	..	..	..	0.1
Spatial distribution				
Population density (per sq. km)	113	114	111	109
Urban population (percentage)	53	60	63	66
Annual urban growth rate (percentage)*	2.1	0.7	0.0	0.1
Annual rural growth rate (percentage)*	-1.4	-1.5	-0.8	-1.6
International migration				
International migrant stock				
Number of migrants (thousands)	402	339	293	316
Percentage of total population	3.8	3.2	2.8	3.1

* For the periods 1970-1975, 1980-1985, 1990-1995 and 2000-2005.
[a] For 1974.
[b] For 1986.
[c] For 1992/1993.

Government views and policies

Population policy variable	*1976*	*1986*	*1996*	*2005*
Population size and growth				
View on growth	Satisfactory	Satisfactory	Satisfactory	Satisfactory
Policy on growth	No intervention	No intervention	No intervention	Maintain
Population age structure				
Level of concern about				
Size of the working-age population	..	..	..	..
Ageing of the population	..	..	..	..
Fertility and family planning				
View on fertility level	Satisfactory	Satisfactory	Satisfactory	Satisfactory
Policy	No intervention	No intervention	No intervention	Maintain
Access to contraceptive methods	Direct support	Direct support	Direct support	Direct support
Adolescent fertility				
Level of concern	..	..	..	..
Policies and programmes	..	..	..	No
Health and mortality				
View				
Expectation of life	Acceptable	Acceptable	Acceptable	Acceptable
Under-five mortality	..	..	..	Acceptable
Maternal mortality	..	..	..	Acceptable
Level of concern about HIV/AIDS	..	..	..	Minor concern
Measures implemented to control HIV/AIDS*	..	..	..	1,2,3,4,5
Grounds on which abortion is permitted**	..	..	1,2,3,4,5,6	1,2,3,4,5,6
Spatial distribution and internal migration				
View on spatial distribution	Minor change desired	Minor change desired	Minor change desired	Major change desired
Policies on internal migration				
From rural to urban areas	..	..	..	Lower
From rural to rural areas	..	..	..	No intervention
From urban to rural areas	..	..	..	No intervention
From urban to urban areas	..	..	..	No intervention
Into urban agglomerations	No intervention	..	..	No intervention
International migration				
Immigration				
View	Satisfactory	Satisfactory	Satisfactory	Satisfactory
Policy	Maintain	Maintain	Maintain	No intervention
Permanent settlement	..	..	..	No intervention
Temporary workers	..	..	..	No intervention
Highly skilled workers	..	..	..	No intervention
Family reunification	..	..	..	No intervention
Integration of non-nationals	..	..	..	No
Emigration				
View	Satisfactory	Satisfactory	Satisfactory	Satisfactory
Policy	Maintain	Maintain	Maintain	No intervention
Encouraging the return of nationals	No	..	..	No

* Measures implemented to control HIV/AIDS: (1) blood screening; (2) information/education campaigns; (3) access to antiretroviral treatment; (4) non-discriminatory policies; (5) promoting condom use.

** Grounds on which abortion is permitted: (1) to save the woman's life; (2) to preserve physical health; (3) to preserve mental health; (4) rape or incest; (5) foetal impairment; (6) economic or social reasons; (7) on request.

Population indicators

Indicator	*1975*	*1985*	*1995*	*2005*
Population size and growth				
Population size (thousands)	218	241	267	295
Annual growth rate (percentage)*	1.3	1.1	1.0	0.9
Population age structure				
Percentage of population under age 15	30	26	24	22
Percentage of population aged 60 or older	13	14	15	16
Fertility and family planning				
Total fertility (births per woman)*	2.8	2.2	2.2	2.0
Teenage fertility rate (per 1,000 women, aged 15 - 19)*	32	26	25	19
Percentage of births to women under age 20*	8	7	6	5
Percentage of births to women aged 35 or older*	11	11	14	16
Percentage of married women using contraception				
Modern methods	..	..	..	..
All methods	..	..	..	..
Health and mortality				
Life expectancy at birth (years)*				
Males	71	74	76	79
Females	77	80	81	83
Both sexes combined	74	77	79	81
Infant mortality rate (per 1,000 births)*	12	6	5	3
Mortality under age 5 (per 1,000 births)*	13	8	6	4
Maternal mortality ratio (per 100,000 births) (2000)	..	..	..	0
HIV/AIDS (2003)				
Number of infected adults (thousands)	..	..	..	<1
Adult prevalence rate (percentage)	..	..	..	0.2
Spatial distribution				
Population density (per sq. km)	2	2	3	3
Urban population (percentage)	87	89	92	93
Annual urban growth rate (percentage)*	1.7	1.4	1.2	0.9
Annual rural growth rate (percentage)*	-1.1	-1.1	-1.3	-1.0
International migration				
International migrant stock				
Number of migrants (thousands)	5	7	11	23
Percentage of total population	2.4	3	3.9	7.8

* For the periods 1970-1975, 1980-1985, 1990-1995 and 2000-2005.

Government views and policies

Population policy variable	*1976*	*1986*	*1996*	*2005*
Population size and growth				
View on growth	Too high	Too high	Too high	Too high
Policy on growth	Lower	Lower	Lower	Lower
Population age structure				
Level of concern about				
Size of the working-age population	..	..	..	Major concern
Ageing of the population	..	..	..	Major concern
Fertility and family planning				
View on fertility level	Too high	Too high	Too high	Too high
Policy	Lower	Lower	Lower	Lower
Access to contraceptive methods	Direct support	Direct support	Direct support	Direct support
Adolescent fertility				
Level of concern	..	..	Major concern	Major concern
Policies and programmes	..	..	Yes	Yes
Health and mortality				
View				
Expectation of life	Unacceptable	Unacceptable	Unacceptable	Unacceptable
Under-five mortality	..	..	Unacceptable	Unacceptable
Maternal mortality	..	..	..	Unacceptable
Level of concern about HIV/AIDS	..	..	Major concern	Major concern
Measures implemented to control HIV/AIDS*	..	..	..	1,2,3,4,5
Grounds on which abortion is permitted**	..	..	1,2,3,4,5,6	1,2,3,4,5,6
Spatial distribution and internal migration				
View on spatial distribution	Major change desired	Minor change desired	Major change desired	Major change desired
Policies on internal migration				
From rural to urban areas	..	..	..	Lower
From rural to rural areas	..	..	..	Maintain
From urban to rural areas	..	..	..	Raise
From urban to urban areas	..	..	..	Maintain
Into urban agglomerations	Lower	..	Lower	Lower
International migration				
Immigration				
View	Satisfactory	Satisfactory	Satisfactory	Satisfactory
Policy	Maintain	Maintain	Maintain	Maintain
Permanent settlement	..	..	..	..
Temporary workers	..	..	..	..
Highly skilled workers	..	..	..	Maintain
Family reunification	..	..	..	..
Integration of non-nationals	..	..	..	..
Emigration				
View	Satisfactory	Satisfactory	Satisfactory	Too low
Policy	Maintain	Maintain	Maintain	Raise
Encouraging the return of nationals	No	..	Yes	..

* Measures implemented to control HIV/AIDS: (1) blood screening; (2) information/education campaigns; (3) access to antiretroviral treatment; (4) non-discriminatory policies; (5) promoting condom use.

** Grounds on which abortion is permitted: (1) to save the woman's life; (2) to preserve physical health; (3) to preserve mental health; (4) rape or incest; (5) foetal impairment; (6) economic or social reasons; (7) on request.

Population indicators

Indicator	*1975*	*1985*	*1995*	*2005*
Population size and growth				
Population size (thousands)	620 701	766 053	935 572	1 103 371
Annual growth rate (percentage)*	2.2	2.1	1.9	1.6
Population age structure				
Percentage of population under age 15	40	38	36	32
Percentage of population aged 60 or older	6	7	7	8
Fertility and family planning				
Total fertility (births per woman)*	5.4	4.5	3.8	3.1
Teenage fertility rate (per 1,000 women, aged 15 - 19)*	179	148	110	80
Percentage of births to women under age 20*	21	21	17	16
Percentage of births to women aged 35 or older*	11	10	9	9
Percentage of married women using contraception				
Modern methods	10[a]	38[b]	43[c]	..
All methods	14[a]	43[b]	48[c]	..
Health and mortality				
Life expectancy at birth (years)*				
Males	51	55	59	62
Females	49	55	60	65
Both sexes combined	50	55	59	63
Infant mortality rate (per 1,000 births)*	132	105	85	68
Mortality under age 5 (per 1,000 births)*	209	165	128	99
Maternal mortality ratio (per 100,000 births) (2000)	..	..	..	540
HIV/AIDS (2003)				
Number of infected adults (thousands)	..	..	..	..
Adult prevalence rate (percentage)	..	..	..	..
Spatial distribution				
Population density (per sq. km)	189	233	285	336
Urban population (percentage)	21	24	27	29
Annual urban growth rate (percentage)*	3.8	3.1	2.7	2.3
Annual rural growth rate (percentage)*	1.8	1.7	1.6	1.2
International migration				
International migrant stock				
Number of migrants (thousands)	8 973	8 131	6 951	5 700
Percentage of total population	1.4	1.1	0.7	0.5

* For the periods 1970-1975, 1980-1985, 1990-1995 and 2000-2005.
[a] For 1970.
[b] For 1988.
[c] For 1998/1999.

Government views and policies

Population policy variable	*1976*	*1986*	*1996*	*2005*
Population size and growth				
View on growth	Too high	Too high	Too high	Too high
Policy on growth	Lower	Lower	Lower	Lower
Population age structure				
Level of concern about				
Size of the working-age population	..	..	..	Major concern
Ageing of the population	..	..	..	Minor concern
Fertility and family planning				
View on fertility level	Too high	Too high	Too high	Too high
Policy	Lower	Lower	Lower	Lower
Access to contraceptive methods	Direct support	Direct support	Direct support	Direct support
Adolescent fertility				
Level of concern	..	..	Major concern	Major concern
Policies and programmes	..	..	Yes	Yes
Health and mortality				
View				
Expectation of life	Unacceptable	Unacceptable	Unacceptable	Unacceptable
Under-five mortality	..	..	Unacceptable	Unacceptable
Maternal mortality	..	..	..	Unacceptable
Level of concern about HIV/AIDS	..	..	Major concern	Major concern
Measures implemented to control HIV/AIDS*	..	..	..	1,2,3,4,5
Grounds on which abortion is permitted**	..	..	1	1
Spatial distribution and internal migration				
View on spatial distribution	Major change desired	Major change desired	Major change desired	Major change desired
Policies on internal migration				
From rural to urban areas	..	..	..	Lower
From rural to rural areas	..	..	..	No intervention
From urban to rural areas	..	..	..	Raise
From urban to urban areas	..	..	..	Maintain
Into urban agglomerations	..	..	Lower	Lower
International migration				
Immigration				
View	Satisfactory	Satisfactory	Too high	Too low
Policy	Maintain	Maintain	Lower	Maintain
Permanent settlement	..	..	Lower	Maintain
Temporary workers	..	..	..	Maintain
Highly skilled workers	..	..	..	Maintain
Family reunification	..	..	..	Maintain
Integration of non-nationals	..	..	..	No
Emigration				
View	Satisfactory	Satisfactory	Satisfactory	Too low
Policy	Maintain	Maintain	No intervention	Raise
Encouraging the return of nationals	..	..	..	No

* Measures implemented to control HIV/AIDS: (1) blood screening; (2) information/education campaigns; (3) access to antiretroviral treatment; (4) non-discriminatory policies; (5) promoting condom use.

** Grounds on which abortion is permitted: (1) to save the woman's life; (2) to preserve physical health; (3) to preserve mental health; (4) rape or incest; (5) foetal impairment; (6) economic or social reasons; (7) on request.

Population indicators

Indicator	*1975*	*1985*	*1995*	*2005*
Population size and growth				
Population size (thousands)	134 395	166 180	195 649	222 781
Annual growth rate (percentage)*	2.3	2.0	1.5	1.3
Population age structure				
Percentage of population under age 15	41	38	33	28
Percentage of population aged 60 or older	5	6	7	8
Fertility and family planning				
Total fertility (births per woman)*	5.2	4.1	2.9	2.4
Teenage fertility rate (per 1,000 women, aged 15 - 19)*	127	96	62	55
Percentage of births to women under age 20*	16	16	14	13
Percentage of births to women aged 35 or older*	14	11	12	10
Percentage of married women using contraception				
Modern methods	17[a]	37	55[b]	57[c]
All methods	18[a]	39	57[b]	60[c]
Health and mortality				
Life expectancy at birth (years)*				
Males	48	55	61	65
Females	51	58	65	69
Both sexes combined	49	56	63	67
Infant mortality rate (per 1,000 births)*	126	89	59	43
Mortality under age 5 (per 1,000 births)*	185	126	79	54
Maternal mortality ratio (per 100,000 births) (2000)	..	..	..	230
HIV/AIDS (2003)				
Number of infected adults (thousands)	..	..	..	110
Adult prevalence rate (percentage)	..	..	..	0.1
Spatial distribution				
Population density (per sq. km)	71	87	103	117
Urban population (percentage)	19	26	36	48
Annual urban growth rate (percentage)*	4.7	5.4	4.6	3.9
Annual rural growth rate (percentage)*	1.7	1.0	0.1	-0.9
International migration				
International migrant stock				
Number of migrants (thousands)	928	593	219	160
Percentage of total population	0.7	0.4	0.1	0.1

* For the periods 1970-1975, 1980-1985, 1990-1995 and 2000-2005.
[a] For 1976.
[b] For 1997.
[c] For 2002/2003.

Government views and policies

Population policy variable	*1976*	*1986*	*1996*	*2005*
Population size and growth				
View on growth	Too high	Satisfactory	Too high	Too high
Policy on growth	Lower	No intervention	Lower	Lower
Population age structure				
Level of concern about				
Size of the working-age population	..	..	..	Major concern
Ageing of the population	..	..	..	Major concern
Fertility and family planning				
View on fertility level	Too high	Satisfactory	Too high	Too high
Policy	Lower	No intervention	Lower	Lower
Access to contraceptive methods	Direct support	Indirect support	Direct support	Direct support
Adolescent fertility				
Level of concern	..	..	Major concern	Major concern
Policies and programmes	..	..	Yes	Yes
Health and mortality				
View				
Expectation of life	Unacceptable	Unacceptable	Unacceptable	Unacceptable
Under-five mortality	..	..	Unacceptable	Unacceptable
Maternal mortality	..	..	..	Unacceptable
Level of concern about HIV/AIDS	..	..	Major concern	Major concern
Measures implemented to control HIV/AIDS*	..	..	..	1,2,3,5
Grounds on which abortion is permitted**	..	..	1	1
Spatial distribution and internal migration				
View on spatial distribution	Major change desired	Minor change desired	Major change desired	Minor change desired
Policies on internal migration				
From rural to urban areas	..	..	..	Lower
From rural to rural areas	..	..	..	Maintain
From urban to rural areas	..	..	..	..
From urban to urban areas	..	..	..	..
Into urban agglomerations	..	Lower	Lower	Lower
International migration				
Immigration				
View	Too low	Too high	Too high	Too high
Policy	Raise	Lower	Lower	Lower
Permanent settlement	..	..	Lower	Maintain
Temporary workers	..	..	No intervention	Maintain
Highly skilled workers	..	..	..	Maintain
Family reunification	..	..	No intervention	..
Integration of non-nationals	..	..	No	..
Emigration				
View	Satisfactory	Too high	Satisfactory	Satisfactory
Policy	Maintain	Lower	Lower	Lower
Encouraging the return of nationals	..	..	Yes	Yes

* Measures implemented to control HIV/AIDS: (1) blood screening; (2) information/education campaigns; (3) access to antiretroviral treatment; (4) non-discriminatory policies; (5) promoting condom use.

** Grounds on which abortion is permitted: (1) to save the woman's life; (2) to preserve physical health; (3) to preserve mental health; (4) rape or incest; (5) foetal impairment; (6) economic or social reasons; (7) on request.

Population indicators

Indicator	*1975*	*1985*	*1995*	*2005*
Population size and growth				
Population size (thousands)	33 344	48 418	62 324	69 515
Annual growth rate (percentage)*	2.9	4.2	1.9	0.9
Population age structure				
Percentage of population under age 15	44	45	43	29
Percentage of population aged 60 or older	5	6	6	6
Fertility and family planning				
Total fertility (births per woman)*	6.4	6.6	4.3	2.1
Teenage fertility rate (per 1,000 women, aged 15 - 19)*	134	139	90	22
Percentage of births to women under age 20*	16	15	15	7
Percentage of births to women aged 35 or older*	16	15	16	8
Percentage of married women using contraception				
Modern methods	..	28[a]	56[b]	..
All methods	36[c]	49[a]	73[b]	..
Health and mortality				
Life expectancy at birth (years)*				
Males	55	59	65	69
Females	55	61	68	72
Both sexes combined	55	60	66	70
Infant mortality rate (per 1,000 births)*	115	88	53	34
Mortality under age 5 (per 1,000 births)*	153	116	64	39
Maternal mortality ratio (per 100,000 births) (2000)	..	..	..	76
HIV/AIDS (2003)				
Number of infected adults (thousands)	..	..	..	31
Adult prevalence rate (percentage)	..	..	..	0.1
Spatial distribution				
Population density (per sq. km)	20	29	38	42
Urban population (percentage)	46	53	60	68
Annual urban growth rate (percentage)*	4.7	5.6	3.2	2.3
Annual rural growth rate (percentage)*	1.5	2.6	0.0	-0.9
International migration				
International migrant stock				
Number of migrants (thousands)	766	2 423	2 478	1 959
Percentage of total population	2.3	5	4	2.8

* For the periods 1970-1975, 1980-1985, 1990-1995 and 2000-2005.
[a] For 1989.
[b] For 1997.
[c] For 1977.

Government views and policies

Population policy variable	*1976*	*1986*	*1996*	*2005*
Population size and growth				
View on growth	Satisfactory	Too low	Too low	Satisfactory
Policy on growth	No intervention	Raise	Raise	Maintain
Population age structure				
Level of concern about				
Size of the working-age population	..	..	..	Major concern
Ageing of the population	..	..	..	Major concern
Fertility and family planning				
View on fertility level	Satisfactory	Too low	Too low	Satisfactory
Policy	Maintain	Raise	Raise	No intervention
Access to contraceptive methods	Direct support	Limits	No support	Direct support
Adolescent fertility				
Level of concern	..	..	..	Minor concern
Policies and programmes	..	..	..	No
Health and mortality				
View				
Expectation of life	Acceptable	Acceptable	Unacceptable	Unacceptable
Under-five mortality	..	..	..	Unacceptable
Maternal mortality	..	..	..	Unacceptable
Level of concern about HIV/AIDS	..	..	..	Major concern
Measures implemented to control HIV/AIDS*	..	..	..	1,2,3
Grounds on which abortion is permitted**	..	..	1,2,3,4,5	1
Spatial distribution and internal migration				
View on spatial distribution	Minor change desired	Minor change desired	Minor change desired	Major change desired
Policies on internal migration				
From rural to urban areas	..	..	..	..
From rural to rural areas	..	..	..	..
From urban to rural areas	..	..	..	..
From urban to urban areas	..	..	..	..
Into urban agglomerations	..	Lower	..	Lower
International migration				
Immigration				
View	Too low	Satisfactory	Satisfactory	Satisfactory
Policy	Raise	Maintain	Maintain	Maintain
Permanent settlement	..	..	Maintain	Maintain
Temporary workers	..	..	..	Maintain
Highly skilled workers	..	..	..	Maintain
Family reunification	..	..	..	..
Integration of non-nationals	..	..	..	Yes
Emigration				
View	Satisfactory	Satisfactory	Satisfactory	Too high
Policy	Maintain	Maintain	Maintain	Lower
Encouraging the return of nationals	..	..	..	..

* Measures implemented to control HIV/AIDS: (1) blood screening; (2) information/education campaigns; (3) access to antiretroviral treatment; (4) non-discriminatory policies; (5) promoting condom use.
** Grounds on which abortion is permitted: (1) to save the woman's life; (2) to preserve physical health; (3) to preserve mental health; (4) rape or incest; (5) foetal impairment; (6) economic or social reasons; (7) on request.

Population indicators

Indicator	*1975*	*1985*	*1995*	*2005*
Population size and growth				
Population size (thousands)	11 972	16 288	21 632	28 807
Annual growth rate (percentage)*	3.4	2.9	3.1	2.8
Population age structure				
Percentage of population under age 15	48	46	44	41
Percentage of population aged 60 or older	5	5	5	5
Fertility and family planning				
Total fertility (births per woman)*	7.2	6.4	5.7	4.8
Teenage fertility rate (per 1,000 women, aged 15 - 19)*	125	65	49	42
Percentage of births to women under age 20*	15	9	7	6
Percentage of births to women aged 35 or older*	14	19	18	17
Percentage of married women using contraception				
Modern methods	13[a]	10[b]	..	..
All methods	15[a]	14[b]	..	..
Health and mortality				
Life expectancy at birth (years)*				
Males	56	61	58	57
Females	58	64	61	60
Both sexes combined	57	62	59	59
Infant mortality rate (per 1,000 births)*	85	60	73	94
Mortality under age 5 (per 1,000 births)*	120	78	101	124
Maternal mortality ratio (per 100,000 births) (2000)	..	..	..	250
HIV/AIDS (2003)				
Number of infected adults (thousands)	..	..	..	<1
Adult prevalence rate (percentage)	..	..	..	<0.1
Spatial distribution				
Population density (per sq. km)	27	37	49	66
Urban population (percentage)	61	69	69	67
Annual urban growth rate (percentage)*	5.1	4.2	2.8	2.4
Annual rural growth rate (percentage)*	0.7	1.3	3.6	3.3
International migration				
International migrant stock				
Number of migrants (thousands)	7	85	134	28
Percentage of total population	0.1	0.5	0.6	0.1

* For the periods 1970-1975, 1980-1985, 1990-1995 and 2000-2005.
[a] For 1974.
[b] For 1989.

Government views and policies

Population policy variable	*1976*	*1986*	*1996*	*2005*
Population size and growth				
View on growth	Too low	Satisfactory	Satisfactory	Satisfactory
Policy on growth	No intervention	Maintain	No intervention	Maintain
Population age structure				
Level of concern about				
Size of the working-age population	..	..	..	Minor concern
Ageing of the population	..	..	..	Major concern
Fertility and family planning				
View on fertility level	Satisfactory	Satisfactory	Satisfactory	Satisfactory
Policy	Maintain	Maintain	Maintain	Maintain
Access to contraceptive methods	No support	Limits	Direct support	Direct support
Adolescent fertility				
Level of concern	..	..	..	Major concern
Policies and programmes	..	..	Yes	Yes
Health and mortality				
View				
Expectation of life	Acceptable	Acceptable	Acceptable	Acceptable
Under-five mortality	..	..	..	Acceptable
Maternal mortality	..	..	..	Acceptable
Level of concern about HIV/AIDS	..	..	Major concern	Minor concern
Measures implemented to control HIV/AIDS*	..	..	..	1,2,3,4,5
Grounds on which abortion is permitted**	..	..	1	1
Spatial distribution and internal migration				
View on spatial distribution	Minor change desired	Minor change desired	Minor change desired	Minor change desired
Policies on internal migration				
From rural to urban areas	..	..	..	Lower
From rural to rural areas	..	..	..	..
From urban to rural areas	..	..	..	..
From urban to urban areas	..	..	..	..
Into urban agglomerations	Lower	..	..	Lower
International migration				
Immigration				
View	Satisfactory	Satisfactory	Satisfactory	Satisfactory
Policy	Maintain	Maintain	Maintain	Maintain
Permanent settlement	..	..	Maintain	Maintain
Temporary workers	..	..	..	Lower
Highly skilled workers	..	..	..	Raise
Family reunification	..	..	..	Maintain
Integration of non-nationals	..	..	..	Yes
Emigration				
View	Too high	Too high	Too high	Satisfactory
Policy	Lower	Lower	Lower	No intervention
Encouraging the return of nationals	No	..	..	Yes

* Measures implemented to control HIV/AIDS: (1) blood screening; (2) information/education campaigns; (3) access to antiretroviral treatment; (4) non-discriminatory policies; (5) promoting condom use.

** Grounds on which abortion is permitted: (1) to save the woman's life; (2) to preserve physical health; (3) to preserve mental health; (4) rape or incest; (5) foetal impairment; (6) economic or social reasons; (7) on request.

Population indicators

Indicator	*1975*	*1985*	*1995*	*2005*
Population size and growth				
Population size (thousands)	3 177	3 539	3 609	4 148
Annual growth rate (percentage)*	1.5	0.8	0.5	1.7
Population age structure				
Percentage of population under age 15	31	30	24	20
Percentage of population aged 60 or older	15	14	15	15
Fertility and family planning				
Total fertility (births per woman)*	3.8	2.9	2.0	1.9
Teenage fertility rate (per 1,000 women, aged 15 - 19)*	34	26	18	15
Percentage of births to women under age 20*	7	6	6	4
Percentage of births to women aged 35 or older*	17	17	20	20
Percentage of married women using contraception				
Modern methods	..	..	..	..
All methods	..	..	..	..
Health and mortality				
Life expectancy at birth (years)*				
Males	69	70	73	75
Females	74	76	78	80
Both sexes combined	71	73	75	78
Infant mortality rate (per 1,000 births)*	18	10	7	5
Mortality under age 5 (per 1,000 births)*	20	12	8	7
Maternal mortality ratio (per 100,000 births) (2000)	..	..	..	5
HIV/AIDS (2003)				
Number of infected adults (thousands)	..	..	..	3
Adult prevalence rate (percentage)	..	..	..	0.1
Spatial distribution				
Population density (per sq. km)	45	50	51	59
Urban population (percentage)	54	56	58	60
Annual urban growth rate (percentage)*	2.2	1.1	0.9	1.5
Annual rural growth rate (percentage)*	0.7	0.4	0.1	0.5
International migration				
International migrant stock				
Number of migrants (thousands)	171	225	264	585
Percentage of total population	5.4	6.4	7.3	14.1

* For the periods 1970-1975, 1980-1985, 1990-1995 and 2000-2005.

Government views and policies

Population policy variable	*1976*	*1986*	*1996*	*2005*
Population size and growth				
View on growth	Too low	Too low	Too low	Too low
Policy on growth	Raise	Raise	Raise	Raise
Population age structure				
Level of concern about				
Size of the working-age population	..	..	..	Major concern
Ageing of the population	..	..	..	Major concern
Fertility and family planning				
View on fertility level	Too low	Too low	Too low	Too low
Policy	Raise	Raise	Raise	Raise
Access to contraceptive methods	Direct support	Direct support	Direct support	Indirect support
Adolescent fertility				
Level of concern	..	..	..	Not a concern
Policies and programmes	..	..	..	Yes
Health and mortality				
View				
Expectation of life	Acceptable	Acceptable	Acceptable	Acceptable
Under-five mortality	..	..	..	Unacceptable
Maternal mortality	..	..	..	Unacceptable
Level of concern about HIV/AIDS	..	..	..	Major concern
Measures implemented to control HIV/AIDS*	..	..	..	1,2,3,4,5
Grounds on which abortion is permitted**	..	..	1,2,3,4,5	1,2,3,4,5
Spatial distribution and internal migration				
View on spatial distribution	Minor change desired	Minor change desired	Minor change desired	Minor change desired
Policies on internal migration				
From rural to urban areas	..	..	..	No intervention
From rural to rural areas	..	..	..	No intervention
From urban to rural areas	..	..	..	Lower
From urban to urban areas	..	..	..	No intervention
Into urban agglomerations	..	..	..	No intervention
International migration				
Immigration				
View	Too low	Too low	Too low	Too low
Policy	Raise	Raise	Raise	Raise
Permanent settlement	..	..	Raise	Raise
Temporary workers	..	..	..	Lower
Highly skilled workers	..	..	..	Maintain
Family reunification	..	..	..	Lower
Integration of non-nationals	..	..	Yes	Yes
Emigration				
View	Satisfactory	Too high	Too high	Too high
Policy	Maintain	Lower	Lower	Lower
Encouraging the return of nationals	..	..	Yes	Yes

* Measures implemented to control HIV/AIDS: (1) blood screening; (2) information/education campaigns; (3) access to antiretroviral treatment; (4) non-discriminatory policies; (5) promoting condom use.

** Grounds on which abortion is permitted: (1) to save the woman's life; (2) to preserve physical health; (3) to preserve mental health; (4) rape or incest; (5) foetal impairment; (6) economic or social reasons; (7) on request.

Population indicators

Indicator	*1975*	*1985*	*1995*	*2005*
Population size and growth				
Population size (thousands)	3 358	4 103	5 374	6 725
Annual growth rate (percentage)*	2.9	1.7	3.5	2.0
Population age structure				
Percentage of population under age 15	33	33	29	28
Percentage of population aged 60 or older	12	12	13	13
Fertility and family planning				
Total fertility (births per woman)*	3.8	3.1	2.9	2.9
Teenage fertility rate (per 1,000 women, aged 15 - 19)*	23	19	18	16
Percentage of births to women under age 20*	4	3	4	3
Percentage of births to women aged 35 or older*	13	13	16	16
Percentage of married women using contraception				
Modern methods	..	52[a]	..	..
All methods	..	68[a]	..	..
Health and mortality				
Life expectancy at birth (years)*				
Males	70	73	75	78
Females	73	76	79	82
Both sexes combined	72	74	77	80
Infant mortality rate (per 1,000 births)*	22	14	9	5
Mortality under age 5 (per 1,000 births)*	24	16	10	6
Maternal mortality ratio (per 100,000 births) (2000)	..	..	..	17
HIV/AIDS (2003)				
Number of infected adults (thousands)	..	..	..	3
Adult prevalence rate (percentage)	..	..	..	0.1
Spatial distribution				
Population density (per sq. km)	152	185	243	304
Urban population (percentage)	87	90	91	92
Annual urban growth rate (percentage)*	3.5	2.0	3.5	2.1
Annual rural growth rate (percentage)*	-0.4	-0.5	2.2	1.4
International migration				
International migrant stock				
Number of migrants (thousands)	1 417	1 523	1 919	2 661
Percentage of total population	42.2	37.1	35.7	39.6

* For the periods 1970-1975, 1980-1985, 1990-1995 and 2000-2005.
[a] For 1987/1988.

Government views and policies

Population policy variable	*1976*	*1986*	*1996*	*2005*
Population size and growth				
View on growth	Satisfactory	Satisfactory	Satisfactory	Too low
Policy on growth	No intervention	No intervention	No intervention	Raise
Population age structure				
Level of concern about				
Size of the working-age population	..	..	..	Major concern
Ageing of the population	..	..	..	Major concern
Fertility and family planning				
View on fertility level	Satisfactory	Satisfactory	Satisfactory	Too low
Policy	No intervention	No intervention	No intervention	Raise
Access to contraceptive methods	Indirect support	Direct support	Direct support	Indirect support
Adolescent fertility				
Level of concern	..	..	Not a concern	Not a concern
Policies and programmes	..	..	No	No
Health and mortality				
View				
Expectation of life	Unacceptable	Unacceptable	Acceptable	Acceptable
Under-five mortality	..	..	Acceptable	Acceptable
Maternal mortality	..	..	..	Acceptable
Level of concern about HIV/AIDS	..	..	Major concern	Major concern
Measures implemented to control HIV/AIDS*	..	..	..	1,2,3,4
Grounds on which abortion is permitted**	..	..	1,2,3,4,5,6	1,2,3,4,5,6,7
Spatial distribution and internal migration				
View on spatial distribution	Minor change desired	Minor change desired	Satisfactory	Minor change desired
Policies on internal migration				
From rural to urban areas	..	..	..	Lower
From rural to rural areas	..	..	..	No intervention
From urban to rural areas	..	..	..	No intervention
From urban to urban areas	..	..	..	No intervention
Into urban agglomerations	Lower	No intervention	No intervention	No intervention
International migration				
Immigration				
View	Satisfactory	Too high	Satisfactory	Too high
Policy	Maintain	Lower	Lower	Lower
Permanent settlement	..	..	Lower	Lower
Temporary workers	..	..	Lower	Raise
Highly skilled workers	..	..	..	No intervention
Family reunification	..	..	Maintain	Maintain
Integration of non-nationals	..	..	Yes	Yes
Emigration				
View	Too high	Satisfactory	Satisfactory	Satisfactory
Policy	Lower	Lower	No intervention	No intervention
Encouraging the return of nationals	No	..	No	No

* Measures implemented to control HIV/AIDS: (1) blood screening; (2) information/education campaigns; (3) access to antiretroviral treatment; (4) non-discriminatory policies; (5) promoting condom use.
** Grounds on which abortion is permitted: (1) to save the woman's life; (2) to preserve physical health; (3) to preserve mental health; (4) rape or incest; (5) foetal impairment; (6) economic or social reasons; (7) on request.

Population indicators

Indicator	*1975*	*1985*	*1995*	*2005*
Population size and growth				
Population size (thousands)	55 441	56 593	57 301	58 093
Annual growth rate (percentage)*	0.6	0.1	0.2	0.1
Population age structure				
Percentage of population under age 15	24	20	15	14
Percentage of population aged 60 or older	17	18	22	26
Fertility and family planning				
Total fertility (births per woman)*	2.3	1.5	1.3	1.3
Teenage fertility rate (per 1,000 women, aged 15 - 19)*	12	8	7	7
Percentage of births to women under age 20*	3	3	2	2
Percentage of births to women aged 35 or older*	18	17	17	21
Percentage of married women using contraception				
Modern methods	32[a]	..	39[b]	..
All methods	78[a]	..	60[b]	..
Health and mortality				
Life expectancy at birth (years)*				
Males	69	71	74	77
Females	75	78	80	83
Both sexes combined	72	75	77	80
Infant mortality rate (per 1,000 births)*	26	13	7	5
Mortality under age 5 (per 1,000 births)*	30	15	9	6
Maternal mortality ratio (per 100,000 births) (2000)	..	..	..	5
HIV/AIDS (2003)				
Number of infected adults (thousands)	..	..	..	140
Adult prevalence rate (percentage)	..	..	..	0.5
Spatial distribution				
Population density (per sq. km)	184	188	190	193
Urban population (percentage)	66	67	67	68
Annual urban growth rate (percentage)*	1.0	0.1	0.3	0.0
Annual rural growth rate (percentage)*	-0.2	-0.1	0.1	-0.3
International migration				
International migrant stock				
Number of migrants (thousands)	1 006	1 222	1 483	2 519
Percentage of total population	1.8	2.2	2.6	4.3

* For the periods 1970-1975, 1980-1985, 1990-1995 and 2000-2005.
[a] For 1979.
[b] For 1995/1996.

Government views and policies

Population policy variable	*1976*	*1986*	*1996*	*2005*
Population size and growth				
View on growth	Too high	Too high	Too high	Satisfactory
Policy on growth	Lower	Lower	Lower	Lower
Population age structure				
Level of concern about				
Size of the working-age population	..	..	..	Minor concern
Ageing of the population	..	..	..	Major concern
Fertility and family planning				
View on fertility level	Too high	Too high	Too high	Too high
Policy	Lower	Lower	Lower	Lower
Access to contraceptive methods	Direct support	Direct support	Direct support	Direct support
Adolescent fertility				
Level of concern	..	..	Major concern	Major concern
Policies and programmes	..	..	Yes	Yes
Health and mortality				
View				
Expectation of life	Acceptable	Unacceptable	Acceptable	Acceptable
Under-five mortality	..	..	Unacceptable	Unacceptable
Maternal mortality	..	..	..	Unacceptable
Level of concern about HIV/AIDS	..	..	Major concern	Major concern
Measures implemented to control HIV/AIDS*	..	..	..	1,2,3,4,5
Grounds on which abortion is permitted**	..	..	1,2,3	1,2,3
Spatial distribution and internal migration				
View on spatial distribution	Major change desired	Major change desired	Major change desired	Major change desired
Policies on internal migration				
From rural to urban areas	..	..	..	No intervention
From rural to rural areas	..	..	..	No intervention
From urban to rural areas	..	..	..	No intervention
From urban to urban areas	..	..	..	No intervention
Into urban agglomerations	Lower	No intervention	Lower	Lower
International migration				
Immigration				
View	Satisfactory	Satisfactory	Satisfactory	Satisfactory
Policy	Maintain	Maintain	Maintain	Maintain
Permanent settlement	..	..	..	Maintain
Temporary workers	..	..	..	Lower
Highly skilled workers	..	..	..	Maintain
Family reunification	..	..	..	Maintain
Integration of non-nationals	..	..	Yes	No
Emigration				
View	Too high	Satisfactory	Too high	Too high
Policy	Lower	Maintain	Lower	No intervention
Encouraging the return of nationals	Yes	..	Yes	Yes

* Measures implemented to control HIV/AIDS: (1) blood screening; (2) information/education campaigns; (3) access to antiretroviral treatment; (4) non-discriminatory policies; (5) promoting condom use.

** Grounds on which abortion is permitted: (1) to save the woman's life; (2) to preserve physical health; (3) to preserve mental health; (4) rape or incest; (5) foetal impairment; (6) economic or social reasons; (7) on request.

Population indicators

Indicator	*1975*	*1985*	*1995*	*2005*
Population size and growth				
Population size (thousands)	2 013	2 297	2 484	2 651
Annual growth rate (percentage)*	1.5	1.5	1.0	0.5
Population age structure				
Percentage of population under age 15	45	37	34	31
Percentage of population aged 60 or older	8	9	10	10
Fertility and family planning				
Total fertility (births per woman)*	5.0	3.6	2.8	2.4
Teenage fertility rate (per 1,000 women, aged 15 - 19)*	182	129	103	82
Percentage of births to women under age 20*	29	26	22	20
Percentage of births to women aged 35 or older*	10	8	9	11
Percentage of married women using contraception				
Modern methods	36[a]	48[b]	63[c]	..
All methods	38[a]	51[b]	66[c]	..
Health and mortality				
Life expectancy at birth (years)*				
Males	67	69	70	69
Females	71	72	74	73
Both sexes combined	69	71	72	71
Infant mortality rate (per 1,000 births)*	45	31	17	15
Mortality under age 5 (per 1,000 births)*	70	45	23	21
Maternal mortality ratio (per 100,000 births) (2000)	..	..	..	87
HIV/AIDS (2003)				
Number of infected adults (thousands)	..	..	..	21
Adult prevalence rate (percentage)	..	..	..	1.2
Spatial distribution				
Population density (per sq. km)	183	209	226	241
Urban population (percentage)	44	49	52	52
Annual urban growth rate (percentage)*	2.7	2.5	1.0	1.0
Annual rural growth rate (percentage)*	0.6	0.5	0.7	0.9
International migration				
International migrant stock				
Number of migrants (thousands)	28	22	20	18
Percentage of total population	1.4	1	0.8	0.7

* For the periods 1970-1975, 1980-1985, 1990-1995 and 2000-2005.
[a] For 1976.
[b] For 1983.
[c] For 1997.

Government views and policies

Population policy variable	*1976*	*1986*	*1996*	*2005*
Population size and growth				
View on growth	Satisfactory	Satisfactory	Satisfactory	Too low
Policy on growth	No intervention	No intervention	No intervention	Raise
Population age structure				
Level of concern about				
Size of the working-age population	..	..	..	Major concern
Ageing of the population	..	..	..	Major concern
Fertility and family planning				
View on fertility level	Satisfactory	Satisfactory	Too low	Too low
Policy	No intervention	No intervention	No intervention	Raise
Access to contraceptive methods	Direct support	Direct support	Direct support	Indirect support
Adolescent fertility				
Level of concern	..	..	Minor concern	Minor concern
Policies and programmes	..	..	..	No
Health and mortality				
View				
Expectation of life	Acceptable	Acceptable	Acceptable	Acceptable
Under-five mortality	..	..	Unacceptable	Unacceptable
Maternal mortality	..	..	..	Unacceptable
Level of concern about HIV/AIDS	..	..	Major concern	Major concern
Measures implemented to control HIV/AIDS*	..	..	..	1,2,3,4,5
Grounds on which abortion is permitted**	..	..	1,2,3,4,6	1,2,4,6
Spatial distribution and internal migration				
View on spatial distribution	Major change desired	Minor change desired	Major change desired	Major change desired
Policies on internal migration				
From rural to urban areas	..	..	..	Lower
From rural to rural areas	..	..	..	No intervention
From urban to rural areas	..	..	..	Raise
From urban to urban areas	..	..	..	No intervention
Into urban agglomerations	..	..	Lower	No intervention
International migration				
Immigration				
View	Satisfactory	Satisfactory	Satisfactory	Satisfactory
Policy	Maintain	Maintain	Maintain	Maintain
Permanent settlement	..	..	Maintain	Maintain
Temporary workers	..	..	Raise	Maintain
Highly skilled workers	..	..	..	Raise
Family reunification	..	..	Maintain	Maintain
Integration of non-nationals	..	..	No	No
Emigration				
View	Satisfactory	Too low	Satisfactory	Satisfactory
Policy	Maintain	Raise	No intervention	No intervention
Encouraging the return of nationals	..	..	..	No

* Measures implemented to control HIV/AIDS: (1) blood screening; (2) information/education campaigns; (3) access to antiretroviral treatment; (4) non-discriminatory policies; (5) promoting condom use.

** Grounds on which abortion is permitted: (1) to save the woman's life; (2) to preserve physical health; (3) to preserve mental health; (4) rape or incest; (5) foetal impairment; (6) economic or social reasons; (7) on request.

Population indicators

Indicator	*1975*	*1985*	*1995*	*2005*
Population size and growth				
Population size (thousands)	111 524	120 837	125 472	128 085
Annual growth rate (percentage)*	1.3	0.7	0.3	0.2
Population age structure				
Percentage of population under age 15	24	22	16	14
Percentage of population aged 60 or older	12	15	21	26
Fertility and family planning				
Total fertility (births per woman)*	2.1	1.8	1.5	1.3
Teenage fertility rate (per 1,000 women, aged 15 - 19)*	7	6	5	4
Percentage of births to women under age 20*	1	2	2	1
Percentage of births to women aged 35 or older*	10	13	12	12
Percentage of married women using contraception				
Modern methods	59	51[a]	53[b]	51[c]
All methods	61	57[a]	59[b]	56[c]
Health and mortality				
Life expectancy at birth (years)*				
Males	71	74	76	78
Females	76	80	82	85
Both sexes combined	73	77	80	82
Infant mortality rate (per 1,000 births)*	12	7	4	3
Mortality under age 5 (per 1,000 births)*	20	10	6	4
Maternal mortality ratio (per 100,000 births) (2000)	..	..	..	10
HIV/AIDS (2003)				
Number of infected adults (thousands)	..	..	..	12
Adult prevalence rate (percentage)	..	..	..	<0.1
Spatial distribution				
Population density (per sq. km)	295	320	332	339
Urban population (percentage)	57	61	65	66
Annual urban growth rate (percentage)*	2.7	1.0	0.8	0.3
Annual rural growth rate (percentage)*	-0.3	0.2	-0.5	-0.1
International migration				
International migrant stock				
Number of migrants (thousands)	640	717	1 261	2 048
Percentage of total population	0.6	0.6	1	1.6

* For the periods 1970-1975, 1980-1985, 1990-1995 and 2000-2005.
[a] For 1984.
[b] For 1994.
[c] For 2000.

Government views and policies

Population policy variable	*1976*	*1986*	*1996*	*2005*
Population size and growth				
View on growth	Satisfactory	Satisfactory	Too high	Too high
Policy on growth	No intervention	No intervention	Lower	Lower
Population age structure				
Level of concern about				
Size of the working-age population	..	..	..	Major concern
Ageing of the population	..	..	..	Minor concern
Fertility and family planning				
View on fertility level	Too high	Satisfactory	Too high	Too high
Policy	No intervention	No intervention	Lower	Lower
Access to contraceptive methods	Direct support	Indirect support	Direct support	Direct support
Adolescent fertility				
Level of concern	..	..	Not a concern	Not a concern
Policies and programmes	..	..	No	No
Health and mortality				
View				
Expectation of life	Acceptable	Unacceptable	Acceptable	Acceptable
Under-five mortality	..	..	Acceptable	Unacceptable
Maternal mortality	..	..	..	Unacceptable
Level of concern about HIV/AIDS	..	..	Major concern	Major concern
Measures implemented to control HIV/AIDS*	..	..	..	1,2,3,4
Grounds on which abortion is permitted**	..	..	1,2,3	1,2,3,5
Spatial distribution and internal migration				
View on spatial distribution	Major change desired	Minor change desired	Satisfactory	Major change desired
Policies on internal migration				
From rural to urban areas	..	..	..	Lower
From rural to rural areas	..	..	..	No intervention
From urban to rural areas	..	..	..	Raise
From urban to urban areas	..	..	..	No intervention
Into urban agglomerations	..	Lower	No intervention	Lower
International migration				
Immigration				
View	Satisfactory	Satisfactory	Satisfactory	Too high
Policy	Maintain	Maintain	Lower	Lower
Permanent settlement	..	..	Lower	Lower
Temporary workers	..	..	No intervention	Lower
Highly skilled workers	..	..	..	Lower
Family reunification	..	..	Lower	Maintain
Integration of non-nationals	..	..	No	No
Emigration				
View	Too high	Too high	Satisfactory	Too low
Policy	Lower	Lower	No intervention	Raise
Encouraging the return of nationals	..	..	No	No

* Measures implemented to control HIV/AIDS: (1) blood screening; (2) information/education campaigns; (3) access to antiretroviral treatment; (4) non-discriminatory policies; (5) promoting condom use.

** Grounds on which abortion is permitted: (1) to save the woman's life; (2) to preserve physical health; (3) to preserve mental health; (4) rape or incest; (5) foetal impairment; (6) economic or social reasons; (7) on request.

Population indicators

Indicator	*1975*	*1985*	*1995*	*2005*
Population size and growth				
Population size (thousands)	1 937	2 706	4 288	5 703
Annual growth rate (percentage)*	3.5	3.9	5.5	2.7
Population age structure				
Percentage of population under age 15	47	47	41	37
Percentage of population aged 60 or older	4	5	4	5
Fertility and family planning				
Total fertility (births per woman)*	7.8	6.8	5.1	3.5
Teenage fertility rate (per 1,000 women, aged 15 - 19)*	71	61	47	27
Percentage of births to women under age 20*	7	8	7	5
Percentage of births to women aged 35 or older*	16	16	13	15
Percentage of married women using contraception				
Modern methods	17[a]	22	27[b]	41[c]
All methods	25[a]	27	35[b]	56[c]
Health and mortality				
Life expectancy at birth (years)*				
Males	55	62	68	70
Females	58	66	70	73
Both sexes combined	57	64	69	71
Infant mortality rate (per 1,000 births)*	82	52	33	23
Mortality under age 5 (per 1,000 births)*	99	62	38	27
Maternal mortality ratio (per 100,000 births) (2000)	..	..	..	41
HIV/AIDS (2003)				
Number of infected adults (thousands)	..	..	..	<1
Adult prevalence rate (percentage)	..	..	..	<0.1
Spatial distribution				
Population density (per sq. km)	22	30	48	64
Urban population (percentage)	58	66	78	79
Annual urban growth rate (percentage)*	4.2	5.9	6.9	2.8
Annual rural growth rate (percentage)*	2.7	0.5	0.4	2.0
International migration				
International migrant stock				
Number of migrants (thousands)	676	942	1 618	2 225
Percentage of total population	34.9	34.8	37.7	39

* For the periods 1970-1975, 1980-1985, 1990-1995 and 2000-2005.
[a] For 1976.
[b] For 1990.
[c] For 2002.

Government views and policies

Population policy variable	*1976*	*1986*	*1996*	*2005*
Population size and growth				
View on growth	..	..	Too low	Too low
Policy on growth	..	..	Raise	Raise
Population age structure				
Level of concern about				
Size of the working-age population	..	..	..	Major concern
Ageing of the population	..	..	..	Major concern
Fertility and family planning				
View on fertility level	..	..	Too low	Too low
Policy	..	..	Raise	Raise
Access to contraceptive methods	..	..	Direct support	Indirect support
Adolescent fertility				
Level of concern	..	..	..	Major concern
Policies and programmes	..	..	Yes	Yes
Health and mortality				
View				
Expectation of life	..	..	Unacceptable	Unacceptable
Under-five mortality	..	..	..	Unacceptable
Maternal mortality	..	..	..	Unacceptable
Level of concern about HIV/AIDS	..	..	..	Major concern
Measures implemented to control HIV/AIDS*	..	..	..	1,2,3,4
Grounds on which abortion is permitted**	..	..	1,2,3,4,5,6,7	1,2,3,4,5,6,7
Spatial distribution and internal migration				
View on spatial distribution	..	..	Satisfactory	Major change desired
Policies on internal migration				
From rural to urban areas	..	..	..	Lower
From rural to rural areas	..	..	..	..
From urban to rural areas	..	..	..	..
From urban to urban areas	..	..	..	..
Into urban agglomerations	..	..	No intervention	Lower
International migration				
Immigration				
View	..	..	Satisfactory	Satisfactory
Policy	..	..	Maintain	Maintain
Permanent settlement	..	..	..	Maintain
Temporary workers	..	..	..	Maintain
Highly skilled workers	..	..	..	Raise
Family reunification	..	..	..	Maintain
Integration of non-nationals	..	..	..	Yes
Emigration				
View	..	..	Too high	Too high
Policy	..	..	Lower	Lower
Encouraging the return of nationals	..	..	Yes	Yes

* Measures implemented to control HIV/AIDS: (1) blood screening; (2) information/education campaigns; (3) access to antiretroviral treatment; (4) non-discriminatory policies; (5) promoting condom use.
** Grounds on which abortion is permitted: (1) to save the woman's life; (2) to preserve physical health; (3) to preserve mental health; (4) rape or incest; (5) foetal impairment; (6) economic or social reasons; (7) on request.

Population indicators

Indicator	*1975*	*1985*	*1995*	*2005*
Population size and growth				
Population size (thousands)	14 136	15 780	15 866	14 825
Annual growth rate (percentage)*	1.5	1.1	-0.8	-0.3
Population age structure				
Percentage of population under age 15	35	32	30	23
Percentage of population aged 60 or older	9	8	10	11
Fertility and family planning				
Total fertility (births per woman)*	3.5	3.0	2.5	2.0
Teenage fertility rate (per 1,000 women, aged 15 - 19)*	72	61	51	31
Percentage of births to women under age 20*	14	12	11	9
Percentage of births to women aged 35 or older*	8	6	9	10
Percentage of married women using contraception				
Modern methods	..	..	53[a]	..
All methods	..	..	66[a]	..
Health and mortality				
Life expectancy at birth (years)*				
Males	58	60	61	58
Females	68	71	70	69
Both sexes combined	63	66	65	63
Infant mortality rate (per 1,000 births)*	77	60	55	61
Mortality under age 5 (per 1,000 births)*	101	76	68	77
Maternal mortality ratio (per 100,000 births) (2000)	..	..	..	210
HIV/AIDS (2003)				
Number of infected adults (thousands)	..	..	..	16
Adult prevalence rate (percentage)	..	..	..	0.2
Spatial distribution				
Population density (per sq. km)	5	6	6	5
Urban population (percentage)	52	56	56	56
Annual urban growth rate (percentage)*	2.2	1.9	-0.5	-0.3
Annual rural growth rate (percentage)*	0.7	0.4	0.0	-0.4
International migration				
International migrant stock				
Number of migrants (thousands)	..	..	3 295	2 502
Percentage of total population	..	..	20.8	16.9

* For the periods 1970-1975, 1980-1985, 1990-1995 and 2000-2005.
[a] For 1999.

Government views and policies

Population policy variable	*1976*	*1986*	*1996*	*2005*
Population size and growth				
View on growth	Too high	Too high	Too high	Too high
Policy on growth	Lower	Lower	Lower	Lower
Population age structure				
Level of concern about				
Size of the working-age population	..	..	..	Major concern
Ageing of the population	..	..	..	Major concern
Fertility and family planning				
View on fertility level	Too high	Too high	Too high	Too high
Policy	Lower	Lower	Lower	Lower
Access to contraceptive methods	Direct support	Direct support	Direct support	Direct support
Adolescent fertility				
Level of concern	..	..	Major concern	Major concern
Policies and programmes	..	..	Yes	Yes
Health and mortality				
View				
Expectation of life	Unacceptable	Unacceptable	Unacceptable	Unacceptable
Under-five mortality	..	..	Unacceptable	Unacceptable
Maternal mortality	..	..	..	Unacceptable
Level of concern about HIV/AIDS	..	..	Major concern	Major concern
Measures implemented to control HIV/AIDS*	..	..	..	1,2,3,4,5
Grounds on which abortion is permitted**	..	..	1	1,2,3
Spatial distribution and internal migration				
View on spatial distribution	Major change desired	Major change desired	Minor change desired	Major change desired
Policies on internal migration				
From rural to urban areas	..	..	..	Lower
From rural to rural areas	..	..	..	No intervention
From urban to rural areas	..	..	..	Raise
From urban to urban areas	..	..	..	No intervention
Into urban agglomerations	No intervention	..	Lower	Lower
International migration				
Immigration				
View	Satisfactory	Satisfactory	Satisfactory	Satisfactory
Policy	Maintain	Maintain	Maintain	No intervention
Permanent settlement	..	..	..	Lower
Temporary workers	..	..	..	No intervention
Highly skilled workers	..	..	..	No intervention
Family reunification	..	..	..	No intervention
Integration of non-nationals	..	..	No	No
Emigration				
View	Satisfactory	Satisfactory	Satisfactory	Satisfactory
Policy	Maintain	Maintain	No intervention	No intervention
Encouraging the return of nationals	No	..	No	No

* Measures implemented to control HIV/AIDS: (1) blood screening; (2) information/education campaigns; (3) access to antiretroviral treatment; (4) non-discriminatory policies; (5) promoting condom use.

** Grounds on which abortion is permitted: (1) to save the woman's life; (2) to preserve physical health; (3) to preserve mental health; (4) rape or incest; (5) foetal impairment; (6) economic or social reasons; (7) on request.

Population indicators

Indicator	*1975*	*1985*	*1995*	*2005*
Population size and growth				
Population size (thousands)	13 512	19 673	27 226	34 256
Annual growth rate (percentage)*	3.6	3.8	3.0	2.2
Population age structure				
Percentage of population under age 15	50	50	46	43
Percentage of population aged 60 or older	5	4	4	4
Fertility and family planning				
Total fertility (births per woman)*	8.0	7.2	5.4	5.0
Teenage fertility rate (per 1,000 women, aged 15 - 19)*	181	163	110	97
Percentage of births to women under age 20*	19	18	16	15
Percentage of births to women aged 35 or older*	15	12	15	12
Percentage of married women using contraception				
Modern methods	4[a]	10[b]	32[c]	32[d]
All methods	7[a]	17[b]	39[c]	39[d]
Health and mortality				
Life expectancy at birth (years)*				
Males	52	57	55	48
Females	56	61	59	46
Both sexes combined	54	59	57	47
Infant mortality rate (per 1,000 births)*	92	69	63	68
Mortality under age 5 (per 1,000 births)*	147	112	104	118
Maternal mortality ratio (per 100,000 births) (2000)	..	..	..	1 000
HIV/AIDS (2003)				
Number of infected adults (thousands)	..	..	..	1 100
Adult prevalence rate (percentage)	..	..	..	6.7
Spatial distribution				
Population density (per sq. km)	23	34	47	59
Urban population (percentage)	13	20	30	42
Annual urban growth rate (percentage)*	8.1	8.2	6.9	4.4
Annual rural growth rate (percentage)*	3.0	2.8	1.5	-0.4
International migration				
International migrant stock				
Number of migrants (thousands)	161	152	366	345
Percentage of total population	1.2	0.8	1.3	1

* For the periods 1970-1975, 1980-1985, 1990-1995 and 2000-2005.
[a] For 1978.
[b] For 1984.
[c] For 1998.
[d] For 2003.

Government views and policies

Population policy variable	*1976*	*1986*	*1996*	*2005*
Population size and growth				
View on growth	..	Too high	Too high	Too high
Policy on growth	..	Lower	Lower	Lower
Population age structure				
Level of concern about				
Size of the working-age population	..	..	..	Major concern
Ageing of the population	..	..	..	..
Fertility and family planning				
View on fertility level	..	Too high	Too high	Too high
Policy	..	Lower	Lower	Lower
Access to contraceptive methods	..	Direct support	Direct support	Direct support
Adolescent fertility				
Level of concern	..	..	..	Minor concern
Policies and programmes	..	..	..	Yes
Health and mortality				
View				
Expectation of life	..	Unacceptable	Unacceptable	Unacceptable
Under-five mortality	..	..	..	Unacceptable
Maternal mortality	..	..	..	Unacceptable
Level of concern about HIV/AIDS	..	..	..	Major concern
Measures implemented to control HIV/AIDS*	..	..	..	2,3
Grounds on which abortion is permitted**	..	..	1	1
Spatial distribution and internal migration				
View on spatial distribution	..	Major change desired	Major change desired	Major change desired
Policies on internal migration				
From rural to urban areas	..	..	..	..
From rural to rural areas	..	..	..	..
From urban to rural areas	..	..	..	..
From urban to urban areas	..	..	..	..
Into urban agglomerations	..	No intervention	..	Lower
International migration				
Immigration				
View	..	Satisfactory	Satisfactory	Satisfactory
Policy	..	Maintain	Maintain	Maintain
Permanent settlement	..	..	..	..
Temporary workers	..	..	..	..
Highly skilled workers	..	..	..	..
Family reunification	..	..	..	..
Integration of non-nationals	..	..	..	..
Emigration				
View	..	Satisfactory	Satisfactory	Satisfactory
Policy	..	Maintain	Maintain	Maintain
Encouraging the return of nationals	..	..	..	..

* Measures implemented to control HIV/AIDS: (1) blood screening; (2) information/education campaigns; (3) access to antiretroviral treatment; (4) non-discriminatory policies; (5) promoting condom use.

** Grounds on which abortion is permitted: (1) to save the woman's life; (2) to preserve physical health; (3) to preserve mental health; (4) rape or incest; (5) foetal impairment; (6) economic or social reasons; (7) on request.

Population indicators

Indicator	*1975*	*1985*	*1995*	*2005*
Population size and growth				
Population size (thousands)	48	63	80	99
Annual growth rate (percentage)*	2.0	2.7	2.2	2.1
Population age structure				
Percentage of population under age 15	..	..	..	..
Percentage of population aged 60 or older	..	..	..	..
Fertility and family planning				
Total fertility (births per woman)*	..	..	..	..
Teenage fertility rate (per 1,000 women, aged 15 - 19)*	..	..	..	..
Percentage of births to women under age 20*	..	..	..	..
Percentage of births to women aged 35 or older*	..	..	..	..
Percentage of married women using contraception				
Modern methods	..	..	..	..
All methods	..	..	..	..
Health and mortality				
Life expectancy at birth (years)*				
Males	..	..	..	..
Females	..	..	..	..
Both sexes combined	..	..	..	..
Infant mortality rate (per 1,000 births)*	..	..	..	..
Mortality under age 5 (per 1,000 births)*	..	..	..	..
Maternal mortality ratio (per 100,000 births) (2000)	..	..	..	..
HIV/AIDS (2003)				
Number of infected adults (thousands)	..	..	..	..
Adult prevalence rate (percentage)	..	..	..	..
Spatial distribution				
Population density (per sq. km)	67	86	111	137
Urban population (percentage)	30	34	36	50
Annual urban growth rate (percentage)*	4.9	3.1	2.6	4.5
Annual rural growth rate (percentage)*	0.4	1.5	1.1	-1.3
International migration				
International migrant stock				
Number of migrants (thousands)	1	2	2	3
Percentage of total population	1.6	3.3	2.9	2.6

* For the periods 1970-1975, 1980-1985, 1990-1995 and 2000-2005.

Government views and policies

Population policy variable	*1976*	*1986*	*1996*	*2005*
Population size and growth				
View on growth	Too low	Too low	Satisfactory	Too low
Policy on growth	No intervention	Raise	Maintain	Maintain
Population age structure				
Level of concern about				
Size of the working-age population	..	..	..	Minor concern
Ageing of the population	..	..	..	Minor concern
Fertility and family planning				
View on fertility level	Satisfactory	Too low	Satisfactory	Too low
Policy	Maintain	Raise	Maintain	Raise
Access to contraceptive methods	No support	No support	No support	Direct support
Adolescent fertility				
Level of concern	..	..	Not a concern	Minor concern
Policies and programmes	..	..	No	Yes
Health and mortality				
View				
Expectation of life	Acceptable	Acceptable	Acceptable	Acceptable
Under-five mortality	..	..	Acceptable	Acceptable
Maternal mortality	..	..	..	Acceptable
Level of concern about HIV/AIDS	..	..	Major concern	Minor concern
Measures implemented to control HIV/AIDS*	..	..	..	1,2,3,4,5
Grounds on which abortion is permitted**	..	..	1,2,3,5	1,2,3,5
Spatial distribution and internal migration				
View on spatial distribution	Satisfactory	Minor change desired	Satisfactory	Satisfactory
Policies on internal migration				
From rural to urban areas	..	..	..	No intervention
From rural to rural areas	..	..	..	No intervention
From urban to rural areas	..	..	..	No intervention
From urban to urban areas	..	..	..	No intervention
Into urban agglomerations	..	No intervention	Lower	No intervention
International migration				
Immigration				
View	Satisfactory	Too high	Satisfactory	Too high
Policy	Maintain	Lower	Lower	Lower
Permanent settlement	..	..	Lower	Lower
Temporary workers	..	..	Lower	Lower
Highly skilled workers	..	..	..	Maintain
Family reunification	..	..	Lower	Maintain
Integration of non-nationals	..	..	No	Yes
Emigration				
View	Satisfactory	Satisfactory	Satisfactory	Too low
Policy	Maintain	Maintain	No intervention	No intervention
Encouraging the return of nationals	..	..	No	No

* Measures implemented to control HIV/AIDS: (1) blood screening; (2) information/education campaigns; (3) access to antiretroviral treatment; (4) non-discriminatory policies; (5) promoting condom use.

** Grounds on which abortion is permitted: (1) to save the woman's life; (2) to preserve physical health; (3) to preserve mental health; (4) rape or incest; (5) foetal impairment; (6) economic or social reasons; (7) on request.

Population indicators

Indicator	*1975*	*1985*	*1995*	*2005*
Population size and growth				
Population size (thousands)	1 007	1 720	1 696	2 687
Annual growth rate (percentage)*	6.0	4.5	-4.7	3.7
Population age structure				
Percentage of population under age 15	44	37	29	24
Percentage of population aged 60 or older	3	2	2	3
Fertility and family planning				
Total fertility (births per woman)*	6.9	4.9	3.2	2.4
Teenage fertility rate (per 1,000 women, aged 15 - 19)*	91	64	42	25
Percentage of births to women under age 20*	8	7	6	4
Percentage of births to women aged 35 or older*	10	11	12	12
Percentage of married women using contraception				
Modern methods	..	32[a]	41[b]	..
All methods	..	35[a]	50[b]	..
Health and mortality				
Life expectancy at birth (years)*				
Males	65	70	74	75
Females	69	74	77	79
Both sexes combined	67	71	75	77
Infant mortality rate (per 1,000 births)*	41	24	13	10
Mortality under age 5 (per 1,000 births)*	55	31	16	12
Maternal mortality ratio (per 100,000 births) (2000)	..	..	..	5
HIV/AIDS (2003)				
Number of infected adults (thousands)	..	..	..	..
Adult prevalence rate (percentage)	..	..	..	..
Spatial distribution				
Population density (per sq. km)	56	97	95	151
Urban population (percentage)	84	94	96	96
Annual urban growth rate (percentage)*	7.5	5.2	-4.6	3.5
Annual rural growth rate (percentage)*	-0.3	-4.9	-7.2	1.4
International migration				
International migrant stock				
Number of migrants (thousands)	662	1 222	996	1 669
Percentage of total population	65.7	71.1	58.7	62.1

* For the periods 1970-1975, 1980-1985, 1990-1995 and 2000-2005.
[a] For 1987.
[b] For 1996.

Government views and policies

Population policy variable	*1976*	*1986*	*1996*	*2005*
Population size and growth				
View on growth	..	..	Satisfactory	Satisfactory
Policy on growth	..	..	No intervention	Maintain
Population age structure				
Level of concern about				
Size of the working-age population	..	..	..	Minor concern
Ageing of the population	..	..	..	Minor concern
Fertility and family planning				
View on fertility level	..	..	Satisfactory	Satisfactory
Policy	..	..	No intervention	Maintain
Access to contraceptive methods	..	..	..	Direct support
Adolescent fertility				
Level of concern	..	..	..	Major concern
Policies and programmes	..	..	..	Yes
Health and mortality				
View				
Expectation of life	..	..	Unacceptable	Unacceptable
Under-five mortality	..	..	..	Unacceptable
Maternal mortality	..	..	..	Unacceptable
Level of concern about HIV/AIDS	..	..	..	Major concern
Measures implemented to control HIV/AIDS*	..	..	..	1,2,3,4,5
Grounds on which abortion is permitted**	..	..	1,2,3,4,5,6,7	1,2,3,4,5,6,7
Spatial distribution and internal migration				
View on spatial distribution	..	..	Minor change desired	Major change desired
Policies on internal migration				
From rural to urban areas	..	..	..	Lower
From rural to rural areas	..	..	..	Maintain
From urban to rural areas	..	..	..	Raise
From urban to urban areas	..	..	..	Maintain
Into urban agglomerations	..	..	..	Lower
International migration				
Immigration				
View	..	..	Satisfactory	Satisfactory
Policy	..	..	No intervention	Maintain
Permanent settlement	..	..	..	Maintain
Temporary workers	..	..	..	Maintain
Highly skilled workers	..	..	..	Maintain
Family reunification	..	..	..	Maintain
Integration of non-nationals	..	..	..	Yes
Emigration				
View	..	..	Too high	Satisfactory
Policy	..	..	Lower	Maintain
Encouraging the return of nationals	..	..	..	Yes

* Measures implemented to control HIV/AIDS: (1) blood screening; (2) information/education campaigns; (3) access to antiretroviral treatment; (4) non-discriminatory policies; (5) promoting condom use.

** Grounds on which abortion is permitted: (1) to save the woman's life; (2) to preserve physical health; (3) to preserve mental health; (4) rape or incest; (5) foetal impairment; (6) economic or social reasons; (7) on request.

Population indicators

Indicator	*1975*	*1985*	*1995*	*2005*
Population size and growth				
Population size (thousands)	3 299	4 013	4 588	5 264
Annual growth rate (percentage)*	2.1	2.0	0.9	1.2
Population age structure				
Percentage of population under age 15	40	37	38	31
Percentage of population aged 60 or older	8	8	8	8
Fertility and family planning				
Total fertility (births per woman)*	4.7	4.1	3.6	2.7
Teenage fertility rate (per 1,000 women, aged 15 - 19)*	60	52	46	34
Percentage of births to women under age 20*	10	8	8	8
Percentage of births to women aged 35 or older*	11	6	9	9
Percentage of married women using contraception				
Modern methods	..	..	49[a]	..
All methods	..	..	60[a]	..
Health and mortality				
Life expectancy at birth (years)*				
Males	57	60	62	63
Females	65	68	70	71
Both sexes combined	61	64	66	67
Infant mortality rate (per 1,000 births)*	100	80	60	55
Mortality under age 5 (per 1,000 births)*	122	97	72	66
Maternal mortality ratio (per 100,000 births) (2000)	..	..	..	110
HIV/AIDS (2003)				
Number of infected adults (thousands)	..	..	..	4
Adult prevalence rate (percentage)	..	..	..	0.1
Spatial distribution				
Population density (per sq. km)	17	20	23	26
Urban population (percentage)	38	38	36	34
Annual urban growth rate (percentage)*	2.4	2.0	-0.2	1.0
Annual rural growth rate (percentage)*	2.0	2.0	1.3	1.6
International migration				
International migrant stock				
Number of migrants (thousands)	..	..	482	288
Percentage of total population	..	..	10.5	5.5

* For the periods 1970-1975, 1980-1985, 1990-1995 and 2000-2005.
[a] For 1997.

Government views and policies

Population policy variable	*1976*	*1986*	*1996*	*2005*
Population size and growth				
View on growth	Too low	Too low	Too low	Too high
Policy on growth	Raise	Raise	Raise	Lower
Population age structure				
Level of concern about				
Size of the working-age population	..	..	..	Major concern
Ageing of the population	..	..	..	Minor concern
Fertility and family planning				
View on fertility level	Satisfactory	Satisfactory	Satisfactory	Too high
Policy	Maintain	Maintain	Maintain	Lower
Access to contraceptive methods	Limits	Limits	No support	Direct support
Adolescent fertility				
Level of concern	..	..	..	Minor concern
Policies and programmes	..	..	..	Yes
Health and mortality				
View				
Expectation of life	Unacceptable	Acceptable	Unacceptable	Unacceptable
Under-five mortality	..	..	..	Unacceptable
Maternal mortality	..	..	..	Unacceptable
Level of concern about HIV/AIDS	..	..	..	Major concern
Measures implemented to control HIV/AIDS*	..	..	..	1,2,5
Grounds on which abortion is permitted**	..	..	1	1,2
Spatial distribution and internal migration				
View on spatial distribution	Major change desired	Major change desired	Major change desired	Major change desired
Policies on internal migration				
From rural to urban areas	..	..	..	Lower
From rural to rural areas	..	..	..	No intervention
From urban to rural areas	..	..	..	Raise
From urban to urban areas	..	..	..	No intervention
Into urban agglomerations	..	..	..	Lower
International migration				
Immigration				
View	Satisfactory	Satisfactory	Satisfactory	Satisfactory
Policy	Maintain	Maintain	Maintain	Maintain
Permanent settlement	..	..	..	Lower
Temporary workers	..	..	..	Raise
Highly skilled workers	..	..	..	Raise
Family reunification	..	..	..	Maintain
Integration of non-nationals	..	..	..	..
Emigration				
View	Satisfactory	Satisfactory	Too high	Too high
Policy	Maintain	Maintain	Lower	No intervention
Encouraging the return of nationals	..	..	..	Yes

* Measures implemented to control HIV/AIDS: (1) blood screening; (2) information/education campaigns; (3) access to antiretroviral treatment; (4) non-discriminatory policies; (5) promoting condom use.

** Grounds on which abortion is permitted: (1) to save the woman's life; (2) to preserve physical health; (3) to preserve mental health; (4) rape or incest; (5) foetal impairment; (6) economic or social reasons; (7) on request.

Population indicators

Indicator	*1975*	*1985*	*1995*	*2005*
Population size and growth				
Population size (thousands)	3 024	3 621	4 686	5 924
Annual growth rate (percentage)*	2.2	2.4	2.5	2.3
Population age structure				
Percentage of population under age 15	42	43	44	41
Percentage of population aged 60 or older	5	6	6	5
Fertility and family planning				
Total fertility (births per woman)*	6.2	6.7	5.8	4.8
Teenage fertility rate (per 1,000 women, aged 15 - 19)*	111	121	105	91
Percentage of births to women under age 20*	13	13	13	14
Percentage of births to women aged 35 or older*	18	17	17	16
Percentage of married women using contraception				
Modern methods	..	..	15[a]	29[b]
All methods	..	..	19[a]	32[b]
Health and mortality				
Life expectancy at birth (years)*				
Males	39	45	50	53
Females	42	47	52	56
Both sexes combined	40	46	51	54
Infant mortality rate (per 1,000 births)*	145	128	104	88
Mortality under age 5 (per 1,000 births)*	247	216	171	141
Maternal mortality ratio (per 100,000 births) (2000)	..	..	..	650
HIV/AIDS (2003)				
Number of infected adults (thousands)	..	..	..	2
Adult prevalence rate (percentage)	..	..	..	0.1
Spatial distribution				
Population density (per sq. km)	13	15	20	25
Urban population (percentage)	11	14	17	22
Annual urban growth rate (percentage)*	5.0	4.6	4.7	4.6
Annual rural growth rate (percentage)*	1.9	2.1	2.1	1.7
International migration				
International migrant stock				
Number of migrants (thousands)	21	23	23	25
Percentage of total population	0.7	0.6	0.5	0.4

* For the periods 1970-1975, 1980-1985, 1990-1995 and 2000-2005.
[a] For 1993.
[b] For 2000.

Government views and policies

Population policy variable	*1976*	*1986*	*1996*	*2005*
Population size and growth				
View on growth	..	..	Too low	Too low
Policy on growth	..	..	No intervention	No intervention
Population age structure				
Level of concern about				
Size of the working-age population	..	..	..	Minor concern
Ageing of the population	..	..	..	Minor concern
Fertility and family planning				
View on fertility level	..	..	Too low	Too low
Policy	..	..	Raise	Raise
Access to contraceptive methods	..	..	Direct support	No support
Adolescent fertility				
Level of concern	..	..	Minor concern	Major concern
Policies and programmes	..	..	No	Yes
Health and mortality				
View				
Expectation of life	..	..	Unacceptable	Unacceptable
Under-five mortality	..	..	Unacceptable	Unacceptable
Maternal mortality	..	..	..	Unacceptable
Level of concern about HIV/AIDS	..	..	Minor concern	Major concern
Measures implemented to control HIV/AIDS*	..	..	..	1,2,3,4,5
Grounds on which abortion is permitted**	..	..	1,2,3,4,5,6,7	1,2,3,4,5,6,7
Spatial distribution and internal migration				
View on spatial distribution	..	..	Major change desired	Minor change desired
Policies on internal migration				
From rural to urban areas	..	..	..	No intervention
From rural to rural areas	..	..	..	No intervention
From urban to rural areas	..	..	..	No intervention
From urban to urban areas	..	..	..	No intervention
Into urban agglomerations	..	..	Lower	No intervention
International migration				
Immigration				
View	..	..	Too high	Satisfactory
Policy	..	..	Lower	Maintain
Permanent settlement	..	..	Lower	Maintain
Temporary workers	..	..	Lower	Lower
Highly skilled workers	..	..	..	Maintain
Family reunification	..	..	Lower	Maintain
Integration of non-nationals	..	..	Yes	Yes
Emigration				
View	..	..	Too low	Satisfactory
Policy	..	..	Raise	No intervention
Encouraging the return of nationals	..	..	Yes	Yes

* Measures implemented to control HIV/AIDS: (1) blood screening; (2) information/education campaigns; (3) access to antiretroviral treatment; (4) non-discriminatory policies; (5) promoting condom use.

** Grounds on which abortion is permitted: (1) to save the woman's life; (2) to preserve physical health; (3) to preserve mental health; (4) rape or incest; (5) foetal impairment; (6) economic or social reasons; (7) on request.

Population indicators

Indicator	*1975*	*1985*	*1995*	*2005*
Population size and growth				
Population size (thousands)	2 456	2 579	2 498	2 307
Annual growth rate (percentage)*	0.8	0.5	-1.7	-0.6
Population age structure				
Percentage of population under age 15	21	21	21	15
Percentage of population aged 60 or older	18	17	19	23
Fertility and family planning				
Total fertility (births per woman)*	2.0	2.0	1.6	1.3
Teenage fertility rate (per 1,000 women, aged 15 - 19)*	52	52	42	18
Percentage of births to women under age 20*	13	12	12	8
Percentage of births to women aged 35 or older*	8	7	7	11
Percentage of married women using contraception				
Modern methods	..	..	39	..
All methods	..	..	48	..
Health and mortality				
Life expectancy at birth (years)*				
Males	65	65	62	66
Females	75	74	74	77
Both sexes combined	70	69	68	71
Infant mortality rate (per 1,000 births)*	21	18	20	10
Mortality under age 5 (per 1,000 births)*	29	25	27	14
Maternal mortality ratio (per 100,000 births) (2000)	..	..	..	42
HIV/AIDS (2003)				
Number of infected adults (thousands)	..	..	..	8
Adult prevalence rate (percentage)	..	..	..	0.6
Spatial distribution				
Population density (per sq. km)	38	40	39	36
Urban population (percentage)	65	70	69	66
Annual urban growth rate (percentage)*	1.9	1.0	-2.1	-1.2
Annual rural growth rate (percentage)*	-1.1	-0.4	-0.5	-0.3
International migration				
International migrant stock				
Number of migrants (thousands)	..	..	713	449
Percentage of total population	..	..	28.5	19.5

* For the periods 1970-1975, 1980-1985, 1990-1995 and 2000-2005.

Government views and policies

Population policy variable	*1976*	*1986*	*1996*	*2005*
Population size and growth				
View on growth	Satisfactory	Satisfactory	Satisfactory	Satisfactory
Policy on growth	No intervention	No intervention	No intervention	No intervention
Population age structure				
Level of concern about				
Size of the working-age population	..	..	..	Minor concern
Ageing of the population	..	..	..	Minor concern
Fertility and family planning				
View on fertility level	Satisfactory	Satisfactory	Satisfactory	Too high
Policy	No intervention	No intervention	No intervention	Lower
Access to contraceptive methods	Indirect support	Indirect support	Indirect support	Direct support
Adolescent fertility				
Level of concern	..	..	..	Minor concern
Policies and programmes	..	..	..	Yes
Health and mortality				
View				
Expectation of life	Unacceptable	Unacceptable	Unacceptable	Acceptable
Under-five mortality	..	..	..	Unacceptable
Maternal mortality	..	..	..	Unacceptable
Level of concern about HIV/AIDS	..	..	..	Major concern
Measures implemented to control HIV/AIDS*	..	..	..	1,2,3,4,5
Grounds on which abortion is permitted**	..	..	1	1
Spatial distribution and internal migration				
View on spatial distribution	Minor change desired	Minor change desired	Major change desired	Major change desired
Policies on internal migration				
From rural to urban areas	..	..	..	Lower
From rural to rural areas	..	..	..	No intervention
From urban to rural areas	..	..	..	Raise
From urban to urban areas	..	..	..	No intervention
Into urban agglomerations	..	..	..	Lower
International migration				
Immigration				
View	Satisfactory	Satisfactory	Too high	Too high
Policy	Maintain	Maintain	Lower	Lower
Permanent settlement	..	..	..	Lower
Temporary workers	..	..	..	Lower
Highly skilled workers	..	..	..	No intervention
Family reunification	..	..	..	No intervention
Integration of non-nationals	..	..	..	No
Emigration				
View	Satisfactory	Satisfactory	Too high	Too high
Policy	Maintain	Maintain	Lower	Lower
Encouraging the return of nationals	..	..	Yes	Yes

* Measures implemented to control HIV/AIDS: (1) blood screening; (2) information/education campaigns; (3) access to antiretroviral treatment; (4) non-discriminatory policies; (5) promoting condom use.

** Grounds on which abortion is permitted: (1) to save the woman's life; (2) to preserve physical health; (3) to preserve mental health; (4) rape or incest; (5) foetal impairment; (6) economic or social reasons; (7) on request.

Population indicators

Indicator	*1975*	*1985*	*1995*	*2005*
Population size and growth				
Population size (thousands)	2 678	2 793	3 177	3 577
Annual growth rate (percentage)*	2.3	0.7	2.9	1.0
Population age structure				
Percentage of population under age 15	40	37	32	29
Percentage of population aged 60 or older	7	8	10	10
Fertility and family planning				
Total fertility (births per woman)*	4.8	3.9	3.0	2.3
Teenage fertility rate (per 1,000 women, aged 15 - 19)*	54	44	34	27
Percentage of births to women under age 20*	9	8	7	7
Percentage of births to women aged 35 or older*	17	14	16	16
Percentage of married women using contraception				
Modern methods	23[a]	..	37[b]	..
All methods	53[a]	..	61[b]	..
Health and mortality				
Life expectancy at birth (years)*				
Males	64	65	67	70
Females	69	70	72	74
Both sexes combined	66	67	69	72
Infant mortality rate (per 1,000 births)*	43	41	31	22
Mortality under age 5 (per 1,000 births)*	55	51	38	26
Maternal mortality ratio (per 100,000 births) (2000)	..	..	..	150
HIV/AIDS (2003)				
Number of infected adults (thousands)	..	..	..	3
Adult prevalence rate (percentage)	..	..	..	0.1
Spatial distribution				
Population density (per sq. km)	258	269	305	344
Urban population (percentage)	67	79	85	88
Annual urban growth rate (percentage)*	4.7	1.5	3.4	1.9
Annual rural growth rate (percentage)*	-1.9	-4.9	0.7	-0.6
International migration				
International migrant stock				
Number of migrants (thousands)	209	344	594	657
Percentage of total population	7.8	12.3	18.7	18.4

* For the periods 1970-1975, 1980-1985, 1990-1995 and 2000-2005.
[a] For 1971.
[b] For 1996.

Government views and policies

Population policy variable	*1976*	*1986*	*1996*	*2005*
Population size and growth				
View on growth	Too high	Too high	Too high	Too high
Policy on growth	Lower	Lower	Lower	Lower
Population age structure				
Level of concern about				
Size of the working-age population	..	..	..	Major concern
Ageing of the population	..	..	..	Minor concern
Fertility and family planning				
View on fertility level	Too high	Too high	Too high	Too high
Policy	Lower	Lower	Lower	Lower
Access to contraceptive methods	Direct support	Direct support	Direct support	Direct support
Adolescent fertility				
Level of concern	..	..	Major concern	Major concern
Policies and programmes	..	..	Yes	Yes
Health and mortality				
View				
Expectation of life	Unacceptable	Unacceptable	Unacceptable	Unacceptable
Under-five mortality	..	..	Unacceptable	Unacceptable
Maternal mortality	..	..	..	Unacceptable
Level of concern about HIV/AIDS	..	..	Major concern	Major concern
Measures implemented to control HIV/AIDS*	..	..	..	1,2,3,4,5
Grounds on which abortion is permitted**	..	..	1	1
Spatial distribution and internal migration				
View on spatial distribution	Minor change desired	Minor change desired	Minor change desired	Major change desired
Policies on internal migration				
From rural to urban areas	..	..	..	Lower
From rural to rural areas	..	..	..	..
From urban to rural areas	..	..	..	..
From urban to urban areas	..	..	..	..
Into urban agglomerations	No intervention	No intervention	No intervention	No intervention
International migration				
Immigration				
View	Satisfactory	Satisfactory	Satisfactory	Satisfactory
Policy	Maintain	Maintain	No intervention	No intervention
Permanent settlement	..	..	No intervention	..
Temporary workers	..	..	No intervention	..
Highly skilled workers	..	..	..	..
Family reunification	..	..	No intervention	..
Integration of non-nationals	..	..	No	..
Emigration				
View	Satisfactory	Too high	Satisfactory	Satisfactory
Policy	Maintain	Lower	No intervention	No intervention
Encouraging the return of nationals	No	..	Yes	Yes

* Measures implemented to control HIV/AIDS: (1) blood screening; (2) information/education campaigns; (3) access to antiretroviral treatment; (4) non-discriminatory policies; (5) promoting condom use.

** Grounds on which abortion is permitted: (1) to save the woman's life; (2) to preserve physical health; (3) to preserve mental health; (4) rape or incest; (5) foetal impairment; (6) economic or social reasons; (7) on request.

Population indicators

Indicator	1975	1985	1995	2005
Population size and growth				
Population size (thousands)	1 145	1 469	1 692	1 795
Annual growth rate (percentage)*	2.1	2.6	1.2	0.1
Population age structure				
Percentage of population under age 15	44	45	44	39
Percentage of population aged 60 or older	6	6	7	7
Fertility and family planning				
Total fertility (births per woman)*	5.7	5.6	4.6	3.6
Teenage fertility rate (per 1,000 women, aged 15 - 19)*	81	79	58	39
Percentage of births to women under age 20*	11	10	10	9
Percentage of births to women aged 35 or older*	18	18	20	15
Percentage of married women using contraception				
Modern methods	2[a]	..	19[b]	30[c]
All methods	5[a]	..	23[b]	30[c]
Health and mortality				
Life expectancy at birth (years)*				
Males	48	53	56	35
Females	51	56	60	38
Both sexes combined	50	54	58	37
Infant mortality rate (per 1,000 births)*	123	97	73	67
Mortality under age 5 (per 1,000 births)*	181	145	107	123
Maternal mortality ratio (per 100,000 births) (2000)	..	..	..	550
HIV/AIDS (2003)				
Number of infected adults (thousands)	..	..	..	300
Adult prevalence rate (percentage)	..	..	..	28.9
Spatial distribution				
Population density (per sq. km)	38	48	56	59
Urban population (percentage)	11	16	17	18
Annual urban growth rate (percentage)*	6.6	6.5	1.6	0.9
Annual rural growth rate (percentage)*	1.6	1.7	1.3	0.0
International migration				
International migrant stock				
Number of migrants (thousands)	4	16	5	6
Percentage of total population	0.3	1.1	0.3	0.3

* For the periods 1970-1975, 1980-1985, 1990-1995 and 2000-2005.
[a] For 1977.
[b] For 1992.
[c] For 2000.

Government views and policies

Population policy variable	*1976*	*1986*	*1996*	*2005*
Population size and growth				
View on growth	Too high	Too high	Too high	Too high
Policy on growth	No intervention	No intervention	Lower	Lower
Population age structure				
Level of concern about				
Size of the working-age population	..	..	..	..
Ageing of the population	..	..	..	..
Fertility and family planning				
View on fertility level	Too high	Too high	Too high	Too high
Policy	No intervention	No intervention	Lower	Lower
Access to contraceptive methods	Direct support	Indirect support	Direct support	Direct support
Adolescent fertility				
Level of concern	..	..	Major concern	Major concern
Policies and programmes	..	..	Yes	Yes
Health and mortality				
View				
Expectation of life	Unacceptable	Unacceptable	Unacceptable	Unacceptable
Under-five mortality	..	..	Unacceptable	Unacceptable
Maternal mortality	..	..	..	Unacceptable
Level of concern about HIV/AIDS	..	..	Major concern	Major concern
Measures implemented to control HIV/AIDS*	..	..	..	1
Grounds on which abortion is permitted**	..	..	1,2,3,4,5	1,2,3,4,5
Spatial distribution and internal migration				
View on spatial distribution	Major change desired	Minor change desired	Major change desired	Major change desired
Policies on internal migration				
From rural to urban areas	..	..	..	..
From rural to rural areas	..	..	..	..
From urban to rural areas	..	..	..	..
From urban to urban areas	..	..	..	..
Into urban agglomerations	No intervention	..	Lower	..
International migration				
Immigration				
View	Satisfactory	Satisfactory	Satisfactory	Satisfactory
Policy	Maintain	Maintain	Maintain	Maintain
Permanent settlement	..	..	Maintain	..
Temporary workers	..	..	Maintain	..
Highly skilled workers	..	..	..	..
Family reunification	..	..	Maintain	..
Integration of non-nationals	..	..	Yes	Yes
Emigration				
View	Satisfactory	Satisfactory	Too high	Satisfactory
Policy	Maintain	Maintain	No intervention	No intervention
Encouraging the return of nationals	No	..	Yes	Yes

* Measures implemented to control HIV/AIDS: (1) blood screening; (2) information/education campaigns; (3) access to antiretroviral treatment; (4) non-discriminatory policies; (5) promoting condom use.

** Grounds on which abortion is permitted: (1) to save the woman's life; (2) to preserve physical health; (3) to preserve mental health; (4) rape or incest; (5) foetal impairment; (6) economic or social reasons; (7) on request.

Population indicators

Indicator	*1975*	*1985*	*1995*	*2005*
Population size and growth				
Population size (thousands)	1 605	2 171	2 141	3 283
Annual growth rate (percentage)*	2.9	3.0	0.1	1.4
Population age structure				
Percentage of population under age 15	46	47	47	47
Percentage of population aged 60 or older	4	4	4	4
Fertility and family planning				
Total fertility (births per woman)*	6.9	6.9	6.9	6.8
Teenage fertility rate (per 1,000 women, aged 15 - 19)*	233	233	233	227
Percentage of births to women under age 20*	25	24	25	25
Percentage of births to women aged 35 or older*	14	14	14	13
Percentage of married women using contraception				
Modern methods	..	6[a]	..	..
All methods	..	6[a]	..	..
Health and mortality				
Life expectancy at birth (years)*				
Males	42	44	39	41
Females	43	46	42	44
Both sexes combined	43	45	41	42
Infant mortality rate (per 1,000 births)*	165	150	178	142
Mortality under age 5 (per 1,000 births)*	247	234	266	224
Maternal mortality ratio (per 100,000 births) (2000)	..	..	..	760
HIV/AIDS (2003)				
Number of infected adults (thousands)	..	..	..	96
Adult prevalence rate (percentage)	..	..	..	5.9
Spatial distribution				
Population density (per sq. km)	14	19	19	29
Urban population (percentage)	30	39	42	48
Annual urban growth rate (percentage)*	6.0	5.3	-0.1	5.3
Annual rural growth rate (percentage)*	1.7	1.6	-0.1	2.9
International migration				
International migrant stock				
Number of migrants (thousands)	64	83	199	50
Percentage of total population	4	3.8	9.3	1.5

* For the periods 1970-1975, 1980-1985, 1990-1995 and 2000-2005.
[a] For 1986.

Government views and policies

Population policy variable	*1976*	*1986*	*1996*	*2005*
Population size and growth				
View on growth	Too low	Satisfactory	Satisfactory	Satisfactory
Policy on growth	Raise	No intervention	No intervention	No intervention
Population age structure				
Level of concern about				
Size of the working-age population	..	..	..	..
Ageing of the population	..	..	..	Minor concern
Fertility and family planning				
View on fertility level	Too low	Satisfactory	Satisfactory	Satisfactory
Policy	Raise	No intervention	No intervention	No intervention
Access to contraceptive methods	No support	No support	No support	No support
Adolescent fertility				
Level of concern	..	..	..	Minor concern
Policies and programmes	..	..	..	Yes
Health and mortality				
View				
Expectation of life	Unacceptable	Acceptable	Acceptable	Acceptable
Under-five mortality	..	..	..	Unacceptable
Maternal mortality	..	..	..	Unacceptable
Level of concern about HIV/AIDS	..	..	..	Not a concern
Measures implemented to control HIV/AIDS*	..	..	..	1,2,3
Grounds on which abortion is permitted**	..	..	1	1
Spatial distribution and internal migration				
View on spatial distribution	Minor change desired	Major change desired	Major change desired	Major change desired
Policies on internal migration				
From rural to urban areas	..	..	..	Lower
From rural to rural areas	..	..	..	..
From urban to rural areas	..	..	..	..
From urban to urban areas	..	..	..	..
Into urban agglomerations	Lower	Lower	..	Lower
International migration				
Immigration				
View	Too low	Too high	Too high	Satisfactory
Policy	Raise	Lower	Lower	Maintain
Permanent settlement	..	..	..	..
Temporary workers	..	..	..	..
Highly skilled workers	..	..	..	..
Family reunification	..	..	..	..
Integration of non-nationals	..	..	..	..
Emigration				
View	Satisfactory	Satisfactory	Satisfactory	Satisfactory
Policy	Maintain	Maintain	Maintain	Maintain
Encouraging the return of nationals	No	..	..	No

* Measures implemented to control HIV/AIDS: (1) blood screening; (2) information/education campaigns; (3) access to antiretroviral treatment; (4) non-discriminatory policies; (5) promoting condom use.
** Grounds on which abortion is permitted: (1) to save the woman's life; (2) to preserve physical health; (3) to preserve mental health; (4) rape or incest; (5) foetal impairment; (6) economic or social reasons; (7) on request.

Population indicators

Indicator	*1975*	*1985*	*1995*	*2005*
Population size and growth				
Population size (thousands)	2 446	3 786	4 808	5 853
Annual growth rate (percentage)*	4.2	4.4	2.1	2.0
Population age structure				
Percentage of population under age 15	46	46	39	30
Percentage of population aged 60 or older	4	4	5	6
Fertility and family planning				
Total fertility (births per woman)*	7.6	7.2	4.1	3.0
Teenage fertility rate (per 1,000 women, aged 15 - 19)*	13	12	7	7
Percentage of births to women under age 20*	1	1	2	2
Percentage of births to women aged 35 or older*	30	30	31	24
Percentage of married women using contraception				
Modern methods	..	..	26	..
All methods	..	..	45	..
Health and mortality				
Life expectancy at birth (years)*				
Males	51	61	67	71
Females	55	64	72	76
Both sexes combined	53	62	69	73
Infant mortality rate (per 1,000 births)*	117	50	30	19
Mortality under age 5 (per 1,000 births)*	140	58	34	21
Maternal mortality ratio (per 100,000 births) (2000)	..	..	..	97
HIV/AIDS (2003)				
Number of infected adults (thousands)	..	..	..	10
Adult prevalence rate (percentage)	..	..	..	0.3
Spatial distribution				
Population density (per sq. km)	1	2	3	3
Urban population (percentage)	61	76	83	87
Annual urban growth rate (percentage)*	10.1	6.2	2.7	2.3
Annual rural growth rate (percentage)*	-2.5	-0.7	-1.2	-0.5
International migration				
International migrant stock				
Number of migrants (thousands)	223	414	506	618
Percentage of total population	9.1	10.9	10.5	10.5

* For the periods 1970-1975, 1980-1985, 1990-1995 and 2000-2005.

Government views and policies

Population policy variable	*1976*	*1986*	*1996*	*2005*
Population size and growth				
View on growth	Too low	Too low	Satisfactory	Too low
Policy on growth	Raise	Raise	No intervention	No intervention
Population age structure				
Level of concern about				
Size of the working-age population	..	..	..	Not a concern
Ageing of the population	..	..	..	Minor concern
Fertility and family planning				
View on fertility level	Too low	Too low	Satisfactory	Too low
Policy	Raise	Raise	No intervention	No intervention
Access to contraceptive methods	No support	No support	No support	No support
Adolescent fertility				
Level of concern	..	..	Not a concern	Not a concern
Policies and programmes	..	..	No	No
Health and mortality				
View				
Expectation of life	Acceptable	Acceptable	Acceptable	Acceptable
Under-five mortality	..	..	..	Acceptable
Maternal mortality	..	..	..	Acceptable
Level of concern about HIV/AIDS	..	..	Minor concern	Minor concern
Measures implemented to control HIV/AIDS*	..	..	..	1,2,3,5
Grounds on which abortion is permitted**	..	..	1,2,3	1,2,3
Spatial distribution and internal migration				
View on spatial distribution	Satisfactory	Satisfactory	Satisfactory	Satisfactory
Policies on internal migration				
From rural to urban areas	..	..	..	No intervention
From rural to rural areas	..	..	..	No intervention
From urban to rural areas	..	..	..	No intervention
From urban to urban areas	..	..	..	No intervention
Into urban agglomerations	..	..	No intervention	No intervention
International migration				
Immigration				
View	Satisfactory	Satisfactory	Satisfactory	Satisfactory
Policy	Maintain	Lower	Lower	Maintain
Permanent settlement	..	..	Lower	Maintain
Temporary workers	..	..	Maintain	Maintain
Highly skilled workers	..	..	..	Maintain
Family reunification	..	..	Maintain	Maintain
Integration of non-nationals	..	..	No	Yes
Emigration				
View	Satisfactory	Satisfactory	Satisfactory	Satisfactory
Policy	Maintain	Maintain	No intervention	No intervention
Encouraging the return of nationals	..	..	No	No

* Measures implemented to control HIV/AIDS: (1) blood screening; (2) information/education campaigns; (3) access to antiretroviral treatment; (4) non-discriminatory policies; (5) promoting condom use.

** Grounds on which abortion is permitted: (1) to save the woman's life; (2) to preserve physical health; (3) to preserve mental health; (4) rape or incest; (5) foetal impairment; (6) economic or social reasons; (7) on request.

Population indicators

Indicator	*1975*	*1985*	*1995*	*2005*
Population size and growth				
Population size (thousands)	23	27	31	35
Annual growth rate (percentage)*	1.7	1.5	1.3	1.0
Population age structure				
Percentage of population under age 15	..	..	..	..
Percentage of population aged 60 or older	..	..	..	..
Fertility and family planning				
Total fertility (births per woman)*	..	..	..	..
Teenage fertility rate (per 1,000 women, aged 15 - 19)*	..	..	..	..
Percentage of births to women under age 20*	..	..	..	..
Percentage of births to women aged 35 or older*	..	..	..	..
Percentage of married women using contraception				
Modern methods	..	..	..	..
All methods	..	..	..	..
Health and mortality				
Life expectancy at birth (years)*				
Males	..	..	..	..
Females	..	..	..	..
Both sexes combined	..	..	..	..
Infant mortality rate (per 1,000 births)*	..	..	..	..
Mortality under age 5 (per 1,000 births)*	..	..	..	..
Maternal mortality ratio (per 100,000 births) (2000)	..	..	..	..
HIV/AIDS (2003)				
Number of infected adults (thousands)	..	..	..	..
Adult prevalence rate (percentage)	..	..	..	..
Spatial distribution				
Population density (per sq. km)	146	170	193	216
Urban population (percentage)	20	20	21	22
Annual urban growth rate (percentage)*	1.6	1.8	1.6	1.2
Annual rural growth rate (percentage)*	1.8	1.3	1.1	0.8
International migration				
International migrant stock				
Number of migrants (thousands)	8	10	12	12
Percentage of total population	34.5	37.3	37.8	33.9

* For the periods 1970-1975, 1980-1985, 1990-1995 and 2000-2005.

Government views and policies

Population policy variable	*1976*	*1986*	*1996*	*2005*
Population size and growth				
View on growth	..	..	Satisfactory	Too low
Policy on growth	..	..	Raise	Raise
Population age structure				
Level of concern about				
Size of the working-age population	..	..	..	Major concern
Ageing of the population	..	..	..	Major concern
Fertility and family planning				
View on fertility level	..	..	Satisfactory	Too low
Policy	..	..	Raise	Raise
Access to contraceptive methods	..	..	Direct support	Indirect support
Adolescent fertility				
Level of concern	..	..	Not a concern	Major concern
Policies and programmes	..	..	No	Yes
Health and mortality				
View				
Expectation of life	..	..	Acceptable	Acceptable
Under-five mortality	..	..	Acceptable	Acceptable
Maternal mortality	..	..	..	Acceptable
Level of concern about HIV/AIDS	..	..	Major concern	Major concern
Measures implemented to control HIV/AIDS*	..	..	..	1,2,3,4,5
Grounds on which abortion is permitted**	..	..	1,2,3,4,5,6,7	1,2,3,4,5,6,7
Spatial distribution and internal migration				
View on spatial distribution	..	..	Satisfactory	Minor change desired
Policies on internal migration				
From rural to urban areas	..	..	..	Lower
From rural to rural areas	..	..	..	..
From urban to rural areas	..	..	..	..
From urban to urban areas	..	..	..	..
Into urban agglomerations	..	..	Lower	Lower
International migration				
Immigration				
View	..	..	Satisfactory	Satisfactory
Policy	..	..	Lower	Maintain
Permanent settlement	..	..	Lower	Maintain
Temporary workers	..	..	No intervention	Maintain
Highly skilled workers	..	..	..	Raise
Family reunification	..	..	No intervention	Maintain
Integration of non-nationals	..	..	Yes	Yes
Emigration				
View	..	..	Satisfactory	Satisfactory
Policy	..	..	Maintain	No intervention
Encouraging the return of nationals	..	..	Yes	No

* Measures implemented to control HIV/AIDS: (1) blood screening; (2) information/education campaigns; (3) access to antiretroviral treatment; (4) non-discriminatory policies; (5) promoting condom use.

** Grounds on which abortion is permitted: (1) to save the woman's life; (2) to preserve physical health; (3) to preserve mental health; (4) rape or incest; (5) foetal impairment; (6) economic or social reasons; (7) on request.

Population indicators

Indicator	*1975*	*1985*	*1995*	*2005*
Population size and growth				
Population size (thousands)	3 302	3 545	3 628	3 431
Annual growth rate (percentage)*	1.0	0.8	-0.4	-0.4
Population age structure				
Percentage of population under age 15	25	23	22	17
Percentage of population aged 60 or older	15	15	18	21
Fertility and family planning				
Total fertility (births per woman)*	2.3	2.0	1.8	1.3
Teenage fertility rate (per 1,000 women, aged 15 - 19)*	56	49	44	22
Percentage of births to women under age 20*	13	12	12	9
Percentage of births to women aged 35 or older*	7	6	6	9
Percentage of married women using contraception				
Modern methods	..	..	31	..
All methods	..	..	47	..
Health and mortality				
Life expectancy at birth (years)*				
Males	67	66	64	66
Females	75	76	75	78
Both sexes combined	71	71	70	72
Infant mortality rate (per 1,000 births)*	22	18	16	9
Mortality under age 5 (per 1,000 births)*	29	24	22	12
Maternal mortality ratio (per 100,000 births) (2000)	..	..	..	13
HIV/AIDS (2003)				
Number of infected adults (thousands)	..	..	..	1
Adult prevalence rate (percentage)	..	..	..	0.1
Spatial distribution				
Population density (per sq. km)	51	54	56	53
Urban population (percentage)	56	65	67	67
Annual urban growth rate (percentage)*	3.3	2.0	-1.1	-0.7
Annual rural growth rate (percentage)*	-1.6	-1.4	-0.8	-0.4
International migration				
International migrant stock				
Number of migrants (thousands)	..	..	272	165
Percentage of total population	..	..	7.5	4.8

* For the periods 1970-1975, 1980-1985, 1990-1995 and 2000-2005.

Government views and policies

Population policy variable	*1976*	*1986*	*1996*	*2005*
Population size and growth				
View on growth	Too low	Satisfactory	Satisfactory	Satisfactory
Policy on growth	Raise	Raise	Maintain	Maintain
Population age structure				
Level of concern about				
Size of the working-age population	..	..	..	Minor concern
Ageing of the population	..	..	..	Minor concern
Fertility and family planning				
View on fertility level	Too low	Too low	Too low	Satisfactory
Policy	Raise	Raise	Raise	Maintain
Access to contraceptive methods	Indirect support	Indirect support	Indirect support	Indirect support
Adolescent fertility				
Level of concern	..	..	..	..
Policies and programmes	..	..	..	..
Health and mortality				
View				
Expectation of life	Acceptable	Acceptable	Acceptable	Acceptable
Under-five mortality	..	..	..	Acceptable
Maternal mortality	..	..	..	Acceptable
Level of concern about HIV/AIDS	..	..	..	Major concern
Measures implemented to control HIV/AIDS*	..	..	..	1,2,3,4,5
Grounds on which abortion is permitted**	..	..	1,2,3,4,5,6	1,2,3,4,5,6
Spatial distribution and internal migration				
View on spatial distribution	Satisfactory	Minor change desired	Major change desired	Satisfactory
Policies on internal migration				
From rural to urban areas	..	..	..	..
From rural to rural areas	..	..	..	..
From urban to rural areas	..	..	..	..
From urban to urban areas	..	..	..	..
Into urban agglomerations	No intervention	..	..	..
International migration				
Immigration				
View	Satisfactory	Too high	Too high	Satisfactory
Policy	Maintain	Lower	Lower	Maintain
Permanent settlement	..	..	..	Maintain
Temporary workers	..	..	..	Maintain
Highly skilled workers	..	..	..	..
Family reunification	..	..	..	..
Integration of non-nationals	..	..	..	Yes
Emigration				
View	Satisfactory	Satisfactory	Satisfactory	Satisfactory
Policy	Maintain	Maintain	No intervention	No intervention
Encouraging the return of nationals	No	..	..	..

* Measures implemented to control HIV/AIDS: (1) blood screening; (2) information/education campaigns; (3) access to antiretroviral treatment; (4) non-discriminatory policies; (5) promoting condom use.

** Grounds on which abortion is permitted: (1) to save the woman's life; (2) to preserve physical health; (3) to preserve mental health; (4) rape or incest; (5) foetal impairment; (6) economic or social reasons; (7) on request.

Population indicators

Indicator	*1975*	*1985*	*1995*	*2005*
Population size and growth				
Population size (thousands)	359	367	405	465
Annual growth rate (percentage)*	1.1	0.1	1.4	1.3
Population age structure				
Percentage of population under age 15	22	17	19	19
Percentage of population aged 60 or older	19	18	18	18
Fertility and family planning				
Total fertility (births per woman)*	2.0	1.5	1.7	1.7
Teenage fertility rate (per 1,000 women, aged 15 - 19)*	14	11	12	9
Percentage of births to women under age 20*	4	3	3	2
Percentage of births to women aged 35 or older*	11	9	11	16
Percentage of married women using contraception				
Modern methods	..	..	..	..
All methods	..	..	..	..
Health and mortality				
Life expectancy at birth (years)*				
Males	67	70	72	75
Females	74	77	79	81
Both sexes combined	71	74	75	78
Infant mortality rate (per 1,000 births)*	17	12	9	5
Mortality under age 5 (per 1,000 births)*	20	14	11	7
Maternal mortality ratio (per 100,000 births) (2000)	..	..	..	28
HIV/AIDS (2003)				
Number of infected adults (thousands)	..	..	..	<1
Adult prevalence rate (percentage)	..	..	..	0.2
Spatial distribution				
Population density (per sq. km)	139	142	157	180
Urban population (percentage)	74	83	89	92
Annual urban growth rate (percentage)*	2.8	1.1	2.1	1.6
Annual rural growth rate (percentage)*	-2.9	-4.1	-3.2	-1.9
International migration				
International migrant stock				
Number of migrants (thousands)	75	104	135	174
Percentage of total population	21	28.3	33.4	37.4

* For the periods 1970-1975, 1980-1985, 1990-1995 and 2000-2005.

Government views and policies

Population policy variable	*1976*	*1986*	*1996*	*2005*
Population size and growth				
View on growth	Too high	Too high	Too high	Too high
Policy on growth	No intervention	No intervention	Lower	Lower
Population age structure				
Level of concern about				
Size of the working-age population	..	..	..	..
Ageing of the population	..	..	..	Major concern
Fertility and family planning				
View on fertility level	Too high	Too high	Too high	Too high
Policy	No intervention	No intervention	Lower	Lower
Access to contraceptive methods	Indirect support	Direct support	Direct support	Direct support
Adolescent fertility				
Level of concern	..	..	Major concern	Major concern
Policies and programmes	..	..	Yes	Yes
Health and mortality				
View				
Expectation of life	Unacceptable	Unacceptable	Unacceptable	Unacceptable
Under-five mortality	..	..	Unacceptable	Unacceptable
Maternal mortality	..	..	..	Unacceptable
Level of concern about HIV/AIDS	..	..	Minor concern	Major concern
Measures implemented to control HIV/AIDS*	..	..	..	1,2,5
Grounds on which abortion is permitted**	..	..	1	1
Spatial distribution and internal migration				
View on spatial distribution	Major change desired	Minor change desired	Major change desired	Minor change desired
Policies on internal migration				
From rural to urban areas	..	..	..	No intervention
From rural to rural areas	..	..	..	..
From urban to rural areas	..	..	..	..
From urban to urban areas	..	..	..	..
Into urban agglomerations	..	No intervention	Lower	No intervention
International migration				
Immigration				
View	Satisfactory	Satisfactory	Satisfactory	Satisfactory
Policy	Maintain	Maintain	No intervention	No intervention
Permanent settlement	..	..	No intervention	..
Temporary workers	..	..	No intervention	..
Highly skilled workers	..	..	..	..
Family reunification	..	..	No intervention	..
Integration of non-nationals	..	..	No	..
Emigration				
View	Satisfactory	Satisfactory	Satisfactory	Satisfactory
Policy	Maintain	Maintain	No intervention	No intervention
Encouraging the return of nationals	Yes	..	No	No

* Measures implemented to control HIV/AIDS: (1) blood screening; (2) information/education campaigns; (3) access to antiretroviral treatment; (4) non-discriminatory policies; (5) promoting condom use.

** Grounds on which abortion is permitted: (1) to save the woman's life; (2) to preserve physical health; (3) to preserve mental health; (4) rape or incest; (5) foetal impairment; (6) economic or social reasons; (7) on request.

Population indicators

Indicator	1975	1985	1995	2005
Population size and growth				
Population size (thousands)	7 909	10 447	13 946	18 606
Annual growth rate (percentage)*	2.6	2.8	2.9	2.8
Population age structure				
Percentage of population under age 15	45	45	45	44
Percentage of population aged 60 or older	5	5	5	5
Fertility and family planning				
Total fertility (births per woman)*	6.7	6.4	6.1	5.4
Teenage fertility rate (per 1,000 women, aged 15 - 19)*	153	151	149	129
Percentage of births to women under age 20*	17	17	18	17
Percentage of births to women aged 35 or older*	17	16	16	14
Percentage of married women using contraception				
Modern methods	..	..	5[a]	17[b]
All methods	..	..	17[a]	27[b]
Health and mortality				
Life expectancy at birth (years)*				
Males	44	48	51	54
Females	46	50	53	57
Both sexes combined	45	49	52	55
Infant mortality rate (per 1,000 births)*	132	111	96	79
Mortality under age 5 (per 1,000 births)*	221	190	165	131
Maternal mortality ratio (per 100,000 births) (2000)	..	..	..	550
HIV/AIDS (2003)				
Number of infected adults (thousands)	..	..	..	130
Adult prevalence rate (percentage)	..	..	..	1.7
Spatial distribution				
Population density (per sq. km)	13	18	24	32
Urban population (percentage)	16	21	25	27
Annual urban growth rate (percentage)*	5.7	5.2	4.4	3.6
Annual rural growth rate (percentage)*	2.1	2.2	2.3	2.6
International migration				
International migrant stock				
Number of migrants (thousands)	54	57	60	63
Percentage of total population	0.7	0.5	0.4	0.3

* For the periods 1970-1975, 1980-1985, 1990-1995 and 2000-2005.
[a] For 1992.
[b] For 2003/2004.

Government views and policies

Population policy variable	*1976*	*1986*	*1996*	*2005*
Population size and growth				
View on growth	Satisfactory	Too high	Too high	Too high
Policy on growth	No intervention	No intervention	No intervention	Lower
Population age structure				
Level of concern about				
Size of the working-age population	..	..	..	Major concern
Ageing of the population	..	..	..	Minor concern
Fertility and family planning				
View on fertility level	Satisfactory	Too high	Too high	Too high
Policy	No intervention	No intervention	Lower	Lower
Access to contraceptive methods	Limits	Direct support	Direct support	Direct support
Adolescent fertility				
Level of concern	..	..	Major concern	Major concern
Policies and programmes	..	..	Yes	Yes
Health and mortality				
View				
Expectation of life	Unacceptable	Unacceptable	Unacceptable	Unacceptable
Under-five mortality	..	..	Unacceptable	Unacceptable
Maternal mortality	..	..	..	Unacceptable
Level of concern about HIV/AIDS	..	..	Major concern	Major concern
Measures implemented to control HIV/AIDS*	..	..	..	1,2,3,5
Grounds on which abortion is permitted**	..	..	1	1
Spatial distribution and internal migration				
View on spatial distribution	Minor change desired	Minor change desired	Minor change desired	Minor change desired
Policies on internal migration				
From rural to urban areas	..	..	..	Lower
From rural to rural areas	..	..	..	..
From urban to rural areas	..	..	..	..
From urban to urban areas	..	..	..	..
Into urban agglomerations	..	..	Lower	Lower
International migration				
Immigration				
View	Satisfactory	Satisfactory	Too high	Satisfactory
Policy	Maintain	Maintain	Lower	Lower
Permanent settlement	..	..	No intervention	Maintain
Temporary workers	..	..	No intervention	Lower
Highly skilled workers	..	..	..	..
Family reunification	..	..	No intervention	Lower
Integration of non-nationals	..	..	No	Yes
Emigration				
View	Satisfactory	Satisfactory	Satisfactory	Satisfactory
Policy	Maintain	Maintain	No intervention	No intervention
Encouraging the return of nationals	..	..	No	Yes

* Measures implemented to control HIV/AIDS: (1) blood screening; (2) information/education campaigns; (3) access to antiretroviral treatment; (4) non-discriminatory policies; (5) promoting condom use.

** Grounds on which abortion is permitted: (1) to save the woman's life; (2) to preserve physical health; (3) to preserve mental health; (4) rape or incest; (5) foetal impairment; (6) economic or social reasons; (7) on request.

Population indicators

Indicator	*1975*	*1985*	*1995*	*2005*
Population size and growth				
Population size (thousands)	5 244	7 250	10 111	12 884
Annual growth rate (percentage)*	3.0	3.2	1.3	2.3
Population age structure				
Percentage of population under age 15	47	48	45	47
Percentage of population aged 60 or older	4	4	5	5
Fertility and family planning				
Total fertility (births per woman)*	7.4	7.5	6.8	6.1
Teenage fertility rate (per 1,000 women, aged 15 - 19)*	183	186	164	163
Percentage of births to women under age 20*	18	19	17	19
Percentage of births to women aged 35 or older*	20	20	17	13
Percentage of married women using contraception				
Modern methods	..	1[a]	14[b]	26[c]
All methods	..	7[a]	22[b]	31[c]
Health and mortality				
Life expectancy at birth (years)*				
Males	41	45	43	40
Females	43	47	47	40
Both sexes combined	42	46	45	40
Infant mortality rate (per 1,000 births)*	185	150	135	111
Mortality under age 5 (per 1,000 births)*	318	257	227	184
Maternal mortality ratio (per 100,000 births) (2000)	..	..	..	1 800
HIV/AIDS (2003)				
Number of infected adults (thousands)	..	..	..	810
Adult prevalence rate (percentage)	..	..	..	14.2
Spatial distribution				
Population density (per sq. km)	44	61	85	109
Urban population (percentage)	8	10	13	17
Annual urban growth rate (percentage)*	7.7	5.6	3.8	4.6
Annual rural growth rate (percentage)*	2.6	2.9	0.8	1.5
International migration				
International migrant stock				
Number of migrants (thousands)	290	285	325	279
Percentage of total population	5.5	3.9	3.2	2.2

* For the periods 1970-1975, 1980-1985, 1990-1995 and 2000-2005.
[a] For 1984.
[b] For 1996.
[c] For 2000.

Government views and policies

Population policy variable	*1976*	*1986*	*1996*	*2005*
Population size and growth				
View on growth	Too high	Satisfactory	Too high	Too high
Policy on growth	Lower	Maintain	Lower	No intervention
Population age structure				
Level of concern about				
Size of the working-age population	..	..	..	Minor concern
Ageing of the population	..	..	..	Minor concern
Fertility and family planning				
View on fertility level	Too high	Satisfactory	Too high	Satisfactory
Policy	Lower	Maintain	Lower	No intervention
Access to contraceptive methods	Direct support	Direct support	Direct support	Direct support
Adolescent fertility				
Level of concern	..	..	Minor concern	Major concern
Policies and programmes	..	..	Yes	Yes
Health and mortality				
View				
Expectation of life	Acceptable	Unacceptable	Acceptable	Acceptable
Under-five mortality	..	..	Acceptable	Acceptable
Maternal mortality	..	..	..	Acceptable
Level of concern about HIV/AIDS	..	..	Major concern	Major concern
Measures implemented to control HIV/AIDS*	..	..	..	1,2,3,4,5
Grounds on which abortion is permitted**	..	..	1,2,3	1,2,3
Spatial distribution and internal migration				
View on spatial distribution	Minor change desired	Minor change desired	Minor change desired	Satisfactory
Policies on internal migration				
From rural to urban areas	..	..	..	Lower
From rural to rural areas	..	..	..	No intervention
From urban to rural areas	..	..	..	Maintain
From urban to urban areas	..	..	..	No intervention
Into urban agglomerations	..	Lower	Lower	Lower
International migration				
Immigration				
View	Satisfactory	Satisfactory	Too high	Satisfactory
Policy	Maintain	Maintain	Lower	Maintain
Permanent settlement	..	..	Lower	Maintain
Temporary workers	..	..	Maintain	Lower
Highly skilled workers	..	..	..	Maintain
Family reunification	..	..	No intervention	Maintain
Integration of non-nationals	..	..	Yes	Yes
Emigration				
View	Too low	Satisfactory	Satisfactory	Satisfactory
Policy	Raise	Maintain	No intervention	No intervention
Encouraging the return of nationals	..	..	No	Yes

* Measures implemented to control HIV/AIDS: (1) blood screening; (2) information/education campaigns; (3) access to antiretroviral treatment; (4) non-discriminatory policies; (5) promoting condom use.

** Grounds on which abortion is permitted: (1) to save the woman's life; (2) to preserve physical health; (3) to preserve mental health; (4) rape or incest; (5) foetal impairment; (6) economic or social reasons; (7) on request.

Population indicators

Indicator	*1975*	*1985*	*1995*	*2005*
Population size and growth				
Population size (thousands)	12 258	15 677	20 362	25 347
Annual growth rate (percentage)*	2.4	2.6	2.6	1.9
Population age structure				
Percentage of population under age 15	42	39	36	32
Percentage of population aged 60 or older	6	6	6	7
Fertility and family planning				
Total fertility (births per woman)*	5.2	4.2	3.6	2.9
Teenage fertility rate (per 1,000 women, aged 15 - 19)*	41	34	29	18
Percentage of births to women under age 20*	7	6	5	4
Percentage of births to women aged 35 or older*	14	13	16	16
Percentage of married women using contraception				
Modern methods	23[a]	30[b]	30[c]	..
All methods	33[a]	51[b]	55[c]	..
Health and mortality				
Life expectancy at birth (years)*				
Males	61	66	69	71
Females	65	70	73	75
Both sexes combined	63	68	71	73
Infant mortality rate (per 1,000 births)*	42	28	15	10
Mortality under age 5 (per 1,000 births)*	57	37	20	13
Maternal mortality ratio (per 100,000 births) (2000)	..	..	..	41
HIV/AIDS (2003)				
Number of infected adults (thousands)	..	..	..	51
Adult prevalence rate (percentage)	..	..	..	0.4
Spatial distribution				
Population density (per sq. km)	37	48	62	77
Urban population (percentage)	38	46	56	65
Annual urban growth rate (percentage)*	4.8	4.4	4.8	3.0
Annual rural growth rate (percentage)*	1.1	1.2	0.2	0.1
International migration				
International migrant stock				
Number of migrants (thousands)	718	908	1 133	1 639
Percentage of total population	5.9	5.8	5.6	6.5

* For the periods 1970-1975, 1980-1985, 1990-1995 and 2000-2005.
[a] For 1974.
[b] For 1984.
[c] For 1994.

Government views and policies

Population policy variable	1976	1986	1996	2005
Population size and growth				
View on growth	Satisfactory	Satisfactory	Too high	Too high
Policy on growth	No intervention	No intervention	Lower	Lower
Population age structure				
Level of concern about				
Size of the working-age population	..	..	..	Major concern
Ageing of the population	..	..	..	Minor concern
Fertility and family planning				
View on fertility level	Satisfactory	Satisfactory	Too high	Too high
Policy	No intervention	No intervention	Lower	Lower
Access to contraceptive methods	No support	Direct support	Direct support	Direct support
Adolescent fertility				
Level of concern	..	..	Minor concern	Major concern
Policies and programmes	..	..	Yes	Yes
Health and mortality				
View				
Expectation of life	Unacceptable	Unacceptable	Unacceptable	Unacceptable
Under-five mortality	..	..	Unacceptable	Unacceptable
Maternal mortality	..	..	..	Unacceptable
Level of concern about HIV/AIDS	..	..	Major concern	Major concern
Measures implemented to control HIV/AIDS*	..	..	..	1,2,3,5
Grounds on which abortion is permitted**	..	..	1,2	1,2
Spatial distribution and internal migration				
View on spatial distribution	Minor change desired	Major change desired	Major change desired	Major change desired
Policies on internal migration				
From rural to urban areas	..	..	..	Lower
From rural to rural areas	..	..	..	..
From urban to rural areas	..	..	..	..
From urban to urban areas	..	..	..	..
Into urban agglomerations	Lower	..	Lower	Lower
International migration				
Immigration				
View	Satisfactory	Satisfactory	Satisfactory	Satisfactory
Policy	Maintain	Maintain	Lower	Lower
Permanent settlement	..	..	Lower	..
Temporary workers	..	..	Lower	..
Highly skilled workers	..	..	..	..
Family reunification	..	..	Lower	Maintain
Integration of non-nationals	..	..	No	..
Emigration				
View	Satisfactory	Satisfactory	Satisfactory	Satisfactory
Policy	Maintain	Maintain	No intervention	No intervention
Encouraging the return of nationals	..	..	No	..

* Measures implemented to control HIV/AIDS: (1) blood screening; (2) information/education campaigns; (3) access to antiretroviral treatment; (4) non-discriminatory policies; (5) promoting condom use.

** Grounds on which abortion is permitted: (1) to save the woman's life; (2) to preserve physical health; (3) to preserve mental health; (4) rape or incest; (5) foetal impairment; (6) economic or social reasons; (7) on request.

Population indicators

Indicator	*1975*	*1985*	*1995*	*2005*
Population size and growth				
Population size (thousands)	137	184	252	329
Annual growth rate (percentage)*	2.5	3.0	3.1	2.5
Population age structure				
Percentage of population under age 15	42	46	46	41
Percentage of population aged 60 or older	7	5	5	5
Fertility and family planning				
Total fertility (births per woman)*	7.0	6.8	6.0	4.3
Teenage fertility rate (per 1,000 women, aged 15 - 19)*	158	154	137	70
Percentage of births to women under age 20*	18	16	17	13
Percentage of births to women aged 35 or older*	18	15	18	13
Percentage of married women using contraception				
Modern methods	..	..	33[a]	..
All methods	..	..	42[a]	..
Health and mortality				
Life expectancy at birth (years)*				
Males	53	58	62	67
Females	50	56	60	66
Both sexes combined	51	57	61	66
Infant mortality rate (per 1,000 births)*	121	94	65	43
Mortality under age 5 (per 1,000 births)*	170	130	90	55
Maternal mortality ratio (per 100,000 births) (2000)	..	..	..	110
HIV/AIDS (2003)				
Number of infected adults (thousands)	..	..	..	..
Adult prevalence rate (percentage)	..	..	..	..
Spatial distribution				
Population density (per sq. km)	461	616	845	1 105
Urban population (percentage)	18	26	26	30
Annual urban growth rate (percentage)*	8.1	5.8	2.8	4.5
Annual rural growth rate (percentage)*	1.4	2.1	3.0	2.4
International migration				
International migrant stock				
Number of migrants (thousands)	2	2	3	3
Percentage of total population	1.5	1.3	1.2	1

* For the periods 1970-1975, 1980-1985, 1990-1995 and 2000-2005.
[a] For 1999.

Government views and policies

Population policy variable	*1976*	*1986*	*1996*	*2005*
Population size and growth				
View on growth	Satisfactory	Satisfactory	Too high	Too high
Policy on growth	No intervention	Maintain	Lower	Lower
Population age structure				
Level of concern about				
Size of the working-age population	..	..	..	Major concern
Ageing of the population	..	..	..	Minor concern
Fertility and family planning				
View on fertility level	Satisfactory	Satisfactory	Too high	Too high
Policy	No intervention	Maintain	Lower	Lower
Access to contraceptive methods	Direct support	Direct support	Direct support	Direct support
Adolescent fertility				
Level of concern	..	..	Minor concern	Minor concern
Policies and programmes	..	..	Yes	No
Health and mortality				
View				
Expectation of life	Unacceptable	Unacceptable	Unacceptable	Unacceptable
Under-five mortality	..	..	Unacceptable	Unacceptable
Maternal mortality	..	..	..	Unacceptable
Level of concern about HIV/AIDS	..	..	Minor concern	Major concern
Measures implemented to control HIV/AIDS*	..	..	..	1,2,3,4,5
Grounds on which abortion is permitted**	..	..	1	1,4
Spatial distribution and internal migration				
View on spatial distribution	Major change desired	Major change desired	Major change desired	Major change desired
Policies on internal migration				
From rural to urban areas	..	..	..	Lower
From rural to rural areas	..	..	..	Maintain
From urban to rural areas	..	..	..	Raise
From urban to urban areas	..	..	..	No intervention
Into urban agglomerations	..	Lower	Lower	Lower
International migration				
Immigration				
View	Satisfactory	Satisfactory	Satisfactory	Too high
Policy	Maintain	Maintain	Maintain	No intervention
Permanent settlement	..	..	Maintain	..
Temporary workers	..	..	Lower	..
Highly skilled workers	..	..	..	..
Family reunification	..	..	Maintain	..
Integration of non-nationals	..	..	No	No
Emigration				
View	Satisfactory	Satisfactory	Satisfactory	Too high
Policy	Maintain	Maintain	Maintain	Lower
Encouraging the return of nationals	..	..	Yes	Yes

* Measures implemented to control HIV/AIDS: (1) blood screening; (2) information/education campaigns; (3) access to antiretroviral treatment; (4) non-discriminatory policies; (5) promoting condom use.

** Grounds on which abortion is permitted: (1) to save the woman's life; (2) to preserve physical health; (3) to preserve mental health; (4) rape or incest; (5) foetal impairment; (6) economic or social reasons; (7) on request.

Population indicators

Indicator	*1975*	*1985*	*1995*	*2005*
Population size and growth				
Population size (thousands)	6 211	7 878	10 147	13 518
Annual growth rate (percentage)*	2.7	2.4	2.6	3.0
Population age structure				
Percentage of population under age 15	46	48	48	48
Percentage of population aged 60 or older	4	4	4	4
Fertility and family planning				
Total fertility (births per woman)*	7.6	7.6	7.4	6.9
Teenage fertility rate (per 1,000 women, aged 15 - 19)*	257	257	206	209
Percentage of births to women under age 20*	23	25	22	23
Percentage of births to women aged 35 or older*	15	15	14	12
Percentage of married women using contraception				
Modern methods	..	1[a]	5	6[b]
All methods	..	5[a]	7	8[b]
Health and mortality				
Life expectancy at birth (years)*				
Males	37	42	46	47
Females	39	44	48	48
Both sexes combined	38	43	47	48
Infant mortality rate (per 1,000 births)*	188	163	142	133
Mortality under age 5 (per 1,000 births)*	334	287	241	220
Maternal mortality ratio (per 100,000 births) (2000)	..	..	..	1 200
HIV/AIDS (2003)				
Number of infected adults (thousands)	..	..	..	120
Adult prevalence rate (percentage)	..	..	..	1.9
Spatial distribution				
Population density (per sq. km)	5	6	8	11
Urban population (percentage)	16	21	27	34
Annual urban growth rate (percentage)*	4.8	5.0	5.1	5.2
Annual rural growth rate (percentage)*	1.9	1.8	1.9	2.0
International migration				
International migrant stock				
Number of migrants (thousands)	82	61	63	46
Percentage of total population	1.3	0.8	0.6	0.3

* For the periods 1970-1975, 1980-1985, 1990-1995 and 2000-2005.
[a] For 1987.
[b] For 2001.

Government views and policies

Population policy variable	*1976*	*1986*	*1996*	*2005*
Population size and growth				
View on growth	Satisfactory	Satisfactory	Satisfactory	Satisfactory
Policy on growth	No intervention	No intervention	No intervention	Maintain
Population age structure				
Level of concern about				
Size of the working-age population	..	..	..	Minor concern
Ageing of the population	..	..	..	Minor concern
Fertility and family planning				
View on fertility level	Satisfactory	Satisfactory	Satisfactory	Too low
Policy	No intervention	No intervention	No intervention	No intervention
Access to contraceptive methods	No support	No support	No support	No support
Adolescent fertility				
Level of concern	..	..	..	Minor concern
Policies and programmes	..	..	..	Yes
Health and mortality				
View				
Expectation of life	Acceptable	Acceptable	Acceptable	Acceptable
Under-five mortality	..	..	..	Acceptable
Maternal mortality	..	..	..	Acceptable
Level of concern about HIV/AIDS	..	..	..	Minor concern
Measures implemented to control HIV/AIDS*	..	..	..	1,2,3,4,5
Grounds on which abortion is permitted**	..	..	Not permitted	Not permitted
Spatial distribution and internal migration				
View on spatial distribution	Satisfactory	Satisfactory	Satisfactory	Minor change desired
Policies on internal migration				
From rural to urban areas	..	..	..	No intervention
From rural to rural areas	..	..	..	No intervention
From urban to rural areas	..	..	..	No intervention
From urban to urban areas	..	..	..	Lower
Into urban agglomerations	..	No intervention	..	No intervention
International migration				
Immigration				
View	Satisfactory	Satisfactory	Satisfactory	Satisfactory
Policy	Maintain	Maintain	Maintain	Maintain
Permanent settlement	..	..	..	Maintain
Temporary workers	..	..	..	Maintain
Highly skilled workers	..	..	..	Maintain
Family reunification	..	..	..	Maintain
Integration of non-nationals	..	..	..	No
Emigration				
View	Satisfactory	Satisfactory	Satisfactory	Satisfactory
Policy	Maintain	Maintain	No intervention	No intervention
Encouraging the return of nationals	..	..	..	No

* Measures implemented to control HIV/AIDS: (1) blood screening; (2) information/education campaigns; (3) access to antiretroviral treatment; (4) non-discriminatory policies; (5) promoting condom use.

** Grounds on which abortion is permitted: (1) to save the woman's life; (2) to preserve physical health; (3) to preserve mental health; (4) rape or incest; (5) foetal impairment; (6) economic or social reasons; (7) on request.

Population indicators

Indicator	*1975*	*1985*	*1995*	*2005*
Population size and growth				
Population size (thousands)	304	344	378	402
Annual growth rate (percentage)*	0.1	1.2	1.0	0.5
Population age structure				
Percentage of population under age 15	25	24	22	18
Percentage of population aged 60 or older	13	14	16	19
Fertility and family planning				
Total fertility (births per woman)*	2.1	2.0	2.0	1.5
Teenage fertility rate (per 1,000 women, aged 15 - 19)*	18	17	18	17
Percentage of births to women under age 20*	5	4	5	6
Percentage of births to women aged 35 or older*	10	11	14	11
Percentage of married women using contraception				
Modern methods	..	..	..	..
All methods	..	..	..	..
Health and mortality				
Life expectancy at birth (years)*				
Males	69	71	74	76
Females	73	76	78	81
Both sexes combined	71	74	76	78
Infant mortality rate (per 1,000 births)*	22	13	9	7
Mortality under age 5 (per 1,000 births)*	24	15	11	8
Maternal mortality ratio (per 100,000 births) (2000)	..	..	..	21
HIV/AIDS (2003)				
Number of infected adults (thousands)	..	..	..	<1
Adult prevalence rate (percentage)	..	..	..	0.2
Spatial distribution				
Population density (per sq. km)	963	1 090	1 196	1 271
Urban population (percentage)	80	86	89	92
Annual urban growth rate (percentage)*	0.9	1.8	1.4	0.7
Annual rural growth rate (percentage)*	-2.8	-1.9	-2.2	-2.4
International migration				
International migrant stock				
Number of migrants (thousands)	8	5	7	11
Percentage of total population	2.7	1.4	1.9	2.7

* For the periods 1970-1975, 1980-1985, 1990-1995 and 2000-2005.

Government views and policies

Population policy variable	*1976*	*1986*	*1996*	*2005*
Population size and growth				
View on growth	..	..	Too high	Too high
Policy on growth	..	..	Lower	Lower
Population age structure				
Level of concern about				
Size of the working-age population	..	..	..	Major concern
Ageing of the population	..	..	..	..
Fertility and family planning				
View on fertility level	..	..	Too high	Too high
Policy	..	..	Lower	Lower
Access to contraceptive methods	..	..	Direct support	Direct support
Adolescent fertility				
Level of concern	..	..	Major concern	Major concern
Policies and programmes	..	..	Yes	Yes
Health and mortality				
View				
Expectation of life	..	..	Unacceptable	Acceptable
Under-five mortality	..	..	Unacceptable	Acceptable
Maternal mortality	..	..	..	Acceptable
Level of concern about HIV/AIDS	..	..	Major concern	Major concern
Measures implemented to control HIV/AIDS*	..	..	..	2,3,4,5
Grounds on which abortion is permitted**	..	..	1	1
Spatial distribution and internal migration				
View on spatial distribution	..	..	Major change desired	Major change desired
Policies on internal migration				
From rural to urban areas	..	..	..	Lower
From rural to rural areas	..	..	..	..
From urban to rural areas	..	..	..	Maintain
From urban to urban areas	..	..	..	Raise
Into urban agglomerations	..	..	No intervention	Lower
International migration				
Immigration				
View	..	..	Satisfactory	Satisfactory
Policy	..	..	Lower	Maintain
Permanent settlement	..	..	Lower	..
Temporary workers	..	..	Lower	Lower
Highly skilled workers	..	..	..	..
Family reunification	..	..	Lower	..
Integration of non-nationals	..	..	No	..
Emigration				
View	..	..	Satisfactory	Satisfactory
Policy	..	..	No intervention	Maintain
Encouraging the return of nationals	..	..	No	No

* Measures implemented to control HIV/AIDS: (1) blood screening; (2) information/education campaigns; (3) access to antiretroviral treatment; (4) non-discriminatory policies; (5) promoting condom use.

** Grounds on which abortion is permitted: (1) to save the woman's life; (2) to preserve physical health; (3) to preserve mental health; (4) rape or incest; (5) foetal impairment; (6) economic or social reasons; (7) on request.

Population indicators

Indicator	*1975*	*1985*	*1995*	*2005*
Population size and growth				
Population size (thousands)	26	38	51	62
Annual growth rate (percentage)*	4.5	4.5	1.5	3.5
Population age structure				
Percentage of population under age 15	..	..	..	..
Percentage of population aged 60 or older	..	..	..	..
Fertility and family planning				
Total fertility (births per woman)*	..	..	..	..
Teenage fertility rate (per 1,000 women, aged 15 - 19)*	..	..	..	..
Percentage of births to women under age 20*	..	..	..	..
Percentage of births to women aged 35 or older*	..	..	..	..
Percentage of married women using contraception				
Modern methods	..	..	..	..
All methods	..	..	..	..
Health and mortality				
Life expectancy at birth (years)*				
Males	..	..	..	..
Females	..	..	..	..
Both sexes combined	..	..	..	..
Infant mortality rate (per 1,000 births)*	..	..	..	..
Mortality under age 5 (per 1,000 births)*	..	..	..	..
Maternal mortality ratio (per 100,000 births) (2000)	..	..	..	..
HIV/AIDS (2003)				
Number of infected adults (thousands)	..	..	..	..
Adult prevalence rate (percentage)	..	..	..	..
Spatial distribution				
Population density (per sq. km)	141	212	282	342
Urban population (percentage)	61	62	65	67
Annual urban growth rate (percentage)*	3.0	5.4	1.6	1.5
Annual rural growth rate (percentage)*	5.0	2.3	1.1	0.7
International migration				
International migrant stock				
Number of migrants (thousands)	1	1	2	2
Percentage of total population	4.5	3.7	3.1	2.7

* For the periods 1970-1975, 1980-1985, 1990-1995 and 2000-2005.

Government views and policies

Population policy variable	*1976*	*1986*	*1996*	*2005*
Population size and growth				
View on growth	Satisfactory	Satisfactory	Satisfactory	Too high
Policy on growth	No intervention	Raise	No intervention	Lower
Population age structure				
Level of concern about				
Size of the working-age population	..	..	..	..
Ageing of the population	..	..	..	Minor concern
Fertility and family planning				
View on fertility level	Satisfactory	Satisfactory	Satisfactory	Too high
Policy	No intervention	No intervention	No intervention	Lower
Access to contraceptive methods	No support	No support	Direct support	Direct support
Adolescent fertility				
Level of concern	..	..	Not a concern	Minor concern
Policies and programmes	..	..	No	No
Health and mortality				
View				
Expectation of life	Unacceptable	Unacceptable	Unacceptable	Unacceptable
Under-five mortality	..	..	Unacceptable	Unacceptable
Maternal mortality	..	..	..	Unacceptable
Level of concern about HIV/AIDS	..	..	Minor concern	Major concern
Measures implemented to control HIV/AIDS*	..	..	..	3
Grounds on which abortion is permitted**	..	..	1	1
Spatial distribution and internal migration				
View on spatial distribution	Major change desired	Major change desired	Major change desired	Major change desired
Policies on internal migration				
From rural to urban areas	..	..	..	Lower
From rural to rural areas	..	..	..	..
From urban to rural areas	..	..	..	..
From urban to urban areas	..	..	..	..
Into urban agglomerations	..	No intervention	Lower	Lower
International migration				
Immigration				
View	Satisfactory	Satisfactory	Satisfactory	Satisfactory
Policy	Maintain	Maintain	No intervention	No intervention
Permanent settlement	..	..	No intervention	..
Temporary workers	..	..	No intervention	..
Highly skilled workers	..	..	..	..
Family reunification	..	..	No intervention	..
Integration of non-nationals	..	..	No	..
Emigration				
View	Satisfactory	Too high	Satisfactory	Satisfactory
Policy	Maintain	Maintain	No intervention	No intervention
Encouraging the return of nationals	..	..	No	..

* Measures implemented to control HIV/AIDS: (1) blood screening; (2) information/education campaigns; (3) access to antiretroviral treatment; (4) non-discriminatory policies; (5) promoting condom use.

** Grounds on which abortion is permitted: (1) to save the woman's life; (2) to preserve physical health; (3) to preserve mental health; (4) rape or incest; (5) foetal impairment; (6) economic or social reasons; (7) on request.

Population indicators

Indicator	*1975*	*1985*	*1995*	*2005*
Population size and growth				
Population size (thousands)	1 423	1 812	2 300	3 069
Annual growth rate (percentage)*	2.4	2.4	2.5	3.0
Population age structure				
Percentage of population under age 15	44	44	44	43
Percentage of population aged 60 or older	5	5	5	5
Fertility and family planning				
Total fertility (births per woman)*	6.5	6.3	6.1	5.8
Teenage fertility rate (per 1,000 women, aged 15 - 19)*	136	134	121	104
Percentage of births to women under age 20*	15	16	15	13
Percentage of births to women aged 35 or older*	23	23	20	18
Percentage of married women using contraception				
Modern methods	..	0[a]	1[b]	5[c]
All methods	..	1[a]	3[b]	8[c]
Health and mortality				
Life expectancy at birth (years)*				
Males	42	46	48	51
Females	45	49	51	54
Both sexes combined	43	47	49	52
Infant mortality rate (per 1,000 births)*	141	120	110	97
Mortality under age 5 (per 1,000 births)*	235	199	181	156
Maternal mortality ratio (per 100,000 births) (2000)	..	..	..	1 000
HIV/AIDS (2003)				
Number of infected adults (thousands)	..	..	..	9
Adult prevalence rate (percentage)	..	..	..	0.6
Spatial distribution				
Population density (per sq. km)	1	2	2	3
Urban population (percentage)	20	36	51	64
Annual urban growth rate (percentage)*	10.3	7.6	5.4	5.1
Annual rural growth rate (percentage)*	0.8	0.0	-0.1	-0.4
International migration				
International migrant stock				
Number of migrants (thousands)	26	44	118	66
Percentage of total population	1.8	2.4	5.1	2.1

* For the periods 1970-1975, 1980-1985, 1990-1995 and 2000-2005.
[a] For 1981.
[b] For 1990.
[c] For 2000/2001.

Government views and policies

Population policy variable	*1976*	*1986*	*1996*	*2005*
Population size and growth				
View on growth	Too high	Too high	Satisfactory	Satisfactory
Policy on growth	Lower	Lower	Maintain	Maintain
Population age structure				
Level of concern about				
Size of the working-age population	..	..	..	Minor concern
Ageing of the population	..	..	..	Major concern
Fertility and family planning				
View on fertility level	Too high	Too high	Satisfactory	Satisfactory
Policy	Lower	Lower	Maintain	Maintain
Access to contraceptive methods	Direct support	Direct support	Direct support	Direct support
Adolescent fertility				
Level of concern	..	..	Major concern	Major concern
Policies and programmes	..	..	Yes	Yes
Health and mortality				
View				
Expectation of life	Acceptable	Unacceptable	Acceptable	Acceptable
Under-five mortality	..	..	Acceptable	Unacceptable
Maternal mortality	..	..	..	Unacceptable
Level of concern about HIV/AIDS	..	..	Major concern	Minor concern
Measures implemented to control HIV/AIDS*	..	..	..	1,2,3,5
Grounds on which abortion is permitted**	..	..	1	1
Spatial distribution and internal migration				
View on spatial distribution	Major change desired	Major change desired	Satisfactory	Satisfactory
Policies on internal migration				
From rural to urban areas	..	..	..	No intervention
From rural to rural areas	..	..	..	No intervention
From urban to rural areas	..	..	..	No intervention
From urban to urban areas	..	..	..	No intervention
Into urban agglomerations	No intervention	No intervention	No intervention	No intervention
International migration				
Immigration				
View	Satisfactory	Satisfactory	Satisfactory	Satisfactory
Policy	Maintain	Maintain	Lower	No intervention
Permanent settlement	..	..	Lower	No intervention
Temporary workers	..	..	Maintain	No intervention
Highly skilled workers	..	..	..	No intervention
Family reunification	..	..	Maintain	No intervention
Integration of non-nationals	..	..	Yes	Yes
Emigration				
View	Satisfactory	Too low	Satisfactory	Satisfactory
Policy	Maintain	Raise	Maintain	No intervention
Encouraging the return of nationals	No	..	Yes	No

* Measures implemented to control HIV/AIDS: (1) blood screening; (2) information/education campaigns; (3) access to antiretroviral treatment; (4) non-discriminatory policies; (5) promoting condom use.
** Grounds on which abortion is permitted: (1) to save the woman's life; (2) to preserve physical health; (3) to preserve mental health; (4) rape or incest; (5) foetal impairment; (6) economic or social reasons; (7) on request.

Population indicators

Indicator	1975	1985	1995	2005
Population size and growth				
Population size (thousands)	892	1 016	1 125	1 245
Annual growth rate (percentage)*	1.5	1.0	1.2	1.0
Population age structure				
Percentage of population under age 15	40	32	27	25
Percentage of population aged 60 or older	5	7	9	10
Fertility and family planning				
Total fertility (births per woman)*	3.2	2.5	2.3	2.0
Teenage fertility rate (per 1,000 women, aged 15 - 19)*	59	44	41	33
Percentage of births to women under age 20*	12	11	10	8
Percentage of births to women aged 35 or older*	7	7	9	10
Percentage of married women using contraception				
Modern methods	29	44	49[a]	..
All methods	46	75	75[a]	..
Health and mortality				
Life expectancy at birth (years)*				
Males	61	64	66	69
Females	65	70	74	76
Both sexes combined	63	67	70	72
Infant mortality rate (per 1,000 births)*	55	28	20	15
Mortality under age 5 (per 1,000 births)*	65	34	24	18
Maternal mortality ratio (per 100,000 births) (2000)	..	..	..	24
HIV/AIDS (2003)				
Number of infected adults (thousands)	..	..	..	..
Adult prevalence rate (percentage)	..	..	..	..
Spatial distribution				
Population density (per sq. km)	437	498	551	610
Urban population (percentage)	43	41	42	44
Annual urban growth rate (percentage)*	2.2	0.5	1.8	1.5
Annual rural growth rate (percentage)*	1.0	1.3	0.9	0.6
International migration				
International migrant stock				
Number of migrants (thousands)	10	9	12	21
Percentage of total population	1.1	0.9	1	1.7

* For the periods 1970-1975, 1980-1985, 1990-1995 and 2000-2005.
[a] For 1991.

Government views and policies

Population policy variable	*1976*	*1986*	*1996*	*2005*
Population size and growth				
View on growth	Too high	Too high	Too high	Too high
Policy on growth	Lower	Lower	Lower	Lower
Population age structure				
Level of concern about				
Size of the working-age population	..	..	..	Major concern
Ageing of the population	..	..	..	Major concern
Fertility and family planning				
View on fertility level	Too high	Too high	Too high	Satisfactory
Policy	Lower	Lower	Lower	Lower
Access to contraceptive methods	Direct support	Direct support	Direct support	Direct support
Adolescent fertility				
Level of concern	..	..	Major concern	Major concern
Policies and programmes	..	..	Yes	Yes
Health and mortality				
View				
Expectation of life	Acceptable	Acceptable	Acceptable	Acceptable
Under-five mortality	..	..	Unacceptable	Unacceptable
Maternal mortality	..	..	..	Unacceptable
Level of concern about HIV/AIDS	..	..	Major concern	Minor concern
Measures implemented to control HIV/AIDS*	..	..	..	1,2,3,4,5
Grounds on which abortion is permitted**	..	..	1,4	1,4
Spatial distribution and internal migration				
View on spatial distribution	Major change desired	Major change desired	Major change desired	Major change desired
Policies on internal migration				
From rural to urban areas	..	..	..	Maintain
From rural to rural areas	..	..	..	Maintain
From urban to rural areas	..	..	..	Maintain
From urban to urban areas	..	..	..	Maintain
Into urban agglomerations	No intervention	Lower	Lower	Lower
International migration				
Immigration				
View	Satisfactory	Satisfactory	Satisfactory	Satisfactory
Policy	Maintain	Maintain	Lower	Maintain
Permanent settlement	..	..	Lower	Maintain
Temporary workers	..	..	Maintain	Maintain
Highly skilled workers	..	..	..	Raise
Family reunification	..	..	Lower	Maintain
Integration of non-nationals	..	..	No	Yes
Emigration				
View	Too high	Satisfactory	Too high	Too high
Policy	Lower	Maintain	Lower	Lower
Encouraging the return of nationals	No	..	Yes	Yes

* Measures implemented to control HIV/AIDS: (1) blood screening; (2) information/education campaigns; (3) access to antiretroviral treatment; (4) non-discriminatory policies; (5) promoting condom use.
** Grounds on which abortion is permitted: (1) to save the woman's life; (2) to preserve physical health; (3) to preserve mental health; (4) rape or incest; (5) foetal impairment; (6) economic or social reasons; (7) on request.

Population indicators

Indicator	*1975*	*1985*	*1995*	*2005*
Population size and growth				
Population size (thousands)	59 287	76 117	92 523	107 029
Annual growth rate (percentage)*	3.2	2.2	1.9	1.3
Population age structure				
Percentage of population under age 15	47	43	36	31
Percentage of population aged 60 or older	6	6	6	8
Fertility and family planning				
Total fertility (births per woman)*	6.6	4.3	3.2	2.4
Teenage fertility rate (per 1,000 women, aged 15 - 19)*	118	96	79	70
Percentage of births to women under age 20*	14	17	17	16
Percentage of births to women aged 35 or older*	15	11	10	10
Percentage of married women using contraception				
Modern methods	23[a]	45[b]	60[c]	..
All methods	30[a]	53[b]	68[c]	..
Health and mortality				
Life expectancy at birth (years)*				
Males	60	64	69	72
Females	65	71	75	77
Both sexes combined	62	68	72	75
Infant mortality rate (per 1,000 births)*	69	47	33	21
Mortality under age 5 (per 1,000 births)*	100	57	40	25
Maternal mortality ratio (per 100,000 births) (2000)	..	..	..	83
HIV/AIDS (2003)				
Number of infected adults (thousands)	..	..	..	160
Adult prevalence rate (percentage)	..	..	..	0.3
Spatial distribution				
Population density (per sq. km)	30	39	47	55
Urban population (percentage)	63	70	73	76
Annual urban growth rate (percentage)*	4.3	3.2	2.1	1.8
Annual rural growth rate (percentage)*	1.2	0.2	1.1	0.4
International migration				
International migrant stock				
Number of migrants (thousands)	230	479	467	644
Percentage of total population	0.4	0.6	0.5	0.6

* For the periods 1970-1975, 1980-1985, 1990-1995 and 2000-2005.
[a] For 1976.
[b] For 1987.
[c] For 1997.

Government views and policies

Population policy variable	*1976*	*1986*	*1996*	*2005*
Population size and growth				
View on growth	..	..	Too high	Too high
Policy on growth	..	..	Lower	Lower
Population age structure				
Level of concern about				
Size of the working-age population	..	..	..	..
Ageing of the population	..	..	..	..
Fertility and family planning				
View on fertility level	..	..	Too high	Too high
Policy	..	..	Lower	Lower
Access to contraceptive methods	..	..	Direct support	Direct support
Adolescent fertility				
Level of concern	..	..	..	Major concern
Policies and programmes	..	..	..	Yes
Health and mortality				
View				
Expectation of life	..	..	Unacceptable	Unacceptable
Under-five mortality	..	..	..	Unacceptable
Maternal mortality	..	..	..	Unacceptable
Level of concern about HIV/AIDS	..	..	..	Major concern
Measures implemented to control HIV/AIDS*	..	..	..	2,3
Grounds on which abortion is permitted**	..	..	..	1
Spatial distribution and internal migration				
View on spatial distribution	..	..	Satisfactory	Major change desired
Policies on internal migration				
From rural to urban areas	..	..	..	..
From rural to rural areas	..	..	..	..
From urban to rural areas	..	..	..	..
From urban to urban areas	..	..	..	..
Into urban agglomerations	..	..	..	..
International migration				
Immigration				
View	..	..	Too high	Too high
Policy	..	..	Lower	Lower
Permanent settlement	..	..	Lower	Lower
Temporary workers	..	..	Lower	Lower
Highly skilled workers	..	..	..	Maintain
Family reunification	..	..	..	..
Integration of non-nationals	..	..	..	..
Emigration				
View	..	..	Too high	Too high
Policy	..	..	Lower	No intervention
Encouraging the return of nationals	..	..	Yes	..

* Measures implemented to control HIV/AIDS: (1) blood screening; (2) information/education campaigns; (3) access to antiretroviral treatment; (4) non-discriminatory policies; (5) promoting condom use.
** Grounds on which abortion is permitted: (1) to save the woman's life; (2) to preserve physical health; (3) to preserve mental health; (4) rape or incest; (5) foetal impairment; (6) economic or social reasons; (7) on request.

Population indicators

Indicator	*1975*	*1985*	*1995*	*2005*
Population size and growth				
Population size (thousands)	63	86	107	110
Annual growth rate (percentage)*	0.5	3.2	2.1	0.6
Population age structure				
Percentage of population under age 15	47	46	43	39
Percentage of population aged 60 or older	6	5	6	5
Fertility and family planning				
Total fertility (births per woman)*	6.9	6.0	4.8	4.4
Teenage fertility rate (per 1,000 women, aged 15 - 19)*	75	64	56	37
Percentage of births to women under age 20*	10	9	10	7
Percentage of births to women aged 35 or older*	18	15	22	19
Percentage of married women using contraception				
Modern methods	..	..	..	..
All methods	..	..	..	..
Health and mortality				
Life expectancy at birth (years)*				
Males	62	65	66	67
Females	63	66	67	68
Both sexes combined	63	65	66	68
Infant mortality rate (per 1,000 births)*	58	47	42	38
Mortality under age 5 (per 1,000 births)*	78	61	54	48
Maternal mortality ratio (per 100,000 births) (2000)	..	..	..	..
HIV/AIDS (2003)				
Number of infected adults (thousands)	..	..	..	..
Adult prevalence rate (percentage)	..	..	..	..
Spatial distribution				
Population density (per sq. km)	90	122	153	157
Urban population (percentage)	25	26	27	30
Annual urban growth rate (percentage)*	0.9	3.8	2.7	2.0
Annual rural growth rate (percentage)*	0.5	3.0	1.9	0.3
International migration				
International migrant stock				
Number of migrants (thousands)	2	3	3	4
Percentage of total population	3.6	3.2	3.2	3.2

* For the periods 1970-1975, 1980-1985, 1990-1995 and 2000-2005.

Government views and policies

Population policy variable	*1976*	*1986*	*1996*	*2005*
Population size and growth				
View on growth	Too low	Too low	Too low	Satisfactory
Policy on growth	Raise	Raise	Raise	No intervention
Population age structure				
Level of concern about				
Size of the working-age population	..	..	..	..
Ageing of the population	..	..	..	Minor concern
Fertility and family planning				
View on fertility level	Too low	Too low	Too low	Satisfactory
Policy	Raise	Raise	Raise	Maintain
Access to contraceptive methods	Direct support	Direct support	No support	No support
Adolescent fertility				
Level of concern	..	..	..	Not a concern
Policies and programmes	..	..	..	No
Health and mortality				
View				
Expectation of life	Acceptable	Acceptable	Acceptable	Acceptable
Under-five mortality	..	..	..	Acceptable
Maternal mortality	..	..	..	Acceptable
Level of concern about HIV/AIDS	..	..	..	Minor concern
Measures implemented to control HIV/AIDS*	..	..	..	1,2,5
Grounds on which abortion is permitted**	..	..	1	1
Spatial distribution and internal migration				
View on spatial distribution	Satisfactory	Satisfactory	Satisfactory	Satisfactory
Policies on internal migration				
From rural to urban areas	..	..	..	No intervention
From rural to rural areas	..	..	..	No intervention
From urban to rural areas	..	..	..	No intervention
From urban to urban areas	..	..	..	No intervention
Into urban agglomerations	..	..	..	No intervention
International migration				
Immigration				
View	Satisfactory	Satisfactory	Satisfactory	Satisfactory
Policy	Maintain	Lower	Lower	Maintain
Permanent settlement	..	..	..	Maintain
Temporary workers	..	..	..	Maintain
Highly skilled workers	..	..	..	..
Family reunification	..	..	..	..
Integration of non-nationals	..	..	..	..
Emigration				
View	Satisfactory	Satisfactory	Satisfactory	Satisfactory
Policy	Maintain	Maintain	Maintain	Maintain
Encouraging the return of nationals	..	..	..	..

* Measures implemented to control HIV/AIDS: (1) blood screening; (2) information/education campaigns; (3) access to antiretroviral treatment; (4) non-discriminatory policies; (5) promoting condom use.

** Grounds on which abortion is permitted: (1) to save the woman's life; (2) to preserve physical health; (3) to preserve mental health; (4) rape or incest; (5) foetal impairment; (6) economic or social reasons; (7) on request.

Population indicators

Indicator	*1975*	*1985*	*1995*	*2005*
Population size and growth				
Population size (thousands)	25	28	32	35
Annual growth rate (percentage)*	1.2	1.7	1.0	1.1
Population age structure				
Percentage of population under age 15	..	..	..	..
Percentage of population aged 60 or older	..	..	..	..
Fertility and family planning				
Total fertility (births per woman)*	..	..	..	..
Teenage fertility rate (per 1,000 women, aged 15 - 19)*	..	..	..	..
Percentage of births to women under age 20*	..	..	..	..
Percentage of births to women aged 35 or older*	..	..	..	..
Percentage of married women using contraception				
Modern methods	..	..	..	..
All methods	..	..	..	..
Health and mortality				
Life expectancy at birth (years)*				
Males	..	..	..	..
Females	..	..	..	..
Both sexes combined	..	..	..	..
Infant mortality rate (per 1,000 births)*	..	..	..	..
Mortality under age 5 (per 1,000 births)*	..	..	..	..
Maternal mortality ratio (per 100,000 births) (2000)	..	..	..	..
HIV/AIDS (2003)				
Number of infected adults (thousands)	..	..	..	..
Adult prevalence rate (percentage)	..	..	..	..
Spatial distribution				
Population density (per sq. km)	16 882	19 036	21 208	23 660
Urban population (percentage)	100	100	100	100
Annual urban growth rate (percentage)*	1.2	1.2	1.2	0.9
Annual rural growth rate (percentage)*	0.0	0.0	0.0	0.0
International migration				
International migrant stock				
Number of migrants (thousands)	16	19	21	25
Percentage of total population	64.8	66	68	69.9

* For the periods 1970-1975, 1980-1985, 1990-1995 and 2000-2005.

Government views and policies

Population policy variable	*1976*	*1986*	*1996*	*2005*
Population size and growth				
View on growth	Too low	Too low	Satisfactory	Too low
Policy on growth	Raise	Raise	Maintain	Raise
Population age structure				
Level of concern about				
Size of the working-age population	..	..	..	Major concern
Ageing of the population	..	..	..	Minor concern
Fertility and family planning				
View on fertility level	Satisfactory	Too low	Satisfactory	Too low
Policy	Maintain	Raise	Maintain	Raise
Access to contraceptive methods	Direct support	Direct support	Direct support	Direct support
Adolescent fertility				
Level of concern	..	..	Minor concern	Major concern
Policies and programmes	..	..	..	Yes
Health and mortality				
View				
Expectation of life	Unacceptable	Unacceptable	Unacceptable	Unacceptable
Under-five mortality	..	..	..	Unacceptable
Maternal mortality	..	..	..	Unacceptable
Level of concern about HIV/AIDS	..	..	Major concern	Minor concern
Measures implemented to control HIV/AIDS*	..	..	..	1,2,4,5
Grounds on which abortion is permitted**	..	..	1,2,3,4,5,6,7	1,2,3,4,5,6,7
Spatial distribution and internal migration				
View on spatial distribution	Minor change desired	Minor change desired	Major change desired	Major change desired
Policies on internal migration				
From rural to urban areas	..	..	..	Lower
From rural to rural areas	..	..	..	Maintain
From urban to rural areas	..	..	..	Raise
From urban to urban areas	..	..	..	Maintain
Into urban agglomerations	..	..	Lower	Lower
International migration				
Immigration				
View	Satisfactory	Satisfactory	Satisfactory	Satisfactory
Policy	Maintain	Maintain	Maintain	Maintain
Permanent settlement	..	..	Maintain	Maintain
Temporary workers	..	..	Lower	Maintain
Highly skilled workers	..	..	..	Raise
Family reunification	..	..	Raise	Maintain
Integration of non-nationals	..	..	No	No
Emigration				
View	Satisfactory	Satisfactory	Satisfactory	Too high
Policy	Maintain	Maintain	No intervention	Maintain
Encouraging the return of nationals	..	..	Yes	Yes

* Measures implemented to control HIV/AIDS: (1) blood screening; (2) information/education campaigns; (3) access to antiretroviral treatment; (4) non-discriminatory policies; (5) promoting condom use.

** Grounds on which abortion is permitted: (1) to save the woman's life; (2) to preserve physical health; (3) to preserve mental health; (4) rape or incest; (5) foetal impairment; (6) economic or social reasons; (7) on request.

Population indicators

Indicator	*1975*	*1985*	*1995*	*2005*
Population size and growth				
Population size (thousands)	1 447	1 909	2 389	2 646
Annual growth rate (percentage)*	2.8	2.8	1.5	1.2
Population age structure				
Percentage of population under age 15	44	42	39	30
Percentage of population aged 60 or older	5	5	6	6
Fertility and family planning				
Total fertility (births per woman)*	7.3	5.7	3.4	2.4
Teenage fertility rate (per 1,000 women, aged 15 - 19)*	129	101	59	54
Percentage of births to women under age 20*	12	12	11	14
Percentage of births to women aged 35 or older*	7	7	6	8
Percentage of married women using contraception				
Modern methods	..	..	25[a]	54[b]
All methods	..	..	61[a]	67[b]
Health and mortality				
Life expectancy at birth (years)*				
Males	53	56	59	62
Females	55	59	63	66
Both sexes combined	54	57	61	64
Infant mortality rate (per 1,000 births)*	98	78	68	58
Mortality under age 5 (per 1,000 births)*	153	119	103	85
Maternal mortality ratio (per 100,000 births) (2000)	..	..	..	110
HIV/AIDS (2003)				
Number of infected adults (thousands)	..	..	..	<1
Adult prevalence rate (percentage)	..	..	..	<0.1
Spatial distribution				
Population density (per sq. km)	1	1	2	2
Urban population (percentage)	49	55	57	57
Annual urban growth rate (percentage)*	4.4	3.9	1.5	1.4
Annual rural growth rate (percentage)*	1.5	1.5	1.6	1.1
International migration				
International migrant stock				
Number of migrants (thousands)	5	6	7	9
Percentage of total population	0.3	0.3	0.3	0.3

* For the periods 1970-1975, 1980-1985, 1990-1995 and 2000-2005.
[a] For 1994.
[b] For 2000.

Government views and policies

Population policy variable	*1976*	*1986*	*1996*	*2005*
Population size and growth				
View on growth	Too high	Too high	Too high	Too high
Policy on growth	Lower	Lower	Lower	Lower
Population age structure				
Level of concern about				
Size of the working-age population	..	..	..	Major concern
Ageing of the population	..	..	..	Minor concern
Fertility and family planning				
View on fertility level	Too high	Too high	Too high	Satisfactory
Policy	Lower	Lower	Lower	Lower
Access to contraceptive methods	Direct support	Direct support	Direct support	Direct support
Adolescent fertility				
Level of concern	..	..	Minor concern	Minor concern
Policies and programmes	..	..	..	Yes
Health and mortality				
View				
Expectation of life	Unacceptable	Unacceptable	Unacceptable	Acceptable
Under-five mortality	..	..	Unacceptable	Unacceptable
Maternal mortality	..	..	..	Unacceptable
Level of concern about HIV/AIDS	..	..	Minor concern	Major concern
Measures implemented to control HIV/AIDS*	..	..	..	1,2,3,4,5
Grounds on which abortion is permitted**	..	..	1,2	1,2,3
Spatial distribution and internal migration				
View on spatial distribution	Major change desired	Major change desired	Minor change desired	Minor change desired
Policies on internal migration				
From rural to urban areas	..	..	..	Lower
From rural to rural areas	..	..	..	..
From urban to rural areas	..	..	..	..
From urban to urban areas	..	..	..	..
Into urban agglomerations	..	Lower	Lower	Lower
International migration				
Immigration				
View	Satisfactory	Satisfactory	Satisfactory	Too high
Policy	Maintain	Maintain	No intervention	Lower
Permanent settlement	..	..	No intervention	Maintain
Temporary workers	..	..	No intervention	Lower
Highly skilled workers	..	..	..	Maintain
Family reunification	..	..	No intervention	Maintain
Integration of non-nationals	..	..	No	Yes
Emigration				
View	Satisfactory	Too low	Satisfactory	Too low
Policy	Maintain	Raise	No intervention	Maintain
Encouraging the return of nationals	..	..	..	Yes

* Measures implemented to control HIV/AIDS: (1) blood screening; (2) information/education campaigns; (3) access to antiretroviral treatment; (4) non-discriminatory policies; (5) promoting condom use.

** Grounds on which abortion is permitted: (1) to save the woman's life; (2) to preserve physical health; (3) to preserve mental health; (4) rape or incest; (5) foetal impairment; (6) economic or social reasons; (7) on request.

Population indicators

Indicator	*1975*	*1985*	*1995*	*2005*
Population size and growth				
Population size (thousands)	17 305	22 193	27 004	31 478
Annual growth rate (percentage)*	2.5	2.6	1.8	1.5
Population age structure				
Percentage of population under age 15	47	42	37	31
Percentage of population aged 60 or older	5	6	6	7
Fertility and family planning				
Total fertility (births per woman)*	6.9	5.4	3.7	2.8
Teenage fertility rate (per 1,000 women, aged 15 - 19)*	72	56	39	25
Percentage of births to women under age 20*	8	8	8	6
Percentage of births to women aged 35 or older*	23	19	23	16
Percentage of married women using contraception				
Modern methods	..	21[a]	42	55[b]
All methods	..	26[a]	50	63[b]
Health and mortality				
Life expectancy at birth (years)*				
Males	51	58	64	67
Females	55	61	67	72
Both sexes combined	53	59	66	70
Infant mortality rate (per 1,000 births)*	123	90	57	38
Mortality under age 5 (per 1,000 births)*	179	133	76	46
Maternal mortality ratio (per 100,000 births) (2000)	..	..	..	220
HIV/AIDS (2003)				
Number of infected adults (thousands)	..	..	..	15
Adult prevalence rate (percentage)	..	..	..	0.1
Spatial distribution				
Population density (per sq. km)	39	50	60	70
Urban population (percentage)	38	45	52	59
Annual urban growth rate (percentage)*	4.2	4.2	3.2	2.8
Annual rural growth rate (percentage)*	1.4	1.3	0.3	0.1
International migration				
International migrant stock				
Number of migrants (thousands)	91	69	103	132
Percentage of total population	0.5	0.3	0.4	0.4

* For the periods 1970-1975, 1980-1985, 1990-1995 and 2000-2005.
[a] For 1984.
[b] For 2003/2004.

Government views and policies

Population policy variable	*1976*	*1986*	*1996*	*2005*
Population size and growth				
View on growth	Too low	Satisfactory	Too high	Too high
Policy on growth	Raise	No intervention	No intervention	No intervention
Population age structure				
Level of concern about				
Size of the working-age population	..	..	..	..
Ageing of the population	..	..	..	Major concern
Fertility and family planning				
View on fertility level	Satisfactory	Satisfactory	Too high	Too high
Policy	Maintain	No intervention	Lower	Lower
Access to contraceptive methods	Direct support	Direct support	Direct support	Direct support
Adolescent fertility				
Level of concern	..	..	Major concern	Major concern
Policies and programmes	..	..	No	Yes
Health and mortality				
View				
Expectation of life	Unacceptable	Unacceptable	Unacceptable	Unacceptable
Under-five mortality	..	..	Unacceptable	Unacceptable
Maternal mortality	..	..	..	Unacceptable
Level of concern about HIV/AIDS	..	..	Major concern	Major concern
Measures implemented to control HIV/AIDS*	..	..	..	1,2,3,4,5
Grounds on which abortion is permitted**	..	..	1	1,2,3
Spatial distribution and internal migration				
View on spatial distribution	Major change desired	Major change desired	Major change desired	Minor change desired
Policies on internal migration				
From rural to urban areas	..	..	..	..
From rural to rural areas	..	..	..	..
From urban to rural areas	..	..	..	..
From urban to urban areas	..	..	..	..
Into urban agglomerations	No intervention	No intervention	No intervention	No intervention
International migration				
Immigration				
View	Satisfactory	Satisfactory	Satisfactory	Satisfactory
Policy	Maintain	Maintain	No intervention	No intervention
Permanent settlement	..	..	No intervention	..
Temporary workers	..	..	No intervention	..
Highly skilled workers	..	..	..	..
Family reunification	..	..	No intervention	..
Integration of non-nationals	..	..	..	..
Emigration				
View	Satisfactory	Satisfactory	Satisfactory	Satisfactory
Policy	Maintain	Lower	No intervention	No intervention
Encouraging the return of nationals	No	..	Yes	..

* Measures implemented to control HIV/AIDS: (1) blood screening; (2) information/education campaigns; (3) access to antiretroviral treatment; (4) non-discriminatory policies; (5) promoting condom use.

** Grounds on which abortion is permitted: (1) to save the woman's life; (2) to preserve physical health; (3) to preserve mental health; (4) rape or incest; (5) foetal impairment; (6) economic or social reasons; (7) on request.

Population indicators

Indicator	*1975*	*1985*	*1995*	*2005*
Population size and growth				
Population size (thousands)	17 305	22 193	27 004	31 478
Annual growth rate (percentage)*	2.5	2.6	1.8	1.5
Population age structure				
Percentage of population under age 15	47	42	37	31
Percentage of population aged 60 or older	5	6	6	7
Fertility and family planning				
Total fertility (births per woman)*	6.9	5.4	3.7	2.8
Teenage fertility rate (per 1,000 women, aged 15 - 19)*	72	56	39	25
Percentage of births to women under age 20*	8	8	8	6
Percentage of births to women aged 35 or older*	23	19	23	16
Percentage of married women using contraception				
Modern methods	..	21[a]	42	55[b]
All methods	..	26[a]	50	63[b]
Health and mortality				
Life expectancy at birth (years)*				
Males	51	58	64	67
Females	55	61	67	72
Both sexes combined	53	59	66	70
Infant mortality rate (per 1,000 births)*	123	90	57	38
Mortality under age 5 (per 1,000 births)*	179	133	76	46
Maternal mortality ratio (per 100,000 births) (2000)	..	..	..	220
HIV/AIDS (2003)				
Number of infected adults (thousands)	..	..	..	15
Adult prevalence rate (percentage)	..	..	..	0.1
Spatial distribution				
Population density (per sq. km)	39	50	60	70
Urban population (percentage)	38	45	52	59
Annual urban growth rate (percentage)*	4.2	4.2	3.2	2.8
Annual rural growth rate (percentage)*	1.4	1.3	0.3	0.1
International migration				
International migrant stock				
Number of migrants (thousands)	91	69	103	132
Percentage of total population	0.5	0.3	0.4	0.4

* For the periods 1970-1975, 1980-1985, 1990-1995 and 2000-2005.
[a] For 1984.
[b] For 2003/2004.

Government views and policies

Population policy variable	*1976*	*1986*	*1996*	*2005*
Population size and growth				
View on growth	Too low	Satisfactory	Too high	Too high
Policy on growth	Raise	No intervention	No intervention	No intervention
Population age structure				
Level of concern about				
Size of the working-age population	..	..	..	..
Ageing of the population	..	..	..	Major concern
Fertility and family planning				
View on fertility level	Satisfactory	Satisfactory	Too high	Too high
Policy	Maintain	No intervention	Lower	Lower
Access to contraceptive methods	Direct support	Direct support	Direct support	Direct support
Adolescent fertility				
Level of concern	..	..	Major concern	Major concern
Policies and programmes	..	..	No	Yes
Health and mortality				
View				
Expectation of life	Unacceptable	Unacceptable	Unacceptable	Unacceptable
Under-five mortality	..	..	Unacceptable	Unacceptable
Maternal mortality	..	..	..	Unacceptable
Level of concern about HIV/AIDS	..	..	Major concern	Major concern
Measures implemented to control HIV/AIDS*	..	..	..	1,2,3,4,5
Grounds on which abortion is permitted**	..	..	1	1,2,3
Spatial distribution and internal migration				
View on spatial distribution	Major change desired	Major change desired	Major change desired	Minor change desired
Policies on internal migration				
From rural to urban areas	..	..	..	..
From rural to rural areas	..	..	..	..
From urban to rural areas	..	..	..	..
From urban to urban areas	..	..	..	..
Into urban agglomerations	No intervention	No intervention	No intervention	No intervention
International migration				
Immigration				
View	Satisfactory	Satisfactory	Satisfactory	Satisfactory
Policy	Maintain	Maintain	No intervention	No intervention
Permanent settlement	..	..	No intervention	..
Temporary workers	..	..	No intervention	..
Highly skilled workers	..	..	..	..
Family reunification	..	..	No intervention	..
Integration of non-nationals	..	..	..	..
Emigration				
View	Satisfactory	Satisfactory	Satisfactory	Satisfactory
Policy	Maintain	Lower	No intervention	No intervention
Encouraging the return of nationals	No	..	Yes	..

* Measures implemented to control HIV/AIDS: (1) blood screening; (2) information/education campaigns; (3) access to antiretroviral treatment; (4) non-discriminatory policies; (5) promoting condom use.

** Grounds on which abortion is permitted: (1) to save the woman's life; (2) to preserve physical health; (3) to preserve mental health; (4) rape or incest; (5) foetal impairment; (6) economic or social reasons; (7) on request.

Population indicators

Indicator	*1975*	*1985*	*1995*	*2005*
Population size and growth				
Population size (thousands)	10 569	13 219	15 854	19 792
Annual growth rate (percentage)*	2.4	1.9	3.3	2.0
Population age structure				
Percentage of population under age 15	44	45	44	44
Percentage of population aged 60 or older	5	5	5	5
Fertility and family planning				
Total fertility (births per woman)*	6.6	6.4	6.2	5.5
Teenage fertility rate (per 1,000 women, aged 15 - 19)*	128	124	117	104
Percentage of births to women under age 20*	13	14	15	14
Percentage of births to women aged 35 or older*	18	17	18	19
Percentage of married women using contraception				
Modern methods	..	..	5[a]	..
All methods	..	..	6[a]	..
Health and mortality				
Life expectancy at birth (years)*				
Males	39	41	42	41
Females	42	44	45	43
Both sexes combined	41	43	44	42
Infant mortality rate (per 1,000 births)*	156	143	134	101
Mortality under age 5 (per 1,000 births)*	260	248	233	182
Maternal mortality ratio (per 100,000 births) (2000)	..	..	..	1 000
HIV/AIDS (2003)				
Number of infected adults (thousands)	..	..	..	1 200
Adult prevalence rate (percentage)	..	..	..	12.2
Spatial distribution				
Population density (per sq. km)	13	16	20	25
Urban population (percentage)	9	17	26	38
Annual urban growth rate (percentage)*	10.5	6.7	7.7	5.1
Annual rural growth rate (percentage)*	1.8	1.0	2.0	0.0
International migration				
International migrant stock				
Number of migrants (thousands)	37	61	246	406
Percentage of total population	0.4	0.5	1.6	2.1

* For the periods 1970-1975, 1980-1985, 1990-1995 and 2000-2005.
[a] For 1997.

Government views and policies

Population policy variable	*1976*	*1986*	*1996*	*2005*
Population size and growth				
View on growth	Satisfactory	Satisfactory	Satisfactory	Satisfactory
Policy on growth	No intervention	No intervention	No intervention	No intervention
Population age structure				
Level of concern about				
Size of the working-age population	..	..	..	Major concern
Ageing of the population	..	..	..	Minor concern
Fertility and family planning				
View on fertility level	Satisfactory	Satisfactory	Too high	Satisfactory
Policy	No intervention	No intervention	No intervention	Maintain
Access to contraceptive methods	No support	Indirect support	Direct support	Direct support
Adolescent fertility				
Level of concern	..	..	Not a concern	Major concern
Policies and programmes	..	..	No	Yes
Health and mortality				
View				
Expectation of life	Unacceptable	Unacceptable	Unacceptable	Unacceptable
Under-five mortality	..	..	Unacceptable	Unacceptable
Maternal mortality	..	..	..	Unacceptable
Level of concern about HIV/AIDS	..	..	Major concern	Major concern
Measures implemented to control HIV/AIDS*	..	..	..	1,2,3,4,5
Grounds on which abortion is permitted**	..	..	1	1
Spatial distribution and internal migration				
View on spatial distribution	Minor change desired	Minor change desired	Satisfactory	Minor change desired
Policies on internal migration				
From rural to urban areas	..	..	..	Lower
From rural to rural areas	..	..	..	..
From urban to rural areas	..	..	..	..
From urban to urban areas	..	..	..	Maintain
Into urban agglomerations	..	..	No intervention	Lower
International migration				
Immigration				
View	Satisfactory	Satisfactory	Satisfactory	Satisfactory
Policy	Maintain	Maintain	Maintain	Lower
Permanent settlement	..	..	Maintain	Lower
Temporary workers	..	..	No intervention	Maintain
Highly skilled workers	..	..	..	Maintain
Family reunification	..	..	No intervention	No intervention
Integration of non-nationals	..	..	No	No
Emigration				
View	Satisfactory	Satisfactory	Satisfactory	Satisfactory
Policy	Maintain	Maintain	Maintain	Maintain
Encouraging the return of nationals	..	..	Yes	Yes

* Measures implemented to control HIV/AIDS: (1) blood screening; (2) information/education campaigns; (3) access to antiretroviral treatment; (4) non-discriminatory policies; (5) promoting condom use.

** Grounds on which abortion is permitted: (1) to save the woman's life; (2) to preserve physical health; (3) to preserve mental health; (4) rape or incest; (5) foetal impairment; (6) economic or social reasons; (7) on request.

Population indicators

Indicator	*1975*	*1985*	*1995*	*2005*
Population size and growth				
Population size (thousands)	30 138	37 237	44 500	50 519
Annual growth rate (percentage)*	2.3	2.0	1.8	1.1
Population age structure				
Percentage of population under age 15	41	39	35	29
Percentage of population aged 60 or older	6	7	7	8
Fertility and family planning				
Total fertility (births per woman)*	5.8	4.7	3.8	2.5
Teenage fertility rate (per 1,000 women, aged 15 - 19)*	91	62	42	21
Percentage of births to women under age 20*	12	9	8	5
Percentage of births to women aged 35 or older*	17	18	17	16
Percentage of married women using contraception				
Modern methods	..	..	28[a]	33[b]
All methods	..	..	33[a]	37[b]
Health and mortality				
Life expectancy at birth (years)*				
Males	47	51	55	57
Females	51	55	59	63
Both sexes combined	49	53	57	60
Infant mortality rate (per 1,000 births)*	122	106	90	75
Mortality under age 5 (per 1,000 births)*	199	169	140	112
Maternal mortality ratio (per 100,000 births) (2000)	..	..	..	360
HIV/AIDS (2003)				
Number of infected adults (thousands)	..	..	..	320
Adult prevalence rate (percentage)	..	..	..	1.2
Spatial distribution				
Population density (per sq. km)	45	55	66	75
Urban population (percentage)	24	24	26	31
Annual urban growth rate (percentage)*	3.3	2.0	2.7	3.1
Annual rural growth rate (percentage)*	2.0	1.9	1.4	0.5
International migration				
International migrant stock				
Number of migrants (thousands)	75	91	112	117
Percentage of total population	0.2	0.2	0.3	0.2

* For the periods 1970-1975, 1980-1985, 1990-1995 and 2000-2005.
[a] For 1997.
[b] For 2001.

Government views and policies

Population policy variable	*1976*	*1986*	*1996*	*2005*
Population size and growth				
View on growth	..	..	Too high	Satisfactory
Policy on growth	..	..	Lower	Lower
Population age structure				
Level of concern about				
Size of the working-age population	..	..	..	Major concern
Ageing of the population	..	..	..	Minor concern
Fertility and family planning				
View on fertility level	..	..	Too high	Satisfactory
Policy	..	..	No intervention	Lower
Access to contraceptive methods	..	..	Direct support	Direct support
Adolescent fertility				
Level of concern	..	..	Major concern	Major concern
Policies and programmes	..	..	Yes	Yes
Health and mortality				
View				
Expectation of life	..	..	Unacceptable	Unacceptable
Under-five mortality	..	..	Unacceptable	Unacceptable
Maternal mortality	..	..	..	Unacceptable
Level of concern about HIV/AIDS	..	..	Major concern	Major concern
Measures implemented to control HIV/AIDS*	..	..	..	1,2,3,4,5
Grounds on which abortion is permitted**	..	..	1,2,3,4,5	1,2,3,4,5
Spatial distribution and internal migration				
View on spatial distribution	..	..	Satisfactory	Major change desired
Policies on internal migration				
From rural to urban areas	..	..	..	Lower
From rural to rural areas	..	..	..	No intervention
From urban to rural areas	..	..	..	Raise
From urban to urban areas	..	..	..	No intervention
Into urban agglomerations	..	..	Maintain	Lower
International migration				
Immigration				
View	..	..	Satisfactory	Satisfactory
Policy	..	..	Raise	Maintain
Permanent settlement	..	..	Raise	Maintain
Temporary workers	..	..	Lower	Maintain
Highly skilled workers	..	..	..	Maintain
Family reunification	..	..	Lower	Maintain
Integration of non-nationals	..	..	No	Yes
Emigration				
View	..	..	Satisfactory	Satisfactory
Policy	..	..	Maintain	No intervention
Encouraging the return of nationals	..	..	No	No

* Measures implemented to control HIV/AIDS: (1) blood screening; (2) information/education campaigns; (3) access to antiretroviral treatment; (4) non-discriminatory policies; (5) promoting condom use.

** Grounds on which abortion is permitted: (1) to save the woman's life; (2) to preserve physical health; (3) to preserve mental health; (4) rape or incest; (5) foetal impairment; (6) economic or social reasons; (7) on request.

Population indicators

Indicator	*1975*	*1985*	*1995*	*2005*
Population size and growth				
Population size (thousands)	891	1 119	1 652	2 031
Annual growth rate (percentage)*	2.9	2.5	3.3	1.4
Population age structure				
Percentage of population under age 15	44	46	44	42
Percentage of population aged 60 or older	6	6	5	5
Fertility and family planning				
Total fertility (births per woman)*	6.6	6.4	5.8	4.0
Teenage fertility rate (per 1,000 women, aged 15 - 19)*	112	107	117	58
Percentage of births to women under age 20*	13	14	15	11
Percentage of births to women aged 35 or older*	23	21	18	14
Percentage of married women using contraception				
Modern methods	..	..	26[a]	..
All methods	..	..	29[a]	..
Health and mortality				
Life expectancy at birth (years)*				
Males	53	58	60	48
Females	55	60	64	49
Both sexes combined	54	59	62	49
Infant mortality rate (per 1,000 births)*	100	73	56	44
Mortality under age 5 (per 1,000 births)*	145	107	79	78
Maternal mortality ratio (per 100,000 births) (2000)	..	..	..	300
HIV/AIDS (2003)				
Number of infected adults (thousands)	..	..	..	200
Adult prevalence rate (percentage)	..	..	..	21.3
Spatial distribution				
Population density (per sq. km)	1	1	2	2
Urban population (percentage)	21	25	29	33
Annual urban growth rate (percentage)*	4.9	3.9	4.5	3.0
Annual rural growth rate (percentage)*	2.3	1.8	2.6	0.6
International migration				
International migrant stock				
Number of migrants (thousands)	42	84	124	143
Percentage of total population	4.7	7.5	7.5	7.1

* For the periods 1970-1975, 1980-1985, 1990-1995 and 2000-2005.
[a] For 1992.

Government views and policies

Population policy variable	*1976*	*1986*	*1996*	*2005*
Population size and growth				
View on growth	Too low	Too low	Too low	Too high
Policy on growth	Raise	Raise	Raise	No intervention
Population age structure				
Level of concern about				
Size of the working-age population	..	..	..	..
Ageing of the population	..	..	..	..
Fertility and family planning				
View on fertility level	Satisfactory	Satisfactory	Satisfactory	Satisfactory
Policy	Maintain	Maintain	Maintain	Maintain
Access to contraceptive methods	Direct support	Direct support	Direct support	Direct support
Adolescent fertility				
Level of concern	..	..	..	..
Policies and programmes	..	..	..	..
Health and mortality				
View				
Expectation of life	Acceptable	Acceptable	Acceptable	Acceptable
Under-five mortality	..	..	..	..
Maternal mortality	..	..	..	..
Level of concern about HIV/AIDS	..	..	..	Major concern
Measures implemented to control HIV/AIDS*	..	..	..	2
Grounds on which abortion is permitted**	..	..	1,2,3	1,2,3
Spatial distribution and internal migration				
View on spatial distribution	Satisfactory	Satisfactory	Satisfactory	Satisfactory
Policies on internal migration				
From rural to urban areas	..	..	..	No intervention
From rural to rural areas	..	..	..	No intervention
From urban to rural areas	..	..	..	No intervention
From urban to urban areas	..	..	..	No intervention
Into urban agglomerations	..	..	..	No intervention
International migration				
Immigration				
View	Satisfactory	Satisfactory	Satisfactory	Satisfactory
Policy	Maintain	Maintain	Maintain	Maintain
Permanent settlement	..	..	Maintain	Maintain
Temporary workers	..	..	..	Lower
Highly skilled workers	..	..	..	..
Family reunification	..	..	..	..
Integration of non-nationals	..	..	..	..
Emigration				
View	Satisfactory	Satisfactory	Satisfactory	Satisfactory
Policy	Maintain	Maintain	Maintain	Maintain
Encouraging the return of nationals	..	..	..	..

* Measures implemented to control HIV/AIDS: (1) blood screening; (2) information/education campaigns; (3) access to antiretroviral treatment; (4) non-discriminatory policies; (5) promoting condom use.

** Grounds on which abortion is permitted: (1) to save the woman's life; (2) to preserve physical health; (3) to preserve mental health; (4) rape or incest; (5) foetal impairment; (6) economic or social reasons; (7) on request.

Population indicators

Indicator	*1975*	*1985*	*1995*	*2005*
Population size and growth				
Population size (thousands)	7	8	11	14
Annual growth rate (percentage)*	1.7	1.8	2.6	2.2
Population age structure				
Percentage of population under age 15	..	..	..	..
Percentage of population aged 60 or older	..	..	..	..
Fertility and family planning				
Total fertility (births per woman)*	..	..	..	..
Teenage fertility rate (per 1,000 women, aged 15 - 19)*	..	..	..	..
Percentage of births to women under age 20*	..	..	..	..
Percentage of births to women aged 35 or older*	..	..	..	..
Percentage of married women using contraception				
Modern methods	..	..	..	..
All methods	..	..	..	..
Health and mortality				
Life expectancy at birth (years)*				
Males	..	..	..	..
Females	..	..	..	..
Both sexes combined	..	..	..	..
Infant mortality rate (per 1,000 births)*	..	..	..	..
Mortality under age 5 (per 1,000 births)*	..	..	..	..
Maternal mortality ratio (per 100,000 births) (2000)	..	..	..	..
HIV/AIDS (2003)				
Number of infected adults (thousands)	..	..	..	..
Adult prevalence rate (percentage)	..	..	..	..
Spatial distribution				
Population density (per sq. km)	336	389	512	649
Urban population (percentage)	100	100	100	100
Annual urban growth rate (percentage)*	1.7	1.7	2.7	2.3
Annual rural growth rate (percentage)*	0.0	0.0	0.0	0.0
International migration				
International migrant stock				
Number of migrants (thousands)	3	4	4	5
Percentage of total population	37.3	44.6	39.3	36.1

* For the periods 1970-1975, 1980-1985, 1990-1995 and 2000-2005.

Government views and policies

Population policy variable	*1976*	*1986*	*1996*	*2005*
Population size and growth				
View on growth	Too high	Too high	Too high	Too high
Policy on growth	Lower	Lower	Lower	Lower
Population age structure				
Level of concern about				
Size of the working-age population	..	..	..	Major concern
Ageing of the population	..	..	..	Minor concern
Fertility and family planning				
View on fertility level	Too high	Too high	Too high	Too high
Policy	Lower	Lower	Lower	Lower
Access to contraceptive methods	Direct support	Direct support	Direct support	Direct support
Adolescent fertility				
Level of concern	..	..	Minor concern	Major concern
Policies and programmes	..	..	No	Yes
Health and mortality				
View				
Expectation of life	Unacceptable	Unacceptable	Unacceptable	Unacceptable
Under-five mortality	..	..	Unacceptable	Unacceptable
Maternal mortality	..	..	..	Unacceptable
Level of concern about HIV/AIDS	..	..	Minor concern	Major concern
Measures implemented to control HIV/AIDS*	..	..	..	1,2,4,5
Grounds on which abortion is permitted**	..	..	1	1,2,3,4,5,6,7
Spatial distribution and internal migration				
View on spatial distribution	Major change desired	Major change desired	Major change desired	Minor change desired
Policies on internal migration				
From rural to urban areas	..	..	..	Raise
From rural to rural areas	..	..	..	No intervention
From urban to rural areas	..	..	..	No intervention
From urban to urban areas	..	..	..	Maintain
Into urban agglomerations	..	No intervention	Lower	No intervention
International migration				
Immigration				
View	Too high	Too high	Too high	Too high
Policy	Lower	Lower	Lower	Maintain
Permanent settlement	..	..	Lower	Maintain
Temporary workers	..	..	No intervention	Maintain
Highly skilled workers	..	..	..	Maintain
Family reunification	..	..	No intervention	Maintain
Integration of non-nationals	..	..	No	No
Emigration				
View	Satisfactory	Satisfactory	Satisfactory	Satisfactory
Policy	Maintain	Lower	No intervention	Raise
Encouraging the return of nationals	..	..	No	Yes

* Measures implemented to control HIV/AIDS: (1) blood screening; (2) information/education campaigns; (3) access to antiretroviral treatment; (4) non-discriminatory policies; (5) promoting condom use.

** Grounds on which abortion is permitted: (1) to save the woman's life; (2) to preserve physical health; (3) to preserve mental health; (4) rape or incest; (5) foetal impairment; (6) economic or social reasons; (7) on request.

Population indicators

Indicator	*1975*	*1985*	*1995*	*2005*
Population size and growth				
Population size (thousands)	13 548	17 003	21 682	27 133
Annual growth rate (percentage)*	2.2	2.3	2.5	2.1
Population age structure				
Percentage of population under age 15	42	42	42	39
Percentage of population aged 60 or older	6	5	5	6
Fertility and family planning				
Total fertility (births per woman)*	5.8	5.5	5.0	3.7
Teenage fertility rate (per 1,000 women, aged 15 - 19)*	127	121	129	123
Percentage of births to women under age 20*	15	15	17	21
Percentage of births to women aged 35 or older*	17	15	12	8
Percentage of married women using contraception				
Modern methods	3[a]	14[b]	22[c]	35[d]
All methods	3[a]	14[b]	23[c]	39[d]
Health and mortality				
Life expectancy at birth (years)*				
Males	44	50	56	61
Females	44	49	56	62
Both sexes combined	44	50	56	61
Infant mortality rate (per 1,000 births)*	156	123	90	64
Mortality under age 5 (per 1,000 births)*	234	182	128	88
Maternal mortality ratio (per 100,000 births) (2000)	..	..	..	740
HIV/AIDS (2003)				
Number of infected adults (thousands)	..	..	..	60
Adult prevalence rate (percentage)	..	..	..	0.5
Spatial distribution				
Population density (per sq. km)	92	116	147	184
Urban population (percentage)	5	8	11	16
Annual urban growth rate (percentage)*	6.9	5.6	6.5	5.2
Annual rural growth rate (percentage)*	1.8	1.9	1.9	1.7
International migration				
International migrant stock				
Number of migrants (thousands)	291	302	615	819
Percentage of total population	2.1	1.8	2.8	3

* For the periods 1970-1975, 1980-1985, 1990-1995 and 2000-2005.
[a] For 1976.
[b] For 1986.
[c] For 1991.
[d] For 2001.

Government views and policies

Population policy variable	*1976*	*1986*	*1996*	*2005*
Population size and growth				
View on growth	Satisfactory	Satisfactory	Satisfactory	Satisfactory
Policy on growth	No intervention	No intervention	No intervention	No intervention
Population age structure				
Level of concern about				
Size of the working-age population	..	..	..	Major concern
Ageing of the population	..	..	..	Major concern
Fertility and family planning				
View on fertility level	Satisfactory	Satisfactory	Satisfactory	Satisfactory
Policy	No intervention	No intervention	No intervention	No intervention
Access to contraceptive methods	Indirect support	Indirect support	Indirect support	Indirect support
Adolescent fertility				
Level of concern	..	..	Major concern	Major concern
Policies and programmes	..	..	Yes	Yes
Health and mortality				
View				
Expectation of life	Acceptable	Acceptable	Acceptable	Unacceptable
Under-five mortality	..	..	Acceptable	Unacceptable
Maternal mortality	..	..	..	Acceptable
Level of concern about HIV/AIDS	..	..	Major concern	Major concern
Measures implemented to control HIV/AIDS*	..	..	..	1,2,3,4,5
Grounds on which abortion is permitted**	..	..	1,2,3,4,5,6,7	1,2,3,4,5,6,7
Spatial distribution and internal migration				
View on spatial distribution	Major change desired	Satisfactory	Satisfactory	Minor change desired
Policies on internal migration				
From rural to urban areas	..	..	..	No intervention
From rural to rural areas	..	..	..	No intervention
From urban to rural areas	..	..	..	No intervention
From urban to urban areas	..	..	..	No intervention
Into urban agglomerations	..	Raise	Maintain	Maintain
International migration				
Immigration				
View	Too high	Too high	Too high	Too high
Policy	Lower	Lower	Lower	Lower
Permanent settlement	..	..	Lower	Lower
Temporary workers	..	..	No intervention	Maintain
Highly skilled workers	..	..	..	Raise
Family reunification	..	..	Maintain	Lower
Integration of non-nationals	..	..	Yes	Yes
Emigration				
View	Satisfactory	Too low	Satisfactory	Satisfactory
Policy	Maintain	Raise	No intervention	No intervention
Encouraging the return of nationals	No	..	No	No

* Measures implemented to control HIV/AIDS: (1) blood screening; (2) information/education campaigns; (3) access to antiretroviral treatment; (4) non-discriminatory policies; (5) promoting condom use.
** Grounds on which abortion is permitted: (1) to save the woman's life; (2) to preserve physical health; (3) to preserve mental health; (4) rape or incest; (5) foetal impairment; (6) economic or social reasons; (7) on request.

Population indicators

Indicator	*1975*	*1985*	*1995*	*2005*
Population size and growth				
Population size (thousands)	13 666	14 492	15 459	16 299
Annual growth rate (percentage)*	0.9	0.5	0.7	0.5
Population age structure				
Percentage of population under age 15	25	19	18	18
Percentage of population aged 60 or older	15	17	18	19
Fertility and family planning				
Total fertility (births per woman)*	2.1	1.5	1.6	1.7
Teenage fertility rate (per 1,000 women, aged 15 - 19)*	7	5	5	5
Percentage of births to women under age 20*	2	2	1	1
Percentage of births to women aged 35 or older*	13	14	15	19
Percentage of married women using contraception				
Modern methods	69	72	76[a]	..
All methods	75	76	79[a]	..
Health and mortality				
Life expectancy at birth (years)*				
Males	71	73	74	76
Females	77	79	80	81
Both sexes combined	74	76	77	78
Infant mortality rate (per 1,000 births)*	12	8	6	5
Mortality under age 5 (per 1,000 births)*	19	13	9	6
Maternal mortality ratio (per 100,000 births) (2000)	..	..	..	16
HIV/AIDS (2003)				
Number of infected adults (thousands)	..	..	..	19
Adult prevalence rate (percentage)	..	..	..	0.2
Spatial distribution				
Population density (per sq. km)	329	349	372	392
Urban population (percentage)	57	59	62	67
Annual urban growth rate (percentage)*	1.3	0.8	1.3	1.3
Annual rural growth rate (percentage)*	0.5	0.0	-0.3	-0.9
International migration				
International migrant stock				
Number of migrants (thousands)	344	761	1 387	1 638
Percentage of total population	2.5	5.3	9	10.1

* For the periods 1970-1975, 1980-1985, 1990-1995 and 2000-2005.
[a] For 1993.

Government views and policies

Population policy variable	*1976*	*1986*	*1996*	*2005*
Population size and growth				
View on growth	Too high	Satisfactory	Satisfactory	Satisfactory
Policy on growth	No intervention	No intervention	No intervention	No intervention
Population age structure				
Level of concern about				
Size of the working-age population	..	..	..	Not a concern
Ageing of the population	..	..	..	Minor concern
Fertility and family planning				
View on fertility level	Satisfactory	Satisfactory	Satisfactory	Satisfactory
Policy	No intervention	No intervention	No intervention	Maintain
Access to contraceptive methods	Direct support	Indirect support	Direct support	Direct support
Adolescent fertility				
Level of concern	..	..	Major concern	Major concern
Policies and programmes	..	..	Yes	Yes
Health and mortality				
View				
Expectation of life	Acceptable	Acceptable	Unacceptable	Acceptable
Under-five mortality	..	..	Unacceptable	Unacceptable
Maternal mortality	..	..	..	Acceptable
Level of concern about HIV/AIDS	..	..	Minor concern	Major concern
Measures implemented to control HIV/AIDS*	..	..	..	1,2,3,4,5
Grounds on which abortion is permitted**	..	..	1,2,3,4,5	1,2,3,4,5
Spatial distribution and internal migration				
View on spatial distribution	Minor change desired	Minor change desired	Minor change desired	Minor change desired
Policies on internal migration				
From rural to urban areas	..	..	..	No intervention
From rural to rural areas	..	..	..	No intervention
From urban to rural areas	..	..	..	No intervention
From urban to urban areas	..	..	..	No intervention
Into urban agglomerations	..	No intervention	No intervention	No intervention
International migration				
Immigration				
View	Too high	Satisfactory	Too low	Satisfactory
Policy	Lower	Maintain	Raise	Maintain
Permanent settlement	..	..	Raise	Raise
Temporary workers	..	..	Maintain	Maintain
Highly skilled workers	..	..	..	Raise
Family reunification	..	..	Maintain	Maintain
Integration of non-nationals	..	..	Yes	Yes
Emigration				
View	Satisfactory	Too high	Too high	Satisfactory
Policy	Maintain	Maintain	No intervention	No intervention
Encouraging the return of nationals	..	..	No	Yes

* Measures implemented to control HIV/AIDS: (1) blood screening; (2) information/education campaigns; (3) access to antiretroviral treatment; (4) non-discriminatory policies; (5) promoting condom use.

** Grounds on which abortion is permitted: (1) to save the woman's life; (2) to preserve physical health; (3) to preserve mental health; (4) rape or incest; (5) foetal impairment; (6) economic or social reasons; (7) on request.

Population indicators

Indicator	*1975*	*1985*	*1995*	*2005*
Population size and growth				
Population size (thousands)	3 083	3 247	3 658	4 028
Annual growth rate (percentage)*	1.8	0.8	1.4	1.1
Population age structure				
Percentage of population under age 15	30	24	23	21
Percentage of population aged 60 or older	13	15	15	17
Fertility and family planning				
Total fertility (births per woman)*	2.8	2.0	2.1	2.0
Teenage fertility rate (per 1,000 women, aged 15 - 19)*	45	31	33	26
Percentage of births to women under age 20*	11	9	8	7
Percentage of births to women aged 35 or older*	11	12	14	17
Percentage of married women using contraception				
Modern methods	62[a]	..	72	..
All methods	70[a]	..	75	..
Health and mortality				
Life expectancy at birth (years)*				
Males	69	71	73	77
Females	75	77	79	81
Both sexes combined	72	74	76	79
Infant mortality rate (per 1,000 births)*	16	12	7	5
Mortality under age 5 (per 1,000 births)*	19	14	9	7
Maternal mortality ratio (per 100,000 births) (2000)	..	..	..	7
HIV/AIDS (2003)				
Number of infected adults (thousands)	..	..	..	1
Adult prevalence rate (percentage)	..	..	..	0.1
Spatial distribution				
Population density (per sq. km)	11	12	14	15
Urban population (percentage)	83	84	85	86
Annual urban growth rate (percentage)*	2.2	0.9	1.5	0.8
Annual rural growth rate (percentage)*	-0.1	0.5	0.6	0.3
International migration				
International migrant stock				
Number of migrants (thousands)	493	531	732	642
Percentage of total population	16	16.3	20	15.9

* For the periods 1970-1975, 1980-1985, 1990-1995 and 2000-2005.
[a] For 1976.

Government views and policies

Population policy variable	*1976*	*1986*	*1996*	*2005*
Population size and growth				
View on growth	Too high	Satisfactory	Too high	Too high
Policy on growth	No intervention	No intervention	Lower	Lower
Population age structure				
Level of concern about				
Size of the working-age population	..	..	..	Major concern
Ageing of the population	..	..	..	Minor concern
Fertility and family planning				
View on fertility level	Too high	Satisfactory	Too high	Too high
Policy	No intervention	No intervention	Lower	Lower
Access to contraceptive methods	Direct support	Indirect support	Direct support	Direct support
Adolescent fertility				
Level of concern	..	..	Major concern	Major concern
Policies and programmes	..	..	Yes	Yes
Health and mortality				
View				
Expectation of life	Unacceptable	Unacceptable	Unacceptable	Unacceptable
Under-five mortality	..	..	Unacceptable	Unacceptable
Maternal mortality	..	..	..	Unacceptable
Level of concern about HIV/AIDS	..	..	Minor concern	Minor concern
Measures implemented to control HIV/AIDS*	..	..	..	1,2,3,4,5
Grounds on which abortion is permitted**	..	..	1	1
Spatial distribution and internal migration				
View on spatial distribution	Minor change desired	Major change desired	Major change desired	Minor change desired
Policies on internal migration				
From rural to urban areas	..	..	..	No intervention
From rural to rural areas	..	..	..	No intervention
From urban to rural areas	..	..	..	No intervention
From urban to urban areas	..	..	..	No intervention
Into urban agglomerations	Lower	Lower	Lower	No intervention
International migration				
Immigration				
View	Satisfactory	Satisfactory	Satisfactory	Satisfactory
Policy	Maintain	Maintain	No intervention	No intervention
Permanent settlement	..	..	No intervention	No intervention
Temporary workers	..	..	No intervention	No intervention
Highly skilled workers	..	..	..	No intervention
Family reunification	..	..	No intervention	No intervention
Integration of non-nationals	..	..	Yes	No
Emigration				
View	Satisfactory	Too high	Satisfactory	Too high
Policy	Maintain	Lower	No intervention	No intervention
Encouraging the return of nationals	No	..	Yes	No

* Measures implemented to control HIV/AIDS: (1) blood screening; (2) information/education campaigns; (3) access to antiretroviral treatment; (4) non-discriminatory policies; (5) promoting condom use.
** Grounds on which abortion is permitted: (1) to save the woman's life; (2) to preserve physical health; (3) to preserve mental health; (4) rape or incest; (5) foetal impairment; (6) economic or social reasons; (7) on request.

Population indicators

Indicator	*1975*	*1985*	*1995*	*2005*
Population size and growth				
Population size (thousands)	2 622	3 526	4 477	5 487
Annual growth rate (percentage)*	3.3	2.8	2.5	2.0
Population age structure				
Percentage of population under age 15	48	47	45	39
Percentage of population aged 60 or older	4	4	4	5
Fertility and family planning				
Total fertility (births per woman)*	6.8	6.0	4.6	3.3
Teenage fertility rate (per 1,000 women, aged 15 - 19)*	158	158	160	125
Percentage of births to women under age 20*	18	20	25	25
Percentage of births to women aged 35 or older*	13	11	10	7
Percentage of married women using contraception				
Modern methods	..	23[a]	45[b]	66[c]
All methods	..	27[a]	49[b]	69[c]
Health and mortality				
Life expectancy at birth (years)*				
Males	54	56	64	67
Females	57	63	69	72
Both sexes combined	55	59	66	70
Infant mortality rate (per 1,000 births)*	98	80	48	30
Mortality under age 5 (per 1,000 births)*	152	117	62	40
Maternal mortality ratio (per 100,000 births) (2000)	..	..	..	230
HIV/AIDS (2003)				
Number of infected adults (thousands)	..	..	..	6
Adult prevalence rate (percentage)	..	..	..	0.2
Spatial distribution				
Population density (per sq. km)	20	27	34	42
Urban population (percentage)	49	52	54	58
Annual urban growth rate (percentage)*	4.0	3.6	3.4	3.1
Annual rural growth rate (percentage)*	2.5	2.5	2.3	1.5
International migration				
International migrant stock				
Number of migrants (thousands)	23	42	27	28
Percentage of total population	0.9	1.2	0.6	0.5

* For the periods 1970-1975, 1980-1985, 1990-1995 and 2000-2005.
[a] For 1981.
[b] For 1992.
[c] For 2001.

Government views and policies

Population policy variable	*1976*	*1986*	*1996*	*2005*
Population size and growth				
View on growth	Satisfactory	Too high	Too high	Too high
Policy on growth	No intervention	Lower	No intervention	Lower
Population age structure				
Level of concern about				
Size of the working-age population	..	..	..	Major concern
Ageing of the population	..	..	..	Minor concern
Fertility and family planning				
View on fertility level	Satisfactory	Too high	Too high	Too high
Policy	No intervention	Lower	Lower	Lower
Access to contraceptive methods	No support	Direct support	Direct support	Direct support
Adolescent fertility				
Level of concern	..	..	Not a concern	Major concern
Policies and programmes	..	..	No	Yes
Health and mortality				
View				
Expectation of life	Unacceptable	Unacceptable	Unacceptable	Unacceptable
Under-five mortality	..	..	Unacceptable	Unacceptable
Maternal mortality	..	..	..	Unacceptable
Level of concern about HIV/AIDS	..	..	Major concern	Major concern
Measures implemented to control HIV/AIDS*	..	..	..	2,3,4,5
Grounds on which abortion is permitted**	..	..	1	1
Spatial distribution and internal migration				
View on spatial distribution	Major change desired	Major change desired	Major change desired	Minor change desired
Policies on internal migration				
From rural to urban areas	..	..	..	No intervention
From rural to rural areas	..	..	..	..
From urban to rural areas	..	..	..	..
From urban to urban areas	..	..	..	..
Into urban agglomerations	No intervention	..	No intervention	No intervention
International migration				
Immigration				
View	Satisfactory	Satisfactory	Satisfactory	Satisfactory
Policy	Maintain	Maintain	No intervention	Lower
Permanent settlement	..	..	No intervention	No intervention
Temporary workers	..	..	No intervention	No intervention
Highly skilled workers	..	..	..	..
Family reunification	..	..	No intervention	No intervention
Integration of non-nationals	..	..	No	No
Emigration				
View	Satisfactory	Satisfactory	Satisfactory	Satisfactory
Policy	Maintain	Maintain	No intervention	No intervention
Encouraging the return of nationals	No	..	No	Yes

* Measures implemented to control HIV/AIDS: (1) blood screening; (2) information/education campaigns; (3) access to antiretroviral treatment; (4) non-discriminatory policies; (5) promoting condom use.

** Grounds on which abortion is permitted: (1) to save the woman's life; (2) to preserve physical health; (3) to preserve mental health; (4) rape or incest; (5) foetal impairment; (6) economic or social reasons; (7) on request.

Population indicators

Indicator	*1975*	*1985*	*1995*	*2005*
Population size and growth				
Population size (thousands)	5 325	7 245	9 929	13 957
Annual growth rate (percentage)*	3.0	3.1	3.2	3.4
Population age structure				
Percentage of population under age 15	48	49	49	49
Percentage of population aged 60 or older	4	4	3	3
Fertility and family planning				
Total fertility (births per woman)*	8.1	8.2	8.2	7.9
Teenage fertility rate (per 1,000 women, aged 15 - 19)*	309	316	270	271
Percentage of births to women under age 20*	28	28	25	25
Percentage of births to women aged 35 or older*	13	12	13	12
Percentage of married women using contraception				
Modern methods	..	..	2[a]	4[b]
All methods	..	..	4[a]	14[b]
Health and mortality				
Life expectancy at birth (years)*				
Males	38	39	40	44
Females	39	39	41	44
Both sexes combined	38	39	41	44
Infant mortality rate (per 1,000 births)*	186	180	173	153
Mortality under age 5 (per 1,000 births)*	329	321	307	264
Maternal mortality ratio (per 100,000 births) (2000)	..	..	..	1 600
HIV/AIDS (2003)				
Number of infected adults (thousands)	..	..	..	64
Adult prevalence rate (percentage)	..	..	..	1.2
Spatial distribution				
Population density (per sq. km)	4	6	8	11
Urban population (percentage)	11	14	18	23
Annual urban growth rate (percentage)*	7.4	5.6	5.8	6.1
Annual rural growth rate (percentage)*	2.4	2.8	2.8	2.9
International migration				
International migrant stock				
Number of migrants (thousands)	85	104	139	124
Percentage of total population	1.6	1.4	1.4	0.9

* For the periods 1970-1975, 1980-1985, 1990-1995 and 2000-2005.
[a] For 1992.
[b] For 2000.

Government views and policies

Population policy variable	*1976*	*1986*	*1996*	*2005*
Population size and growth				
View on growth	Satisfactory	Too high	Too high	Too high
Policy on growth	No intervention	Lower	Lower	Lower
Population age structure				
Level of concern about				
Size of the working-age population	..	..	..	Major concern
Ageing of the population	..	..	..	Minor concern
Fertility and family planning				
View on fertility level	Satisfactory	Too high	Too high	Too high
Policy	No intervention	Lower	Lower	Lower
Access to contraceptive methods	Direct support	Direct support	Direct support	Direct support
Adolescent fertility				
Level of concern	..	..	..	Major concern
Policies and programmes	..	..	..	..
Health and mortality				
View				
Expectation of life	Unacceptable	Unacceptable	Unacceptable	Unacceptable
Under-five mortality	..	..	..	Unacceptable
Maternal mortality	..	..	..	Unacceptable
Level of concern about HIV/AIDS	..	..	..	Major concern
Measures implemented to control HIV/AIDS*	..	..	..	2,3,4,5
Grounds on which abortion is permitted**	..	..	1	1,2,3
Spatial distribution and internal migration				
View on spatial distribution	Major change desired	Major change desired	Major change desired	Major change desired
Policies on internal migration				
From rural to urban areas	..	..	..	Lower
From rural to rural areas	..	..	..	..
From urban to rural areas	..	..	..	..
From urban to urban areas	..	..	..	..
Into urban agglomerations	..	..	..	Lower
International migration				
Immigration				
View	Satisfactory	Satisfactory	Satisfactory	Satisfactory
Policy	Maintain	Maintain	Maintain	Maintain
Permanent settlement	..	..	Maintain	Maintain
Temporary workers	..	..	..	..
Highly skilled workers	..	..	..	..
Family reunification	..	..	..	..
Integration of non-nationals	..	..	..	..
Emigration				
View	Satisfactory	Satisfactory	Satisfactory	Satisfactory
Policy	Maintain	Maintain	No intervention	No intervention
Encouraging the return of nationals	No	..	..	Yes

* Measures implemented to control HIV/AIDS: (1) blood screening; (2) information/education campaigns; (3) access to antiretroviral treatment; (4) non-discriminatory policies; (5) promoting condom use.

** Grounds on which abortion is permitted: (1) to save the woman's life; (2) to preserve physical health; (3) to preserve mental health; (4) rape or incest; (5) foetal impairment; (6) economic or social reasons; (7) on request.

Population indicators

Indicator	*1975*	*1985*	*1995*	*2005*
Population size and growth				
Population size (thousands)	58 950	78 435	103 914	131 530
Annual growth rate (percentage)*	2.6	2.7	2.8	2.2
Population age structure				
Percentage of population under age 15	45	45	46	44
Percentage of population aged 60 or older	5	5	5	5
Fertility and family planning				
Total fertility (births per woman)*	6.9	6.9	6.6	5.8
Teenage fertility rate (per 1,000 women, aged 15 - 19)*	156	182	179	153
Percentage of births to women under age 20*	17	19	20	20
Percentage of births to women aged 35 or older*	21	16	16	13
Percentage of married women using contraception				
Modern methods	..	1[a]	9[b]	8[c]
All methods	..	5[a]	15[b]	13[c]
Health and mortality				
Life expectancy at birth (years)*				
Males	41	44	45	43
Females	44	47	48	44
Both sexes combined	43	46	46	43
Infant mortality rate (per 1,000 births)*	144	127	119	114
Mortality under age 5 (per 1,000 births)*	240	221	206	200
Maternal mortality ratio (per 100,000 births) (2000)	..	..	..	800
HIV/AIDS (2003)				
Number of infected adults (thousands)	..	..	..	3 300
Adult prevalence rate (percentage)	..	..	..	5.4
Spatial distribution				
Population density (per sq. km)	64	85	112	142
Urban population (percentage)	23	31	40	48
Annual urban growth rate (percentage)*	5.5	5.5	5.4	4.4
Annual rural growth rate (percentage)*	1.9	1.7	1.5	1.0
International migration				
International migrant stock				
Number of migrants (thousands)	704	348	582	971
Percentage of total population	1.2	0.4	0.6	0.7

* For the periods 1970-1975, 1980-1985, 1990-1995 and 2000-2005.
[a] For 1982.
[b] For 1999.
[c] For 2003.

Government views and policies

Population policy variable	*1976*	*1986*	*1996*	*2005*
Population size and growth				
View on growth	..	..	Too low	Too low
Policy on growth	..	..	Raise	Raise
Population age structure				
Level of concern about				
Size of the working-age population	..	..	..	..
Ageing of the population	..	..	..	..
Fertility and family planning				
View on fertility level	..	..	Too low	Too low
Policy	..	..	Raise	Raise
Access to contraceptive methods	..	..	..	Indirect support
Adolescent fertility				
Level of concern	..	..	..	Major concern
Policies and programmes	..	..	No	Yes
Health and mortality				
View				
Expectation of life	..	..	Acceptable	Acceptable
Under-five mortality	..	..	..	Acceptable
Maternal mortality	..	..	..	Acceptable
Level of concern about HIV/AIDS	..	..	..	Major concern
Measures implemented to control HIV/AIDS*	..	..	..	..
Grounds on which abortion is permitted**	..	..	1,2,3	1,2,3
Spatial distribution and internal migration				
View on spatial distribution	..	..	Satisfactory	Satisfactory
Policies on internal migration				
From rural to urban areas	..	..	..	..
From rural to rural areas	..	..	..	..
From urban to rural areas	..	..	..	..
From urban to urban areas	..	..	..	..
Into urban agglomerations	..	..	..	..
International migration				
Immigration				
View	..	..	Satisfactory	Too low
Policy	..	..	No intervention	Raise
Permanent settlement	..	..	..	Raise
Temporary workers	..	..	..	Raise
Highly skilled workers	..	..	..	..
Family reunification	..	..	..	..
Integration of non-nationals	..	..	..	..
Emigration				
View	..	..	Too high	Too high
Policy	..	..	Lower	Lower
Encouraging the return of nationals	..	..	Yes	Yes

* Measures implemented to control HIV/AIDS: (1) blood screening; (2) information/education campaigns; (3) access to antiretroviral treatment; (4) non-discriminatory policies; (5) promoting condom use.

** Grounds on which abortion is permitted: (1) to save the woman's life; (2) to preserve physical health; (3) to preserve mental health; (4) rape or incest; (5) foetal impairment; (6) economic or social reasons; (7) on request.

Population indicators

Indicator	*1975*	*1985*	*1995*	*2005*
Population size and growth				
Population size (thousands)	4	2	2	1
Annual growth rate (percentage)*	-4.7	-5.5	-2.2	-2.2
Population age structure				
Percentage of population under age 15	..	..	..	..
Percentage of population aged 60 or older	..	..	..	..
Fertility and family planning				
Total fertility (births per woman)*	..	..	..	..
Teenage fertility rate (per 1,000 women, aged 15 - 19)*	..	..	..	..
Percentage of births to women under age 20*	..	..	..	..
Percentage of births to women aged 35 or older*	..	..	..	..
Percentage of married women using contraception				
Modern methods	..	..	..	..
All methods	..	..	..	..
Health and mortality				
Life expectancy at birth (years)*				
Males	..	..	..	..
Females	..	..	..	..
Both sexes combined	..	..	..	..
Infant mortality rate (per 1,000 births)*	..	..	..	..
Mortality under age 5 (per 1,000 births)*	..	..	..	..
Maternal mortality ratio (per 100,000 births) (2000)	..	..	..	..
HIV/AIDS (2003)				
Number of infected adults (thousands)	..	..	..	..
Adult prevalence rate (percentage)	..	..	..	..
Spatial distribution				
Population density (per sq. km)	15	9	7	6
Urban population (percentage)	23	31	31	37
Annual urban growth rate (percentage)*	-2.1	-1.9	-1.2	0.5
Annual rural growth rate (percentage)*	-4.7	-5.8	-1.7	-2.2
International migration				
International migrant stock				
Number of migrants (thousands)	0	0	0	0
Percentage of total population	10.9	11.9	10	7.6

* For the periods 1970-1975, 1980-1985, 1990-1995 and 2000-2005.

Government views and policies

Population policy variable	*1976*	*1986*	*1996*	*2005*
Population size and growth				
View on growth	Satisfactory	Satisfactory	Satisfactory	Satisfactory
Policy on growth	No intervention	No intervention	No intervention	No intervention
Population age structure				
Level of concern about				
Size of the working-age population	..	..	..	Minor concern
Ageing of the population	..	..	..	Minor concern
Fertility and family planning				
View on fertility level	Satisfactory	Satisfactory	Satisfactory	Satisfactory
Policy	No intervention	No intervention	No intervention	Maintain
Access to contraceptive methods	Direct support	Direct support	Direct support	Direct support
Adolescent fertility				
Level of concern	..	..	Minor concern	Minor concern
Policies and programmes	..	..	Yes	Yes
Health and mortality				
View				
Expectation of life	Acceptable	Acceptable	Unacceptable	Acceptable
Under-five mortality	..	..	Unacceptable	Acceptable
Maternal mortality	..	..	..	Acceptable
Level of concern about HIV/AIDS	..	..	Minor concern	Minor concern
Measures implemented to control HIV/AIDS*	..	..	..	1,2,3,5
Grounds on which abortion is permitted**	..	..	1,2,3,4,5,6,7	1,2,3,4,5,6,7
Spatial distribution and internal migration				
View on spatial distribution	Minor change desired	Satisfactory	Minor change desired	Major change desired
Policies on internal migration				
From rural to urban areas	..	..	..	Lower
From rural to rural areas	..	..	..	No intervention
From urban to rural areas	..	..	..	No intervention
From urban to urban areas	..	..	..	No intervention
Into urban agglomerations	Lower	Maintain	Lower	Lower
International migration				
Immigration				
View	Too high	Satisfactory	Satisfactory	Satisfactory
Policy	Lower	Maintain	Lower	Maintain
Permanent settlement	..	..	Lower	Maintain
Temporary workers	..	..	Lower	Maintain
Highly skilled workers	..	..	..	Raise
Family reunification	..	..	Maintain	Lower
Integration of non-nationals	..	..	Yes	Yes
Emigration				
View	Satisfactory	Satisfactory	Satisfactory	Satisfactory
Policy	Maintain	Maintain	No intervention	No intervention
Encouraging the return of nationals	No	..	No	No

* Measures implemented to control HIV/AIDS: (1) blood screening; (2) information/education campaigns; (3) access to antiretroviral treatment; (4) non-discriminatory policies; (5) promoting condom use.

** Grounds on which abortion is permitted: (1) to save the woman's life; (2) to preserve physical health; (3) to preserve mental health; (4) rape or incest; (5) foetal impairment; (6) economic or social reasons; (7) on request.

Population indicators

Indicator	*1975*	*1985*	*1995*	*2005*
Population size and growth				
Population size (thousands)	4 007	4 153	4 359	4 620
Annual growth rate (percentage)*	0.7	0.3	0.5	0.5
Population age structure				
Percentage of population under age 15	24	20	19	20
Percentage of population aged 60 or older	19	21	20	20
Fertility and family planning				
Total fertility (births per woman)*	2.2	1.7	1.9	1.8
Teenage fertility rate (per 1,000 women, aged 15 - 19)*	15	11	13	10
Percentage of births to women under age 20*	4	4	3	2
Percentage of births to women aged 35 or older*	10	12	13	16
Percentage of married women using contraception				
Modern methods	65[a]	69[b]	..	..
All methods	71[a]	74[b]	..	..
Health and mortality				
Life expectancy at birth (years)*				
Males	71	73	74	77
Females	78	80	80	82
Both sexes combined	74	76	77	79
Infant mortality rate (per 1,000 births)*	12	8	6	4
Mortality under age 5 (per 1,000 births)*	14	10	7	5
Maternal mortality ratio (per 100,000 births) (2000)	..	..	..	16
HIV/AIDS (2003)				
Number of infected adults (thousands)	..	..	..	2
Adult prevalence rate (percentage)	..	..	..	0.1
Spatial distribution				
Population density (per sq. km)	10	11	11	12
Urban population (percentage)	68	71	73	80
Annual urban growth rate (percentage)*	1.5	0.5	0.9	1.6
Annual rural growth rate (percentage)*	-1.0	-0.2	-0.5	-3.8
International migration				
International migrant stock				
Number of migrants (thousands)	107	154	231	344
Percentage of total population	2.7	3.7	5.3	7.4

* For the periods 1970-1975, 1980-1985, 1990-1995 and 2000-2005.
[a] For 1977.
[b] For 1988/1989.

Government views and policies

Population policy variable	*1976*	*1986*	*1996*	*2005*
Population size and growth				
View on growth	Too low	Too low	Too low	Too high
Policy on growth	Raise	Raise	Raise	Lower
Population age structure				
Level of concern about				
Size of the working-age population	..	..	..	Major concern
Ageing of the population	..	..	..	..
Fertility and family planning				
View on fertility level	Satisfactory	Satisfactory	Satisfactory	Too high
Policy	Maintain	Maintain	Maintain	Lower
Access to contraceptive methods	No support	No support	No support	Direct support
Adolescent fertility				
Level of concern	..	..	..	Minor concern
Policies and programmes	..	..	..	Yes
Health and mortality				
View				
Expectation of life	Unacceptable	Unacceptable	Unacceptable	Acceptable
Under-five mortality	..	..	..	Unacceptable
Maternal mortality	..	..	..	Acceptable
Level of concern about HIV/AIDS	..	..	..	Major concern
Measures implemented to control HIV/AIDS*	..	..	..	1,2,3,4,5
Grounds on which abortion is permitted**	..	..	1	1
Spatial distribution and internal migration				
View on spatial distribution	Minor change desired	Minor change desired	Minor change desired	Major change desired
Policies on internal migration				
From rural to urban areas	..	..	..	Lower
From rural to rural areas	..	..	..	No intervention
From urban to rural areas	..	..	..	Raise
From urban to urban areas	..	..	..	No intervention
Into urban agglomerations	..	..	..	Lower
International migration				
Immigration				
View	Satisfactory	Satisfactory	Too high	Too high
Policy	Maintain	Maintain	Lower	Lower
Permanent settlement	..	..	..	Lower
Temporary workers	..	..	..	Lower
Highly skilled workers	..	..	..	Maintain
Family reunification	..	..	..	Maintain
Integration of non-nationals	..	..	..	No
Emigration				
View	Satisfactory	Satisfactory	Satisfactory	Satisfactory
Policy	Maintain	Maintain	Maintain	No intervention
Encouraging the return of nationals	..	..	..	No

* Measures implemented to control HIV/AIDS: (1) blood screening; (2) information/education campaigns; (3) access to antiretroviral treatment; (4) non-discriminatory policies; (5) promoting condom use.

** Grounds on which abortion is permitted: (1) to save the woman's life; (2) to preserve physical health; (3) to preserve mental health; (4) rape or incest; (5) foetal impairment; (6) economic or social reasons; (7) on request.

Population indicators

Indicator	*1975*	*1985*	*1995*	*2005*
Population size and growth				
Population size (thousands)	917	1 527	2 177	2 567
Annual growth rate (percentage)*	4.1	5.0	3.3	1.0
Population age structure				
Percentage of population under age 15	47	45	40	34
Percentage of population aged 60 or older	4	3	3	4
Fertility and family planning				
Total fertility (births per woman)*	7.2	7.2	6.3	3.8
Teenage fertility rate (per 1,000 women, aged 15 - 19)*	122	122	86	50
Percentage of births to women under age 20*	13	12	11	10
Percentage of births to women aged 35 or older*	13	14	21	15
Percentage of married women using contraception				
Modern methods	..	8[a]	18	..
All methods	..	9[a]	24	..
Health and mortality				
Life expectancy at birth (years)*				
Males	51	61	70	73
Females	53	64	73	76
Both sexes combined	52	63	71	74
Infant mortality rate (per 1,000 births)*	110	58	24	16
Mortality under age 5 (per 1,000 births)*	159	78	28	18
Maternal mortality ratio (per 100,000 births) (2000)	..	..	..	87
HIV/AIDS (2003)				
Number of infected adults (thousands)	..	..	..	1
Adult prevalence rate (percentage)	..	..	..	0.1
Spatial distribution				
Population density (per sq. km)	3	5	7	8
Urban population (percentage)	20	47	73	79
Annual urban growth rate (percentage)*	14.9	12.8	7.0	3.6
Annual rural growth rate (percentage)*	2.2	0.1	-2.7	0.6
International migration				
International migrant stock				
Number of migrants (thousands)	75	327	573	628
Percentage of total population	8.2	21.4	26.3	24.4

* For the periods 1970-1975, 1980-1985, 1990-1995 and 2000-2005.
[a] For 1988.

Government views and policies

Population policy variable	*1976*	*1986*	*1996*	*2005*
Population size and growth				
View on growth	Too high	Too high	Too high	Too high
Policy on growth	Lower	Lower	Lower	Lower
Population age structure				
Level of concern about				
Size of the working-age population	..	..	..	Major concern
Ageing of the population	..	..	..	Minor concern
Fertility and family planning				
View on fertility level	Too high	Too high	Too high	Too high
Policy	Lower	Lower	Lower	Lower
Access to contraceptive methods	Direct support	Direct support	Direct support	Direct support
Adolescent fertility				
Level of concern	..	..	Not a concern	Major concern
Policies and programmes	..	..	No	Yes
Health and mortality				
View				
Expectation of life	Unacceptable	Unacceptable	Acceptable	Unacceptable
Under-five mortality	..	..	Unacceptable	Unacceptable
Maternal mortality	..	..	..	Unacceptable
Level of concern about HIV/AIDS	..	..	Major concern	Major concern
Measures implemented to control HIV/AIDS*	..	..	..	1,2,3,4,5
Grounds on which abortion is permitted**	..	..	1,2,3	1,2,3
Spatial distribution and internal migration				
View on spatial distribution	Major change desired	Major change desired	Satisfactory	Major change desired
Policies on internal migration				
From rural to urban areas	..	..	..	Lower
From rural to rural areas	..	..	..	No intervention
From urban to rural areas	..	..	..	Raise
From urban to urban areas	..	..	..	Maintain
Into urban agglomerations	..	Lower	Lower	Lower
International migration				
Immigration				
View	Satisfactory	Too high	Satisfactory	Too high
Policy	Maintain	Lower	No intervention	Lower
Permanent settlement	..	..	No intervention	Lower
Temporary workers	..	..	No intervention	Maintain
Highly skilled workers	..	..	..	Maintain
Family reunification	..	..	No intervention	Lower
Integration of non-nationals	..	..	No	No
Emigration				
View	Satisfactory	Satisfactory	Too low	Satisfactory
Policy	Maintain	Raise	Raise	Raise
Encouraging the return of nationals	..	..	Yes	Yes

* Measures implemented to control HIV/AIDS: (1) blood screening; (2) information/education campaigns; (3) access to antiretroviral treatment; (4) non-discriminatory policies; (5) promoting condom use.
** Grounds on which abortion is permitted: (1) to save the woman's life; (2) to preserve physical health; (3) to preserve mental health; (4) rape or incest; (5) foetal impairment; (6) economic or social reasons; (7) on request.

Population indicators

Indicator	*1975*	*1985*	*1995*	*2005*
Population size and growth				
Population size (thousands)	68 294	94 719	126 075	157 935
Annual growth rate (percentage)*	2.7	3.6	2.4	2.0
Population age structure				
Percentage of population under age 15	43	43	44	38
Percentage of population aged 60 or older	6	5	6	6
Fertility and family planning				
Total fertility (births per woman)*	6.6	6.6	5.7	4.3
Teenage fertility rate (per 1,000 women, aged 15 - 19)*	101	102	95	70
Percentage of births to women under age 20*	11	11	12	12
Percentage of births to women aged 35 or older*	23	18	17	13
Percentage of married women using contraception				
Modern methods	4	6	13	20[a]
All methods	5	8	18	28[a]
Health and mortality				
Life expectancy at birth (years)*				
Males	52	56	61	63
Females	51	56	61	63
Both sexes combined	52	56	61	63
Infant mortality rate (per 1,000 births)*	128	108	87	79
Mortality under age 5 (per 1,000 births)*	203	167	128	114
Maternal mortality ratio (per 100,000 births) (2000)	..	..	..	500
HIV/AIDS (2003)				
Number of infected adults (thousands)	..	..	..	73
Adult prevalence rate (percentage)	..	..	..	0.1
Spatial distribution				
Population density (per sq. km)	86	119	158	198
Urban population (percentage)	26	29	32	35
Annual urban growth rate (percentage)*	3.7	4.2	3.2	3.4
Annual rural growth rate (percentage)*	2.1	2.9	2.0	1.9
International migration				
International migrant stock				
Number of migrants (thousands)	4 574	6 288	4 077	3 254
Percentage of total population	6.7	6.6	3.2	2.1

* For the periods 1970-1975, 1980-1985, 1990-1995 and 2000-2005.
[a] For 2000/2001.

Government views and policies

Population policy variable	*1976*	*1986*	*1996*	*2005*
Population size and growth				
View on growth	..	..	Satisfactory	Satisfactory
Policy on growth	..	..	No intervention	No intervention
Population age structure				
Level of concern about				
Size of the working-age population	..	..	..	..
Ageing of the population	..	..	..	..
Fertility and family planning				
View on fertility level	..	..	Satisfactory	Satisfactory
Policy	..	..	No intervention	No intervention
Access to contraceptive methods	..	..	..	Indirect support
Adolescent fertility				
Level of concern	..	..	..	Minor concern
Policies and programmes	..	..	No	No
Health and mortality				
View				
Expectation of life	..	..	Acceptable	Acceptable
Under-five mortality	..	..	..	Acceptable
Maternal mortality	..	..	..	Acceptable
Level of concern about HIV/AIDS	..	..	..	Major concern
Measures implemented to control HIV/AIDS*	..	..	..	2,3
Grounds on which abortion is permitted**	..	..	1	1
Spatial distribution and internal migration				
View on spatial distribution	..	..	Minor change desired	Minor change desired
Policies on internal migration				
From rural to urban areas	..	..	..	..
From rural to rural areas	..	..	..	..
From urban to rural areas	..	..	..	..
From urban to urban areas	..	..	..	..
Into urban agglomerations	..	..	..	..
International migration				
Immigration				
View	..	..	Too high	Too high
Policy	..	..	No intervention	No intervention
Permanent settlement	..	..	..	..
Temporary workers	..	..	..	Lower
Highly skilled workers	..	..	..	..
Family reunification	..	..	..	..
Integration of non-nationals	..	..	..	..
Emigration				
View	..	..	Too high	Too high
Policy	..	..	No intervention	Lower
Encouraging the return of nationals	..	..	Yes	Yes

* Measures implemented to control HIV/AIDS: (1) blood screening; (2) information/education campaigns; (3) access to antiretroviral treatment; (4) non-discriminatory policies; (5) promoting condom use.

** Grounds on which abortion is permitted: (1) to save the woman's life; (2) to preserve physical health; (3) to preserve mental health; (4) rape or incest; (5) foetal impairment; (6) economic or social reasons; (7) on request.

Population indicators

Indicator	*1975*	*1985*	*1995*	*2005*
Population size and growth				
Population size (thousands)	12	14	17	20
Annual growth rate (percentage)*	1.3	2.6	2.6	0.7
Population age structure				
Percentage of population under age 15	..	..	..	..
Percentage of population aged 60 or older	..	..	..	..
Fertility and family planning				
Total fertility (births per woman)*	..	..	..	..
Teenage fertility rate (per 1,000 women, aged 15 - 19)*	..	..	..	..
Percentage of births to women under age 20*	..	..	..	..
Percentage of births to women aged 35 or older*	..	..	..	..
Percentage of married women using contraception				
Modern methods	..	..	..	..
All methods	..	..	..	..
Health and mortality				
Life expectancy at birth (years)*				
Males	..	..	..	..
Females	..	..	..	..
Both sexes combined	..	..	..	..
Infant mortality rate (per 1,000 births)*	..	..	..	..
Mortality under age 5 (per 1,000 births)*	..	..	..	..
Maternal mortality ratio (per 100,000 births) (2000)	..	..	..	..
HIV/AIDS (2003)				
Number of infected adults (thousands)	..	..	..	..
Adult prevalence rate (percentage)	..	..	..	..
Spatial distribution				
Population density (per sq. km)	26	30	38	43
Urban population (percentage)	62	68	71	68
Annual urban growth rate (percentage)*	3.0	3.2	2.9	1.7
Annual rural growth rate (percentage)*	0.5	0.7	1.1	2.9
International migration				
International migrant stock				
Number of migrants (thousands)	1	2	2	3
Percentage of total population	10.2	11.9	12.9	15.2

* For the periods 1970-1975, 1980-1985, 1990-1995 and 2000-2005.

Government views and policies

Population policy variable	*1976*	*1986*	*1996*	*2005*
Population size and growth				
View on growth	Satisfactory	Satisfactory	Satisfactory	Satisfactory
Policy on growth	No intervention	No intervention	No intervention	Maintain
Population age structure				
Level of concern about				
Size of the working-age population	..	..	..	Minor concern
Ageing of the population	..	..	..	Major concern
Fertility and family planning				
View on fertility level	Too high	Satisfactory	Satisfactory	Satisfactory
Policy	No intervention	No intervention	No intervention	Maintain
Access to contraceptive methods	Direct support	Direct support	Direct support	Direct support
Adolescent fertility				
Level of concern	..	..	Major concern	Major concern
Policies and programmes	..	..	Yes	Yes
Health and mortality				
View				
Expectation of life	Acceptable	Acceptable	Acceptable	Acceptable
Under-five mortality	..	..	Unacceptable	Unacceptable
Maternal mortality	..	..	..	Unacceptable
Level of concern about HIV/AIDS	..	..	Major concern	Major concern
Measures implemented to control HIV/AIDS*	..	..	..	1,2,3,4,5
Grounds on which abortion is permitted**	..	..	1,4,5	1,3,4
Spatial distribution and internal migration				
View on spatial distribution	Major change desired	Major change desired	Major change desired	Minor change desired
Policies on internal migration				
From rural to urban areas	..	..	..	Lower
From rural to rural areas	..	..	..	..
From urban to rural areas	..	..	..	..
From urban to urban areas	..	..	..	Raise
Into urban agglomerations	No intervention	Lower	No intervention	Lower
International migration				
Immigration				
View	Satisfactory	Satisfactory	Satisfactory	Satisfactory
Policy	Maintain	Maintain	Maintain	Lower
Permanent settlement	..	..	Maintain	Lower
Temporary workers	..	..	No intervention	Lower
Highly skilled workers	..	..	..	..
Family reunification	..	..	No intervention	Lower
Integration of non-nationals	..	..	Yes	..
Emigration				
View	Satisfactory	Satisfactory	Satisfactory	Satisfactory
Policy	Maintain	Maintain	No intervention	No intervention
Encouraging the return of nationals	No	..	No	Yes

* Measures implemented to control HIV/AIDS: (1) blood screening; (2) information/education campaigns; (3) access to antiretroviral treatment; (4) non-discriminatory policies; (5) promoting condom use.

** Grounds on which abortion is permitted: (1) to save the woman's life; (2) to preserve physical health; (3) to preserve mental health; (4) rape or incest; (5) foetal impairment; (6) economic or social reasons; (7) on request.

Population indicators

Indicator	*1975*	*1985*	*1995*	*2005*
Population size and growth				
Population size (thousands)	1 723	2 176	2 670	3 232
Annual growth rate (percentage)*	2.7	2.2	2.0	1.8
Population age structure				
Percentage of population under age 15	43	38	33	30
Percentage of population aged 60 or older	7	7	7	9
Fertility and family planning				
Total fertility (births per woman)*	4.9	3.5	2.9	2.7
Teenage fertility rate (per 1,000 women, aged 15 - 19)*	135	108	91	89
Percentage of births to women under age 20*	19	21	19	18
Percentage of births to women aged 35 or older*	10	9	8	9
Percentage of married women using contraception				
Modern methods	46[a]	54[b]	..	..
All methods	54[a]	58[b]	..	..
Health and mortality				
Life expectancy at birth (years)*				
Males	65	68	70	72
Females	68	73	76	77
Both sexes combined	66	70	72	75
Infant mortality rate (per 1,000 births)*	44	32	27	21
Mortality under age 5 (per 1,000 births)*	68	43	34	27
Maternal mortality ratio (per 100,000 births) (2000)	..	..	..	160
HIV/AIDS (2003)				
Number of infected adults (thousands)	..	..	..	15
Adult prevalence rate (percentage)	..	..	..	0.9
Spatial distribution				
Population density (per sq. km)	23	29	35	43
Urban population (percentage)	49	52	55	58
Annual urban growth rate (percentage)*	3.3	2.8	2.5	2.4
Annual rural growth rate (percentage)*	2.1	1.5	1.5	1.1
International migration				
International migrant stock				
Number of migrants (thousands)	53	54	73	102
Percentage of total population	3.1	2.5	2.7	3.2

* For the periods 1970-1975, 1980-1985, 1990-1995 and 2000-2005.
[a] For 1976.
[b] For 1984.

Government views and policies

Population policy variable	*1976*	*1986*	*1996*	*2005*
Population size and growth				
View on growth	Too high	Too high	Too high	Too high
Policy on growth	Lower	Lower	Lower	Lower
Population age structure				
Level of concern about				
Size of the working-age population	..	..	..	Major concern
Ageing of the population	..	..	..	..
Fertility and family planning				
View on fertility level	Too high	Too high	Too high	Too high
Policy	Lower	No intervention	Lower	Lower
Access to contraceptive methods	Direct support	Direct support	Direct support	Direct support
Adolescent fertility				
Level of concern	..	..	..	Major concern
Policies and programmes	..	..	..	Yes
Health and mortality				
View				
Expectation of life	Unacceptable	Unacceptable	Unacceptable	Unacceptable
Under-five mortality	..	..	..	Unacceptable
Maternal mortality	..	..	..	Unacceptable
Level of concern about HIV/AIDS	..	..	..	Major concern
Measures implemented to control HIV/AIDS*	..	..	..	1,2,3,4,5
Grounds on which abortion is permitted**	..	..	1,2,3	1,2,3
Spatial distribution and internal migration				
View on spatial distribution	Major change desired	Minor change desired	Minor change desired	Major change desired
Policies on internal migration				
From rural to urban areas	..	..	..	Lower
From rural to rural areas	..	..	..	..
From urban to rural areas	..	..	..	..
From urban to urban areas	..	..	..	..
Into urban agglomerations	..	No intervention	..	Lower
International migration				
Immigration				
View	Satisfactory	Satisfactory	Satisfactory	Satisfactory
Policy	Maintain	Maintain	Maintain	Maintain
Permanent settlement	..	..	..	No intervention
Temporary workers	..	..	..	Maintain
Highly skilled workers	..	..	..	Raise
Family reunification	..	..	..	Maintain
Integration of non-nationals	..	..	..	Yes
Emigration				
View	Satisfactory	Satisfactory	Satisfactory	Satisfactory
Policy	Maintain	Maintain	Maintain	No intervention
Encouraging the return of nationals	..	..	..	Yes

* Measures implemented to control HIV/AIDS: (1) blood screening; (2) information/education campaigns; (3) access to antiretroviral treatment; (4) non-discriminatory policies; (5) promoting condom use.
** Grounds on which abortion is permitted: (1) to save the woman's life; (2) to preserve physical health; (3) to preserve mental health; (4) rape or incest; (5) foetal impairment; (6) economic or social reasons; (7) on request.

Population indicators

Indicator	*1975*	*1985*	*1995*	*2005*
Population size and growth				
Population size (thousands)	2 866	3 655	4 687	5 887
Annual growth rate (percentage)*	2.3	2.4	2.6	2.1
Population age structure				
Percentage of population under age 15	44	43	42	40
Percentage of population aged 60 or older	4	4	4	4
Fertility and family planning				
Total fertility (births per woman)*	6.1	5.5	5.0	4.1
Teenage fertility rate (per 1,000 women, aged 15 - 19)*	106	95	87	67
Percentage of births to women under age 20*	13	13	12	10
Percentage of births to women aged 35 or older*	17	16	15	14
Percentage of married women using contraception				
Modern methods	..	..	20[a]	..
All methods	..	..	26[a]	..
Health and mortality				
Life expectancy at birth (years)*				
Males	44	49	52	55
Females	46	51	54	56
Both sexes combined	45	50	52	55
Infant mortality rate (per 1,000 births)*	112	91	80	71
Mortality under age 5 (per 1,000 births)*	163	131	113	98
Maternal mortality ratio (per 100,000 births) (2000)	..	..	..	300
HIV/AIDS (2003)				
Number of infected adults (thousands)	..	..	..	16
Adult prevalence rate (percentage)	..	..	..	0.6
Spatial distribution				
Population density (per sq. km)	6	8	10	13
Urban population (percentage)	12	13	13	13
Annual urban growth rate (percentage)*	6.2	2.5	2.7	2.3
Annual rural growth rate (percentage)*	1.8	2.4	2.7	2.2
International migration				
International migrant stock				
Number of migrants (thousands)	44	40	32	25
Percentage of total population	1.5	1.1	0.7	0.4

* For the periods 1970-1975, 1980-1985, 1990-1995 and 2000-2005.
[a] For 1996.

Government views and policies

Population policy variable	*1976*	*1986*	*1996*	*2005*
Population size and growth				
View on growth	Too low	Satisfactory	Satisfactory	Too high
Policy on growth	No intervention	No intervention	No intervention	No intervention
Population age structure				
Level of concern about				
Size of the working-age population	..	..	..	Major concern
Ageing of the population	..	..	..	Major concern
Fertility and family planning				
View on fertility level	Satisfactory	Satisfactory	Satisfactory	Too high
Policy	No intervention	No intervention	No intervention	No intervention
Access to contraceptive methods	Direct support	Indirect support	Direct support	Direct support
Adolescent fertility				
Level of concern	..	..	Major concern	Major concern
Policies and programmes	..	..	No	..
Health and mortality				
View				
Expectation of life	Unacceptable	Acceptable	Acceptable	Acceptable
Under-five mortality	..	..	Unacceptable	Unacceptable
Maternal mortality	..	..	..	Unacceptable
Level of concern about HIV/AIDS	..	..	Major concern	Major concern
Measures implemented to control HIV/AIDS*	..	..	..	1,2,4,5
Grounds on which abortion is permitted**	..	..	1	1
Spatial distribution and internal migration				
View on spatial distribution	Major change desired	Major change desired	Satisfactory	Minor change desired
Policies on internal migration				
From rural to urban areas	..	..	..	Lower
From rural to rural areas	..	..	..	..
From urban to rural areas	..	..	..	..
From urban to urban areas	..	..	..	..
Into urban agglomerations	..	Lower	No intervention	Lower
International migration				
Immigration				
View	Satisfactory	Too low	Too low	Satisfactory
Policy	Maintain	Raise	Raise	Maintain
Permanent settlement	..	..	..	Maintain
Temporary workers	..	..	..	Maintain
Highly skilled workers	..	..	..	Maintain
Family reunification	..	..	..	Maintain
Integration of non-nationals	..	..	Yes	No
Emigration				
View	Too high	Satisfactory	Satisfactory	Satisfactory
Policy	Lower	Lower	No intervention	No intervention
Encouraging the return of nationals	..	..	Yes	Yes

* Measures implemented to control HIV/AIDS: (1) blood screening; (2) information/education campaigns; (3) access to antiretroviral treatment; (4) non-discriminatory policies; (5) promoting condom use.
** Grounds on which abortion is permitted: (1) to save the woman's life; (2) to preserve physical health; (3) to preserve mental health; (4) rape or incest; (5) foetal impairment; (6) economic or social reasons; (7) on request.

Population indicators

Indicator	*1975*	*1985*	*1995*	*2005*
Population size and growth				
Population size (thousands)	2 659	3 609	4 829	6 158
Annual growth rate (percentage)*	2.5	3.0	2.7	2.4
Population age structure				
Percentage of population under age 15	44	42	42	38
Percentage of population aged 60 or older	7	6	5	6
Fertility and family planning				
Total fertility (births per woman)*	5.7	5.3	4.6	3.9
Teenage fertility rate (per 1,000 women, aged 15 - 19)*	96	94	87	68
Percentage of births to women under age 20*	15	13	13	12
Percentage of births to women aged 35 or older*	17	14	17	16
Percentage of married women using contraception				
Modern methods	23[a]	29[b]	41	61[c]
All methods	29[a]	45[b]	56	73[c]
Health and mortality				
Life expectancy at birth (years)*				
Males	64	65	66	69
Females	68	69	71	73
Both sexes combined	66	67	69	71
Infant mortality rate (per 1,000 births)*	53	49	43	37
Mortality under age 5 (per 1,000 births)*	72	63	54	45
Maternal mortality ratio (per 100,000 births) (2000)	..	..	..	170
HIV/AIDS (2003)				
Number of infected adults (thousands)	..	..	..	15
Adult prevalence rate (percentage)	..	..	..	0.5
Spatial distribution				
Population density (per sq. km)	7	9	12	15
Urban population (percentage)	39	45	52	58
Annual urban growth rate (percentage)*	3.5	4.5	4.1	3.5
Annual rural growth rate (percentage)*	1.8	1.8	1.3	0.9
International migration				
International migrant stock				
Number of migrants (thousands)	101	174	183	168
Percentage of total population	3.8	4.8	3.8	2.7

* For the periods 1970-1975, 1980-1985, 1990-1995 and 2000-2005.
[a] For 1977.
[b] For 1987.
[c] For 2004.

Government views and policies

Population policy variable	*1976*	*1986*	*1996*	*2005*
Population size and growth				
View on growth	Satisfactory	Too high	Too high	Too high
Policy on growth	No intervention	Lower	Lower	Lower
Population age structure				
Level of concern about				
Size of the working-age population	..	..	..	Major concern
Ageing of the population	..	..	..	Major concern
Fertility and family planning				
View on fertility level	Satisfactory	Too high	Too high	Too high
Policy	No intervention	Lower	Lower	Lower
Access to contraceptive methods	Direct support	Direct support	Direct support	Direct support
Adolescent fertility				
Level of concern	..	..	Major concern	Major concern
Policies and programmes	..	..	Yes	Yes
Health and mortality				
View				
Expectation of life	Unacceptable	Unacceptable	Unacceptable	Unacceptable
Under-five mortality	..	..	..	Unacceptable
Maternal mortality	..	..	..	Unacceptable
Level of concern about HIV/AIDS	..	..	Minor concern	Major concern
Measures implemented to control HIV/AIDS*	..	..	..	1,2,3,4,5
Grounds on which abortion is permitted**	..	..	1,2	1,2,3
Spatial distribution and internal migration				
View on spatial distribution	Major change desired	Major change desired	Major change desired	Major change desired
Policies on internal migration				
From rural to urban areas	..	..	..	Lower
From rural to rural areas	..	..	..	..
From urban to rural areas	..	..	..	..
From urban to urban areas	..	..	..	Raise
Into urban agglomerations	..	Lower	Lower	Lower
International migration				
Immigration				
View	Satisfactory	Satisfactory	Satisfactory	Satisfactory
Policy	Maintain	Maintain	No intervention	Maintain
Permanent settlement	..	..	No intervention	Maintain
Temporary workers	..	..	No intervention	Maintain
Highly skilled workers	..	..	..	Maintain
Family reunification	..	..	No intervention	Maintain
Integration of non-nationals	..	..	Yes	No
Emigration				
View	Satisfactory	Satisfactory	Too high	Satisfactory
Policy	Maintain	Maintain	No intervention	No intervention
Encouraging the return of nationals	..	..	Yes	Yes

* Measures implemented to control HIV/AIDS: (1) blood screening; (2) information/education campaigns; (3) access to antiretroviral treatment; (4) non-discriminatory policies; (5) promoting condom use.

** Grounds on which abortion is permitted: (1) to save the woman's life; (2) to preserve physical health; (3) to preserve mental health; (4) rape or incest; (5) foetal impairment; (6) economic or social reasons; (7) on request.

Population indicators

Indicator	*1975*	*1985*	*1995*	*2005*
Population size and growth				
Population size (thousands)	15 161	19 516	23 837	27 968
Annual growth rate (percentage)*	2.8	2.4	1.8	1.5
Population age structure				
Percentage of population under age 15	43	40	36	32
Percentage of population aged 60 or older	6	6	7	8
Fertility and family planning				
Total fertility (births per woman)*	6.0	4.7	3.7	2.9
Teenage fertility rate (per 1,000 women, aged 15 - 19)*	86	74	71	55
Percentage of births to women under age 20*	11	12	13	12
Percentage of births to women aged 35 or older*	19	17	15	16
Percentage of married women using contraception				
Modern methods	11[a]	23[b]	33[c]	50[d]
All methods	31[a]	46[b]	59[c]	69[d]
Health and mortality				
Life expectancy at birth (years)*				
Males	54	59	64	67
Females	57	64	69	72
Both sexes combined	55	61	66	70
Infant mortality rate (per 1,000 births)*	110	82	55	33
Mortality under age 5 (per 1,000 births)*	169	117	77	52
Maternal mortality ratio (per 100,000 births) (2000)	..	..	..	410
HIV/AIDS (2003)				
Number of infected adults (thousands)	..	..	..	80
Adult prevalence rate (percentage)	..	..	..	0.5
Spatial distribution				
Population density (per sq. km)	12	15	19	22
Urban population (percentage)	61	67	71	75
Annual urban growth rate (percentage)*	4.1	3.1	2.4	2.0
Annual rural growth rate (percentage)*	0.8	1.0	0.5	0.1
International migration				
International migrant stock				
Number of migrants (thousands)	67	62	51	42
Percentage of total population	0.4	0.3	0.2	0.1

* For the periods 1970-1975, 1980-1985, 1990-1995 and 2000-2005.
[a] For 1977.
[b] For 1986.
[c] For 1992.
[d] For 2000.

Government views and policies

Population policy variable	*1976*	*1986*	*1996*	*2005*
Population size and growth				
View on growth	Too high	Too high	Too high	Too high
Policy on growth	Lower	Lower	Lower	Lower
Population age structure				
Level of concern about				
Size of the working-age population	..	..	..	Major concern
Ageing of the population	..	..	..	Minor concern
Fertility and family planning				
View on fertility level	Too high	Too high	Too high	Too high
Policy	Lower	Lower	Lower	Lower
Access to contraceptive methods	Direct support	Direct support	Direct support	Direct support
Adolescent fertility				
Level of concern	..	..	Major concern	Major concern
Policies and programmes	..	..	Yes	Yes
Health and mortality				
View				
Expectation of life	Acceptable	Acceptable	Unacceptable	Acceptable
Under-five mortality	..	..	Unacceptable	Unacceptable
Maternal mortality	..	..	..	Unacceptable
Level of concern about HIV/AIDS	..	..	Minor concern	Major concern
Measures implemented to control HIV/AIDS*	..	..	..	1,2,4,5
Grounds on which abortion is permitted**	..	..	1	1
Spatial distribution and internal migration				
View on spatial distribution	Major change desired	Major change desired	Major change desired	Major change desired
Policies on internal migration				
From rural to urban areas	..	..	..	Lower
From rural to rural areas	..	..	..	No intervention
From urban to rural areas	..	..	..	Raise
From urban to urban areas	..	..	..	Raise
Into urban agglomerations	Lower	Lower	Lower	Lower
International migration				
Immigration				
View	Satisfactory	Satisfactory	Satisfactory	Satisfactory
Policy	Maintain	Maintain	Lower	Maintain
Permanent settlement	..	..	Lower	Maintain
Temporary workers	..	..	No intervention	Maintain
Highly skilled workers	..	..	..	Maintain
Family reunification	..	..	No intervention	Maintain
Integration of non-nationals	..	..	No	Yes
Emigration				
View	Satisfactory	Satisfactory	Satisfactory	Satisfactory
Policy	Maintain	Maintain	No intervention	Maintain
Encouraging the return of nationals	Yes	..	No	Yes

* Measures implemented to control HIV/AIDS: (1) blood screening; (2) information/education campaigns; (3) access to antiretroviral treatment; (4) non-discriminatory policies; (5) promoting condom use.

** Grounds on which abortion is permitted: (1) to save the woman's life; (2) to preserve physical health; (3) to preserve mental health; (4) rape or incest; (5) foetal impairment; (6) economic or social reasons; (7) on request.

Population indicators

Indicator	*1975*	*1985*	*1995*	*2005*
Population size and growth				
Population size (thousands)	42 019	54 266	68 396	83 054
Annual growth rate (percentage)*	2.8	2.4	2.3	1.8
Population age structure				
Percentage of population under age 15	44	42	39	35
Percentage of population aged 60 or older	5	5	5	6
Fertility and family planning				
Total fertility (births per woman)*	6.0	5.0	4.1	3.2
Teenage fertility rate (per 1,000 women, aged 15 - 19)*	56	52	48	39
Percentage of births to women under age 20*	8	8	8	8
Percentage of births to women aged 35 or older*	19	16	16	15
Percentage of married women using contraception				
Modern methods	11[a]	21[b]	28[c]	33[d]
All methods	18[a]	44[b]	47[c]	49[d]
Health and mortality				
Life expectancy at birth (years)*				
Males	56	60	65	68
Females	60	64	69	72
Both sexes combined	58	62	66	70
Infant mortality rate (per 1,000 births)*	80	61	43	28
Mortality under age 5 (per 1,000 births)*	112	83	54	34
Maternal mortality ratio (per 100,000 births) (2000)	..	..	..	200
HIV/AIDS (2003)				
Number of infected adults (thousands)	..	..	..	9
Adult prevalence rate (percentage)	..	..	..	<0.1
Spatial distribution				
Population density (per sq. km)	140	181	228	277
Urban population (percentage)	36	43	54	63
Annual urban growth rate (percentage)*	4.3	5.2	4.3	3.1
Annual rural growth rate (percentage)*	2.0	0.6	0.1	-0.3
International migration				
International migrant stock				
Number of migrants (thousands)	162	148	214	374
Percentage of total population	0.4	0.3	0.3	0.5

* For the periods 1970-1975, 1980-1985, 1990-1995 and 2000-2005.
[a] For 1973.
[b] For 1986.
[c] For 1998.
[d] For 2003.

Government views and policies

Population policy variable	*1976*	*1986*	*1996*	*2005*
Population size and growth				
View on growth	Satisfactory	Satisfactory	Satisfactory	Too low
Policy on growth	No intervention	No intervention	No intervention	No intervention
Population age structure				
Level of concern about				
Size of the working-age population	..	..	..	Major concern
Ageing of the population	..	..	..	Major concern
Fertility and family planning				
View on fertility level	Satisfactory	Satisfactory	Satisfactory	Too low
Policy	Maintain	Maintain	No intervention	No intervention
Access to contraceptive methods	Direct support	Direct support	Direct support	Indirect support
Adolescent fertility				
Level of concern	..	..	Minor concern	Major concern
Policies and programmes	..	..	No	No
Health and mortality				
View				
Expectation of life	Acceptable	Unacceptable	Unacceptable	Acceptable
Under-five mortality	..	..	Unacceptable	Acceptable
Maternal mortality	..	..	..	Acceptable
Level of concern about HIV/AIDS	..	..	Major concern	Major concern
Measures implemented to control HIV/AIDS*	..	..	..	1,2,3,4,5
Grounds on which abortion is permitted**	..	..	1,2,4,5	1,2,3,4,5
Spatial distribution and internal migration				
View on spatial distribution	Minor change desired	Minor change desired	Minor change desired	Satisfactory
Policies on internal migration				
From rural to urban areas	..	..	..	Lower
From rural to rural areas	..	..	..	No intervention
From urban to rural areas	..	..	..	No intervention
From urban to urban areas	..	..	..	No intervention
Into urban agglomerations	Raise	Lower	Lower	No intervention
International migration				
Immigration				
View	Satisfactory	Satisfactory	Satisfactory	Satisfactory
Policy	Maintain	Maintain	Maintain	Maintain
Permanent settlement	..	..	Maintain	Maintain
Temporary workers	..	..	Maintain	Maintain
Highly skilled workers	..	..	..	Maintain
Family reunification	..	..	No intervention	Maintain
Integration of non-nationals	..	..	Yes	Yes
Emigration				
View	Satisfactory	Satisfactory	Too high	Satisfactory
Policy	Maintain	Maintain	No intervention	No intervention
Encouraging the return of nationals	No	..	No	No

* Measures implemented to control HIV/AIDS: (1) blood screening; (2) information/education campaigns; (3) access to antiretroviral treatment; (4) non-discriminatory policies; (5) promoting condom use.

** Grounds on which abortion is permitted: (1) to save the woman's life; (2) to preserve physical health; (3) to preserve mental health; (4) rape or incest; (5) foetal impairment; (6) economic or social reasons; (7) on request.

Population indicators

Indicator	*1975*	*1985*	*1995*	*2005*
Population size and growth				
Population size (thousands)	34 015	37 202	38 595	38 530
Annual growth rate (percentage)*	0.8	0.9	0.3	-0.1
Population age structure				
Percentage of population under age 15	24	26	23	16
Percentage of population aged 60 or older	14	14	16	17
Fertility and family planning				
Total fertility (births per woman)*	2.3	2.3	1.9	1.3
Teenage fertility rate (per 1,000 women, aged 15 - 19)*	30	31	25	15
Percentage of births to women under age 20*	9	6	7	6
Percentage of births to women aged 35 or older*	8	7	11	9
Percentage of married women using contraception				
Modern methods	26[a]	..	19[b]	..
All methods	75[a]	..	49[b]	..
Health and mortality				
Life expectancy at birth (years)*				
Males	67	67	67	70
Females	74	75	76	78
Both sexes combined	70	71	72	74
Infant mortality rate (per 1,000 births)*	27	20	15	9
Mortality under age 5 (per 1,000 births)*	30	22	17	10
Maternal mortality ratio (per 100,000 births) (2000)	..	..	..	13
HIV/AIDS (2003)				
Number of infected adults (thousands)	..	..	..	14
Adult prevalence rate (percentage)	..	..	..	0.1
Spatial distribution				
Population density (per sq. km)	105	115	119	119
Urban population (percentage)	55	59	61	62
Annual urban growth rate (percentage)*	2.0	1.4	0.4	0.0
Annual rural growth rate (percentage)*	-0.5	0.2	0.0	-0.3
International migration				
International migrant stock				
Number of migrants (thousands)	1 808	1 319	963	703
Percentage of total population	5.3	3.5	2.5	1.8

* For the periods 1970-1975, 1980-1985, 1990-1995 and 2000-2005.
[a] For 1977.
[b] For 1991.

Government views and policies

Population policy variable	*1976*	*1986*	*1996*	*2005*
Population size and growth				
View on growth	Satisfactory	Satisfactory	Too low	Satisfactory
Policy on growth	No intervention	No intervention	No intervention	No intervention
Population age structure				
Level of concern about				
Size of the working-age population	..	..	..	Minor concern
Ageing of the population	..	..	..	Major concern
Fertility and family planning				
View on fertility level	Satisfactory	Satisfactory	Too low	Too low
Policy	No intervention	No intervention	No intervention	Raise
Access to contraceptive methods	Direct support	Direct support	Direct support	Direct support
Adolescent fertility				
Level of concern	..	..	Major concern	Major concern
Policies and programmes	..	..	Yes	Yes
Health and mortality				
View				
Expectation of life	Acceptable	Unacceptable	Acceptable	Acceptable
Under-five mortality	..	..	Acceptable	Acceptable
Maternal mortality	..	..	..	Acceptable
Level of concern about HIV/AIDS	..	..	Minor concern	Major concern
Measures implemented to control HIV/AIDS*	..	..	..	1,2,3,4,5
Grounds on which abortion is permitted**	..	..	1,2,3,4,5	1,2,3,4,5
Spatial distribution and internal migration				
View on spatial distribution	Minor change desired	Major change desired	Major change desired	Major change desired
Policies on internal migration				
From rural to urban areas	..	..	..	Lower
From rural to rural areas	..	..	..	Maintain
From urban to rural areas	..	..	..	Raise
From urban to urban areas	..	..	..	No intervention
Into urban agglomerations	No intervention	..	No intervention	No intervention
International migration				
Immigration				
View	Satisfactory	Satisfactory	Satisfactory	Satisfactory
Policy	Maintain	Maintain	Lower	Maintain
Permanent settlement	..	..	Lower	Maintain
Temporary workers	..	..	Maintain	Maintain
Highly skilled workers	..	..	..	Maintain
Family reunification	..	..	Maintain	Maintain
Integration of non-nationals	..	..	Yes	Yes
Emigration				
View	Too low	Satisfactory	Satisfactory	Satisfactory
Policy	Raise	Maintain	No intervention	Maintain
Encouraging the return of nationals	No	..	No	No

* Measures implemented to control HIV/AIDS: (1) blood screening; (2) information/education campaigns; (3) access to antiretroviral treatment; (4) non-discriminatory policies; (5) promoting condom use.
** Grounds on which abortion is permitted: (1) to save the woman's life; (2) to preserve physical health; (3) to preserve mental health; (4) rape or incest; (5) foetal impairment; (6) economic or social reasons; (7) on request.

Population indicators

Indicator	*1975*	*1985*	*1995*	*2005*
Population size and growth				
Population size (thousands)	9 093	10 011	10 030	10 495
Annual growth rate (percentage)*	0.9	0.5	0.1	0.5
Population age structure				
Percentage of population under age 15	28	24	18	16
Percentage of population aged 60 or older	14	17	20	22
Fertility and family planning				
Total fertility (births per woman)*	2.7	2.0	1.5	1.5
Teenage fertility rate (per 1,000 women, aged 15 - 19)*	38	28	21	20
Percentage of births to women under age 20*	8	8	7	6
Percentage of births to women aged 35 or older*	11	10	11	14
Percentage of married women using contraception				
Modern methods	33[a]	..	..	..
All methods	66[a]	..	..	..
Health and mortality				
Life expectancy at birth (years)*				
Males	65	69	71	74
Females	71	76	78	81
Both sexes combined	68	72	75	77
Infant mortality rate (per 1,000 births)*	45	20	9	6
Mortality under age 5 (per 1,000 births)*	64	29	12	7
Maternal mortality ratio (per 100,000 births) (2000)	..	..	..	5
HIV/AIDS (2003)				
Number of infected adults (thousands)	..	..	..	22
Adult prevalence rate (percentage)	..	..	..	0.4
Spatial distribution				
Population density (per sq. km)	99	109	109	114
Urban population (percentage)	28	37	50	56
Annual urban growth rate (percentage)*	2.2	5.2	1.6	1.1
Annual rural growth rate (percentage)*	0.5	-1.8	-1.4	-1.0
International migration				
International migrant stock				
Number of migrants (thousands)	164	346	528	764
Percentage of total population	1.8	3.5	5.3	7.3

* For the periods 1970-1975, 1980-1985, 1990-1995 and 2000-2005.
[a] For 1979/1980.

Government views and policies

Population policy variable	*1976*	*1986*	*1996*	*2005*
Population size and growth				
View on growth	Too low	Too low	Too low	Satisfactory
Policy on growth	Raise	Raise	Raise	Maintain
Population age structure				
Level of concern about				
Size of the working-age population	..	..	..	..
Ageing of the population	..	..	..	Minor concern
Fertility and family planning				
View on fertility level	Satisfactory	Satisfactory	Satisfactory	Satisfactory
Policy	Maintain	Maintain	Maintain	Maintain
Access to contraceptive methods	No support	No support	No support	Direct support
Adolescent fertility				
Level of concern	..	..	..	..
Policies and programmes	..	..	..	No
Health and mortality				
View				
Expectation of life	Acceptable	Acceptable	Acceptable	Acceptable
Under-five mortality	..	..	..	Acceptable
Maternal mortality	..	..	..	Acceptable
Level of concern about HIV/AIDS	..	..	..	Major concern
Measures implemented to control HIV/AIDS*	..	..	..	1,3
Grounds on which abortion is permitted**	..	..	1,2,5	1,2,3,5
Spatial distribution and internal migration				
View on spatial distribution	Satisfactory	Satisfactory	Satisfactory	Minor change desired
Policies on internal migration				
From rural to urban areas	..	..	..	..
From rural to rural areas	..	..	..	..
From urban to rural areas	..	..	..	..
From urban to urban areas	..	..	..	..
Into urban agglomerations	..	Lower	..	..
International migration				
Immigration				
View	Satisfactory	Satisfactory	Satisfactory	Too high
Policy	Maintain	Maintain	Maintain	Lower
Permanent settlement	..	..	..	..
Temporary workers	..	..	..	Lower
Highly skilled workers	..	..	..	Maintain
Family reunification	..	..	..	Lower
Integration of non-nationals	..	..	..	..
Emigration				
View	Satisfactory	Satisfactory	Satisfactory	Satisfactory
Policy	Maintain	Maintain	Maintain	No intervention
Encouraging the return of nationals	..	..	..	..

* Measures implemented to control HIV/AIDS: (1) blood screening; (2) information/education campaigns; (3) access to antiretroviral treatment; (4) non-discriminatory policies; (5) promoting condom use.

** Grounds on which abortion is permitted: (1) to save the woman's life; (2) to preserve physical health; (3) to preserve mental health; (4) rape or incest; (5) foetal impairment; (6) economic or social reasons; (7) on request.

Population indicators

Indicator	*1975*	*1985*	*1995*	*2005*
Population size and growth				
Population size (thousands)	171	361	526	813
Annual growth ratc (pcrccntagc)*	8.6	9.1	2.4	5.9
Population age structure				
Percentage of population under age 15	33	28	27	22
Percentage of population aged 60 or older	3	2	2	3
Fertility and family planning				
Total fertility (births per woman)*	6.8	5.5	4.1	3.0
Teenage fertility rate (per 1,000 women, aged 15 - 19)*	41	33	25	19
Percentage of births to women under age 20*	4	3	3	3
Percentage of births to women aged 35 or older*	19	19	26	23
Percentage of married women using contraception				
Modern methods	..	29[a]	32[b]	..
All methods	..	32[a]	43[b]	..
Health and mortality				
Life expectancy at birth (years)*				
Males	61	65	68	71
Females	64	70	73	76
Both sexes combined	62	67	70	73
Infant mortality rate (per 1,000 births)*	57	33	17	12
Mortality under age 5 (per 1,000 births)*	69	40	20	14
Maternal mortality ratio (per 100,000 births) (2000)	..	..	..	7
HIV/AIDS (2003)				
Number of infected adults (thousands)	..	..	..	..
Adult prevalence rate (percentage)	..	..	..	..
Spatial distribution				
Population density (per sq. km)	16	33	48	74
Urban population (percentage)	85	88	90	92
Annual urban growth rate (percentage)*	9.0	9.4	2.5	1.7
Annual rural growth rate (percentage)*	6.3	6.7	0.0	-0.6
International migration				
International migrant stock				
Number of migrants (thousands)	119	282	406	637
Percentage of total population	69.6	78.2	77.2	78.3

* For the periods 1970-1975, 1980-1985, 1990-1995 and 2000-2005.
[a] For 1987.
[b] For 1998.

Government views and policies

Population policy variable	*1976*	*1986*	*1996*	*2005*
Population size and growth				
View on growth	Too high	Too high	Satisfactory	Too low
Policy on growth	Lower	Lower	No intervention	Raise
Population age structure				
Level of concern about				
Size of the working-age population	..	..	..	Minor concern
Ageing of the population	..	..	..	Major concern
Fertility and family planning				
View on fertility level	Too high	Too high	Satisfactory	Too low
Policy	Lower	Lower	No intervention	Raise
Access to contraceptive methods	Direct support	Direct support	Direct support	Direct support
Adolescent fertility				
Level of concern	..	..	Minor concern	Major concern
Policies and programmes	..	..	Yes	Yes
Health and mortality				
View				
Expectation of life	Unacceptable	Unacceptable	Unacceptable	Acceptable
Under-five mortality	..	..	..	Unacceptable
Maternal mortality	..	..	..	Unacceptable
Level of concern about HIV/AIDS	..	..	Major concern	Major concern
Measures implemented to control HIV/AIDS*	..	..	..	1,2,3,4,5
Grounds on which abortion is permitted**	..	..	1,2,3,4,5	1,2,3,4,5
Spatial distribution and internal migration				
View on spatial distribution	Minor change desired	Major change desired	Major change desired	Minor change desired
Policies on internal migration				
From rural to urban areas	..	..	..	..
From rural to rural areas	..	..	..	..
From urban to rural areas	..	..	..	..
From urban to urban areas	..	..	..	Maintain
Into urban agglomerations	..	Lower	Lower	Lower
International migration				
Immigration				
View	Satisfactory	Satisfactory	Satisfactory	Satisfactory
Policy	Maintain	Maintain	Lower	Raise
Permanent settlement	..	..	Lower	Raise
Temporary workers	..	..	Lower	Raise
Highly skilled workers	..	..	..	Raise
Family reunification	..	..	Lower	Maintain
Integration of non-nationals	..	..	Yes	Yes
Emigration				
View	Too low	Too low	Too low	Too high
Policy	Raise	Raise	Raise	No intervention
Encouraging the return of nationals	..	..	No	No

* Measures implemented to control HIV/AIDS: (1) blood screening; (2) information/education campaigns; (3) access to antiretroviral treatment; (4) non-discriminatory policies; (5) promoting condom use.

** Grounds on which abortion is permitted: (1) to save the woman's life; (2) to preserve physical health; (3) to preserve mental health; (4) rape or incest; (5) foetal impairment; (6) economic or social reasons; (7) on request.

Population indicators

Indicator	*1975*	*1985*	*1995*	*2005*
Population size and growth				
Population size (thousands)	35 281	40 806	45 007	47 817
Annual growth rate (percentage)*	2.0	1.4	1.0	0.4
Population age structure				
Percentage of population under age 15	38	30	23	19
Percentage of population aged 60 or older	6	7	9	14
Fertility and family planning				
Total fertility (births per woman)*	4.3	2.2	1.7	1.2
Teenage fertility rate (per 1,000 women, aged 15 - 19)*	10	5	4	3
Percentage of births to women under age 20*	2	2	1	1
Percentage of births to women aged 35 or older*	3	3	3	8
Percentage of married women using contraception				
Modern methods	27[a]	59	67[b]	..
All methods	35[a]	70	81[b]	..
Health and mortality				
Life expectancy at birth (years)*				
Males	59	63	68	73
Females	66	71	77	80
Both sexes combined	63	67	72	77
Infant mortality rate (per 1,000 births)*	38	23	13	4
Mortality under age 5 (per 1,000 births)*	50	31	18	5
Maternal mortality ratio (per 100,000 births) (2000)	..	..	..	20
HIV/AIDS (2003)				
Number of infected adults (thousands)	..	..	..	8
Adult prevalence rate (percentage)	..	..	..	<0.1
Spatial distribution				
Population density (per sq. km)	354	410	452	480
Urban population (percentage)	48	65	78	81
Annual urban growth rate (percentage)*	5.3	4.0	2.1	0.9
Annual rural growth rate (percentage)*	-0.6	-2.8	-2.7	-0.6
International migration				
International migrant stock				
Number of migrants (thousands)	305	560	584	551
Percentage of total population	0.9	1.4	1.3	1.2

* For the periods 1970-1975, 1980-1985, 1990-1995 and 2000-2005.
[a] For 1974.
[b] For 1997.

Government views and policies

Population policy variable	*1976*	*1986*	*1996*	*2005*
Population size and growth				
View on growth	..	..	Too low	Too low
Policy on growth	..	..	Raise	Raise
Population age structure				
Level of concern about				
Size of the working-age population	..	..	..	..
Ageing of the population	..	..	..	..
Fertility and family planning				
View on fertility level	..	..	Satisfactory	Too low
Policy	..	..	No intervention	Raise
Access to contraceptive methods	..	..	Direct support	Direct support
Adolescent fertility				
Level of concern	..	..	..	Not a concern
Policies and programmes	..	..	..	No
Health and mortality				
View				
Expectation of life	..	..	Unacceptable	Unacceptable
Under-five mortality	..	..	..	Unacceptable
Maternal mortality	..	..	..	Unacceptable
Level of concern about HIV/AIDS	..	..	..	Major concern
Measures implemented to control HIV/AIDS*	..	..	..	1,2,3,4,5
Grounds on which abortion is permitted**	..	..	1,2,3,4,5,6,7	1,2,3,4,5,6,7
Spatial distribution and internal migration				
View on spatial distribution	..	..	Major change desired	Satisfactory
Policies on internal migration				
From rural to urban areas	..	..	..	..
From rural to rural areas	..	..	..	..
From urban to rural areas	..	..	..	..
From urban to urban areas	..	..	..	..
Into urban agglomerations	..	..	..	..
International migration				
Immigration				
View	..	..	Satisfactory	Satisfactory
Policy	..	..	No intervention	Maintain
Permanent settlement	..	..	..	Maintain
Temporary workers	..	..	..	Lower
Highly skilled workers	..	..	..	..
Family reunification	..	..	..	Lower
Integration of non-nationals	..	..	..	..
Emigration				
View	..	..	Too high	Too high
Policy	..	..	Lower	No intervention
Encouraging the return of nationals	..	..	..	..

* Measures implemented to control HIV/AIDS: (1) blood screening; (2) information/education campaigns; (3) access to antiretroviral treatment; (4) non-discriminatory policies; (5) promoting condom use.

** Grounds on which abortion is permitted: (1) to save the woman's life; (2) to preserve physical health; (3) to preserve mental health; (4) rape or incest; (5) foetal impairment; (6) economic or social reasons; (7) on request.

Population indicators

Indicator	*1975*	*1985*	*1995*	*2005*
Population size and growth				
Population size (thousands)	3 839	4 215	4 339	4 206
Annual growth rate (percentage)*	1.3	1.0	-0.1	-0.3
Population age structure				
Percentage of population under age 15	29	27	27	18
Percentage of population aged 60 or older	11	12	13	14
Fertility and family planning				
Total fertility (births per woman)*	2.6	2.6	2.1	1.2
Teenage fertility rate (per 1,000 women, aged 15 - 19)*	87	87	72	33
Percentage of births to women under age 20*	22	17	18	15
Percentage of births to women aged 35 or older*	5	4	6	6
Percentage of married women using contraception				
Modern methods	..	..	..	43[a]
All methods	..	..	..	62[a]
Health and mortality				
Life expectancy at birth (years)*				
Males	62	62	64	64
Females	69	68	71	71
Both sexes combined	65	65	67	67
Infant mortality rate (per 1,000 births)*	46	35	29	26
Mortality under age 5 (per 1,000 births)*	53	41	35	31
Maternal mortality ratio (per 100,000 births) (2000)	..	..	..	36
HIV/AIDS (2003)				
Number of infected adults (thousands)	..	..	..	6
Adult prevalence rate (percentage)	..	..	..	0.2
Spatial distribution				
Population density (per sq. km)	113	125	128	124
Urban population (percentage)	36	44	46	46
Annual urban growth rate (percentage)*	3.7	2.9	-0.4	0.1
Annual rural growth rate (percentage)*	0.1	-0.4	0.2	-0.3
International migration				
International migrant stock				
Number of migrants (thousands)	..	..	473	440
Percentage of total population	..	..	10.9	10.5

* For the periods 1970-1975, 1980-1985, 1990-1995 and 2000-2005.
[a] For 2000.

Government views and policies

Population policy variable	*1976*	*1986*	*1996*	*2005*
Population size and growth				
View on growth	Satisfactory	Satisfactory	Too low	Too low
Policy on growth	No intervention	Raise	No intervention	Raise
Population age structure				
Level of concern about				
Size of the working-age population	..	..	..	Minor concern
Ageing of the population	..	..	..	Major concern
Fertility and family planning				
View on fertility level	Satisfactory	Too low	Too low	Too low
Policy	Maintain	Raise	Raise	Raise
Access to contraceptive methods	Direct support	Limits	Direct support	Direct support
Adolescent fertility				
Level of concern	..	..	Not a concern	Minor concern
Policies and programmes	..	..	Yes	Yes
Health and mortality				
View				
Expectation of life	Acceptable	Acceptable	Unacceptable	Unacceptable
Under-five mortality	..	..	Unacceptable	Unacceptable
Maternal mortality	..	..	..	Unacceptable
Level of concern about HIV/AIDS	..	..	Major concern	Major concern
Measures implemented to control HIV/AIDS*	..	..	..	1,2,3,4,5
Grounds on which abortion is permitted**	..	..	1,2,3,4,5,6,7	1,2,3,4,5,6,7
Spatial distribution and internal migration				
View on spatial distribution	Minor change desired	Satisfactory	Satisfactory	Minor change desired
Policies on internal migration				
From rural to urban areas	..	..	..	Lower
From rural to rural areas	..	..	..	Maintain
From urban to rural areas	..	..	..	Raise
From urban to urban areas	..	..	..	..
Into urban agglomerations	Lower	Lower	No intervention	No intervention
International migration				
Immigration				
View	Satisfactory	Satisfactory	Satisfactory	Satisfactory
Policy	Maintain	Maintain	Lower	Lower
Permanent settlement	..	..	Lower	Lower
Temporary workers	..	..	Lower	Lower
Highly skilled workers	..	..	..	No intervention
Family reunification	..	..	Lower	Raise
Integration of non-nationals	..	..	No	Yes
Emigration				
View	Satisfactory	Satisfactory	Too high	Too high
Policy	Maintain	Maintain	No intervention	Lower
Encouraging the return of nationals	No	..	Yes	No

* Measures implemented to control HIV/AIDS: (1) blood screening; (2) information/education campaigns; (3) access to antiretroviral treatment; (4) non-discriminatory policies; (5) promoting condom use.

** Grounds on which abortion is permitted: (1) to save the woman's life; (2) to preserve physical health; (3) to preserve mental health; (4) rape or incest; (5) foetal impairment; (6) economic or social reasons; (7) on request.

Population indicators

Indicator	*1975*	*1985*	*1995*	*2005*
Population size and growth				
Population size (thousands)	21 245	22 725	22 681	21 711
Annual growth rate (percentage)*	1.0	0.5	-0.5	-0.4
Population age structure				
Percentage of population under age 15	25	25	20	15
Percentage of population aged 60 or older	14	14	17	19
Fertility and family planning				
Total fertility (births per woman)*	2.6	2.3	1.5	1.3
Teenage fertility rate (per 1,000 women, aged 15 - 19)*	79	68	45	36
Percentage of births to women under age 20*	17	16	16	14
Percentage of births to women aged 35 or older*	6	5	5	6
Percentage of married women using contraception				
Modern methods	5[a]	..	30[b]	..
All methods	58[a]	..	64[b]	..
Health and mortality				
Life expectancy at birth (years)*				
Males	67	67	66	68
Females	71	73	73	75
Both sexes combined	69	70	69	71
Infant mortality rate (per 1,000 births)*	40	26	23	18
Mortality under age 5 (per 1,000 births)*	50	33	29	22
Maternal mortality ratio (per 100,000 births) (2000)	..	..	..	49
HIV/AIDS (2003)				
Number of infected adults (thousands)	..	..	..	3
Adult prevalence rate (percentage)	..	..	..	<0.1
Spatial distribution				
Population density (per sq. km)	89	95	95	91
Urban population (percentage)	43	50	55	55
Annual urban growth rate (percentage)*	2.2	2.0	0.2	-0.2
Annual rural growth rate (percentage)*	0.1	-0.9	-1.2	-0.3
International migration				
International migrant stock				
Number of migrants (thousands)	239	170	135	133
Percentage of total population	1.1	0.7	0.6	0.6

* For the periods 1970-1975, 1980-1985, 1990-1995 and 2000-2005.
[a] For 1978.
[b] For 1999.

Government views and policies

Population policy variable	*1976*	*1986*	*1996*	*2005*
Population size and growth				
View on growth	..	..	Satisfactory	Too low
Policy on growth	..	..	No intervention	Raise
Population age structure				
Level of concern about				
Size of the working-age population	..	..	..	Major concern
Ageing of the population	..	..	..	Major concern
Fertility and family planning				
View on fertility level	..	..	Too low	Too low
Policy	..	..	No intervention	Raise
Access to contraceptive methods	..	..	Direct support	Indirect support
Adolescent fertility				
Level of concern	..	..	Minor concern	Major concern
Policies and programmes	..	..	Yes	No
Health and mortality				
View				
Expectation of life	..	..	Unacceptable	Unacceptable
Under-five mortality	..	..	Unacceptable	Unacceptable
Maternal mortality	..	..	..	Unacceptable
Level of concern about HIV/AIDS	..	..	Minor concern	Major concern
Measures implemented to control HIV/AIDS*	..	..	..	1,2,3,4,5
Grounds on which abortion is permitted**	..	..	1,2,3,4,5,6,7	1,2,3,4,5,6,7
Spatial distribution and internal migration				
View on spatial distribution	..	..	Major change desired	Major change desired
Policies on internal migration				
From rural to urban areas	..	..	..	..
From rural to rural areas	..	..	..	..
From urban to rural areas	..	..	..	..
From urban to urban areas	..	..	..	..
Into urban agglomerations	..	..	No intervention	..
International migration				
Immigration				
View	..	..	Too high	Too low
Policy	..	..	Lower	Raise
Permanent settlement	..	..	Lower	Raise
Temporary workers	..	..	Maintain	Raise
Highly skilled workers	..	..	..	Raise
Family reunification	..	..	No intervention	No intervention
Integration of non-nationals	..	..	Yes	Yes
Emigration				
View	..	..	Too high	Too high
Policy	..	..	Lower	No intervention
Encouraging the return of nationals	..	..	Yes	..

* Measures implemented to control HIV/AIDS: (1) blood screening; (2) information/education campaigns; (3) access to antiretroviral treatment; (4) non-discriminatory policies; (5) promoting condom use.

** Grounds on which abortion is permitted: (1) to save the woman's life; (2) to preserve physical health; (3) to preserve mental health; (4) rape or incest; (5) foetal impairment; (6) economic or social reasons; (7) on request.

Population indicators

Indicator	*1975*	*1985*	*1995*	*2005*
Population size and growth				
Population size (thousands)	134 233	143 329	148 189	143 202
Annual growth rate (percentage)*	0.6	0.7	0.0	-0.5
Population age structure				
Percentage of population under age 15	23	23	21	15
Percentage of population aged 60 or older	14	14	17	17
Fertility and family planning				
Total fertility (births per woman)*	2.0	2.0	1.6	1.3
Teenage fertility rate (per 1,000 women, aged 15 - 19)*	58	58	44	30
Percentage of births to women under age 20*	17	13	14	12
Percentage of births to women aged 35 or older*	6	4	6	6
Percentage of married women using contraception				
Modern methods	..	..	..	..
All methods	..	..	..	..
Health and mortality				
Life expectancy at birth (years)*				
Males	64	63	61	59
Females	74	74	73	72
Both sexes combined	70	69	67	65
Infant mortality rate (per 1,000 births)*	28	26	21	17
Mortality under age 5 (per 1,000 births)*	35	33	26	22
Maternal mortality ratio (per 100,000 births) (2000)	..	..	..	67
HIV/AIDS (2003)				
Number of infected adults (thousands)	..	..	..	860
Adult prevalence rate (percentage)	..	..	..	1.1
Spatial distribution				
Population density (per sq. km)	8	8	9	8
Urban population (percentage)	66	72	73	73
Annual urban growth rate (percentage)*	1.8	1.3	0.0	-0.6
Annual rural growth rate (percentage)*	-1.6	-0.8	0.0	-0.5
International migration				
International migrant stock				
Number of migrants (thousands)	..	..	11 707	12 080
Percentage of total population	..	..	7.9	8.4

* For the periods 1970-1975, 1980-1985, 1990-1995 and 2000-2005.

Government views and policies

Population policy variable	*1976*	*1986*	*1996*	*2005*
Population size and growth				
View on growth	Satisfactory	Too high	Too high	Too high
Policy on growth	No intervention	Lower	Lower	Lower
Population age structure				
Level of concern about				
Size of the working-age population	..	..	..	Major concern
Ageing of the population	..	..	..	Major concern
Fertility and family planning				
View on fertility level	Too high	Too high	Too high	Too high
Policy	No intervention	Lower	Lower	Lower
Access to contraceptive methods	No support	Direct support	Direct support	Direct support
Adolescent fertility				
Level of concern	..	..	Minor concern	Major concern
Policies and programmes	..	..	Yes	Yes
Health and mortality				
View				
Expectation of life	Acceptable	Acceptable	Unacceptable	Unacceptable
Under-five mortality	..	..	Unacceptable	Unacceptable
Maternal mortality	..	..	..	Unacceptable
Level of concern about HIV/AIDS	..	..	Major concern	Major concern
Measures implemented to control HIV/AIDS*	..	..	..	1,2,3,4,5
Grounds on which abortion is permitted**	..	..	1,2	1,2,3
Spatial distribution and internal migration				
View on spatial distribution	Major change desired	Major change desired	Major change desired	Major change desired
Policies on internal migration				
From rural to urban areas	..	..	..	Lower
From rural to rural areas	..	..	..	Raise
From urban to rural areas	..	..	..	No intervention
From urban to urban areas	..	..	..	Raise
Into urban agglomerations	No intervention	No intervention	No intervention	Lower
International migration				
Immigration				
View	Satisfactory	Satisfactory	Satisfactory	Satisfactory
Policy	Maintain	Maintain	No intervention	Maintain
Permanent settlement	..	..	No intervention	..
Temporary workers	..	..	No intervention	No intervention
Highly skilled workers	..	..	..	No intervention
Family reunification	..	..	No intervention	Raise
Integration of non-nationals	..	..	No	Yes
Emigration				
View	Satisfactory	Too low	Too high	Satisfactory
Policy	Maintain	Maintain	Lower	Maintain
Encouraging the return of nationals	No	..	Yes	Yes

* Measures implemented to control HIV/AIDS: (1) blood screening; (2) information/education campaigns; (3) access to antiretroviral treatment; (4) non-discriminatory policies; (5) promoting condom use.
** Grounds on which abortion is permitted: (1) to save the woman's life; (2) to preserve physical health; (3) to preserve mental health; (4) rape or incest; (5) foetal impairment; (6) economic or social reasons; (7) on request.

Population indicators

Indicator	*1975*	*1985*	*1995*	*2005*
Population size and growth				
Population size (thousands)	4 410	6 061	5 439	9 038
Annual growth rate (percentage)*	3.1	3.1	-5.3	2.4
Population age structure				
Percentage of population under age 15	48	49	50	43
Percentage of population aged 60 or older	4	4	4	4
Fertility and family planning				
Total fertility (births per woman)*	8.3	8.5	6.9	5.7
Teenage fertility rate (per 1,000 women, aged 15 - 19)*	77	79	48	49
Percentage of births to women under age 20*	8	8	6	8
Percentage of births to women aged 35 or older*	22	21	21	17
Percentage of married women using contraception				
Modern methods	..	1[a]	13[b]	4[c]
All methods	..	10[a]	21[b]	13[c]
Health and mortality				
Life expectancy at birth (years)*				
Males	43	44	22	42
Females	46	48	26	45
Both sexes combined	45	46	24	44
Infant mortality rate (per 1,000 births)*	134	124	129	116
Mortality under age 5 (per 1,000 births)*	227	199	223	190
Maternal mortality ratio (per 100,000 births) (2000)	..	..	..	1 400
HIV/AIDS (2003)				
Number of infected adults (thousands)	..	..	..	230
Adult prevalence rate (percentage)	..	..	..	5.1
Spatial distribution				
Population density (per sq. km)	167	230	207	343
Urban population (percentage)	4	5	8	22
Annual urban growth rate (percentage)*	7.6	4.1	3.0	11.6
Annual rural growth rate (percentage)*	2.9	2.8	-6.1	0.2
International migration				
International migrant stock				
Number of migrants (thousands)	46	80	60	121
Percentage of total population	1	1.3	1.1	1.3

* For the periods 1970-1975, 1980-1985, 1990-1995 and 2000-2005.
[a] For 1983.
[b] For 1992.
[c] For 2000.

Government views and policies

Population policy variable	*1976*	*1986*	*1996*	*2005*
Population size and growth				
View on growth	..	Too high	Too high	Satisfactory
Policy on growth	..	Lower	Lower	No intervention
Population age structure				
Level of concern about				
Size of the working-age population	..	..	..	Minor concern
Ageing of the population	..	..	..	Minor concern
Fertility and family planning				
View on fertility level	..	Too high	Too high	Satisfactory
Policy	..	Lower	Lower	No intervention
Access to contraceptive methods	..	Direct support	Direct support	Direct support
Adolescent fertility				
Level of concern	..	..	..	Minor concern
Policies and programmes	..	..	..	Yes
Health and mortality				
View				
Expectation of life	..	Unacceptable	Unacceptable	Unacceptable
Under-five mortality	..	..	..	..
Maternal mortality	..	..	..	Acceptable
Level of concern about HIV/AIDS	..	..	..	Major concern
Measures implemented to control HIV/AIDS*	..	..	..	1,2,3,5
Grounds on which abortion is permitted**	..	..	1,2,3	1,2,3,4
Spatial distribution and internal migration				
View on spatial distribution	..	Minor change desired	Minor change desired	Minor change desired
Policies on internal migration				
From rural to urban areas	..	..	..	..
From rural to rural areas	..	..	..	..
From urban to rural areas	..	..	..	..
From urban to urban areas	..	..	..	Raise
Into urban agglomerations	..	..	..	Lower
International migration				
Immigration				
View	..	Satisfactory	Satisfactory	Satisfactory
Policy	..	Maintain	Maintain	Maintain
Permanent settlement	..	..	..	Maintain
Temporary workers	..	..	..	..
Highly skilled workers	..	..	..	Maintain
Family reunification	..	..	..	..
Integration of non-nationals	..	..	..	..
Emigration				
View	..	Satisfactory	Satisfactory	Too high
Policy	..	Maintain	Maintain	No intervention
Encouraging the return of nationals	..	..	..	Yes

* Measures implemented to control HIV/AIDS: (1) blood screening; (2) information/education campaigns; (3) access to antiretroviral treatment; (4) non-discriminatory policies; (5) promoting condom use.

** Grounds on which abortion is permitted: (1) to save the woman's life; (2) to preserve physical health; (3) to preserve mental health; (4) rape or incest; (5) foetal impairment; (6) economic or social reasons; (7) on request.

Population indicators

Indicator	*1975*	*1985*	*1995*	*2005*
Population size and growth				
Population size (thousands)	44	42	40	43
Annual growth rate (percentage)*	-0.3	-0.5	-0.2	1.1
Population age structure				
Percentage of population under age 15	..	..	..	..
Percentage of population aged 60 or older	..	..	..	..
Fertility and family planning				
Total fertility (births per woman)*	..	..	..	..
Teenage fertility rate (per 1,000 women, aged 15 - 19)*	..	..	..	..
Percentage of births to women under age 20*	..	..	..	..
Percentage of births to women aged 35 or older*	..	..	..	..
Percentage of married women using contraception				
Modern methods	..	37[a]	..	..
All methods	..	41[a]	..	..
Health and mortality				
Life expectancy at birth (years)*				
Males	..	..	..	..
Females	..	..	..	..
Both sexes combined	..	..	..	..
Infant mortality rate (per 1,000 births)*	..	..	..	..
Mortality under age 5 (per 1,000 births)*	..	..	..	..
Maternal mortality ratio (per 100,000 births) (2000)	..	..	..	..
HIV/AIDS (2003)				
Number of infected adults (thousands)	..	..	..	..
Adult prevalence rate (percentage)	..	..	..	..
Spatial distribution				
Population density (per sq. km)	170	161	154	164
Urban population (percentage)	35	35	34	32
Annual urban growth rate (percentage)*	-0.2	-1.1	0.7	-0.9
Annual rural growth rate (percentage)*	-0.9	-0.6	1.5	0.0
International migration				
International migrant stock				
Number of migrants (thousands)	4	4	4	4
Percentage of total population	8.3	9.3	10.3	10.4

* For the periods 1970-1975, 1980-1985, 1990-1995 and 2000-2005.
[a] For 1984.

Government views and policies

Population policy variable	*1976*	*1986*	*1996*	*2005*
Population size and growth				
View on growth	..	Too high	Too high	Too high
Policy on growth	..	Lower	Lower	Lower
Population age structure				
Level of concern about				
Size of the working-age population	..	..	..	Minor concern
Ageing of the population	..	..	..	Major concern
Fertility and family planning				
View on fertility level	..	Too high	Too high	Too high
Policy	..	Lower	Lower	Lower
Access to contraceptive methods	..	Direct support	Direct support	Direct support
Adolescent fertility				
Level of concern	..	..	Major concern	Major concern
Policies and programmes	..	..	Yes	Yes
Health and mortality				
View				
Expectation of life	..	Unacceptable	Unacceptable	Unacceptable
Under-five mortality	..	..	Unacceptable	Unacceptable
Maternal mortality	..	..	..	Unacceptable
Level of concern about HIV/AIDS	..	..	Major concern	Major concern
Measures implemented to control HIV/AIDS*	..	..	..	1,2
Grounds on which abortion is permitted**	..	..	1,2,3	1,2,3,4
Spatial distribution and internal migration				
View on spatial distribution	..	Minor change desired	Satisfactory	Satisfactory
Policies on internal migration				
From rural to urban areas	..	..	..	..
From rural to rural areas	..	..	..	..
From urban to rural areas	..	..	..	..
From urban to urban areas	..	..	..	..
Into urban agglomerations	..	..	No intervention	..
International migration				
Immigration				
View	..	Satisfactory	Satisfactory	Satisfactory
Policy	..	Maintain	Lower	Maintain
Permanent settlement	..	..	Lower	Maintain
Temporary workers	..	..	Lower	Maintain
Highly skilled workers	..	..	..	Maintain
Family reunification	..	..	Lower	..
Integration of non-nationals	..	..	No	..
Emigration				
View	..	Satisfactory	Satisfactory	Satisfactory
Policy	..	Maintain	No intervention	No intervention
Encouraging the return of nationals	..	..	No	..

* Measures implemented to control HIV/AIDS: (1) blood screening; (2) information/education campaigns; (3) access to antiretroviral treatment; (4) non-discriminatory policies; (5) promoting condom use.

** Grounds on which abortion is permitted: (1) to save the woman's life; (2) to preserve physical health; (3) to preserve mental health; (4) rape or incest; (5) foetal impairment; (6) economic or social reasons; (7) on request.

Population indicators

Indicator	*1975*	*1985*	*1995*	*2005*
Population size and growth				
Population size (thousands)	110	127	148	161
Annual growth rate (percentage)*	1.0	1.4	1.4	0.8
Population age structure				
Percentage of population under age 15	47	41	35	29
Percentage of population aged 60 or older	7	8	9	10
Fertility and family planning				
Total fertility (births per woman)*	5.7	4.2	3.3	2.2
Teenage fertility rate (per 1,000 women, aged 15 - 19)*	164	121	95	63
Percentage of births to women under age 20*	23	23	19	17
Percentage of births to women aged 35 or older*	14	12	13	15
Percentage of married women using contraception				
Modern methods	..	46[a]	..	..
All methods	..	47[a]	..	..
Health and mortality				
Life expectancy at birth (years)*				
Males	62	67	69	71
Females	68	74	74	74
Both sexes combined	65	71	71	72
Infant mortality rate (per 1,000 births)*	39	23	17	15
Mortality under age 5 (per 1,000 births)*	55	31	22	20
Maternal mortality ratio (per 100,000 births) (2000)	..	..	..	..
HIV/AIDS (2003)				
Number of infected adults (thousands)	..	..	..	..
Adult prevalence rate (percentage)	..	..	..	..
Spatial distribution				
Population density (per sq. km)	204	235	274	298
Urban population (percentage)	24	26	28	31
Annual urban growth rate (percentage)*	1.9	2.2	2.1	2.1
Annual rural growth rate (percentage)*	0.8	1.1	1.0	0.2
International migration				
International migrant stock				
Number of migrants (thousands)	3	4	6	9
Percentage of total population	2.9	3.4	4.3	5.4

* For the periods 1970-1975, 1980-1985, 1990-1995 and 2000-2005.
[a] For 1988.

Government views and policies

Population policy variable	*1976*	*1986*	*1996*	*2005*
Population size and growth				
View on growth	..	Too high	Too high	Satisfactory
Policy on growth	..	Lower	Lower	Maintain
Population age structure				
Level of concern about				
Size of the working-age population	..	..	..	Major concern
Ageing of the population	..	..	..	Minor concern
Fertility and family planning				
View on fertility level	..	Too high	Too high	Satisfactory
Policy	..	Lower	Lower	Maintain
Access to contraceptive methods	..	Direct support	Direct support	Direct support
Adolescent fertility				
Level of concern	..	..	Major concern	Major concern
Policies and programmes	..	..	Yes	Yes
Health and mortality				
View				
Expectation of life	..	Unacceptable	Acceptable	Acceptable
Under-five mortality	..	..	Unacceptable	Unacceptable
Maternal mortality	..	..	..	Acceptable
Level of concern about HIV/AIDS	..	..	Major concern	Major concern
Measures implemented to control HIV/AIDS*	..	..	..	1,2,3,5
Grounds on which abortion is permitted**	..	..	1,2,3,4,5	1,2,3,4,5,6
Spatial distribution and internal migration				
View on spatial distribution	..	Minor change desired	Satisfactory	Minor change desired
Policies on internal migration				
From rural to urban areas	..	..	..	Lower
From rural to rural areas	..	..	..	..
From urban to rural areas	..	..	..	..
From urban to urban areas	..	..	..	..
Into urban agglomerations	..	..	No intervention	Lower
International migration				
Immigration				
View	..	Satisfactory	Satisfactory	Satisfactory
Policy	..	Maintain	No intervention	Maintain
Permanent settlement	..	..	No intervention	Maintain
Temporary workers	..	..	No intervention	Maintain
Highly skilled workers	..	..	..	Maintain
Family reunification	..	..	No intervention	No intervention
Integration of non-nationals	..	..	No	..
Emigration				
View	..	Satisfactory	Satisfactory	Satisfactory
Policy	..	Maintain	No intervention	No intervention
Encouraging the return of nationals	..	..	No	..

* Measures implemented to control HIV/AIDS: (1) blood screening; (2) information/education campaigns; (3) access to antiretroviral treatment; (4) non-discriminatory policies; (5) promoting condom use.

** Grounds on which abortion is permitted: (1) to save the woman's life; (2) to preserve physical health; (3) to preserve mental health; (4) rape or incest; (5) foetal impairment; (6) economic or social reasons; (7) on request.

Population indicators

Indicator	*1975*	*1985*	*1995*	*2005*
Population size and growth				
Population size (thousands)	96	104	113	119
Annual growth rate (percentage)*	1.1	0.8	0.7	0.5
Population age structure				
Percentage of population under age 15	47	40	37	29
Percentage of population aged 60 or older	8	8	9	9
Fertility and family planning				
Total fertility (births per woman)*	5.5	3.6	2.8	2.3
Teenage fertility rate (per 1,000 women, aged 15 - 19)*	164	110	87	67
Percentage of births to women under age 20*	25	24	21	19
Percentage of births to women aged 35 or older*	9	7	8	10
Percentage of married women using contraception				
Modern methods	..	55[a]	..	..
All methods	..	58[a]	..	..
Health and mortality				
Life expectancy at birth (years)*				
Males	60	65	67	68
Females	63	69	72	74
Both sexes combined	62	67	70	71
Infant mortality rate (per 1,000 births)*	64	42	30	26
Mortality under age 5 (per 1,000 births)*	87	53	36	31
Maternal mortality ratio (per 100,000 births) (2000)	..	..	..	..
HIV/AIDS (2003)				
Number of infected adults (thousands)	..	..	..	..
Adult prevalence rate (percentage)	..	..	..	..
Spatial distribution				
Population density (per sq. km)	246	269	291	307
Urban population (percentage)	27	34	48	60
Annual urban growth rate (percentage)*	1.1	5.0	4.1	2.5
Annual rural growth rate (percentage)*	1.1	-1.1	-2.0	-2.1
International migration				
International migrant stock				
Number of migrants (thousands)	2	3	5	10
Percentage of total population	2.3	2.8	4.9	8.7

* For the periods 1970-1975, 1980-1985, 1990-1995 and 2000-2005.
[a] For 1988.

Government views and policies

Population policy variable	*1976*	*1986*	*1996*	*2005*
Population size and growth				
View on growth	Too high	Too high	Too high	Too high
Policy on growth	Lower	Lower	Lower	Lower
Population age structure				
Level of concern about				
Size of the working-age population	..	..	..	Major concern
Ageing of the population	..	..	..	Minor concern
Fertility and family planning				
View on fertility level	Too high	Too high	Too high	Too high
Policy	Lower	Lower	Lower	Lower
Access to contraceptive methods	Direct support	Direct support	Direct support	Direct support
Adolescent fertility				
Level of concern	..	..	..	Major concern
Policies and programmes	..	..	..	Yes
Health and mortality				
View				
Expectation of life	Acceptable	Unacceptable	Unacceptable	Unacceptable
Under-five mortality	..	..	..	..
Maternal mortality	..	..	..	..
Level of concern about HIV/AIDS	..	..	..	Major concern
Measures implemented to control HIV/AIDS*	..	..	..	2
Grounds on which abortion is permitted**	..	..	1,2,3	1,2,3
Spatial distribution and internal migration				
View on spatial distribution	Major change desired	Major change desired	Major change desired	Major change desired
Policies on internal migration				
From rural to urban areas	..	..	..	..
From rural to rural areas	..	..	..	..
From urban to rural areas	..	..	..	..
From urban to urban areas	..	..	..	..
Into urban agglomerations	..	..	..	..
International migration				
Immigration				
View	Satisfactory	Too high	Too high	Satisfactory
Policy	Maintain	Maintain	Maintain	Maintain
Permanent settlement	..	..	..	Maintain
Temporary workers	..	..	..	Maintain
Highly skilled workers	..	..	..	Maintain
Family reunification	..	..	..	Maintain
Integration of non-nationals	..	..	..	..
Emigration				
View	Satisfactory	Satisfactory	Satisfactory	Satisfactory
Policy	Maintain	Maintain	Maintain	Maintain
Encouraging the return of nationals	..	..	..	..

* Measures implemented to control HIV/AIDS: (1) blood screening; (2) information/education campaigns; (3) access to antiretroviral treatment; (4) non-discriminatory policies; (5) promoting condom use.

** Grounds on which abortion is permitted: (1) to save the woman's life; (2) to preserve physical health; (3) to preserve mental health; (4) rape or incest; (5) foetal impairment; (6) economic or social reasons; (7) on request.

Population indicators

Indicator	*1975*	*1985*	*1995*	*2005*
Population size and growth				
Population size (thousands)	150	157	168	185
Annual growth rate (percentage)*	1.1	0.2	0.8	0.8
Population age structure				
Percentage of population under age 15	45	40	39	41
Percentage of population aged 60 or older	3	4	6	7
Fertility and family planning				
Total fertility (births per woman)*	5.7	4.9	4.7	4.4
Teenage fertility rate (per 1,000 women, aged 15 - 19)*	39	33	32	37
Percentage of births to women under age 20*	7	6	6	6
Percentage of births to women aged 35 or older*	19	16	20	20
Percentage of married women using contraception				
Modern methods	..	..	..	..
All methods	..	..	..	..
Health and mortality				
Life expectancy at birth (years)*				
Males	53	58	63	67
Females	60	65	70	74
Both sexes combined	56	61	66	70
Infant mortality rate (per 1,000 births)*	69	52	36	26
Mortality under age 5 (per 1,000 births)*	89	66	45	31
Maternal mortality ratio (per 100,000 births) (2000)	..	..	..	130
HIV/AIDS (2003)				
Number of infected adults (thousands)	..	..	..	..
Adult prevalence rate (percentage)	..	..	..	..
Spatial distribution				
Population density (per sq. km)	53	55	59	65
Urban population (percentage)	21	21	22	22
Annual urban growth rate (percentage)*	1.8	0.3	0.9	1.3
Annual rural growth rate (percentage)*	0.9	0.2	0.6	0.9
International migration				
International migrant stock				
Number of migrants (thousands)	4	5	7	9
Percentage of total population	2.5	3.2	4.1	5

* For the periods 1970-1975, 1980-1985, 1990-1995 and 2000-2005.

Government views and policies

Population policy variable	*1976*	*1986*	*1996*	*2005*
Population size and growth				
View on growth	Satisfactory	Satisfactory	Satisfactory	Satisfactory
Policy on growth	No intervention	Maintain	Maintain	No intervention
Population age structure				
Level of concern about				
Size of the working-age population	..	..	..	Not a concern
Ageing of the population	..	..	..	Minor concern
Fertility and family planning				
View on fertility level	Satisfactory	Satisfactory	Satisfactory	Satisfactory
Policy	No intervention	No intervention	No intervention	No intervention
Access to contraceptive methods	No support	No support	No support	No support
Adolescent fertility				
Level of concern	..	..	..	Not a concern
Policies and programmes	..	..	..	No
Health and mortality				
View				
Expectation of life	Acceptable	Acceptable	Acceptable	Acceptable
Under-five mortality	..	..	..	Acceptable
Maternal mortality	..	..	..	Acceptable
Level of concern about HIV/AIDS	..	..	..	Major concern
Measures implemented to control HIV/AIDS*	..	..	..	1,2,5
Grounds on which abortion is permitted**	..	..	1	1
Spatial distribution and internal migration				
View on spatial distribution	Satisfactory	Satisfactory	Satisfactory	Satisfactory
Policies on internal migration				
From rural to urban areas	..	..	..	..
From rural to rural areas	..	..	..	..
From urban to rural areas	..	..	..	..
From urban to urban areas	..	..	..	..
Into urban agglomerations	No intervention	..	..	No intervention
International migration				
Immigration				
View	Too high	Too high	Too high	Satisfactory
Policy	Lower	Lower	Lower	No intervention
Permanent settlement	..	..	..	No intervention
Temporary workers	..	..	..	No intervention
Highly skilled workers	..	..	..	No intervention
Family reunification	..	..	..	No intervention
Integration of non-nationals	..	..	..	No
Emigration				
View	Satisfactory	Satisfactory	Satisfactory	Satisfactory
Policy	Maintain	Maintain	Maintain	No intervention
Encouraging the return of nationals	No	..	..	No

* Measures implemented to control HIV/AIDS: (1) blood screening; (2) information/education campaigns; (3) access to antiretroviral treatment; (4) non-discriminatory policies; (5) promoting condom use.

** Grounds on which abortion is permitted: (1) to save the woman's life; (2) to preserve physical health; (3) to preserve mental health; (4) rape or incest; (5) foetal impairment; (6) economic or social reasons; (7) on request.

Population indicators

Indicator	*1975*	*1985*	*1995*	*2005*
Population size and growth				
Population size (thousands)	20	23	26	28
Annual growth rate (percentage)*	0.6	1.3	1.2	0.9
Population age structure				
Percentage of population under age 15	..	..	..	..
Percentage of population aged 60 or older	..	..	..	..
Fertility and family planning				
Total fertility (births per woman)*	..	..	..	..
Teenage fertility rate (per 1,000 women, aged 15 - 19)*	..	..	..	..
Percentage of births to women under age 20*	..	..	..	..
Percentage of births to women aged 35 or older*	..	..	..	..
Percentage of married women using contraception				
Modern methods	..	..	..	..
All methods	..	..	..	..
Health and mortality				
Life expectancy at birth (years)*				
Males	..	..	..	..
Females	..	..	..	..
Both sexes combined	..	..	..	..
Infant mortality rate (per 1,000 births)*	..	..	..	..
Mortality under age 5 (per 1,000 births)*	..	..	..	..
Maternal mortality ratio (per 100,000 births) (2000)	..	..	..	..
HIV/AIDS (2003)				
Number of infected adults (thousands)	..	..	..	..
Adult prevalence rate (percentage)	..	..	..	..
Spatial distribution				
Population density (per sq. km)	324	374	421	461
Urban population (percentage)	72	87	89	89
Annual urban growth rate (percentage)*	3.8	2.4	1.4	0.9
Annual rural growth rate (percentage)*	-5.9	-7.3	3.1	1.4
International migration				
International migrant stock				
Number of migrants (thousands)	8	9	9	9
Percentage of total population	41.1	37.4	34.9	33.5

* For the periods 1970-1975, 1980-1985, 1990-1995 and 2000-2005.

Government views and policies

Population policy variable	*1976*	*1986*	*1996*	*2005*
Population size and growth				
View on growth	Satisfactory	Satisfactory	Satisfactory	Satisfactory
Policy on growth	No intervention	Maintain	No intervention	No intervention
Population age structure				
Level of concern about				
Size of the working-age population	..	..	..	Major concern
Ageing of the population	..	..	..	..
Fertility and family planning				
View on fertility level	Satisfactory	Satisfactory	Too high	Too high
Policy	No intervention	Maintain	No intervention	No intervention
Access to contraceptive methods	No support	Direct support	Direct support	Direct support
Adolescent fertility				
Level of concern	..	..	Not a concern	Not a concern
Policies and programmes	..	..	..	..
Health and mortality				
View				
Expectation of life	Unacceptable	Unacceptable	Acceptable	Unacceptable
Under-five mortality	..	..	Unacceptable	Unacceptable
Maternal mortality	..	..	..	Unacceptable
Level of concern about HIV/AIDS	..	..	Major concern	Major concern
Measures implemented to control HIV/AIDS*	..	..	..	..
Grounds on which abortion is permitted**	..	..	1	1
Spatial distribution and internal migration				
View on spatial distribution	Major change desired	Major change desired	Satisfactory	Minor change desired
Policies on internal migration				
From rural to urban areas	..	..	..	Lower
From rural to rural areas	..	..	..	..
From urban to rural areas	..	..	..	..
From urban to urban areas	..	..	..	..
Into urban agglomerations	..	..	No intervention	..
International migration				
Immigration				
View	Satisfactory	Satisfactory	Satisfactory	Satisfactory
Policy	Maintain	Maintain	No intervention	No intervention
Permanent settlement	..	..	No intervention	..
Temporary workers	..	..	No intervention	..
Highly skilled workers	..	..	..	..
Family reunification	..	..	No intervention	..
Integration of non-nationals	..	..	No	..
Emigration				
View	Satisfactory	Satisfactory	Satisfactory	Satisfactory
Policy	Maintain	Maintain	No intervention	No intervention
Encouraging the return of nationals	..	..	No	..

* Measures implemented to control HIV/AIDS: (1) blood screening; (2) information/education campaigns; (3) access to antiretroviral treatment; (4) non-discriminatory policies; (5) promoting condom use.

** Grounds on which abortion is permitted: (1) to save the woman's life; (2) to preserve physical health; (3) to preserve mental health; (4) rape or incest; (5) foetal impairment; (6) economic or social reasons; (7) on request.

Population indicators

Indicator	*1975*	*1985*	*1995*	*2005*
Population size and growth				
Population size (thousands)	82	104	128	157
Annual growth rate (percentage)*	2.2	1.9	1.8	2.3
Population age structure				
Percentage of population under age 15	47	47	45	39
Percentage of population aged 60 or older	6	7	6	6
Fertility and family planning				
Total fertility (births per woman)*	6.5	6.2	5.0	4.1
Teenage fertility rate (per 1,000 women, aged 15 - 19)*	140	133	107	71
Percentage of births to women under age 20*	18	18	17	13
Percentage of births to women aged 35 or older*	9	9	9	8
Percentage of married women using contraception				
Modern methods	..	..	..	27[a]
All methods	..	..	..	29[a]
Health and mortality				
Life expectancy at birth (years)*				
Males	55	59	61	62
Females	58	62	63	64
Both sexes combined	56	60	62	63
Infant mortality rate (per 1,000 births)*	75	74	86	82
Mortality under age 5 (per 1,000 births)*	100	98	119	112
Maternal mortality ratio (per 100,000 births) (2000)	..	..	..	..
HIV/AIDS (2003)				
Number of infected adults (thousands)	..	..	..	..
Adult prevalence rate (percentage)	..	..	..	..
Spatial distribution				
Population density (per sq. km)	85	108	132	162
Urban population (percentage)	27	34	37	38
Annual urban growth rate (percentage)*	4.9	3.7	2.9	2.6
Annual rural growth rate (percentage)*	1.2	1.1	2.2	2.4
International migration				
International migrant stock				
Number of migrants (thousands)	6	7	7	7
Percentage of total population	7.5	6.5	5.6	4.8

* For the periods 1970-1975, 1980-1985, 1990-1995 and 2000-2005.
[a] For 2000.

Government views and policies

Population policy variable	*1976*	*1986*	*1996*	*2005*
Population size and growth				
View on growth	Too low	Too low	Too low	Satisfactory
Policy on growth	Raise	Raise	Raise	Maintain
Population age structure				
Level of concern about				
Size of the working-age population	..	..	..	Major concern
Ageing of the population	..	..	..	Minor concern
Fertility and family planning				
View on fertility level	Satisfactory	Satisfactory	Satisfactory	Satisfactory
Policy	Maintain	Maintain	Maintain	Raise
Access to contraceptive methods	Limits	Limits	Limits	Indirect support
Adolescent fertility				
Level of concern	..	..	..	Major concern
Policies and programmes	..	..	..	Yes
Health and mortality				
View				
Expectation of life	Unacceptable	Unacceptable	Unacceptable	Acceptable
Under-five mortality	..	..	..	Acceptable
Maternal mortality	..	..	..	Acceptable
Level of concern about HIV/AIDS	..	..	..	Major concern
Measures implemented to control HIV/AIDS*	..	..	..	1,2,3,4,5
Grounds on which abortion is permitted**	..	..	1,2	1,2,3
Spatial distribution and internal migration				
View on spatial distribution	Minor change desired	Minor change desired	Minor change desired	Minor change desired
Policies on internal migration				
From rural to urban areas	..	..	..	Lower
From rural to rural areas	..	..	..	Raise
From urban to rural areas	..	..	..	..
From urban to urban areas	..	..	..	..
Into urban agglomerations	..	..	..	Lower
International migration				
Immigration				
View	Too low	Satisfactory	Too high	Too high
Policy	Raise	Maintain	Lower	Lower
Permanent settlement	..	..	..	No intervention
Temporary workers	..	..	..	Lower
Highly skilled workers	..	..	..	Lower
Family reunification	..	..	..	Lower
Integration of non-nationals	..	..	..	Yes
Emigration				
View	Satisfactory	Satisfactory	Satisfactory	Satisfactory
Policy	Maintain	Maintain	Maintain	Lower
Encouraging the return of nationals	..	..	..	Yes

* Measures implemented to control HIV/AIDS: (1) blood screening; (2) information/education campaigns; (3) access to antiretroviral treatment; (4) non-discriminatory policies; (5) promoting condom use.

** Grounds on which abortion is permitted: (1) to save the woman's life; (2) to preserve physical health; (3) to preserve mental health; (4) rape or incest; (5) foetal impairment; (6) economic or social reasons; (7) on request.

Population indicators

Indicator	*1975*	*1985*	*1995*	*2005*
Population size and growth				
Population size (thousands)	7 251	12 880	18 682	24 573
Annual growth rate (percentage)*	4.7	5.9	2.6	2.7
Population age structure				
Percentage of population under age 15	44	42	41	37
Percentage of population aged 60 or older	5	4	3	5
Fertility and family planning				
Total fertility (births per woman)*	7.3	7.1	5.6	4.1
Teenage fertility rate (per 1,000 women, aged 15 - 19)*	63	61	49	35
Percentage of births to women under age 20*	7	7	7	6
Percentage of births to women aged 35 or older*	25	23	23	24
Percentage of married women using contraception				
Modern methods	..	..	29[a]	..
All methods	..	..	32[a]	..
Health and mortality				
Life expectancy at birth (years)*				
Males	52	62	67	70
Females	56	65	71	74
Both sexes combined	54	63	69	72
Infant mortality rate (per 1,000 births)*	105	56	32	23
Mortality under age 5 (per 1,000 births)*	141	75	39	27
Maternal mortality ratio (per 100,000 births) (2000)	..	..	..	23
HIV/AIDS (2003)				
Number of infected adults (thousands)	..	..	..	..
Adult prevalence rate (percentage)	..	..	..	..
Spatial distribution				
Population density (per sq. km)	3	6	9	11
Urban population (percentage)	58	73	83	88
Annual urban growth rate (percentage)*	8.3	7.9	3.9	3.4
Annual rural growth rate (percentage)*	0.5	1.5	-2.1	-0.8
International migration				
International migrant stock				
Number of migrants (thousands)	929	3 401	4 611	6 361
Percentage of total population	12.8	26.4	24.7	25.9

* For the periods 1970-1975, 1980-1985, 1990-1995 and 2000-2005.
[a] For 1996.

Government views and policies

Population policy variable	*1976*	*1986*	*1996*	*2005*
Population size and growth				
View on growth	Too high	Too high	Too high	Too high
Policy on growth	No intervention	Lower	Lower	Lower
Population age structure				
Level of concern about				
Size of the working-age population	..	..	..	..
Ageing of the population	..	..	..	Major concern
Fertility and family planning				
View on fertility level	Too high	Too high	Too high	Too high
Policy	No intervention	Lower	Lower	Lower
Access to contraceptive methods	No support	Direct support	Direct support	Direct support
Adolescent fertility				
Level of concern	..	..	Major concern	Major concern
Policies and programmes	..	..	Yes	Yes
Health and mortality				
View				
Expectation of life	Unacceptable	Unacceptable	Unacceptable	Unacceptable
Under-five mortality	..	..	Unacceptable	Unacceptable
Maternal mortality	..	..	..	Unacceptable
Level of concern about HIV/AIDS	..	..	Major concern	Major concern
Measures implemented to control HIV/AIDS*	..	..	..	1,2,3,5
Grounds on which abortion is permitted**	..	..	1	1
Spatial distribution and internal migration				
View on spatial distribution	Major change desired	Minor change desired	Major change desired	Major change desired
Policies on internal migration				
From rural to urban areas	..	..	..	Lower
From rural to rural areas	..	..	..	..
From urban to rural areas	..	..	..	..
From urban to urban areas	..	..	..	..
Into urban agglomerations	Lower	No intervention	Lower	Lower
International migration				
Immigration				
View	Satisfactory	Satisfactory	Satisfactory	Satisfactory
Policy	Maintain	Maintain	No intervention	No intervention
Permanent settlement	..	..	No intervention	..
Temporary workers	..	..	No intervention	..
Highly skilled workers	..	..	..	..
Family reunification	..	..	No intervention	..
Integration of non-nationals	..	..	Yes	..
Emigration				
View	Satisfactory	Satisfactory	Satisfactory	Satisfactory
Policy	Maintain	Maintain	No intervention	No intervention
Encouraging the return of nationals	..	..	Yes	Yes

* Measures implemented to control HIV/AIDS: (1) blood screening; (2) information/education campaigns; (3) access to antiretroviral treatment; (4) non-discriminatory policies; (5) promoting condom use.

** Grounds on which abortion is permitted: (1) to save the woman's life; (2) to preserve physical health; (3) to preserve mental health; (4) rape or incest; (5) foetal impairment; (6) economic or social reasons; (7) on request.

Population indicators

Indicator	*1975*	*1985*	*1995*	*2005*
Population size and growth				
Population size (thousands)	5 262	6 870	9 120	11 658
Annual growth rate (percentage)*	2.8	2.8	2.7	2.4
Population age structure				
Percentage of population under age 15	45	46	46	43
Percentage of population aged 60 or older	6	5	5	5
Fertility and family planning				
Total fertility (births per woman)*	7.0	7.0	6.2	5.0
Teenage fertility rate (per 1,000 women, aged 15 - 19)*	127	127	113	87
Percentage of births to women under age 20*	13	14	14	13
Percentage of births to women aged 35 or older*	20	20	19	16
Percentage of married women using contraception				
Modern methods	1[a]	2[b]	8[c]	..
All methods	4[a]	11[b]	11[c]	..
Health and mortality				
Life expectancy at birth (years)*				
Males	39	47	53	54
Females	41	49	55	57
Both sexes combined	40	48	54	56
Infant mortality rate (per 1,000 births)*	170	116	90	83
Mortality under age 5 (per 1,000 births)*	291	193	144	133
Maternal mortality ratio (per 100,000 births) (2000)	..	..	..	690
HIV/AIDS (2003)				
Number of infected adults (thousands)	..	..	..	41
Adult prevalence rate (percentage)	..	..	..	0.8
Spatial distribution				
Population density (per sq. km)	27	35	46	59
Urban population (percentage)	34	37	44	51
Annual urban growth rate (percentage)*	3.3	3.8	4.3	3.9
Annual rural growth rate (percentage)*	2.7	2.3	1.3	1.0
International migration				
International migrant stock				
Number of migrants (thousands)	155	170	320	326
Percentage of total population	2.9	2.5	3.5	2.8

* For the periods 1970-1975, 1980-1985, 1990-1995 and 2000-2005.
[a] For 1978.
[b] For 1986.
[c] For 1999.

Government views and policies

Population policy variable	*1976*	*1986*	*1996*	*2005*
Population size and growth				
View on growth	..	..	Satisfactory	Too low
Policy on growth	..	..	Maintain	Raise
Population age structure				
Level of concern about				
Size of the working-age population	..	..	..	Minor concern
Ageing of the population	..	..	..	Major concern
Fertility and family planning				
View on fertility level	..	..	Satisfactory	Too low
Policy	..	..	Maintain	Raise
Access to contraceptive methods	..	..	Indirect support	Direct support
Adolescent fertility				
Level of concern	..	..	Minor concern	Minor concern
Policies and programmes	..	..	Yes	No
Health and mortality				
View				
Expectation of life	..	..	Acceptable	Unacceptable
Under-five mortality	..	..	Unacceptable	Acceptable
Maternal mortality	..	..	..	Unacceptable
Level of concern about HIV/AIDS	..	..	Major concern	Major concern
Measures implemented to control HIV/AIDS*	..	..	..	1,2,3,5
Grounds on which abortion is permitted**	..	..	1,2,3,4,5,6,7	1,2,3,4,5,6,7
Spatial distribution and internal migration				
View on spatial distribution	..	..	Major change desired	Major change desired
Policies on internal migration				
From rural to urban areas	..	..	..	Lower
From rural to rural areas	..	..	..	..
From urban to rural areas	..	..	..	..
From urban to urban areas	..	..	..	..
Into urban agglomerations	..	..	No intervention	Maintain
International migration				
Immigration				
View	..	..	Satisfactory	Satisfactory
Policy	..	..	No intervention	Maintain
Permanent settlement	..	..	..	Lower
Temporary workers	..	..	..	Lower
Highly skilled workers	..	..	..	Raise
Family reunification	..	..	..	Raise
Integration of non-nationals	..	..	..	Yes
Emigration				
View	..	..	Too high	Too high
Policy	..	..	Lower	Lower
Encouraging the return of nationals	..	..	Yes	Yes

* Measures implemented to control HIV/AIDS: (1) blood screening; (2) information/education campaigns; (3) access to antiretroviral treatment; (4) non-discriminatory policies; (5) promoting condom use.

** Grounds on which abortion is permitted: (1) to save the woman's life; (2) to preserve physical health; (3) to preserve mental health; (4) rape or incest; (5) foetal impairment; (6) economic or social reasons; (7) on request.

Population indicators

Indicator	*1975*	*1985*	*1995*	*2005*
Population size and growth				
Population size (thousands)	9 085	9 848	10 548	10 503
Annual growth rate (percentage)*	0.9	0.7	0.8	-0.1
Population age structure				
Percentage of population under age 15	25	24	22	18
Percentage of population aged 60 or older	13	13	17	18
Fertility and family planning				
Total fertility (births per woman)*	2.4	2.3	2.0	1.7
Teenage fertility rate (per 1,000 women, aged 15 - 19)*	45	44	37	25
Percentage of births to women under age 20*	11	9	10	8
Percentage of births to women aged 35 or older*	7	6	8	9
Percentage of married women using contraception				
Modern methods	12[a]	..	..	33[b]
All methods	55[a]	..	..	55[b]
Health and mortality				
Life expectancy at birth (years)*				
Males	67	68	69	71
Females	71	73	74	76
Both sexes combined	69	70	72	73
Infant mortality rate (per 1,000 births)*	47	34	17	13
Mortality under age 5 (per 1,000 births)*	54	39	20	15
Maternal mortality ratio (per 100,000 births) (2000)	..	..	..	11
HIV/AIDS (2003)				
Number of infected adults (thousands)	..	..	..	10
Adult prevalence rate (percentage)	..	..	..	0.2
Spatial distribution				
Population density (per sq. km)	89	96	103	103
Urban population (percentage)	43	49	51	52
Annual urban growth rate (percentage)*	2.7	1.7	1.0	0.2
Annual rural growth rate (percentage)*	-0.4	-0.2	0.6	-0.4
International migration				
International migrant stock				
Number of migrants (thousands)	..	..	760	512
Percentage of total population	..	..	7.2	4.9

* For the periods 1970-1975, 1980-1985, 1990-1995 and 2000-2005.
[a] For 1976.
[b] For 2000.

Government views and policies

Population policy variable	*1976*	*1986*	*1996*	*2005*
Population size and growth				
View on growth	Too high	Too high	Too high	Satisfactory
Policy on growth	Lower	Lower	Lower	No intervention
Population age structure				
Level of concern about				
Size of the working-age population	..	..	..	Major concern
Ageing of the population	..	..	..	Minor concern
Fertility and family planning				
View on fertility level	Too high	Too high	Too high	Satisfactory
Policy	Lower	Lower	Lower	No intervention
Access to contraceptive methods	Direct support	Direct support	Direct support	Direct support
Adolescent fertility				
Level of concern	..	..	..	Major concern
Policies and programmes	..	..	..	Yes
Health and mortality				
View				
Expectation of life	Unacceptable	Acceptable	Acceptable	Acceptable
Under-five mortality	..	..	..	Acceptable
Maternal mortality	..	..	..	Acceptable
Level of concern about HIV/AIDS	..	..	..	Major concern
Measures implemented to control HIV/AIDS*	..	..	..	1,2,3,5
Grounds on which abortion is permitted**	..	..	1,2,3,4,5	1,2,3,4,5
Spatial distribution and internal migration				
View on spatial distribution	Major change desired	Major change desired	Major change desired	Minor change desired
Policies on internal migration				
From rural to urban areas	..	..	..	..
From rural to rural areas	..	..	..	..
From urban to rural areas	..	..	..	..
From urban to urban areas	..	..	..	..
Into urban agglomerations	..	..	..	..
International migration				
Immigration				
View	Satisfactory	Satisfactory	Satisfactory	Satisfactory
Policy	Maintain	Maintain	Maintain	Maintain
Permanent settlement	..	..	..	..
Temporary workers	..	..	..	..
Highly skilled workers	..	..	..	..
Family reunification	..	..	..	..
Integration of non-nationals	..	..	..	..
Emigration				
View	Satisfactory	Too high	Too high	Satisfactory
Policy	Maintain	Maintain	Maintain	Maintain
Encouraging the return of nationals	..	..	..	..

* Measures implemented to control HIV/AIDS: (1) blood screening; (2) information/education campaigns; (3) access to antiretroviral treatment; (4) non-discriminatory policies; (5) promoting condom use.

** Grounds on which abortion is permitted: (1) to save the woman's life; (2) to preserve physical health; (3) to preserve mental health; (4) rape or incest; (5) foetal impairment; (6) economic or social reasons; (7) on request.

Population indicators

Indicator	*1975*	*1985*	*1995*	*2005*
Population size and growth				
Population size (thousands)	60	69	75	81
Annual growth rate (percentage)*	1.8	1.1	0.9	0.9
Population age structure				
Percentage of population under age 15	..	..	..	..
Percentage of population aged 60 or older	..	..	..	..
Fertility and family planning				
Total fertility (births per woman)*	..	..	..	..
Teenage fertility rate (per 1,000 women, aged 15 - 19)*	..	..	..	..
Percentage of births to women under age 20*	..	..	..	..
Percentage of births to women aged 35 or older*	..	..	..	..
Percentage of married women using contraception				
Modern methods	..	..	..	..
All methods	..	..	..	..
Health and mortality				
Life expectancy at birth (years)*				
Males	..	..	..	..
Females	..	..	..	..
Both sexes combined	..	..	..	..
Infant mortality rate (per 1,000 births)*	..	..	..	..
Mortality under age 5 (per 1,000 births)*	..	..	..	..
Maternal mortality ratio (per 100,000 births) (2000)	..	..	..	..
HIV/AIDS (2003)				
Number of infected adults (thousands)	..	..	..	..
Adult prevalence rate (percentage)	..	..	..	..
Spatial distribution				
Population density (per sq. km)	131	151	166	177
Urban population (percentage)	33	47	50	50
Annual urban growth rate (percentage)*	7.2	3.9	1.1	1.1
Annual rural growth rate (percentage)*	0.4	-1.2	1.1	0.7
International migration				
International migrant stock				
Number of migrants (thousands)	3	4	4	5
Percentage of total population	4.9	5.1	5.5	6.1

* For the periods 1970-1975, 1980-1985, 1990-1995 and 2000-2005.

Government views and policies

Population policy variable	*1976*	*1986*	*1996*	*2005*
Population size and growth				
View on growth	Too high	Too high	Too high	Too high
Policy on growth	No intervention	No intervention	No intervention	No intervention
Population age structure				
Level of concern about				
Size of the working-age population	..	..	..	Minor concern
Ageing of the population	..	..	..	..
Fertility and family planning				
View on fertility level	Too high	Too high	Too high	Too high
Policy	No intervention	No intervention	Lower	Lower
Access to contraceptive methods	Direct support	Indirect support	Indirect support	Indirect support
Adolescent fertility				
Level of concern	..	..	Major concern	Major concern
Policies and programmes	..	..	Yes	Yes
Health and mortality				
View				
Expectation of life	Unacceptable	Unacceptable	Unacceptable	Unacceptable
Under-five mortality	..	..	Unacceptable	Unacceptable
Maternal mortality	..	..	..	Unacceptable
Level of concern about HIV/AIDS	..	..	Major concern	Major concern
Measures implemented to control HIV/AIDS*	..	..	..	2,3,5
Grounds on which abortion is permitted**	..	..	1,2,3	1,2,3
Spatial distribution and internal migration				
View on spatial distribution	Minor change desired	Major change desired	Minor change desired	Major change desired
Policies on internal migration				
From rural to urban areas	..	..	..	Lower
From rural to rural areas	..	..	..	..
From urban to rural areas	..	..	..	..
From urban to urban areas	..	..	..	..
Into urban agglomerations	No intervention	No intervention	No intervention	Lower
International migration				
Immigration				
View	Satisfactory	Satisfactory	Satisfactory	Satisfactory
Policy	Maintain	Maintain	Lower	No intervention
Permanent settlement	..	..	No intervention	..
Temporary workers	..	..	..	..
Highly skilled workers	..	..	..	..
Family reunification	..	..	..	..
Integration of non-nationals	..	..	No	..
Emigration				
View	Satisfactory	Satisfactory	Satisfactory	Satisfactory
Policy	Maintain	Maintain	No intervention	No intervention
Encouraging the return of nationals	No	..	No	..

* Measures implemented to control HIV/AIDS: (1) blood screening; (2) information/education campaigns; (3) access to antiretroviral treatment; (4) non-discriminatory policies; (5) promoting condom use.

** Grounds on which abortion is permitted: (1) to save the woman's life; (2) to preserve physical health; (3) to preserve mental health; (4) rape or incest; (5) foetal impairment; (6) economic or social reasons; (7) on request.

Population indicators

Indicator	*1975*	*1985*	*1995*	*2005*
Population size and growth				
Population size (thousands)	2 945	3 580	4 137	5 525
Annual growth rate (percentage)*	1.8	2.0	0.3	4.1
Population age structure				
Percentage of population under age 15	41	40	42	43
Percentage of population aged 60 or older	6	6	6	5
Fertility and family planning				
Total fertility (births per woman)*	6.5	6.5	6.5	6.5
Teenage fertility rate (per 1,000 women, aged 15 - 19)*	80	79	192	192
Percentage of births to women under age 20*	9	9	20	21
Percentage of births to women aged 35 or older*	21	21	18	18
Percentage of married women using contraception				
Modern methods	..	..	..	4[a]
All methods	..	..	..	4[a]
Health and mortality				
Life expectancy at birth (years)*				
Males	34	37	37	39
Females	37	40	40	42
Both sexes combined	35	38	38	41
Infant mortality rate (per 1,000 births)*	203	186	187	165
Mortality under age 5 (per 1,000 births)*	363	333	331	290
Maternal mortality ratio (per 100,000 births) (2000)	..	..	..	2 000
HIV/AIDS (2003)				
Number of infected adults (thousands)	..	..	..	..
Adult prevalence rate (percentage)	..	..	..	..
Spatial distribution				
Population density (per sq. km)	41	50	58	77
Urban population (percentage)	21	27	33	40
Annual urban growth rate (percentage)*	6.0	4.3	2.2	5.6
Annual rural growth rate (percentage)*	1.0	1.2	-0.8	2.7
International migration				
International migrant stock				
Number of migrants (thousands)	80	98	55	119
Percentage of total population	2.7	2.7	1.3	2.2

* For the periods 1970-1975, 1980-1985, 1990-1995 and 2000-2005.
[a] For 2000.

Government views and policies

Population policy variable	*1976*	*1986*	*1996*	*2005*
Population size and growth				
View on growth	Satisfactory	Too low	Satisfactory	Too low
Policy on growth	No intervention	Raise	Maintain	Raise
Population age structure				
Level of concern about				
Size of the working-age population	..	..	..	Major concern
Ageing of the population	..	..	..	Major concern
Fertility and family planning				
View on fertility level	Satisfactory	Too low	Too low	Too low
Policy	No intervention	Raise	Raise	Raise
Access to contraceptive methods	Direct support	Direct support	Direct support	Direct support
Adolescent fertility				
Level of concern	..	..	Minor concern	Minor concern
Policies and programmes	..	..	Yes	Yes
Health and mortality				
View				
Expectation of life	Acceptable	Acceptable	Acceptable	Acceptable
Under-five mortality	..	..	Acceptable	Acceptable
Maternal mortality	..	..	..	Acceptable
Level of concern about HIV/AIDS	..	..	Minor concern	Major concern
Measures implemented to control HIV/AIDS*	..	..	..	1,2,3,5
Grounds on which abortion is permitted**	..	..	1,2,3,4,5,6,7	1,2,3,4,5,6,7
Spatial distribution and internal migration				
View on spatial distribution	Satisfactory	Satisfactory	Satisfactory	Satisfactory
Policies on internal migration				
From rural to urban areas	..	..	..	No intervention
From rural to rural areas	..	..	..	No intervention
From urban to rural areas	..	..	..	No intervention
From urban to urban areas	..	..	..	No intervention
Into urban agglomerations	..	..	No intervention	No intervention
International migration				
Immigration				
View	Satisfactory	Satisfactory	Satisfactory	Too low
Policy	Maintain	Maintain	Raise	Raise
Permanent settlement	..	..	Raise	Raise
Temporary workers	..	..	No intervention	Maintain
Highly skilled workers	..	..	..	Raise
Family reunification	..	..	No intervention	Maintain
Integration of non-nationals	..	..	No	Yes
Emigration				
View	Satisfactory	Satisfactory	Satisfactory	Too high
Policy	Maintain	Maintain	No intervention	Lower
Encouraging the return of nationals	..	..	No	Yes

* Measures implemented to control HIV/AIDS: (1) blood screening; (2) information/education campaigns; (3) access to antiretroviral treatment; (4) non-discriminatory policies; (5) promoting condom use.

** Grounds on which abortion is permitted: (1) to save the woman's life; (2) to preserve physical health; (3) to preserve mental health; (4) rape or incest; (5) foetal impairment; (6) economic or social reasons; (7) on request.

Population indicators

Indicator	*1975*	*1985*	*1995*	*2005*
Population size and growth				
Population size (thousands)	2 263	2 709	3 478	4 326
Annual growth rate (percentage)*	1.7	2.3	2.8	1.5
Population age structure				
Percentage of population under age 15	33	24	22	20
Percentage of population aged 60 or older	7	8	9	12
Fertility and family planning				
Total fertility (births per woman)*	2.6	1.7	1.8	1.4
Teenage fertility rate (per 1,000 women, aged 15 - 19)*	12	7	8	6
Percentage of births to women under age 20*	4	2	2	2
Percentage of births to women aged 35 or older*	11	10	14	21
Percentage of married women using contraception				
Modern methods	53[a]	73[b]	53[c]	..
All methods	60[a]	74[b]	62[c]	..
Health and mortality				
Life expectancy at birth (years)*				
Males	67	69	74	77
Females	72	75	78	81
Both sexes combined	70	72	76	79
Infant mortality rate (per 1,000 births)*	19	8	6	3
Mortality under age 5 (per 1,000 births)*	21	10	7	4
Maternal mortality ratio (per 100,000 births) (2000)	..	..	..	30
HIV/AIDS (2003)				
Number of infected adults (thousands)	..	..	..	4
Adult prevalence rate (percentage)	..	..	..	0.2
Spatial distribution				
Population density (per sq. km)	3 313	3 966	5 092	6 333
Urban population (percentage)	100	100	100	100
Annual urban growth rate (percentage)*	1.7	2.3	2.8	1.7
Annual rural growth rate (percentage)*	0.0	0.0	0.0	0.0
International migration				
International migrant stock				
Number of migrants (thousands)	528	619	992	1 843
Percentage of total population	23.3	22.9	28.5	42.6

* For the periods 1970-1975, 1980-1985, 1990-1995 and 2000-2005.
[a] For 1973.
[b] For 1982.
[c] For 1997.

Government views and policies

Population policy variable	*1976*	*1986*	*1996*	*2005*
Population size and growth				
View on growth	..	..	Too low	Satisfactory
Policy on growth	..	..	Raise	Maintain
Population age structure				
Level of concern about				
Size of the working-age population	..	..	..	Major concern
Ageing of the population	..	..	..	Major concern
Fertility and family planning				
View on fertility level	..	..	Too low	Too low
Policy	..	..	Raise	Raise
Access to contraceptive methods	..	..	No support	No support
Adolescent fertility				
Level of concern	..	..	Not a concern	Not a concern
Policies and programmes	..	..	No	No
Health and mortality				
View				
Expectation of life	..	..	Unacceptable	Acceptable
Under-five mortality	..	..	..	Acceptable
Maternal mortality	..	..	..	Acceptable
Level of concern about HIV/AIDS	..	..	..	Major concern
Measures implemented to control HIV/AIDS*	..	..	..	1,2,3,5
Grounds on which abortion is permitted**	..	..	1,2,3,4,5,6,7	1,2,3,4,5,6,7
Spatial distribution and internal migration				
View on spatial distribution	..	..	Satisfactory	Major change desired
Policies on internal migration				
From rural to urban areas	..	..	..	No intervention
From rural to rural areas	..	..	..	No intervention
From urban to rural areas	..	..	..	No intervention
From urban to urban areas	..	..	..	No intervention
Into urban agglomerations	..	..	..	No intervention
International migration				
Immigration				
View	..	..	Satisfactory	Satisfactory
Policy	..	..	Lower	Maintain
Permanent settlement	..	..	Lower	Maintain
Temporary workers	..	..	Lower	Maintain
Highly skilled workers	..	..	..	Maintain
Family reunification	..	..	Lower	Maintain
Integration of non-nationals	..	..	Yes	Yes
Emigration				
View	..	..	Satisfactory	Satisfactory
Policy	..	..	No intervention	No intervention
Encouraging the return of nationals	..	..	No	No

* Measures implemented to control HIV/AIDS: (1) blood screening; (2) information/education campaigns; (3) access to antiretroviral treatment; (4) non-discriminatory policies; (5) promoting condom use.
** Grounds on which abortion is permitted: (1) to save the woman's life; (2) to preserve physical health; (3) to preserve mental health; (4) rape or incest; (5) foetal impairment; (6) economic or social reasons; (7) on request.

Population indicators

Indicator	*1975*	*1985*	*1995*	*2005*
Population size and growth				
Population size (thousands)	4 735	5 140	5 364	5 401
Annual growth rate (percentage)*	0.9	0.6	0.4	0.0
Population age structure				
Percentage of population under age 15	26	27	23	17
Percentage of population aged 60 or older	14	14	15	16
Fertility and family planning				
Total fertility (births per woman)*	2.5	2.3	1.9	1.2
Teenage fertility rate (per 1,000 women, aged 15 - 19)*	50	45	37	21
Percentage of births to women under age 20*	12	9	11	9
Percentage of births to women aged 35 or older*	5	5	7	7
Percentage of married women using contraception				
Modern methods	..	..	41[a]	..
All methods	..	..	74[a]	..
Health and mortality				
Life expectancy at birth (years)*				
Males	67	67	68	70
Females	73	75	76	78
Both sexes combined	70	71	72	74
Infant mortality rate (per 1,000 births)*	24	18	12	8
Mortality under age 5 (per 1,000 births)*	30	22	15	10
Maternal mortality ratio (per 100,000 births) (2000)	..	..	..	3
HIV/AIDS (2003)				
Number of infected adults (thousands)	..	..	..	<1
Adult prevalence rate (percentage)	..	..	..	<0.1
Spatial distribution				
Population density (per sq. km)	97	105	109	110
Urban population (percentage)	46	54	57	58
Annual urban growth rate (percentage)*	3.3	1.6	0.5	0.5
Annual rural growth rate (percentage)*	-1.0	-0.4	0.3	-0.5
International migration				
International migrant stock				
Number of migrants (thousands)	..	..	114	124
Percentage of total population	..	..	2.1	2.3

* For the periods 1970-1975, 1980-1985, 1990-1995 and 2000-2005.
[a] For 1991.

Government views and policies

Population policy variable	*1976*	*1986*	*1996*	*2005*
Population size and growth				
View on growth	..	..	Too low	Too low
Policy on growth	..	..	Raise	Raise
Population age structure				
Level of concern about				
Size of the working-age population	..	..	..	Major concern
Ageing of the population	..	..	..	Major concern
Fertility and family planning				
View on fertility level	..	..	Too low	Too low
Policy	..	..	Raise	Raise
Access to contraceptive methods	..	..	Direct support	Direct support
Adolescent fertility				
Level of concern	..	..	..	Minor concern
Policies and programmes	..	..	No	Yes
Health and mortality				
View				
Expectation of life	..	..	Acceptable	Unacceptable
Under-five mortality	..	..	..	Acceptable
Maternal mortality	..	..	..	Unacceptable
Level of concern about HIV/AIDS	..	..	..	Minor concern
Measures implemented to control HIV/AIDS*	..	..	..	1,2,3,4,5
Grounds on which abortion is permitted**	..	..	1,2,3,4,5,6,7	1,2,3,4,5,6,7
Spatial distribution and internal migration				
View on spatial distribution	..	..	Minor change desired	Minor change desired
Policies on internal migration				
From rural to urban areas	..	..	..	Lower
From rural to rural areas	..	..	..	..
From urban to rural areas	..	..	..	..
From urban to urban areas	..	..	..	..
Into urban agglomerations	..	..	..	Lower
International migration				
Immigration				
View	..	..	Satisfactory	Satisfactory
Policy	..	..	Lower	Maintain
Permanent settlement	..	..	..	Maintain
Temporary workers	..	..	..	Lower
Highly skilled workers	..	..	..	Maintain
Family reunification	..	..	..	Maintain
Integration of non-nationals	..	..	..	Yes
Emigration				
View	..	..	Satisfactory	Satisfactory
Policy	..	..	No intervention	No intervention
Encouraging the return of nationals	..	..	Yes	Yes

* Measures implemented to control HIV/AIDS: (1) blood screening; (2) information/education campaigns; (3) access to antiretroviral treatment; (4) non-discriminatory policies; (5) promoting condom use.
** Grounds on which abortion is permitted: (1) to save the woman's life; (2) to preserve physical health; (3) to preserve mental health; (4) rape or incest; (5) foetal impairment; (6) economic or social reasons; (7) on request.

Population indicators

Indicator	*1975*	*1985*	*1995*	*2005*
Population size and growth				
Population size (thousands)	1 742	1 884	1 964	1 967
Annual growth rate (percentage)*	0.8	0.6	0.4	0.0
Population age structure				
Percentage of population under age 15	24	22	18	14
Percentage of population aged 60 or older	15	15	18	20
Fertility and family planning				
Total fertility (births per woman)*	2.2	1.9	1.4	1.2
Teenage fertility rate (per 1,000 women, aged 15 - 19)*	55	47	18	6
Percentage of births to women under age 20*	13	12	7	2
Percentage of births to women aged 35 or older*	5	5	6	10
Percentage of married women using contraception				
Modern methods	..	..	59[a]	..
All methods	..	..	74[a]	..
Health and mortality				
Life expectancy at birth (years)*				
Males	66	67	70	73
Females	74	75	77	80
Both sexes combined	70	71	73	76
Infant mortality rate (per 1,000 births)*	22	14	7	5
Mortality under age 5 (per 1,000 births)*	28	18	9	7
Maternal mortality ratio (per 100,000 births) (2000)	..	..	..	17
HIV/AIDS (2003)				
Number of infected adults (thousands)	..	..	..	<1
Adult prevalence rate (percentage)	..	..	..	<0.1
Spatial distribution				
Population density (per sq. km)	86	93	97	97
Urban population (percentage)	42	50	51	51
Annual urban growth rate (percentage)*	3.6	1.2	0.8	-0.1
Annual rural growth rate (percentage)*	-0.9	-0.1	0.7	-0.1
International migration				
International migrant stock				
Number of migrants (thousands)	..	..	200	167
Percentage of total population	..	..	10.2	8.5

* For the periods 1970-1975, 1980-1985, 1990-1995 and 2000-2005.
[a] For 1994.

Government views and policies

Population policy variable	*1976*	*1986*	*1996*	*2005*
Population size and growth				
View on growth	..	Too high	Too high	Too high
Policy on growth	..	No intervention	Lower	Lower
Population age structure				
Level of concern about				
Size of the working-age population	..	..	..	Major concern
Ageing of the population	..	..	..	Minor concern
Fertility and family planning				
View on fertility level	..	Too high	Too high	Too high
Policy	..	No intervention	Lower	Lower
Access to contraceptive methods	..	Direct support	Direct support	No support
Adolescent fertility				
Level of concern	..	..	..	Minor concern
Policies and programmes	..	..	..	Yes
Health and mortality				
View				
Expectation of life	..	Unacceptable	Unacceptable	Unacceptable
Under-five mortality	..	..	..	Unacceptable
Maternal mortality	..	..	..	Unacceptable
Level of concern about HIV/AIDS	..	..	..	Major concern
Measures implemented to control HIV/AIDS*	..	..	..	1,2
Grounds on which abortion is permitted**	..	..	1	1
Spatial distribution and internal migration				
View on spatial distribution	..	Minor change desired	Minor change desired	Minor change desired
Policies on internal migration				
From rural to urban areas	..	..	..	Lower
From rural to rural areas	..	..	..	..
From urban to rural areas	..	..	..	..
From urban to urban areas	..	..	..	..
Into urban agglomerations	..	..	..	Lower
International migration				
Immigration				
View	..	Satisfactory	Satisfactory	Satisfactory
Policy	..	Maintain	Maintain	Maintain
Permanent settlement	..	..	..	..
Temporary workers	..	..	..	Maintain
Highly skilled workers	..	..	..	Maintain
Family reunification	..	..	..	..
Integration of non-nationals	..	..	..	..
Emigration				
View	..	Satisfactory	Satisfactory	Satisfactory
Policy	..	Maintain	Maintain	Maintain
Encouraging the return of nationals	..	..	..	..

* Measures implemented to control HIV/AIDS: (1) blood screening; (2) information/education campaigns; (3) access to antiretroviral treatment; (4) non-discriminatory policies; (5) promoting condom use.
** Grounds on which abortion is permitted: (1) to save the woman's life; (2) to preserve physical health; (3) to preserve mental health; (4) rape or incest; (5) foetal impairment; (6) economic or social reasons; (7) on request.

Population indicators

Indicator	*1975*	*1985*	*1995*	*2005*
Population size and growth				
Population size (thousands)	193	272	364	478
Annual growth rate (percentage)*	3.6	3.4	2.8	2.6
Population age structure				
Percentage of population under age 15	48	47	44	41
Percentage of population aged 60 or older	5	5	4	4
Fertility and family planning				
Total fertility (births per woman)*	7.2	6.4	5.1	4.3
Teenage fertility rate (per 1,000 women, aged 15 - 19)*	107	94	71	51
Percentage of births to women under age 20*	11	12	11	8
Percentage of births to women aged 35 or older*	18	17	15	12
Percentage of married women using contraception				
Modern methods	..	..	..	..
All methods	..	..	..	..
Health and mortality				
Life expectancy at birth (years)*				
Males	55	60	60	62
Females	56	61	62	63
Both sexes combined	56	60	61	62
Infant mortality rate (per 1,000 births)*	61	38	37	34
Mortality under age 5 (per 1,000 births)*	113	65	63	58
Maternal mortality ratio (per 100,000 births) (2000)	..	..	..	130
HIV/AIDS (2003)				
Number of infected adults (thousands)	..	..	..	..
Adult prevalence rate (percentage)	..	..	..	..
Spatial distribution				
Population density (per sq. km)	7	9	13	17
Urban population (percentage)	9	12	15	17
Annual urban growth rate (percentage)*	4.0	6.7	4.6	4.5
Annual rural growth rate (percentage)*	3.6	3.0	3.0	2.6
International migration				
International migrant stock				
Number of migrants (thousands)	5	4	4	3
Percentage of total population	2.5	1.6	1	0.7

* For the periods 1970-1975, 1980-1985, 1990-1995 and 2000-2005.

Government views and policies

Population policy variable	*1976*	*1986*	*1996*	*2005*
Population size and growth				
View on growth	Satisfactory	Satisfactory	Satisfactory	Satisfactory
Policy on growth	No intervention	No intervention	No intervention	No intervention
Population age structure				
Level of concern about				
Size of the working-age population	..	..	..	..
Ageing of the population	..	..	..	..
Fertility and family planning				
View on fertility level	Satisfactory	Satisfactory	Satisfactory	Satisfactory
Policy	No intervention	No intervention	No intervention	No intervention
Access to contraceptive methods	No support	Indirect support	Indirect support	Indirect support
Adolescent fertility				
Level of concern	..	..	..	..
Policies and programmes	..	..	..	..
Health and mortality				
View				
Expectation of life	Unacceptable	Unacceptable	Unacceptable	Unacceptable
Under-five mortality	..	..	..	Unacceptable
Maternal mortality	..	..	..	Unacceptable
Level of concern about HIV/AIDS	..	..	..	..
Measures implemented to control HIV/AIDS*	..	..	..	1,2
Grounds on which abortion is permitted**	..	..	1	1
Spatial distribution and internal migration				
View on spatial distribution	Major change desired	Major change desired	Minor change desired	Minor change desired
Policies on internal migration				
From rural to urban areas	..	..	..	..
From rural to rural areas	..	..	..	..
From urban to rural areas	..	..	..	..
From urban to urban areas	..	..	..	..
Into urban agglomerations	No intervention	No intervention	..	..
International migration				
Immigration				
View	Satisfactory	Too high	Satisfactory	Satisfactory
Policy	Maintain	Lower	No intervention	No intervention
Permanent settlement	..	..	..	..
Temporary workers	..	..	..	..
Highly skilled workers	..	..	..	..
Family reunification	..	..	..	..
Integration of non-nationals	..	..	..	..
Emigration				
View	Satisfactory	Too high	Satisfactory	Satisfactory
Policy	Maintain	Lower	No intervention	No intervention
Encouraging the return of nationals	No	..	..	..

* Measures implemented to control HIV/AIDS: (1) blood screening; (2) information/education campaigns; (3) access to antiretroviral treatment; (4) non-discriminatory policies; (5) promoting condom use.

** Grounds on which abortion is permitted: (1) to save the woman's life; (2) to preserve physical health; (3) to preserve mental health; (4) rape or incest; (5) foetal impairment; (6) economic or social reasons; (7) on request.

Population indicators

Indicator	*1975*	*1985*	*1995*	*2005*
Population size and growth				
Population size (thousands)	4 134	6 470	6 312	8 228
Annual growth rate (percentage)*	2.8	-0.1	-1.1	3.2
Population age structure				
Percentage of population under age 15	46	46	44	44
Percentage of population aged 60 or older	5	5	4	4
Fertility and family planning				
Total fertility (births per woman)*	7.3	7.2	6.6	6.4
Teenage fertility rate (per 1,000 women, aged 15 - 19)*	213	86	72	71
Percentage of births to women under age 20*	22	10	9	8
Percentage of births to women aged 35 or older*	14	23	20	20
Percentage of married women using contraception				
Modern methods	..	..	..	..
All methods	..	..	..	..
Health and mortality				
Life expectancy at birth (years)*				
Males	39	41	38	45
Females	43	45	41	47
Both sexes combined	41	43	40	46
Infant mortality rate (per 1,000 births)*	155	143	163	126
Mortality under age 5 (per 1,000 births)*	258	239	270	211
Maternal mortality ratio (per 100,000 births) (2000)	..	..	..	1 100
HIV/AIDS (2003)				
Number of infected adults (thousands)	..	..	..	..
Adult prevalence rate (percentage)	..	..	..	..
Spatial distribution				
Population density (per sq. km)	6	10	10	13
Urban population (percentage)	25	28	31	36
Annual urban growth rate (percentage)*	5.1	1.4	1.7	5.7
Annual rural growth rate (percentage)*	2.0	0.1	0.0	3.4
International migration				
International migrant stock				
Number of migrants (thousands)	14	775	18	282
Percentage of total population	0.3	12	0.3	3.4

* For the periods 1970-1975, 1980-1985, 1990-1995 and 2000-2005.

Government views and policies

Population policy variable	*1976*	*1986*	*1996*	*2005*
Population size and growth				
View on growth	Too high	Too high	Too high	Satisfactory
Policy on growth	Lower	Lower	Lower	Maintain
Population age structure				
Level of concern about				
Size of the working-age population	..	..	..	Major concern
Ageing of the population	..	..	..	Major concern
Fertility and family planning				
View on fertility level	Too high	Too high	Too high	Satisfactory
Policy	Lower	Lower	Lower	Maintain
Access to contraceptive methods	Direct support	Direct support	Direct support	Direct support
Adolescent fertility				
Level of concern	..	..	Major concern	Major concern
Policies and programmes	..	..	Yes	Yes
Health and mortality				
View				
Expectation of life	Unacceptable	Unacceptable	Unacceptable	Unacceptable
Under-five mortality	..	..	Unacceptable	Unacceptable
Maternal mortality	..	..	..	Unacceptable
Level of concern about HIV/AIDS	..	..	Major concern	Major concern
Measures implemented to control HIV/AIDS*	..	..	..	1,2,3,4,5
Grounds on which abortion is permitted**	..	..	1,2,3,4,5,6,7	1,2,3,4,5,6,7
Spatial distribution and internal migration				
View on spatial distribution	Minor change desired	Minor change desired	Major change desired	Major change desired
Policies on internal migration				
From rural to urban areas	..	..	..	Lower
From rural to rural areas	..	..	..	No intervention
From urban to rural areas	..	..	..	Raise
From urban to urban areas	..	..	..	Maintain
Into urban agglomerations	Lower	..	..	Lower
International migration				
Immigration				
View	Too low	Too high	Satisfactory	Too high
Policy	Raise	Lower	Maintain	Lower
Permanent settlement	..	..	..	Lower
Temporary workers	..	..	..	Maintain
Highly skilled workers	..	..	..	Maintain
Family reunification	..	..	..	Maintain
Integration of non-nationals	..	..	..	Yes
Emigration				
View	Satisfactory	Too high	Satisfactory	Too high
Policy	Maintain	Lower	No intervention	Lower
Encouraging the return of nationals	No	..	..	Yes

* Measures implemented to control HIV/AIDS: (1) blood screening; (2) information/education campaigns; (3) access to antiretroviral treatment; (4) non-discriminatory policies; (5) promoting condom use.
** Grounds on which abortion is permitted: (1) to save the woman's life; (2) to preserve physical health; (3) to preserve mental health; (4) rape or incest; (5) foetal impairment; (6) economic or social reasons; (7) on request.

Population indicators

Indicator	*1975*	*1985*	*1995*	*2005*
Population size and growth				
Population size (thousands)	25 854	33 178	41 894	47 432
Annual growth rate (percentage)*	2.6	2.5	2.6	0.8
Population age structure				
Percentage of population under age 15	42	40	36	33
Percentage of population aged 60 or older	5	5	5	7
Fertility and family planning				
Total fertility (births per woman)*	5.5	4.6	3.3	2.8
Teenage fertility rate (per 1,000 women, aged 15 - 19)*	76	94	91	71
Percentage of births to women under age 20*	10	15	17	15
Percentage of births to women aged 35 or older*	21	17	14	14
Percentage of married women using contraception				
Modern methods	35[a]	48[b]	55[c]	..
All methods	37[a]	50[b]	56[c]	..
Health and mortality				
Life expectancy at birth (years)*				
Males	51	55	58	47
Females	57	62	66	51
Both sexes combined	54	58	62	49
Infant mortality rate (per 1,000 births)*	77	60	46	43
Mortality under age 5 (per 1,000 births)*	109	83	61	74
Maternal mortality ratio (per 100,000 births) (2000)	..	..	..	230
HIV/AIDS (2003)				
Number of infected adults (thousands)	..	..	..	5 100
Adult prevalence rate (percentage)	..	..	..	21.5
Spatial distribution				
Population density (per sq. km)	21	27	34	39
Urban population (percentage)	48	48	53	58
Annual urban growth rate (percentage)*	2.7	2.6	3.6	1.4
Annual rural growth rate (percentage)*	2.5	2.4	0.6	-0.5
International migration				
International migrant stock				
Number of migrants (thousands)	962	1 815	1 098	1 106
Percentage of total population	3.7	5.5	2.6	2.3

* For the periods 1970-1975, 1980-1985, 1990-1995 and 2000-2005.
[a] For 1976.
[b] For 1988.
[c] For 1998.

Government views and policies

Population policy variable	*1976*	*1986*	*1996*	*2005*
Population size and growth				
View on growth	Satisfactory	Satisfactory	Satisfactory	Satisfactory
Policy on growth	No intervention	No intervention	No intervention	No intervention
Population age structure				
Level of concern about				
Size of the working-age population	..	..	..	Minor concern
Ageing of the population	..	..	..	Minor concern
Fertility and family planning				
View on fertility level	Satisfactory	Satisfactory	Satisfactory	Too low
Policy	No intervention	No intervention	No intervention	Raise
Access to contraceptive methods	Limits	Direct support	Direct support	Indirect support
Adolescent fertility				
Level of concern	..	..	..	Minor concern
Policies and programmes	..	..	..	Yes
Health and mortality				
View				
Expectation of life	Acceptable	Acceptable	Acceptable	Acceptable
Under-five mortality	..	..	..	Acceptable
Maternal mortality	..	..	..	Acceptable
Level of concern about HIV/AIDS	..	..	..	Major concern
Measures implemented to control HIV/AIDS*	..	..	..	1,2,3,4,5
Grounds on which abortion is permitted**	..	..	1,2,3,4,5	1,2,3,4,5
Spatial distribution and internal migration				
View on spatial distribution	Minor change desired	Minor change desired	Satisfactory	Satisfactory
Policies on internal migration				
From rural to urban areas	..	..	..	No intervention
From rural to rural areas	..	..	..	No intervention
From urban to rural areas	..	..	..	No intervention
From urban to urban areas	..	..	..	No intervention
Into urban agglomerations	..	No intervention	..	No intervention
International migration				
Immigration				
View	Satisfactory	Satisfactory	Satisfactory	Satisfactory
Policy	Maintain	Lower	Lower	Maintain
Permanent settlement	..	..	..	Maintain
Temporary workers	..	..	..	Maintain
Highly skilled workers	..	..	..	Maintain
Family reunification	..	..	..	Maintain
Integration of non-nationals	..	..	Yes	Yes
Emigration				
View	Too high	Too high	Satisfactory	Too high
Policy	Lower	Lower	Lower	Lower
Encouraging the return of nationals	..	..	Yes	Yes

* Measures implemented to control HIV/AIDS: (1) blood screening; (2) information/education campaigns; (3) access to antiretroviral treatment; (4) non-discriminatory policies; (5) promoting condom use.

** Grounds on which abortion is permitted: (1) to save the woman's life; (2) to preserve physical health; (3) to preserve mental health; (4) rape or incest; (5) foetal impairment; (6) economic or social reasons; (7) on request.

Population indicators

Indicator	*1975*	*1985*	*1995*	*2005*
Population size and growth				
Population size (thousands)	35 596	38 474	39 921	43 064
Annual growth rate (percentage)*	1.0	0.5	0.3	1.1
Population age structure				
Percentage of population under age 15	28	23	16	14
Percentage of population aged 60 or older	14	17	21	21
Fertility and family planning				
Total fertility (births per woman)*	2.9	1.9	1.3	1.3
Teenage fertility rate (per 1,000 women, aged 15 - 19)*	19	12	8	10
Percentage of births to women under age 20*	4	4	3	3
Percentage of births to women aged 35 or older*	17	15	15	21
Percentage of married women using contraception				
Modern methods	20[a]	38	67	..
All methods	51[a]	59	81	..
Health and mortality				
Life expectancy at birth (years)*				
Males	70	73	74	76
Females	76	79	81	83
Both sexes combined	73	76	77	79
Infant mortality rate (per 1,000 births)*	21	11	7	5
Mortality under age 5 (per 1,000 births)*	24	13	8	6
Maternal mortality ratio (per 100,000 births) (2000)	..	..	..	4
HIV/AIDS (2003)				
Number of infected adults (thousands)	..	..	..	130
Adult prevalence rate (percentage)	..	..	..	0.7
Spatial distribution				
Population density (per sq. km)	70	76	79	85
Urban population (percentage)	70	74	76	77
Annual urban growth rate (percentage)*	2.1	0.9	0.5	0.3
Annual rural growth rate (percentage)*	-1.1	-0.6	-0.1	-0.1
International migration				
International migrant stock				
Number of migrants (thousands)	300	406	1 009	4 790
Percentage of total population	0.8	1.1	2.5	11.1

* For the periods 1970-1975, 1980-1985, 1990-1995 and 2000-2005.
[a] For 1977.

Government views and policies

Population policy variable	*1976*	*1986*	*1996*	*2005*
Population size and growth				
View on growth	Too high	Too high	Too high	Too high
Policy on growth	Lower	Lower	Lower	Lower
Population age structure				
Level of concern about				
Size of the working-age population	..	..	..	..
Ageing of the population	..	..	..	Minor concern
Fertility and family planning				
View on fertility level	Too high	Too high	Too high	Satisfactory
Policy	Lower	Lower	Lower	Maintain
Access to contraceptive methods	Direct support	Direct support	Direct support	Direct support
Adolescent fertility				
Level of concern	..	..	Minor concern	Minor concern
Policies and programmes	..	..	Yes	Yes
Health and mortality				
View				
Expectation of life	Acceptable	Unacceptable	Unacceptable	Acceptable
Under-five mortality	..	..	Unacceptable	Unacceptable
Maternal mortality	..	..	..	Unacceptable
Level of concern about HIV/AIDS	..	..	Major concern	Major concern
Measures implemented to control HIV/AIDS*	..	..	..	1,2,3,4,5
Grounds on which abortion is permitted**	..	..	1	1
Spatial distribution and internal migration				
View on spatial distribution	Major change desired	Major change desired	Minor change desired	Minor change desired
Policies on internal migration				
From rural to urban areas	..	..	..	Raise
From rural to rural areas	..	..	..	..
From urban to rural areas	..	..	..	..
From urban to urban areas	..	..	..	Maintain
Into urban agglomerations	..	Lower	No intervention	Raise
International migration				
Immigration				
View	Satisfactory	Satisfactory	Satisfactory	Satisfactory
Policy	Maintain	Maintain	Maintain	Maintain
Permanent settlement	..	..	Maintain	Maintain
Temporary workers	..	..	Maintain	..
Highly skilled workers	..	..	..	Maintain
Family reunification	..	..	Maintain	..
Integration of non-nationals	..	..	Yes	..
Emigration				
View	Satisfactory	Satisfactory	Satisfactory	Too high
Policy	Maintain	Maintain	No intervention	Maintain
Encouraging the return of nationals	..	..	Yes	..

* Measures implemented to control HIV/AIDS: (1) blood screening; (2) information/education campaigns; (3) access to antiretroviral treatment; (4) non-discriminatory policies; (5) promoting condom use.

** Grounds on which abortion is permitted: (1) to save the woman's life; (2) to preserve physical health; (3) to preserve mental health; (4) rape or incest; (5) foetal impairment; (6) economic or social reasons; (7) on request.

Population indicators

Indicator	*1975*	*1985*	*1995*	*2005*
Population size and growth				
Population size (thousands)	14 042	16 437	18 872	20 743
Annual growth rate (percentage)*	2.0	1.5	1.2	0.9
Population age structure				
Percentage of population under age 15	38	34	29	24
Percentage of population aged 60 or older	6	7	9	11
Fertility and family planning				
Total fertility (births per woman)*	4.1	3.4	2.4	2.0
Teenage fertility rate (per 1,000 women, aged 15 - 19)*	41	46	37	20
Percentage of births to women under age 20*	8	9	9	6
Percentage of births to women aged 35 or older*	16	12	12	11
Percentage of married women using contraception				
Modern methods	20	41[a]	44[b]	50[c]
All methods	43	62[a]	66[b]	70[c]
Health and mortality				
Life expectancy at birth (years)*				
Males	62	67	69	71
Females	65	71	74	77
Both sexes combined	63	68	71	74
Infant mortality rate (per 1,000 births)*	56	34	23	17
Mortality under age 5 (per 1,000 births)*	75	41	28	20
Maternal mortality ratio (per 100,000 births) (2000)	..	..	..	92
HIV/AIDS (2003)				
Number of infected adults (thousands)	..	..	..	4
Adult prevalence rate (percentage)	..	..	..	<0.1
Spatial distribution				
Population density (per sq. km)	214	251	288	316
Urban population (percentage)	22	21	21	21
Annual urban growth rate (percentage)*	2.0	1.3	1.0	0.7
Annual rural growth rate (percentage)*	1.8	1.5	1.1	0.8
International migration				
International migrant stock				
Number of migrants (thousands)	714	533	428	368
Percentage of total population	5.1	3.2	2.3	1.8

* For the periods 1970-1975, 1980-1985, 1990-1995 and 2000-2005.
[a] For 1987.
[b] For 1993.
[c] For 2000.

Government views and policies

Population policy variable	*1976*	*1986*	*1996*	*2005*
Population size and growth				
View on growth	Satisfactory	Satisfactory	Too high	Too high
Policy on growth	No intervention	No intervention	Lower	Lower
Population age structure				
Level of concern about				
Size of the working-age population	..	..	..	..
Ageing of the population	..	..	..	Minor concern
Fertility and family planning				
View on fertility level	Satisfactory	Satisfactory	Too high	Too high
Policy	No intervention	No intervention	Lower	Lower
Access to contraceptive methods	Direct support	Direct support	Direct support	Direct support
Adolescent fertility				
Level of concern	..	..	Not a concern	Not a concern
Policies and programmes	..	..	No	No
Health and mortality				
View				
Expectation of life	Unacceptable	Unacceptable	Unacceptable	Unacceptable
Under-five mortality	..	..	Unacceptable	Unacceptable
Maternal mortality	..	..	..	Unacceptable
Level of concern about HIV/AIDS	..	..	Major concern	Major concern
Measures implemented to control HIV/AIDS*	..	..	..	1,2
Grounds on which abortion is permitted**	..	..	1,4	1,4
Spatial distribution and internal migration				
View on spatial distribution	Major change desired	Major change desired	Major change desired	Major change desired
Policies on internal migration				
From rural to urban areas	..	..	..	..
From rural to rural areas	..	..	..	..
From urban to rural areas	..	..	..	..
From urban to urban areas	..	..	..	..
Into urban agglomerations	Lower	..	Lower	..
International migration				
Immigration				
View	Too low	Too high	Satisfactory	Satisfactory
Policy	Raise	Lower	Raise	Maintain
Permanent settlement	..	..	Raise	..
Temporary workers	..	..	Raise	Maintain
Highly skilled workers	..	..	..	..
Family reunification	..	..	Raise	..
Integration of non-nationals	..	..	No	..
Emigration				
View	Satisfactory	Satisfactory	Too high	Too high
Policy	Maintain	Maintain	Lower	Lower
Encouraging the return of nationals	Yes	..	Yes	..

* Measures implemented to control HIV/AIDS: (1) blood screening; (2) information/education campaigns; (3) access to antiretroviral treatment; (4) non-discriminatory policies; (5) promoting condom use.

** Grounds on which abortion is permitted: (1) to save the woman's life; (2) to preserve physical health; (3) to preserve mental health; (4) rape or incest; (5) foetal impairment; (6) economic or social reasons; (7) on request.

Population indicators

Indicator	*1975*	*1985*	*1995*	*2005*
Population size and growth				
Population size (thousands)	17 056	23 382	29 352	36 233
Annual growth rate (percentage)*	3.0	3.2	2.4	1.9
Population age structure				
Percentage of population under age 15	45	45	42	39
Percentage of population aged 60 or older	5	5	5	6
Fertility and family planning				
Total fertility (births per woman)*	6.7	6.3	5.4	4.4
Teenage fertility rate (per 1,000 women, aged 15 - 19)*	126	105	72	55
Percentage of births to women under age 20*	13	12	10	9
Percentage of births to women aged 35 or older*	16	18	17	14
Percentage of married women using contraception				
Modern methods	4[a]	6[b]	7[c]	..
All methods	5[a]	9[b]	10[c]	..
Health and mortality				
Life expectancy at birth (years)*				
Males	44	49	52	55
Females	47	52	55	58
Both sexes combined	45	50	53	56
Infant mortality rate (per 1,000 births)*	131	106	90	72
Mortality under age 5 (per 1,000 births)*	220	181	151	119
Maternal mortality ratio (per 100,000 births) (2000)	..	..	..	590
HIV/AIDS (2003)				
Number of infected adults (thousands)	..	..	..	380
Adult prevalence rate (percentage)	..	..	..	2.3
Spatial distribution				
Population density (per sq. km)	7	9	12	14
Urban population (percentage)	19	22	31	41
Annual urban growth rate (percentage)*	5.8	5.3	5.7	4.6
Annual rural growth rate (percentage)*	2.3	2.4	1.0	0.7
International migration				
International migrant stock				
Number of migrants (thousands)	322	1 408	1 111	639
Percentage of total population	1.9	6	3.8	1.8

* For the periods 1970-1975, 1980-1985, 1990-1995 and 2000-2005.
[a] For 1979.
[b] For 1989.
[c] For 1992/1993.

Government views and policies

Population policy variable	*1976*	*1986*	*1996*	*2005*
Population size and growth				
View on growth	Satisfactory	Satisfactory	Satisfactory	Satisfactory
Policy on growth	No intervention	No intervention	No intervention	Maintain
Population age structure				
Level of concern about				
Size of the working-age population	..	..	..	Not a concern
Ageing of the population	..	..	..	Minor concern
Fertility and family planning				
View on fertility level	Satisfactory	Satisfactory	Satisfactory	Satisfactory
Policy	No intervention	No intervention	No intervention	Maintain
Access to contraceptive methods	No support	Direct support	Direct support	Indirect support
Adolescent fertility				
Level of concern	..	..	Major concern	Major concern
Policies and programmes	..	..	No	Yes
Health and mortality				
View				
Expectation of life	Unacceptable	Unacceptable	Acceptable	Acceptable
Under-five mortality	..	..	..	Unacceptable
Maternal mortality	..	..	..	Unacceptable
Level of concern about HIV/AIDS	..	..	Major concern	Major concern
Measures implemented to control HIV/AIDS*	..	..	..	1,2,3,5
Grounds on which abortion is permitted**	..	..	1	1
Spatial distribution and internal migration				
View on spatial distribution	Major change desired	Major change desired	Major change desired	Major change desired
Policies on internal migration				
From rural to urban areas	..	..	..	Lower
From rural to rural areas	..	..	..	Raise
From urban to rural areas	..	..	..	Maintain
From urban to urban areas	..	..	..	No intervention
Into urban agglomerations	..	..	No intervention	Lower
International migration				
Immigration				
View	Satisfactory	Satisfactory	Too high	Too low
Policy	Maintain	Maintain	Lower	Raise
Permanent settlement	..	..	No intervention	Raise
Temporary workers	..	..	Lower	No intervention
Highly skilled workers	..	..	..	Raise
Family reunification	..	..	Maintain	No intervention
Integration of non-nationals	..	..	No	Yes
Emigration				
View	Too high	Too high	Too high	Too high
Policy	Lower	Lower	Lower	Lower
Encouraging the return of nationals	..	..	Yes	No

* Measures implemented to control HIV/AIDS: (1) blood screening; (2) information/education campaigns; (3) access to antiretroviral treatment; (4) non-discriminatory policies; (5) promoting condom use.

** Grounds on which abortion is permitted: (1) to save the woman's life; (2) to preserve physical health; (3) to preserve mental health; (4) rape or incest; (5) foetal impairment; (6) economic or social reasons; (7) on request.

Population indicators

Indicator	*1975*	*1985*	*1995*	*2005*
Population size and growth				
Population size (thousands)	364	383	415	449
Annual growth rate (percentage)*	-0.4	1.5	0.6	0.7
Population age structure				
Percentage of population under age 15	48	38	34	30
Percentage of population aged 60 or older	6	6	8	9
Fertility and family planning				
Total fertility (births per woman)*	5.3	3.7	2.6	2.6
Teenage fertility rate (per 1,000 women, aged 15 - 19)*	116	81	50	45
Percentage of births to women under age 20*	18	17	11	11
Percentage of births to women aged 35 or older*	9	7	8	11
Percentage of married women using contraception				
Modern methods	..	..	..	41[a]
All methods	..	..	..	42[a]
Health and mortality				
Life expectancy at birth (years)*				
Males	62	65	65	66
Females	67	69	71	73
Both sexes combined	64	67	68	69
Infant mortality rate (per 1,000 births)*	49	40	34	26
Mortality under age 5 (per 1,000 births)*	61	50	40	31
Maternal mortality ratio (per 100,000 births) (2000)	..	..	..	110
HIV/AIDS (2003)				
Number of infected adults (thousands)	..	..	..	5
Adult prevalence rate (percentage)	..	..	..	1.7
Spatial distribution				
Population density (per sq. km)	2	2	3	3
Urban population (percentage)	49	60	70	77
Annual urban growth rate (percentage)*	1.1	3.4	1.8	1.6
Annual rural growth rate (percentage)*	-1.8	-1.0	-2.6	-1.8
International migration				
International migrant stock				
Number of migrants (thousands)	14	10	7	5
Percentage of total population	3.8	2.6	1.8	1.2

* For the periods 1970-1975, 1980-1985, 1990-1995 and 2000-2005.
[a] For 2000.

Government views and policies

Population policy variable	*1976*	*1986*	*1996*	*2005*
Population size and growth				
View on growth	Too high	Too high	Too high	Too high
Policy on growth	Lower	No intervention	Lower	No intervention
Population age structure				
Level of concern about				
Size of the working-age population	..	..	..	Minor concern
Ageing of the population	..	..	..	Minor concern
Fertility and family planning				
View on fertility level	Too high	Too high	Too high	Too high
Policy	Lower	Lower	Lower	Lower
Access to contraceptive methods	Direct support	Direct support	Direct support	Direct support
Adolescent fertility				
Level of concern	..	..	..	Minor concern
Policies and programmes	..	..	..	Yes
Health and mortality				
View				
Expectation of life	Unacceptable	Unacceptable	Unacceptable	Unacceptable
Under-five mortality	..	..	..	Unacceptable
Maternal mortality	..	..	..	Unacceptable
Level of concern about HIV/AIDS	..	..	..	Major concern
Measures implemented to control HIV/AIDS*	..	..	..	1,2,3,5
Grounds on which abortion is permitted**	..	..	1	1,2,3,5
Spatial distribution and internal migration				
View on spatial distribution	Major change desired	Major change desired	Minor change desired	Major change desired
Policies on internal migration				
From rural to urban areas	..	..	..	Lower
From rural to rural areas	..	..	..	Raise
From urban to rural areas	..	..	..	..
From urban to urban areas	..	..	..	Lower
Into urban agglomerations	No intervention	No intervention	..	Lower
International migration				
Immigration				
View	Satisfactory	Satisfactory	Satisfactory	Satisfactory
Policy	Maintain	Maintain	Maintain	Maintain
Permanent settlement	..	..	..	..
Temporary workers	..	..	..	..
Highly skilled workers	..	..	..	..
Family reunification	..	..	..	..
Integration of non-nationals	..	..	..	..
Emigration				
View	Satisfactory	Satisfactory	Satisfactory	Satisfactory
Policy	Maintain	Maintain	No intervention	No intervention
Encouraging the return of nationals	No	..	..	..

* Measures implemented to control HIV/AIDS: (1) blood screening; (2) information/education campaigns; (3) access to antiretroviral treatment; (4) non-discriminatory policies; (5) promoting condom use.

** Grounds on which abortion is permitted: (1) to save the woman's life; (2) to preserve physical health; (3) to preserve mental health; (4) rape or incest; (5) foetal impairment; (6) economic or social reasons; (7) on request.

Population indicators

Indicator	*1975*	*1985*	*1995*	*2005*
Population size and growth				
Population size (thousands)	528	717	953	1 032
Annual growth rate (percentage)*	3.0	3.0	1.9	0.2
Population age structure				
Percentage of population under age 15	48	49	46	41
Percentage of population aged 60 or older	4	4	4	5
Fertility and family planning				
Total fertility (births per woman)*	6.9	6.5	5.3	4.0
Teenage fertility rate (per 1,000 women, aged 15 - 19)*	165	114	56	39
Percentage of births to women under age 20*	19	13	8	9
Percentage of births to women aged 35 or older*	15	16	19	15
Percentage of married women using contraception				
Modern methods	..	17[a]	..	26[b]
All methods	..	20[a]	..	28[b]
Health and mortality				
Life expectancy at birth (years)*				
Males	48	54	52	32
Females	52	57	59	33
Both sexes combined	50	56	56	33
Infant mortality rate (per 1,000 births)*	124	91	74	73
Mortality under age 5 (per 1,000 births)*	182	136	109	143
Maternal mortality ratio (per 100,000 births) (2000)	..	..	..	370
HIV/AIDS (2003)				
Number of infected adults (thousands)	..	..	..	200
Adult prevalence rate (percentage)	..	..	..	38.8
Spatial distribution				
Population density (per sq. km)	30	41	55	59
Urban population (percentage)	14	22	23	24
Annual urban growth rate (percentage)*	10.3	7.3	2.2	1.4
Annual rural growth rate (percentage)*	2.0	2.3	2.0	0.6
International migration				
International migrant stock				
Number of migrants (thousands)	28	41	38	45
Percentage of total population	5.3	5.7	4	4.4

* For the periods 1970-1975, 1980-1985, 1990-1995 and 2000-2005.
[a] For 1988.
[b] For 2000.

Government views and policies

Population policy variable	*1976*	*1986*	*1996*	*2005*
Population size and growth				
View on growth	Satisfactory	Satisfactory	Satisfactory	Satisfactory
Policy on growth	No intervention	No intervention	No intervention	No intervention
Population age structure				
Level of concern about				
Size of the working-age population	..	..	..	Major concern
Ageing of the population	..	..	..	Major concern
Fertility and family planning				
View on fertility level	Satisfactory	Too low	Satisfactory	Satisfactory
Policy	No intervention	No intervention	No intervention	No intervention
Access to contraceptive methods	Direct support	Direct support	Direct support	Direct support
Adolescent fertility				
Level of concern	..	..	Minor concern	Minor concern
Policies and programmes	..	..	Yes	Yes
Health and mortality				
View				
Expectation of life	Acceptable	Acceptable	Acceptable	Acceptable
Under-five mortality	..	..	Acceptable	Acceptable
Maternal mortality	..	..	..	Acceptable
Level of concern about HIV/AIDS	..	..	Major concern	Major concern
Measures implemented to control HIV/AIDS*	..	..	..	1,2,3,4,5
Grounds on which abortion is permitted**	..	..	1,2,3,4,5,6,7	1,2,3,4,5,6,7
Spatial distribution and internal migration				
View on spatial distribution	Satisfactory	Minor change desired	Minor change desired	Satisfactory
Policies on internal migration				
From rural to urban areas	..	..	..	No intervention
From rural to rural areas	..	..	..	No intervention
From urban to rural areas	..	..	..	No intervention
From urban to urban areas	..	..	..	No intervention
Into urban agglomerations	Lower	Lower	No intervention	No intervention
International migration				
Immigration				
View	Too high	Satisfactory	Satisfactory	Satisfactory
Policy	Lower	Lower	Lower	Maintain
Permanent settlement	..	..	Lower	Maintain
Temporary workers	..	..	Maintain	Maintain
Highly skilled workers	..	..	..	Maintain
Family reunification	..	..	Maintain	Maintain
Integration of non-nationals	..	..	Yes	Yes
Emigration				
View	Satisfactory	Satisfactory	Satisfactory	Satisfactory
Policy	Maintain	Maintain	No intervention	No intervention
Encouraging the return of nationals	No	..	No	No

* Measures implemented to control HIV/AIDS: (1) blood screening; (2) information/education campaigns; (3) access to antiretroviral treatment; (4) non-discriminatory policies; (5) promoting condom use.

** Grounds on which abortion is permitted: (1) to save the woman's life; (2) to preserve physical health; (3) to preserve mental health; (4) rape or incest; (5) foetal impairment; (6) economic or social reasons; (7) on request.

Population indicators

Indicator	*1975*	*1985*	*1995*	*2005*
Population size and growth				
Population size (thousands)	7 538	10 836	14 755	19 043
Annual growth rate (percentage)*	3.3	3.8	2.8	2.5
Population age structure				
Percentage of population under age 15	49	49	45	37
Percentage of population aged 60 or older	4	4	4	5
Fertility and family planning				
Total fertility (births per woman)*	7.5	7.3	4.6	3.5
Teenage fertility rate (per 1,000 women, aged 15 - 19)*	125	120	57	36
Percentage of births to women under age 20*	14	14	10	8
Percentage of births to women aged 35 or older*	19	17	13	11
Percentage of married women using contraception				
Modern methods	15[a]	..	28[b]	..
All methods	20[a]	..	40[b]	..
Health and mortality				
Life expectancy at birth (years)*				
Males	56	63	68	71
Females	59	66	71	75
Both sexes combined	57	65	69	73
Infant mortality rate (per 1,000 births)*	83	50	31	18
Mortality under age 5 (per 1,000 births)*	117	66	37	21
Maternal mortality ratio (per 100,000 births) (2000)	..	..	..	160
HIV/AIDS (2003)				
Number of infected adults (thousands)	..	..	..	<1
Adult prevalence rate (percentage)	..	..	..	<0.1
Spatial distribution				
Population density (per sq. km)	41	59	80	103
Urban population (percentage)	45	48	50	50
Annual urban growth rate (percentage)*	4.1	4.2	3.1	2.5
Annual rural growth rate (percentage)*	2.7	3.2	2.4	2.3
International migration				
International migrant stock				
Number of migrants (thousands)	447	621	801	985
Percentage of total population	5.9	5.7	5.4	5.2

* For the periods 1970-1975, 1980-1985, 1990-1995 and 2000-2005.
[a] For 1978.
[b] For 1993.

Government views and policies

Population policy variable	*1976*	*1986*	*1996*	*2005*
Population size and growth				
View on growth	..	..	Satisfactory	Too high
Policy on growth	..	..	No intervention	Lower
Population age structure				
Level of concern about				
Size of the working-age population	..	..	..	Major concern
Ageing of the population	..	..	..	..
Fertility and family planning				
View on fertility level	..	..	Too high	Too high
Policy	..	..	Lower	Lower
Access to contraceptive methods	..	..	Direct support	Direct support
Adolescent fertility				
Level of concern	..	..	Not a concern	Minor concern
Policies and programmes	..	..	No	Yes
Health and mortality				
View				
Expectation of life	..	..	Acceptable	Unacceptable
Under-five mortality	..	..	Unacceptable	Unacceptable
Maternal mortality	..	..	..	Unacceptable
Level of concern about HIV/AIDS	..	..	Not a concern	Major concern
Measures implemented to control HIV/AIDS*	..	..	..	1,2,4,5
Grounds on which abortion is permitted**	..	..	1,2,3,4,5,6,7	1,2,3,4,5,6,7
Spatial distribution and internal migration				
View on spatial distribution	..	..	Minor change desired	Minor change desired
Policies on internal migration				
From rural to urban areas	..	..	..	No intervention
From rural to rural areas	..	..	..	..
From urban to rural areas	..	..	..	..
From urban to urban areas	..	..	..	..
Into urban agglomerations	..	..	No intervention	No intervention
International migration				
Immigration				
View	..	..	Satisfactory	Satisfactory
Policy	..	..	No intervention	Maintain
Permanent settlement	..	..	No intervention	Maintain
Temporary workers	..	..	No intervention	Maintain
Highly skilled workers	..	..	..	..
Family reunification	..	..	No intervention	..
Integration of non-nationals	..	..	Yes	..
Emigration				
View	..	..	Too high	Too high
Policy	..	..	No intervention	No intervention
Encouraging the return of nationals	..	..	Yes	Yes

* Measures implemented to control HIV/AIDS: (1) blood screening; (2) information/education campaigns; (3) access to antiretroviral treatment; (4) non-discriminatory policies; (5) promoting condom use.

** Grounds on which abortion is permitted: (1) to save the woman's life; (2) to preserve physical health; (3) to preserve mental health; (4) rape or incest; (5) foetal impairment; (6) economic or social reasons; (7) on request.

Population indicators

Indicator	*1975*	*1985*	*1995*	*2005*
Population size and growth				
Population size (thousands)	3 442	4 567	5 770	6 507
Annual growth rate (percentage)*	3.1	2.9	1.7	1.1
Population age structure				
Percentage of population under age 15	45	43	44	39
Percentage of population aged 60 or older	7	6	6	5
Fertility and family planning				
Total fertility (births per woman)*	6.8	5.5	4.9	3.8
Teenage fertility rate (per 1,000 women, aged 15 - 19)*	57	47	41	32
Percentage of births to women under age 20*	7	6	6	6
Percentage of births to women aged 35 or older*	16	9	11	12
Percentage of married women using contraception				
Modern methods	..	..	..	27[a]
All methods	..	..	..	34[a]
Health and mortality				
Life expectancy at birth (years)*				
Males	58	60	60	61
Females	63	65	66	66
Both sexes combined	61	63	63	64
Infant mortality rate (per 1,000 births)*	125	107	91	89
Mortality under age 5 (per 1,000 births)*	170	142	119	116
Maternal mortality ratio (per 100,000 births) (2000)	..	..	..	100
HIV/AIDS (2003)				
Number of infected adults (thousands)	..	..	..	<1
Adult prevalence rate (percentage)	..	..	..	<0.1
Spatial distribution				
Population density (per sq. km)	24	32	40	45
Urban population (percentage)	36	33	29	24
Annual urban growth rate (percentage)*	2.4	2.3	-0.4	-0.4
Annual rural growth rate (percentage)*	3.6	3.2	2.4	1.3
International migration				
International migrant stock				
Number of migrants (thousands)	..	..	305	306
Percentage of total population	..	..	5.3	4.7

* For the periods 1970-1975, 1980-1985, 1990-1995 and 2000-2005.
[a] For 2000.

Government views and policies

Population policy variable	*1976*	*1986*	*1996*	*2005*
Population size and growth				
View on growth	Too high	Satisfactory	Too high	Too low
Policy on growth	Lower	Lower	Lower	Maintain
Population age structure				
Level of concern about				
Size of the working-age population	..	..	..	Major concern
Ageing of the population	..	..	..	Major concern
Fertility and family planning				
View on fertility level	Too high	Too high	Too high	Satisfactory
Policy	Lower	Lower	Lower	Maintain
Access to contraceptive methods	Direct support	Direct support	Direct support	Direct support
Adolescent fertility				
Level of concern	..	..	Major concern	Major concern
Policies and programmes	..	..	Yes	Yes
Health and mortality				
View				
Expectation of life	Acceptable	Acceptable	Unacceptable	Acceptable
Under-five mortality	..	..	Unacceptable	Unacceptable
Maternal mortality	..	..	..	Unacceptable
Level of concern about HIV/AIDS	..	..	Major concern	Major concern
Measures implemented to control HIV/AIDS*	..	..	..	1,2,3,4,5
Grounds on which abortion is permitted**	..	..	1,2,4,5	1,2,3,4
Spatial distribution and internal migration				
View on spatial distribution	Major change desired	Minor change desired	Major change desired	Major change desired
Policies on internal migration				
From rural to urban areas	..	..	..	Lower
From rural to rural areas	..	..	..	No intervention
From urban to rural areas	..	..	..	No intervention
From urban to urban areas	..	..	..	No intervention
Into urban agglomerations	..	Lower	Lower	Lower
International migration				
Immigration				
View	Satisfactory	Too high	Satisfactory	Satisfactory
Policy	Maintain	Lower	Lower	Maintain
Permanent settlement	..	..	..	Maintain
Temporary workers	..	..	..	Maintain
Highly skilled workers	..	..	..	Maintain
Family reunification	..	..	..	Lower
Integration of non-nationals	..	..	..	No
Emigration				
View	Satisfactory	Satisfactory	Satisfactory	Too low
Policy	Maintain	Raise	Maintain	Raise
Encouraging the return of nationals	..	..	..	No

* Measures implemented to control HIV/AIDS: (1) blood screening; (2) information/education campaigns; (3) access to antiretroviral treatment; (4) non-discriminatory policies; (5) promoting condom use.

** Grounds on which abortion is permitted: (1) to save the woman's life; (2) to preserve physical health; (3) to preserve mental health; (4) rape or incest; (5) foetal impairment; (6) economic or social reasons; (7) on request.

Population indicators

Indicator	*1975*	*1985*	*1995*	*2005*
Population size and growth				
Population size (thousands)	41 292	50 612	58 336	64 233
Annual growth rate (percentage)*	2.6	1.8	1.3	0.9
Population age structure				
Percentage of population under age 15	43	36	28	24
Percentage of population aged 60 or older	5	6	8	10
Fertility and family planning				
Total fertility (births per woman)*	5.0	3.1	2.1	1.9
Teenage fertility rate (per 1,000 women, aged 15 - 19)*	68	66	55	49
Percentage of births to women under age 20*	11	15	15	13
Percentage of births to women aged 35 or older*	18	11	9	11
Percentage of married women using contraception				
Modern methods	30	59[a]	70[b]	..
All methods	33	59[a]	72[b]	..
Health and mortality				
Life expectancy at birth (years)*				
Males	59	63	66	66
Females	64	67	72	74
Both sexes combined	61	65	69	70
Infant mortality rate (per 1,000 births)*	66	47	29	20
Mortality under age 5 (per 1,000 births)*	90	63	37	25
Maternal mortality ratio (per 100,000 births) (2000)	..	..	..	44
HIV/AIDS (2003)				
Number of infected adults (thousands)	..	..	..	560
Adult prevalence rate (percentage)	..	..	..	1.5
Spatial distribution				
Population density (per sq. km)	80	99	114	125
Urban population (percentage)	24	28	30	32
Annual urban growth rate (percentage)*	5.2	2.7	1.8	1.9
Annual rural growth rate (percentage)*	1.9	1.4	1.0	0.6
International migration				
International migrant stock				
Number of migrants (thousands)	388	436	568	1 050
Percentage of total population	0.9	0.9	1	1.6

* For the periods 1970-1975, 1980-1985, 1990-1995 and 2000-2005.
[a] For 1984.
[b] For 1996/1997.

Government views and policies

Population policy variable	*1976*	*1986*	*1996*	*2005*
Population size and growth				
View on growth	..	..	Too high	Satisfactory
Policy on growth	..	..	Lower	No intervention
Population age structure				
Level of concern about				
Size of the working-age population	..	..	..	Major concern
Ageing of the population	..	..	..	Major concern
Fertility and family planning				
View on fertility level	..	..	Too high	Satisfactory
Policy	..	..	Lower	No intervention
Access to contraceptive methods	..	..	Direct support	Direct support
Adolescent fertility				
Level of concern	..	..	Major concern	..
Policies and programmes	..	..	Yes	..
Health and mortality				
View				
Expectation of life	..	..	Unacceptable	Unacceptable
Under-five mortality	..	..	Unacceptable	Unacceptable
Maternal mortality	..	..	..	Unacceptable
Level of concern about HIV/AIDS	..	..	Minor concern	Major concern
Measures implemented to control HIV/AIDS*	..	..	..	1
Grounds on which abortion is permitted**	..	..	1,2,3,4,5,6,7	1,2,3,4,5,6,7
Spatial distribution and internal migration				
View on spatial distribution	..	..	Minor change desired	Major change desired
Policies on internal migration				
From rural to urban areas	..	..	..	Lower
From rural to rural areas	..	..	..	..
From urban to rural areas	..	..	..	..
From urban to urban areas	..	..	..	..
Into urban agglomerations	..	..	Lower	Lower
International migration				
Immigration				
View	..	..	Too high	Satisfactory
Policy	..	..	Lower	Maintain
Permanent settlement	..	..	Lower	Maintain
Temporary workers	..	..	Lower	Maintain
Highly skilled workers	..	..	..	..
Family reunification	..	..	Lower	Maintain
Integration of non-nationals	..	..	Yes	No
Emigration				
View	..	..	Too high	Too high
Policy	..	..	Lower	Lower
Encouraging the return of nationals	..	..	Yes	No

* Measures implemented to control HIV/AIDS: (1) blood screening; (2) information/education campaigns; (3) access to antiretroviral treatment; (4) non-discriminatory policies; (5) promoting condom use.

** Grounds on which abortion is permitted: (1) to save the woman's life; (2) to preserve physical health; (3) to preserve mental health; (4) rape or incest; (5) foetal impairment; (6) economic or social reasons; (7) on request.

Population indicators

Indicator	*1975*	*1985*	*1995*	*2005*
Population size and growth				
Population size (thousands)	1 676	1 828	1 963	2 034
Annual growth rate (percentage)*	1.3	0.4	0.6	0.2
Population age structure				
Percentage of population under age 15	31	27	25	20
Percentage of population aged 60 or older	9	10	13	15
Fertility and family planning				
Total fertility (births per woman)*	3.0	2.3	1.9	1.5
Teenage fertility rate (per 1,000 women, aged 15 - 19)*	55	43	36	25
Percentage of births to women under age 20*	11	10	10	8
Percentage of births to women aged 35 or older*	4	4	5	6
Percentage of married women using contraception				
Modern methods	..	..	..	..
All methods	..	..	..	..
Health and mortality				
Life expectancy at birth (years)*				
Males	66	68	69	71
Females	69	72	74	76
Both sexes combined	67	70	72	74
Infant mortality rate (per 1,000 births)*	74	45	27	16
Mortality under age 5 (per 1,000 births)*	85	52	30	18
Maternal mortality ratio (per 100,000 births) (2000)	..	..	..	23
HIV/AIDS (2003)				
Number of infected adults (thousands)	..	..	..	<1
Adult prevalence rate (percentage)	..	..	..	<0.1
Spatial distribution				
Population density (per sq. km)	65	71	76	79
Urban population (percentage)	51	56	60	60
Annual urban growth rate (percentage)*	2.8	1.2	1.2	0.6
Annual rural growth rate (percentage)*	0.0	-0.6	-0.4	0.4
International migration				
International migrant stock				
Number of migrants (thousands)	..	..	114	121
Percentage of total population	..	..	5.8	6

* For the periods 1970-1975, 1980-1985, 1990-1995 and 2000-2005.

Government views and policies

Population policy variable	*1976*	*1986*	*1996*	*2005*
Population size and growth				
View on growth	Satisfactory	Satisfactory	Too high	Too high
Policy on growth	No intervention	Maintain	No intervention	Lower
Population age structure				
Level of concern about				
Size of the working-age population	..	..	..	..
Ageing of the population	..	..	..	Minor concern
Fertility and family planning				
View on fertility level	Satisfactory	Satisfactory	Satisfactory	Too high
Policy	No intervention	Maintain	Maintain	Lower
Access to contraceptive methods	Indirect support	Direct support	Direct support	Direct support
Adolescent fertility				
Level of concern	..	..	Major concern	Minor concern
Policies and programmes	..	..	No	Yes
Health and mortality				
View				
Expectation of life	Unacceptable	Unacceptable	Unacceptable	Unacceptable
Under-five mortality	..	..	Unacceptable	Unacceptable
Maternal mortality	..	..	..	Unacceptable
Level of concern about HIV/AIDS	..	..	Major concern	Major concern
Measures implemented to control HIV/AIDS*	..	..	..	1,2,3,4,5
Grounds on which abortion is permitted**	..	..	1	1
Spatial distribution and internal migration				
View on spatial distribution	Major change desired	Major change desired	Major change desired	Satisfactory
Policies on internal migration				
From rural to urban areas	..	..	..	No intervention
From rural to rural areas	..	..	..	No intervention
From urban to rural areas	..	..	..	No intervention
From urban to urban areas	..	..	..	No intervention
Into urban agglomerations	No intervention	..	No intervention	No intervention
International migration				
Immigration				
View	Satisfactory	Satisfactory	Satisfactory	Satisfactory
Policy	Maintain	Maintain	No intervention	No intervention
Permanent settlement	..	..	No intervention	No intervention
Temporary workers	..	..	No intervention	No intervention
Highly skilled workers	..	..	..	No intervention
Family reunification	..	..	No intervention	No intervention
Integration of non-nationals	..	..	No	Yes
Emigration				
View	Satisfactory	Satisfactory	Satisfactory	Satisfactory
Policy	Maintain	Maintain	No intervention	No intervention
Encouraging the return of nationals	No	..	No	..

* Measures implemented to control HIV/AIDS: (1) blood screening; (2) information/education campaigns; (3) access to antiretroviral treatment; (4) non-discriminatory policies; (5) promoting condom use.
** Grounds on which abortion is permitted: (1) to save the woman's life; (2) to preserve physical health; (3) to preserve mental health; (4) rape or incest; (5) foetal impairment; (6) economic or social reasons; (7) on request.

Population indicators

Indicator	*1975*	*1985*	*1995*	*2005*
Population size and growth				
Population size (thousands)	2 446	3 355	4 512	6 145
Annual growth rate (percentage)*	2.7	3.7	2.6	2.7
Population age structure				
Percentage of population under age 15	46	47	46	43
Percentage of population aged 60 or older	5	5	5	5
Fertility and family planning				
Total fertility (births per woman)*	7.1	6.9	6.2	5.4
Teenage fertility rate (per 1,000 women, aged 15 - 19)*	154	148	127	104
Percentage of births to women under age 20*	16	16	16	15
Percentage of births to women aged 35 or older*	18	17	17	15
Percentage of married women using contraception				
Modern methods	..	3[a]	..	9[b]
All methods	..	12[a]	..	26[b]
Health and mortality				
Life expectancy at birth (years)*				
Males	48	54	56	52
Females	51	57	60	56
Both sexes combined	50	56	58	54
Infant mortality rate (per 1,000 births)*	134	110	99	93
Mortality under age 5 (per 1,000 births)*	218	170	148	137
Maternal mortality ratio (per 100,000 births) (2000)	..	..	..	570
HIV/AIDS (2003)				
Number of infected adults (thousands)	..	..	..	96
Adult prevalence rate (percentage)	..	..	..	4.1
Spatial distribution				
Population density (per sq. km)	43	59	79	108
Urban population (percentage)	16	27	31	36
Annual urban growth rate (percentage)*	6.7	6.3	3.8	4.0
Annual rural growth rate (percentage)*	1.6	2.4	1.6	1.4
International migration				
International migrant stock				
Number of migrants (thousands)	149	156	169	183
Percentage of total population	6.1	4.7	3.8	3

* For the periods 1970-1975, 1980-1985, 1990-1995 and 2000-2005.
[a] For 1988.
[b] For 2000.

Government views and policies

Population policy variable	*1976*	*1986*	*1996*	*2005*
Population size and growth				
View on growth	Too high	Too high	Too low	Too low
Policy on growth	Lower	Lower	No intervention	No intervention
Population age structure				
Level of concern about				
Size of the working-age population	..	..	..	Minor concern
Ageing of the population	..	..	..	..
Fertility and family planning				
View on fertility level	Too high	Too high	Satisfactory	Satisfactory
Policy	Lower	Lower	Maintain	Maintain
Access to contraceptive methods	Direct support	Direct support	Direct support	Direct support
Adolescent fertility				
Level of concern	..	..	Minor concern	Minor concern
Policies and programmes	..	..	No	No
Health and mortality				
View				
Expectation of life	Unacceptable	Unacceptable	Unacceptable	Unacceptable
Under-five mortality	..	..	..	Unacceptable
Maternal mortality	..	..	..	Unacceptable
Level of concern about HIV/AIDS	..	..	Major concern	Major concern
Measures implemented to control HIV/AIDS*	..	..	..	1
Grounds on which abortion is permitted**	..	..	1	1
Spatial distribution and internal migration				
View on spatial distribution	Minor change desired	Minor change desired	Satisfactory	Minor change desired
Policies on internal migration				
From rural to urban areas	..	..	..	Lower
From rural to rural areas	..	..	..	..
From urban to rural areas	..	..	..	..
From urban to urban areas	..	..	..	..
Into urban agglomerations	..	..	Maintain	Lower
International migration				
Immigration				
View	Satisfactory	Satisfactory	Satisfactory	Satisfactory
Policy	Maintain	Maintain	Maintain	Maintain
Permanent settlement	..	..	Maintain	..
Temporary workers	..	..	Maintain	Lower
Highly skilled workers	..	..	..	Maintain
Family reunification	..	..	Maintain	..
Integration of non-nationals	..	..	No	..
Emigration				
View	Satisfactory	Satisfactory	Satisfactory	Satisfactory
Policy	Maintain	Maintain	Maintain	Maintain
Encouraging the return of nationals	..	..	No	..

* Measures implemented to control HIV/AIDS: (1) blood screening; (2) information/education campaigns; (3) access to antiretroviral treatment; (4) non-discriminatory policies; (5) promoting condom use.

** Grounds on which abortion is permitted: (1) to save the woman's life; (2) to preserve physical health; (3) to preserve mental health; (4) rape or incest; (5) foetal impairment; (6) economic or social reasons; (7) on request.

Population indicators

Indicator	*1975*	*1985*	*1995*	*2005*
Population size and growth				
Population size (thousands)	92	92	97	102
Annual growth rate (percentage)*	-1.3	-0.9	0.5	0.4
Population age structure				
Percentage of population under age 15	47	41	40	36
Percentage of population aged 60 or older	4	6	8	9
Fertility and family planning				
Total fertility (births per woman)*	5.5	5.5	4.5	3.5
Teenage fertility rate (per 1,000 women, aged 15 - 19)*	24	24	20	13
Percentage of births to women under age 20*	4	4	4	3
Percentage of births to women aged 35 or older*	24	25	22	19
Percentage of married women using contraception				
Modern methods	..	..	..	..
All methods	..	..	..	..
Health and mortality				
Life expectancy at birth (years)*				
Males	65	67	69	71
Females	67	70	71	73
Both sexes combined	66	68	70	72
Infant mortality rate (per 1,000 births)*	37	31	25	21
Mortality under age 5 (per 1,000 births)*	47	38	31	25
Maternal mortality ratio (per 100,000 births) (2000)	..	..	..	..
HIV/AIDS (2003)				
Number of infected adults (thousands)	..	..	..	..
Adult prevalence rate (percentage)	..	..	..	..
Spatial distribution				
Population density (per sq. km)	142	142	149	157
Urban population (percentage)	24	30	32	34
Annual urban growth rate (percentage)*	1.9	2.0	0.5	1.7
Annual rural growth rate (percentage)*	-0.8	-0.8	-0.2	0.6
International migration				
International migrant stock				
Number of migrants (thousands)	1	3	2	1
Percentage of total population	1	3.7	2.3	1.1

* For the periods 1970-1975, 1980-1985, 1990-1995 and 2000-2005.

Government views and policies

Population policy variable	*1976*	*1986*	*1996*	*2005*
Population size and growth				
View on growth	Too high	Too high	Too high	Satisfactory
Policy on growth	Lower	Lower	Lower	Maintain
Population age structure				
Level of concern about				
Size of the working-age population	..	..	..	Major concern
Ageing of the population	..	..	..	Major concern
Fertility and family planning				
View on fertility level	Too high	Too high	Too high	Satisfactory
Policy	Lower	Lower	Lower	Maintain
Access to contraceptive methods	Direct support	Direct support	Direct support	Direct support
Adolescent fertility				
Level of concern	..	..	..	Major concern
Policies and programmes	..	..	..	Yes
Health and mortality				
View				
Expectation of life	Acceptable	Acceptable	Acceptable	Acceptable
Under-five mortality	..	..	Acceptable	Unacceptable
Maternal mortality	..	..	..	Unacceptable
Level of concern about HIV/AIDS	..	..	Major concern	Major concern
Measures implemented to control HIV/AIDS*	..	..	..	1,2,3,5
Grounds on which abortion is permitted**	..	..	1,2,3	1,2,3
Spatial distribution and internal migration				
View on spatial distribution	Major change desired	Major change desired	Major change desired	Minor change desired
Policies on internal migration				
From rural to urban areas	..	..	..	Lower
From rural to rural areas	..	..	..	..
From urban to rural areas	..	..	..	..
From urban to urban areas	..	..	..	..
Into urban agglomerations	No intervention	..	..	Lower
International migration				
Immigration				
View	Satisfactory	Satisfactory	Satisfactory	Satisfactory
Policy	Maintain	Maintain	Maintain	Maintain
Permanent settlement	..	..	..	No intervention
Temporary workers	..	..	..	No intervention
Highly skilled workers	..	..	..	Maintain
Family reunification	..	..	..	Maintain
Integration of non-nationals	..	..	..	Yes
Emigration				
View	Too high	Too high	Too high	Too high
Policy	Lower	Lower	Lower	No intervention
Encouraging the return of nationals	Yes	..	..	No

* Measures implemented to control HIV/AIDS: (1) blood screening; (2) information/education campaigns; (3) access to antiretroviral treatment; (4) non-discriminatory policies; (5) promoting condom use.

** Grounds on which abortion is permitted: (1) to save the woman's life; (2) to preserve physical health; (3) to preserve mental health; (4) rape or incest; (5) foetal impairment; (6) economic or social reasons; (7) on request.

Population indicators

Indicator	*1975*	*1985*	*1995*	*2005*
Population size and growth				
Population size (thousands)	1 012	1 178	1 259	1 305
Annual growth rate (percentage)*	0.8	1.7	0.7	0.3
Population age structure				
Percentage of population under age 15	38	34	30	22
Percentage of population aged 60 or older	8	8	9	11
Fertility and family planning				
Total fertility (births per woman)*	3.5	3.2	2.1	1.6
Teenage fertility rate (per 1,000 women, aged 15 - 19)*	90	84	55	37
Percentage of births to women under age 20*	20	17	15	14
Percentage of births to women aged 35 or older*	8	8	10	11
Percentage of married women using contraception				
Modern methods	46[a]	44[b]	..	33[c]
All methods	52[a]	53[b]	..	38[c]
Health and mortality				
Life expectancy at birth (years)*				
Males	64	67	69	67
Females	68	73	75	73
Both sexes combined	66	70	71	70
Infant mortality rate (per 1,000 births)*	41	25	17	14
Mortality under age 5 (per 1,000 births)*	52	33	19	19
Maternal mortality ratio (per 100,000 births) (2000)	..	..	..	160
HIV/AIDS (2003)				
Number of infected adults (thousands)	..	..	..	28
Adult prevalence rate (percentage)	..	..	..	3.2
Spatial distribution				
Population density (per sq. km)	197	230	245	254
Urban population (percentage)	63	66	72	76
Annual urban growth rate (percentage)*	0.8	2.7	1.5	0.9
Annual rural growth rate (percentage)*	0.8	0.0	-1.1	-1.4
International migration				
International migrant stock				
Number of migrants (thousands)	61	56	46	38
Percentage of total population	6	4.7	3.6	2.9

* For the periods 1970-1975, 1980-1985, 1990-1995 and 2000-2005.
[a] For 1977.
[b] For 1987.
[c] For 2000.

Government views and policies

Population policy variable	*1976*	*1986*	*1996*	*2005*
Population size and growth				
View on growth	Too high	Too high	Satisfactory	Satisfactory
Policy on growth	Lower	Lower	Lower	Lower
Population age structure				
Level of concern about				
Size of the working-age population	..	..	..	Major concern
Ageing of the population	..	..	..	Minor concern
Fertility and family planning				
View on fertility level	Too high	Too high	Too high	Satisfactory
Policy	Lower	Lower	Lower	Lower
Access to contraceptive methods	Direct support	Direct support	Direct support	Direct support
Adolescent fertility				
Level of concern	..	..	Not a concern	Not a concern
Policies and programmes	..	..	No	No
Health and mortality				
View				
Expectation of life	Unacceptable	Unacceptable	Acceptable	Acceptable
Under-five mortality	..	..	..	Acceptable
Maternal mortality	..	..	..	Unacceptable
Level of concern about HIV/AIDS	..	..	..	Minor concern
Measures implemented to control HIV/AIDS*	..	..	..	1,2,3,4,5
Grounds on which abortion is permitted**	..	..	1,2,3,4,5,6,7	1,2,3,4,5,6,7
Spatial distribution and internal migration				
View on spatial distribution	Minor change desired	Major change desired	Major change desired	Minor change desired
Policies on internal migration				
From rural to urban areas	..	..	..	Lower
From rural to rural areas	..	..	..	No intervention
From urban to rural areas	..	..	..	No intervention
From urban to urban areas	..	..	..	No intervention
Into urban agglomerations	Lower	Lower	Lower	Lower
International migration				
Immigration				
View	Satisfactory	Satisfactory	Satisfactory	Satisfactory
Policy	Maintain	Maintain	Maintain	No intervention
Permanent settlement	..	..	..	No intervention
Temporary workers	..	..	..	No intervention
Highly skilled workers	..	..	..	No intervention
Family reunification	..	..	..	No intervention
Integration of non-nationals	..	..	..	No
Emigration				
View	Satisfactory	Satisfactory	Satisfactory	Satisfactory
Policy	Maintain	Maintain	Raise	Raise
Encouraging the return of nationals	Yes	..	No	No

* Measures implemented to control HIV/AIDS: (1) blood screening; (2) information/education campaigns; (3) access to antiretroviral treatment; (4) non-discriminatory policies; (5) promoting condom use.

** Grounds on which abortion is permitted: (1) to save the woman's life; (2) to preserve physical health; (3) to preserve mental health; (4) rape or incest; (5) foetal impairment; (6) economic or social reasons; (7) on request.

Population indicators

Indicator	*1975*	*1985*	*1995*	*2005*
Population size and growth				
Population size (thousands)	5 668	7 332	8 977	10 102
Annual growth rate (percentage)*	2.0	2.6	1.8	1.1
Population age structure				
Percentage of population under age 15	44	40	35	26
Percentage of population aged 60 or older	6	6	8	9
Fertility and family planning				
Total fertility (births per woman)*	6.2	4.9	3.1	2.0
Teenage fertility rate (per 1,000 women, aged 15 - 19)*	37	30	18	7
Percentage of births to women under age 20*	5	5	4	2
Percentage of births to women aged 35 or older*	21	15	17	19
Percentage of married women using contraception				
Modern methods	25[a]	34[b]	51[c]	53[d]
All methods	31[a]	41[b]	60[c]	63[d]
Health and mortality				
Life expectancy at birth (years)*				
Males	55	63	68	71
Females	56	66	72	75
Both sexes combined	56	64	70	73
Infant mortality rate (per 1,000 births)*	119	64	34	22
Mortality under age 5 (per 1,000 births)*	151	80	40	25
Maternal mortality ratio (per 100,000 births) (2000)	..	..	..	120
HIV/AIDS (2003)				
Number of infected adults (thousands)	..	..	..	1
Adult prevalence rate (percentage)	..	..	..	<0.1
Spatial distribution				
Population density (per sq. km)	35	45	55	62
Urban population (percentage)	50	54	61	64
Annual urban growth rate (percentage)*	4.3	3.4	2.9	1.6
Annual rural growth rate (percentage)*	0.0	1.6	0.0	0.2
International migration				
International migrant stock				
Number of migrants (thousands)	38	38	38	38
Percentage of total population	0.7	0.5	0.4	0.4

* For the periods 1970-1975, 1980-1985, 1990-1995 and 2000-2005.
[a] For 1978.
[b] For 1983.
[c] For 1994.
[d] For 2001.

Government views and policies

Population policy variable	*1976*	*1986*	*1996*	*2005*
Population size and growth				
View on growth	Too high	Too high	Too high	Satisfactory
Policy on growth	Lower	Lower	Lower	Maintain
Population age structure				
Level of concern about				
Size of the working-age population	..	..	..	Major concern
Ageing of the population	..	..	..	Minor concern
Fertility and family planning				
View on fertility level	Too high	Too high	Too high	Satisfactory
Policy	Lower	Lower	Lower	Maintain
Access to contraceptive methods	Direct support	Direct support	Direct support	Direct support
Adolescent fertility				
Level of concern	..	..	Not a concern	Minor concern
Policies and programmes	..	..	No	Yes
Health and mortality				
View				
Expectation of life	Unacceptable	Unacceptable	Unacceptable	Unacceptable
Under-five mortality	..	..	Unacceptable	Unacceptable
Maternal mortality	..	..	..	Unacceptable
Level of concern about HIV/AIDS	..	..	Minor concern	Minor concern
Measures implemented to control HIV/AIDS*	..	..	..	1,2,3,5
Grounds on which abortion is permitted**	..	..	1,2,3,4,5,6,7	1,2,3,4,5,6,7
Spatial distribution and internal migration				
View on spatial distribution	Major change desired	Minor change desired	Minor change desired	Major change desired
Policies on internal migration				
From rural to urban areas	..	..	..	Lower
From rural to rural areas	..	..	..	No intervention
From urban to rural areas	..	..	..	Raise
From urban to urban areas	..	..	..	Raise
Into urban agglomerations	Lower	Lower	Lower	Lower
International migration				
Immigration				
View	Satisfactory	Satisfactory	Satisfactory	Too high
Policy	Maintain	Maintain	Lower	Lower
Permanent settlement	..	..	Lower	Maintain
Temporary workers	..	..	Maintain	Lower
Highly skilled workers	..	..	..	Raise
Family reunification	..	..	Maintain	Maintain
Integration of non-nationals	..	..	No	No
Emigration				
View	Too low	Too low	Satisfactory	Satisfactory
Policy	Raise	Raise	Maintain	Maintain
Encouraging the return of nationals	No	..	No	No

* Measures implemented to control HIV/AIDS: (1) blood screening; (2) information/education campaigns; (3) access to antiretroviral treatment; (4) non-discriminatory policies; (5) promoting condom use.

** Grounds on which abortion is permitted: (1) to save the woman's life; (2) to preserve physical health; (3) to preserve mental health; (4) rape or incest; (5) foetal impairment; (6) economic or social reasons; (7) on request.

Population indicators

Indicator	*1975*	*1985*	*1995*	*2005*
Population size and growth				
Population size (thousands)	41 211	52 150	62 620	73 193
Annual growth rate (percentage)*	2.6	2.4	1.8	1.4
Population age structure				
Percentage of population under age 15	41	38	33	29
Percentage of population aged 60 or older	7	6	7	8
Fertility and family planning				
Total fertility (births per woman)*	5.3	4.2	2.9	2.5
Teenage fertility rate (per 1,000 women, aged 15 - 19)*	131	103	72	45
Percentage of births to women under age 20*	18	16	15	10
Percentage of births to women aged 35 or older*	9	8	8	8
Percentage of married women using contraception				
Modern methods	14[a]	23[b]	38[c]	..
All methods	38[a]	51[b]	64[c]	..
Health and mortality				
Life expectancy at birth (years)*				
Males	55	59	64	66
Females	59	63	69	71
Both sexes combined	57	61	66	69
Infant mortality rate (per 1,000 births)*	138	93	54	42
Mortality under age 5 (per 1,000 births)*	174	116	65	49
Maternal mortality ratio (per 100,000 births) (2000)	..	..	..	70
HIV/AIDS (2003)				
Number of infected adults (thousands)	..	..	..	..
Adult prevalence rate (percentage)	..	..	..	..
Spatial distribution				
Population density (per sq. km)	53	67	80	93
Urban population (percentage)	42	52	62	67
Annual urban growth rate (percentage)*	4.1	6.0	2.8	2.2
Annual rural growth rate (percentage)*	1.4	-1.0	0.3	-0.1
International migration				
International migrant stock				
Number of migrants (thousands)	121	926	1 210	1 328
Percentage of total population	0.3	1.8	1.9	1.8

* For the periods 1970-1975, 1980-1985, 1990-1995 and 2000-2005.
[a] For 1978.
[b] For 1983.
[c] For 1998.

Government views and policies

Population policy variable	*1976*	*1986*	*1996*	*2005*
Population size and growth				
View on growth	..	..	Satisfactory	Satisfactory
Policy on growth	..	..	No intervention	Maintain
Population age structure				
Level of concern about				
Size of the working-age population	..	..	..	..
Ageing of the population	..	..	..	..
Fertility and family planning				
View on fertility level	..	..	Satisfactory	Satisfactory
Policy	..	..	No intervention	Maintain
Access to contraceptive methods	..	..	No support	Indirect support
Adolescent fertility				
Level of concern	..	..	..	..
Policies and programmes	..	..	Yes	..
Health and mortality				
View				
Expectation of life	..	..	Unacceptable	Unacceptable
Under-five mortality	..	..	..	Unacceptable
Maternal mortality	..	..	..	Unacceptable
Level of concern about HIV/AIDS	..	..	..	Major concern
Measures implemented to control HIV/AIDS*	..	..	..	1,2,4
Grounds on which abortion is permitted**	..	..	1,2,3,4,5,6,7	1,2,3,4,5,6,7
Spatial distribution and internal migration				
View on spatial distribution	..	..	Minor change desired	Minor change desired
Policies on internal migration				
From rural to urban areas	..	..	..	..
From rural to rural areas	..	..	..	..
From urban to rural areas	..	..	..	..
From urban to urban areas	..	..	..	..
Into urban agglomerations	..	..	..	..
International migration				
Immigration				
View	..	..	Satisfactory	Satisfactory
Policy	..	..	No intervention	Lower
Permanent settlement	..	..	..	Lower
Temporary workers	..	..	..	Lower
Highly skilled workers	..	..	..	..
Family reunification	..	..	..	..
Integration of non-nationals	..	..	..	No
Emigration				
View	..	..	Too high	Too high
Policy	..	..	No intervention	Lower
Encouraging the return of nationals	..	..	..	..

* Measures implemented to control HIV/AIDS: (1) blood screening; (2) information/education campaigns; (3) access to antiretroviral treatment; (4) non-discriminatory policies; (5) promoting condom use.
** Grounds on which abortion is permitted: (1) to save the woman's life; (2) to preserve physical health; (3) to preserve mental health; (4) rape or incest; (5) foetal impairment; (6) economic or social reasons; (7) on request.

Population indicators

Indicator	*1975*	*1985*	*1995*	*2005*
Population size and growth				
Population size (thousands)	2 520	3 230	4 193	4 833
Annual growth rate (percentage)*	2.8	2.4	2.7	1.4
Population age structure				
Percentage of population under age 15	43	41	40	32
Percentage of population aged 60 or older	7	6	6	6
Fertility and family planning				
Total fertility (births per woman)*	6.2	4.8	4.0	2.8
Teenage fertility rate (per 1,000 women, aged 15 - 19)*	35	27	23	17
Percentage of births to women under age 20*	5	4	4	4
Percentage of births to women aged 35 or older*	14	8	11	11
Percentage of married women using contraception				
Modern methods	..	..	..	53[a]
All methods	..	..	..	62[a]
Health and mortality				
Life expectancy at birth (years)*				
Males	56	58	59	58
Females	63	65	68	67
Both sexes combined	59	62	63	62
Infant mortality rate (per 1,000 births)*	111	91	74	78
Mortality under age 5 (per 1,000 births)*	143	117	94	99
Maternal mortality ratio (per 100,000 births) (2000)	..	..	..	31
HIV/AIDS (2003)				
Number of infected adults (thousands)	..	..	..	<1
Adult prevalence rate (percentage)	..	..	..	<0.1
Spatial distribution				
Population density (per sq. km)	5	7	9	10
Urban population (percentage)	48	46	45	46
Annual urban growth rate (percentage)*	2.7	1.9	2.5	2.0
Annual rural growth rate (percentage)*	2.9	2.8	2.9	1.2
International migration				
International migrant stock				
Number of migrants (thousands)	..	..	260	224
Percentage of total population	..	..	6.2	4.6

* For the periods 1970-1975, 1980-1985, 1990-1995 and 2000-2005.
[a] For 2000.

Government views and policies

Population policy variable	*1976*	*1986*	*1996*	*2005*
Population size and growth				
View on growth	..	Too high	Too high	Too high
Policy on growth	..	Lower	Lower	Lower
Population age structure				
Level of concern about				
Size of the working-age population	..	..	..	..
Ageing of the population	..	..	..	..
Fertility and family planning				
View on fertility level	..	Too high	Too high	Too high
Policy	..	Lower	Lower	Lower
Access to contraceptive methods	..	Direct support	Direct support	Direct support
Adolescent fertility				
Level of concern	..	..	..	Major concern
Policies and programmes	..	..	..	Yes
Health and mortality				
View				
Expectation of life	..	Unacceptable	Unacceptable	Unacceptable
Under-five mortality	..	..	..	Unacceptable
Maternal mortality	..	..	..	Acceptable
Level of concern about HIV/AIDS	..	..	..	Major concern
Measures implemented to control HIV/AIDS*	..	..	..	1,2,5
Grounds on which abortion is permitted**	..	..	1	1
Spatial distribution and internal migration				
View on spatial distribution	..	Minor change desired	Major change desired	Major change desired
Policies on internal migration				
From rural to urban areas	..	..	..	Lower
From rural to rural areas	..	..	..	..
From urban to rural areas	..	..	..	..
From urban to urban areas	..	..	..	..
Into urban agglomerations	..	..	..	Lower
International migration				
Immigration				
View	..	Satisfactory	Satisfactory	Satisfactory
Policy	..	Maintain	Maintain	Maintain
Permanent settlement	..	..	..	..
Temporary workers	..	..	..	..
Highly skilled workers	..	..	..	..
Family reunification	..	..	..	..
Integration of non-nationals	..	..	..	..
Emigration				
View	..	Satisfactory	Satisfactory	Too low
Policy	..	Maintain	Maintain	Raise
Encouraging the return of nationals	..	..	..	..

* Measures implemented to control HIV/AIDS: (1) blood screening; (2) information/education campaigns; (3) access to antiretroviral treatment; (4) non-discriminatory policies; (5) promoting condom use.

** Grounds on which abortion is permitted: (1) to save the woman's life; (2) to preserve physical health; (3) to preserve mental health; (4) rape or incest; (5) foetal impairment; (6) economic or social reasons; (7) on request.

Population indicators

Indicator	*1975*	*1985*	*1995*	*2005*
Population size and growth				
Population size (thousands)	8	9	10	10
Annual growth rate (percentage)*	1.0	1.4	0.8	0.5
Population age structure				
Percentage of population under age 15	..	..	..	..
Percentage of population aged 60 or older	..	..	..	..
Fertility and family planning				
Total fertility (births per woman)*	..	..	..	..
Teenage fertility rate (per 1,000 women, aged 15 - 19)*	..	..	..	..
Percentage of births to women under age 20*	..	..	..	..
Percentage of births to women aged 35 or older*	..	..	..	..
Percentage of married women using contraception				
Modern methods	..	..	..	..
All methods	..	..	..	..
Health and mortality				
Life expectancy at birth (years)*				
Males	..	..	..	..
Females	..	..	..	..
Both sexes combined	..	..	..	..
Infant mortality rate (per 1,000 births)*	..	..	..	..
Mortality under age 5 (per 1,000 births)*	..	..	..	..
Maternal mortality ratio (per 100,000 births) (2000)	..	..	..	..
HIV/AIDS (2003)				
Number of infected adults (thousands)	..	..	..	..
Adult prevalence rate (percentage)	..	..	..	..
Spatial distribution				
Population density (per sq. km)	296	333	377	402
Urban population (percentage)	25	35	47	57
Annual urban growth rate (percentage)*	5.2	4.9	4.2	3.0
Annual rural growth rate (percentage)*	0.4	0.1	-0.6	-0.9
International migration				
International migrant stock				
Number of migrants (thousands)	0	0	0	0
Percentage of total population	3.1	3.3	3.2	3.1

* For the periods 1970-1975, 1980-1985, 1990-1995 and 2000-2005.

Government views and policies

Population policy variable	*1976*	*1986*	*1996*	*2005*
Population size and growth				
View on growth	Too high	Too high	Too high	Too high
Policy on growth	Lower	Lower	Lower	Lower
Population age structure				
Level of concern about				
Size of the working-age population	..	..	..	Major concern
Ageing of the population	..	..	..	Major concern
Fertility and family planning				
View on fertility level	Too high	Too high	Too high	Too high
Policy	Lower	Lower	Lower	Lower
Access to contraceptive methods	Direct support	Direct support	Direct support	Direct support
Adolescent fertility				
Level of concern	..	..	Major concern	Major concern
Policies and programmes	..	..	Yes	Yes
Health and mortality				
View				
Expectation of life	Unacceptable	Unacceptable	Unacceptable	Unacceptable
Under-five mortality	..	..	Unacceptable	Unacceptable
Maternal mortality	..	..	..	Unacceptable
Level of concern about HIV/AIDS	..	..	Major concern	Major concern
Measures implemented to control HIV/AIDS*	..	..	..	1,2,3,4,5
Grounds on which abortion is permitted**	..	..	1,2,3	1,2,3
Spatial distribution and internal migration				
View on spatial distribution	Minor change desired	Minor change desired	Minor change desired	Minor change desired
Policies on internal migration				
From rural to urban areas	..	..	..	Lower
From rural to rural areas	..	..	..	..
From urban to rural areas	..	..	..	..
From urban to urban areas	..	..	..	..
Into urban agglomerations	Lower	No intervention	Lower	Lower
International migration				
Immigration				
View	Satisfactory	Satisfactory	Satisfactory	Satisfactory
Policy	Maintain	Maintain	Maintain	Maintain
Permanent settlement	..	..	No intervention	..
Temporary workers	..	..	Maintain	..
Highly skilled workers	..	..	..	..
Family reunification	..	..	No intervention	..
Integration of non-nationals	..	..	Yes	No
Emigration				
View	Satisfactory	Satisfactory	Satisfactory	Satisfactory
Policy	Maintain	Maintain	No intervention	No intervention
Encouraging the return of nationals	No	..	Yes	..

* Measures implemented to control HIV/AIDS: (1) blood screening; (2) information/education campaigns; (3) access to antiretroviral treatment; (4) non-discriminatory policies; (5) promoting condom use.

** Grounds on which abortion is permitted: (1) to save the woman's life; (2) to preserve physical health; (3) to preserve mental health; (4) rape or incest; (5) foetal impairment; (6) economic or social reasons; (7) on request.

Population indicators

Indicator	*1975*	*1985*	*1995*	*2005*
Population size and growth				
Population size (thousands)	10 766	14 772	20 892	28 816
Annual growth rate (percentage)*	3.0	3.2	3.3	3.4
Population age structure				
Percentage of population under age 15	48	48	50	50
Percentage of population aged 60 or older	4	4	4	4
Fertility and family planning				
Total fertility (births per woman)*	7.1	7.1	7.1	7.1
Teenage fertility rate (per 1,000 women, aged 15 - 19)*	211	211	211	211
Percentage of births to women under age 20*	22	22	23	23
Percentage of births to women aged 35 or older*	13	13	12	10
Percentage of married women using contraception				
Modern methods	..	3[a]	8	18[b]
All methods	..	5[a]	15	23[b]
Health and mortality				
Life expectancy at birth (years)*				
Males	50	48	42	46
Females	53	52	45	47
Both sexes combined	51	50	44	47
Infant mortality rate (per 1,000 births)*	103	107	90	81
Mortality under age 5 (per 1,000 births)*	167	180	162	139
Maternal mortality ratio (per 100,000 births) (2000)	..	..	..	880
HIV/AIDS (2003)				
Number of infected adults (thousands)	..	..	..	450
Adult prevalence rate (percentage)	..	..	..	4.1
Spatial distribution				
Population density (per sq. km)	45	61	87	120
Urban population (percentage)	8	10	12	12
Annual urban growth rate (percentage)*	3.6	5.5	3.9	3.9
Annual rural growth rate (percentage)*	2.6	2.8	3.0	3.2
International migration				
International migrant stock				
Number of migrants (thousands)	777	634	610	518
Percentage of total population	7.2	4.3	2.9	1.8

* For the periods 1970-1975, 1980-1985, 1990-1995 and 2000-2005.
[a] For 1988.
[b] For 2000/2001.

Government views and policies

Population policy variable	*1976*	*1986*	*1996*	*2005*
Population size and growth				
View on growth	Too low	Satisfactory	Too low	Too low
Policy on growth	Raise	Maintain	Raise	Raise
Population age structure				
Level of concern about				
Size of the working-age population	..	..	..	Not a concern
Ageing of the population	..	..	..	Major concern
Fertility and family planning				
View on fertility level	Satisfactory	Satisfactory	Too low	Too low
Policy	Maintain	Maintain	Raise	Raise
Access to contraceptive methods	Direct support	Direct support	Direct support	Indirect support
Adolescent fertility				
Level of concern	..	..	Major concern	Major concern
Policies and programmes	..	..	Yes	Yes
Health and mortality				
View				
Expectation of life	Unacceptable	Acceptable	Unacceptable	Unacceptable
Under-five mortality	..	..	Unacceptable	Unacceptable
Maternal mortality	..	..	..	Unacceptable
Level of concern about HIV/AIDS	..	..	Major concern	Major concern
Measures implemented to control HIV/AIDS*	..	..	..	1,2,3,4,5
Grounds on which abortion is permitted**	..	..	1,2,3,4,5,6,7	1,2,3,4,5,6,7
Spatial distribution and internal migration				
View on spatial distribution	Minor change desired	Minor change desired	Minor change desired	Minor change desired
Policies on internal migration				
From rural to urban areas	..	..	..	Maintain
From rural to rural areas	..	..	..	No intervention
From urban to rural areas	..	..	..	No intervention
From urban to urban areas	..	..	..	No intervention
Into urban agglomerations	..	Lower	Lower	No intervention
International migration				
Immigration				
View	Satisfactory	Satisfactory	Satisfactory	Satisfactory
Policy	Maintain	Maintain	No intervention	Maintain
Permanent settlement	..	..	No intervention	Maintain
Temporary workers	..	..	No intervention	Maintain
Highly skilled workers	..	..	..	Maintain
Family reunification	..	..	No intervention	Maintain
Integration of non-nationals	..	..	No	No
Emigration				
View	Satisfactory	Satisfactory	Too high	Too high
Policy	Maintain	Maintain	Lower	Lower
Encouraging the return of nationals	..	..	Yes	No

* Measures implemented to control HIV/AIDS: (1) blood screening; (2) information/education campaigns; (3) access to antiretroviral treatment; (4) non-discriminatory policies; (5) promoting condom use.
** Grounds on which abortion is permitted: (1) to save the woman's life; (2) to preserve physical health; (3) to preserve mental health; (4) rape or incest; (5) foetal impairment; (6) economic or social reasons; (7) on request.

Population indicators

Indicator	*1975*	*1985*	*1995*	*2005*
Population size and growth				
Population size (thousands)	49 016	50 941	51 531	46 481
Annual growth rate (percentage)*	0.7	0.4	-0.1	-1.1
Population age structure				
Percentage of population under age 15	23	22	20	15
Percentage of population aged 60 or older	16	16	18	21
Fertility and family planning				
Total fertility (births per woman)*	2.2	2.0	1.6	1.1
Teenage fertility rate (per 1,000 women, aged 15 - 19)*	81	75	61	30
Percentage of births to women under age 20*	21	18	19	14
Percentage of births to women aged 35 or older*	5	4	5	5
Percentage of married women using contraception				
Modern methods	..	..	38[a]	..
All methods	..	..	68[a]	..
Health and mortality				
Life expectancy at birth (years)*				
Males	65	64	62	60
Females	74	73	72	72
Both sexes combined	70	69	67	66
Infant mortality rate (per 1,000 births)*	22	20	18	16
Mortality under age 5 (per 1,000 births)*	24	22	20	18
Maternal mortality ratio (per 100,000 births) (2000)	..	..	..	35
HIV/AIDS (2003)				
Number of infected adults (thousands)	..	..	..	360
Adult prevalence rate (percentage)	..	..	..	1.4
Spatial distribution				
Population density (per sq. km)	81	84	85	77
Urban population (percentage)	58	65	67	67
Annual urban growth rate (percentage)*	2.0	1.3	-0.1	-0.7
Annual rural growth rate (percentage)*	-1.0	-1.3	-0.3	-0.9
International migration				
International migrant stock				
Number of migrants (thousands)	..	..	7 063	6 833
Percentage of total population	..	..	13.7	14.7

* For the periods 1970-1975, 1980-1985, 1990-1995 and 2000-2005.
[a] For 1999.

Government views and policies

Population policy variable	*1976*	*1986*	*1996*	*2005*
Population size and growth				
View on growth	Too low	Satisfactory	Too high	Satisfactory
Policy on growth	Raise	Raise	No intervention	Lower
Population age structure				
Level of concern about				
Size of the working-age population	..	..	..	Minor concern
Ageing of the population	..	..	..	Minor concern
Fertility and family planning				
View on fertility level	Satisfactory	Satisfactory	Satisfactory	Satisfactory
Policy	Maintain	Raise	No intervention	Maintain
Access to contraceptive methods	No support	No support	No support	No support
Adolescent fertility				
Level of concern	..	..	..	Not a concern
Policies and programmes	..	..	..	No
Health and mortality				
View				
Expectation of life	Acceptable	Acceptable	Acceptable	Acceptable
Under-five mortality	..	..	..	Acceptable
Maternal mortality	..	..	..	Acceptable
Level of concern about HIV/AIDS	..	..	..	Minor concern
Measures implemented to control HIV/AIDS*	..	..	..	1,2,3,4
Grounds on which abortion is permitted**	..	..	1	1
Spatial distribution and internal migration				
View on spatial distribution	Minor change desired	Minor change desired	Satisfactory	Satisfactory
Policies on internal migration				
From rural to urban areas	..	..	..	No intervention
From rural to rural areas	..	..	..	No intervention
From urban to rural areas	..	..	..	No intervention
From urban to urban areas	..	..	..	No intervention
Into urban agglomerations	..	No intervention	..	No intervention
International migration				
Immigration				
View	Satisfactory	Too high	Too high	Too high
Policy	Maintain	Lower	Lower	Lower
Permanent settlement	..	..	..	..
Temporary workers	..	..	..	Lower
Highly skilled workers	..	..	..	Lower
Family reunification	..	..	..	Lower
Integration of non-nationals	..	..	..	..
Emigration				
View	Satisfactory	Satisfactory	Satisfactory	Satisfactory
Policy	Maintain	Maintain	No intervention	No intervention
Encouraging the return of nationals	..	..	..	Yes

* Measures implemented to control HIV/AIDS: (1) blood screening; (2) information/education campaigns; (3) access to antiretroviral treatment; (4) non-discriminatory policies; (5) promoting condom use.

** Grounds on which abortion is permitted: (1) to save the woman's life; (2) to preserve physical health; (3) to preserve mental health; (4) rape or incest; (5) foetal impairment; (6) economic or social reasons; (7) on request.

Population indicators

Indicator	*1975*	*1985*	*1995*	*2005*
Population size and growth				
Population size (thousands)	530	1 410	2 435	4 496
Annual growth rate (percentage)*	17.2	6.6	5.3	6.5
Population age structure				
Percentage of population under age 15	28	30	28	22
Percentage of population aged 60 or older	3	2	2	2
Fertility and family planning				
Total fertility (births per woman)*	6.4	5.2	3.9	2.5
Teenage fertility rate (per 1,000 women, aged 15 - 19)*	122	100	55	22
Percentage of births to women under age 20*	11	8	7	4
Percentage of births to women aged 35 or older*	13	11	18	15
Percentage of married women using contraception				
Modern methods	..	..	24	..
All methods	..	..	28	..
Health and mortality				
Life expectancy at birth (years)*				
Males	61	67	72	76
Females	64	71	76	81
Both sexes combined	62	69	74	78
Infant mortality rate (per 1,000 births)*	57	32	16	9
Mortality under age 5 (per 1,000 births)*	68	37	18	10
Maternal mortality ratio (per 100,000 births) (2000)	..	..	..	54
HIV/AIDS (2003)				
Number of infected adults (thousands)	..	..	..	..
Adult prevalence rate (percentage)	..	..	..	..
Spatial distribution				
Population density (per sq. km)	6	17	29	54
Urban population (percentage)	84	82	84	85
Annual urban growth rate (percentage)*	17.0	8.6	4.3	2.1
Annual rural growth rate (percentage)*	12.5	7.8	3.0	0.8
International migration				
International migrant stock				
Number of migrants (thousands)	312	1 008	1 716	3 212
Percentage of total population	58.9	71.5	70.5	71.4

* For the periods 1970-1975, 1980-1985, 1990-1995 and 2000-2005.

Government views and policies

Population policy variable	*1976*	*1986*	*1996*	*2005*
Population size and growth				
View on growth	Satisfactory	Satisfactory	Satisfactory	Satisfactory
Policy on growth	No intervention	No intervention	No intervention	No intervention
Population age structure				
Level of concern about				
Size of the working-age population	..	..	..	Major concern
Ageing of the population	..	..	..	Major concern
Fertility and family planning				
View on fertility level	Satisfactory	Satisfactory	Satisfactory	Satisfactory
Policy	No intervention	No intervention	No intervention	No intervention
Access to contraceptive methods	Direct support	Indirect support	Direct support	Direct support
Adolescent fertility				
Level of concern	..	..	Major concern	Major concern
Policies and programmes	..	..	Yes	Yes
Health and mortality				
View				
Expectation of life	Unacceptable	Unacceptable	Unacceptable	Unacceptable
Under-five mortality	..	..	Unacceptable	Unacceptable
Maternal mortality	..	..	..	Acceptable
Level of concern about HIV/AIDS	..	..	Major concern	Major concern
Measures implemented to control HIV/AIDS*	..	..	..	1,2,3,4,5
Grounds on which abortion is permitted**	..	..	1,2,3,5,6	1,2,3,5,6
Spatial distribution and internal migration				
View on spatial distribution	Minor change desired	Minor change desired	Satisfactory	Major change desired
Policies on internal migration				
From rural to urban areas	..	..	..	Raise
From rural to rural areas	..	..	..	..
From urban to rural areas	..	..	..	Lower
From urban to urban areas	..	..	..	..
Into urban agglomerations	Lower	No intervention	Raise	Raise
International migration				
Immigration				
View	Too high	Too high	Too high	Satisfactory
Policy	Lower	Lower	Lower	Maintain
Permanent settlement	..	..	Lower	Maintain
Temporary workers	..	..	Lower	Maintain
Highly skilled workers	..	..	..	Raise
Family reunification	..	..	Lower	Maintain
Integration of non-nationals	..	..	Yes	Yes
Emigration				
View	Satisfactory	Satisfactory	Satisfactory	Satisfactory
Policy	Maintain	Maintain	No intervention	No intervention
Encouraging the return of nationals	No	..	No	No

* Measures implemented to control HIV/AIDS: (1) blood screening; (2) information/education campaigns; (3) access to antiretroviral treatment; (4) non-discriminatory policies; (5) promoting condom use.

** Grounds on which abortion is permitted: (1) to save the woman's life; (2) to preserve physical health; (3) to preserve mental health; (4) rape or incest; (5) foetal impairment; (6) economic or social reasons; (7) on request.

Population indicators

Indicator	*1975*	*1985*	*1995*	*2005*
Population size and growth				
Population size (thousands)	55 426	56 008	57 670	59 668
Annual growth rate (percentage)*	0.2	0.2	0.3	0.3
Population age structure				
Percentage of population under age 15	23	19	19	18
Percentage of population aged 60 or older	20	21	21	21
Fertility and family planning				
Total fertility (births per woman)*	2.0	1.8	1.8	1.7
Teenage fertility rate (per 1,000 women, aged 15 - 19)*	34	30	30	28
Percentage of births to women under age 20*	9	9	7	8
Percentage of births to women aged 35 or older*	14	14	15	18
Percentage of married women using contraception				
Modern methods	69	78[a]	82[b]	81[c]
All methods	76	81[a]	82[b]	84[c]
Health and mortality				
Life expectancy at birth (years)*				
Males	69	71	74	76
Females	75	77	79	81
Both sexes combined	72	74	76	78
Infant mortality rate (per 1,000 births)*	17	11	8	5
Mortality under age 5 (per 1,000 births)*	19	12	10	6
Maternal mortality ratio (per 100,000 births) (2000)	..	..	..	13
HIV/AIDS (2003)				
Number of infected adults (thousands)	..	..	..	47
Adult prevalence rate (percentage)	..	..	..	0.2
Spatial distribution				
Population density (per sq. km)	228	231	237	246
Urban population (percentage)	83	89	89	89
Annual urban growth rate (percentage)*	1.6	0.3	0.3	0.4
Annual rural growth rate (percentage)*	-5.3	-1.0	0.2	-0.3
International migration				
International migrant stock				
Number of migrants (thousands)	3 197	3 623	4 198	5 408
Percentage of total population	5.8	6.5	7.3	9.1

* For the periods 1970-1975, 1980-1985, 1990-1995 and 2000-2005.
[a] For 1986.
[b] For 1993.
[c] For 2002.

Government views and policies

Population policy variable	*1976*	*1986*	*1996*	*2005*
Population size and growth				
View on growth	Satisfactory	Too high	Too high	Too high
Policy on growth	No intervention	No intervention	Lower	Lower
Population age structure				
Level of concern about				
Size of the working-age population	..	..	..	Major concern
Ageing of the population	..	..	..	Major concern
Fertility and family planning				
View on fertility level	Satisfactory	Too high	Too high	Too high
Policy	No intervention	No intervention	Lower	Lower
Access to contraceptive methods	Direct support	Direct support	Direct support	Direct support
Adolescent fertility				
Level of concern	..	..	Minor concern	Major concern
Policies and programmes	..	..	Yes	Yes
Health and mortality				
View				
Expectation of life	Unacceptable	Unacceptable	Unacceptable	Unacceptable
Under-five mortality	..	..	Unacceptable	Unacceptable
Maternal mortality	..	..	..	Unacceptable
Level of concern about HIV/AIDS	..	..	Major concern	Major concern
Measures implemented to control HIV/AIDS*	..	..	..	1,2,3,4,5
Grounds on which abortion is permitted**	..	..	1,2,3	1,2,3
Spatial distribution and internal migration				
View on spatial distribution	Major change desired	Major change desired	Major change desired	Major change desired
Policies on internal migration				
From rural to urban areas	..	..	..	Lower
From rural to rural areas	..	..	..	..
From urban to rural areas	..	..	..	..
From urban to urban areas	..	..	..	..
Into urban agglomerations	No intervention	Lower	Lower	Lower
International migration				
Immigration				
View	Satisfactory	Satisfactory	Satisfactory	Satisfactory
Policy	Maintain	Maintain	Lower	No intervention
Permanent settlement	..	..	No intervention	No intervention
Temporary workers	..	..	Lower	No intervention
Highly skilled workers	..	..	..	..
Family reunification	..	..	No intervention	No intervention
Integration of non-nationals	..	..	Yes	No
Emigration				
View	Satisfactory	Satisfactory	Too high	Satisfactory
Policy	Maintain	Maintain	Lower	No intervention
Encouraging the return of nationals	No	..	Yes	No

* Measures implemented to control HIV/AIDS: (1) blood screening; (2) information/education campaigns; (3) access to antiretroviral treatment; (4) non-discriminatory policies; (5) promoting condom use.

** Grounds on which abortion is permitted: (1) to save the woman's life; (2) to preserve physical health; (3) to preserve mental health; (4) rape or incest; (5) foetal impairment; (6) economic or social reasons; (7) on request.

Population indicators

Indicator	*1975*	*1985*	*1995*	*2005*
Population size and growth				
Population size (thousands)	55 426	56 008	57 670	59 668
Annual growth rate (percentage)*	0.2	0.2	0.3	0.3
Population age structure				
Percentage of population under age 15	23	19	19	18
Percentage of population aged 60 or older	20	21	21	21
Fertility and family planning				
Total fertility (births per woman)*	2.0	1.8	1.8	1.7
Teenage fertility rate (per 1,000 women, aged 15 - 19)*	34	30	30	28
Percentage of births to women under age 20*	9	9	7	8
Percentage of births to women aged 35 or older*	14	14	15	18
Percentage of married women using contraception				
Modern methods	69	78[a]	82[b]	81[c]
All methods	76	81[a]	82[b]	84[c]
Health and mortality				
Life expectancy at birth (years)*				
Males	69	71	74	76
Females	75	77	79	81
Both sexes combined	72	74	76	78
Infant mortality rate (per 1,000 births)*	17	11	8	5
Mortality under age 5 (per 1,000 births)*	19	12	10	6
Maternal mortality ratio (per 100,000 births) (2000)	..	..	..	13
HIV/AIDS (2003)				
Number of infected adults (thousands)	..	..	..	47
Adult prevalence rate (percentage)	..	..	..	0.2
Spatial distribution				
Population density (per sq. km)	228	231	237	246
Urban population (percentage)	83	89	89	89
Annual urban growth rate (percentage)*	1.6	0.3	0.3	0.4
Annual rural growth rate (percentage)*	-5.3	-1.0	0.2	-0.3
International migration				
International migrant stock				
Number of migrants (thousands)	3 197	3 623	4 198	5 408
Percentage of total population	5.8	6.5	7.3	9.1

* For the periods 1970-1975, 1980-1985, 1990-1995 and 2000-2005.
[a] For 1986.
[b] For 1993.
[c] For 2002.

Government views and policies

Population policy variable	*1976*	*1986*	*1996*	*2005*
Population size and growth				
View on growth	Satisfactory	Too high	Too high	Too high
Policy on growth	No intervention	No intervention	Lower	Lower
Population age structure				
Level of concern about				
Size of the working-age population	..	..	..	Major concern
Ageing of the population	..	..	..	Major concern
Fertility and family planning				
View on fertility level	Satisfactory	Too high	Too high	Too high
Policy	No intervention	No intervention	Lower	Lower
Access to contraceptive methods	Direct support	Direct support	Direct support	Direct support
Adolescent fertility				
Level of concern	..	..	Minor concern	Major concern
Policies and programmes	..	..	Yes	Yes
Health and mortality				
View				
Expectation of life	Unacceptable	Unacceptable	Unacceptable	Unacceptable
Under-five mortality	..	..	Unacceptable	Unacceptable
Maternal mortality	..	..	..	Unacceptable
Level of concern about HIV/AIDS	..	..	Major concern	Major concern
Measures implemented to control HIV/AIDS*	..	..	..	1,2,3,4,5
Grounds on which abortion is permitted**	..	..	1,2,3	1,2,3
Spatial distribution and internal migration				
View on spatial distribution	Major change desired	Major change desired	Major change desired	Major change desired
Policies on internal migration				
From rural to urban areas	..	..	..	Lower
From rural to rural areas	..	..	..	..
From urban to rural areas	..	..	..	..
From urban to urban areas	..	..	..	..
Into urban agglomerations	No intervention	Lower	Lower	Lower
International migration				
Immigration				
View	Satisfactory	Satisfactory	Satisfactory	Satisfactory
Policy	Maintain	Maintain	Lower	No intervention
Permanent settlement	..	..	No intervention	No intervention
Temporary workers	..	..	Lower	No intervention
Highly skilled workers	..	..	..	..
Family reunification	..	..	No intervention	No intervention
Integration of non-nationals	..	..	Yes	No
Emigration				
View	Satisfactory	Satisfactory	Too high	Satisfactory
Policy	Maintain	Maintain	Lower	No intervention
Encouraging the return of nationals	No	..	Yes	No

* Measures implemented to control HIV/AIDS: (1) blood screening; (2) information/education campaigns; (3) access to antiretroviral treatment; (4) non-discriminatory policies; (5) promoting condom use.

** Grounds on which abortion is permitted: (1) to save the woman's life; (2) to preserve physical health; (3) to preserve mental health; (4) rape or incest; (5) foetal impairment; (6) economic or social reasons; (7) on request.

Population indicators

Indicator	*1975*	*1985*	*1995*	*2005*
Population size and growth				
Population size (thousands)	16 044	22 268	30 930	38 329
Annual growth rate (percentage)*	3.3	3.3	3.3	2.0
Population age structure				
Percentage of population under age 15	46	46	45	43
Percentage of population aged 60 or older	4	4	5	5
Fertility and family planning				
Total fertility (births per woman)*	6.8	6.6	5.9	5.0
Teenage fertility rate (per 1,000 women, aged 15 - 19)*	151	147	141	118
Percentage of births to women under age 20*	16	17	18	18
Percentage of births to women aged 35 or older*	17	17	15	12
Percentage of married women using contraception				
Modern methods	..	..	17[a]	..
All methods	..	..	25[a]	..
Health and mortality				
Life expectancy at birth (years)*				
Males	48	53	50	46
Females	51	57	55	46
Both sexes combined	50	55	52	46
Infant mortality rate (per 1,000 births)*	128	113	107	104
Mortality under age 5 (per 1,000 births)*	203	174	165	164
Maternal mortality ratio (per 100,000 births) (2000)	..	..	..	1 500
HIV/AIDS (2003)				
Number of infected adults (thousands)	..	..	..	1 500
Adult prevalence rate (percentage)	..	..	..	8.8
Spatial distribution				
Population density (per sq. km)	17	24	33	41
Urban population (percentage)	10	18	27	38
Annual urban growth rate (percentage)*	11.4	6.8	7.7	4.9
Annual rural growth rate (percentage)*	2.5	2.6	2.0	0.3
International migration				
International migrant stock				
Number of migrants (thousands)	608	548	1 130	792
Percentage of total population	3.8	2.5	3.7	2.1

* For the periods 1970-1975, 1980-1985, 1990-1995 and 2000-2005.
[a] For 1999.

Government views and policies

Population policy variable	*1976*	*1986*	*1996*	*2005*
Population size and growth				
View on growth	Satisfactory	Satisfactory	Satisfactory	Satisfactory
Policy on growth	No intervention	No intervention	No intervention	No intervention
Population age structure				
Level of concern about				
Size of the working-age population	..	..	..	Major concern
Ageing of the population	..	..	..	Major concern
Fertility and family planning				
View on fertility level	Satisfactory	Satisfactory	Satisfactory	Satisfactory
Policy	No intervention	No intervention	No intervention	No intervention
Access to contraceptive methods	Direct support	Direct support	Direct support	Direct support
Adolescent fertility				
Level of concern	..	..	Major concern	Major concern
Policies and programmes	..	..	Yes	Yes
Health and mortality				
View				
Expectation of life	Acceptable	Acceptable	Unacceptable	Unacceptable
Under-five mortality	..	..	Unacceptable	Unacceptable
Maternal mortality	..	..	..	Unacceptable
Level of concern about HIV/AIDS	..	..	Major concern	Major concern
Measures implemented to control HIV/AIDS*	..	..	..	1,2,3,4,5
Grounds on which abortion is permitted**	..	..	1,2,3,4,5,6,7	1,2,3,4,5,6,7
Spatial distribution and internal migration				
View on spatial distribution	Satisfactory	Satisfactory	Satisfactory	Satisfactory
Policies on internal migration				
From rural to urban areas	..	..	..	No intervention
From rural to rural areas	..	..	..	No intervention
From urban to rural areas	..	..	..	No intervention
From urban to urban areas	..	..	..	No intervention
Into urban agglomerations	..	No intervention	No intervention	No intervention
International migration				
Immigration				
View	Satisfactory	Too high	Satisfactory	Satisfactory
Policy	Maintain	Maintain	Maintain	Maintain
Permanent settlement	..	..	Maintain	Maintain
Temporary workers	..	..	Maintain	Maintain
Highly skilled workers	..	..	..	Maintain
Family reunification	..	..	Maintain	Maintain
Integration of non-nationals	..	..	Yes	Yes
Emigration				
View	Satisfactory	Satisfactory	Satisfactory	Satisfactory
Policy	Maintain	Maintain	No intervention	No intervention
Encouraging the return of nationals	..	..	No	No

* Measures implemented to control HIV/AIDS: (1) blood screening; (2) information/education campaigns; (3) access to antiretroviral treatment; (4) non-discriminatory policies; (5) promoting condom use.
** Grounds on which abortion is permitted: (1) to save the woman's life; (2) to preserve physical health; (3) to preserve mental health; (4) rape or incest; (5) foetal impairment; (6) economic or social reasons; (7) on request.

Population indicators

Indicator	*1975*	*1985*	*1995*	*2005*
Population size and growth				
Population size (thousands)	220 165	243 056	269 603	298 213
Annual growth rate (percentage)*	0.9	1.0	1.1	1.0
Population age structure				
Percentage of population under age 15	25	22	22	21
Percentage of population aged 60 or older	15	16	16	17
Fertility and family planning				
Total fertility (births per woman)*	2.0	1.8	2.0	2.0
Teenage fertility rate (per 1,000 women, aged 15 - 19)*	59	53	54	51
Percentage of births to women under age 20*	18	14	11	13
Percentage of births to women aged 35 or older*	6	7	11	12
Percentage of married women using contraception				
Modern methods	61[a]	64[b]	71	..
All methods	68[a]	70[b]	76	..
Health and mortality				
Life expectancy at birth (years)*				
Males	68	71	72	75
Females	75	78	79	80
Both sexes combined	72	74	75	77
Infant mortality rate (per 1,000 births)*	18	10	8	7
Mortality under age 5 (per 1,000 births)*	22	13	10	8
Maternal mortality ratio (per 100,000 births) (2000)	..	..	..	17
HIV/AIDS (2003)				
Number of infected adults (thousands)	..	..	..	940
Adult prevalence rate (percentage)	..	..	..	0.6
Spatial distribution				
Population density (per sq. km)	23	25	28	31
Urban population (percentage)	74	74	77	81
Annual urban growth rate (percentage)*	0.9	1.2	1.6	1.4
Annual rural growth rate (percentage)*	0.9	0.4	-0.6	-0.6
International migration				
International migrant stock				
Number of migrants (thousands)	11 749	18 223	28 522	38 355
Percentage of total population	5.3	7.5	10.6	12.9

* For the periods 1970-1975, 1980-1985, 1990-1995 and 2000-2005.
[a] For 1976.
[b] For 1982.

Government views and policies

Population policy variable	*1976*	*1986*	*1996*	*2005*
Population size and growth				
View on growth	Too low	Too low	Too low	Too low
Policy on growth	Raise	No intervention	Raise	No intervention
Population age structure				
Level of concern about				
Size of the working-age population	..	..	..	Major concern
Ageing of the population	..	..	..	Major concern
Fertility and family planning				
View on fertility level	Too low	Too low	Too low	Too low
Policy	Raise	No intervention	Raise	No intervention
Access to contraceptive methods	No support	Direct support	Direct support	Direct support
Adolescent fertility				
Level of concern	..	..	..	Major concern
Policies and programmes	..	..	..	Yes
Health and mortality				
View				
Expectation of life	Acceptable	Acceptable	Acceptable	Acceptable
Under-five mortality	..	..	..	Acceptable
Maternal mortality	..	..	..	Acceptable
Level of concern about HIV/AIDS	..	..	..	Major concern
Measures implemented to control HIV/AIDS*	..	..	..	1,2,3,4,5
Grounds on which abortion is permitted**	..	..	1,2	1,2,3,4
Spatial distribution and internal migration				
View on spatial distribution	Major change desired	Major change desired	Major change desired	Minor change desired
Policies on internal migration				
From rural to urban areas	..	..	..	Lower
From rural to rural areas	..	..	..	..
From urban to rural areas	..	..	..	Raise
From urban to urban areas	..	..	..	No intervention
Into urban agglomerations	No intervention	No intervention	..	Lower
International migration				
Immigration				
View	Satisfactory	Too low	Too low	Satisfactory
Policy	Maintain	Raise	Raise	Maintain
Permanent settlement	..	..	..	Maintain
Temporary workers	..	..	..	Maintain
Highly skilled workers	..	..	..	Maintain
Family reunification	..	..	..	Maintain
Integration of non-nationals	..	..	..	No
Emigration				
View	Too high	Too high	Too high	Too high
Policy	Lower	Lower	Lower	No intervention
Encouraging the return of nationals	No	..	Yes	No

* Measures implemented to control HIV/AIDS: (1) blood screening; (2) information/education campaigns; (3) access to antiretroviral treatment; (4) non-discriminatory policies; (5) promoting condom use.

** Grounds on which abortion is permitted: (1) to save the woman's life; (2) to preserve physical health; (3) to preserve mental health; (4) rape or incest; (5) foetal impairment; (6) economic or social reasons; (7) on request.

Population indicators

Indicator	*1975*	*1985*	*1995*	*2005*
Population size and growth				
Population size (thousands)	2 829	3 009	3 218	3 463
Annual growth rate (percentage)*	0.1	0.6	0.7	0.7
Population age structure				
Percentage of population under age 15	28	27	25	24
Percentage of population aged 60 or older	14	16	17	17
Fertility and family planning				
Total fertility (births per woman)*	3.0	2.6	2.5	2.3
Teenage fertility rate (per 1,000 women, aged 15 - 19)*	65	63	71	70
Percentage of births to women under age 20*	13	14	16	15
Percentage of births to women aged 35 or older*	14	12	12	10
Percentage of married women using contraception				
Modern methods	..	..	..	..
All methods	..	..	..	..
Health and mortality				
Life expectancy at birth (years)*				
Males	66	68	69	72
Females	72	75	77	79
Both sexes combined	69	71	73	75
Infant mortality rate (per 1,000 births)*	46	33	20	13
Mortality under age 5 (per 1,000 births)*	52	37	23	15
Maternal mortality ratio (per 100,000 births) (2000)	..	..	..	27
HIV/AIDS (2003)				
Number of infected adults (thousands)	..	..	..	6
Adult prevalence rate (percentage)	..	..	..	0.3
Spatial distribution				
Population density (per sq. km)	16	17	18	20
Urban population (percentage)	83	87	91	93
Annual urban growth rate (percentage)*	0.4	1.1	1.1	0.9
Annual rural growth rate (percentage)*	-1.0	-2.0	-2.4	-2.1
International migration				
International migrant stock				
Number of migrants (thousands)	131	103	93	84
Percentage of total population	4.6	3.4	2.9	2.4

* For the periods 1970-1975, 1980-1985, 1990-1995 and 2000-2005.

Government views and policies

Population policy variable	1976	1986	1996	2005
Population size and growth				
View on growth	..	..	Too high	Satisfactory
Policy on growth	..	..	Lower	Maintain
Population age structure				
Level of concern about				
Size of the working-age population	..	..	..	Minor concern
Ageing of the population	..	..	..	Major concern
Fertility and family planning				
View on fertility level	..	..	Satisfactory	Satisfactory
Policy	..	..	Maintain	Maintain
Access to contraceptive methods	..	..	Direct support	Direct support
Adolescent fertility				
Level of concern	..	..	..	Minor concern
Policies and programmes	..	..	Yes	Yes
Health and mortality				
View				
Expectation of life	..	..	Unacceptable	Unacceptable
Under-five mortality	..	..	..	Unacceptable
Maternal mortality	..	..	..	Unacceptable
Level of concern about HIV/AIDS	..	..	..	Major concern
Measures implemented to control HIV/AIDS*	..	..	..	1,2,4,5
Grounds on which abortion is permitted**	..	..	1,2,3,4,5,6,7	1,2,3,4,5,6,7
Spatial distribution and internal migration				
View on spatial distribution	..	..	Satisfactory	Satisfactory
Policies on internal migration				
From rural to urban areas	..	..	..	..
From rural to rural areas	..	..	..	..
From urban to rural areas	..	..	..	..
From urban to urban areas	..	..	..	..
Into urban agglomerations	..	..	..	..
International migration				
Immigration				
View	..	..	Satisfactory	Satisfactory
Policy	..	..	No intervention	Maintain
Permanent settlement	..	..	..	Maintain
Temporary workers	..	..	..	Maintain
Highly skilled workers	..	..	..	Maintain
Family reunification	..	..	..	..
Integration of non-nationals	..	..	..	..
Emigration				
View	..	..	Too high	Satisfactory
Policy	..	..	No intervention	Maintain
Encouraging the return of nationals	..	..	..	..

* Measures implemented to control HIV/AIDS: (1) blood screening; (2) information/education campaigns; (3) access to antiretroviral treatment; (4) non-discriminatory policies; (5) promoting condom use.

** Grounds on which abortion is permitted: (1) to save the woman's life; (2) to preserve physical health; (3) to preserve mental health; (4) rape or incest; (5) foetal impairment; (6) economic or social reasons; (7) on request.

Population indicators

Indicator	*1975*	*1985*	*1995*	*2005*
Population size and growth				
Population size (thousands)	13 981	18 174	22 918	26 593
Annual growth rate (percentage)*	3.1	2.6	2.2	1.5
Population age structure				
Percentage of population under age 15	43	40	40	33
Percentage of population aged 60 or older	8	6	6	6
Fertility and family planning				
Total fertility (births per woman)*	6.3	4.7	3.9	2.7
Teenage fertility rate (per 1,000 women, aged 15 - 19)*	116	87	71	37
Percentage of births to women under age 20*	15	12	11	9
Percentage of births to women aged 35 or older*	6	3	5	6
Percentage of married women using contraception				
Modern methods	..	..	..	63[a]
All methods	..	..	..	68[a]
Health and mortality				
Life expectancy at birth (years)*				
Males	60	63	63	63
Females	67	70	69	70
Both sexes combined	64	66	66	66
Infant mortality rate (per 1,000 births)*	84	71	59	58
Mortality under age 5 (per 1,000 births)*	102	86	71	70
Maternal mortality ratio (per 100,000 births) (2000)	..	..	..	24
HIV/AIDS (2003)				
Number of infected adults (thousands)	..	..	..	11
Adult prevalence rate (percentage)	..	..	..	0.1
Spatial distribution				
Population density (per sq. km)	31	41	51	59
Urban population (percentage)	39	41	38	36
Annual urban growth rate (percentage)*	4.4	2.6	1.2	1.0
Annual rural growth rate (percentage)*	2.3	2.6	2.7	1.8
International migration				
International migrant stock				
Number of migrants (thousands)	..	..	1 474	1 268
Percentage of total population	..	..	6.4	4.8

* For the periods 1970-1975, 1980-1985, 1990-1995 and 2000-2005.
[a] For 2002.

Government views and policies

Population policy variable	*1976*	*1986*	*1996*	*2005*
Population size and growth				
View on growth	..	Satisfactory	Satisfactory	Too high
Policy on growth	..	No intervention	No intervention	Lower
Population age structure				
Level of concern about				
Size of the working-age population	..	..	..	..
Ageing of the population	..	..	..	..
Fertility and family planning				
View on fertility level	..	Satisfactory	Satisfactory	Too high
Policy	..	No intervention	No intervention	Lower
Access to contraceptive methods	..	Direct support	Direct support	Direct support
Adolescent fertility				
Level of concern	..	..	..	Major concern
Policies and programmes	..	..	..	Yes
Health and mortality				
View				
Expectation of life	..	Unacceptable	Unacceptable	Unacceptable
Under-five mortality	..	..	..	Unacceptable
Maternal mortality	..	..	..	Unacceptable
Level of concern about HIV/AIDS	..	..	..	Major concern
Measures implemented to control HIV/AIDS*	..	..	..	..
Grounds on which abortion is permitted**	..	..	1,2	1,2,3
Spatial distribution and internal migration				
View on spatial distribution	..	Minor change desired	Satisfactory	Minor change desired
Policies on internal migration				
From rural to urban areas	..	..	..	Lower
From rural to rural areas	..	..	..	..
From urban to rural areas	..	..	..	..
From urban to urban areas	..	..	..	..
Into urban agglomerations	..	No intervention	..	Lower
International migration				
Immigration				
View	..	Satisfactory	Satisfactory	Satisfactory
Policy	..	Maintain	No intervention	No intervention
Permanent settlement	..	..	..	..
Temporary workers	..	..	..	Maintain
Highly skilled workers	..	..	..	..
Family reunification	..	..	..	..
Integration of non-nationals	..	..	..	..
Emigration				
View	..	Satisfactory	Satisfactory	Satisfactory
Policy	..	Maintain	No intervention	No intervention
Encouraging the return of nationals	..	..	..	..

* Measures implemented to control HIV/AIDS: (1) blood screening; (2) information/education campaigns; (3) access to antiretroviral treatment; (4) non-discriminatory policies; (5) promoting condom use.
** Grounds on which abortion is permitted: (1) to save the woman's life; (2) to preserve physical health; (3) to preserve mental health; (4) rape or incest; (5) foetal impairment; (6) economic or social reasons; (7) on request.

Population indicators

Indicator	*1975*	*1985*	*1995*	*2005*
Population size and growth				
Population size (thousands)	101	132	172	211
Annual growth rate (percentage)*	3.2	2.4	2.8	2.0
Population age structure				
Percentage of population under age 15	45	45	43	40
Percentage of population aged 60 or older	4	5	5	5
Fertility and family planning				
Total fertility (births per woman)*	6.1	5.4	4.8	4.2
Teenage fertility rate (per 1,000 women, aged 15 - 19)*	82	73	65	52
Percentage of births to women under age 20*	10	10	9	9
Percentage of births to women aged 35 or older*	15	14	15	15
Percentage of married women using contraception				
Modern methods	..	..	..	..
All methods	..	..	..	..
Health and mortality				
Life expectancy at birth (years)*				
Males	52	58	63	67
Females	56	62	66	70
Both sexes combined	54	60	65	68
Infant mortality rate (per 1,000 births)*	99	70	38	34
Mortality under age 5 (per 1,000 births)*	130	90	47	42
Maternal mortality ratio (per 100,000 births) (2000)	..	..	..	130
HIV/AIDS (2003)				
Number of infected adults (thousands)	..	..	..	..
Adult prevalence rate (percentage)	..	..	..	..
Spatial distribution				
Population density (per sq. km)	8	11	14	17
Urban population (percentage)	16	18	20	24
Annual urban growth rate (percentage)*	6.8	2.6	4.4	4.1
Annual rural growth rate (percentage)*	2.6	2.3	2.5	1.9
International migration				
International migrant stock				
Number of migrants (thousands)	4	3	2	1
Percentage of total population	3.5	2.1	1	0.5

* For the periods 1970-1975, 1980-1985, 1990-1995 and 2000-2005.

Government views and policies

Population policy variable	*1976*	*1986*	*1996*	*2005*
Population size and growth				
View on growth	Satisfactory	Satisfactory	Satisfactory	Satisfactory
Policy on growth	No intervention	No intervention	No intervention	No intervention
Population age structure				
Level of concern about				
Size of the working-age population	..	..	..	Major concern
Ageing of the population	..	..	..	Major concern
Fertility and family planning				
View on fertility level	Satisfactory	Satisfactory	Satisfactory	Satisfactory
Policy	No intervention	No intervention	Lower	Lower
Access to contraceptive methods	Direct support	Direct support	Direct support	Direct support
Adolescent fertility				
Level of concern	..	..	Major concern	Major concern
Policies and programmes	..	..	Yes	Yes
Health and mortality				
View				
Expectation of life	Unacceptable	Unacceptable	Acceptable	Acceptable
Under-five mortality	..	..	..	Unacceptable
Maternal mortality	..	..	..	Unacceptable
Level of concern about HIV/AIDS	..	..	Minor concern	Major concern
Measures implemented to control HIV/AIDS*	..	..	..	1,2,3
Grounds on which abortion is permitted**	..	..	1	1
Spatial distribution and internal migration				
View on spatial distribution	Major change desired	Major change desired	Major change desired	Major change desired
Policies on internal migration				
From rural to urban areas	..	..	..	Lower
From rural to rural areas	..	..	..	..
From urban to rural areas	..	..	..	..
From urban to urban areas	..	..	..	..
Into urban agglomerations	..	..	No intervention	Lower
International migration				
Immigration				
View	Too high	Too high	Satisfactory	Satisfactory
Policy	Lower	Lower	No intervention	Maintain
Permanent settlement	..	..	No intervention	Maintain
Temporary workers	..	..	No intervention	Maintain
Highly skilled workers	..	..	..	Maintain
Family reunification	..	..	No intervention	Maintain
Integration of non-nationals	..	..	No	..
Emigration				
View	Satisfactory	Satisfactory	Satisfactory	Satisfactory
Policy	Maintain	Maintain	No intervention	No intervention
Encouraging the return of nationals	..	..	No	No

* Measures implemented to control HIV/AIDS: (1) blood screening; (2) information/education campaigns; (3) access to antiretroviral treatment; (4) non-discriminatory policies; (5) promoting condom use.

** Grounds on which abortion is permitted: (1) to save the woman's life; (2) to preserve physical health; (3) to preserve mental health; (4) rape or incest; (5) foetal impairment; (6) economic or social reasons; (7) on request.

Population indicators

Indicator	*1975*	*1985*	*1995*	*2005*
Population size and growth				
Population size (thousands)	12 734	17 318	22 087	26 749
Annual growth rate (percentage)*	3.4	2.8	2.3	1.8
Population age structure				
Percentage of population under age 15	43	39	36	31
Percentage of population aged 60 or older	5	5	6	8
Fertility and family planning				
Total fertility (births per woman)*	4.9	4.0	3.3	2.7
Teenage fertility rate (per 1,000 women, aged 15 - 19)*	103	101	98	92
Percentage of births to women under age 20*	15	17	18	20
Percentage of births to women aged 35 or older*	14	11	11	11
Percentage of married women using contraception				
Modern methods	38[a]	..	..	..
All methods	49[a]	..	..	..
Health and mortality				
Life expectancy at birth (years)*				
Males	63	66	69	70
Females	69	72	74	76
Both sexes combined	66	69	71	73
Infant mortality rate (per 1,000 births)*	49	34	23	18
Mortality under age 5 (per 1,000 births)*	67	42	30	29
Maternal mortality ratio (per 100,000 births) (2000)	..	..	..	96
HIV/AIDS (2003)				
Number of infected adults (thousands)	..	..	..	100
Adult prevalence rate (percentage)	..	..	..	0.7
Spatial distribution				
Population density (per sq. km)	14	19	24	29
Urban population (percentage)	76	82	86	88
Annual urban growth rate (percentage)*	4.6	3.2	2.7	2.1
Annual rural growth rate (percentage)*	0.3	-0.1	0.3	-0.1
International migration				
International migrant stock				
Number of migrants (thousands)	731	1 033	1 019	1 010
Percentage of total population	5.7	6	4.6	3.8

* For the periods 1970-1975, 1980-1985, 1990-1995 and 2000-2005.
[a] For 1977.

Government views and policies

Population policy variable	*1976*	*1986*	*1996*	*2005*
Population size and growth				
View on growth	Too high	Too high	Too high	Too high
Policy on growth	Lower	Lower	Lower	Lower
Population age structure				
Level of concern about				
Size of the working-age population	..	..	..	Major concern
Ageing of the population	..	..	..	Major concern
Fertility and family planning				
View on fertility level	Too high	Too high	Too high	Satisfactory
Policy	Lower	Lower	Lower	Maintain
Access to contraceptive methods	Direct support	Direct support	Direct support	Direct support
Adolescent fertility				
Level of concern	..	..	Minor concern	Major concern
Policies and programmes	..	..	Yes	Yes
Health and mortality				
View				
Expectation of life	Unacceptable	Unacceptable	Acceptable	Acceptable
Under-five mortality	..	..	Acceptable	Unacceptable
Maternal mortality	..	..	..	Unacceptable
Level of concern about HIV/AIDS	..	..	Major concern	Major concern
Measures implemented to control HIV/AIDS*	..	..	..	1,2,3,4,5
Grounds on which abortion is permitted**	..	..	1,2,3,4,5,6,7	1,2,3,4,5,6,7
Spatial distribution and internal migration				
View on spatial distribution	Major change desired	Major change desired	Minor change desired	Major change desired
Policies on internal migration				
From rural to urban areas	..	..	..	No intervention
From rural to rural areas	..	..	..	Maintain
From urban to rural areas	..	..	..	No intervention
From urban to urban areas	..	..	..	No intervention
Into urban agglomerations	..	..	Lower	Maintain
International migration				
Immigration				
View	Satisfactory	Satisfactory	Satisfactory	Satisfactory
Policy	Maintain	Maintain	Lower	Maintain
Permanent settlement	..	..	No intervention	Maintain
Temporary workers	..	..	Lower	Lower
Highly skilled workers	..	..	..	Maintain
Family reunification	..	..	Lower	Maintain
Integration of non-nationals	..	..	No	Yes
Emigration				
View	Satisfactory	Satisfactory	Satisfactory	Too low
Policy	Maintain	Maintain	No intervention	Raise
Encouraging the return of nationals	..	..	No	Yes

* Measures implemented to control HIV/AIDS: (1) blood screening; (2) information/education campaigns; (3) access to antiretroviral treatment; (4) non-discriminatory policies; (5) promoting condom use.

** Grounds on which abortion is permitted: (1) to save the woman's life; (2) to preserve physical health; (3) to preserve mental health; (4) rape or incest; (5) foetal impairment; (6) economic or social reasons; (7) on request.

Population indicators

Indicator	*1975*	*1985*	*1995*	*2005*
Population size and growth				
Population size (thousands)	47 974	59 136	73 163	84 238
Annual growth rate (percentage)*	2.2	2.2	2.0	1.4
Population age structure				
Percentage of population under age 15	43	40	37	30
Percentage of population aged 60 or older	7	7	7	7
Fertility and family planning				
Total fertility (births per woman)*	6.7	4.5	3.3	2.3
Teenage fertility rate (per 1,000 women, aged 15 - 19)*	62	53	46	21
Percentage of births to women under age 20*	8	9	9	6
Percentage of births to women aged 35 or older*	26	8	8	10
Percentage of married women using contraception				
Modern methods	..	35[a]	44[b]	57[c]
All methods	..	53[a]	65[b]	79[c]
Health and mortality				
Life expectancy at birth (years)*				
Males	48	57	65	68
Females	53	62	69	72
Both sexes combined	50	59	66	70
Infant mortality rate (per 1,000 births)*	107	69	42	30
Mortality under age 5 (per 1,000 births)*	174	107	60	39
Maternal mortality ratio (per 100,000 births) (2000)	..	..	..	130
HIV/AIDS (2003)				
Number of infected adults (thousands)	..	..	..	200
Adult prevalence rate (percentage)	..	..	..	0.4
Spatial distribution				
Population density (per sq. km)	145	178	221	254
Urban population (percentage)	19	20	22	27
Annual urban growth rate (percentage)*	2.9	2.4	3.8	3.2
Annual rural growth rate (percentage)*	2.1	2.1	1.5	0.7
International migration				
International migrant stock				
Number of migrants (thousands)	5	28	27	21
Percentage of total population	0	0	0	0

* For the periods 1970-1975, 1980-1985, 1990-1995 and 2000-2005.
[a] For 1988.
[b] For 1994.
[c] For 2002.

Government views and policies

Population policy variable	*1976*	*1986*	*1996*	*2005*
Population size and growth				
View on growth	Satisfactory	Satisfactory	Too high	Too high
Policy on growth	No intervention	No intervention	Lower	Lower
Population age structure				
Level of concern about				
Size of the working-age population	..	..	..	Major concern
Ageing of the population	..	..	..	..
Fertility and family planning				
View on fertility level	Satisfactory	Too high	Too high	Too high
Policy	No intervention	Lower	Lower	Lower
Access to contraceptive methods	Direct support	Direct support	Direct support	Direct support
Adolescent fertility				
Level of concern	..	..	Major concern	Major concern
Policies and programmes	..	..	..	Yes
Health and mortality				
View				
Expectation of life	Unacceptable	Acceptable	Unacceptable	Unacceptable
Under-five mortality	..	..	Unacceptable	Unacceptable
Maternal mortality	..	..	..	Unacceptable
Level of concern about HIV/AIDS	..	..	Minor concern	Major concern
Measures implemented to control HIV/AIDS*	..	..	..	1,2
Grounds on which abortion is permitted**	..	..	1	1
Spatial distribution and internal migration				
View on spatial distribution	Minor change desired	Minor change desired	Major change desired	Major change desired
Policies on internal migration				
From rural to urban areas	..	..	..	Lower
From rural to rural areas	..	..	..	..
From urban to rural areas	..	..	..	..
From urban to urban areas	..	..	..	..
Into urban agglomerations	..	..	Lower	Lower
International migration				
Immigration				
View	Satisfactory	Satisfactory	Too high	Too high
Policy	Maintain	Maintain	Lower	Lower
Permanent settlement	..	..	Lower	..
Temporary workers	..	..	Lower	Lower
Highly skilled workers	..	..	..	Maintain
Family reunification	..	..	Maintain	..
Integration of non-nationals	..	..	No	..
Emigration				
View	Satisfactory	Too high	Satisfactory	Satisfactory
Policy	Maintain	Lower	Raise	Raise
Encouraging the return of nationals	..	..	No	..

Note: Views and policies for 1976 and 1986 are those of the former Yemen Arab Republic. The views and policies of the former People's Democratic Republic of Yemen may have been different.

* Measures implemented to control HIV/AIDS: (1) blood screening; (2) information/education campaigns; (3) access to antiretroviral treatment; (4) non-discriminatory policies; (5) promoting condom use.

** Grounds on which abortion is permitted: (1) to save the woman's life; (2) to preserve physical health; (3) to preserve mental health; (4) rape or incest; (5) foetal impairment; (6) economic or social reasons; (7) on request.

Population indicators

Indicator	*1975*	*1985*	*1995*	*2005*
Population size and growth				
Population size (thousands)	6 968	9 951	15 219	20 975
Annual growth rate (percentage)*	1.9	3.9	4.6	3.1
Population age structure				
Percentage of population under age 15	50	51	50	46
Percentage of population aged 60 or older	4	3	4	4
Fertility and family planning				
Total fertility (births per woman)*	8.5	8.7	7.6	6.2
Teenage fertility rate (per 1,000 women, aged 15 - 19)*	139	143	125	98
Percentage of births to women under age 20*	14	13	13	14
Percentage of births to women aged 35 or older*	17	15	18	17
Percentage of married women using contraception				
Modern methods	1[a]	..	10[b]	..
All methods	1[a]	..	21[b]	..
Health and mortality				
Life expectancy at birth (years)*				
Males	40	49	55	59
Females	40	49	57	62
Both sexes combined	40	49	56	60
Infant mortality rate (per 1,000 births)*	184	126	91	69
Mortality under age 5 (per 1,000 births)*	276	186	130	95
Maternal mortality ratio (per 100,000 births) (2000)	..	..	..	570
HIV/AIDS (2003)				
Number of infected adults (thousands)	..	..	..	12
Adult prevalence rate (percentage)	..	..	..	0.1
Spatial distribution				
Population density (per sq. km)	13	19	29	40
Urban population (percentage)	15	18	24	26
Annual urban growth rate (percentage)*	4.1	5.9	6.7	4.8
Annual rural growth rate (percentage)*	1.5	3.3	4.1	3.1
International migration				
International migrant stock				
Number of migrants (thousands)	56	67	228	265
Percentage of total population	0.8	0.7	1.5	1.3

* For the periods 1970-1975, 1980-1985, 1990-1995 and 2000-2005.
[a] For 1979.
[b] For 1997.

Government views and policies

Population policy variable	*1976*	*1986*	*1996*	*2005*
Population size and growth				
View on growth	Satisfactory	Too high	Too high	Too high
Policy on growth	No intervention	No intervention	Lower	Maintain
Population age structure				
Level of concern about				
Size of the working-age population	..	..	..	Major concern
Ageing of the population	..	..	..	Minor concern
Fertility and family planning				
View on fertility level	Satisfactory	Too high	Too high	Too high
Policy	No intervention	No intervention	Lower	Lower
Access to contraceptive methods	Direct support	Direct support	Direct support	Direct support
Adolescent fertility				
Level of concern	..	..	..	Major concern
Policies and programmes	..	..	..	Yes
Health and mortality				
View				
Expectation of life	Unacceptable	Unacceptable	Unacceptable	Unacceptable
Under-five mortality	..	..	..	Unacceptable
Maternal mortality	..	..	..	Unacceptable
Level of concern about HIV/AIDS	..	..	..	Major concern
Measures implemented to control HIV/AIDS*	..	..	..	1,2,3,4,5
Grounds on which abortion is permitted**	..	..	1,2,3,5,6	1,2,3,5,6
Spatial distribution and internal migration				
View on spatial distribution	Major change desired	Major change desired	Major change desired	Major change desired
Policies on internal migration				
From rural to urban areas	..	..	..	Lower
From rural to rural areas	..	..	..	No intervention
From urban to rural areas	..	..	..	Raise
From urban to urban areas	..	..	..	No intervention
Into urban agglomerations	Lower	Lower	..	No intervention
International migration				
Immigration				
View	Satisfactory	Satisfactory	Too high	Satisfactory
Policy	Maintain	Maintain	Lower	Raise
Permanent settlement	..	..	..	No intervention
Temporary workers	..	..	..	Maintain
Highly skilled workers	..	..	..	Maintain
Family reunification	..	..	..	No intervention
Integration of non-nationals	..	..	..	Yes
Emigration				
View	Satisfactory	Satisfactory	Satisfactory	Satisfactory
Policy	Maintain	Maintain	No intervention	Lower
Encouraging the return of nationals	No	..	..	Yes

* Measures implemented to control HIV/AIDS: (1) blood screening; (2) information/education campaigns; (3) access to antiretroviral treatment; (4) non-discriminatory policies; (5) promoting condom use.

** Grounds on which abortion is permitted: (1) to save the woman's life; (2) to preserve physical health; (3) to preserve mental health; (4) rape or incest; (5) foetal impairment; (6) economic or social reasons; (7) on request.

Population indicators

Indicator	*1975*	*1985*	*1995*	*2005*
Population size and growth				
Population size (thousands)	5 151	7 150	9 559	11 668
Annual growth rate (percentage)*	3.6	3.3	2.6	1.7
Population age structure				
Percentage of population under age 15	48	47	47	46
Percentage of population aged 60 or older	4	4	4	5
Fertility and family planning				
Total fertility (births per woman)*	7.8	6.9	6.4	5.7
Teenage fertility rate (per 1,000 women, aged 15 - 19)*	153	159	165	133
Percentage of births to women under age 20*	15	18	20	19
Percentage of births to women aged 35 or older*	21	19	14	11
Percentage of married women using contraception				
Modern methods	..	..	9[a]	23[b]
All methods	..	..	15[a]	34[b]
Health and mortality				
Life expectancy at birth (years)*				
Males	49	50	42	38
Females	52	53	45	37
Both sexes combined	50	51	43	37
Infant mortality rate (per 1,000 births)*	107	98	102	95
Mortality under age 5 (per 1,000 births)*	175	165	179	173
Maternal mortality ratio (per 100,000 births) (2000)	..	..	..	750
HIV/AIDS (2003)				
Number of infected adults (thousands)	..	..	..	830
Adult prevalence rate (percentage)	..	..	..	16.5
Spatial distribution				
Population density (per sq. km)	7	10	13	16
Urban population (percentage)	35	40	37	37
Annual urban growth rate (percentage)*	6.5	3.2	1.6	1.9
Annual rural growth rate (percentage)*	2.2	3.3	3.4	0.7
International migration				
International migrant stock				
Number of migrants (thousands)	297	282	271	275
Percentage of total population	5.8	3.9	2.8	2.4

* For the periods 1970-1975, 1980-1985, 1990-1995 and 2000-2005.
[a] For 1992.
[b] For 2001/2002.

Government views and policies

Population policy variable	*1976*	*1986*	*1996*	*2005*
Population size and growth				
View on growth	..	Too high	Too high	Too high
Policy on growth	..	Lower	Lower	Lower
Population age structure				
Level of concern about				
Size of the working-age population	..	..	..	Major concern
Ageing of the population	..	..	..	Major concern
Fertility and family planning				
View on fertility level	..	Too high	Too high	Too high
Policy	..	Lower	Lower	Lower
Access to contraceptive methods	..	Direct support	Direct support	Direct support
Adolescent fertility				
Level of concern	..	..	Minor concern	Minor concern
Policies and programmes	..	..	Yes	No
Health and mortality				
View				
Expectation of life	..	Unacceptable	Unacceptable	Unacceptable
Under-five mortality	..	..	Unacceptable	Unacceptable
Maternal mortality	..	..	..	Unacceptable
Level of concern about HIV/AIDS	..	..	Major concern	Major concern
Measures implemented to control HIV/AIDS*	..	..	..	1,2,3,4,5
Grounds on which abortion is permitted**	..	..	1,2,4,5	1,2,4,5
Spatial distribution and internal migration				
View on spatial distribution	..	Minor change desired	Major change desired	Major change desired
Policies on internal migration				
From rural to urban areas	..	..	..	Lower
From rural to rural areas	..	..	..	..
From urban to rural areas	..	..	..	..
From urban to urban areas	..	..	..	..
Into urban agglomerations	..	Lower	No intervention	Lower
International migration				
Immigration				
View	..	Too high	Satisfactory	Satisfactory
Policy	..	Lower	Lower	No intervention
Permanent settlement	..	..	Lower	..
Temporary workers	..	..	Lower	..
Highly skilled workers	..	..	..	Raise
Family reunification	..	..	Lower	..
Integration of non-nationals	..	..	Yes	..
Emigration				
View	..	Satisfactory	Too high	Too high
Policy	..	Maintain	Lower	Lower
Encouraging the return of nationals	..	..	No	..

* Measures implemented to control HIV/AIDS: (1) blood screening; (2) information/education campaigns; (3) access to antiretroviral treatment; (4) non-discriminatory policies; (5) promoting condom use.

** Grounds on which abortion is permitted: (1) to save the woman's life; (2) to preserve physical health; (3) to preserve mental health; (4) rape or incest; (5) foetal impairment; (6) economic or social reasons; (7) on request.

Population indicators

Indicator	*1975*	*1985*	*1995*	*2005*
Population size and growth				
Population size (thousands)	6 212	8 888	11 820	13 010
Annual growth rate (percentage)*	3.5	3.9	2.2	0.6
Population age structure				
Percentage of population under age 15	49	48	45	40
Percentage of population aged 60 or older	5	4	5	5
Fertility and family planning				
Total fertility (births per woman)*	7.7	6.7	4.8	3.6
Teenage fertility rate (per 1,000 women, aged 15 - 19)*	147	129	110	97
Percentage of births to women under age 20*	16	16	17	21
Percentage of births to women aged 35 or older*	17	14	13	9
Percentage of married women using contraception				
Modern methods	..	27[a]	50[b]	..
All methods	..	38[a]	54[b]	..
Health and mortality				
Life expectancy at birth (years)*				
Males	54	59	53	38
Females	57	62	60	37
Both sexes combined	56	60	56	37
Infant mortality rate (per 1,000 births)*	83	63	50	62
Mortality under age 5 (per 1,000 births)*	131	101	85	117
Maternal mortality ratio (per 100,000 births) (2000)	..	..	..	1 100
HIV/AIDS (2003)				
Number of infected adults (thousands)	..	..	..	1 600
Adult prevalence rate (percentage)	..	..	..	24.6
Spatial distribution				
Population density (per sq. km)	16	23	30	33
Urban population (percentage)	20	25	32	36
Annual urban growth rate (percentage)*	6.0	6.5	4.1	1.8
Annual rural growth rate (percentage)*	2.9	3.1	1.5	-0.2
International migration				
International migrant stock				
Number of migrants (thousands)	548	662	638	511
Percentage of total population	8.8	7.4	5.4	3.9

* For the periods 1970-1975, 1980-1985, 1990-1995 and 2000-2005.
[a] For 1984.
[b] For 1999.